Images of the Recent Past

Readings in Historical Archaeology

Images of the Recent Past

Readings in Historical Archaeology

edited by
Charles E. Orser, Jr.

ALTAMIRA
PRESS

A Division of Sage Publications, Inc.

Walnut Creek ■ *London* ■ *New Delhi*

For information address:

AltaMira Press
A Division of Sage Publications, Inc.
1630 North Main Street, Suite 367
Walnut Creek, CA 94596

SAGE Publications Ltd.
6 Bonhill Street
London EC2A 4PU
United Kingdom

SAGE Publications India Pvt. Ltd.
M-32 Market
Greater Kailash 1
New Delhi 110 048 India

PRINTED IN THE UNITED STATES OF AMERICA

Library of Congress Cataloging-in-Publication Data

Orser, Charles E., Jr.
    Images of the recent past: readings in historical archaeology / edited by Charles E. Orser, Jr.
        p.   cm.
    Includes bibliographical references
    ISBN 0–7619–9141–7 (cloth : acid-free paper). — ISBN 0–7619–9142–5 (pbk. : acid-free paper)
    1. Archaeology and history. 2. Archaeology and history—United States. 3. United States—Antiquities. I. Orser, Charles E., Jr.
CC77.H5I45 1996
930.1—dc20   96–10102 CIP

Production Services: Carole Bernard, ECS
Editorial Management: Erik Hanson
Cover Design: Denise M. Santoro

99 00 01 02   6 5 4 3 2

Contents

About the Editor

Charles E. Orser, Jr. is professor of anthropology at Illinois State University. He is the founding editor of the *International Journal of Historical Archaeology* and of a book series entitled "Contributions to Global Historical Archaeology." His most recent books are *Historical Archaeology* (with Brian M. Fagan, 1995) and *A Historical Archaeology of the Modern World* (1996). His research interests are in global historical archaeology and the archaeology of disenfranchised groups, and he is currently conducting a long-term research project in Ireland.

Introduction

Images of the Recent Past

August 1856—Leaving the steaming cotton fields of south Georgia behind, a middle-aged slave approaches his tiny, square cabin. His back is bent and his hair shows flecks of gray. He tiredly props his long-handled hoe against the outer wall of the cabin and pushes open the narrow, wooden door. Inside the single room stands a square, rough-hewn table and two wobbly, three-legged stools. An odd assortment of bowls sits on the table. Most of them are yellow and encircled with thin bands of blue and brown. One or two sit in stark contrast, white and plain. A blackened iron kettle hangs in the yawning fireplace, and folded down from the wall to the right is a two-legged wooden bed. It is on this simple platform that the man seeks refuge from his daily ordeal.

May 1776—A well-dressed gentleman in his fifties leans over and smells a delicate pink rose. He straightens and gazes out across the symmetrical, formal garden stretching before him. Among the various shades of green, he sees an occasional floral splash of blue, pink, and violet. In the distance, a silvery pond roughly shaped like a fish brightly reflects the sun's midmorning light. The man heaves a contented sigh and thinks to himself that the cost of this garden was worth every penny. Few aristocrats in the Chesapeake can afford a garden such as this. "Life is truly good," thinks the man.

October 1920—A woman with chestnut-colored hair emerges from the back door of the house lugging a bluish-gray tin bucket filled with pork ribs and other refuse from the dinner table. Pork is a rare treat in northeastern Arizona—where beef, mutton, and goat are much more common—and her family quickly stripped these bones of their meat. Walking about 400 ft to the northwest, the woman unthinkingly heaves the bucket's contents onto the growing pile of refuse that serves as her family's trash pit. As she does, her mind wanders to dinner and she hopes that she will soon taste this rare meat again.

These three little vignettes, though largely imaginary, show ordinary men and women in the past living their lives surrounded by physical things. You will meet men and women such as these throughout this book. Each individual portrayed, though acting alone, behaved in a way that made sense to the culture in which he or she lived. Both the objects and the activities were firmly rooted to larger cultural patterns. These three make-believe individuals, and thousands of others who lived alongside them in the same culture, would have been amazed to learn that archaeologists today have a deep interest in both their daily lives and the cultures in which they lived.

Even today, when most people think about archaeology, they seldom envision the sort of people we have just met. Instead, their minds generally leap to distant places, exotic cultures, and the deepest recesses of antiquity. For most people, the stuff of archaeology is replete with powerful pharaohs with peculiar-sounding names, crumbling, vine-covered monuments in remote jungles, and golden idols gathering dust in ancient temples.

This exotic image of archaeology is not necessarily incorrect. Archaeology has a long and venerable history of investigating the seemingly strange cultures of the past and of poking its head into the world's most remote corners. During the past 50 years, however, archaeology has been changing. A growing number of excavators have turned away from deepest antiquity to pursue a new and unchartered course. They have decided to investigate the lives and cultures of their own closest ancestors. Instead of peeling back the dusty layers of ancient history, historical archaeologists around the world are lifting the veil of mystery that surrounds the histories and cultures of the post-Columbian era.

Why would archaeologists wish to study so recent a past? You may think that historians have already told us everything we need to know about historical times. In their copious volumes, historians have sketched the lives of famous people and described history's most monumental events in painstaking detail. They have opened many windows to the past, but have they told us everything we may wish to know?

Think for a moment. What do you really know about the daily lives of your grandparents and the times in which they lived? If they were like most people, they did not write laws or build monuments to honor themselves. Nor did they lead cavalry charges or write classic works of fiction. Most men and women simply went about their daily chores, remaining fairly anonymous in the process, lost to today's history books. Census rolls, marriage and death certificates, school records, and other official documents may sketch the basic outlines of their lives, but the same records are often vague or even silent when it comes to disclosing the human side of their everyday lives. By the same token, a person's personal letters, memoirs, and diaries usually present only tiny pieces of history. In many cases, eyewitnesses are misleading, are ambiguous, and even downright wrong. Public documents are often of little help because they usually say nothing at all about culture as a whole or the little details of a person's life.

Only archaeology has the power to resurrect the daily lives and cultural patterns of the invisible men and women of the past. By piecing together the often scant evidence left behind by a people in their artifacts and building remains, archaeologists can construct pictures of the past that are unique, insightful, and intimately human. This is as true about recent history as it is for antiquity. Archaeology cannot tell us everything, but it can provide valuable clues that exist in no other discipline. For example, as you will see in this collection of essays, archaeologists can tell what foods people ate on a daily basis, they can learn how men and women symbolized their identities, and they can even identify specific individuals from their bones. By exploring abandoned sites and probing the surface of the earth, archaeology opens narrow thresholds to the past across which historians, relying on written words alone, typically cannot traverse. Historical archaeology, as the term is used in this book, opens doors to the past 500 years.

Today's archaeologists use "historical archaeology" in two ways. In the broadest sense, they use the term to refer to the archaeology of any period for which written records exist. Under this definition, an archaeologist studying the ancient Aztecs or the dynastic Egyptians would be considered historical archaeologists because both cultures used writing and were literate. In this sense, all historical arch-aeologists are linked through their method of using a combination of historical and archaeological sources of information to reconstruct the past. In the second sense of the term, historical archaeology is considered to be the archaeology of post-Columbian history. The theoretical basis of this perspective is the idea that the world became a different place when colonizing Europeans began to travel across the globe, meeting and interacting with diverse indigenous peoples as they went. The hybrid cultures that were subsequently created in the Americas, Asia, Africa, the South Seas, and even in Europe are the outcomes of these dramatic cultural exchanges.

The second sense of historical archaeology is used in this book. The roots of this kind of historical archaeology extend only to the 1930s, when archaeologists began to study famous colonial forts and settlements in North America—Jamestown, Williamsburg, and Fortress Louisbourg in Canada. Since then, historical archaeolo-gists have examined sites associated with the rich and the famous, the poor and the dispossessed, and those in between. They have pushed their spades into the soil at fortifications and encampments, farmsteads and plantations, Native American villages, urban town lots, factories, cemeteries, and many other kinds of sites. And, they have taken historical archaeology around the world.

The number of sites excavated by historical archaeologists grows with amazing speed every year. In addition to pure research efforts, historical archaeologists investigate many sites as part of rescue operations designed to preserve the past from the irreparable damage that can be caused by urban renewal and new con-struction projects. The science of archaeology owes much to the scores of archaeologists who spend their careers in cultural resource management, rescuing sites from destruction. Nowhere is this debt greater than in historical archaeology.

Much of the recent growth experienced in the field can be directly related to preservation legislation that mandates the protection of both prehistoric- *and* historic-period archaeological sites. Several of the chapters in this book were the direct result of cultural resource management or rescue excavations.

No single volume about historical archaeology could ever give you the full breadth of this fast-moving field. What I have tried to do in this book is to introduce you to several aspects of historical archaeology through the writings of practicing archaeologists. The book is divided into six parts.

In Part I, two prominent historical archaeologists present their views of the history and future directions of the field. Like most scholars, historical archaeologists often disagree about the interpretations they formulate. This difference of opinion is healthy because it keeps the field fresh, exciting, and interesting. These two chapters will give you a good understanding of how historical archaeology has developed up to the early 1990s.

Part II introduces you to some of the diverse peoples and cultures historical archaeologists study. Focusing in turn on Spanish missionaries and Native Americans, Revolutionary War soldiers, African-American slaves, Chinese immigrants, and urban prostitutes, this section demonstrates how historical archaeologists actually approach the study of the past and how they piece together past cultures through the physical remains left behind.

Historical archaeologists study a wide spectrum of artifacts. Much of the variety stems from the mass manufacturing that accompanied the Industrial Revolution. All historical archaeologists are trained to analyze post-Columbian material culture, and many have become highly skilled specialists, renowned for their expertise and experience. Among all artifacts, ceramics have fascinated archaeologists for generations, and historical archaeologists are no exception. Ceramics are important to archaeologists for three reasons. First, ceramics—particularly the glazed wares most studied by historical archaeologists—generally preserve well in the ground, often under extremely harsh environmental conditions. Second, ceramics can be used to date archaeological deposits and even whole sites, often quite precisely. Third, as you will see, archaeologists can use ceramics to investigate social variables, such as socioeconomic class, as well as certain specific aspects of behavior. But historical archaeologists do not always agree on the best way to analyze ceramics, and many perspectives exist. This book presents four of them: a type-variety approach adapted from prehistory, a consumer choice approach, a perspective that sees ceramics as capable of promoting and maintaining cultural cohesion, pride, and resistance, and an approach that is rooted in the concept of social power and control. Historical archaeologists study more than just ceramics, but the full range of studies cannot be presented here. Instead, these four chapters are intended to represent of the perspectives that can be used to analyze all artifacts regardless of their physical properties and past functions.

Historical archaeologists, like all archaeologists, extend their analyses beyond artifacts. In truth, they normally rely on a broad array of disciplines, each of which requires specialized training and years of experience. In Part IV I present three studies that illustrate three specializations routinely used in historical archaeology: pollen analysis, faunal analysis, and physical anthropology. You will see that each of these specializations adds a powerful dimension to our understanding of the past.

Part V, focused on landscapes, shows that historical archaeologists understand that the sites they investigate are part of larger environments shaped by men and women to fit their culturally perceived needs, hopes, and visions. Landscapes encompass several diverse natural and cultural elements. The three chapters presented here focus on spatial units of increasing size: a garden in Maryland, a settlement pattern at a cotton plantation in South Carolina, and an entire region of Canada involved in the fur trade.

Historical archaeology is rapidly expanding across the globe. Part VI of this book illustrates the state of research in three places that have a developing tradition of historical archaeology: Mexico, South Africa, and the Middle East. One of the great challenges facing today's historical archaeologists is to take theories and methods designed for one place and to apply them somewhere else. Many historical archaeologists now realize the advantage of a global perspective. Their reasons are both practical and research oriented. Historical archaeologists living in one country, by virtue of their experience and knowledge, have much to teach those living in other countries. By working together and exchanging ideas, historical archaeologists have an opportunity to move their field forward in exciting ways. This vision of working together is more than just a utopian wish for a better world. Cooperative, international research efforts help historical archaeologists to unravel the interconnections of the past. The reason is simple. Many of the products made in the industrial mills of history's great superpowers were widely disbursed as traders and merchants circled the globe. Ideas, perceptions, biases, and cultural attitudes also accompanied these physical objects into the world, creating links that sometimes stretched thousands of miles. Thus, to understand the life and culture of one place, an archaeologist must often know about a completely different place. The post-Columbian world was a place of complex cultural connections and interactions, and a growing number of historical archaeologists now recognize the need to think globally.

The sites inhabited by men and women like the three individuals we met at the beginning of this section give historical archaeologists important clues about the past. This volume is a starting point for your journey into the exciting and ever-unfolding world of historical archaeology. As you learn about the people and cultures interpreted in these pages, remember that sites inhabited by countless men and women from the past still remain to be probed for archaeological information. Perhaps you too will play a part in rescuing some slice of time from historical oblivion.

PART I

Recent Perspectives

Archaeologists often find they must pause to take stock of where their discipline has been and where it seems to be headed. The need for periodic assessment may be more pressing in historical archaeology because the field, being relatively new, is developing and changing so rapidly. The goal of review articles is generally to evaluate the research of practicing historical archaeologists in order to discern their general patterns of thought and to discover if they are focusing their efforts on any particular kinds of sites. The first two chapters in this book are overviews of historical archaeology as it appeared to two archaeologists at the beginning of the 1980s and the 1990s.

In the first chapter, published initially in 1982, Kathleen Deagan, an archaeologist with the Florida Museum of Natural History, examines the history of historical archaeology. As part of this history, she explores the often tortured debates held by historical archaeologists as they attempted to understand whether historical archaeology was history, anthropology, or some special combination of the two. Deagan notes that this controversy has never truly been resolved, even though most American historical archaeologists today are trained in departments of anthropology. To explain the growth of historical archaeology into the broad field it is today, Deagan highlights three important avenues: historical archaeology as a way to add to what is currently known about the past from the work of historians (historical supplementation); historical archaeology as a kind of cultural anthropology that seeks to provide ethnographies of past cultures (reconstruction of past lifeways); and historical archaeology as a kind of anthropology that seeks to provide unique information about cultural processes (processual studies). Deagan then looks to the future and identifies two areas in which historical archaeologists will undoubtedly contribute to general archaeology: in the development of archaeological science and in the archaeological understanding of the cognitive elements of human life.

In the second chapter, Barbara Little, an archaeologist with the National Park Service in Washington, DC, uses Deagan's article as a starting point. Little's objective in this 1994 article is to chart the growth of historical archaeology in the decade after Deagan wrote. Little assesses the advancements in the areas noted by Deagan and takes the discussion in a new direction: the archaeology of capitalism. After Deagan's article first appeared, the archaeology of capitalism became a major topic of study for many historical archaeologists. Though not all historical archaeologists today would agree with this focus, Little shows the relevance of this perspective by concentrating on several subjects of archaeological interest: capitalist development in cross-cultural perspective, production, consumption, industrialism, and ideology, and power. In the final section, Little presents a case study of the 19th-century Cherokee to demonstrate the relationship between ideology and material culture.

Taken together, these two articles indicate the breadth and scope of modern historical archaeology as it appeared in 1982 and in 1994. Although the two essays do not exhaust all possible subjects currently being studied by historical archaeologists, the authors' comments and their extensive references demonstrate that historical archaeology is an important kind of archaeology that is branching out in many directions.

Chapter One

Avenues of Inquiry
in Historical Archaeology

Introduction

Historical archaeology is not a new subfield of archaeology, although its emergence as a legitimate subfield in the consciousnesses of most American archaeologists is relatively recent. Much of the earliest archaeology conducted in Europe was historical archaeology because it was concerned with civilizations documented in some form by written records. The origins of archaeology in the 15th century resulted in a tradition emphasizing the classical sites of Greece, Rome, and the Bible lands (Braidwood 1960:6–8; Daniel 1967:15; Rowe 1965) using both documents and objects as research tools. Other branches of archaeology have, of course, developed in Europe since then, emphasizing the study of both prehistory and history from a developmental, cultural-historical orientation.

In North America as well, some of the earliest archaeological research concerned historic-period sites, such as the excavation of an historic-period Algonquian grave in 1622 by the settlers at Plymouth (Schuyler 1976:27; Young 1841). Applied historical archaeological methods in a quite modern sense were used in 1797 to settle a political dispute between Britain and the newly established United States. The dispute concerned the course of the St. Croix River as mapped by Champlain, which established the boundary separating American from British territory after the Revolutionary War. To help solve this problem, a survey and test excavation were undertaken to find the French settlement of St. Croix, which was recorded by Champlain but later abandoned. The remains of structures and artifacts were located and helped to solve the dispute over the boundary (Schuyler 1976:27–28).

This article was originally published in *Advances in Archaeological Method and Theory*, Vol. 5, pp. 151–177, Orlando: Academic Press, ©1982.

Despite these examples of early historical archaeology in North America, the field has not had a continuous and active role since that time. Not until the mid-1960s did historical archaeology gain formal status, and even then, there was considerable confusion as to what historical archaeology actually was, did, or even ought to do. This resulted in the "crisis of identity" discussed in the following, which has remained with us to some extent.

This crisis of identity was reflected in the lack of agreement among historical archaeologists upon the proper name and proper definition of the field. These discussions resulted in the assignment of labels, with varying degrees of restrictiveness, to the potential subject matter of the field (Schuyler 1970). *Historical archaeology* has emerged as the most generally used term today, largely on the premise that the closest, and somewhat more cumbersome competitor, *historic sites archaeology*, implies that the field concentrates on sites of historical significance, as opposed to cultural significance.

A number of definitions of the field can be found, which more or less emphasize the presence of a documentary record as the distinguishing feature of historical archaeology. Examples include "the study of material remains from any historic period" (Schuyler 1970:119) and "the archaeology of the spread of European cultures throughout the world since the fifteenth century, and its impact on the indigenous people" (Deetz 1977a:5). Noël Hume defines archaeology as "the study of material remains from both the remote and recent past in relationship to documentary history and the stratigraphy of the ground in which they are found" (1969:12); whereas according to Stanley South, "those studies using both archaeological and historical data have come to be called historical archaeology" (1977:1).

None of these definitions have been entirely satisfactory to all historical archaeologists for various reasons of emphasis and subject-matter restriction. Schuyler's definition, for example, is perhaps too elegant, implying to the unwary that material remains themselves are the focus of historical archaeology, rather than the cultural systems that produced them. Likewise, South's statement could also describe several contemporary historical studies that use both historical and archaeological data (Hall 1981; Manucy 1978). Since the time when Deetz's definition was offered, several emphases in historical archaeology have emerged that would be difficult to encompass within that definition, such as the study of African-American culture, Asian-American culture, and the Victorian period. Noël Hume's suggestion, aside from its puzzling construction, implies a stronger emphasis on documentary history as the focus of organization than many contemporary historical archaeologists are comfortable with.

All of these definitions, however, include reference to the use of both archaeological and historical data in research, and are thus in agreement that the time period covered by this discipline begins after 1492 for North America. The subject matter suggested includes material remains and past behavior. Thus, most historical archaeologists would probably agree that the field includes the study of human behavior through material remains, for which written history in some way affects its interpretation.

In only two decades, historical archaeology has made a rapid theoretical progression from descriptive and chronological concerns, through cultural historical studies, to problems of culture process, cognition, and archaeological principles. The process has been in a sense additive in that the earlier goals continue to be addressed by historical archaeologists even as they pursue more contemporary problems and issues. Historical archaeology is today a complex discipline that incorporates principles from, and makes contributions to, a number of other disciplines both within and outside anthropology.

Because of its unique command of all the contexts of human behavior (Schuyler's "spoken word, written word, preserved behavior, and observed behavior" [1977]) (see also Brown 1974), historical archaeology has been able to make contributions that would not be possible through any other avenue of inquiry. Documented information about past social, temporal, and economic variables allows investigation of the cultural processes that affect those variables, and which are in turn affected by them. Furthermore, the simultaneous access by historical archaeologists to both emic statements (documents) and etic statements (archaeological data) about conditions in the past allows the study of behavioral processes involved in human perception, and the manipulation and means of coping with the environment.

It is partly due to these same circumstances, however, that historical archaeology today is in a difficult position. Most contemporary historical archaeologists are trying to establish the field as a subdiscipline of anthropology, both because of its unique potentials for understanding human behavior and because most American archaeologists are trained in anthropology departments. At the same time, however, the field is closely associated with other, nonanthropological disciplines that frequently can recover information relevant to their concerns only through historical archaeology. This is particularly true of such fields as applied history and architecture. Because historical archaeology, unlike prehistoric archaeology, shares its subject matter with other disciplines that ask very different kinds of questions about the same subject matter, the process of self-definition has been somewhat more complex.

The complexities involved in the recognition and understanding of historical archaeology as a field of scholarship were underscored also by the relationships between prehistoric and historical archaeologists during the early development of these fields. Although by the 1960s most historical archaeologists had been trained in the same departments as prehistoric archaeologists, there remained a certain ambivalence toward historic-period sites in American archaeology. Part of this was the bias in anthropological archaeology toward non-Western cultures as the proper focus of research (cf. Fontana 1965). This bias was due, at least in part, to the relatively abrupt and intrusive appearance of literate societies in the culture history of North America, providing a natural historical division of subject matter. The directions of American anthropology tended to support this division in that from the 19th-century origins of the field through the middle of the 20th century, the major emphases in American anthropology were Native American studies and the development of cultural-historical syntheses (Willey and Sabloff 1974:Chs. 3 and 4). The ambivalent attitude toward European-American sites as a legitimate emphasis has, however, been reduced and perhaps resolved since the earliest decades of 20th-century historical archaeology. This has been largely due to the American Bicentennial effort, which not only made colonial America a popular and timely subject, but provided funds for historical archaeology on a major scale.

The strict separation of *history* from *prehistory* is in contrast to the attitudes of many archaeologists trained in Europe (cf. Noël Hume 1969). Probably due in part to the more gradual and variable spread of literacy in the Old World, many European archaeologists do not use a specific point in time, or even the presence of documents, to differentiate between history and prehistory. Christopher Hawkes, for example, suggested in 1951 that "prehistory, from the neolithic colonization of Europe onward, is classified according to the degree (as we ascend the scale) in which our knowledge of it stands indebted to historic materials" (Hawkes 1951:1). Grahame Clark, commenting on Hawke's discussion, offered a classification of prehistory and history, which included *autonomous prehistory* (data for which no written references exist), *secondary prehistory* (nonliterate cultures that need to be studied in reference to contemporary civilization), and *history* (civilization) (Clark 1954:7–9).

Among archaeologists in the United States during the early decades of this century, there was little doubt that autonomous prehistory was the domain of prehistoric archaeologists, and that history was the domain of historical archaeologists. Secondary prehistory was somewhat less well defined, and was studied by both prehistoric and historical archaeologists.

The following discussion assesses the development of historical archaeology and the effects of this development on the work historical archaeologists are doing today. It also identifies and evaluates the several approaches to historical archaeology that are currently being taken, and that are contributing to a range of scholarly concerns.

Development and Emergence of Historical Archaeology in America

Isolated examples of historical archaeology can be found throughout the 19th century. Such work as that of James Hill in 1856 at Miles Standish's home (Deetz 1977a:29–30) is characteristic of that early period in that the site was the home of an important historical figure, and Hall himself was a civil engineer rather than an archaeologist.

Near the end of the 19th century, investigations were undertaken by the New York Historical Society to recover information about military camp life and objects from the Revolutionary War and the War of 1812. Excavations were carried out in what are now the Washington Heights and Kingsbridge districts of the Bronx by officers of the Society, who carefully recorded and reported their finds (Calver and Bolton 1950).

Emphasis on historically important sites and the involvement of non-archaeologists in the excavation of these also characterized studies in the early 20th century. The development of a national program of Historic Preservation in the early decades of the 20th century resulted in the entrenchment of historical archaeology as a recognized field of endeavor in this country. During the 1930s, particularly, programs aimed at relieving the effects of the Great Depression resulted in the first serious and large-scale investigations of historic-period sites (Harrington 1952). These covered a wide range of subjects, including British colonies such as Fort Frederica (Fairbanks 1956), Spanish missions (Montgomery 1949; Smith 1948), 19th-century forts (Smith 1939), and trading posts (Kelley 1939; Lombard 1953). These projects were particularly notable because of the serious emphasis on European-American sites for the first time in American archaeology.

Nearly all of these studies, however, were oriented toward recovering specific details useful for architectural reconstruction and the interpretation of what happened at the site. "The aim of the excavating was much the same as the Jamestown project, namely to rescue data that would permit the best possible interpretation of the site to the visitor" (Harrington 1952:342). Occasionally, such studies also solved problems of documentary ambiguity or the absence of information needed for reconstruction, such as Fairbanks's location of the Frederica town lot plan by locating the common wall between a duplex structure, thus pinning down the physical location of a known lot line (Fairbanks 1956).

While these projects brought recognition to historical archaeology as a field of research, their primary orientation toward questions of historical reconstruction rather than anthropological questions laid the groundwork for later conflict in the field. During the early decades of historical archaeology's development, prehistoric archaeology in North America was emerging in solid alignment with anthropology (Willey and Sabloff 1974:Ch. 2). Most American archaeologists were trained in departments of anthropology; however, it was not until the decades of the 1930s and 1940s that such anthropologically trained archaeologists became involved on a serious scale in the archaeology of historic-period sites. They have not, however, always dominated the field, and even today there are non-anthropologically trained archaeologists doing historical archaeology in America (Noël Hume 1969; Webster 1974).

The first formal recognition in this country of historical archaeology as a discipline came in 1960, with the establishment of the Conference on Historic Sites Archaeology and the publication of its proceedings. This was followed in 1965 by the formation of the Society for Historical Archaeology and the publication of its journal, *Historical Archaeology*. Both of these organizations and publications remain the primary foci of professional activity in historical archaeology.

One of the first issues to be addressed in the early stages of the formalized discipline was the apparent "crisis of identity" (Cleland and Fitting 1968). This crisis revolved around the definition of what historical archaeology actually was, what its parent discipline was, and what its proper orientation should be.

The opposing points of view in the identity crisis were grounded in the question of whether history or anthropology was the parent discipline of the field, and by extension, whether historical archaeology was historical and particularizing in scope or anthropological and generalizing in scope. Anthropologically trained historical archaeologists, such as Cleland and Fitting (1968) and Griffin (1958), pointed out that there was little difference between the methods of observation, recovery, control, and analysis used by prehistoric and historical archaeologists. Most importantly, they pointed out that both areas of archaeology could (and should) ultimately address questions of human cultural adaptation and evolution. In this sense, historical archaeology shared the same guiding processual questions as cultural anthropology and anthropological prehistoric archaeology.

Another point of view was offered by several archaeologists (not all of whom were trained in departments of anthropology) and historians involved in historical archaeology. Dollar (1968), Harrington (1952, 1955), Noël Hume (1964), and Walker (1967) have suggested that the nature and extent of documentary information on historic sites render the analytical methods used by prehistoric archaeology inappropriate for historical archaeology (see particularly Dollar 1968). It was also suggested that due to the short time periods frequently characteristic of historical sites, some of the basic tools of archaeology—stratigraphy and seriation—are not as useful on these sites as on prehistoric ones (Harrington 1952:342). The basic point of view of the historically oriented researchers in this debate was that the best questions and most reliable answers in historical archaeological research were those organized around the need to "fill in the gaps" in history. This need included providing details of architecture and material culture that were not available in documents, such as Harrington's work at Fort Necessity (1957), as well as bringing to light the details of nonelite life so essential to the interpretation of the past.

The debate over the proper orientation of historical archaeology has not altogether been resolved, although most historical archaeologists today appear to claim an anthropological orientation (Deagan 1979:369). The needs of historians, however, and the goals of historically oriented archaeologists cannot be ignored, particularly since historical archaeology is often the only way to satisfy such needs and goals. The issue today resulting from the "crisis-of-identity" debates that marked the formal emergence of historical archaeology is to learn how to integrate the needs of both anthropology and history, rather than determining which of the two will emerge as a winner.

There are several practical and developmental reasons why this should be so. Cleland and Fitting (1968), Schuyler (1979:201), South (1977:5–13), and others have discussed the basic divisions of scholarship and the relationship of historical archaeology to them. They have identified these divisions as scientific (generalizing), historical (particularizing), and humanistic (aesthetic). If historical archaeology is a scientific discipline, it should be concerned with developing general principles that can explain regularities and variability in human culture and behavior. If it is essentially an historical discipline, it should be concerned with studying and illuminating the attributes, events, and processes of a particular time, place, and society; however, this does not preclude the use of scientific methods in the approach to these concerns. Finally, if historical archaeology is a humanistic discipline, it should impart an aesthetic appreciation of and an empathy with the human conditions of the past.

During the first decades of historical archaeological research in this country, one could confidently place historical archaeology in the historical category. Since the 1960s however, the placement has become somewhat confused, both because of the work done by historical archaeologists, and because of the fact that the same kind of confusion existed in the field of archaeology in general.

Prehistoric archaeology underwent a "crisis of identity" of sorts at about the same time as historical archaeology did; the main issue being whether culture history (particularizing) or culture process (generalizing) was the proper focus of archaeology (cf. Binford 1962; Deetz 1970; Willey and Sabloff 1974:Chs. 5 and 6). Attempting to share the goals and orientations of prehistoric archaeologists trained in anthropology departments did not help the newly emergent field of historical archaeology to resolve its basic crisis of identity. Anthropologists and archaeologists alike were studying and describing particular cultures at particular times and places, and in that sense, what anthropology was doing in 1960 was often little different from social history. This tended to confuse further the determination of whether historical archaeology was historical or anthropological in origin, because in practice, it was frequently difficult to precisely distinguish between the two.

One result of these circumstances and developments is that historical archaeology today encompasses several different orientations. Not only have the "handmaiden-to-history," "reconstruction-of-past-lifeways," and "culture-process" concerns been retained both in stated intent and in practice, but certain newer emphases, unique to historical archaeology, have been added in recent years. These include the investigation of the relationships between patterned human behavior and patterned archaeological remains (cf. Deetz 1977b; Schiffer 1976, 1977; South 1977) and the testing of traditional archaeological principles developed to account for those relationships (cf. South 1977).

Some historical archaeologists have turned to questions that depend on the unique access of the field to both written and material by-products of behavior (Brown 1974; Schuyler 1977). These questions concern human perceptual systems and the role of patterned cognition in shaping the material world (see Deetz 1974, 1977a; Glassie 1969, 1975). This marks an unusual departure from the traditionally materialist explanatory framework of archaeology.

These new avenues of inquiry, as well as the research being conducted from the earlier orientations, are considered in the following sections. The emphases and accomplishments of this research and the mutual compatibility of these various approaches within the field as a whole are also discussed.

Historical Supplementation

Historical archaeology as a "handmaiden to history" (Noël Hume 1964), that is, as a provider of supplementation for the historical record of the past, is most visible today in those projects carried out in support of historic recon-struction and restoration.

The large-scale retention of the historical supplementation goals in the field has also been influenced by the rapid expansion of cultural resource management needs during the 1970s. Historical archaeology conducted in support of architectural and historical reconstruction shares many of the potential contract-related problems faced by prehistoric archaeologists in that artificial restrictions are often placed on the scope of research because of the terms of a contract. Many historical arch-aeologists working on contracts, however, are doing research in conjunction with historians and architects in order to provide information on which to base the recon-struction interpretation of a site, which is frequently not endangered by anything other than the reconstruction activities. Unlike prehistoric archaeological contract work, the data recovered by the historical archaeologists under contract very often is crucially important to the successful completion of the project that provoked the issuance of the contract in the first place. Instead of (and occasionally in addition to) the narrow geographic restrictions often placed on prehistoric archaeological contracts, historical archaeologists are restricted in the questions they can ask: When was the east wing added? What was the evolution of the floor plan? There are hundreds of single-instance projects throughout the country that contractually restrict the historical archaeologist to supplemental data gathering, and historical archaeology to a service industry (Swannack 1975). It is difficult to gauge the full extent of such work because it is usually not published or presented at professional meetings. One suspects that if it were all gathered in one place, the major contribution of these projects would not even be to history, but rather to historical architecture. The many problems resulting from these circumstances in historical archaeology as well as in prehistoric archaeology can only be resolved through the ethical orientation of the archaeologists, who, as Schiffer and Gumerman (1977:16) and South (1977:294) have pointed out, must be willing to insist on the integration in the project design of problem-related goals with reconstruction needs.

That such integration is indeed possible has been demonstrated at a number of sites in the 1970s. Such contributions as Deetz's La Purisima study discussed previously, Lewis's study of frontier patterning (1977), House's documentation of squatters in the Ozarks (1977), Ferguson's work on the interpretation of artifact distributions at Fort Watson (1977b), Otto's status variability study on St. Simon's Island (1975), Honerkamp's study of frontier adaptations at Frederica, Georgia (1980), and the community-patterning and acculturation studies at St. Augustine (Deagan 1978) have all been carried out within a cultural resource management framework.

This integration is perhaps most evident at major centers for public interpretation, such as Plimouth Plantation, St. Augustine, St. Mary's City, and Ft. Michili-mackinac. At these centers, archaeology is generally supported specifically to recover data necessary for the reconstruction and interpretation of the sites. Because these sites represent communities, however, and because they have both long-term research and development plans and long-term commitments by academic institutions, it has been possible to integrate historical and anthropological studies into the framework of resource management (see also Stephenson 1977).

That there have also been positive contributions through a primarily historical orientation in historical archaeology cannot be denied. Archaeology has probably reached more nonarchaeologists through programs of public interpretation than through any other means, combating the field's potential for an "Ivory Tower" image. There is also certain historical information which simply cannot be retrieved through any means other than archaeology. This information can often enhance or even change traditional interpretations of social history. Such changes can include physical plans or constructions at a site, such as Harrington's at Ft. Necessity and Ferguson's discovery through archaeological data of the tactics involved in the battle at Ft. Watson (1977b:69). In St. Augustine, archaeological remains have indicated the extent to which colonists, despite claims to the contrary, indulged in illegal trade with the British colonies (Deagan 1978), and the foodways of the Spanish colonists in Florida (Reitz 1979). South (1977) has determined archaeologically that British colonists in the South disposed of their trash in a predictably patterned manner, a fact that could be of importance in the reconstruction of British colonial sites. The growth and expansion of settlement patterns in historic communities are also frequently documented only through archaeology (Deetz 1968; Fairbanks 1956). Another example of the illumination of historical interpretation through archaeology is found on slave sites, where documentary indications that firearms were prohibited and that food was cooked communally have been refuted archaeologically (Fairbanks 1972). The approach to historical issues through archaeological research can result in a more objective standard of measurement, as opposed to the frequently subjective standard of written history. This cannot be denied as one facet of modern historical archaeology.

Reconstruction of Past Lifeways

Another orientation from which research is currently being conducted in historical archaeology addresses the reconstruction of a past society and conditions of the past. Although this orientation is certainly in keeping with anthropological tradition and practice, it is essentially similar to social history and to ethnography in that the focus of research is most often, although not always exclusively, on a particular time, place, and society. This is in contrast to the "processual" orientation, which has a primary research focus on general principles of behavior of culture process.

The emphasis on reconstruction of past lifeways in historical archaeology was paralleled by the methodological shift toward "backyard archaeology" proposed by Fairbanks in 1971 (Fairbanks 1977). This method deemphasized historic structures and foundations, and the "Barnum and Bailey" syndrome (Noël Hume 1969:10) of concentration on the "oldest" or "largest" or "most historically significant" site. Instead, emphasis was to be placed on the by-products of all aspects of behavior in the past, which were found most frequently in those locations where the behavior took place, namely the backyard.

One of the most visible and significant results of this emphasis on specific societies in historical archaeology has been the documentation of historically disenfranchised groups in our own culture, providing alternative images of national identity from those provided by written history (Schuyler 1976). The study of the roots of African-American culture—the written history of which has most often been incomplete and distorted—is a particularly evident example of this. Work done by Fairbanks in 1968 at the Kingsley Plantation slave cabins in Florida (Fairbanks 1972) was one of the first archaeological studies of American slavery from a nondocumentary point of view, and has been followed by numerous studies concentrating on African-American culture both in freedom and slavery (Deetz 1977a; Handler and Lange 1978; Otto 1979; Schuyler 1980; Singleton 1980, among others). Other undocumented, disenfranchised groups have also been the focus of historical archaeology, including Asian-Americans (Schuyler 1980); Native Americans of the historic period (Goodyear 1977; Kirkpatrick et al. 1980); Hispanic-American Creoles (Shephard 1975); and groups disenfranchised by poverty or disreputability such as mountaineers (House 1977; Price and Price 1978), hobos (Klein 1977), and miners (Deetz 1981).

With a few exceptions, such as the Hispanic-American sites in the southern and western United States, and some slave sites, such as those at Kingsley Plantation, Florida, most of the research on these groups has not been applied in the intensive public interpretation programs that characterize Anglo-American sites. These studies of disenfranchised groups are, however, being gradually included in the popular media (for example, *Odyssey*, a television series that communicates the contributions of anthropology to the general public) and in the research of other disciplines (Hall 1980, for example).

Such studies are quite often closely interrelated with processual concerns. Cross-cultural comparisons, for example, can reveal striking parallels and differences in the ways by which various groups adapted to relocation in a new environment and the mechanisms by which different groups became integrated into or excluded from American society. Archaeology has demonstrated, for example, that Spaniards in North America physically integrated themselves with the indigenous inhabitants of the New World, while British colonists resisted such integration. This resulted in a very different kind of adaptive pattern between the two groups (Deagan 1980).

Such ethnographically oriented studies have also occasionally resulted in a new perspective on historical and social processes traditionally cherished in those fields. "The melting pot" concept of the formation of America's national identity, for example, has recently been cast into doubt as an explanatory model. Deetz (1977b) and Schuyler (1976) have both suggested that the formation of American society was instead a process of systematic exclusion of non-Anglo groups from the mainstream of Anglo-American life, much in the same way that such exclusion is evident today. Research at the non-Anglo site of St. Augustine, however, has somewhat ironically indicated that the melting pot concept did indeed describe the process of formation for Hispanic-American society in the New World (Deagan 1980).

Processual Studies

A third orientation in contemporary historical archaeology can be seen in those studies with a primary focus on the investigation of a cultural process, rather than on the investigation of a specific social group or set of events. The development of this orientation parallels the same development in American archaeology in general (Willey and Sabloff 1974:Ch. 6).

Processual studies in historical archaeology have most often concentrated on cultural processes operating at specific times and places, and are thus, strictly speaking, particularizing in result. They provide, however, the building blocks on which more general processual questions about human culture may be investigated.

Most often, the studies have been approached through a hypothetico-deductive method of investigation.

The great advantage of historical archaeology in this research effort is the presence of the documentary record. In many cases, such social variables as ethnic affiliation, income, religious affiliation, occupation, family composition, economic network, and political restrictions of the social unit are known. Thus, it is frequently possible to investigate the specific mechanics of specific processes in a given unit, rather than simply identifying the presence of a certain phenomenon that might help interpret an archaeological pattern.

The use of documents as controls in this manner is, of course, subject to a considerably cautious assessment of their veracity and validity. Problems related to the nature of documentary evidence, and methods to cope with them have been concerns of archaeologists and historians alike (Barzun and Graff 1970).

One processual area to which historical archaeology has made particularly significant contributions is that of understanding acculturation. Many studies have been oriented, at least in part, toward the elucidation of this process due to the obvious advantage of having European–Native American contact sites available. Studies have concentrated on acculturation through trading relations (Brown 1978; Deetz 1965; Fairbanks 1962; Irwin-Mason 1963), religious conversion (Cheek 1974; Deetz 1963; Loucks 1979), and racial intermarriage (Deagan 1974).

These studies have suggested that the sex of the people who provide the links between the two cultures in contact is a critical factor in determining the end results of acculturation. Among the 18th-century Creek Indians, for example, the primary link with Europeans was through the deerskin trade. In this trade, European men came into contact with the Creek men, and archaeological evidence indicates that it was the male activities among the 18th-century Creeks that showed evidence of European acculturation and alteration (Fairbanks 1962; Irwin-Mason 1963). Female-related activities, such as food production, pottery, and basketry, were little altered, and it has been suggested that the lag between technological change in male and female areas of 18th-century Creek culture was a causal factor in the personal stress leading to the Prophet's revitalization movement among the Creeks (Fairbanks 1962:53).

At the Spanish La Purisima mission, Deetz also found that male activity areas were subject to more intensive and rapid alteration through European influence than were women's activities (1963). This was also the case at the Florida missions (Loucks 1979). At these missions, however, both men and women were in direct contact with the male European friars.

These studies imply that because the Europeans who came into contact with Native American cultures were nearly always males, little innovative technology relating directly to female activities would result from European contact. In the Native American cultures, therefore, technological innovation took place in male activity areas through trade and occasionally through gift giving. In the European-American cultures, little alteration occurred through contact with Native Americans in male activity areas, but in those activity areas traditionally associated with women, the Europeans frequently incorporated the technologies of Native American women. This was particularly evident in situations involving concubinage or intermarriage (Deagan 1974).

Historical archaeology is also in a strong position with regard to revealing the impact of European technological innovation upon Native American social systems. Social change in Native American groups resulting from European interaction has been shown to be more closely linked to alteration of economic patterns than to either religious conversion or intermarriage. The example of the Arikara, cited previously, revealed a shift in kinship structure in response to a change from a farming economy to an economy based on middleman trade (Deetz 1965). Among the Algonquians, the implementation of the fur trade resulted in both a shift from small lineage-based villages to larger clan-based settlements; and a more pronounced structure of social differentiation, based in large part on differential access to European goods (Mainfort 1979).

Several other historical archaeological studies have investigated processes related to colonization and the establishment of European-American society. Lewis's work with the process of expansion by an established society into a wilderness has indicated that the frontier model developed by social scientists over the years (Lewis 1977:153–156) is an appropriate framework through which to understand the mechanisms and results of colonization. The frontier model and other studies based on it (for example, Honerkamp's application of the model at Frederica, Georgia [1980]) have not only illuminated the mechanics of adaptation by early New World colonists but also provided a model for the interpretation of early American history.

Certain other processual issues have also been noted as particularly appropriate foci for historical archaeology; however, little work has been directly oriented toward these. One of these processes is that of imperialism (Schuyler 1976). The circumstances under which imperialist expansion does or does not succeed, and the ultimate results of such expansion are relevant issues throughout much of the world. Such results can be objectively studied and assessed through historical archaeology. Another little-studied area in historical archaeology is that of the Marxian-derived dialectical relationships by which contemporary society is economically and socially organized, that is, production, distribution, and exchange mechanisms (Leone 1977b). Through historical archaeology's potential control through documents over the economic variables of past societies, the specific mechanisms of this dialectic could be predicted and tested in the archaeological record. Leone points out that historical archaeology's particular potential for explicating this dynamic process in the past can directly explicate the same processes as they operate in our own society.

Archaeological Science

One of the most uniquely productive and important aspects of historical archaeology is its ability to test principles of archaeological interpretation under controlled conditions. Although this is not a recent application in the field (for example, Deetz 1965:1), it has only been in recent years that studies concentrating on testing and verifying relationships between patterning in the material and behavioral spheres have become explicit (Ferguson 1977a; South 1977).

Historical archaeology studies oriented toward this end have been able to demonstrate that the associations between archaeological data and past behavior are indeed patterned and predictable in specific ways. Such studies focus on the development, testing, and verification of interpretive principles necessary for the scientific investigation of specific processes and events. Historical archaeology has been applied to the testing of a number of methods and assumptions commonly used in archaeological analysis and interpretation. One of the most prominent of these applications has been in testing the well-known assumption of a normal frequency distribution for stylistic traits through time (Flannery 1973; Kroeber 1919), or the *battleship curve of popularity*. In combination with the principles of stratigraphy and seriation, this assumption is basic to the description and interpretation of events in culture history. At least two historical archaeological studies using well-dated materials—gravestones (Deetz and Dethlefson 1967) and historic ceramics (South 1972)—have demonstrated that the battleship curve of popularity is a true description of a real and predictable diachronic phenomenon in the material world. It is a phenomenon that exists regardless of spatial and temporal location, and thus may constitute one of the very few general laws derived solely through archaeology. The most explicit proponent of this approach in contemporary historical archaeology has been South (1977). South has demonstrated that specific cultural phenomena are recognizably patterned and can be predicted in the archaeological record. Intersite function and intrasite activities, for example, are revealed through a statistical analysis pattern in South's discussion of the Carolina and frontier patterns (1977).

In his discussion of the Brunswick pattern of refuse disposal—a horizontal distributional pattern of artifacts associated with British colonists—South lays the groundwork for, and comes tantalizingly close to, explicating a basic postulate for archaeological interpretation; that is, the way in which refuse is disposed of is distinctly and recognizably patterned for specific groups of different ethnic background or cultural heritage. Such a postulate, if demonstrated and verified, could have considerable value in the interpretation of ethnic differentiation in the archaeological record, including that of prehistoric sites. Additional archaeological evidence related to this issue, such as Carillo's (1977) investigation of the German-American pattern, provides increasing support that the link between cultural heritage and patterned refuse disposal is indeed a valid observation.

Many historical archaeological studies have attempted to demonstrate the ways in which certain sociocultural variables are manifested in the archaeological record, using documentation about the nature of these variables as controls. One of the most frequently studied phenomena is the way in which variability in social status is reflected archaeologically. Otto's work at a Georgia plantation site (1975, 1977) indicated that ceramic type and form provided a reliable reflection of the status differences known to have been present in that society among planters, overseers, and slaves. Because of different dietary patterns among the groups, different ceramic forms related to type were used by each group despite the fact that the same basic ceramic assemblage was shared by all of the groups.

Similar results were obtained by Poe (1979) in Spanish Florida, where it was found that economic variability, as measured by income and occupation, was predictably linked to specific proportions of Hispanic, aboriginal, and other European wares within the ceramic assemblage of each household. In this case, the patterns were believed to have been a function of differential access to scarce Hispanic goods.

Several historical archaeological studies have also tested the strength with which dietary remains reflect certain social subsystems. Work such as Cumbaa's (1975), Mudar's (1978), and Reitz's (1979) have shown that there is a predictable relationship between the specific components and proportions in a given faunal assemblage, and the function of the site from which it came, the ethnic affiliation of the site's inhabitants, and the economic status of the inhabitants.

Historic-period burial populations have also been tested through comparison with documentation to reveal their facility in reflecting certain social phenomena. Analysis of 17th- and 18th-century St. Augustine burial data has revealed that specific and sharply distinct mortuary patterns are associated with British-Protestant and Spanish-Catholic burials (Koch 1980), and Algonquian burial populations have been shown to reflect social changes, particularly status differentiation, brought about through the introduction of the European fur trade (Mainfort 1979).

In the pursuit of scientific principles that can help explain the relationship between behavioral variability and the archaeological record, historical archaeologists have turned to the study of contemporary groups. Such ethnoarchaeological studies in historical archaeology can simultaneously make use of material remains, oral accounts, documentation, and ethnographic observation. This has emerged in historical archaeology through the increasing awareness that the spoken word and observed behavior constitute categories of data equivalent to that of documents in the implementation of the many goals of the field (Brown 1974; Deetz 1977a, 1977b; Schuyler 1977).

One of the best-known studies of this type is the Tucson garbage project (Rathje 1977; Rathje and McCarthy 1977). Using a combination of interviews and analyses of household garbage in Tucson, Rathje was able to directly observe and record the processes of discard in specific households over time. These households were sampled to reflect ethnic and economic differences within the community. Results of the study provided an indication of the ways in which economic stress was reflected in consumption patterns. In the case of Tucson, economic stress was accompanied by increased waste due to unfamiliarity with new and cheaper resources, and also by increased alcohol consumption. The project also suggested that while social variability was indeed visible after the formation of the archaeological record, the specific relationships between sociocultural variables, such as income or family size, and material patterns are not immutable, and are interrelated in ways that are not always recognizable in contemporary archaeological studies (Rathje and McCarthy 1977:284).

The observation of contemporary social and archaeological processes has considerably expanded the scope and potential of historical archaeology during the past decade. Not only can this allow cross-checking and verifications of principles developed through observation of the archaeological and written records (and vice versa), but it is the basis for the unique potential of historical archaeology toward understanding the relationships between material patterning, human behavior, and human perception.

The inclusion of contemporary societies in the focus of historical archaeology is related to a relatively recent conceptual self-image in the field, that of historical archaeology as the "science of material culture" (Deetz 1977b). This term describes archaeology essentially as the study of relationships between human beings and material things. One rather early statement of this point was provided by James Deetz in 1968 when he suggested that "archaeology must concern itself with material culture, regardless of its provenience, be it archaeological in the excavated sense or ethnographic in terms of present use" (1968:129).

An expanded statement of this point of view is found in Deetz's paper as well as in many of the other papers included in Ferguson (1977a). In these papers, material culture was treated as that segment of our physical environment that we modify through culturally determined behavior. While this expansion of the subject matter of the field has not received universal acclaim in the discipline, it has greatly expanded its scope, and created the potential for discovering enduring principles of behavioral-material relationships in human culture. As the garbage project has demonstrated, and as Leone (1977b) and Schuyler (1976) have pointed out, historical archaeology contributions are not restricted to our understanding of the past, but can help us to understand ourselves today, and possibly even predict our future behavior with regard to material things. This is not an insignificant potential when one considers the problems facing us from misuse or overconsumption of material resources.

Another important avenue toward archaeological science is also a potential focus for historical archaeology. This is the delineation of archaeological formation processes, the behavioral archaeology most visibly associated with Schiffer (1976, 1977). Although this was not a direct development from historical archaeological concerns, historical archaeology offers an important avenue of inquiry and investigation in support of it. Clearly, an understanding of the transformations through which the living material world passes in becoming an archaeological site is essential both to recognizing patterns in the archaeological record, and in understanding what those processes reflect. The controls offered by historical archaeology through its involvement in direct and indirect observation are of considerable potential for the definition of archaeological formation processes.

This orientation within historical archaeology toward the development, testing, and refinement of interpretive principles for archaeology is one of the field's more recent developments and one of the most useful for nonhistorical archaeologists. It also, however, presents a potential danger if it becomes the predominant goal in the field in that historical archaeology could evolve from a "handmaiden to history" to a "handmaiden to archaeology." The simple demonstration that material-behavioral patterns exist in a predictable manner (many of which are in any case intuitively obvious) is not in itself a desirable end result of research. Rather, these demonstrations hopefully will serve as a foundation for explaining why patterns and pattern variations exist in terms of human cultural adaptive behavior.

Cognitive Studies

A more recently evolved orientation in historical archaeology, also based on the simultaneous observation of the spoken, written, observed, and preserved contexts of behavior, is the attempt to discover and define the mental structures and cognitive systems of people through material culture. This, as noted above, is an extension of the "science-of-material-culture" definition of archaeology. Although in a very initial stage of development, if this approach can reveal general principles governing the relationships between cognitive processes and the shaping of the material world, it could offer tremendous potentials for contributing to explanation in many fields of the social sciences.

Much of the emphasis on cognitive studies has been due to the work of Deetz (1974, 1977a) and Glassie (1969, 1975). Glassie used principles of generative grammar to explain architectural regularity. Particular cultures hold in their collective unconscious basic units and deep structures (in the Lévi-Straussian sense). These units are combined according to a set of transformations (rules) to generate all culturally acceptable forms and patterns. Glassie used folk housing as an example of this (1975), and Deetz extended the approach to ceramics, gravestones, and meals (1977a). The task of the archaeologist working from this stance is to reveal through archaeological methods such as quantification and pattern recognition these deep structures and cognitive systems.

The application of these ideas in historical archaeology has been extended to the concept of *mind set* by Glassie, Deetz, and their students. Mind set refers to a set of basic units which comprise a cognitive orientation. Such an orientation is shared by members of a group, and determines the way in which the material world is organized and shaped. It is, as yet, unclear whether the mind set is a racially, societally, culturally, or geographically specific phenomenon. Leone, in his work with Mormon material patterning, has suggested that religious affiliation carries with it a set of cognitive principles that are reflected in both sacred and secular architecture (1973, 1977a).

Deetz (1977a), in one of the principle statements regarding this orientation in historical archaeology, suggests that prior to the mid-18th century, British-American colonists in New England had an essentially *medieval* mind set. This was characterized by an organic, informal, and unstructured pattern of organizing the material world. Houses were asymmetrical and grew in response to need rather than plan. Existence was corporate and privacy was not highly valued. This was reflected, according to Deetz, in house floor plans and the material culture of foodways, which did not emphasize individual place settings or serving pieces.

This cognitive model was replaced in the mid-18th century by a new one known as the *Georgian* mind set, and characterized by an emphasis on the individual, separation of components, and tripartite symmetry. Symmetrical, Georgian-style formal houses, matched individual place settings at the table, and tripartite meat-potato-vegetable meals are suggested as examples of the manifestation of the Georgian mind set.

Two immediately apparent questions about this model are, why do the mind sets change? and how do they come to exist in the first place? In these questions, however, lies a possibility for the reconciliation of the mentalist approach taken by the proponents of the cognitive orientation and the materialist approach shared by the majority of American archaeologists. An obvious suggestion is that these cognitive structures function as part of the adaptive strategy of a group dealing with a specific set of techno-environmental circumstances. As Deetz (1977a) pointed out, as we come closer in time to the present the fit between humans and their physical environment becomes less tight, and social and ideological factors assume more obvious roles in the adaptive strategies of historic populations. Deetz, for example, noted that a distinctly American colonial cultural pattern developed in the mid-17th century in response to the isolation of communities, the separation in time and space from the Old World origins, and the use and overuse of certain resources such as wood (1977a:37–43, 107–108). With the advent of better communications systems and the more effective dissemination of ideas through books—ultimately a result of the technological innovation of the printing press—the pattern of isolation and organic growth in response to need changed to a pattern of shared ideas and planned, formal growth.

Such a change is not only historically documented, but can be seen archaeologically in the patterns of the material world. The causal relationships between that material world and the cognitive structures behind it, however, remain unclear.

Another provocative aspect of the cognitive orientation can be seen in Deetz's treatment of the Parting Ways site, a black community in New England (1977a). Material patterns at Parting Ways did not reflect the mainstream American-Georgian mind set, but was instead a separate and distinct pattern. The implication here is that different racial and social groups have different basic cognitive units and mental structures. Such a principle could be applied in contemporary society with unpredictable results. It could be interpreted to justify the separation and differential treatment of certain ethnic groups, or it could perhaps result in a heightened awareness of cultural differences and promote a spirit of understanding and compromise.

Whatever the ultimate application of such suggestions might be, the cognitive orientation in historical archaeology—made possible by access to written statements reflecting perception in the past—could offer a potential for the explanation of pattern. Shared cognitive orientations in a group, for example, might account for the different patterned refuse disposal practices of British, Spanish, and German- American colonists. It could also be offered as an explanation of why the "melting pot" concept discussed previously is an inaccurate description of the formation of American society, and why the systematic exclusion of minorities might be a more appropriate description of that process. Furthermore, this avenue of inquiry offers one of the very few possibilities in archaeology for investigating the interrelationships among the techno-environmental and ideological sectors of culture in shaping human cultural adaptations. Patterns reflecting such adaptation can be revealed and recognized through the application of scientific archaeological methods, exemplified by South's explication of quantification and pattern recognition (1977).

The programs of the 1980 and 1981 Society for Historical Archaeology meetings reflect the increasing and continuing interest in cognitive studies, with several sessions devoted to such questions, although there is some question about the assumption that "the proper emphasis of historical archaeology is the intellectual climates in which the artifacts and patterns our excavations discover once existed" (Hudgins 1980).

Conclusions

Historical archaeology today is actively contributing to a variety of problems and disciplines. From its emergence as a recognized area of research in the 1930s, the field has advanced from being essentially a set of techniques providing supplemental data for other disciplines, through being an anthropological tool for the reconstruction of past lifeways and the study of cultural process, to being a means of discovering predictable relationships between human adaptive strategies, ideology, and patterned variability in the archaeological record.

Certain aspects of historical archaeology should be particularly noted as having the potential for making contributions not possible through any other discipline. These contributions result from historical archaeology's unique ability to simultaneously observe written statements about what people said they did, what observers said people did, and what the archaeological record said people did. Inconsistencies and inaccuracies in the records of the past provided by written sources may be detected and ultimately predicted. Insights into past perceptions of human conditions provided by such written sources may be compared to the more objective archaeological record of actual conditions in the past in order to provide insight into cognitive processes. The simultaneous access to varied sources of information about the past also allows the historical archaeologist to match the archaeological patterning of a given unit against the documented social, economic, and ideological attributes of the same unit in order to arrive at a better understanding of how the archaeological record reflects human behavior.

The unique potential of historical archaeology lies not only in its ability to answer questions of archaeological and anthropological interest, but also in its ability to provide historical data not available through documentation or any other source. The adequate treatment of the disenfranchised groups in America's past, excluded from historical sources because of race, religion, isolation, or poverty, is an important function of contemporary historical archaeology and one that cannot be ignored.

It is this very quality of relevance to a wide variety of problems and disciplines that is both a unique strength and an inherent danger to historical archaeology. Simultaneous attention to historical, anthropological, archaeological, and ideological questions has caused the field to be somewhat unfocused and erratic. The increased influence of reconstruction-oriented cultural resource management programs in historical archaeology has additionally exacerbated this condition. Different historical archaeologists ask very different kinds of questions, with little exchange of ideas in many cases. In this lies the possibility that historical archaeology could become a set of techniques applicable to a wide variety of concerns, but with no primary focus of its own.

On the other hand, the best studies in the field, and many of those discussed in the preceding sections, have not been restricted to a single orientation, but rather have made significant contributions to the concerns of anthropology, history, the humanities, and cultural resource management programs, all through the combined use of documented and archaeological sources and careful research design. Historical archaeology is in a state of rapid and unpredictable change, characterized by a hybridization of goals and ideas. The resulting hybrid vigor in the field has provoked its three-decade advance from a handmaiden to history to a branch of scientific archaeology that can pursue questions beyond the scope of any other subfield of archaeology, or of history. Although Schuyler's question, "Is historical archaeology a technique or a discipline?" (1979:202) cannot be finally and conclusively answered today, contemporary advances suggest that a distinct discipline is indeed emerging.

REFERENCES

Barzun, J. and H. Graff. 1970. *The Modern Researcher.* Revised ed. New York: Harcourt.

Binford, L. 1962. Archeology as Anthropology. *American Antiquity* 28:217–225.

Braidwood, R. 1960. *Archaeologists and What They Do.* New York: Franklin Watts.

Brown, I. 1978. Early 18th Century French-Indian Culture Contact in the Yazoo Bluffs Region of the Lower Mississippi Valley. Unpublished Ph.D. dissertation, Department of Anthropology, Brown University.

Brown, M. 1974. The Use of Oral and Documentary Sources in Historical Archaeology: Ethnohistory at the Mott Farm. *Ethnohistory* 20:347–360.

Calver, W. and R. Bolton. 1950. *History Written with Pick and Shovel.* New York: New York Historical Society.

Carillo, R. 1977. Archaeological Variability—Socio-cultural Variability. In *Research Strategies in Historical Archaeology*, S. South (ed.), pp. 73–90. New York: Academic Press.

Cheek, A. 1974. The Evidence for Acculturation in Artifacts: Indians and Non-Indians at San Xavier del Bac, Arizona. Unpublished Ph.D. dissertation, Department of Anthropology, University of Arizona.

Clark, G. 1954. *The Study of Prehistory.* New York: Cambridge University Press.

Cleland, C. and J. Fitting. 1968. The Crisis in Identity: Theory in Historic Sites Archeology. *Conference on Historic Sites Archeology Papers* 2(2):124–138.

Cotter, J. L. (ed.). 1958. Symposium on the Role of Archaeology in Historical Research. Washington, DC: National Park Service.

Cumbaa, S. 1975. Patterns of Resource Use and Cross-cultural Dietary Change in the Spanish Colonial Period. Unpublished Ph.D. dissertation, Department of Anthropology, University of Florida.

Daniel, G. 1967. *The Origins and Growth of Archaeology.* Baltimore: Penguin.

Deagan, K. 1974. Sex, Status, and Role in the Mestizaje of Spanish Colonial Florida. Unpublished Ph.D. dissertation, Department of Anthropology, University of Florida.

Deagan, K. 1978. The Archaeological Investigation of First Spanish Period St. Augustine. *El Escribano* 14:1–351.

Deagan, K. 1979. Self-awareness and Coming of Age in Historical Archaeology: Review of Schuyler's *Historical Archaeology: A Guide to Substantive and Theoretical Contributions. Reviews in Anthropology* 6(3):365–372.

Deagan, K. 1980. Spanish St. Augustine: America's First "Melting Pot." *Archaeology* 33(5):22–30.

Deetz, J. 1963. Archaeological Investigations at La Purisima Mission. *Annual Report of the Archeological Survey of the University of California Los Angeles*, pp. 165–209.

Deetz, J. 1965. The Dynamics of Stylistic Change in Arikara Ceramics. *Illinois Studies in Anthropology* No. 4. Urbana: University of Illinois Press.

Deetz, J. 1968. Late Man in North America: Archaeology of European-Americans. In *Anthropological Archaeology in the Americas*, B. Meggers (ed.), pp. 121–130. Washington, DC: Anthropological Society of Washington.

Deetz, J. 1970. Archaeology as a Social Science. In *Current Directions in Anthropology. American Anthropological Association Bulletin* 3(2):115–125.

Deetz, J. 1974. A Cognitive Model for American Culture: 1620–1835. In *Reconstructing Complex Societies*, C. Moore (ed.), pp. 21–29. Chicago: American School of Oriental Research.

Deetz, J. 1977a. *In Small Things Forgotten.* Garden City, NY: Anchor Books.

Deetz, J. 1977b. Material Culture and Archaeology—What's the Difference? In *Historical Archaeology and the Importance of Material Things*, L. Ferguson (ed.) *Society for Historical Archaeology Special Publication* No. 2.

Deetz, J. 1981. Resurrecting the Mining Community of Somerville: Mapping as a Research Strategy. Paper presented at the Society for Historical Archaeology Conference, New Orleans.

Deetz, J. and E. Dethlefson. 1967. Death's Head, Cherub, Urn and Willow. *Natural History* 76(3):29–37.

Dollar, C. 1968. Some Thoughts on Method and Theory in Historical Archaeology. *Conference on Historic Sites Archaeology Papers* 2(2):3–30.

Fairbanks, C. 1956. The Excavation of the Hawkins-Davison Houses. *Georgia Historical Quarterly* 40:213–229.

Fairbanks, C. 1962. Excavations at Horseshoe Bend, Alabama. *Florida Anthropologist* 15(2):41–56.

Fairbanks, C. 1972. The Kingsley Slave Cabins in Duval County, Florida, 1968. *Conference on Historic Sites Archaeology Papers* 7:62–93.

Fairbanks, C. 1977. Backyard Archaeology as a Research Strategy. *Conference on Historic Sites Archaeology Papers* 11:133–139.

Ferguson, L. (ed.). 1977. Historical Archaeology and the Importance of Material Things. *Society for Historical Archaeology Special Publication* No. 2.

Ferguson, L. 1977b. An Archaeological-Historical Analysis of Fort Watson: December 1780–April 1981. In *Research Strategies in Historical Archeology*, S. South (ed.), pp. 41–72. New York: Academic Press.

Flannery, K. 1973. Archeology with a Capital S. In *Research and Theory in Current Archeology*. C. Redman (ed.), pp. 47–53. New York: Wiley.

Fontana, B. 1965. On the Meaning of Historic Sites Archaeology. *American Antiquity* 31:61–65. Reprinted in *Historical Archaeology: A Guide to Substantive and Theoretical Contributions* (1979), R. Schuyler (ed.), pp. 23–26. Farmingdale, NY: Baywood.

Glassie, H. 1969. Pattern in the Material Folk Culture of the Eastern United States. *Folklore and Folklife*, 1. Philadelphia: University of Pennsylvania Press.

Glassie, H. 1975. *Folk Housing in Middle Virginia: A Structural Analysis of Historical Artifacts*. Knoxville: University of Tennessee Press.

Goodyear, A. C. 1977. The Historical and Ecological Position of Protohistoric Sites in the Slate Mountains, South Central Arizona. In *Research Strategies in Historical Archaeology*, S. South (ed.), pp. 203–240. New York: Academic Press.

Griffin, J. W. 1958. End Products of Historic Sites Archeology. In *Symposium on the Role of Archaeology in Historical Research*, J. Cotter (ed.), pp. 1–6. Reprinted in *Historical Archaeology: A Guide to Substantive and Theoretical Contributions* (1979), R. Schuyler (ed.), pp. 20–22. Farmingdale, NY: Baywood.

Hall, R. 1981. Varieties of Black Religious Experience in Florida, 1565–1906. Unpublished Ph.D. dissertation, Department of History, Florida State University.

Handler, J. and F. Lange, 1978. *Plantation Slavery in Barbados: An Archaeological and Historical Investigation*. Cambridge: Harvard University Press.

Harrington, J. C. 1952. Historic Sites Archeology in the United States. In *Archeology of Eastern North America*, J. B. Griffin (ed.), pp. 295–315. Chicago: University of Chicago Press.

Harrington, J. C. 1955. Archaeology as an Auxiliary Science to American History. *American Anthropologist* 57:1121–1130.

Harrington, J. C. 1957. *New Light on Washington's Fort Necessity*. Richmond: Eastern National Park and Monument Association. Reprinted in *Historical Archaeology: A Guide to Substantive and Theoretical Contributions* (1979), R. Schuyler (ed.), pp. 91–138. Farmingdale, NY: Baywood.

Hawkes, C. 1951. British Prehistory Half-way Through the Century. *Proceedings of the Prehistoric Society* 17:1–9.

Honerkamp, N. 1980. Frontier Process in Eighteenth-Century Colonial Georgia: An Archeological Approach. Unpublished Ph.D. dissertation, Department of Anthropology, University of Florida. Ann Arbor, MI: University Microfilms.

House, J. 1977. Survey Data and Regional Models in Historical Archeology. In *Research Strategies in Historical Archaeology*, S. South (ed.), pp. 214–260. New York: Academic Press.

Hudgins, C. 1980. Every Man's House and Home: Archaeological Perspectives on the Mental Life of Earlier Generations (abstract). Symposium presented at the Society for Historical Archaeology meetings, Albuquerque.

Irwin-Mason, C. 1963. Eighteenth Century Culture Change Among the Lower Creeks. *Florida Anthropologist* 16(3):65–80.

Kelley, A. R. 1939. The Macon Trading Post, An Historical Foundling. *American Antiquity* 4(4):328–333.

Kirkpatrick, D. et al. 1980. Studies of Navajo Culture from Northwestern New Mexico. Symposium presented at the annual meeting of the Society for Historical Archaeology, Albuquerque.

Klein, J. 1977. 20th Century Archeological Sites: Are They Eligible for the National Register? Paper presented at the annual meeting of the Society for Historical Archaeology, Ottawa.

Koch, J. 1980. Mortuary Behavior Patterning in Colonial St. Augustine. Unpublished M.A. thesis, Department of Anthropology, Florida State University.

Kroeber, A. 1919. On the Order of Change in Civilization as Exemplified by Changes in Fashion. *American Anthropologist* 21:235–263.

Leone, M. 1973. Archaeology as the Science of Technology: Mormon Town Plans and Fences. In *Research and Theory in Current Archaeology*, C. Redman (ed.), pp. 125–150. New York: Wiley.

Leone, M. 1977a. The New Mormon Temple in Washington, D.C. In *Historical Archaeology and the Importance of Material Things*, L. Ferguson (ed.), pp. 43–61. *Society for Historical Archaeology Special Publication* No. 2.

Leone, M. 1977b. Foreword. In *Research Strategies in Historical Archaeology*, S. South (ed.), pp. xvii–xxi. New York: Academic Press, New York.

Lewis, K. 1977. Sampling the Archaeological Frontier: Regional Models and Component Analysis. In *Research Strategies in Historical Archaeology*, S. South (ed.), pp. 151–202. New York: Academic Press.

Lombard, P. 1953. *The Aptucxet Trading Post.* Bourne, MA: Bourne Historical Society.

Loucks, L. J. 1979. Political and Economic Interactions Between Spaniards and Indians: Archaeological and Ethnohistorical Perspectives of the Mission System in Florida. Unpublished Ph.D. dissertation, Department of Anthropology, University of Florida.

Mainfort, R. C. 1979. Indian Social Dynamics in the Period of European Contact. *Publications of the Museum, Michigan State University* 1(4):269–418.

Manucy, A. 1978. Toward Recreation of 16th century St. Augustine. *El Escribano* 14:1–5.

Montgomery, R., W. Smith, and J. Brew. 1949. Franciscan Awatovi. *Papers of the Peabody Museum, Harvard University* 36.

Mudar, K. 1978. The Effects of Socio-Cultural Variables on Food Preferences in 19th century Detroit. *Conference on Historic Sites Archaeology Papers* 12:323–391.

Noël Hume, I. 1964. Archaeology: Handmaiden to History. *The North Carolina Historical Review* 41(2):215–225.

Noël Hume, I. 1969. *Historical Archaeology.* New York: Knopf.

Otto, J. S. 1975. Status Differences and the Archeological Record: A Comparison of Planter, Overseer and Slave Sites from Cannon's Point Plantation (1794–1861), St. Simon's Island, Georgia. Unpublished Ph.D. dissertation, Department of Anthropology, University of Florida.

Otto, J. S. 1977. Artifacts and Status Differences—A Comparison of Ceramics from Planter, Overseer, and Slave Sites on an Antebellum Plantation. In *Research*

Strategies in Historical Archaeology, S. South (ed.), pp. 91–118. New York: Academic Press.

Otto, J. S. 1979. A New Look at Slave Life. *Natural History* 88(1):8–30.

Poe, C. 1979. The Manifestation of Status in 18th Century Criollo Culture in Colonial St. Augustine. Paper presented at the annual meeting of the Society for Historical Archaeology, Nashville.

Price, C. and J. Price. 1978. Investigation of Settlement and Subsistence Systems in the Ozark Border Region of Southeast Missouri During the First Half of the Nineteenth Century. Paper presented at the annual meeting of the Society for Historical Archaeology, San Antonio.

Rathje, W. 1977. In Praise of Archaeology: Le Projet du Garbage. In *Historical Archaeology and the Importance of Material Things*, L. Ferguson (ed.), pp. 36–42. *Society for Historical Archaeology Special Publications* No. 2.

Rathje, W. and M. McCarthy. 1977. Regularity and Variability in Contemporary Garbage. In *Research Strategies in Historical Archaeology*, S. South (ed.), pp. 261–286. New York: Academic Press.

Reitz, E. 1979. Spanish and British Subsistence Strategies at St. Augustine, Florida and Frederica, Georgia, between 1563 and 1783. Unpublished Ph.D. dissertation, Department of Anthropology, University of Florida.

Rowe, J. H. 1965. The Renaissance Foundations of Anthropology. *American Anthropologist* 67(1):1–20.

Schiffer, M. 1976. *Behavioral Archaeology*. New York: Academic Press.

Schiffer, M. 1977. Toward a Unified Science of the Cultural Past. In *Research Strategies in Historical Archeology*, S. South (ed.), pp. 13–40. New York: Academic Press.

Schiffer, M. and G. Gumerman (eds.). 1977. *Conservation Archaeology*. New York: Academic Press.

Schuyler, R. 1970. Historical and Historic Sites Archaeology as Anthropology: Basic Definitions and Relationships. *Historical Archaeology* 4:83–89.

Schuyler, R. 1976. Images of America: The Contribution of Historical Archaeology to National Identity. *Southwestern Lore* 42(4):27–39.

Schuyler, R. 1977. The Spoken Word, the Written Word, Observed Behavior and Preserved Behavior: The Contexts Available to the Archaeologist. *Conference on Historic Sites Archaeology Papers* 10(2):99–120.

Schuyler, R. (ed.). 1979. *Historical Archaeology: A Guide to Substantive and Theoretical Contributions*. Farmingdale, NY: Baywood.

Schuyler, R. (ed.). 1980. *Archaeological Perspectives on Ethnicity in America*. Farmingdale, NY: Baywood.

Shephard, S. 1975. The Geronimo de Hita y Salazar Site: A Study of Criollo Culture in Colonial St. Augustine. Unpublished M.A. thesis, Department of Anthropology, Florida State University.

Singleton, T. 1980. The Archaeology of Afro-American Slavery in Coastal Georgia: A Regional Perception of Slave Households and Community Patterns. Unpublished Ph.D. dissertation, Department of Anthropology, University of Florida.

Smith, G. H. 1939. Excavating the Site of Old Fort Ridgely. *Minnesota History: A Quarterly Magazine* 20(2):146–155.

Smith, H. C. 1948. Two Historical Archeological Periods in Florida. *American Antiquity* 13(4):313–319.

South, S. 1972. Evolution and Horizon as Revealed in Ceramic Analysis in Historical Archaeology. *Conference on Historic Sites Archaeology Papers* 6:71–116.

South, S. 1977. *Method and Theory in Historical Archaeology*. New York: Academic Press.

Stephenson, R. 1977. A Strategy for Getting the Job Done. In *Research Strategies in Historical Archaeology*, S. South (ed.), pp. 307–321. New York: Academic Press.

Swannack, J. 1975. Mission-Oriented Agencies: Means and Ends of Historic Sites Archaeology. *Historical Archaeology* 9:80–81.

Walker, I. 1967. Historical Archaeology—Methods and Principles. *Historical Archaeology* 1:23–34.

Webster, D. 1974. On the Digging of Potteries. *Antiques* 430–433.

Willey, G. and J. Sabloff. 1974. *A History of American Archaeology*. San Francisco: Freeman.

Young, A. 1841. Chronicles of the Pilgrim Fathers. Boston: A Young.

Chapter Two

People with History:
An Update on Historical Archaeology in the United States

Introduction

In the same year in which Kathleen Deagan's (1982) article "Avenues of Inquiry in Historical Archaeology" was published in *Advances in Archaeological Method and Theory*, Eric Wolf's (1982) *Europe and the People Without History* appeared. Wolf focused anthropologists' attention on a number of issues simultaneously: the modern world system, capitalism, history, and the variable political uses of "history." Historical archaeology concerns both people "with history," those who commonly have written stories about the past, and people "without history," those who often have been excluded from those stories. A focus on people with history highlights Europeans' history in relation to that of other peoples', creating an archaeology of the Age of Discovery, colonization, and the development of the modern world system. A focus on people without history considers those issues from another viewpoint and not only is crucial to building a fuller European-American archaeology, but also has the desirable consequence of adding many more voices to our perception of the past. Historical archaeology often has concentrated on people with history but has made serious efforts to restore some of the diversity of the past to our versions of it. This goal is furthered by the discipline's recent grappling with concepts such as capitalism, ideology, inequality, power, and heterogeneity and by paying serious attention to interpreting the meanings and uses of material culture.

This essay discusses some of the trends and themes that have become important or promising in historical archaeology since Deagan's article of over a decade ago.

This article was originally published in the *Journal of Archaeological Method and Theory* (1994) 1(1): 5–40.

Many of the issues that dominated the field in 1982 remain. The rapid theoretical development that characterized the discipline from 1960 to 1980 continues, in conjunction with developments in archaeology and in anthropology as a whole. One set of issues that remains important is the professional, institutional, and intellectual relations between historical and prehistoric archaeology and between historical archaeology and sociocultural anthropology. Historical archaeology may still be characterized as additive. Early goals such as recovering details of historic architecture continue; newer goals such as the elucidation of power and ideology appear and are engaged. Historical archaeology is beginning to assess more effectively and more critically analytic categories such as gender and race. The following section in this essay takes stock of trends in the discipline over the last decade and considers currently recognized issues and problems. The next section discusses capitalism as one theme with the potential to unify research, and the final section, through an example, offers some threads that are integral to the interpretation of material culture if the broad context of capitalism and related issues are to be addressed successfully.

Assessment

The contributions of historical archaeology that Deagan (1982) summarized from the literature include historical supplementation, reconstructions of past lifeways, processual studies, cognitive studies, and contributions to archaeological science. These contributions all continue and it is worth summarizing some of the questions that are being addressed. Deagan's second, third, and fourth categories are subsumed here under the heading of historical ethnography.

Historical Supplementation—Historical Challenge

Archaeology still functions as historical supplementation, in the large sense that prehistory might be considered "the best we can do" given the lack of written records and in the more restricted sense of filling in the gaps in documented societies. There is no question that this function continues to be important. But archaeologists need not be content with providing details or "facts" that documentary historians may or may not find useful. Archaeology is not "handmaiden to history," as Ivor Noël Hume (1964) insisted 30 years ago, but is colleague to history.

While much historical archaeology continues to be restricted by the specific needs of cultural resource management (CRM) and by the demands of architectural reconstruction, innovative and important research continues to be done under these conditions. One illustration among many examples comes from work done at the

Hermitage, Andrew Jackson's estate in Tennessee (e.g., Smith 1976). During a routine investigation, archaeologists uncovered architectural details that necessitated a revised understanding of the sequence of building at the site (McKee et al. 1992). It may not seem anthropologically significant that the present kitchen was separated from the main house a few years later than originally thought, or that other remodeling was carried out, until one considers the broader context and the meanings attached to the built environment. In this particular case previously unasked questions were raised about the implications of occupants' physical proximity and tensions within a household made up of white owners living in the main house and black slaves living in the kitchen. The apparent attempts to decrease social and personal tensions through physical separation raise further questions about the efficacy of architectural solutions to social problems.

In addition to suggesting further avenues of inquiry into social relations, the reinterpretation prompted by the archaeology also encourages an examination of by whom and for whom the history of a house and its occupants is structured. As it is told at the Hermitage, the story of Andrew Jackson and even his house implicitly denies contradictions or unsolved conflicts (McKee et al. 1992), a situation that seems extraordinary given Jackson's career, but that is similar to other "great man" exhibits. Decisions about what parts of history are told, embellished, excluded, or glossed over are current choices. Historical archaeologists have some input and responsibility for those choices.

The supplementation function of historical archaeology must be explicitly expanded to address the writing of histories and often may correct history derived from documents. I do not mean to resurrect the idea that archaeology is objective while history is subjective. Instead I mean to emphasize that archaeology may provide alternative questions and interpretations. Part of historical supplementation, then, includes creating ways of writing about the past that do not rely on historical documents or documentary historians as final arbiters of meaningful or accurate history. For example, McDonald et al. (1991) describe an archaeological project commissioned by the Northern Cheyenne to document escape routes taken during the outbreak from Fort Robinson, Nebraska, in 1879. Archaeological results successfully challenged official Army-based accounts of the escape by providing data that bolstered Cheyenne oral tradition. Oral history and archaeology thus may be mutually supportive in providing data and perspectives that contribute to a more accurate history in which biases and the politics of knowledge are acknowledged.

Supplementing history by filling in gaps calls attention to those gaps and to an appreciation of their importance. Historical archaeology is in a position to create analytic links among written, oral, and material forms of expressions as it continues intertwining history and anthropology. The function of supplementation, then, is more usefully thought of as historical challenge. History thus supplemented is history reconceptualized.

Historical Ethnography

Everyday life, cognition, and cultural process all must be considered in constructing historical ethnography. The trend of pursuing cognitive studies of the sort exemplified by Deetz (1977) and Glassie (1975) was taking firm hold by the time Deagan (1982) wrote that this orientation could be a way to reconcile mentalist and materialist perspectives. This pursuit is indeed an extension of the "science of material culture" definition of archaeology and requires that material-culture interpretations be more adequately theorized. The expressed aim in "cognitive studies" is cultural rather than behavioral reconstruction or functional interpretation. It is open to debate whether a focus on structuralist interpretation could be accurately termed a cognitive approach, since critiques of Lévi-Strauss structuralism point out its inherent emphasis on ahistoricity and meaninglessness. Diamond (1974:303), for example, writes, "There is, obviously, an inconsistency in the presumably highly symbolic categories of structuralism and the reduction inherent in its explanatory principle." Nevertheless, investigations of "worldview," however framed, serve both to direct archaeological attention to culture and to provide some insight into ideology, broadly defined. Struggles to understand links between worldview and material culture have furthered immeasurably the potential for historical archaeologists to perform historical ethnography. Deetz (1988a) makes this point by suggesting that the term archaeography more accurately describes the work that archaeologists do that is parallel to ethnography.

The separate categories of lifeway studies and cognitive or cultural studies reflected real trends in the discipline 15 years ago, but it no longer makes sense to attempt one without the other. Nor does it make sense to separate the goals of historical archaeology from those of anthropology as a whole. As historical archaeology was being defined professionally, Schuyler (1970) commented on its potential as a laboratory for anthropology, particularly concerning processes such as colonization and acculturation. Potential for consideration of such processes continues to expand in the discipline. The idea of colonization, for example, may be dissected into dynamically related packages of power, domination, hegemonic negotiation, and resistance on many levels. Acculturation, discussed in the case study below, is more usefully investigated as complicated economic and symbolic mediations between ethnocide and ethnogenesis. The reconstruction of past cultures and lifeways, or historical ethnography, and the description of processes such as acculturation, frontier adaptation, imperialism, and capitalism continue to contribute to the histories of disenfranchised people as well as to those of the privileged.

Historical archaeologists categorize their research in several different, overlapping ways. For example, I may simultaneously describe my work as focused primarily on the 18th century, the eastern United States, urban contexts, capitalism, ideology, and a feminist approach. I could offer an assessment of current work organized chronologically, geographically, thematically, philosophically, or technically. Both the geographic and the analytic scales at which historical archaeologists work vary considerably. Scholars have argued for fruitful scales of analysis from the global world system (e.g., Falk 1991), to community (e.g., Schuyler 1988), to household (e.g., Beaudry 1984). Such variety may be interpreted as hopeless fragmentation or, optimistically, as healthy diversity that may be directed by suggesting some guiding themes.

Since 1982 significant work by many scholars has contributed to topical and regional interests in the United States. The following citations are not exhaustive. For the sake of brevity, I cite mostly monographs and collections rather than articles and individual chapters and include few references to CRM reports. My purpose is to underscore both the enormous amount of work in the past dozen years and the topics that have been investigated as historical archaeology has grown and matured as a discipline. Research within the context of colonization and capitalist expansion includes contact among European, African, Asian, and indigenous peoples; the development of superordinate and subordinate cultures, including the establishment of plantation economy, cities, and industry; interethnic and interracial conflicts and cooperation; changing gender roles, relations, and ideologies; and myriad related topics.

The unique perspective of historical archaeology provides the organizing theme for several edited volumes of varying geographic, temporal, and thematic coverage (Beaudry 1988; Cotter 1984; Falk 1991; Little 1992b; Neuman 1983; Ward 1983; Yentsch 1987). Urban archaeology has received specific attention (Dickens 1982; Schuyler 1982; Staski 1987). Both Leone and Potter (1988a) and Yentsch and Beaudry (1992) have edited collections devoted to symbolic analysis and meaning. These themes also are considered by Shackel (1993a) in his analysis of the creation of modern personal discipline.

Inequality is a condition of the ethnographic settings studied by most historical archaeologists and it serves as the topic for McGuire and Paynter's (1991) volume. Related to inequality are race, ethnicity, class, gender, and other social and economic factors important in historical ethnography. Gender, in particular, is a rapidly growing research focus (Seifert 1991; Walde and Willows 1991). Several authors have recently discussed the treatment of ethnicity (Leone et al. 1994; McGuire 1982; Staski 1990). It is difficult to sort out race and ethnicity because the nature of group boundaries shifts within cultural contexts. Anglo, Spanish, African, and Native Americans have received a great deal of attention. Extensive archaeological and historical research has been performed in the Spanish borderlands from California to Florida (e.g., Farnsworth and Williams 1992; Thomas 1989, 1990, 1991). For example, the city of St. Augustine (e.g., Deagan 1983; Reitz and Scarry 1985) and California's missions (e.g., Farnsworth 1989; Hoover and Costello 1985) are subjects of numerous studies. Racially and ethnically defined Asians are also researched (Costello and Maniery 1988; Wegars 1993).

Archaeology of African-Americans often has focused on plantation slavery but has expanded to consider the changing roles and situations of black Americans as slave and free, rural and urban. Plantation studies have undertaken to provide accounts of single plantations (e.g., Kelso 1984; Otto 1984), experiment with South's pattern-recognition technique (Singleton 1985), illuminate material expressions such as colono ware (Ferguson 1992), and critique the archaeological treatment of slavery (Orser 1990a). Postbellum tenant plantations and southern farms and the varying situations of free blacks have also been studied (Geismar 1982; Orser 1988a, 1990b; Singleton 1994).

The effects of colonization on native peoples (as well as on settlers) is an important area of overlap for prehistorians and historical archaeologists. Extensive work has been done on Native American depopulation and demography (Dobyns 1983; Ramenofsky 1987; Smith 1987; Verano and Ubelaker 1992). European explorations, processes of colonization, and postcontact change form essential frameworks for the interpretation of sites and regions (Dyson 1985; Ewen 1991; Fitzhugh 1985; Fitzhugh and Olin 1993; McGhee 1984; Rogers and Wilson 1993). Some of the research involving contact between Europeans and indigenous people has been carried out in the Southeast (Blakely 1988; Keegan 1992; Potter 1993; Wood et al. 1989), in the Northeast (Faulkner and Faulkner 1987), and in the midcontinent (Gums 1988; Walthall 1990; Walthall and Emerson 1992). Rogers (1990) concentrates on culture change among the Arikara. Trigger (1985) reexamines standard accounts and myths of the settlement of Canada by Europeans, crediting Native Americans with a creative role in shaping that country.

The variety of other topics explored is quite broad. The frontier (Lewis 1984) and changing core-periphery relations (Paynter 1982) are significant issues. Westward movement and extracting wealth from the land are integral to topics such as the California gold rush (Pastron and Hattori 1990) and silver mining in Nevada (Hardesty 1988). Focusing on consumer choice in the marketplace, Spencer-Wood (1987) collects research that extends Miller's technique of economic scaling to examine issues of socioeconomic status and its archaeological interpretation. Landscape has received increasing attention in many disciplines and has proved fruitful for historical archaeology (Kelso and Most 1990). The American Civil War, which has always received a good deal of attention from historians, presents a challenge to archaeologists (Geier and Winter 1994). Other military research includes that on the Battle of Little Bighorn (Scott and Fox 1987; Scott et al. 1989).

Some other region-specific works include that on the Carolinas (Wilson 1985), the Chesapeake (Shackel and Little 1994), Long Island (Stone and Ottusch-Kianka 1987), and Rockbridge County, Virginia (McDaniel and Russ 1984). Locally focused work includes that on St. Mary's City in Maryland (Miller 1986), Martins Hundred in Virginia (Noël Hume 1983), Philadelphia (Cotter et al. 1992), 18th-century New York City (Rothschild 1990), and 19th-century Monterey, California (Felton and Schulz 1983).

Although admittedly underrepresented in the last few paragraphs, the breadth of the historical ethnography produced in historical archaeology, along with the volume of literature, continues to grow dramatically.

Testing Ground for Prehistoric Principles

The use of historical archaeology as a laboratory for more general archaeological science to be perfected through ethnoarchaeology and a "science of material culture" has been widely noted (e.g., Deagan 1982; Schuyler 1970). A similar contribution is made by modern material culture studies (e.g., Gould and Schiffer 1981; Rathje 1979). Such work includes tests of seriation, refuse patterning as a mirror of ethnicity, status indicators, and the observation of formation processes. Many historical archaeologists remain explicit about their hope to develop methods that will further the aims of prehistory and contribute to cross-cultural research, particularly among complex societies (e.g., McGuire and Paynter 1991; Mrozowski 1988; Paynter 1982, 1985; South 1988a, 1988b; Stevenson 1982). Paynter (1985), for example, sets up a model of frontier-homeland relations that is meant to be widely applicable to stratified societies. In considering the local environment, primary producers, regional elites, and core elites, Paynter creates a political-economic approach that explicitly rejects a diffusionist model and instead focuses on the production and distribution of surplus. One important insight to studies of phenomena such as frontiers, colonialism, and acculturation is that contact tends to create differences and conflict rather than a melting pot of uniformity. This insight of heterogeneity is broadly applicable to the internal as well as external affairs of states (see Brumfiel 1992).

Many historical archaeologists use evolutionary and ecological frameworks for explanation. In describing the industrial frontier of 19th-century America by analogy to an ecosystem, Hardesty (1985) describes niche structures. He advocates the use of scientific evolutionary theory in historical archaeology but he also writes that "it is clear that we presently lack a set of explanatory principles capable of dealing with the *creative* behavior of organisms [people] toward their environment, such as the 'imported' environment of industrial societies" (Hardesty 1985:226).

There is both an advantage and a disadvantage to such an approach. Using the same language, models, and research questions that prehistorians employ encourages historical archaeology to fit itself into a temporal continuum and offer itself as a laboratory for prehistoric models and concepts. However, instead of truly acting as a laboratory, historical archaeology often offers itself only as a confirmation of models already created and applied to other data. The function of historical archaeology as "handmaiden to prehistory" is an essential contribution of historical archaeology, yet it is a mistake to dismiss goals that may not necessarily advance more general method. Imagine the poverty of our field if ethnologists were unconcerned with the abstract expressions of cognition, myth, intention, and culture because such information could not be sought through prehistoric data.

New Crisis and Questions of Method

In 1982 archaeology as a whole was beginning a new period of critical self-examination and, some would say, reactionary entrenchment. In this year were published Hodder's *Symbolic and Structural Archaeology* (1982a) and *Symbols in Action* (1982b) and Leone's (1982) "Some Opinions on Recovering Mind." Since then numerous debates have taken place about the pros and cons of processual and "postprocessual" archaeology (e.g., Earle and Preucel 1987; Gibbon 1989; Hodder 1985, 1986, 1991; Leone et al. 1987; Miller and Tilley 1984; Patterson 1990a, 1990b; Preucel 1991; Schiffer 1988; Shanks and Tilley 1987; Watson 1990; Watson and Fotiadis 1990). Historical archaeology has gone through its own periods of growth and change, and it has been no less affected by the turmoil of the 1980s and early 1990s than has prehistory. In fact, its practitioners have often been the most successful proponents of an approach that seeks to uncover intention, social relations, and ideology along with economy, function, and structure. Watson and Fotiadis (1990:615) note that "it has not escaped the notice of processualists, and others who are not persuaded by the symbolic-structuralist postprocessualists, that virtually all of their published work so far has been within or has relied heavily upon ethnographic and historical data (e.g., Leone and Potter 1988)." It is obvious that the kinds of goals espoused by postprocessualism—concerns with meanings, symbols, cognition, power, and historical context—are much more completely and convincingly achieved within historical archaeology. Hodder (1986:141) writes, "It is partly for this reason [need for great deal of contextual data] that historical archaeology is an 'easier' approach . . . the richer data allow more similarities and differences to be sought along more relevant dimensions of variation."

Of course, historical archaeologists laughingly dismiss such observations on the "ease" of their work. They are instead all too aware of the numerous difficulties in maneuvering through both documents and other material culture and in accommodating cross-cultural concepts and historically particular situations while recognizing the complexities and dynamism of their data and their models. The creation of appropriate method is still under way and is a constant focus of discussion in the discipline.

In 1987 the plenary session at the annual Society for Historical Archaeology meetings focused on "Questions that Count in Historical Archaeology." The opinions expressed at that meeting emphasize the need for conscious attention to method and the need for connecting method and theory. The critiques that were leveled at the discipline by its practitioners identify long-standing problems. Promises of the vast yet imperfectly realized potential of historical archaeology were also reiterated. The plenary session papers appeared in the journal the following year (see *Historical Archaeology* 22 [1]).

In that forum, Honerkamp (1988) characterizes historical-archaeological research as routinized and atheoretical. Some of the plenary participants seek solutions in traditional anthropological concerns. For example, the use of energy theory as an organizing concept to describe and categorize societies is advised by South (1988b). Mrozowski (1988) emphasizes that a cross-cultural perspective may provide the sense of purpose that the discipline lacks.

It is not, however, difficult to find questions that count concerning the modern world after A.D. 1500; what is difficult is finding a unique way of addressing them (Deagan 1988). Methodology is seen as the primary stumbling block. Two levels of method may be distinguished: the procedural or technical, which often is dwelt upon; and the method informed by theory that structures research, of which there is a dearth and for which there is a desperate need (Cleland 1988). One major methodological issue is one of using both the archaeological and the documentary records effectively (Beaudry 1988; Leone 1988; Little 1992a; Schuyler 1988).

There are at least five approaches used in the discipline to combine text and material culture. These strategies consider the two data sources as contradictory, complementary, sources for hypotheses, ripe for debunking, and needed for context (Little 1992b). In the first case, documents and archaeological data may be played off against one another. Looking for anomalies in databases is inspired by the ethnoarchaeological approach of "middle range theory" (e.g., Binford 1977, 1981; Schiffer 1976) adapted for historical contexts (e.g., Leone 1988; Potter 1992). The data sources in the second approach may be used to complement each other and fill in where each lacks detail or trustworthiness. In the third case, either data set, commonly the documentary, may give rise to hypotheses, which are then tested against the other data set, usually the archaeological. In the fourth approach, either data set may be used to debunk some version of the past provided by the other. Archaeologists have been more concerned with debunking historical myths than vice versa, a situation that may well change as historians begin to pay more attention to the results of archaeology. Finally, either database, but usually the documentary one, may be used as a source of context that provides the basis for interpretation. In each of these approaches material culture must be accorded full status as a primary database.

There is no question that methods developed specifically for historical archaeology have helped both to describe data and to establish research problems within the discipline. Two particularly widely used methods are pattern recognition of functionally defined artifact categories, created by South (1977a, 1977b, 1988b), and the economic-scaling index created for English ceramic vessels by Miller (1980, 1991). Each of these approaches provides ways of coherently organizing and comparing data. Critiques of the methods help to refine the questions we ask and better theorize the meaning and relevance of both the categories and the comparisons. Orser (1989) critiques South's pattern-recognition technique, which is widely applied. Yentsch (1991a, 1991b) critiques the widespread focus on measures of economic scaling inspired by Miller's index and the analytical limitations of South's categories. She sees each method as promoting certain questions at the expense of those with more potential to inform on gender and the material correlates of gender relations. The careful documentation of prices for consumer goods and the comparison of relative original costs of assemblages have encouraged the description of consumer choices (Spencer-Wood 1987) and should continue to spark critical analysis of the meaning and expression of social status, consumption, and developing economic practices.

While it is generally recognized that methodology—in structuring research, in connecting theory to data, and in effectively using both documentary and archaeological information—is in need of attention, there is little agreement over how method is to be improved or applied to broader questions. And the questions themselves are not altogether obvious. Should archaeologists rely on social historians and cultural anthropologists to define the questions that count? Are questions that count those of race, class, and gender? Of current political and sociological import? Of traditional anthropological concern? Of historical detail? The obvious answer, that all of these count, forces us again to emphasize appropriate methods for addressing these questions.

Deagan (1982:171) notes particular potentials of the field owing to the nature of the databases available:

It is this very quality of relevance to a wide variety of problems and disciplines that is both a unique strength and an inherent danger to historical archaeology. Simultaneous attention to historical, anthropological, archaeological, and ideological questions has caused the field to be somewhat unfocused and erratic. The increased influence of reconstruction-oriented cultural resource management programs in historical archaeology has additionally exacerbated this condition. Different historical archaeologists ask very different kinds of questions, with little exchange of ideas in many cases. In this lies the possibility that historical archaeology could become a set of techniques applicable to a wide variety of concerns, but with no primary focus of its own.

Several archaeologists have suggested that capitalism be considered the proper primary focus of the discipline (Leone 1977; Leone and Potter 1988b; Orser 1988b; Paynter 1988). Orser (1988b) advises that this focus solves the long-standing problem of an atheoretical and eclectic stance in the discipline. A focus on capitalism, on the development of the current dominant ideology of the modern Western world, is important. There are weaknesses though, not the least of which is a Western/European-centered viewpoint that may serve to omit from "historical archaeology" cross-culturally relevant work incorporating written documentation such as that on Old World precapitalist states (e.g., Boone et al. 1990; Redman 1986); political maneuvering between Native American groups (e.g., Hantman 1990); medieval Europe (e.g., Young 1992); or African cultures documented through oral history (e.g., Schmidt 1977).

It remains a reality in the field, however, that historical archaeology is defined as "the archaeology of the spread of European culture throughout the world since the fifteenth century and its impact on indigenous peoples" (Deetz 1977:5). I want to echo the protest that others (Posnansky and Decorse 1986) have made of the one-sidedness of such a definition. The European emphasis in it comes from the history parentage of historical archaeology. The anthropology parent provides an emphasis on the "other." Historical archaeology need not shortchange either outlook but may examine the dynamic interplay between and within worlds with and without history. In the United States such an historical archaeology is nearly always centered on time periods and people embedded in or buffeted by the complex context of capitalism.

An Archaeology of Capitalism?

Leone and Potter (1988b:19) write,

> Whether or not historical archaeology is to be an archaeology of the emergence and development of capitalism has been settled in the affirmative. There has never been a choice even for those who were indifferent or hostile to the issue. . . . In other words, we can either know our social context, which is the context of advanced industrial capitalism, or be prisoners of it.

There are two issues: the archaeology of capitalist context as that context has emerged and developed and the social context of archaeology itself within a capitalist culture. Leone and Potter (1988b) identify two concepts that need to be incorporated into our work: ideology—both in historical development and as the current ideology that uses the "pasts" constructed by archaeologists; and consciousness—as awareness of the ideological constructions and constraints within which we as archaeologists work. Several scholars (Blakey 1983; Handsman 1983; Schuyler 1976) have raised the issue of historical archaeology as serving current ideology, a role that might be dubbed "handmaiden to capitalism." Others too have insisted on the necessity of archaeology's social and ideological role (e.g., Gathercole 1984). The disadvantage of such an insistence, if taken out of a Marxist context, is the risk of overstating relativism. The more convincing advantage is the potential for a real assessment of our own biases and interpretations as well as their social impacts. Consciousness and current ideological context cannot be adequately discussed here, although their importance is assumed in this essay. Instead, investigation of the historical development of the context(s) of capitalism, a compelling research topic due to our current social and cultural situation, is the subject of the rest of this section.

Research on the culture of capitalism seeks to understand the most pervasive changes of the past half-millennium: How did people make sense of capitalism's economic, technical, and social transformations and their cultural effects? Of course, a focus on capitalism in this case begins with mercantile capitalism from the 15th century rather than solely forms of industrial capitalism from the 18th century. Capitalism as a world system serves as a way to keep myriad issues connected. Within the world system of capitalism there are certainly different spatial and temporal scales of analysis and different foci for research. Within the United States the phenomenon of capitalism is not necessarily specific to region or time period; it is not unique to East Coast industrialism. Although capitalism supports and is supported by a dominant cultural ideology, neither it nor the ideology is transcendent or all-encompassing; they are challenged, changed, and embraced. In seeking to understand the roots and development of capitalism as the roots of much of our modern American society and culture, we must be careful not to treat its history and development as inevitable To deny the contingencies of historical events would be a disservice to those who resisted and a denial of other possible outcomes or possible futures.

The culture of capitalism as an issue requires consideration in several ways, few of which have received more than preliminary consideration in the literature. There need to be comparative work on different capitalist and noncapitalist cultures; careful linking of production, distribution, and consumption; and innovative analyses of industrialism. There also need to be continued refinement and application of central concepts such as power and ideology.

Cross-Cultural Research

Paynter (1989:372) writes, "A true archaeology of capitalism would be worldwide in scope, and would have to understand the intricate trajectories various parts of the world were following prior to the arrival of Europeans." It is essential that the development of a modern world system be considered in cross-cultural perspective. In looking to capitalism and the development of con-temporary society and the modern world as unifying concepts, historical archaeologists need to turn their attention around the globe to areas colonized or otherwise affected by Europeans. Capitalism will begin to seem less monolithic a concept as regional differences in indigenous culture, historical contingencies, and ecological setting are seen to influence the European adventure. The cross-cultural approach is needed to understand the contemporary "modern world," which is truly diverse.

Several provocative studies highlight the variability of dynamics between colonizers and colonized. For example, Sichone (1989) discusses colonial effects on indigenous populations in the Rhodesian Copperbelt, arguing that colonialism forced new cultural forms instead of allowing indigenous "survivals." His call for a new vocabulary and new ways of looking at colonized peoples' reactions needs to be taken seriously. "Acculturation" and its material-culture clues must be reconceptualized. Howson (1990) also argues for this need to refine our approaches to acculturation in looking at African-American social and cultural adaptation in plantation settings in the American South. Rogers (1990) emphasizes the complexities of cultural survival in his analysis of contact between the Arikara and European settlers. Material conditions, material culture, and the uses to which objects are put vary widely within indigenous stratified societies. They vary as well within a global system such as developing capitalism that consists of interdependent but separate parts.

Intent on identifying similarities and unifying some of the British experience, Deetz (1977, 1983) has turned his attention to South Africa, searching there for parallel developments to those described for Anglo-American society. Winer and Deetz (1990) describe the formulation of a distinctive Eastern Cape culture from the parent British culture from 1820 to 1860. Scott and Deetz (1990:76) write,

> [W]hile each of these "little Englands" had its own distinctive character, the result of different environments and interaction with a rich diversity of indigenous peoples, they all shared a common general form and quality. Language, custom and a distinctive shaping of the physical environment tie together places as outwardly disparate as southern Africa, the United States and Australia, all sharing a common English cultural heritage.

Such homogeneity may well be overstated, yet it is vital to recognize the similarities as well as the differences within world systems. Comparing like and dislike, Schrire and Merwick (1991), for example, contrast the different purposes and outcomes of Dutch activity in New Netherlands in the Americas and on the South African Cape.

Production, Consumption, Industrialism

In promoting a class model for connecting material change and capitalism, Paynter (1988) argues that production and consumption, although often investigated as separate processes, need to be explicitly connected. It is not altogether clear how these phenomena are to be analytically linked, especially as we operate within the culture of capitalism, which implicitly demands such separations (e.g., Barnett and Silverman 1979:41–81). The separate consideration of work and domestic life would be foreign in many times and places but the separations are enforced within modern capitalism by both gender ideology, which has attempted to define home as a place where valued "work" is not done, and class ideology, wherein it is essential to keep the alienated worker and the consuming worker unaware that they are identical.

Work affects what there is to be consumed and the conditions under which it is produced. There is an overarching cultural change that accompanies the social changes in the organization of work and connects the conditions of production with the circumstances of consumption; that is, there is a change in cultural expectations and control. The study of work is a potential area of contribution for industrial archaeology. Merging accounts of workers' tasks with descriptions of workplace and equipment should provide a "comprehensive picture of daily routines within a particular trade," an orientation Leary (1979:176) terms "industrial ecology." An historical archaeology of work need not be limited to echoing an ecosystem approach, but will make valuable contributions to political economy of the sort promoted by McGuire and Paynter (1991).

There is a large and growing body of literature on industrial archaeology, particularly on that done in Great Britain and the United States (e.g., Greenwood 1985; Rapp and Beranek 1984; Sande 1976) but also on that done around the world (e.g., Hudson 1979; Vance 1984). Much of industrial archaeology suffers from antiquarianism and lacks a coherent theoretical structure. Therefore, the subdiscipline stands to gain an enormous amount of intellectual stimulation from the explicit consideration of capitalism as a unifying construct. Although the effects of industrial capitalism are apparent outside the workplace as well as within it, the locus of work, the physical conditions, and the organization of the process of labor and production offer intellectual inroads into the negotiation between people who were laborers and people who were managers.

There are a few examples of explicit linking of discipline in the workplace with personal discipline of the individual. One has been offered by Shackel (1993a) in describing the standardization of the toothbrush. Standardized manufacturing of toothbrushes began in Great Britain by the early 19th century. Artisan judgment in placing and drilling holes for the bristles was replaced in stages by machine precision introduced with reorganization of manufacturing. The change in the workplace is correlated with the use of toothbrushes as part of an individualizing routine involving hygiene and the careful presentation of self. Production and consumption of a particular artifact, then, are linked within overall culture change emphasizing discipline. Outside of historical archaeology, but of use to the field, is the link between standardized routines of workers—authors and printers—in emerging print culture and both the standardized products of the press and the standardizing influence of printing on consumers of printed, standard items (Eisenstein 1983; Little 1988).

Linking workers' production and workers' housing is particularly important in gaining a comprehensive interpretation of early industrial towns. Beaudry and Mrozowski (1988, 1989; Beaudry 1989) discuss the role of corporate paternalism and its effects on workers' lives in Lowell, Massachusetts. The work being done at Harpers Ferry, West Virginia (Shackel 1993b), explicitly considers relations between technology and culture change. Domestic material culture, food choice, health-related practices, and treatment of the landscape are investigated to interpret resistance to and acceptance of discipline both in the factory itself and within households.

Ideology and Power

It is clear that one of the important concepts in an archaeology of capitalism is that of ideology. This concern is no less important in the (pre-) history of institutionalized states and mechanisms of power and control. The term ideology has many different and sometimes conflicting meanings. Eagleton (1991) discusses the ambiguity and changing meanings, offers six increasingly focused definitions, and identifies six characteristics or strategies of ideology. Historical archaeologists will find that distinguishing among these levels of specificity and strategies is useful but need to recognize that the distinctions in any situation often may not be clear and that ideology may remain ambiguous. Often several kinds of ideologies operate simultaneously. The strategies of various players are not necessarily mutually exclusive or clearly defined by the players themselves, let alone the researchers viewing a dynamic situation from another cultural context.

At the risk of oversimplification, only the essence of these definitions of ideology follows, from broadest to most focused:

1. ideas, beliefs, and values produced by material processes (stressing social production of thought);
2. ideas and beliefs (false or true) of a specific, socially significant group or class;
3. promotion or legitimation of such a group's concerns;
4. promotion of a dominant group's interests;
5. legitimation of the dominant group's interests through distortion and dissimulation; and
6. deceptive beliefs arising not from the interests of a dominant group, but from the material structure of society, such as fetishism of commodities.

Ideologies, then, are not necessarily false, nor are they characteristic only of the ruling class. Depending on their focus, ideologies may further six kinds of strategies. These are unifying and hegemonic; action oriented, i.e., practical; rationalizing; legitimizing; universalizing; and naturalizing. The latter two aspects are part of a dehistoricizing thrust that attempts to erase social context and remove any human basis for critique.

Eagleton's carefully argued definitions are helpful in sorting out the different uses of "ideology" in historical archaeology, particularly in distinguishing between ideology as "false consciousness," the definition attributed to "standard" Marxism, and ideology as the totality of social consciousness, a definition that equates ideology with culture (see McGuire 1988, 1991). The latter definition often is too broad to allow meaningful analyses of ideologies per se. Although the concept of ideology as false consciousness has fallen into disfavor (Abercrombie et al. 1980; Eagleton 1991:10), it has been used successfully within historical archaeology, particularly to stimulate ongoing discussion about the interplay between social groups and between ideology and material culture. For example, Leone (1984) uses this idea in his analysis of naturalizing ideology through the material culture of gardens in 18th-century Annapolis, Maryland. Hodder (1986:63–70) has critiqued Leone's (1984) use of Althusser's (1971) dominant ideology thesis and the critique has been echoed by others (Beaudry et al. 1991; Hall 1992; Johnson 1989). Yet the proffered alternative based on Abercrombie and co-authors' (1980) critique—that subordinates are constantly aware of dominant attempts at ideological obfuscation and that only the elite are misled by their own legitimation strategies—seems an alternative oversimplification. Instead, Eagleton's layered definitions explain that ideologies may be true or false or, more likely, a blend of both, and may be held by groups of varying structural power. Ideologies are not necessarily consciously articulated. Wolf (1990:592–593) draws on Wallace's (1970) insights that social actors do not need to understand the meaning behind others' actions, but they do need to know how to respond appropriately. "Issues of meaning need not ever rise into consciousness" (Wolf 1990:593). Practical knowledge and action must be contrasted against discursive knowledge, which is consciously theorized (Feierman 1990:27).

Kryder-Reid (1994), for example, is careful to distinguish among the several "readings" that any particular built landscape may prompt. There are messages for different audiences, both the dominant and the dominated: The large house and elaborate garden of Charles Carroll of Carrollton in Annapolis may fail to impress upon the untutored the necessary geometric principles and their relation to the laws of nature but could not fail to impress with the amount of money and coercive power needed to build and maintain such a place. Whether individuals are "duped" by dominant justifications for the claiming of power, they are not likely to be confused as to whether some groups actually *possess* power.

This landscape example also emphasizes a distinction that has been used in archaeology between vulgar and nonvulgar ideology. Vulgar ideology is subjective knowledge and explanation that serves some social class (Meltzer 1981:114, following Handsman 1977). Vulgar ideology, encompassing the third, fourth, and fifth of Eagleton's definitions, is potentially obvious and penetrable by members of a culture who can recognize, if not effectively resist, the ideological "arguments" used to promote certain interests. An explicit message of a geometric Georgian garden that material wealth is a legitimation as well as an expression of social power may be questioned but not necessarily effectively resisted. Nonvulgar ideology, akin to Eagleton's most focused definition of deceptive beliefs arising from the material structure of society, is knowledge thought to be objective and beyond question. Nonvulgar ideology is much more difficult to penetrate because it forms the basis for accepted truth, for example, supernatural and natural prescription. The same "wealth equals power" argument holds implicit messages, as wealthy individuals embed their power in natural right and the laws of nature and express it materially through, for example, scientific instruments (e.g., Leone and Shackel 1987) as well as formal gardens (e.g., Leone 1984).

Resistance to dominant ideology does not necessitate the complete piercing of dominant ideology but does require understanding what the dominant ideology demands and fulfilling or avoiding those demands. In forming their own ideologies, subordinate groups incorporate, reform, manipulate, and appeal to dominant ideology. The dominant ideology in turn, if operating hegemonically, will incorporate and reform, coopting subordinate concerns into its own constructs. Women's domestic reform movements of the 19th century (e.g., Spencer-Wood 1991) provide an example of this process within gender ideology.

The theme of power is implicit in the manipulation of ideologies and is increasingly offered as a central focus in the examination of capitalism or, indeed, in any context where inequality is an issue (Paynter 1989; Paynter and McGuire 1991). Wolf (1990) acknowledges the discomfort that the very term "power" creates and finds it useful to distinguish among four modes to bring more precision to discussion of the concept. The first is power as the capability of a person; the second is power as the ability of a person to impose upon another interpersonally; the third is tactical power, which controls social settings; and the fourth is structural power, which allocates social labor. The first is what Miller and Tilley (1984) and Paynter and McGuire (1991) call "power to," while the latter three are increasing degrees of "power over." The theme of "power" would be trivial in its universality were it not for this explicit consideration of its inherent heterogeneity. The contrast between a universal notion of power and a pluralistic notion of various sorts of power, contextualized, is the contrast that makes the notion useful. Another sense of the heterogeneity of power must also be recognized. Domination may be carried out through coercion, legitimation, or a combination of these. Similarly, resistance may be overt and violent or hidden in everyday defiance (Scott 1985).

By considering different kinds of power in different contexts, one may also avoid the trap of considering power from a primarily male viewpoint since the usual focus on power may be a peculiarly male focus. As Conkey and Gero (1991) note, the attempt to engender archaeology may require paying closer attention to interpersonal relations and analytically privileging less the centralized state and centralized power. Appraising various scales of power and various forms of resistance and subversion is a key to successfully addressing social relations.

Historical archaeology has a largely untapped but increasingly recognized potential for theorizing, analyzing, and describing strategies of power, expressions of all levels of ideology, and dynamic interactions among those attempting to dominate and those attempting to resist. Within the archaeology of slavery in the United States, for example, Epperson (1990) analyzes covert slave resistance on a Virginia plantation. There are many promising historical contexts for such analyses, including the 16th-century European onslaught in the Caribbean, 18th-century rise of industrialism, 19th-century expansion of Manifest Destiny, and 20th-century indigenous resurgence. None of these concerns can be addressed, however, without a thorough investigation of material culture: the objects that both express social relationships and reify cultural constructs and metaphors.

Material Culture in the Negotiation of Ideology: An Example from the Historic Cherokee

In the past several years there have been a number of studies on the meanings of goods. These are from museum studies (e.g., Craven 1986; Lubar and Kingery 1993), folklore (e.g., St. George 1988), social history (e.g., Isaac 1982; Schama 1987), American studies (e.g., Lears 1981; Schlereth 1985), and architectural and landscape history (e.g., Herman 1984; Stilgoe 1982; Upton 1986; Upton and Vlach 1986), in addition to cultural anthropology (e.g., Appadurai 1986; Bourdieu 1984; Douglas and Isherwood 1979; Fowler 1987; Ingersoll and Bronitsky 1987; McCracken 1988; McKendrick et al. 1982; Reynolds and Stott 1987; Scott 1985). There also have been a large number of studies in archaeology (e.g., Burley 1989; Deetz 1988b; Hodder 1979, 1989; Little and Shackel 1992; Neiman 1978; Schiffer 1991; Tilley 1990; Wobst 1977; Yentsch 1991b). Serious material culture studies have escalated in the past decade.

No longer confined to questions of chronology or function, historical archaeology is now beginning to focus on meaning in context. Contexts are defined at different spatial scales as mentioned above—global, regional, local, household—and temporal scales—*longue durée*, social time, event (e.g., Little and Shackel 1989; Paynter 1988; Shackel 1993a). Many of these studies draw upon the work of Pierre Bourdieu and Mary Douglas as well as Anthony Giddens and Michel Foucault (see Shackel and Little 1992).

A short case study of 19th-century Cherokee in Georgia integrates meanings of material culture with a group's resistance to and attempted negotiation of dominant ideology. Part of a dominant nonvulgar ideology in this case is the avowed progress of civilization; the vulgar ideology that is challenged through both material and nonmaterial culture is the rigidity of the expression of civilization. All of Wolf's modes of power come into play, but particularly important is tactical power as dominant and dominated struggle over acceptable social settings. The heterogeneity that the resistant group attempts to enforce within the dominant culture's hegemony fails. Rather than incorporating an effective and compelling challenge to its own ideology, the dominant group resorts to brute force to eliminate the threat. This example is offered not as an illustration of premier historical-archaeological research—the archaeology done decades ago is poorly documented and difficult to interpret—but as a case of broadly examining a context in which a culture of capitalism impacted and was challenged by people "without history." I have simplified the challenge and response. Neither the dominant nor the dominated group acted uniformly; their actions and desires were not monolithic. Rather, there were factions on each side involved in intragroup power dynamics and ideological struggles.

In considering contact between Native Americans and European-Americans during the early 19th century, themes of civilization, ideology, and acculturation are useful. The Cherokee found it necessary to present themselves so as to be understood by whites as "civilized" and simultaneously to maintain their identity as Cherokee (e.g., Perdue 1979; Persico 1979). They selectively accepted and manipulated the foreign idea of civilization, expressing through material culture both the adoption of "white ways" and the preservation of their own tradition. Their situation was complicated by the coalescence of nationalism in the United States: The quintessential citizen was in the process of being defined, and the Indian was not He.

The Cherokee capital of New Echota established in northwest Georgia is an embodiment of the Cherokee's most explicit demonstration of this white ideology of civilization and a final, desperate effort to preserve their land and nation. New Echota was in many ways the culmination of long intercultural contact. By the first decades of the 19th century the Cherokee had undergone extensive change. As in other native societies, all aspects of life were affected. Economy changed as Cherokee hunted to supply the skin trade, began raising stock, and intensified agriculture. Intermarriage brought in outsiders. Gender relations changed as European patriarchy gained influence. Naming and inheritance rules changed. The community of autonomous villages transformed into a "priest-state" and then a nation. Traditional ceremonies were altered and diminished. Missionaries promoted not only Christianity but also behavior and material culture appropriate to their own civilization. Missions established schools and churches and taught the values of individualism and capitalism as well as acceptable styles of dress, hair, speech, and demeanor. Property and wealth became valued and egalitarianism faded. Plantation economy, holding of black slaves, and racism were adopted (Gearing 1962; Mooney 1900, 1975; Perdue 1979; Ronda and Axtell 1978).

Beginning with a treaty in 1721, Cherokee landholdings steadily diminished. By the end of the 18th century there was little left of the original territory, which was further diminished by cessions in 1804, 1805, 1806, 1816, 1817, and 1819. By 1808 governmental pressure increased for the Cherokee to exchange their land for property west of the Mississippi, and by 1817 a few thousand Cherokee had emigrated to Arkansas.

The Cherokee responded to such pressure with political moves. It is hardly coincidental that the first rules of the Cherokee National Council were established in 1808, and the "Articles of 1817" created a Grand Council. In 1820 the council established a republican government, with eight districts electing representatives to the council. In 1825 plans were made for the permanent capital at New Echota, which was surveyed and established a year later. The Presbyterian minister

Worcester moved from nearby Brainerd to the new capital and established a mission house.

Cherokee literacy was also made possible in the 1820s. Sequoyah submitted his syllabary to the council in 1821 and within a few years it was resolved to establish a national newspaper published at the capital in both Cherokee and English. The first issue of the *Cherokee Phoenix* was published on February 28, 1828. Printed in both English and the newly available Cherokee, the newspaper promoted literacy but insisted on equal status of its two languages and cultures. The title itself was taken from Western mythology but refers to the rebirth of the Cherokee people out of an earlier way of life that had become impossible to maintain.

New Echota, then, was created by the Cherokee as the capital of an independent nation with a constitution (in 1827) and a republican government, literacy, printing, a national newspaper, Christianity, and a police force to protect property—in short, all the explicit ingredients for what was understood to be "civilization."

New Echota contained the concrete material-culture evidence of a people presenting themselves as civilized. It also contained evidence of a people who saw themselves as separate from white culture, as distinctly Cherokee [see, for example, writings of Elias Boudinot, editor of the *Phoenix* (cited in Perdue 1983)]. Preliminary evidence suggests that while some of the most external and visible elements of material culture, especially architecture and planned settlement pattern (Pillsbury 1983; Wilms 1974), followed white rules, less visible elements, particularly objects used within households or within activities of limited audience, preserved traditional culture.

Such division itself has implications for adoption of the white dichotomy of public and private and for the role of women and men in separate spheres. Other historical archaeologists' studies of Native-European contact (e.g., Deagan 1983; Deetz 1963) have attributed maintenance of traditional culture, kept private within households, to women. As Perdue (1979) mentions, Cherokee women's roles had already changed drastically by the 19th century. It is likely that one of women's new roles involved the discreet maintenance of certain traditional practices, including the manufacture and decoration of ceramics.

Archaeological excavations were conducted at the site of New Echota in 1954 (DeBaillou 1955) and 1969 (Baker 1970). Descriptions of domestic materials recovered are brief but provocative and imply both coexistence of European- and native-manufactured ceramics and building technology combining native and European attributes. Cherokee ceramics were found throughout one of the excavations in direct conjunction with European ceramics, at least some of which were presumably high-status teawares (Baker 1970:22; DeBaillou 1955:26). Anglo-produced building timbers were used in "old Indian fashion" according to DeBaillou (1955:21).

There are some notes and maps and a brief report on the extensive 1954 excavations. Eighteen "units" were explored, each of which apparently measured at least 100 ft on a side. Several of the units are noted simply as having yielded "nothing important" or as being meager. Features such as wells, cellars, and refuse pits were excavated within six of the large units. Stratigraphic control may have been practiced in the field, but the recorded provenience of artifacts was specific only to the features as a whole. After examining the available material from 11 of 21 features in five units, I found that 9 features exhibited a mix of traditional and European-derived materials. Retouched flakes and retouched sherds of glass probably served similar purposes. Part of an incised slate palette and grit-tempered Lamar-like ceramic sherds, most undecorated but a few with complicated stamping, appeared with handpainted pearlware teacup fragments and an occasional sherd of glazed stoneware from a storage vessel. A stone pipe and pewter table utensils were found together in a refuse pit. (A fully quantified assessment of the material culture must await a full-scale reconstruction of the archaeology performed at New Echota. I examined artifacts that had been curated at New Echota State Park and moved to the Office of the State Archaeologist at West Georgia College in the summer of 1992. Although there are references to a full report of the excavations supervised by Baker, no copy could be located. I have confined my observations to the earlier work for which I could correlate artifacts with provenience.)

Material culture was used both to adopt and to reject white objects and their uses. The Cherokee invention of an alphabet exemplifies this dual strategic function. An alphabet was adopted but it was not the correct, i.e., civilized English, language. Sequoyah's invention of letters for the Cherokee tongue has been seen as progressive and as an indication of intelligence (e.g., McGinty 1955; Self 1955), but it was more than an example of "catching on" to civilization. It was an adoption and adaptation of one part of white civilization in Cherokee terms.

A native people's counteractions and adaptations to the continuing demands of an invading and dominating culture provide insight into the ideological perspective of the nondominant on the issue of acculturation. Ethnocide and ethnogenesis are of central concern to both the dominant culture and the resisters. The Cherokee resisted both the total destruction of their culture and the creation of a new culture that would be defined solely by missionaries, government agents, and other whites. Instead the Cherokee's own ethnogenesis was of an altered Cherokee identity.

The case of New Echota provides an example of alternative uses and meanings of material culture, including but not limited to the use of symbolic artifacts in negotiation for political or social rights. After the American Revolutionary War the Cherokee were compelled to invent peaceful methods for negotiating in a desperate situation and in the face of racism. One method promoted the adoption of the symbols and structures of white civilization. Other types of material culture were used to maintain and create a Cherokee version of civilization.

A great deal of historical and anthropological scholarship has been published on the historic Cherokee (e.g., Gearing 1962; King 1979; McLoughlin 1984, 1986; Mooney 1900, 1975; Perdue 1979, 1983, 1989). There is, however, little specific attention to New Echota as a place of importance in the Cherokee strategy for survival. But it is an essential place, especially for understanding the strategies of a culture that traditionally placed great emphasis on places in the landscape.

Because New Echota was occupied by the Cherokee only briefly (1826–1838), it provides a material environment focused on a period of great political and social importance in their history. The material culture of the capital embodies an attempt at the creation of a syncretic, Cherokee and White, civilization.

Summary

Conflicts in relations among Native, African, European, and Asian Americans began with first contacts and continued through the 18th and 19th centuries and beyond. Capitalism's increasingly pervasive promises were being made: In return for market participation, cultural assimilation, and conformity were to be had individual liberty and a place in the new republic. But racism, nationalism, and ethnocentrism were used to deny the promise to Native Americans as well as to blacks and women. The native was a special sort of "other" in the New World but there was no room in the dominant ideology for another version of the promise; there was no place for what could be perceived as a distorted imitation or reflection of "us." Because cultural conformity could not be complete, capitalism's manifest destiny could not tolerate the challenge. In spite of a United States Supreme Court ruling in favor of the Cherokee maintaining title and possession of their lands, President Andrew Jackson ordered their removal. Nearly all of the Cherokee were forcibly removed to reservations in Oklahoma on the "Trail of Tears" from 1838 to 1839. Their land was distributed by lottery to white Georgians. For most Cherokee, ethnogenesis had to continue on foreign soil.

Using acculturation leading to assimilation as an explanatory process to measure cultural influence leads to an interpretation of the Cherokee as Native Americans trying to be "white" and "civilized" but not quite getting it—missing the point by retaining survivals from the prehistoric, Indian past. Instead, an approach that incorporates ideology, hegemony, and negotiation may reveal and create more satisfying interpretations that admit human agency as individuals and groups compete and attempt to "work the system to their minimum disadvantage" (Scott 1985:xv).

Sider (1976) points out that there are two usual views of indigenous peoples' options in the face of colonizing powers. One is stagnation, wherein culture is statically preserved and people impoverished. The other is progress or economic development, with its attendant pressures for complete assimilation. The absence of ethnogenesis from these options, he writes, is a failing of capitalism. I suggest instead that the failure to recognize ethnogenesis as an option and a process is a direct result of failing to consider the dynamics of the contexts of capitalism in our analyses.

Prospect

Deagan (1982:170) acknowledges a question about whether or not historical archaeology should concern itself with the "intellectual climate" that existed when sites were created. The question is still heard, but by now there should be little debate that intellectual climate in the form of social and political relationships, ideology, and worldview—in short, the whole of culture rather than decontextualized artifacts—is indeed the proper emphasis of historical archaeology. Increasing attention will be paid to the complex contexts illuminated by historical archaeology as cultural anthropology continues to recognize the need not only for historical context (e.g., Dening 1988; Sahlins 1981, 1985; Wolf 1982), but also for material culture (e.g., Fowler 1987; Reynolds and Stott 1987).

Historical archaeology had long been practiced in the United States by the time the new archaeology discovered it and insisted on its incorporation into anthropological archaeology. Since the 1960s, and particularly since 1967, when the Society for Historical Archaeology was formed, historical archaeology has been growing. In spite of its incorporation into anthropological archaeology, its acceptance into the same has been lagging. Often poor cousin and handmaiden to prehistory, itself suffering reduced status under the anthropological parent discipline, historical archaeology repeatedly has been relegated to the role of providing cautionary tales, illustrations, and controlled laboratories for methods to be refined for use with the "real" data of prehistoric sites. Despite Deagan's (1982:154) optimism that ambivalence toward the legitimacy of historical archaeology has been resolved, the attitude may still be found that historical archaeology is something of a junior varsity where simple confirmation of historical "fact" is the main goal.

In 1982 Deagan (1982:172) could reasonably write that "contemporary advances suggest that a distinct discipline is indeed emerging." There is indeed a discipline of historical archaeology; it has emerged as historical material anthropology. The crisis in the discipline that raged in the 1960s, over whether history or anthropology would be the appropriate parent discipline, is over. "In their approaches to the past there is often little difference today among studies in historical archaeology, cultural anthropology, and social history" (Deagan 1988:7). There are plenty of questions that count; there are methods being refined and developed to address them, and there is a strong sense of the contemporary context of archaeology and the scholarly responsibility that such a recognition demands. Given the promise and the productivity of the field, why is there still a crisis in historical archaeology? The current crisis is one of professional placement. Historical archaeology is interdisciplinary; it is interloper still. Its own disciplinary genesis as a social and historical endeavor, one useful to but not beholden to method seeking by prehistorians, is painfully under way.

Acknowledgments

Several people read, commented on, and improved this article through their encouragement and critique. I thank Mike Schiffer for inviting me to contribute to this series and for his helpful comments. I also want to thank Chuck Orser and several anonymous reviewers for their insight and enthusiasm. I thank Kathy Deagan, Eric Larsen, Mark Leone, Mike Lucas, Terry Majewski, Bob Schuyler, Paul Shackel, Suzanne Spencer-Wood, Bruce Trigger, and Kirsti Uunila for taking the time to read the manuscript and offer comments. Thanks go to George Stuart for directing me to the New Echota material in the first place and to Lewis Larson for very kindly collecting the artifacts and providing a place to examine them at West Georgia College. Very special thanks are due to Tom Patterson, who directed me to literature I had overlooked and whose careful reading and comments have expanded my own thinking. I cannot blame any of these individuals for shortcomings in this work, and I thank them for helping to improve it.

REFERENCES

Abercrombie, N., S. Hill, and B. S. Turner. 1980. *The Dominant Ideology Thesis*. London: George Allen & Unwin.

Althusser, L. 1971. *Lenin and Philosophy*. New York: Monthly Review Press.

Appadurai, A. 1986. *The Social Life of Things: Commodities in Cultural Perspective*. Cambridge: Cambridge University Press.

Baker, S. G. 1970. New Echota Archaeology 1969: A Progress Report. Submitted to Georgia Historical Commission.

Barnett, S. and M. G. Silverman. 1979. *Ideology and Everyday Life: Anthropology, Neomarxist Thought and the Problem of Ideology and the Social Whole*. Ann Arbor: University of Michigan Press.

Beaudry, M. C. 1984. Archaeology and the Historic Household. *Man in the Northeast* 28:27–38.

Beaudry, M. C. (ed.). 1988. *Documentary Archaeology in the New World*. Cambridge: Cambridge University Press.

Beaudry, M. C. 1989. The Lowell Boott Mills Complex and Its Housing: Material Expressions of Corporate Ideology. *Historical Archaeology* 23(1):19–33.

Beaudry, M. C. and S. Mrozowski. 1988. The Archaeology of Work and Home Life in Lowell, Massachusetts: An Interdisciplinary Study of the Boott Cotton Mills Corporation. *Industrial Archaeology* 19(2):1–22.

Beaudry, M. C. and S. Mrozowski. 1989. *Interdisciplinary Investigations of the Boott Mills, Lowell, Massachusetts, Vol. 3: The Boarding House System as a Way of Life.* Cultural Resources Management Series 21, National Park Service, North Atlantic Regional Office, Boston.

Beaudry, M., L. J. Cook, and S. A. Mrozowski. 1991. Artifacts and Active Voices: Material Culture as Social Discourse. In *The Archaeology of Inequality*, R. H. McGuire and R. Paynter (eds.), pp. 150–191. Oxford: Basil Blackwell.

Binford, L. R. 1977. Introduction. In *For Theory Building in Archaeology*, L. R. Binford (ed.). New York: Academic Press.

Binford, L. R. 1981. *Bones: Ancient Men and Modem Myths.* New York: Academic Press.

Blakely, R. L. (ed.). 1988. *The King Site: Continuity and Contact in Sixteenth-Century Georgia.* Athens: University of Georgia Press.

Blakey, R. L. 1983. Socio-political Bias and Ideological Production in Historical Archaeology. In *The Socio-Politics of Archaeology*, J. M. Gero, D. M. Lacy, and M. L. Blakey (eds.), pp. 5–16. Research Reports No. 23, Department of Anthropology, University of Massachusetts, Amherst.

Boone, J. L., J. E. Myers, and C. L. Redman. 1990. Archeological and Historical Approaches to Complex Societies. *American Anthropologist* 92: 630–646.

Bourdieu, P. 1984. *Distinctions: A Social Critique of the Judgement of Taste*, R. Nice (trans.), Cambridge: Harvard University Press.

Brumfiel, E. 1992. Distinguished Lecture in Archaeology: Breaking and Entering the Ecosystem—Gender, Class, and Faction Steal the Show. *American Anthropologist* 94:551–567.

Burley, D. V. 1989. Function, Meaning and Context: Ambiguities in Ceramic Use by the Hivernant Metis of the Northwest Plains. *Historical Archaeology* 23(1):97–106.

Cleland, C. E. 1988. Questions of Substance, Questions that Count. *Historical Archaeology* 22(1):13–17.

Conkey, M. W. and J. M. Gero. 1991. Tensions, Pluralities, and Engendering Archaeology: An Introduction to Women and Prehistory. In *Engendering Archaeology: Women and Prehistory*, J. Gero and M. W. Conkey (eds.), pp. 3–30. Oxford: Basil Blackwell.

Costello, J. G. and M. L. Maniery. 1988. Rice Bowls in the Delta: Artifacts Recovered from the 1915 Asian Community of Walnut Grove, California. *Occasional Paper 16*, UCLA Institute of Archaeology, Los Angeles.

Cotter, J. (ed.). 1984. *The Scope of Historical Archaeology*. Philadelphia: Temple University Press.

Cotter, J. L., D. G. Roberts, and M. Parrington. 1992. *The Buried Past: An Archaeological History of Philadelphia.* Philadelphia: University of Pennsylvania Press.

Craven, W. 1986. *Colonial American Portraiture.* Cambridge: Cambridge University Press.

DeBaillou, C. 1955. Excavations at New Echota in 1954. *Early Georgia* 1:18–29.

Deagan, K. 1982. Avenues of Inquiry in Historical Archaeology. In *Advances in Archaeological Method and Theory, Vol. 5,* M. B. Schiffer (ed.), pp. 151–177. New York: Academic Press.

Deagan, K. 1983. *Spanish St. Augustine: The Archaeology of a Colonial Creole Community.* New York: Academic Press.

Deagan, K. 1988. Neither History nor Prehistory: The Questions that Count in Historical Archaeology. *Historical Archaeology* 22(1):7–12.

Deetz, J. 1963. *Archaeological Investigations at La Purisima Mission.* UCLA Archaeological Survey Annual Report 1962–1963, pp. 163–208.

Deetz, J. 1963. 1977. *In Small Things Forgotten: The Archaeology of Early American Life.* Garden City, NY: Anchor Press/Doubleday.

Deetz, J. 1983. Scientific Humanism and Humanistic Science: A Plea for Paradigmatic Pluralism in Historical Archaeology. *Geoscience and Man* 23:27–34.

Deetz, J. 1988a. History and Archaeological Theory: Walter Taylor Revisited. *American Antiquity* 53:13–22.

Deetz, J. 1988b. American Historical Archaeology: Method and Results. *Science* 239:362–367.

Dening, G. 1988. *History's Anthropology: The Death of William Gooch.* Special Publication of the Association for Social Anthropology in Oceania No. 2, Lanham, MD: University Press of America.

Diamond, S. 1974. *In Search of the Primitive: A Critique of Civilization.* New Brunswick, NJ: Transaction Books.

Dickens, R. (ed.). 1982. *Archaeology of Urban America: The Search for Pattern and Process.* New York: Academic Press.

Dobyns, H. 1983. *Their Number Become Thinned: Native American Population Dynamics in Eastern North America.* Knoxville: University of Tennessee Press.

Douglas, M. and B. Isherwood. 1979. *The World of Goods.* New York: Basic Books.

Dyson, S. L. (ed.). 1985. *Comparative Studies in the Archaeology of Colonialism.* BAR International Series 233, Oxford.

Eagleton, T. 1991. *Ideology: An Introduction.* New York: Verso.

Earle, T. and R. Preucel. 1987. Processual Archaeology and the Radical Critique. *Current Anthropology* 28: 501–527.

Eisenstein, E. 1983. *The Printing Revolution in Early Modern Europe.* Cambridge: Cambridge University Press.

Epperson, T. W. 1990. Race and Discipline of the Plantation. In *Historical Archaeology on Southern Plantations and Farms,* C. E. Orser (ed.), *Historical Archaeology* 24(4):29–36.

Ewen, C. R. 1991. *From Spaniard to Creole: The Archaeology of Cultural Formation at Puerto Real, Haiti.* Tuscaloosa: University of Alabama Press.

Falk, L. (ed.). 1991. *Historical Archaeology in Global Perspective.* Washington, DC: Smithsonian Institution Press.

Farnsworth, P. 1989. Native American Acculturation in the Spanish Colonial Empire: The Franciscan Missions of Alta California. In *Centre and Periphery: Comparative Studies in Archaeology*, T. C. Champion (ed.). London: Unwin Hyman.

Farnsworth, P. and J. S. Williams (eds.). 1992. The Archaeology of the Spanish Colonial and Mexican Republican Periods. *Historical Archaeology* 26(1).

Faulkner, A. and G. Faulkner. 1987. *The French at Pentagoet 1625–1674: An Archaeological Portrait of the Acadian Frontier.* Augusta: Maine Historic Preservation Commission; St. Johns: New Brunswick Museum.

Feierman, S.. 1990. *Peasant Intellectuals: Anthropology and History in Tanzania.* Madison: University of Wisconsin Press.

Felton, L. and P. Schulz. 1983. *The Diaz Collection: Material Culture and Social Change in Mid-Nineteenth-Century Monterey.* California Archaeological Reports No. 23, State of California Department of Parks and Recreation, Cultural Resource Unit, Sacramento.

Ferguson, L. G. 1992. *Uncommon Ground: Archaeology and Colonial African-America.* Washington, DC: Smithsonian Institution Press.

Fitzhugh, W. W. (ed.). 1985. *Cultures in Contact: The Impact of European Contacts on Native American Cultural Institutions A.D. 1000–1800.* Washington, DC: Smithsonian Institution Press.

Fitzhugh, W. W. and J. S. Olin (eds.). 1993. *Archaeology of the Frobisher Voyages.* Washington, DC: Smithsonian Institution Press.

Fowler, L. 1987. *Shared Symbols, Contested Meanings: Gros Ventre Culture and History, 1778–1984.* Ithaca, NY: Cornell University Press.

Gathercole, P. 1984. A Consideration of Ideology. In *Marxist Perspectives in Archaeology*, M. Spriggs (ed.), pp. 149–54. Cambridge: Uiversity Press.

Gearing, F. 1962. *Priests and Warriors: Social Structures for Cherokee Politics in the 18th Century.* Memoir No. 93, American Anthropological Association.

Geier, C. and S. Winter (eds.). 1994. *Look to the Earth: The Archaeology of the Civil War.* Knoxville: University of Tennessee Press.

Geismar, J. H. 1982. *The Archaeology of Social Disintegration in Skunk Hollow.* New York: Academic Press.

Gibbon G. 1989. *Explanation in Archaeology.* Oxford: Basil Blackwell.

Glassie H. 1975. *Folk Housing in Middle Virginia.* Knoxville: University of Tennessee Press.

Gould, R. A. and M. B. Schiffer (eds.). 1981. *Modern Material Culture: The Archaeology of Us.* New York: Academic Press.

Greenwood, J. 1985. *The Industrial Archaeology and Industrial History of Northern England: A Bibliography.* Cranfield, England: Open University.

Gums, B. L. 1988. *Archaeology at French Colonial Cahokia.* Studies in Illinois Archaeology No. 3, Illinois Historic Preservation Agency, Springfield.

Hall, M. 1992. Small Things and the Mobile, Conflictual Fusion of Power, Fear, and Desire. In *Art and Mystery of Historical Archaeology: Essays in Honor of James Deetz*, A. E. Yentsch and M. C. Beaudry (eds.), pp. 373–399. Boca Raton, FL: CRC Press.

Handsman, R. G. 1977. The Bushkill Complex as an Anomaly: Unmasking the Ideology of American Archaeology. Unpublished Ph.D. dissertation, Department of Anthropology, American University, Washington, DC. Ann Arbor, MI: University Microfilms.

Handsman, R. G. 1983. Historical Archaeology and Capitalism, Subscriptions and Separations: The Production of Individualism. *North American Archaeologist* 4(1):63–79.

Hantman, J. 1990. Between Powhatan and Quirank: Reconstructing Monacan Culture and History in the Context of Jamestown. *American Anthropologist* 92:676–690.

Hardesty, D. L. 1985. Evolution on the Industrial Frontier. In *The Archaeology of Frontiers and Boundaries*, S. W. Green and S. M. Perlman (eds.), pp. 213–230. Orlando: Academic Press.

Hardesty, D. L. 1988. *The Archaeology of Mining and Miners: A View from the Silver State.* Special Publication No. 6, Society for Historical Archaeology, California, PA.

Herman, B. L. 1984. Multiple Materials, Multiple Meanings: The Fortunes of Thomas Mendenhall. *Winterthur Portfolio* 19(1):67–86.

Hodder, I. 1979. Economic and Social Stress and Material Culture Patterning. *American Antiquity* 44:446–454.

Hodder, I. (ed.). 1982a. *Symbolic and Structural Archaeology.* Cambridge: Cambridge University Press.

Hodder, I. 1982b. *Symbols in Action.* Cambridge: Cambridge University Press.

Hodder, I. 1985. Postprocessual Archaeology. In *Advances in Archaeological Methods and Theory, Vol. 8*, M. B. Schiffer (ed.), pp. 1–26. New York: Academic Press.

Hodder, I. 1986. *Reading the Past.* Cambridge: Cambridge University Press.

Hodder, I. (ed.). 1989. *The Meaning of Things: Material Culture and Symbolic Expressions.* London: Unwin Hyman.

Hodder, I. 1991. Interpretive Archaeology and Its Role. *American Antiquity* 56:7–18.

Honerkamp, N. 1988. Preface: Questions that Count in Historical Archaeology. *Historical Archaeology* 22(1):5–6.

Hoover, R. L. and J. G. Costello (eds.). 1985. *Excavations at Mission San Antonio, 1976–1978.* UCLA Institute of Archaeology No. 26, Los Angeles.

Howson, J. E. 1990. Social Relations and Material Culture: A Critique of the Archaeology of Plantation Slavery. In *Historical Archaeology on Southern Plantations and Farms*, C. E. Orser (ed.), *Historical Archaeology* 24(4):78–91.

Hudson, K. 1979. *World Industrial Archaeology*. Cambridge: Cambridge University Press.

Ingersoll, D. W, Jr., and G. Bronitsky (eds.). 1987. *Mirror and Metaphor: Material and Social Constructions of Reality*. Lanham, MD: University Press of America.

Isaac, R. 1982. *The Transformation of Virginia 1740–1790*. Chapel Hill: University of North Carolina Press.

Johnson, M. H. 1989. Conceptions of Agency in Archaeological Interpretation. *Journal of Anthropological Archaeology* 8:189–211.

Keegan, W. F. 1992. *The People Who Discovered Columbus*. Gainesville: University Press of Florida.

Kelso, W. M. 1984. *Kingsmill Plantations 1619-1800: Archaeology of Country Life in Colonial Virginia*. New York: Academic Press.

Kelso, W. and R. Most (eds.). 1990. *Earth Patterns: Essays in Landscape Archaeology*. Charlottesville: University Press of Virginia.

King, D. (ed.). 1979. *The Cherokee Indian Nation*. Knoxville: University of Tennessee Press.

Kryder-Reid, E. 1994. "As the Gardener, So Is the Garden": The Archaeology of Landscape as Myth. In *The Historical Archaeology of the Chesapeake*, P. A. Shackel and B. J. Little (eds.), pp. 131–148. Washington, DC: Smithsonian Institution Press.

Lears, T. J. J. 1981. *No Place of Grace: Antimodernism and the Transformation of American Culture 1880–1920*. New York: Pantheon Books.

Leary, T. E. 1979. Industrial Archaeology and Industrial Ecology. *Radical History Review* 21:171–182.

Leone, M. P. 1977. Foreword. In *Research Strategies in Historical Archaeology*, S. South (ed.), pp. xvii–xxi. New York: Academic Press.

Leone, M. P. 1982. Some Opinions about Recovering Mind. *American Antiquity* 47:742–760.

Leone, M. P. 1984. Interpreting Ideology in Historical Archaeology: Using the Rules of Perspective in the William Paca Garden in Annapolis, Maryland. In *Ideology, Power, and Prehistory*, D. Miller and C. Tilley (eds.), pp. 25–36. London: Cambridge University Press.

Leone, M. P. 1988. The Relationship Between Archaeological Data and the Documentary Record: 18th-century Gardens in Annapolis, Maryland. *Historical Archaeology* 22(1):29–35.

Leone, M. P. and P. B. Potter, Jr. (eds.). 1988a. *The Recovery of Meaning in Historical Archaeology in the Eastern United States*. Washington, DC: Smithsonian Institution Press.

Leone, M. P. and P. B. Potter, Jr. (eds.). 1988b Introduction: Issues in Historical Archaeology. In *The Recovery of Meaning in Historical Archaeology in the Eastern United States*, M. P. Leone and P. B. Potter, Jr. (eds.), pp. 1–22. Washington, DC: Smithsonian Institution Press.

Leone, M. P. and P. A. Shackel. 1987. Forks, Clocks, and Power. In *Mirror and Metaphor: Material and Social Constructions of Reality*, D. Ingersoll (ed.), pp. 45–62. Lanham, MD: University Press of America.

Leone, M. P., P. B. Potter, Jr., and P. A. Shackel. 1987. Toward a Critical Archaeology. *Current Anthropology* 28:283–302.

Leone, M. P., B. J. Little, M. S. Warner, P. B. Potter, Jr., P. A. Shackel, G. C. Logan, P. R. Mullins, and J. A. Ernstein. 1994. The Constituencies for an Archaeology of African Americans in Annapolis, Maryland. In *"I Too Am America": Studies in African American Archaeology*, T. Singleton (ed.). Charlottesville: University Press of Virginia.

Lewis, K. 1984. *The American Frontier: An Archaeological Study of Settlement Pattern and Process*. New York: Academic Press.

Little, B. J. 1988. Craft and Culture Change in the Eighteenth-century Chesapeake. In *The Recovery of Meaning*, M. P. Leone and P. B. Potter, Jr. (eds.), pp. 263–292. Washington, DC: Smithsonian Institution Press.

Little, B. J. 1992a. Text-Aided Archaeology. In *Text-Aided Archaeology*, B. J. Little (ed.), pp. 1–6. Boca Raton, FL: CRC Press.

Little, B. J. (ed.). 1992b. *Text-Aided Archaeology*. Boca Raton, FL: CRC Press.

Little, B. J. and P. A. Shackel. 1989. Scales of Historical Anthropology: An Archaeology of Colonial Anglo-America. *Antiquity* 63:495–509.

Little, B. J. and P. A. Shackel (eds.). 1992. Meanings and Uses of Material Culture. *Historical Archaeology* 26(3).

Lubar, S. and W. D. Kingery (eds.). 1993. *History from Things: Essays on Material Culture*. Washington, DC: Smithsonian Institution Press.

McCracken, G. 1988. *Culture and Consumption, New Approaches to the Symbolic Character of Consumer Goods and Activities*. Bloomington: Indiana University Press.

McDaniel, J. M. and K. C. Russ (eds.). 1984. *Historical Archaeology West of the Blue Ridge: A Regional Example from Rockbridge County*. The James G. Leyburn Papers in Anthropology, Vol. 1. Lexington, VA: Liberty Hall Press, Washington and Lee University.

McDonald, J. D., L. J. Zimmerman, A. L. McDonald, W. Tall Bull, and T. Rising Sun. 1991. The Northern Cheyenne Outbreak of 1879: Using Oral History and Archaeology as Tools of Resistance. In *The Archaeology of Inequality*, R. H. McGuire and R. Paynter (eds.), pp. 64–78. Oxford: Basil Blackwell.

McGhee, R. 1984. Contact Between Native North Americans and the Medieval Norse: A Review of the Evidence. *American Antiquity* 49:4–26.

McGinty, J. R. 1955. Symbols of a Civilization that Perished in Its Infancy. *Early Georgia* 1(4):14–17.

McGuire, R. H. 1982. The Study of Ethnicity in Historical Archaeology. *Journal of Anthropological Archaeology* 1:159–178.

McGuire, R. H. 1988. Dialogues with the Dead: Ideology and the Cemetery. In *The Recovery of Meaning Historical Archaeology in the Eastern United States*, M. P. Leone and P. B. Potter, Jr. (eds.), pp. 435–480. Washington, DC: Smithsonian Institution Press.

McGuire, R. H. 1991. Building Power in the Cultural Landscape of Broome County, New York, 1880 to 1940. In *The Archaeology of Inequality*, R. H. McGuire and R. Paynter (eds.), pp. 102–124. Oxford: Basil Blackwell.

McGuire, R. H. and R. Paynter (eds.). 1991. *The Archaeology of Inequality*. Oxford: Basil Blackwell.

McKee, L., V. P. Hood, and S. Macpherson. 1992. Reinterpreting the Construction History of the Service Area of the Hermitage Mansion. In *Text-Aided Archaeology*, B. J. Little (ed.), pp. 163–180. Boca Raton, FL: CRC Press.

McKendrick, N., J. Brewer, and J. H. Plumb. 1982. *The Birth of a Consumer Society: The Commercialization of the Eighteenth Century*. Bloomington: Indiana University Press.

McLoughlin, W. G. 1984. *Cherokees and Missionaries 1789–1839*. New Haven: Yale University Press.

McLoughlin, W. G. 1986. *Cherokee Renascence in the New Republic*. Princeton: Princeton University Press.

Meltzer, D. J. 1981. Ideology and material culture. In *Modern Material Culture: The Archaeology of Us*, R. A. Gould and M. B. Schiffer (eds.), pp. 113–125. New York: Academic Press.

Miller, D. and C. Tilley. 1984. Ideology, Power, and Prehistory: An Introduction. In *Ideology, Power, and Prehistory*, D. Miller and C. Tilley (eds.), pp. 1–15. Cambridge: Cambridge University Press.

Miller, G. 1980. Classification and Economic Scaling of 19th-century Ceramics. *Historical Archaeology* 14:1–41.

Miller, G. 1991. A Revised Set of CC Index Values for Classification and Economic Scaling of English Ceramics from 1787 to 1880. *Historical Archaeology* 25(1):1–25.

Miller H. 1986. *Discovering Maryland's First City: A Summary Report on the 1981–1984 Archaeological Investigations in St. Mary's City Maryland*. St. Mary's City Archaeology Series No. 2, St. Mary's City, MD.

Mooney, J. 1900. *Myths of the Cherokee*. Bureau of American Ethnography, 19th Annual Report, 1897–1898, Washington, DC.

Mooney, J. 1975. *Historical Sketch of the Cherokee*. Chicago: Aldine.

Mrozowski, S. L. 1988. Historical Archaeology as Anthropology. *Historical Archaeology* 22(1):18–24.

Neiman, F. D. 1978. Domestic Architecture at the Clifts Plantation: The Social Context of Early Virginia Building. *Northern Neck of Virginia Historical Magazine* 28:3096–3128. Reprinted in *Common Places: Readings in American Vernacular Architecture* (1986), D. Upton and J. M. Vlach (eds.), pp. 292–314. Athens: University of Georgia Press.

Neuman, R. W. (ed.). 1983. Historical Archaeology of the Eastern United States: Papers from the R. J. Russell Symposium. *Geoscience and Man* 26.

Noël Hume, I. 1964. Archaeology: Handmaiden to History. *The North Carolina Historical Review* 41(2): 215–225.

Noël Hume, I. 1983. *Martin's Hundred*. New York: Alfred A. Knopf.

Orser, C. E., Jr. 1988a. *The Material Basis of the Postbellum Tenant Plantation: Historical Archaeology in the South Carolina Piedmont*. Athens: University of Georgia Press.

Orser, C. E., Jr. 1988b. Toward a Theory of Power for Historical Archaeology: Plantation and Space. In *The Recovery of Meaning: Historical Archaeology in the Eastern United States*, M. P. Leone and P. B. Potter, Jr. (eds.), pp. 313–343. Washington, DC: Smithsonian Institution Press.

Orser, C. E., Jr. 1989. On Plantations and Patterns. *Historical Archaeology* 23(2): 28–40.

Orser, C. E., Jr. 1990a. Archaeological Approaches to New World Plantation Slavery. In *Archaeological Method and Theory, Vol. 2*, M. B. Schiffer (ed.), pp. 111–154. Tucson: University of Arizona Press.

Orser, C. E., Jr. (ed.). 1990b. Historical Archaeology on Southern Plantations and Farms. *Historical Archaeology* 24(4).

Otto, J. S. 1984. *Cannon's Point Plantation 1794-1860: Living Conditions and Status Patterns in the Old South.* Orlando: Academic Press.

Pastron, A. G. and E. M. Hattori (eds.). 1990. *The Hoff Store Site and Gold Rush Merchandise from San Francisco, California.* Special Publication No. 7, Society for Historical Archaeology, California, Pennsylvania.

Patterson, T. 1990a. History and the Post-processual Archaeologies. *Man* 24:555–566.

Patterson, T. 1990b. Some Theoretical Tensions Within and Between the Processual and Postprocessual Archaeologies. *Journal of Anthropological Archaeology* 9:189–200.

Paynter, R. 1982. *Models of Spatial Inequality: Settlement Patterns in Historical Archaeology.* New York: Academic Press.

Paynter, R. 1985. Surplus Flow Between Frontiers and Homelands. In *The Archaeology of Frontiers and Boundaries*, S. W. Green and S. M. Perlman (eds.), pp. 163–211. Orlando: Academic Press.

Paynter, R. 1988. Steps to an Archaeology of Capitalism. In *The Recovery of Meaning Historical Archaeology in the Eastern United States*, M. P. Leone and P. B. Potter, Jr. (eds.), pp. 407–433. Washington, DC: Smithsonian Institution Press.

Paynter, R. 1989. The Archaeology of Equality and Inequality. *Annual Review of Anthropology* 18:369–399.

Paynter, R. and R. H. McGuire. 1991. The Archaeology of Inequality: Material Culture, Domination and Resistance. In *The Archaeology of Inequality*, McGuire, R. H., and Paynter, R. (eds.), pp. 1–27. Oxford: Basil Blackwell.

Perdue, T. 1979. *Slavery and the Evolution of Cherokee Society 1540–1866.* Knoxville: University of Tennessee Press.

Perdue, T. (ed.). 1983. *Cherokee Editor, The Writings of Elias Boudinot.* Knoxville: University of Tennessee Press.

Perdue, T. 1989. *The Cherokee.* New York: Chelsea House.

Persico, V. R., Jr. 1979. Early Nineteenth-Century Cherokee Political Organization. In *The Cherokee Indian Nation*, D. H. King (ed.), pp. 92–109. Knoxville: University of Tennessee Press.

Pillsbury, R. 1983. The Europeanization of the Cherokee Settlement Landscape Prior to Removal: A Georgia Case Study. *Geoscience and Man* 23:59–69.

Posnansky, M. and C. R. Decorse. 1986. Historical Archaeology in Sub-Saharan Africa—A Review. *Historical Archaeology* 20(1):1–14.

Potter, P. B., Jr. 1992. Middle-Range Theory, Ceramics, and Capitalism in 19th-century Rockbridge County, Virginia. In *Text-Aided Archaeology*, B. J. Little (ed.), pp. 9–24. Boca Raton, FL: CRC Press.

Potter, S. R. 1993. *Commoners, Tribute, and Chiefs; the Development of Algonquian Culture in the Potomac Valley.* Charlottesville: University Press of Virginia.

Preucel, R. W. (ed.). 1991. *Processual and Postprocessual Archaeologies: Multiple Ways of Knowing the Past*, Occasional Paper No. 10, Center for Archaeological Investigations, Southern Illinois University, Carbondale.

Ramenofsky, A. 1987. *Vectors of Death: The Archaeology of European Contact.* Albuquerque: University of New Mexico Press.

Rapp, W. F. and S. K. Beranek. 1984. *The Industrial Archaeology of Nebraska.* Crete, NE: J-B.

Rathje, W. L. 1979. Modern Material Culture Studies. In *Advances in Archaeological Method and Theory, Vol. 2.* M. B. Schiffer (ed.), pp. 1–29. New York: Academic Press.

Redman, C. L. 1986. *Qsar es-Seghir: An Archaeological View of Medieval Life.* New York: Academic Press.

Reitz, E. J. and M. Scarry. 1985. *Reconstructing Historic Subsistence with an Example from Sixteenth-Century Spanish Florida.* Special Publication, No. 3, Society for Historical Archaeology, California, PA.

Reynolds, B. and M. A. Stott (eds.). 1987. *Material Anthropology, Contemporary Approaches to Material Culture.* Lanham, MD: University Press of America.

Rogers, J. D. 1990. *Objects of Change: The Archaeology and History of Arikara Contact with Europeans.* Washington, DC: Smithsonian Institution Press.

Rogers, J. D. and S. M. Wilson. 1993. *Ethnohistory and Archaeology: Approaches to Postcontact Change in the Americas.* New York: Plenum.

Ronda, J. P. and J. Axtell. 1978. *Indian Missions: A Critical Bibliography.* Bloomington: Indiana University Press.

Rothschild, N. A. 1990. *New York City Neighborhoods, The 18th Century.* New York: Academic Press.

Sahlins, M. 1981. *Historical Metaphors and Mythical Realities.* Special Publication of the Association for Social Anthropology in Oceania No. 1, University of Michigan, Ann Arbor.

Sahlins, M. 1985. *Islands of History.* Chicago: University of Chicago Press.

Sande, T. A. 1976. *Industrial Archaeology: A New Look at the American Heritage.* Brattleboro, VT: S. Greene Press.

Schama, S. 1987. *The Embarrassment of Riches: An Interpretation of Dutch Culture in the Golden Age.* New York: Alfred Knopf.

Schiffer, M. B. 1976. *Behavioral Archaeology.* New York: Academic Press.

Schiffer, M. B. 1988. The Structure of Archaeological Theory. *American Antiquity* 53: 461–485.

Schiffer, M. B. 1991. *The Portable Radio in American Life.* Tucson: University of Arizona Press.

Schlereth, T. J. (ed.). 1985. *Material Culture: A Research Guide.* Lawrence: University Press of Kansas.

Schmidt, P. 1977. *Historical Archaeology: A Structural Approach in African Culture.* Westport, CT: Greenwood Press.

Schrire, C. and D. Merwick. 1991. Dutch-Indigenous Relations in New Netherland and the Cape in the Seventeenth Century. In *Historical Archaeology in Global Perspective*, L. Falk (ed.), pp. 11–20. Washington, DC: Smithsonian Institution Press.

Schuyler, R. L. 1970. Historical and Historic Sites Archaeology as Anthropology: Basic Definitions and Relationships. *Historical Archaeology* 4:83–89.

Schuyler, R. L. 1976. Images of America: The Contribution of Historical Archaeology to National Identity. *Southwestern Lore* 42(4):27–39.

Schuyler, R. L. (ed.). 1982. Urban Archaeology in America. *North American Archaeologist* 3(3).

Schuyler, R. L. 1988. Archaeological Remains, Documents, and Anthropology: A Call for a New Culture History. *Historical Archaeology* 22(1):36–42.

Scott, D. D., and R. A. Fox, Jr. 1987. *Archaeological Insights into the Custer Battle: An Assessment of the 1984 Field Season.* Norman: University of Oklahoma Press.

Scott, D. D., R. A. Fox, Jr., M. A. Conner, and D. Harmon. 1989. *Archaeological Perspectives on the Battle of the Little Bighorn.* Norman: University of Oklahoma Press.

Scott, J. C. 1985. *Weapons of the Weak: The Everyday Forms of Peasant Resistance.* New Haven: Yale University Press.

Scott, P. E. and J. Deetz. 1990. Building, Furnishings and Social Change in Early Victorian Grahamstown. *Social Dynamics* 16(1):76–89.

Seifert, D. J. (ed.). 1991. Gender in Historical Archaeology. *Historical Archaeology* 25(4).

Self, R. D. 1955. Chronology of New Echota. *Early Georgia* 1(4):3–5.

Shackel, P. 1993a. *A Historical Archaeology of Personal Discipline and Material Culture in the Chesapeake.* Knoxville: University of Tennessee Press.

Shackel, P. (ed.). 1993b. *Interdisciplinary Investigations of Domestic Life in Government Block B: Perspectives on Harpers Ferry's Armory and Commercial District.* Occasional Report No. 6. National Park Service, National Capital Region.

Shackel, P. A. and B. J. Little. 1992. Post-Processual Approaches to Meanings and Uses of Material Culture in Historical Archaeology. In *Meanings and Uses of Material Culture*, B. J. Little and P. A. Shackel (eds.). *Historical Archaeology* 26(3):5–11.

Shackel, P. A. and B. J. Little (eds.). 1994. *The Historical Archaeology of the Chesapeake.* Washington, DC: Smithsonian Institution Press.

Shanks, M. and C. Tilley. 1987. *Re-Constructing Archaeology Theory and Practice.* Cambridge: Cambridge University Press.

Sichone, O. B. 1989. The Development of an Urban Working-Class Culture on the Rhodesian Copperbelt. In *Domination and Resistance*, D. Miller, M. Rowlands, and C. Tilley (eds.), pp. 290–298. London: Unwin Hyman.

Sider, G. M. 1976. Lumbee Indian Cultural Nationalism and Ethnogenesis. *Dialectical Anthropology* 1:161–172.

Singleton, T. (ed.) 1985. *The Archaeology of Slavery and Plantation Life.* New York: Academic Press.

Singleton, T. In press. *"I Too Am America": Studies in African American Archaeology.* Charlottesville: University of Virginia Press.

Smith, M. T. 1987. *Archaeology of Aboriginal Culture Change in the Interior Southeast: Depopulation During the Early Historic Period.* Gainesville: University Press of Florida.

Smith, S. D. 1976. *An Archaeological and Historical Assessment of the First Hermitage.* Research Series No. 2, Tennessee Department of Conservation, Division of Archaeology.

South, S. 1977a. *Method and Theory in Historical Archaeology.* New York: Academic Press.

South, S. 1977b. *Research Strategies in Historical Archeology.* New York: Academic Press.

South, S. 1988a. Santa Elena: Threshold of Conquest. In *The Recovery of Meaning: Historical Archaeology in the Eastern United States*, M. P. Leone and P. B. Potter, Jr. (eds.), pp. 27–72. Washington, DC: Smithsonian Institution Press.

South, S. 1988b. Whither Pattern? *Historical Archaeology* 22(1):25–28.

Spencer-Wood, S. (ed.) 1987. *Consumer Choice in Historical Archaeology.* New York: Plenum.

Spencer-Wood, S. 1991.Toward an Historical Archaeology of Materialistic Domestic Reform. In *The Archaeology of Inequality*, R. H. McGuire and R. Paynter (eds.), pp. 231–286. Oxford: Basil Blackwell.

Staski, E. (ed.). 1987. *Living in Cities: Current Research in Urban Archaeology.* Special Publication No. 5, Society for Historical Archaeology, California, Pennsylvania.

Staski, E. 1990. Studies of Ethnicity in North American Historical Archaeology. *North American Archaeologist* 11(2):121–145.

Stevenson, M. G. 1982. Toward an Understanding of Site Abandonment Behavior: Evidence from Historic Mining Camps in the Southwest Yukon. *Journal of Anthropological Archaeology* 1:236–265.

St. George, R. B. (ed.). 1988. *Material Life in America, 1600–1860.* Boston: Northeastern University Press.

Stilgoe, J. R. 1982. *Common Landscapes of America, 1580 to 1845.* New Haven: Yale University Press.

Stone, G. and D. Ottusch-Kianka (eds.). 1987. *The Historical Archaeology of Long Island, Vol. 7, Part 1: The Sites.* Suffolk County Archaeological Association and Nassau County Archaeological Committee, Stony Brook, NY.

Thomas, D. H. (ed.). 1989. *Columbian Consequences, Vol. 1: Archaeological and Historical Perspectives on the Spanish Borderlands West.* Washington, DC: Smithsonian Institution Press.

Thomas, D. H. 1990. *Columbian Consequences, Vol. 2: Archaeological and Historical Perspectives on the Spanish Borderlands East.* Washington, DC: Smithsonian Institution Press.

Thomas, D. H. 1991. *Columbian Consequences, Vol. 3: The Spanish Borderlands in Pan-American Perspective.* Washington, DC: Smithsonian Institution Press.

Tilley, C. (ed.). 1990. *Reading Material Culture.* Oxford: Basil Blackwell.

Trigger, B. G. 1985. *Natives and Newcomers: Canada's "Heroic Age" Reconsidered.* Montreal: McGill-Queen's University Press.

Upton, D. 1986. *Holy Things and Profane: Anglican Parish Churches in Colonial Virginia.* Cambridge: Harvard University Press.

Upton, D. and J. M. Vlach (eds.). 1986. *Common Places: Readings in American Vernacular Architecture.* Athens: University of Georgia Press.

Vance, M. 1984. *Monographs on Industrial Archaeology.* Bibliography A1286, Vance Bibliographies, Architecture Series, Monticello, IL.

Verano, J. W. and D. H. Ubelaker (eds.). 1992. *Disease and Demography in the Americas.* Washington, DC: Smithsonian Institution Press.

Walde, D. and N. D. Willows (eds.). 1991. *The Archaeology of Gender.* Proceedings of the 22nd Annual Chacmool Conference, Archaeological Association of the University of Calgary, Calgary.

Wallace, A. F. C. 1970. *Culture and Personality.* New York: Random House.

Walthall, J. A. (ed.). 1990. *French Colonial Archaeology of the Illinois Country.* Urbana: University of Illinois Press.

Walthall, J. A. and T. E. Emerson (eds.). 1992. *Calumet and Fleur-de-Lys: Archaeology of the Indian and French Contact in the Midcontinent.* Washington, DC: Smithsonian Institution Press.

Ward, A. E. (ed.). 1983. *Forgotten Places and Things, Archaeological Perspectives on American History.* Center for Anthropological Studies, Albuquerque.

Watson, P. J. and M. Fotiadis. 1990. The Razor's Edge: Symbolic-structuralist Archeology and the Expansion of Archeological Inference. *American Anthropologist* 92:613–629.

Watson R. A. 1990. Ozymandias, King of Kings: Postprocessual Radical Archaeology as Critique. *American Antiquity* 55:673–689.

Wegars, P. (ed.). 1993. *Hidden Heritage, Historical Archaeology of the Overseas Chinese.* Amityville, NY: Baywood.

Wilms, D. 1974. Cherokee Indian Land Use in Georgia 1800–1888. Ph.D. dissertation. University of Georgia.

Wilson, J. H., Jr. (ed.). 1985. *Current Research in the Historical Archaeology of the Carolinas.* Chicora Foundation Research Series No. 4, Columbia, SC.

Winer, M. and J. Deetz. 1990. The Transformation of British Culture in the Eastern Cape, 1820–1860. *Social Dynamics* 16(1):55–75.

Wobst, H. M. 1977. Stylistic Behavior and Information Exchange. In *For the Director: Research Essays in Honor of James B. Griffin*, C. E. Cleland (ed.), Museum of Anthropology Publication 61, University of Michigan, Ann Arbor.

Wolf, E. 1982. *Europe and the People Without History.* Berkeley: University of California Press.

Wolf. E. 1990. Distinguished Lecture: Facing Power—Old Insights, New Questions. *American Anthropologist* 92:586–596.

Wood, P., G. A. Waselkov, and T. Hantley (eds.). 1989. *Powhatan's Mantle: Indians in the Colonial Southeast.* Lincoln: University of Nebraska Press.

Yentsch, A. (ed.). 1987. Humanism and Revisionism in Historical Archaeology. *American Archaeology* 6(1).

Yentsch, A. 1991a. Engendering Visible and Invisible Ceramic Artifacts, Especially Dairy Vessels. *Historical Archaeology* 25(4):132–155.

Yentsch, A. 1991b. The Symbolic Divisions of Pottery: Sex-related Attributes of English and Anglo-American Household Pots. In *The Archaeology of Inequality*, R. H. McGuire and R. Paynter (eds.), pp. 192–230. Oxford: Basil Blackwell.

Yentsch, A. E. and M. C. Beaudry (eds.). 1992. *Art and Mystery of Historical Archaeology: Essays in Honor of James Deetz.* Boca Raton, FL: CRC Press.

Young, B. K. 1992. Text Aided or Text Misled? Reflections on the Uses of Archaeology in Medieval History. In *Text-Aided Archaeology*, B. J. Little (ed.), pp. 135–150. Boca Raton, FL: CRC Press.

PART II

People and Places

Historical archaeologists conduct research at a vast variety of sites. Sites studied can range in date from the late 15th to the late 20th centuries, and can examine men and women from many cultural traditions. Though the true scope of the cultures examined by historical archaeologists is impossible to present in this book, I have selected five articles that will give you a good idea of the diverse people and places historical archaeologists regularly study. At the same time, these chapters will introduce you to the kinds of research questions historical archaeologists pose.

In the first chapter, archaeologist David Hurst Thomas, from the American Museum of Natural History in New York, explains his 15 years of research at Mission Santa Catalina de Guale, a Spanish colonial outpost on an island off the coast of Georgia. Thomas details the methods he used to search for the lost mission site and describes the material culture used by the people who once lived there. Thomas points out that colonial Europeans, when they went in search of "new" lands to settle, did not enter empty landscapes devoid of human habitation. On the contrary, everywhere they went, exploring Europeans met and interacted with numerous indigenous cultures that had been developing for generations. Though Americanist historical archaeology is often incorrectly perceived as focusing only on European colonists and their ancestors, many historical archaeologists regularly study the ways in which native peoples interacted, resisted, and succumbed to European influence. Thomas's article demonstrates the complexities of cultural interaction, and illustrates why historical archaeologists must consider both Europeans and indigenous peoples when they study culture contact.

We next travel north to a famous site, Valley Forge, Pennsylvania. This site has entered the world's imagination because of an event that occurred there for six months during the winter of 1777–78: the bivouacking of the Continental Army during the American Revolution. Archaeologists began investigating the site in the 1960s with an eye toward using the excavated information to improve the interpretation presented to the site's visitors. When Michael Parrington, an archaeologist with Helen Schenck Associates—a private archaeological consulting firm—and his colleagues Helen Schenck and Jacqueline Thibaut, began to study the encampment, their goal was to provide concrete, physical information about the actual material conditions faced by Washington's beleaguered troops during that fateful winter. Their examination highlights the important role that historical archaeology plays in understanding sites and properties that at first seem so well known. The data presented by Parrington and his colleagues about the habitation huts and the objects used by the soldiers give us a behind-the-scenes peek at a common soldier's life during the American Revolution. Without archaeology, this picture would remain forever blank. At the same time, this article exemplifies the importance of historical archaeology for site interpretors, even at the world's most famous places.

The issue of remaining blank is taken up by Theresa Singleton, an archaeologist with the Smithsonian Institution, in her overview of the archaeology of African-American slavery in the American South and the Caribbean. Though the history of New World slavery has been and continues to be well told by historians, most of the mundane elements of this cruel institution remained hidden from view until archaeologists started probing the soils of former slave sites. Singleton indicates that archaeologists who have examined slavery have uncovered a wealth of information about several elements of everyday African-American life. Archaeological research has shown, for example, that slaves brought to the New World aspects of their African cultures, and that they often combined these cultural traits with those of Native Americans and Europeans. Archaeologists also have unearthed evidence for the most basic material conditions of the slaves' physical existence, relating to food, clothing, and housing. As Singleton also shows, several archaeologists have begun to delve into the world of slave religion, a subject frequently kept hidden from slave masters and plantation owners. Singleton's portrait of archaeological research demonstrates the limitless future of African-American archaeology as a way of discovering the details of a way of life that was for too long thought unknowable.

From African-American slaves we move in the next chapter to the Chinese immigrants of El Paso, Texas. Here, archaeologist Edward Staski, from New Mexico State University, addresses the difficult archaeological subjects of changing ethnic relations and multiculturalism. Archaeologists find ethnicity a difficult subject because they must first understand how social attributes, like ethnicity, are represented in the silent archaeological remains they excavate. Once they are confident they have reached this level of understanding, they must then examine how ethnic relations have evolved over time. Historical archaeologists, of course, have recourse to written records that they can use to guide their research, but these documents often do not make their task any easier. Archaeologists must still understand the material expressions of ethnic group maintenance and change. In this chapter, Staski examines the social conditions experienced by Chinese immigrants, with an eye toward understanding how they adapted, as an ethnic group, to their new surroundings. Staski contributes to the anthropological understanding of ethnic boundary maintenance by showing that these men and women did not become completely absorbed by the dominant American culture around them. He shows that the Chinese had little impact on the power structure in the city and that the discrimination they faced encouraged them to maintain strong ethnic boundaries. Staski's article demonstrates how historical archaeologists can tackle complex anthropological subjects like ethnicity and through detailed site investigation provide important insights into their material dimensions.

In the final chapter of this section, we travel from Texas to Washington, DC, at a roughly contemporaneous time. Donna Seifert, an archaeologist with John Milner Associates, a private archaeological consulting firm, explores the archaeological nature of a subject seldom mentioned in academic settings: prostitution. Seifert's research gives a glimpse at the everyday, material conditions of women in Hooker's Division, a section of Washington within sight of the White House. Typically, the lives of prostitutes are only documented in bland, often unemotional terms in census rolls, city directories, and police blotters. Seifert instills life into prostitution, and rather than attempting to envision it as some kind of social aberration, shows that prostitution was largely an economic decision made by working-class women who had few other choices. Seifert's article also illustrates an important side of historical archaeology. Because of the nature of their research, archaeologists are usually permitted to examine history and culture as they unfolded over time, often over vast generations. Historical archaeologists, however, generally do not study huge blocks of time. In most cases their analyses usually cover only decades. But there is much to be said in favor of this ability to examine such short time frames. As an example, Seifert investigates the changes that occurred among the women of Hooker's Division from 1870 to 1890 and from 1890 to 1920. The excavated artifacts revealed that prostitution became more lucrative in the later period. Seifert's look at women who are not usually the focus of archaeological research again illustrates the important role that historical archaeologists play in bringing to light the lives and cultures of many different kinds of people and places, many of whom are often ignored by documentary history.

DAVID HURST THOMAS ■

Chapter Three

The Archaeology of Mission Santa Catalina de Guale:

Our First 15 Years

In 1977 the American Museum of Natural History began searching for Mission Santa Catalina de Guale, located somewhere on St. Catherines Island, Georgia. Four years later we found that site and have been excavating the 16th- and 17th-century archaeological remains ever since. Here we review how we located Santa Catalina, summarize the findings to date, and set out the research framework for additional work. We have learned much, but we caution the reader that despite our 15 years of archaeological investigations, the human story played out at Mission Santa Catalina remains very much a work in progress (see Thomas 1987, 1988a, 1988b).[1]

Ethnohistorical Background

The Guale Indians living at Santa Catalina and elsewhere along the Georgia coast were among the first indigenous peoples met by Europeans exploring north of Mexico (Jones 1978; Larson 1978; Sturtevant 1962; Swanton 1922:81, 1946:603; Thomas 1990). In 1526 the Spanish made brief contact with this Muskhogean-speaking group and the French encountered them in 1562–1563. Then, beginning in 1566, the Guale were exposed to a long, intensive period of Spanish colonization. By 1684 the gradual withdrawal of the Spanish to the south and the correlative southward expansion of the Carolina colony prompted relocation and reorganization of the vastly reduced Guale population.

This article was originally published in *The Spanish Missions of La Florida*, Bonnie G. McEwan, ed., pp. 1–34, Gainesville: University Press of Florida, ©1993.

St. Catherines Island may (or may not) have been an important settlement during the earliest phase of European contact, but there is no doubt that an important Guale town existed there by at least 1576 (Jones 1978:203). Spanish mission efforts were minimal at this point; the year 1584 found only four Franciscan friars stationed throughout all of *La Florida*, and they spent their time ministering to Spanish needs at St. Augustine and Santa Elena, with little time for missionizing the Guale and Timucua.

The Spanish named the Guale Indians for the chiefdom centered at the principal town on St. Catherines Island; the associated Franciscan mission eventually became known as Santa Catalina de Guale. By 1597, a decade after the abandonment of Santa Elena, 14 friars were stationed in *La Florida* and several of these served in Guale (Geiger 1940). That year, the Indians of Guale staged a major revolt partly played out on St. Catherines Island—an uprising with distinctly nativistic overtones (Sturtevant 1962:58).

For a time the missions were abandoned, but after their resettlement in the early 17th century (Ross 1926), Spanish hegemony remained unchallenged until 1670, when the English established Charles Town, South Carolina. Spanish missions on the barrier islands of coastal Georgia became the first victims in the so-called conflict over the "debatable land" (Bolton and Ross 1925). After the Spanish launched an unsuccessful expedition to attack and destroy Charles Town, the southernmost British settlement, the British retaliated in force, steadily pushing down the coast and across the interior toward the Mississippi.

In 1680 the British forces attacked the fortified mission at Santa Catalina, which was defended by a small and hastily organized band of Spaniards and Guale Indians (Bolton and Ross 1925:36). Although the Guale successfully held off the invaders, they were horrified by the attack and St. Catherines Island was soon abandoned. British travelers in 1687 and 1738 described the ruins of Santa Catalina (Dunlop 1929:131; Hvidt 1980:39), but the mission site was "lost" soon thereafter.

Previous Attempts to Find Santa Catalina

We were hardly the first to look for Santa Catalina de Guale. Historians and ethnographers have debated the whereabouts of the site of Santa Catalina for decades. Swanton (1922:50–55) thought that the principal town of Guale and its associated mission were initially established on St. Catherines Island in the spring of 1566. A member of our research team, Grant Jones (1978:203), has argued that prior to 1575 the town of Guale was *not* on St. Catherines Island but rather to the north, either near Skidaway Island or on Ossabaw. There was no question, however, that by 1587 both the Guale chiefdom and the associated Franciscan mission existed somewhere on St. Catherines Island (Bolton and Ross 1925; Gannon 1965:39; Jones 1978:204; Lyon 1976:154; Ross 1926).

Such conjecture was then supplemented by hands-on archaeology in the 1950s and 1960s (Figure 3.1). As part of the Georgia Historical Commission search for 16th–17th-century Spanish mission sites along the Georgia coast, Lewis Larson visited St. Catherines Island in 1952. Among the "good candidates for the location of a mission," Larson (1952:2) listed "Wamassee Head on St. Catherines as the location of Santa Catherina de Guale," but he cautioned that "no final and conclusive identification of a mission site can be made until adequate excavation . . . has been undertaken."

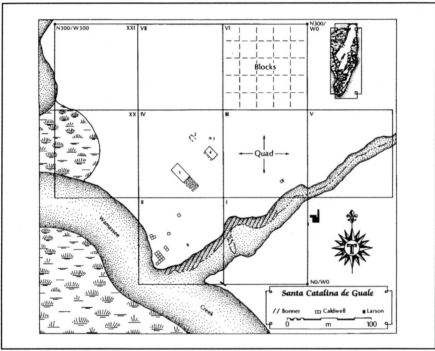

Figure 3.1. Map showing the location of Mission Santa Catalina on St. Catherines Island, Georgia. The numbered mission buildings in Quad IV were excavated by the American Museum of Natural History (1981–1990). Previous archaeological investigations by Larson, Bonner, and Caldwell are also indicated. Reproduced with the permission of the American Museum of Natural History.

Larson returned to excavate at Wamassee Creek six years later. The recovered sherd sample consisted primarily of aboriginal wares dating to the Spanish period, and majolica was found comparable to that from Spanish mission sites in Florida. But no structural evidence of Santa Catalina emerged in these limited tests.

In the mid-1950s the general location of Santa Catalina was "rediscovered" by John W. Bonner and Carrol Hart, who had been retained by Edward John Noble to prepare a historical overview of St. Catherines Island. Apparently unaware of Larson's earlier work, Hart and Bonner used the 1687 account (Dunlop 1929) to look for Santa Catalina. Before long, Bonner and Gaffney Blalock photographed several olive jar and majolica sherds eroding from the creek bed, correctly pinpointing Wamassee Creek as the probable location of Santa Catalina de Guale.

In April 1965 John W. Grifffin (then staff archaeologist, National Park Service) visited St. Catherines Island to gather information regarding the eligibility of the site of Santa Catalina mission as a Registered National Historic Landmark. Although he subsequently reported that "further work on the site of Santa Catalina mission is in some respects of the highest priority" (Griffin 1965a:10–11), Griffin also warned that given "the perishable nature of the structures themselves—they were of poles and thatch, not masonry—it can readily be seen that extensive archaeological work would be needed to pinpoint individual buildings of the settlement" (Griffin 1965b:5–7).

Joseph R. Caldwell and students from the University of Georgia conducted three seasons of archaeological fieldwork on St. Catherines Island in 1969–1971. Although they excavated mostly in mounds elsewhere on the island (see Larsen and Thomas 1982:271–342), they sank several test pits in the Wamassee Creek area. In unpublished field notes Caldwell concluded: "There is no reason to believe, at present, that this is not the site of the mission of Santa Catalina. So far, however, our excavations have yielded little structural detail" (J. R. Caldwell n.d.).

Such was the state of knowledge regarding the location of Mission Santa Catalina when the American Museum of Natural History started working on St. Catherines Island in 1974. The combined French, English, and Spanish historic documentation available in the late 1970s supplied little more than general geographic clues. The limited archaeological evidence suggested only that *if* any mission structures remained intact they were likely to be buried somewhere near the southwestern marsh on St. Catherines Island.

Discovering Mission Santa Catalina: 1977–1981

We began our own search for Santa Catalina with an extensive program of reconnaissance and site evaluation for all of St. Catherines Island; here we briefly summarize that research (see Thomas 1987, 1988a).

The Regional Random Sample

We initially employed a research design deliberately patterned after our earlier work at Pleistocene Lake Tonopah, Nevada. This survey generated a 20 percent sample of the island, obtained in a series of 31 east-west transects, each 100 m wide. We found 135 archaeological sites, ranging from massive shell heaps to small, isolated shell scatters; each "site" was explored with two or more 1-m-square test units; more than 400 such test pits were dug in this phase of excavation. We are presently completing a book-length treatment of these survey findings (Thomas n.d.; see also Thomas 1989:228–230).

In addition to providing extensive data on the settlement pattern and cultural ecology of St. Catherines Island during the precontact period, the survey sampling also clearly demonstrated that 16th–17th-century Spanish period remains occurred at only a handful of the 135 archaeological sites investigated. Significantly, relevant mission-period materials showed up only around Wamassee Creek (as earlier investigators had correctly surmised).

Abortive Efforts at Randomized Test Pitting

This regional approach confirmed and complemented earlier archaeological investigations by Larson, Bonner, Griffin, and Caldwell: Mission Santa Catalina almost certainly was in a 10-ha tract near Wamassee Creek. But the nature of the mission ruins remained unknown. Did Santa Catalina survive merely as 16th- and 17th-century garbage middens, or was structural evidence buried somewhere nearby?

In 1980 the research focus shifted from systematic regional to intrasite sampling. Where in these 10 ha should we begin digging? Although we tried randomized test pitting, such blind testing was slow, tedious, and rather unproductive. Roughly 200 person-days were invested in the randomized test pit procedures at Santa Catalina, but we soon recognized that to understand the structure of this site, a huge sampling fraction would be required. We dug up plenty of intriguing material—mostly from the Spanish period—but these excavations lacked any sense of context because of the relatively small "window" provided by each 1-m test pit. At Santa Catalina, randomized test pitting told us little more than where not to dig.

Auger Sampling

Looking around for better ways to find the needle hidden somewhere in this haystack, we were inspired by Kathleen Deagan's successful search for 16th-century St. Augustine. Following her example, we initiated a systematic auger test survey throughout the high-probability area at Wamassee Creek (Deagan 1981; see also Shapiro 1987).

Auger testing quickly generated the data we needed. Once field testing was complete (by mid-1981), we plotted the distribution of Spanish-period materials in a series of simple dot-density maps. Sherd density varied considerably across the 10 ha sampled, with the central and western zones containing extremely high densities of Spanish period aboriginal sherds and Hispanic ceramics. Accepting the conventional wisdom that Hispanic/aboriginal sherd ratios reflect social status (e.g., Deagan 1983:114–116; South 1977:172–175), a single 100-m-by-100-m tract emerged as the most probable location for the central mission complex (Figure 3.1).

This area, termed Quad IV, was a totally unremarkable piece of real estate, covered by the same scrub palmetto/live oak forest typical of the western margin of St. Catherines. The only evidence of any human occupation was a little-used field road for island research vehicles. Although shell midden scatters were evident here and there, Quad IV contained absolutely no surface evidence distinguishing it from its surroundings. In effect, the simple and expedient auger testing had narrowed the focus from 10 ha to 1 ha.

Significantly, Quad IV contained relatively little shell midden compared with surrounding areas. After all, if this was a "sacred" precinct, then it should have been (and apparently was) kept fairly clear of everyday (secular) garbage. Ironically, had we followed the conventional search strategy (find the largest shell midden and center punch it), we would certainly have missed the mission church, cemetery, and associated *convento* complex.

A Successful Appeal to Remote Sensing Technology

At this point we shifted methods once again—from relatively destructive subsurface testing to more noninvasive, nondestructive remote sensing. We followed three specific objectives in this phase of our work at Santa Catalina: (1) to locate and define the mission complex, (2) to determine the general size and configuration of buried features and structures before they were excavated, and (3) to build a baseline library of geophysical signatures to be projected against the independent evidence of future archaeological excavation.

The initial instrument prospection at Santa Catalina was a proton magnetometer survey, conducted in May 1981 by Ervan G. Garrison and James Tribble; subsequent surveys took place over the next two years. Although several computer graphic techniques helped filter and refine the magnetic survey data (see Garrison, Baker, and Thomas 1985; Thomas 1987:47–161), such remote sensing paid off significantly even before the computer plots were available.

We explored three major magnetic anomalies in the few remaining days of our May 1981 field season. The first such anomaly, located near an auger hole that had previously produced daub, turned out to be the well-preserved Franciscan church (*iglesia*), which we identified as Structure 1. The second anomaly was the mission kitchen (*cocina*), now denoted as Structure 2. The third magnetic anomaly was a mission-period barrel well.

Although the magnetometer survey yielded accurate indications of daub wall segments, subsequent soil resistivity studies provided a better way to define the configuration and extent of the unexcavated buildings. In the spring of 1982, Gary Shapiro and Mark Williams conducted a pilot study to determine the potential and feasibility of large-scale resistivity prospection at Santa Catalina (Thomas 1987: 47–161, 1989:238–241; see also Shapiro 1984). Not only did soil resistivity provide a general projection of site structure across the central mission precinct, but it also gave us excellent structure-by-structure resolution, defining the shape, orientation, and extent of several unexcavated buildings at Santa Catalina. This soil resistivity survey also disclosed the presence of a previously unknown building, the mission *convento* (Structure 4). These projections were then tested against independent data generated from ground-penetrating radar studies across Quad IV, conducted in 1984.

We believe that today's remote sensing technology provides archaeologists with powerful, cost-effective means of generating noninvasive, nondestructive assessments of the archaeological record (Weymouth 1986:311), and we are at present expanding our remote sensing efforts at Santa Catalina (see below).

Excavating at Santa Catalina: 1981–1990

We have been digging at Santa Catalina for a decade, and our field investigations continue. Although future excavations and analysis will doubtless refine our interpretations, the basics of site structure are now quite apparent.

The entire mission complex and the Guale pueblo that surrounded it followed a rigid grid system in which the long axis of the church was oriented 45° west of magnetic north (see Thomas 1987:47–161, 1988b). The central plaza was rectangular, measuring 23 m by approximately 40 m. The church (Structure 1) defined the western margin of the central plaza; the *cocina* and *convento(s)* defined the eastern margin (Figures 3.1 and 3.2).

The Churches of Santa Catalina

The church at Santa Catalina has been completely exposed; except for the eastern wall, preserved as a witness section, the entire church deposit was excavated. We can recognize two sequential church structures. The late 16th-century *iglesia* was destroyed by fire, probably in September 1597. These ruins were personally inspected Governor Gonzalo Méndez de Canzo, who had traveled north from St. Augustine to observe for himself the aftermath of the Guale rebellion (Geiger 1937:103–104). Unfortunately, later building episodes have largely obscured the appearance of the earlier church.

Figure 3.2. Low-level aerial photograph showing excavations in Quad IV at Santa Catalina de Guale (as of May 1984). The top of the photograph is magnetic north, and the white tick marks are spaced at 20-m intervals. Toward the bottom center is the church (Structure 1); the two dark linear daub concentrations (upper right) form the *convento/cocina* complex (see also structure placement in Figure 3.1). The light-colored vertical stripes are 4-m-wide shallow test trenches. Reproduced with the permission of the American Museum of Natural History (photography by Dennis O'Brien).

After a period of abandonment, Santa Catalina was resettled by the Spanish in 1604 and the mission church was reconstructed (apparently on the 16th-century site). Most of what we term Structure 1 at Santa Catalina is the primary 17th-century church, abandoned shortly after the British siege in 1680. This later church was constructed on a single nave plan, lacking both transept and chancel. The rectangular structure is 20 m long and 11 m wide. The facade, facing southeast, was the only one built strictly of wattlework; it was anchored to four round uprights set into shell-lined postholes. Either a pointed gable was elevated to support a steep thatch roof (as in Manucy 1985:Fig. 5), or the facade sported a false front projecting above the single-story construction of the nave.

The lateral church walls were constructed of both wattlework and pine planking. The nave portion of the church was 16 m long and decorated in places by figures sculpted in clay (as in Figure 3.3, right).

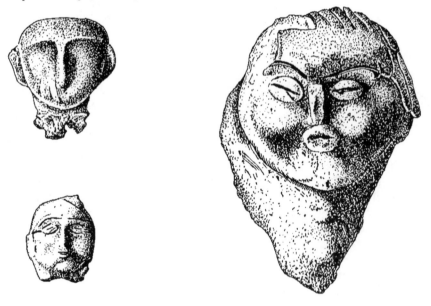

Figure 3.3. Selected Guale Indian human sculptures found at Mission Santa Catalina. Reproduced with the permission of the American Museum of Natural History.

The symbolic separation between nave and sanctuary was emphasized by a composite construction technique. The sanctuary (northwestern) end of the church, constructed entirely of wooden planking, was apparently elevated above the lateral wattle-and-daub walls of the nave. Some evidence suggests that the interior of the sanctuary may have been decorated with a reredos, several ornamental metal panels that were apparently not removed before the church was abandoned.

Although we have relied heavily on the available historical documentation to date the various daub walls encountered at Mission Santa Catalina, independent and *strictly archaeological* evidence is also desirable. Ceramic evidence helps, but we were looking for something more precise. In consultation with Robert Dunnell (Department of Anthropology, University of Washington), we have conducted a pilot study of thermoluminescence dating of these wall daub deposits. The first step was to determine the chemical composition of daub at Santa Catalina by X-ray fluorescence analysis; Dunnell's analysis indicates that the daub was almost certainly obtained from nearby marsh mud sources. Several dosimeters were buried over two-year intervals around the site to monitor the degree of contemporary thermoluminescent activity. Numerous archaeological samples, which were then taken from the collapsed walls of the *iglesia, convento,* and *cocina,* are currently being processed in the thermoluminescence laboratory of the University of Washington.

A clearly demarcated sacristy, measuring 5 m wide by 3 m deep, was built on the Gospel side of the church (the left-hand side of the sanctuary as one faces the altar). This room was presumably used for storage of vestments, linens, candles, processional materials, and other ritual paraphernalia essential to celebration of the Mass (Bushnell 1990). Inside we found a cache of charred wheat, which was probably destined to be baked into the "host," the flat bread used in the Eucharist. Donna L. Ruhl (Department of Anthropology, University of Florida) is currently analyzing these materials as part of her more extensive analysis of paleobotanical remains recovered from Santa Catalina (see also Ruhl 1990).

Although wheat had never assumed great dietary importance to Spaniards living in *La Florida*, this inglorious cache inside the sacristy underscores the effectiveness of the Franciscan order in obtaining the supplies necessary for the proper conduct of church ritual—even on the most remote northern frontier of the Guale province. Amy Bushnell (research associate, American Museum of Natural History and Department of History, Johns Hopkins University) is pursuing this matter in detail, analyzing the documentary evidence of the economic support systems necessary to sustain Mission Santa Catalina (Bushnell 1992).

The Churchyard *(Atrio)*

Fronting the church at Santa Catalina is a square shell-covered subplaza, measuring about 15 m on a side. This *atrio* was probably a low-walled enclosure demarcating the public entrance to the church. Ubiquitous features of New World religious architecture, such churchyards not only served as decorous entryways into the church but also functioned as outdoor chapels, areas to contain overflow congregations, and sometimes as cemeteries (Kubler 1940:73–75; Montgomery, Smith, and Brew 1949:54).

The churchyard at Santa Catalina was constructed of water-rolled marine shell, available from naturally occurring deposits scattered along the intracoastal waterway; today these massive shell bars, accessible only by watercraft, continue to provide building aggregate to an island lacking local stone.

The Cemetery (Campo Santo)

The only known cemetery at Santa Catalina was found inside the church, where we encountered a minimum of 431 individuals buried beneath the floor of the nave and sanctuary. Clark Spencer Larsen (research associate, American Museum of Natural History, and professor of anthropology, University of North Carolina) supervised the complete excavation of this cemetery between 1982 and 1986; the extensive biocultural evidence from Santa Catalina has been discussed elsewhere (see Larsen 1990:8–10; Larsen et al. 1990).[2]

The *campo santo* at Santa Catalina also contained a truly astounding array of associated grave goods, including nearly three dozen crosses (Figure 3.4), medallions (Figure 3.5), small medals (Figure 3.6), so-called Jesuit finger rings (with unique sculpted Sacred Heart castings), and a cast figurine depicting the infant Jesus holding a cross in one hand and raising the other in a gesture of blessing. The material, form, and iconography of nearly three dozen Catholic religious items have been analyzed by Richard E. Ahlborn (curator, National Museum of American History, Smithsonian Institution).

Additional grave goods in the *campo santo* include four complete majolica vessels, several projectile points, a chunkey stone, a rattlesnake shell gorget in the "Tellico" style, two complete glass cruets, two mirrors, two hawk's bells, one rosary, eight shroud pins, two copper plaque fragments, and one large piece of shroud cloth. The cemetery also contained literally tens of thousands of glass beads, which are currently being analyzed. Most were embroidery beads sewn onto clothing and sashes; other beads were portions of jewelry and ornaments. Rosary beads were commonly found accompanying burials. The remainder of the beads are aboriginal shell beads and lapidary beads.

The Friary (Convento) *Complex*

Eastward across the plaza stood the *convento* and *cocina* complex. The *convento* (usually translated as monastery, convent, or friary) comprised one or more subsidiary buildings in which friars and lay brothers lived cloistered lives according to the rules of their Franciscan order.

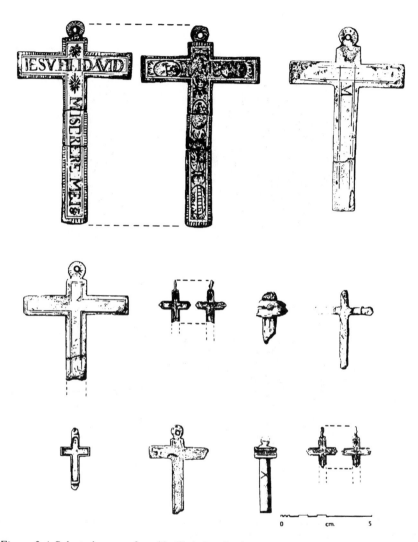

Figure 3.4. Selected crosses found in Christian Guale graves at Santa Catalina. Note the variety in means of manufacture, design, and size (particularly when compared to the uniformity of the small religious medals in Figure 3.6). Latin inscription on upper left cross translates "Jesus, son of David, have mercy on me." On the reverse side of this cross are six oval reserves with symbols and instruments of the Passion (suffering) of Jesus. Left to right: crossed hammer and pliers; wounds of hands, feet, and side; three crossed nails; crown of thorns and stars (?); two dice, lance, and staff with vinegar in sponge; ladder and the six (?) pieces of silver to pay Judas (Ahlborn 1991). Reproduced with the permission of the American Museum of Natural History.

Figure 3.5. Three medallions recovered from the *campo santo* at Santa Catalina. Richard Ahlborn (1991) offers the following iconographic interpretations:
(a) Cast and glass enameled medallion with Spanish inscription that translates "Hail, Mary, conceived without original sin." High mercury content suggests that this medallion may have been gilded. The scene recalls the popular image of Our Lady of Guadalupe, which the Franciscan order had successfully established in Mexico after 1531 before the first friar reached Santa Catalina.
(b) Silver medallion with mercury gilding, found near the altar and associated with the phalanx of a 2 year old, some copper links, and a textile fragment with three seed beads woven into it. It depicts the heavily robed and hooded "Sorrowing Mother" of Jesus, seated in grief on rocks at Golgatha. In the background in a cross with three nails and a (continued)

At least two superimposed *conventos* exist at Santa Catalina. The earlier structure was probably built in the late 1580s shortly after the Franciscans arrived. Second only in size to the church itself, it measured at least 10 m by 20 m, the long axis running roughly northwest-southeast (at an angle of 310°). Construction was entirely of rough wattle and daub (considerably coarser than that employed in building the church). This early building was supported by relatively large posts set in holes with clean sand fill. It appears to have been divided into at least three rooms. The kitchen and refectory were probably housed inside the 16th-century *convento*, the other rooms were probably used for living quarters and storage. Kitchen debris and table scraps were tossed out the back door, where a fringe of shell midden accumulated against the rear wall well out of sight from the church. A clearly incised drip line demonstrates that the 16th-century *convento* had eaves extending about a meter beyond the rear wall.

This building was probably burnt by rebellious Guale in the fall of 1597. When Fray Ruiz supervised the reconstruction in 1604, he apparently separated sacred from secular, for a distinct *cocina* was erected 20 m to the north of the new *convento*. The detached kitchen was also a common feature within urban St. Augustine (Deagan 1983:247).

The southeastern wall of both 16th- and 17th-century *conventos* was built on the same location. But the later structure was somewhat smaller, measuring only about 10 m by 9 m. Moreover, the long axis of the 17th-century *convento* is 325°; the ± 15° difference in orientation greatly facilitated separating the two buildings during excavation.

The western wall was enclosed by a well-defined arcade, probably a colonnaded porch marking the eastern margin of the central plaza. At least three doorways faced the church to the west. This porch was exactly aligned with the western wall of the *cocina*. An addition of some sort, apparently not of wattle and daub, was appended to the southern wall.

---

shroud. Similar to *veneras* worn on clothing by fashionable women in 17th-century Spain (Muller 1972:124).

(c) Made of sandy micaceous clay, low fired, and cast from two molds, this medallion could have been used to impress wax seals. *Left side*: The lengthy circumferential and basal inscriptions, probably in Latin, have not yet been transcribed. A standing male in a hooded habit holds in one hand a thin, vertical device (a cross?) over a small kneeling figure; his lowered hand holds a chain. Below a basal inscription (perhaps abbreviated) is a winged angel's head. This scene recalls Jesus and Franciscan missionaries martyred in the 16th century while evangelizing in Asia. Right side: This design in similar to the obverse, but the large figure has his cowl back and his head radiates light. He also raises a cross over the kneeling figure. To one side is a thin plant and above is a birdlike form; at the bottom, below an inscription, is a winged angel's head. Reproduced with the permission of the American Museum of Natural History.

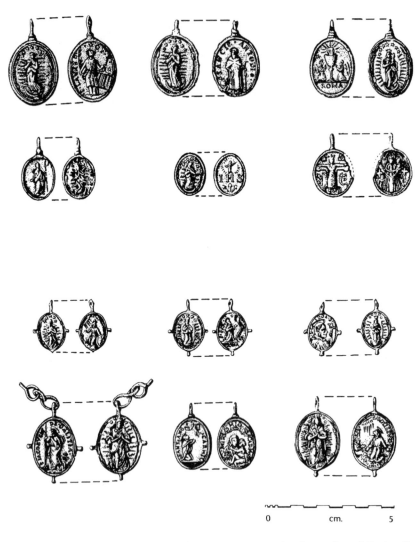

Figure 3.6. Selected small medals with cross-set suspension loops from Mission Santa Catalina de Guale. They contain various inscriptions referring to specific religious concepts or identities, generally involving a prayer for protection from a holy personage such as Jesus, his mother in several advocations, and various saints (Ahlborn 1991). Reproduced with the permission of the American Museum of Natural History.

The later friary consists of three well-defined and one less well-preserved daub walls, accompanied in all cases by in situ wall posts. Set into the clay floor of the central room was a curious feature: a rectangular clay foundation, standing 25 cm above the floor, scooped out to receive an oval metallic receptacle. Although this floor font might have held holy water, it was more likely employed for personal hygiene, perhaps as a foot bath.[3]

Immediately outside the back of the *convento*, we found a concentration of nearly four dozen bronze bell fragments (other fragments have been found haphazardly scattered about Santa Catalina). Several pieces show punch and axe marks, indicating that the bells were deliberately destroyed; at least four different bells are represented. The mission bell always held a special significance, at times symbolizing the entire mission enterprise. Like all sacred vessels of the church, bells were consecrated and blessed, this status continuing even after the breaking of a bell; bell fragments were collected at missions San Miguel and San Luis Rey in Alta California and sent to Mexico, ultimately to be recast into new bells (Walsh 1934:32).

Elsewhere (Thomas 1988a:104) I have speculated that the fragments found behind the 17th-century *convento* were from bells broken by rebellious Guale during the uprising of 1597. Friars who returned to Santa Catalina some years later undoubtedly came upon some of these fragments, and the broken bells found behind the *convento* may be a deliberate cache of still-consecrated fragments, perhaps intended for recycling into new bells.

The Kitchen (Cocina)

The new friary was about 15 percent smaller than its predecessor, but this size differential was more than counterbalanced by the new *cocina* (kitchen) built 20 m to the northwest. The 17th-century kitchen, measuring 4.5 m by 6 m, was constructed of wattle and daub on three sides. These walls were supported by squared-off pine posts placed in pits. The southern end of the kitchen was apparently left open, presumably to facilitate both access and ventilation.

The cooking for the friars was probably shifted to this new structure early in the 17th century. Although most kitchen debris was discarded some distance away (probably outside the walled mission compound), some midden accumulated in pits near the *cocina*, and occasional smaller pieces of garbage were trampled underfoot, being thus incorporated in the kitchen floor. Elizabeth J. Reitz (Museum of Natural History, University of Georgia) and her students have completed the identification of the nonhuman bones from the *cocina* and elsewhere in the Mission Santa Catalina excavations; these results, when published, will enhance the already growing body of zooarchaeological data from the missions of *La Florida* (Reitz 1990).

The Mission Wells

Two wells were found on the eastern side of the plaza. The first, initially located by the magnetometer survey, was a simple barrel well consisting of seven decomposing iron rings above the well-preserved remains of an oak casing (item 3 in Figure 3.1). The construction pit was relatively small, perhaps 1.5 m in diameter, with the much smaller barrel well located inside. Relatively little was found in the construction pit and well fill (some olive jar and majolica sherds, plus a metal plate). This well obviously had a relatively short use-life, and we think it likely that it dates from the 16th century.

A second, much larger well was encountered later, directly between the *cocina* and the *convento* (Figure 3.7). When first recognized, the large circular construction pit was more than 4 m in diameter, with a dark, largely circular stain in the middle. As we excavated downward, the construction pit narrowed, with distinct "steps" on both sides; a 17th-century cave-in is recorded in the southern sidewall, where one of the sand steps apparently collapsed. Although the well and its contents are still being analyzed, some details are now available.

The well was originally much smaller, having been first constructed with standard barrels. It was subsequently renovated using a casement constructed of two U-shaped cypress logs that were lowered into the construction pit, then nailed together. This later, handmade well casing was at least 2 m in diameter, considerably larger than any of the mission-period wells encountered in Spanish Florida. This well clearly crosscuts surrounding features in the *convento/cocina* complex; it was one of the last features built at the mission and was probably in use until the final mission abandonment in the 1680s.

The well reached a depth of roughly 2.5 m. A fair amount of cultural and botanical remains were included in both the construction pit and well fill. A quantity of waterlogged items found at the base of the well includes a broken iron hatchet (with a partial wooden handle still intact, possibly broken during the carving of the casement), two wooden balls (roughly the size of pool balls), at least five reconstructible aboriginal vessels (two are unbroken, and one is painted on the interior and exterior), most of two olive jars, and many seeds and pits including grape, peach, and squash. At the bottom of the well were quantities of burnt cut wood, which may have been part of a superstructure that once covered the well.

Exploring the Guale Pueblo and Beyond

Although we have learned a great deal about the central mission compound at Santa Catalina, the surrounding Guale Indian pueblo remains a mystery—both because

Figure 3.7. Photograph of 1988 excavation of the primary well at Mission Santa Catalina.

the Hispanic documents gloss over such mundane matters and because of limited archaeological exploration of the entire mission context.

Within the past year, we shifted the archaeological focus of attention at Santa Catalina from the Hispanic core to the Native American outskirts. We tested the surrounding Guale pueblo in several places, but our concern was primarily chronological—to be certain that this extensive habitation area surrounding the mission buildings was occupied during the 16th and 17th centuries.

Responding to our interest in establishing this broader context, the St. Catherines Island Foundation and the Edward John Noble Foundation have generously granted us three additional years of excavation and analysis designed specifically to learn more about the mission-period Indians on St. Catherines Island. In this newest research phase, begun in January 1991, our primary goal is to define the nature and extent of the Guale pueblo at Mission Santa Catalina and to find out how Guale lifeways were modified by interactions with Europeans.

What Are We Looking For?

Reliable evidence regarding the appearance of either precontact or mission-period Guale settlements is rare in the documentary sources. Perhaps the following account of the town of Orista in 1666 can be applied to most Guale towns: "The Ttowne is scituate on the side or rather in the skirts of a faire forrest, in which at several distances are diverse fields of maiz with many little houses straglingly amongst them for the habitations of the particular families" (Sandford 1911).

In a letter dated 22 September 1602, Governor Gonzalo Méndez de Canzo commented that in the Guale settlements "the natives that there are in these provinces do not have cities nor towns or organized villages [*pueblos avezindados*] amounting to anything more than that each cacique has a community house where the Indians came together to hold their dances and assemblies and to drink a brew [*brevage*] of casina, which cannot be done in any other place except in the said house of the said cacique and they are all scattered about with their little houses [*casillas*] at intervals on the edges of the woods" (Méndez de Canzo 1602). This account can probably be considered a credible description because it was written by a governor who was well acquainted with the coastal Guale villages, having destroyed a considerable number of them.

Both accounts suggest a "dispersed town" settlement pattern, with horticultural plots and residences scattered in the vicinity of the town center. The maize plots would have been located behind the town center itself. The households of the *mico*, or village chief, and other principal leaders were located near the center of the Guale towns (Jones 1978:198) and perhaps in the mission pueblos as well. Such towns also contained large plazas used for public activities including the ritual chunkey game, performed with poles and a disk-shaped stone and common to many southeastern aboriginal groups (Hudson 1976; Sandford 1911; San Miguel 1902). Such a playing field would certainly be expected in the precontact Guale town and perhaps at Guale missions as well.

We know that missionaries and other Spanish officials permitted the Apalachee neophytes to participate in their ritual ball game in the mission context (Bushnell 1978; Hann 1988). If the chunkey game was viewed in similar fashion in Guale territory, then we might expect to find a plaza/chunkey field in the pueblo at Santa Catalina. In fact, Governor Rebolledo explicitly stipulated in his regulatory code for Apalachee that the ball game be permitted (Hann 1986:89).

Clearly the most remarkable feature of any Guale town was the large community building (*buhío*) in which periodic councils and intercommunity feasts were held. The council house, in mission times and well before, symbolized and enshrined critical sociopolitical bonds. Friars recognized the importance of the council house and sanctioned its construction on the mission grounds—encouraging local Indians to think of the mission as "their home."

Nobody knows what a Guale council house looked like. Ayllón's expedition of 1526 into Guale territory reported an abandoned, rectangular *buhío* (measuring about 4–8 m wide by at least 80 m long) constructed of lashed pine uprights and big enough to accommodate 300 men, but this description has been discounted by Swanton (1946:406), Jones (1978:199), and Shapiro and Hann (1990:515). Subsequent accounts consistently describe Guale council houses as round structures, varying in size from less than 25 m to more than 60 m in diameter (Jones 1978; Shapiro and Hann 1990). These would have been conspicuous features on the mission landscape, and evidence must have been preserved at the Guale missions.

The nature of aboriginal domestic dwellings along the Georgia coast is even more uncertain. Laudonnière (1975:43) described one Guale house with a lavish interior "decorated with tapestries of various colored feathers up to the height of a pike. The place where the king slept was covered with white coverlets embroidered with fine workmanship and fringed in scarlet." In 1595 Fray Andrés de San Miguel (1902) noted that Guale houses at Asao were constructed of wooden timbers and covered with palmettos. Jones (1978:199) suggests that the precontact Guale houses were circular, built on the same general principle as the *buhío* only smaller.

Limited archaeological evidence suggests otherwise for Guale dwellings during the mission period. At the north end of Harris Neck, Larson (1980) encountered several squarish and overlapping Spanish period aboriginal structures aligned on a grid system approximately 10° west of north. Several wall trench outlines of Spanish period aboriginal domestic structures were also uncovered by S. K. Caldwell at Fort King George, near Darien (S. K. Caldwell 1953, 1954; see also Larson 1980; Thomas 1987:95–97) These seem to be wattle-and-daub structures built with shallow wall trenches and small round postholes and divided into several rooms. Incidentally, we are currently reanalyzing all mission-period materials recovered by Caldwell from Fort King George, in the hope of defining more firmly the context of these important structures.

These skimpy data suggest that the pueblo at Santa Catalina probably consisted of rectangular buildings constructed of wattle and daub and/or wall trenches and perhaps separated by "streets." The Native American sector was probably built as an extension of the initial Spanish gridwork.

So How Do We Find
These Things Archaeologically?

Virtually all we know about Santa Catalina comes from a decade of digging around the plaza in the central part of Santa Catalina—the church, *convento*, and *cocina* complex—an area of about 5000 m². If we are to address the pueblo periphery, the research frame must be expanded to *at least* 10 ha, and this is a very conservative estimate. Because our proposed pueblo project must cover at least twenty times the area investigated in our 1980–1990 research and because this work must be completed within just three years, a different archaeological strategy is clearly in order.

Once again we think that remote sensing provides part of the solution. In collaboration with John Weymouth (Department of Physics and Astronomy, University of Nebraska), we are at present developing a multivariate approach to geophysical prospection at Santa Catalina. We feel that the value of remote sensing studies has not been fully realized in modern archaeology and hope that the pueblo at Santa Catalina can serve as a case study to demonstrate the potential of such methods.

In our initial search for Santa Catalina 15 years ago, we employed three primary remote sensing techniques: proton precession magnetometry, soil resistivity, and ground-penetrating radar (Thomas 1987:47–161, 1989:Ch. 7). In the ongoing work at the pueblo, we will continue to use these techniques but will also employ several others—not only to learn more about the pueblo but also to understand better the strengths and weaknesses of various geophysical currencies and approaches. Our most recent efforts (1990–1991) on the Santa Catalina pueblo have utilized paired proton precession magnetometry, gradiometry, high-speed soil resistivity, and soil conductivity; other techniques are being considered as well. We have every confidence that at least some of this technology will prove fruitful.

Preliminary testing also suggests that the pueblo contains huge samples of faunal remains. In continued collaboration with Elizabeth J. Reitz, we are expanding our investigation of vertebrate utilization during the late prehistoric and mission periods. We are particularly interested in exploring the nature of intrasite variability at

Mission Santa Catalina. Relatively large zooarchaeological samples have already been studied from the *cocina* and other "central" mission contexts; the proposed 1991–1993 excavations should produce comparable samples from the Mission Santa Catalina pueblo.

We also think that important data lie outside the mission compound proper and even outside the pueblo. When Captain Dunlop visited the ruins of Santa Catalina in 1687, he reported "the ruins of severall houses which we were informed the Spaniards had deserted for ffear of the English about 3 years agoe; the Setlement was great, much clear ground in our view for 7 or 8 miles together" (Dunlop 1929: 131). Even allowing for considerable exaggeration, this rare eyewitness account indicates that Mission Santa Catalina was surrounded by a huge agricultural field complex. But what did these fields look like? How were they organized? What crops were grown there?

Once again, we are required to shift the scale: the 5000 m^2 around the mission plaza covers only the religious precinct; the 10-ha area surrounding the plaza contains only the aboriginal pueblo. But in order to obtain a more complete view of Mission Santa Catalina as an economic entity, we must be willing to operate on the scale of several dozen hectares.

Large-scale patterning is one way to look for the potential residues left from mission-period agriculture. Recent investigators using the techniques of landscape archaeology have enjoyed some success by analyzing the distribution of plant opal phytoliths; an example is Irwin Rovner's (1988) successful reconstruction of Thomas Jefferson's gardens and fodder fields at Monticello, Virginia. We would like to do the same at Santa Catalina.

But in these days of conservation-oriented archaeology, *no one* should contemplate digging several hectares (even if the resources and the sites were available). Instead, we should be seeking ways to monitor variability on a scale previously unattainable in archaeology. Our specific objective here is to reconstruct the distribution and configuration of the agricultural field systems surrounding Mission Santa Catalina. To do so, we are required to conduct considerable baseline studies of phytolith taxonomy and depositional processes. In collaboration with Irwin Rovner (North Carolina State University), we have begun a comprehensive study of plant phytoliths at Santa Catalina (and other contact period sites on St. Catherines Island).

Although this landscape approach is far-reaching indeed, we wish to expand the scope still further. In collaboration with Joseph Jimenez (City University of New York), we intend to explore the nature of socioeconomic change between the late prehistoric and the early contact periods. To complement our expanded studies at the Santa Catalina pueblo, we have selected five additional sites on St. Catherines Island for detailed investigation: three mission-period sites plus two Irene-period (late precontact) sites. We are at present using geophysical techniques at these sites, and they will be further mapped and tested in conjunction with our expanded work at the Santa Catalina pueblo.

We also continue our collaboration with Clark Spencer Larsen to further refine our previous biocultural findings. In 1991 Larsen returned to South End Mound, previously excavated by C. B. Moore and retested by the American Museum of Natural History (Larsen and Thomas 1986:1–46), in hopes of expanding the Irene-period mortuary sample. We are simultaneously exploring several other late pre-historic and mission-period St. Catherines Island sites in the search for additional mortuary evidence.

We hope that this expanded regional approach will enable us not only to determine the nature of precontact Guale adaptations but also to see whether the mission system was able to exert significant social and economic control beyond the confines of Mission Santa Catalina proper. We also believe that intensive inves-tigations at these key sites will enable us to assess changing social relations between precontact and contact period villages, to trace intravillage changes through micro-analysis of ceramic traits, to refine the late precontact and contact period ceramic chronologies, and to perfect archaeological indicators of seasonality. Without question, our inquiry will not prove equally successful in all these potential directions. But we are confident that by extending our mission research far beyond the Hispanic hub, we can learn more about the lifeways of the majority of people living under the umbrella of Mission Santa Catalina de Guale.

Acknowledgments

I express my sincerest thanks to the trustees of the St. Catherines Island and Edward John Noble foundations for providing both the opportunity and the support to conduct the archaeological research described here. We are particularly grateful to Mr. and Mrs. Frank Y. Larkin for their truly extraordinary level of interest and benefaction. Additional funding for our excavations has been provided by the Richard K. Lounsbery Foundation, the National Science Foundation, the Georgia Endowment or the Humanities, Donald McClain, the James Ruel Smith Fund, the Geiger Lumber Company, the Sander and Ray Epstein Charitable Foundation, the General William Mayer Foundation, the Ogden Mills Fund, and Earthwatch.

I also thank Royce Hayes, superintendent of St. Catherines Island, who made our work both effective and pleasurable; we are also grateful to his able-bodied staff for always being willing to lend a hand. I am likewise grateful to the special people who helped supervise the excavations at Mission Santa Catalina de Guale: Stacy Goodman, Debra Guerrero, Joseph Jimenez, Clark Spencer Larsen, Deborah Mayer O'Brien, Dennis O'Brien, Lorann S. A. Pendleton, Donna Ruhl, William Sandy, and Rebecca Saunders. This manuscript benefited considerably from the editorial and substantive suggestions provided by Margot Dembo, Lorann Pendleton, and three anonymous reviewers. Nicholas Amorosi and Dennis O'Brien prepared the artwork for this article. We also thank Richard Ahlborn (National Museum of American History, Smithsonian Institution) for allowing us to draw upon his iconographic research on the Santa Catalina religious artifacts.

NOTES

1. Some years ago we published an overview of the natural and cultural history of St. Catherines Island (Thomas et al. 1978:155–248), and that monograph serves as a backdrop for this discussion as well.

Although the archaeology of Mission Santa Catalina has consumed much of our research energies on St. Catherines Island, we have spent considerable effort looking at the precontact archaeological remains as well. We began our research on the island in 1974, by focusing on the Refuge and Deptford phase mortuary complex (Thomas and Larsen 1979:1–180). Larsen (1982:155–270) subsequently conducted a detailed examination of prehistoric biocultural adaptations on St. Catherines Island. This program in mortuary archaeology continued in 1977 and 1978, when two St. Catherines period burial mounds (Johns and Marys Mounds) were also studied. Both mounds were initially excavated by Joseph Caldwell and his students at the University of Georgia, and we combined their results with our own (Larsen and Thomas 1982:271–342). More recently we reported on excavations at two additional prehistoric burial mounds (Larsen and Thomas 1986:1–46). South End Mound I, an Irene period mortuary site, had been initially excavated by C. B. Moore during the winter of 1896–1897. South End Mound II, a previously unrecorded St. Catherines/Savannah period burial mound, was discovered not far from Moore's excavations. Other related mortuary excavations are reported elsewhere (Thomas, South, and Larsen 1977:393–420).

2. We must emphasize the sensitivity required when excavating such mission-period human remains (see Thomas 1987:147–148, 1988b:124–125). Because we could establish no biological descendants of those buried at Santa Catalina—the Guale people disappeared in the 18th century—we focused on working with those who maintained the closest cultural and religious affinity with the remains. From our earliest tests in the *campo santo*, it was clear that this was a Catholic cemetery, containing the remains of hundreds of Guale Indians who had explicitly opted for Christian burial.

Accordingly, we established contact with Father Raymond Lessard, bishop of Savannah. Bishop Lessard assured us that the Catholic church supported and encouraged our excavations. On 25 May 1984 Bishop Lessard returned to St. Catherines Island to conduct a service dedicated to "reblessing the ground and reburial of remains," and he has assisted in the on-site reburial of remains. Further, recognizing that two Franciscans had been martyred at Santa Catalina in 1597, the Franciscan order also sent a representative, Fr. Conrad Harkins, to participate in the excavations at the *iglesia* and *convento* (see Harkins 1990).

3. It remains possible, however, that this unusual feature was a brazier, designed to hold glowing embers to ward off the wintertime cold; but a more likely charcoal-filled "brazier" was discovered along the southern margin of the *convento*.

REFERENCES

Ahlborn, R. E. 1991. Religious Devices from Santa Catalina de Guale, Georgia: 1566–1686. Anthropological Papers of the American Museum of Natural History, New York. In preparation.

Bolton, H. E., and M. Ross. 1925. *The Debatable Land.* Berkeley: University of California Press.

Bushnell, A. T. 1978. "That Demonic Game": The Campaign to Stop Indian *Pelota* Playing in Spanish Florida, 1675–1684. *The Americas* 35:1–19.

Bushnell, A. T. 1990. The Sacramental Imperative: Catholic Ritual and Indian Sedentism in the Provinces of Florida. In *Columbian Consequences. Vol. 2: Archaeological and Historical Perspectives on the Spanish Borderlands East,* D. H. Thomas (ed.), pp. 475–490. Washington, DC: Smithsonian Institution Press.

Bushnell, A. T. In press. *The Archaeology of Mission Santa Catalina de Guale: 3. The Support System of a Spanish Maritime Periphery.* New York: Anthropological Papers of the American Museum of Natural History.

Caldwell, J. R. n.d.. Unpublished field notes on file, Laboratory of Anthropology, St. Catherines Island, Georgia.

Caldwell, S. K. 1953. Excavations at a Spanish Mission Site in Georgia. *Southeastern Archaeological Conference Newsletter* 3(3):31–32.

Caldwell, S. K. 1954. A Spanish Mission House near Darien. *Early Georgia* 1(3):13–17.

Deagan, K. 1981. Downtown Survey: The Discovery of Sixteenth-Century St. Augustine in an Urban Area. *American Antiquity* 46(3):626–634.

Deagan, K. 1983. *Spanish St. Augustine: The Archaeology of a Colonial Creole Community.* New York: Academic Press.

Dunlop, Captain. 1929. Journall Capt. Dunlop's Voyage to the Southward, 1687. *South Carolina Historical and Genealogical Magazine* 30(3):127–133.

Gannon, M. V. 1965. *The Cross in the Sand: The Early Catholic Church in Florida, 1513–1870.* Gainesville: University of Florida Press.

Garrison, E. G., J. G. Baker, and D. H. Thomas. 1985. Magnetic Prospection and the Discovery of Mission Santa Catalina de Guile. *Journal of Field Archaeology* 12: 299–313.

Geiger, M. J., O.I.M. 1937. *The Franciscan Conquest of Florida, 1573–1618.* Studies in Hispanic American History, Vol. 1. Washington, DC: Catholic University of America.

Geiger, M. J., O.I.M. 1940. *Biographical Dictionary of the Franciscans in Spanish Florida and Cuba (1528–1841).* Franciscan Studies, 21. Patterson, NJ: St. Anthony's Guild Press.

Griffin, J. 1965a. Notes on the Archeology of St. Catherines Island, Georgia. Report to the Edward John Noble Foundation. Manuscript on file, Department of Anthropology, American Museum of Natural History, New York.

Griffin, J. 1965b. Santa Catalina Mission, Liberty County, Georgia. Documentation for Consideration as a Registered National Historic Landmark. Manuscript on file, Department of Anthropology, American Museum of Natural History, New York.

Hann, J. 1986. Translation of Governor Rebolledo's 1637 Visitation of Three Florida Provinces and Related Documents. In *Spanish Translations*, 81–145. Florida Archaeology no. 2. Tallahassee: Florida Bureau of Archaeological Research.

Hann, J. 1988. *Apalachee: The Land between the Rivers*. Ripley P. Bullen Monographs in Anthropology and History, no. 7. Gainesville: University Press of Florida.

Harkins, C. 1990. On Franciscans, Archaeology, and Old Missions. In *Columbian Consequences. Vol. 2: Archaeological and Historical Perspectives on the Spanish Borderlands East*, D. H. Thomas (ed.), pp. 459–474. Washington, DC: Smithsonian Institution Press.

Hudson, C. 1976. *The Southeastern Indians*. Knoxville: University of Tennessee Press.

Hvidt, K. 1980. *Von Reck's Voyage: Drawings and Journal of Philip Georg Friedrich von Reck*. Savannah: Beehive Press.

Jones, G. 1978. The Ethnohistory of the Guale Coast through 1684. In *The Anthropology of St. Catherines Island: I. Natural and Cultural History*, by D. H. Thomas, G. D. Jones, R. S. Durham, and C. S. Larsen, pp. 178–210, Vol. 55, pt. 2. New York: Anthropological Papers of the American Museum of Natural History.

Kubler, G. 1940. *The Religious Architecture of New Mexico in the Colonial Period and Since the American Occupation*. Colorado Springs: Taylor Museum.

Larsen, C. 1982. *The Anthropology of St. Catherines Island: 3. Prehistoric Human Biological Adaptation*, Vol. 57, pt. 3. New York: Anthropological Papers of the American Museum of Natural History.

Larsen, C. S., (ed.). 1990. *The Archaeology of Mission Santa Catalina de Cuale: 2. Biocultural Interpretations of a Population in Transition*, no. 68. New York: Anthropological Papers of the American Museum of Natural History.

Larsen, C. S. and D. H. Thomas. 1982. *The Anthropology of St. Catherines Island: 4. The St. Catherines Period Mortuary Complex*, Vol. 57, pt. 4. New York: Anthropological Papers of the American Museum of Natural History.

Larsen, C. S. and D. H. Thomas. 1986. *The Archaeology of St. Catherines Island: 5. The South End Complex*, Vol. 63, pt. 1. New York: Anthropological Papers of the American Museum of Natural History.

Larsen, C. S., M. J. Schoeninger, D. L. Hutchinson, K. F. Russell, and C. B. Ruff. 1990. Beyond Demographic Collapse: Biological Adaptation and Change in Native Populations of *La Florida*. In *Columbian Consequences. Vol. 2: Archaeological and Historical Perspectives on the Spanish Borderlands East*, D. H. Thomas (ed.). pp. 409–428. Washington, DC: Smithsonian Institution Press.

Larson, L. H., Jr. 1952. 1952 Season. Georgia Historical Commission, Archaeological Survey of the Georgia Coast. Manuscript on file, University of Georgia, Athens.

Larson, L. H., Jr. 1978. Historic Guale Indians of the Georgia Coast and the Impact of the Spanish Mission Effort. In *Tacachale: Essays on the Indians of Florida and Southeastern Georgia during the Historic Period*, J. Milanich and S. Proctor (eds.), pp. 120–140. Ripley P. Bullen Monographs in Anthropology and History, no. 1. Gainesville: University Press of Florida.

Larson, L. H. 1980. The Spanish on Sapelo. In *Sapelo Papers: Researches in the History and Prehistory of Sapelo Island*, Georgia, D. P. Juengst (ed.), pp. 77–87, no. 19. Carrollton: West Georgia College Studies in the Social Sciences.

Laudonnière, R. 1975. *Three Voyages*. C. E. Bennett (trans.). Gainesville: University Press of Florida.

Lyon, E. 1976. *The Enterprise of Florida: Pedro Menendez de Aviles and the Spanish Conquest of 1565–1568*. Gainesville: University Presses of Florida.

Manucy, A. 1985. *The Houses of St. Augustine*. St. Augustine: St. Augustine Historical Society.

Mendez de Canzo, G. 1602. Letter to the King, St. Augustine, 22 September 1602. Archivo General de Indias, Santo Domingo 226, reel 2, Jeannette Thurber Connor Collection. P. K. Yonge Library of Florida History, University of Florida, Gainesville.

Montgomery, R. G., W. Smith, and J. O. Brew. 1949. *Franciscan Awatovi*. Papers of the Peabody Museum of American Archaeology and Ethnology, no. 36. Cambridge: Harvard University.

Muller, P. E. 1972. *Jewels of Spain, 1500–1800*. New York: Hispanic Society of America.

Reitz, E. J. 1990. Zooarchaeological Evidence for Subsistence at La Florida Missions. In *Columbian Consequences. Vol. 2: Archaeological and Historical Perspectives on the Spanish Borderlands East*, D. H. Thomas (ed.), pp. 543–554. Washington, DC: Smithsonian Institution Press.

Ross, M. 1926. The Restoration of the Spanish Missions in Georgia, 1598–1606. *Georgia Historical Quarterly* 10(3):171–199.

Rovner, I. 1988. Macro- and Micro-Ecological Reconstruction Using Plant Opal Phytolith Data from Archaeological Sediments. *Geoarchaeology* 3(2):155–163.

Ruhl, D. L. 1990. Spanish Mission Paleoethnobotany and Culture Change: A Survey of the Archaeobotanical Data and Some Speculations on Aboriginal and Spanish Agrarian Interactions in *La Florida*. In *Columbian Consequences. Vol. 2: Archaeological and Historical Perspectives on the Spanish Borderlands East*, D. H. Thomas (ed.), pp. 555–580. Washington, DC: Smithsonian Institution Press.

Sandford, R. 1911. A Relation of a Voyage on the Coast of the Province of Carolina [1666]. In *Original Narratives of Early American History, Vol. 15*, A. S. Salley (ed.), pp. 82–108. New York: Charles Scribner's Sons.

San Miguel, Andres de. 1902. Relación de las Trabajos que la Gente de una nao llamada Nra Señora de l a Merced Padeció y de algunas Cosas que en Aquella Flota Sucedieron. In *Dos Antiguas Relaciones de la Florida*, G. García (ed.), pp. 153–226. Mexico City: J. Aguilar Vera y Compañía.

Shapiro, G. 1984. Soil Resistivity Survey of Sixteenth-Century Puerto Real, Haiti. *Journal of Field Archaeology* 11(1):101–110.

Shapiro, G. 1987. *Archaeology at San Luis: Broad-Scale Testing, 1984–1985*. Florida Archaeology no. 3. Tallahassee: Florida Bureau of Archaeological Research.

Shapiro, G. N. and J. H. Hann. 1990. The Documentary Image of the Council Houses of Spanish Florida Tested by Excavations at the Mission of San Luis de Talimali. In

Columbian Consequences. Vol. 2: Archaeological and Historical Perspectives on the Spanish Borderlands East, D. H. Thomas (ed.), pp. 491–510. Washington, DC: Smithsonian Institution Press.

South, S. 1977. *Method and Theory in Historical Archaeology*. New York: Academic Press.

Sturtevant, W. C. 1962. Spanish-Indian Relations in Southeastern North America. *Ethnohistory* 9(1):41–94.

Swanton, J. R. 1922. *Early History of the Creek Indians and Their Neighbors*. Bureau of American Ethnology Bulletin no. 73. Washington, DC: Smithsonian Institution Press.

Swanton, J. R. 1946. *The Indians of the Southeastern United States*. Bureau of American Ethnology Bulletin no. 137. Washington, DC: Smithsonian Institution Press.

Thomas, D. H. 1987. *The Archaeology of Mission Santa Catalina de Guale: 1. Search and Discovery*, Vol. 63, pt. 2. New York: Anthropological Papers of the American Museum of Natural History.

Thomas, D. H. 1988a. *St. Catherines: An Island in Time*. Atlanta: Georgia Endowment for the Humanities (Georgia History and Culture Series).

Thomas, D. H. 1988b. Saints and Soldiers at Santa Catalina: Hispanic Designs for Colonial America. In *The Recovery of Meaning: Historical Archaeology in the Eastern United States*, M. P. Leone and P. B. Potter, Jr. (eds.), pp. 73–140. Washington, DC: Smithsonian Institution Press.

Thomas, D. H. 1989. *Archaeology*, 2nd ed. Fort Worth: Holt, Rinehart and Winston.

Thomas, D. H. 1990. The Spanish Missions of *La Florida*: An Overview. In *Columbian Consequences. Vol. 2: Archaeological and Historical Perspectives on the Spanish Borderlands East*, D. H. Thomas (ed.), pp. 357–397. Washington, DC: Smithsonian Institution Press.

Thomas, D. H. n.d. The Regional Archaeology of St. Catherines Island. In preparation.

Thomas, D. H. and C. S. Larsen. 1979.*The Anthropology of St. Catherines Island: 2. The Refuge-Deptford Mortuary Complex*, Vol. 56, pt. 1. New York: Anthropological Papers of the American Museum of Natural History.

Thomas, D. H., S. South, and C. S. Larsen. 1977. *Rich Man, Poor Men: Observations on Three Antebellum Burials from the Georgia Coast*, Vol. 54, pt. 3. New York: Anthropological Papers of the American Museum of Natural History.

Thomas, D. H., G. D. Jones, R. S. Durham, and C. S. Larsen. 1978. *The Anthropology of St. Catherines Island: 1. The Natural and Cultural History*, Vol. 55. pt. 2. New York: Anthropological Papers of the American Museum of Natural History.

Walsh, M. T. 1934. *The Mission Bells of California*. San Francisco: Hart Wagner.

Weymouth, J. W. 1986. Geophysical Methods of Archaeological Site Surveying. In *Advances in Archaeological Method and Theory, Vol. 9*, M. B. Schiffer (ed), pp. 311–395. Orlando: Academic Press.

MICHAEL PARRINGTON ■
HELEN SCHENCK
JACQUELINE THIBAUT

Chapter Four

The Material World of the Revolutionary War Soldier at Valley Forge

Introduction

The encampment of the Continental Army at Valley Forge in the winter of 1777–1778 remains one of the most celebrated events of the American Revolution. Over the past two centuries it has become, through the ministrations of popular historians, a potent symbol of patriotic devotion and sacrifice. From December 19, 1777 to June 19, 1778, the main body of the Continental Army lodged in makeshift huts on a cluster of barren hills and ridges above the west bank of the Schuylkill River, 18 miles northwest of Philadelphia. The British army under Sir William Howe occupied the city throughout this period, and Congress, in exile at York, Pennsylvania, charged Washington with the near-impossible task of containing depredations and parrying the forages launched by his English adversary.

Through the winter the troops under Washington's command were plagued by logistical breakdown and the consequent failure of the supply mechanisms serving the Army. The departments of the Quarter Master, Commissary, Clothier General, and Commissary of Military Stores were thrown into disarray by weather, attrition of horses and wagons, spot shortages, lack of funds, political wrangling, and administrative incompetency. These afflictions, which fed upon themselves and multiplied, precipitated the hardships which would make Valley Forge synonymous in the minds of American schoolchildren with hunger, disease, and death (Thibaut 1980).

Valley Forge did not cease to function as a military post immediately upon the evacuation of the Main Army in June of 1778. There remained numerous sick in

This article was originally published in *The Scope of Historical Archaeology: Essays in Honor of John L. Cotter*, David G. Orr and Daniel G. Crozier, eds., pp. 125–161. Philadelphia: Laboratory of Anthropology, Temple University, ©1984.

camp, and Colonel Van Cortlandt and a portion of the 2nd New York Regiment were detailed to stay behind and guard the invalids (Thibaut 1979:34–39). The Artillery branch of the army continued to use Valley Forge as an ammunition store until at least 1780, and a Quarter Master's store remained at Moore Hall, just west of camp, well into the summer of 1778.

The encampment was used briefly by British prisoners from the battle of Saratoga on their way south to internment in Winchester, Virginia, during December 1778. In November 1778, the Continental Barrack Master General had inspected the site, and recommended to Congress that they should dispose of (presumably sell) the ". . . logs, timber, Shingles etc. . . ." left by the departed Continental Army. There is no evidence that this was ever undertaken (Thibaut 1979:34).

The importance of Valley Forge as a site of national historical significance resulted in May of 1893 in the creation of a state park designed to preserve undeveloped the ground on which the Continental Army had camped. From 1929 on, in excavations of varying levels of scientific rigor, investigators have sought to uncover the physical traces of that encampment, especially the earthen fortifications and redoubts, and the huts of the soldiers (Figure 4.1).

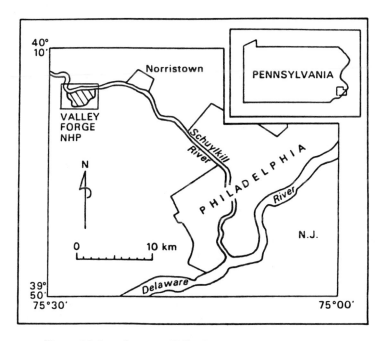

Figure 4.1. Location map, Valley Forge National Historic Park, Pennsylvania.

An attempt is made in this paper to correlate the historical evidence of the subsistence and equipage of the troops at Valley Forge with the archaeological evidence from four brigade encampment sites: those of General Anthony Wayne, General Thomas Conway, General William Maxwell, and that located at the eastern end of Outer Line Drive. It is uncertain if the troops quartered there were under the command of General Peter Muhlenberg or General George Weedon. In the discussion of the excavations and artifactual remains which follows this site will be referred to as the Virginia Brigade area.

Brigade Encampments at Valley Forge

Introduction

Evidence for the positioning of the brigades at Valley Forge derives from the rough map drafted by the engineer-general of the Continental Army, Louis Lebèque Duportail, in late December or early January, and from several variants (Duportail Map, Historical Society of Pennsylvania) (Figure 4.2). The boundaries of the brigade sites are not precisely delineated on any of the maps, nor are their exact configurations. The two Pennsylvania brigades comprising General Anthony Wayne's Division were located on a rise toward the southwestern extremity of the outer line of defenses. The troops in this division were of the 1st, 2nd, 4th, 5th, 7th, 8th, 10th, and 11th Pennsylvania Regiments. Wayne, acting division commander in the absence of Arthur St. Clair, was present in camp for the preponderance of the winter, lobbying actively for supplies with State and Continental authorities.

Conway's Brigade, positioned towards the center of the inner line, included the 3rd, 6th, 9th, and 12th Pennsylvania Regiments, along with Malcolm's and Spencer's Additional Continental Regiments (units without official state affiliations). This brigade, unfortunate in that General Thomas Conway was not in camp to foster its welfare, was probably commanded in his stead by Colonel Oliver Spencer. In the contentious, not to say desperate, matter of clothing issuances, the Pennsylvania regiments in Conway's Brigade did not fare nearly so well as did those in Wayne's division, causing considerable animosity among the men.

General William Maxwell's Brigade, situated to the west of Conway's on the inner line, consisted of the 1st, 2nd, 3rd, and 4th New Jersey Regiments.

General Peter Muhlenberg's and General George Weedon's brigades, consisting principally of Virginia troops, were located on the far left of the outer line of defense. Muhlenberg's men were at the easternmost extremity, with Weedon's troops bordering them on the west. It is impossible to establish through known documentary sources precisely where the dividing line between the two encampments lay. Muhlenberg commanded the 1st, 5th, 6th, 9th, and 13th Virginia Regiments, along with the so-called German (Pennsylvania German) Regiment.

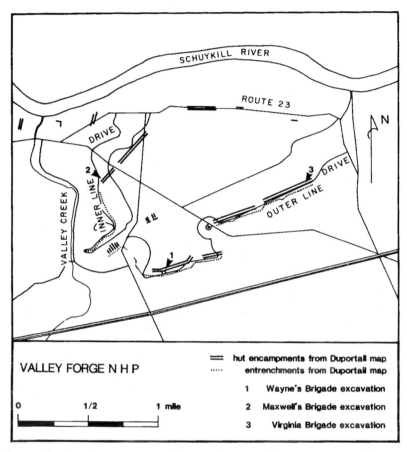

Figure 4.2. Plan of encampment with entrenchments and hut encampments from the Duportail map added. (This and subsequent figures in this chapter were drafted by H. Schenck.)

Weedon's Brigade included the 2nd, 3rd, 4th, 10th, and 14th Virginia Regiments, and in addition the 13th Pennsylvania (Trussell 1976:128–129).

The brigade encampments included huts and auxiliary structures built by the men for themselves, by regiment, 12 men to a hut measuring roughly 16 by 18 ft (Thibaut 1979:25, 26, 29). Six officers shared a hut, while those of the rank of colonel and above had log structures to themselves or lived in appropriated farm dwellings. Each brigade built a hospital hut, isolated to the rear of their encampment. Brigades and regiments had commissary stores, Quarter Master stores, slaughter pens, suttlers' booths, and probably bake ovens. Tools for all of this construction were in short supply, the most commonly encountered in documents being spades, axes, and froes (Thibaut 1979:20–23).

Huts

General orders governing the construction of the huts were issued by Washington's headquarters on 18 December 1777, including the stipulation that the huts were to measure 14 by 16 ft (Fitzpatrick 1933, 10:170–171). Surviving accounts indicate that some were built slightly larger, 16 by 18 ft being the most commonly cited dimensions. Certainly the additional two feet in length and width would have more adequately accommodated the 12 men who were to inhabit each structure. Two accounts for a site under consideration survive, both for Maxwell's brigade encampment. Captain William Gifford of the 3rd New Jersey wrote that by January 20 the men of his regiment were sheltered ". . . in huts 16 by 18 covered with Oak Shingles . . ." (Thibaut 1979:26). Ensign George Ewing, of the same regiment, recorded in his diary the only description of the arrangement of huts which has come to light for the Valley Forge encampment: ". . . the huts are built in three lines each four deep five yards asunder the huts eighteen by sixteen feet long six feet to the eves built of loggs and covered with staves the chimney in the east end the door in the South side the Officers huts in the rear of the mens twelve men in each hut and two cores of Officers in a hut" (Ewing 1928:25).

It is quite likely that not all regimental encampments were this orderly, nor perhaps were all the huts so commodious. During the next winter, with the army grouped loosely about Middlebrook, New Jersey, and later in 1779–1780 at the Morristown encampment, regulations for the proper alignment and construction of huts were much more rigorously enforced than seems to have been the case at Valley Forge (Thibaut 1979:107).

Archaeological Excavations at Hut Encampments

Wayne's Brigade (Figure 4.3)

The hut sites within Wayne's Woods, north of Outer Line Drive, have been extensively probed. Systematic excavation began there in 1966 when John Cotter directed a summer field school from the University of Pennsylvania in excavating two hut sites as well as locating and mapping others. Cotter reported in full on this excavation (Cotter 1966). That summer and subsequently, Stanley Landis, collector and amateur archaeologist, hunted through Wayne's Woods with a metal detector, investigating suspicious depressions and digging wherever the detector signaled the presence of metal. His summary reports on the activities of only three of these summers have been located (Landis in Cotter 1966; Landis 1968, 1969).

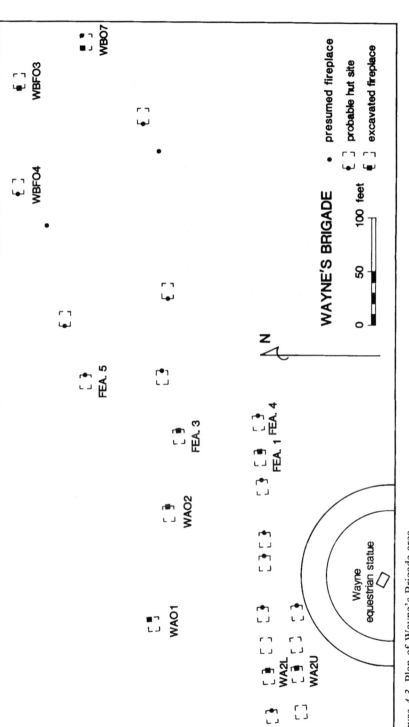

Figure 4.3. Plan of Wayne's Brigade area.

Cotter's detailed description of the two hut floors excavated by his class, in conjunction with the sparse notes left by Landis, enable us to make some general comments on some aspects of hut construction and encampment layout for this brigade location. The size of the floors, which were terraced into the hillside, varied greatly, although it was difficult to distinguish the fill from the subsoil. The fireplaces were mostly of stone slab construction, with the wings slanting out from the back wall to a 5-ft width. In two cases cited by Landis the fireplace was constructed of log cribbing plastered with clay; he also describes one door sill constructed of flat stones (Landis in Cotter 1966:5, 3). The fireplaces of the huts were uniformly oriented to the east with three exceptions. One of these was an unusually long hut (12 by 22 ft) and appeared to have a fireplace at either end; Landis interpreted it as a double hut (Landis in Cotter 1966:4). The excavated hut floors lay more or less in rows parallel to the crest of the hill (along which the outer line entrenchment is postulated to have run).

In Landis' later meanderings through the area he located and tested numerous pits, identified by him as trash, offal and ash pits, and latrine pits. These are not located; he gives only details of dimensions for them, and they vary widely from 9 to 3 ft in diameter, conforming to various shapes and depths. A wealth of artifacts came from these pits.

During the University of Pennsylvania Museum Applied Science Center for Archaeology's survey in 1978, one hut floor was encountered in the area between Outer Line Drive and the woods, but was not excavated beyond what was necessary to define the roughly rectangular and indistinct outline of the floor fill (8 by 6.5 ft). The hearth in this case consisted solely of a fire-reddened burnt clay surface (Parrington in Ralph and Parrington 1979:126).

Conway's Brigade

For Conway's Brigade area the only information available on the excavation is that supplied on the artifact bag labels, where the pieces are described as coming, in most cases, from a "burned hut," or a "tent fireplace." The artifacts were catalogued in Harrisburg at the William Penn Memorial Museum as part of the "Landis Collection"; presumably they were excavated by Landis during some unreported summer. This brigade encampment is therefore not discussed further in this section.

Maxwell's Brigade (Figure 4.4)

For four weeks in 1962 Duncan Campbell, then state archaeologist, with three other people, one of whom was Stanley Landis, excavated five hut floors in the wooded area between Camp Road and the Inner Line Drive, a short distance to the east of the inner line entrenchment. A two-page summary report on these excavations was submitted by Campbell (1962).

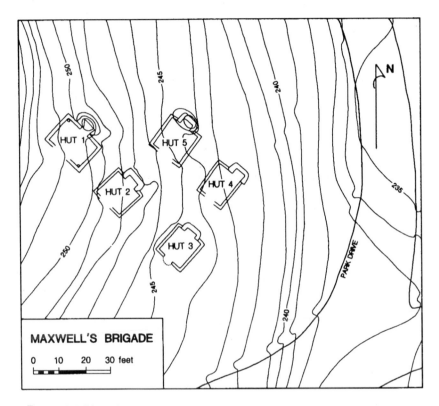

Figure 4.4. Plan of Maxwell's Brigade area (drafted by H. Schenck 1980).

The hut floors were found in two rows running northwest and southeast, three in one line and two in a parallel line to the northeast. The huts varied in size (between 16 by 14 to 12 ft square) but had hearths uniformly centered (with one exception) on the northeast wall. Clay had been used to level the floors between the stones of the hillside in all cases. The depths of the hut floors and construction of the fireplaces were not recorded.

Virginia Brigade (Figure 4.5)

The history of the excavations at this site is bewilderingly complex. In the spring of 1972 an area on the level unwooded ground to the north of Outer Line Drive and to the west of two lines of uniformly sized and oriented huts (which had been reconstructed around 1950) was designated for construction of a new parking lot of 60 by 100 ft. Before construction took place the area was entirely excavated under the direction of Brian Egloff and Vance Packard, using students from Lower Merion High School and the University of Delaware. Four hut floors were uncovered (Egloff et al. n.d.).

To follow up this success Egloff conducted a soil resistivity survey over a large area to the west of the parking lot. To test out the results of the survey an area of approximately 5000 ft^2 was totally excavated in the summers of 1972 and 1973 and a total of 13 more hut floors and four pits located. These excavations, with one exception, took place under the overall direction of Vance Packard. In the summer of 1972 a University of Pennsylvania field school under John Cotter was responsible for the excavation of one of these huts. Joseph Hall and Cotter wrote a report on this single hut (Cotter 1972; Hall 1972b). The site report on the other huts was written by Michael Parrington (1979a). In 1978 the remains of a structure tentatively identified as a bread oven were encountered in the course of the survey conducted by the Museum Applied Science Center for Archaeology (MASCA). This was located directly to the west of these hut floors, but the structure was not excavated (Parrington in Ralph and Parrington 1979:127).

Despite the large numbers of people and organizations digging here and the difficulties in integrating their field records, the relatively good descriptions and plans of the hut floors and associated features allow us to say more about hut construction here than at the other brigade sites. Again there is a marked discrepancy between the floors in overall dimensions as well as in shape. The largest measured 12.5 by 12 ft and the smallest, 7.5 by 6.5 ft. The depth that the floors had been excavated into the subsoil varied as well, from 8 in to 1.5 ft. Most of the hut depressions contained post holes of varying shapes and sizes. Substantial ones located along the edges of the depressions possibly indicate doorway location, while the smaller internal post holes may have been for bunk supports. The orientation of the fireplaces was totally nonuniform; they showed up on north, south, east, and west walls. Three huts had corner fireplaces, one had none at all. While stones were used to line the backs of the hearths in a few instances, a fireplace constructed of log cribbing covered with daub must have been common. Just as the orientation of the individual huts was most irregular, so their overall layout seems without plan or purpose, though at least three north-south rows, running perpendicular to the probable course of the Outer Line entrenchment, can perhaps be discerned.

The possible bread oven consisted of a rectangular area 12 by 6 ft packed with stone with an associated hearth or area of burning.

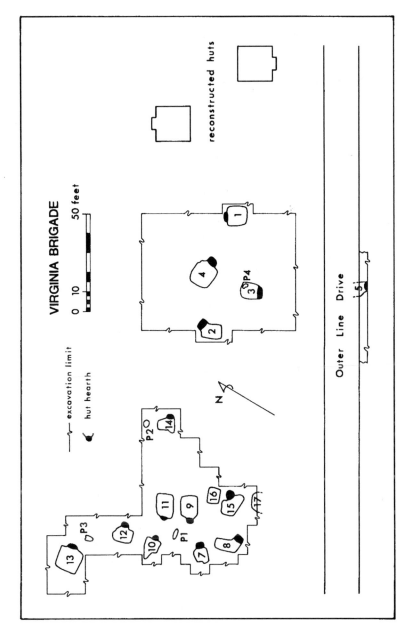

Figure 4.5. Plan of Virginia Brigade area.

Discussion of Excavated Features

Both the differing excavation strategies, with the concomitant variation in quality of field records, and the varying degree of preservation of the features, make it difficult to compare construction methods and systems of spatial organization across the three brigade areas for which we have reports. For example, at Maxwell's Brigade, while the use of clay as a filler to level the floor made it possible to make quite accurate measurements (in one case) of the hut's interior dimensions, the lack of field records or a substantial report means we have no information on depth of the floors or fireplace construction.

In Wayne's Woods, the method of terracing the floors into the pronounced grade of the hill meant that the uphill side of a floor was well-preserved, but the downhill side lost. The steepness of the slope guaranteed that this area had not been subject to plowing in the 19th century (cf. map, Garrigues 1897); while the ground cover therefore facilitated the preservation of the features, extensive root action was responsible for displacing the stones of the fireplaces. Again, while the two hut floors excavated by Cotter are well reported, very few of the floors and pits recorded by Landis are even located. This is perhaps the most regrettable loss of information, because Wayne's Brigade area is the one for which we have the largest number of various types of pits, and therefore the best hope of perceiving the way in which an encampment would have been laid out in its totality. Proper recording would have indicated not only how the huts stood in relation to each other, but also where facilities such as latrines, ash, offal and trash pits were located, and the patterns of communication between them. Landis does give basic dimensions and shapes for most of the pits and has loosely organized them according to the hut they were closest to in each case.

The flat, arable ground occupied by the Virginia Brigade was plowed probably throughout the 19th century (plow scars were observed across a hut floor outline excavated by MASCA in 1978 further to the west along Outer Line Drive [Parrington in Ralph and Parrington 1979:119]). Thus in this area, in contrast to Maxwell's Brigade and Wayne's Brigade, all that remains of the Revolutionary War period features are the portions that the soldiers excavated into the subsoil, below the depth of the plow zone. It is unlikely that the dimensions preserved accurately represent the true length and breadth of the superstructure of the hut. On the other hand these features are well-preserved and stand out well against the bright yellow clay of the subsoil, and good reports exist for almost all the features excavated in this area.

Perhaps the most striking feature of the three hut encampments is the variation in size, shape, and layout of the excavated hut floors. The Virginia Brigade has both the smallest (the largest floor outline measures 13 by 9 ft) and the most irregular hut outlines, but, as indicated above, we cannot be confident that they represent the true interior hut dimensions. In Wayne's Brigade, since the floor fill could not easily be distinguished from the subsoil, accurate measurements were difficult.

However, the hut floors from Maxwell's Brigade were apparently all good rectangles, and they were generally both larger and more uniform in size.

The plan of the hut floors in the Virginia Brigade shows none of the regimentation that might be expected in a military camp. The huts appear to have been laid out in haphazard fashion with little apparent order, and the fireplaces are located randomly around the sides of the huts. In contrast, the huts in Maxwell's Brigade are laid out along two parallel northwest/southeast azimuths, at uniform distances apart. Since no area excavation took place in Wayne's Woods it is uncertain what form the plan of that encampment took; however at present we may conjecture that it would have fallen between the symmetry of Maxwell's Brigade and the dissymmetry of the Virginia Brigade.

The orientation of each brigade to the defensive system varied as well. Maxwell's Brigade huts are in front of (to the east of) the inner line defenses, remnants of which remain to this day. The huts in both the Virginia Brigade and Wayne's Brigade are behind (to the north of) the outer line defenses, but the huts in the former run roughly perpendicular to the course of the entrenchments, while those in the latter run roughly parallel to it.

As for details on actual hut construction, the most information comes from the Virginia Brigade, but is confined to the subterranean support system. It seems likely that the single large post hole found in the outline of the hut fill in at least 10 cases would have supported a door post doubling as main supporting beam. A compacted clay floor was found in two of the huts. Finds of nails, hinges and flat (window?) glass tell us something of the wooden superstructure, while the pieces of burnt clay daub found here must have come from the log-crib fireplaces.

In Wayne's Woods there was little evidence of compaction of the floor. The ready availability of the stone slabs (the crest of Wayne's Woods is created by a Cambrian quartzite very resistant to weathering) (Bermingham in Ralph and Parrington 1979:7) resulted in the men building stone fireplaces, but the log-crib fireplaces prescribed by Washington were also in evidence here.

Even with the incomplete record so far recovered it is evident that hut construction and layout varied markedly from one brigade to the next, and indeed, within one brigade. Ewing's account does correlate fairly well with the archaeological evidence from excavations at Maxwell's Brigade, but it is clear that it is not permissible to extrapolate from either Washington's orders or from Ewing's single description to a picture of what all the brigade encampments would have looked like.

Military and Camp Equipage at Valley Forge

Introduction

The material world of the Continental soldier at Valley Forge encompassed not only the makeshift wooden shelters and low earthen defenses of the camp, but also the clothing on his back, the musket at his side and the redware mug in his hands. Some remnants of the assemblage of military and camp equipage and of personal items that every soldier would have owned or have been issued have been recovered in the archaeological excavations, and in less systematic collecting. The following section attempts to integrate the information from the documentary record about that assemblage with the actual objects recovered from the earth.

Historical Background

From early 1777 the Military Stores Department was under the direction of Colonel Benjamin Flower, who was subject to recurring bouts of severe and incapacitating illness. One such episode occurred early in 1778, leaving the direction of his department in the hands of an unscrupulous subordinate. Flower's deputies, however, who superintended the various military stores depots scattered through interior Pennsylvania, were generally a conscientious and efficient group. The Quarter Master's Department, first under the supervision of Thomas Mifflin and then, from late February 1778, directed by Nathanael Greene, shared with the Military Stores Department the responsibility for the manufacture of certain items of military equipage.

Prior to the occupation of Philadelphia by the British in late September 1777, the capital had been an important depot for military stores belonging to the State of Pennsylvania and to the Continental government. The precipitous evacuation of the supplies scattered and confused these resources, along with the personnel who manufactured and repaired arms, accoutrements and camp equipage. Despite Washington's avowed intention to make Carlisle, Pennsylvania, the principal "grand arsenal" for the Army west of the Hudson River, stores remained at several locations throughout the winter, from which sporadic shipments would proceed to camp at Valley Forge.

Allentown, designated as a temporary depot following the evacuation, sheltered large quantities of material under the supervision of Deputy Commissary Jonathan Gostelowe, a noted Philadelphia cabinetmaker. Small arms ammunition was manufactured principally at Lebanon, while Carlisle housed artillery stores and ordnance. Rhiemstown (now Reamstown), situated between Lebanon and Ephrata, was a staging area where material would be collected from more remote stores in readiness to send to the army. This was apparently occasioned by the reliable network of roads between Reamstown and the area of the Valley Forge encampment. At camp Samuel French, commissary of military stores with the Army, received arms, ammunition and accoutrements for distribution to the troops. (At the same time, individual states were contracting for similar supplies, many of which were manufactured at distant locations.)

The Quarter Master's Department, aside from its key function of transporting baggage and supplies, had an arm responsible for the manufacture and repair of such things as tents, knapsacks, haversacks, canteens, and camp kettles. During the Valley Forge winter these items were stored, repaired and manufactured at Reading and subsidiary locations. In March of 1778 Nathanael Greene installed James Abeel at Reading as deputy quarter master for military stores. Abeel gathered in items of equipage from the domains of other deputies, contracted for the manufacture of canteens, hired local women to sew knapsacks and haversacks by the thousand, supervised displaced sail-makers from Philadelphia in the repair and manufacture of tents, and engaged a small army of blacksmiths, whose anvils rang day and night fashioning trace-chains and harness for the wagons of the Continental Army. The items, desperately needed before the opening of the campaign, were dispatched by flat-bottomed boats down the Schuylkill to Valley Forge (Thibaut 1980, Part Three).

Artifact Provenience

The finds from Duncan Campbell's excavation at Maxwell's Brigade were recorded and catalogued by their location within his grid system, and not stratigraphically nor, except in a few cases, by feature association. The finds from John Cotter's excavation at two hut sites in Wayne's Brigade were recovered and catalogued stratigraphically, and their feature associations were recorded, as were the artifacts retrieved during the various excavations at the Virginia Brigade.

Those artifacts collected in Wayne's Woods by Stanley Landis, however, were identified only according to the contexts they came from. Landis gave every feature he encountered a designation assigned according to its postulated place within the (ideal) layout of a military encampment: thus, WAO5 means Wayne's 1st Pennsylvania Regiment, officer's hut #5 (from the right facing out). Pits were numbered as they were discovered and identified with the nearest hut (hut WBO6, for example, had five pits identified with it, numbers 1–5). Landis was quite meticulous in his artifact collection and it is probably safe to assume that the artifacts catalogued as from one of these contexts actually came from it. Landis did not, however, fully excavate most of the features he encountered. Artifacts that Landis and others recovered using the metal detector were so identified. (Artifacts from all of these excavations are currently dispersed between Harrisburg, at the William Penn Memorial Museum, and Valley Forge. It is certain that some artifacts, judging by extant preliminary catalogues, are missing.)

In some cases poor preservation of the artifacts due to the acidic soil of Valley Forge, which has a pH range of 6.5–4.4 (Soil Survey of Montgomery County 1967: 154–155, 179) and subsequent, postexcavation deterioration (especially of iron objects) has made identification impossible. Despite these problems, much of the total sample of material found is identifiable as to function, and can be paralleled in the numerous published reports on military sites, both British and American, which cover the Revolutionary War period. (Rather than burden this text with frequently cited references to comparanda it was felt that the artifacts should be discussed in general terms, as their significance for this paper lies in their presence at Valley Forge during the encampment and not in their similarity to other objects of the same period.)

The artifacts from the Wayne's Brigade area are listed in Table 4.1, from Maxwell's Brigade area in Table 4.2, from Conway's Brigade area in Table 4.3, and from the Virginia Brigade area in Table 4.4. In compiling the tables an attempt was made to list minimum numbers of artifacts rather than actual fragments so that, for example, many more fragments of buttons were found than appear in the tables and the number given represents a reasonable estimate of the total number found. An exception to this rule was made in the case of glass and ceramic sherds as insufficient time was available to analyze this material using minimum numbers.

TABLE 4.1
Total Artifact Tabulation: Wayne's Brigade

Artifact	No.	Artifact	No.	Artifact	No.	Artifact	No.
Lead shot	53	Tomahawks	—	Ceramic	281	Unid. iron	49
Buck shot	9	Spades	—	Vessel glass	580	Unid. copper	3
Lead sprue	40	Files	1	Knives	6	Unid. lead	1
Gun flints	13	Nails	285	Spoons	3	Unid. pewter	1
Flint grips	6	Sheet lead	16	Forks	1	Unid. alloy	5
Gun parts	1	Copper tags	6	Barrel hoops	—	Copper ferrules	1
Barrel bands	4	Horse shoes	4	Camp kettles	—	Tubular copper	1
Musket worms	1	Hinges	3	Pot hooks	1	Copper rings	5
Ramrods	1	Spikes	1	Pewter vessels	1	Sulphur	1
Rammer caps	1	Copper rivets	3	Tin cups	1	Clay seals	1
Screwdrivers	1	Iron chain links	2	Hickory nuts	—	Aboriginal points	—
Sling swivels	2	Flat glass	—	Peach pits	1		
Cartridge boxes	1	Iron staples	—	Coins	4		
Scabbard clips	1	Iron bolts	1	Lead pencils	6		
Scabbard tips	—	Fish hooks	—	Slate pencils	—		
Iron shot	—	Iron buckets	1	Clay pipes	1		
Buttons	63	Iron wire	1	Thimbles	1		
Buckles	16	Copper wire	6	Marbles	1		
Cufflinks	2	Brass handles	—	Signet rings	1		
Hook and eyes	—	Brass lock plates	1				
Iron shoe cleats	—	Iron screws	1				
Bale seals	1						
Leather	1						
Textile	1						

TABLE 4.2
Total Artifact Tabulation: Maxwell's Brigade

Artifact	No.	Artifact	No.	Artifact	No.	Artifact	No.
Lead shot	4	Tomahawks	—	Ceramic	12	Unid. iron	2
Buck shot	1	Spades	—	Vessel glass	5	Unid. copper	—
Lead sprue	28	Files	—	Knives	4	Unid. lead	3
Gun flints	4	Nails	50	Spoons	—	Unid. pewter	—
Flint grips	—	Sheet lead	—	Forks	—	Unid. alloy	—
Gun parts	—	Copper tags	—	Barrel hoops	—	Copper ferrules	—
Barrel bands	—	Horse shoes	—	Camp kettles	—	Tubular copper	—
Musket worms	—	Hinges	—	Pot hooks	—	Copper rings	—
Ramrods	—	Spikes	—	Pewter vessels	—	Sulphur	—
Rammer caps	—	Copper rivets	—	Tin cups	—	Clay seals	—
Screwdrivers	—	Iron chain links	—	Hickory nuts	—	Aboriginal points	2
Sling swivels	—	Flat glass	—	Peach pits	—		
Cartridge boxes	—	Iron staples	—	Coins	1		
Scabbard clips	—	Iron bolts	—	Lead pencils	—		
Scabbard tips	2	Fish hooks	1	Slate pencils	—		
Iron shot	1	Iron buckets	—	Clay pipes	1		
Buttons	17	Iron wire	—	Thimbles	—		
Buckles	3	Copper wire	—	Marbles	—		
Cufflinks	1	Brass handles	—	Signet rings	—		
Hook and eyes	—	Brass lock plates	—				
Iron shoe cleats	—	Iron screws	—				
Bale seals	—						
Leather	—						
Textile	—						

Artifact Discussion

The differing quality of the excavations, and incomplete recovery of the artifactual assemblage from any one feature, together with the problem of provenience control, must be regarded as important factors in assessing the significance of statistical proportions of the total sample from brigade area to brigade area. Since any conclusions based on these skewed proportions alone would be invalid and meaningless, we have chosen to analyze the artifacts descriptively, focusing on the classes of artifacts for which we have good documentation.

Guns and Ammunition

Twenty-nine gun flints came from three of the brigade areas, none being found at Conway's. Of this total 23 were honey-colored French flints, 3 were gray (Dutch or English flints), and 3 had been burned white. This high proportion of French flints is to be expected on Revolutionary War period sites (Hanson and Hsu (1975:

TABLE 4.3
Total Artifact Tabulation: Conway's Brigade

Artifact	No.	Artifact	No.	Artifact	No.	Artifact	No.
Lead shot	20	Tomahawks	—	Ceramic	1	Unid. iron	20
Buck shot	—	Spades	—	Vessel glass	4[a]	Unid. copper	10
Lead sprue	53	Files	—	Knives	3	Unid. lead	7
Gun flints	—	Nails	331	Spoons	1	Unid. pewter	1
Flint grips	—	Sheet lead	—	Forks	1	Unid. alloy	—
Gun parts	3	Copper tags	—	Barrel hoops	—	Copper ferrules	—
Barrel bands	—	Horse shoes	—	Camp kettles	—	Tubular copper	—
Musket worms	—	Hinges	1	Pot hooks	—	Copper rings	—
Ramrods	—	Spikes	3	Pewter vessels	—	Sulphur	—
Rammer caps	—	Copper rivets	—	Tin cups	—	Clay seals	—
Screwdrivers	—	Iron chain links	—	Hickory nuts	9	Aboriginal points	—
Sling swivels	—	Flat glass	—	Peach pits	—		
Cartridge boxes	—	Iron staples	—	Coins	—		
Scabbard clips	—	Iron bolts	—	Lead pencils	—		
Scabbard tips	2	Fish hooks	—	Slate pencils	—		
Iron shot	—	Iron buckets	—	Clay pipes	—		
Buttons	30	Iron wire	—	Thimbles	—		
Buckles	8	Copper wire	—	Marbles	—		
Cufflinks	1	Brass handles	1	Signet rings	1		
Hook and eyes	—	Brass lock plates	—				
Iron shoe cleats	—	Iron screws	—				
Bale seals	—						
Leather	—						
Textile	—						

[a] Not including several hundred sherds from one context which were not individually counted.

76), since flints in use by the American army were commonly the honey-colored variety imported from France (Peterson 1968:63). Most of the gun flints found would have been suitable for muskets and a few were small enough for rifles and pistols.

In order for the flint to remain firmly in the jaws of the cock, it had to be sheathed either in a piece of leather or flattened lead. Lead flint grips were relatively common finds at the brigade areas, as were fragments of sheet lead which are presumably waste from the production of flint grips. The grips were frequently circular and had been bent double around the area of the flint as it fit in the jaws. Such pieces are often pierced in the middle, which derives from the abrasion of the cock screw at the rear of the flint (cf. illustration, Calver and Bolton 1950:217). Several examples of flattened musket balls used as flint grips were found.

Seventeen artifacts from the four brigade areas were classified as gun parts and these included iron barrel bands, fragments of gun locks and a butt plate. Other

TABLE 4.4
Total Artifact Tabulation: Virginia Brigade

Artifact	No.	Artifact	No.	Artifact	No.	Artifact	No.
Lead shot	24	Tomahawks	2	Ceramic	67	Unid. iron	70
Buck shot	20	Spades	2	Vessel glass	85	Unid. copper	1
Lead sprue	a	Files	—	Knives	5	Unid. lead	22
Gun flints	12	Nails	65	Spoons	—	Unid. pewter	1
Flint grips	6	Sheet lead	—	Forks	—	Unid. alloy	—
Gun parts	5	Copper tags	—	Barrel hoops	1	Copper ferrules	—
Barrel bands	4	Horse shoes	—	Camp kettles	3	Tubular copper	—
Musket worms	—	Hinges	—	Pot hooks	1	Copper rings	—
Ramrods	—	Spikes	—	Pewter vessels	—	Sulphur	1
Rammer caps	—	Copper rivets	—	Tin cups	—	Clay seals	—
Screwdrivers	1	Iron chain links	1	Hickory nuts	—	Aboriginal points	1
Sling swivels	1	Flat glass	4	Peach pits	—		
Cartridge boxes	1	Iron staples	1	Coins	1		
Scabbard clips	—	Iron bolts	1	Lead pencils	1		
Scabbard tips	8	Fish hooks	—	Slate pencils	1		
Iron shot	—	Iron buckets	—	Clay pipes	1		
Buttons	44	Iron wire	—	Thimbles	—		
Buckles	7	Copper wire	—	Marbles	—		
Cufflinks	—	Brass handles	—	Signet rings	—		
Hook and eyes	1	Brass lock plates	—				
Iron shoe cleats	1	Iron screws	—				
Bale seals	—						
Leather	—						
Textile	—						

a Present in quantity, not individually counted.

items concerned with firearms comprised an iron ramrod, ramrod caps, two screwdrivers of the type used to change gun flints and a musketworm. The so-called worm, used to clean and clear debris from a fouled musket barrel, was part of every soldier's military kit and was essential to the proper maintenance of his shoulder arm. Screwed to the end of the ramrod, the worm was used to extract paper residue from spent cartridges, and, used with a bit of rag or flax, to swab the barrel to clean it. The "screw and wiper," a variation of the worm, had a screw which could be used in extracting a round from the musket without firing the piece. Military stores of the Valley Forge period show no shortage of these implements. Five hundred and seventy-five of them were delivered to Valley Forge from the stores at Lebanon in March 1778, as were 405 more in April, most of these probably going to supply new recruits (Thibaut 1980:489, 503, 508).

The only identifiable gun part found was a gun lock from the 1763 model "Charleville." By the spring of 1778, the Continental army was receiving substantial shipments of new French .69 calibre muskets of the "Charleville" pattern. They were on hand in the principal stores, and more were enroute from New England. Three hundred and sixty-two of the new muskets were issued to the Army in mid-June, just before the Army marched for the Delaware (Thibaut 1980:429).

While this paper is mainly concerned with the artifact assemblage from the four brigade encampment sites where reliable archaeological evidence exists for the provenience of the various artifacts discussed, a fairly large amount of material exists which was located with the use of a metal detector by Stanley Landis. Although it is likely that the majority of this material is associated with the encampment it seems wise, with certain exceptions, to avoid any discussion of artifacts without a good provenience.

One exception which it seems reasonable to make is that of small arms ammunition found at Valley Forge. It seems probable that most of these lead balls date from the Revolutionary War period, and an analysis of them should indicate the calibre or the various muskets and rifles in use at Valley Forge. The diameters of 288 lead balls and buckshot are shown in Table 4.5.

TABLE 4.5

Diameters in Hundredths of Inches of Lead Balls and Buckshot from Valley Forge

British/American .75 Calibre		French .69 Calibre		Rifle Balls		Buckshot	
Diameter	Number	Diameter	Number	Diameter	Number	Diameter	Number
70/100	73	65/100	29	57/100	4	34/100	4
69/100	64	64/100	25	54/100	1	33/100	1
68/100	9	63/100	17	47/100	3	32/100	1
67/100	7	62/100	10	46/100	2	31/100	3
66/100	4	61/100	2	45/100	1	30/100	9
		60/100	6	44/100	2	29/100	10
		59/100	1				
TOTAL	157		90		13		28

As well as the French "Charleville" musket, the army still employed English .75 calibre "Brown Bess" pattern muskets, muskets from Holland, and domestic contract muskets commonly referred to as "Committee of Safety" arms. The diversity of arms in use, including not only muskets, but smaller calibre rifles, would presuppose the use of lead projectiles of varying calibers. Because black powder rapidly fouled the barrel, balls used in muskets had to be considerably smaller than the calibre of the arm. Thus balls of about .70 calibre or less would be used in the muskets of .75 calibre, and the French muskets would employ balls of about .65 calibre or less. Small calibre balls characterized as buckshot were often used in prepared paper cartridges supplied by the Military Stores Department to the Army. Joseph Watkins was manufacturing these at Lebanon in the spring of 1778 (Thibaut 1980:407).

The proportions of .75 calibre ammunition to .69 calibre suggest that there were more of the larger calibre weapons in use at Valley Forge. However, 123 of the larger calibre balls came from the area around General Jedediah Huntington's quarters where they were located by Stanley Landis using a metal detector. This may indicate that the men quartered there were equipped with a larger proportion of British or American muskets than French. In contrast, out of 39 measurable musket balls from Wayne's Brigade area 32 were .69 calibre suggesting that the troops quartered there had a high proportion of French muskets. At the Virginia Brigade area the proportions of .69 and .75 balls were more or less equal.

The proper maintenance of musket ammunition at camp posed recurring problems. Until curtailed by general orders, soldiers were prone to shoot off random rounds within the boundaries of the encampment. During January of 1778 alone, 77,537 rounds of musket ammunition were delivered to Valley Forge. This is hardly an extravagant amount, considering the size of the Army at the time (about 12,000), but certainly it was enough to supply a variety of extraneous uses (Thibaut 1980:376). Although Washington attempted to control wastage by ordering all spare ammunition to be collected together and stored, it is evident that quantities of lead escaped the stores, to serve a variety of unauthorized purposes (Thibaut 1980:382).

Among the musket balls recovered were three examples which had been cut in half, presumably to increase their destructive properties (Peterson 1968:61). Thirty-three musket balls had been chewed or bitten which recalls the reminiscences of Joseph Moore, who wrote of two soldiers biting on lead balls in 1776 when being whipped (in Hanson and Hsu 1975:80–81). Twenty-one of the bitten balls came from the area around Huntington's quarters and it is tempting to suggest that they may be associated with an area where punishment was administered. Unfortunately as there is no record of the circumstances in which the bitten balls were found, this premise must remain a speculation. Lead pencils found at the Virginia Brigade area and in Wayne's Woods had been created from lead musket balls in some cases. Finds of lead sprue were common at all four brigade areas indicating that musket balls were cast in, or in the vicinity of, the huts.

Other Camp Equipage

Iron and copper alloy buckles and suspensory equipment included sling swivels suitable for use on the "Brown Bess" musket, and cross belt buckles. Fragments of tinned iron found may represent cartridge canisters of the new type first issued in 1777 (Peterson 1968:67–68).

Two tomahawks came from the Virginia Brigade area, one of which was split where the bit had been welded on. This recalls a complaint made by General John

Sullivan regarding the poor quality of the axes supplied at Valley Forge (Thibaut 1979:16). Tomahawks and hatchets appear in quantity in returns of military stores for the Valley Forge period. There were, for instance, 860 at Allentown in October of 1777, 800 at Carlisle in February of 1778, and 3620 at Lebanon in March of 1778 (Thibaut 1980:Appendix D). There remains no known record of actual issuances at camp, but they were in ubiquitous use.

One of the more curious groups of artifacts from Valley Forge is a series of nine copper alloy tags with numerals on them. Three of the tags were found with a metal detector, the remainder were excavated. All the tags came from the Wayne's Brigade area and with the exception of one round tag, all the others were octagonal measuring 7/8 in in diameter. All the tags were holed at the top for suspension and several retained the original suspension nails. The octagonal tags were numbered: 1 (two examples), 2, 3 (two examples), 4, 9, and 14, and the round tag was numbered 16. No parallels have been found for these objects and the tentative hypothesis is advanced here that they were used to number the hut doors in Wayne's Brigade.

Clothing

A wide variety of buttons was found in all four brigade areas: 63 came from Wayne's Brigade, 44 from the Virginia Brigade, 30 from Conway's Brigade, and 17 from Maxwell's Brigade. The most common type of button was cast in pewter and closely resembles Stanley South's (1964) Type 11. Twenty-six examples of this type were identified out of the total of 171 examined; 1 of these had the initials USA on it. It seems likely that this type was the official army button, at least of enlisted men. The remaining buttons were mostly of copper alloy, many with embossed geometric, plaited and floral designs on them, and a few examples of silver and gilded buttons were found.

Among the artifacts found by Landis were two cast pewter buttons with regimental designations on them: 14 and 22. There is no recorded provenience for these buttons within the encampment other than that they came from Valley Forge. There is no record of a 22nd regiment being at Valley Forge, which raises the possibility that this button came from a captured British uniform or alternatively that it was lost by one of the Convention troops who were briefly housed at Valley Forge in 1778. The button with 14 on it may be from the 14th Virginia Regiment.

The diversity of buttons encountered is attributable to irregularities in the manufacture of military clothing during the Revolutionary War. Uniform clothing came from contractors in the states, from the Continental Clothier's Department, and from abroad. It was supplemented in times of particular hardship by collections and seizures of civilian raiment. The State of Connecticut, for instance, initiated a collection system by township in the autumn of 1777, when Congress reported to the states that the clothier general would not be able to supply the Army's wants

(Thibaut 1980:281, 560). Thus a considerable quantity of civilian clothing found its way to Valley Forge.

Anthony Wayne was particularly concerned with having his Pennsylvania troops clothed in a neat and uniform fashion, not only for reasons of health, but also to bolster morale and improve *esprit* in the field. When his men fell short of clothing, he contracted with Lancaster manufacturer Paul Zantzinger in late 1777 for regimental coats, jackets, breeches, waistcoats, shirts, stockings, shoes, and hats. These arrived periodically in camp through the winter and spring to replace worn-out clothing from the clothier's store. For buttons, Zantzinger would have employed what was locally available, but his correspondence with Wayne does not reveal a source (Thibaut 1980:266).

The Pennsylvania soldiers of Conway's Brigade were not so well served, and resented their inequality with Wayne's comparatively well-clad troops. Colonel Richard Butler of the 9th Pennsylvania Regiment assumed the task of pleading with the state government for clothing, and in late February 1778 his efforts were rewarded with some success. The two "additional" regiments in Conway's Brigade were entirely dependent upon the flagging efforts of the clothier general, and little is known of their condition (Thibaut 1980:304–305, 308).

Maxwell's Brigade had its clothing complaints as well, although they were probably not so severe as those afflicting Conway's. There was certainly no surplus of clothing available to the New Jersey troops, for their state had, like Pennsylvania, undertaken the seizure of clothing from disaffected civilians. How much of this made its way to camp, however, is uncertain (Thibaut 1980:286).

Washington, as the senior officer of the State of Virginia, felt himself bound to plead with Governor Patrick Henry to provide clothing for the Virginia line. Governor Henry presided over clothing collections taken up among the civilian populace, supplemented by some French uniform materials smuggled past the British squadron. Because sea transport had become so dangerous as to be prohibitive, however, these materials had to be sent north by overland route, a process which was painfully slow. The shipment arrived on the west bank of the Susquehanna in January, only to be stalled there by ice floes in the river. When a crossing was attempted the sledges broke through the ice, and although much of the shipment was rescued, the fabrics were damaged by freezing (Thibaut 1980:286–287).

The 13th Pennsylvania, attached to Weedon's Brigade, fell victim to similar ill-luck, when local materials being made up into uniforms for them at Newtown, Bucks County, were seized in a British dragoon raid (Thibaut 1980:307). The Virginia regiments, and the 13th Pennsylvania, were eventually supplied by their respective states, but their raiment was doubtless of a makeshift and diverse order.

Buttons had a variety of applications in the uniforms and clothing normally worn. The 2nd Pennsylvania Regiment, for instance was issued regimental coats, short jackets, breeches, and overalls (linen leggings), all of which would have required buttons (Thibaut 1980:556).

Other clothing items included pewter, silver and copper stock buckles, shoe buckles and belt buckles. The majority of the buckles were plain military types, but some were more ornate civilian-type buckles.

A signet ring with a Masonic emblem came from the Wayne's Brigade area. A substantial number of the officers of the Continental line were active Freemasons (of the 293 officers of the Pennsylvania Line who joined the Society of the Cincinnati in 1783, the majority had become Freemasons by that date) (Thibaut, unpublished research).

Food and Drink

The only brigade area where large numbers of ceramic sherds were found was Wayne's, where out of 281 sherds 238 were redware and presumably locally produced. The remaining sherds were more exotic and included four fragments of a purple tortoise-shell pattern Whieldon ware teapot lid, a porcelain teacup sherd, a number of joining sherds from a gray/blue stoneware mug with a GR medallion, and two sherds of black stoneware.

The majority of the sherds from the Virginia Brigade area were also redware, 46 out of a total of 67. The other sherds comprised delftware, stoneware, and one sherd of porcelain. Most of the sherds were very small. The few other identifiable vessels were drug pots, two in redware and two in delftware. Only 12 sherds were in the artifact assemblage examined from Maxwell's Brigade and one sherd was recorded from Conway's Brigade. These small numbers are probably a reflection of the excavation techniques used in these brigade areas or may be due to post-excavation loss of sherds.

One of the drug pots from the Virginia Brigade contained a greenish-yellow residue identified as sulphur, and a lump of sulphur was also found in the Wayne's Brigade area. The use of sulphur for medical purposes at Valley Forge is demonstrated by an extract from General George Weedon's orderly book, which requests the regimental surgeons to obtain sulphur "for the use of their Regiments" (Weedon 1902:183). Sulphur is also an ingredient of gunpowder but it seems likely that the excavated example of sulphur had a medicinal use and was probably employed to alleviate the after-effects of smallpox vaccination or for skin disorders such as scabies (Trussell 1976:40–43).

Glass forms the largest component of the assemblage from the Wayne and Virginia Brigade areas and also from Conway's Brigade, from which a large quantity of several hundred glass sherds (uncounted), some of which were melted, was excavated. Wine, spirit, and case bottles formed a large proportion of the glass found in all three areas, and medicine bottles and vials were also well represented, especially in the Wayne's Brigade area. Only five glass fragments came from Maxwell's Brigade but again this may be due to post-excavation loss.

Eighteen knives, four spoons, and two forks were found at the four brigade encampments. Other items concerned with food were camp kettle fragments, a tin cup fragment and a portion of a pewter vessel. Several examples of iron barrel bands which may have been used as grills were recorded (Calver and Bolton 1950:216; Olsen 1964:508).

The principal items of camp equipage that were supplied by the Quarter Master's Department were camp kettles and tents. Knives, eating utensils, plates, trenchers, and other items of a more domestic nature would have been supplied by the men, and thus came from an infinite number of sources.

The ration issued by the commissary of the Continental Army over the winter of 1777–78 was supposed to have supplied 1.25 lb beef, *or* 1 lb pork, *or* 1.25 lb salt fish per man per day, with 1.25 lb soft or hard bread and .5 gill of whiskey or rum per day. From late December 1777, the men were responsible for supplementing the ration with whatever vegetable or other food they could purchase. A market operated in camp from late January, to which neighboring farmers could bring their produce. The price regulations established by the Army suggest a wide variety of provender, including wild and domestic fowl, dairy products, and root vegetables. Soldiers and officers who could afford steep prices could also purchase from sutlers who hovered about the camp. They caught shad in the Schuylkill during the spring run, and according to tradition, raided the chicken coops of neighboring farmers (Thibaut 1980:130–131).

The winter was punctuated by periods of near-famine, when for days at a time the commissary failed to provide parts of the ration. At such times, and even when food was more plentiful, the officers and men were thrown back upon their own devices.

Faunal Analysis

Numbers of bones were recovered from the Wayne's Woods and Outer Line Drive excavations but little of that has been systematically analyzed. While we were unable to identify and analyze the boxes of bone at Harrisburg, a brief summary of the results of earlier faunal analyses at Valley Forge ties in well with the information on the ration issued to the soldiers. The information comes from the Virginia Brigade area (Hall 1972a; Parrington 1979a), from all the Revolutionary War period features excavated by MASCA (Hall in Ralph and Parrington 1979:136f), from Cotter's excavations in Wayne's Brigade (Hall 1972a), and from Maxwell's Brigade (Olsen 1964) (the latter discussion includes bones excavated by Duncan Campbell from Morristown as well).

The vast majority of the bones are of the domestic cow (*Bos taurus*) with the domestic sheep (*Ovis aries*) and domestic pig (*Sus scrofa*) represented in fewer numbers. Minimum numbers for the Virginia Brigade consist of eight cattle, two sheep and one pig. Remains of other animals included deer (*Odocoileus virginianus*), snapping turtle (*Chelydra serpentina*), and unidentified fish and bird from the Virginia Brigade, goat (*Capra hircus*), rabbit (*Lepus sylvagicus*), squirrel (*Sciurus carolinus*), and unidentified bird from the Wayne's Wood huts.

A point noted by both Hall and Olsen is the nearly complete destruction of the bone, presumably by cracking, chopping and splitting to extract the marrow, although damage may also have followed from disposal of bones on the living surfaces of the huts. The bones from the Virginia Brigade showing butcher marks had all been dismembered with an axe or cleaver; there were no saw marks on the bones. The beef bones generally came from parts designated (at present) by butchers as too poor for quality cuts, as, for example, the lower limbs (metapodials and carpals/tarsals). Their presence indicates that "the feet were not removed in butchering before distribution, and . . . whatever nutritional value was present in the meat/bones of cattle feet was utilized" (Hall in Parrington 1979a:65).

Another point of interest is the relative lack of remains of game animals, when one would have postulated foraging activities would have been essential for survival during the periods of scarcity.

Conclusions

Excavations for which published information is available have taken place at few sites directly comparable to Valley Forge. (Archaeological work has taken place at New Windsor, New York and at Pluckemin, New Jersey, both sites comparable to Valley Forge, but no published reports are available for either site.) Morristown, New Jersey, and Camp Reading, Connecticut are two exceptions. Three brigades went into winter quarters (in 1778–79) in three locations at Reading, Connecticut; one of those locations, within Putnam Memorial State Park, was the subject of limited archaeological excavation in 1973 and 1974 (Poirier 1976).

Morristown saw a major winter cantonment in 1779–80 of the "Main Army"; and in later winters (1780–81 and 1781–82) the Pennsylvania and New Jersey Brigades reoccupied the huts built in 1779 (Rutsch and Peters 1977:15–26). The sites of Morristown and Valley Forge are also directly comparable in that Morristown has been subjected to an equivalent series of intermittent and small-scale excavations by myriad archaeologists (including Duncan Campbell, Stanley Landis and John Cotter) from the 1930s to the 1970s, as detailed in Rutsch and Peters' admirable summary (1976).

The plan of the encampment (Poirier 1976:Fig. 2) at Camp Reading is based on a walking survey which mapped two parallel rows of depressions filled with fieldstones. There are about 50 putative hut floors in each row, and they seem to have been ordered in pairs across the "street," and in groups of three and six along the street. The rows lie along exact north-south azimuths, the depressions are all more or less the same size, and the whole impression is of an impressively symmetrical layout.

Testing of two of these depressions, however, revealed no occupational floor or distinctive hearth area in either case, although recovery of numerous Revolutionary War period artifacts and the discovery of three indisputable Revolutionary War period pits—two refuse, one a possible lead shot manufacturing area—demonstrated unequivocally that the area had been occupied by the soldiers (Poirier 1976:47). Given that the depressions had been identified and preserved in that form by the park commissioners (Poirier 1976:43), and given the indeterminate archaeological findings at the tested depressions, the regularity of the layout cannot be unquestionably accepted, until confirmed by more extensive excavation.

The layout of the brigade lines at Morristown was apparently based on that used by the Pennsylvania troops at Middlebrook the previous winter (1778–79, the year after Valley Forge) (Fitzpatrick in Rutsch and Peters 1977:21), and there exists a contemporary sketch of the cantonment of General Stark's Brigade (in Rutsch and Peters 1977:Fig. 3a) which shows four groups of about 24 huts, each three rows deep, the huts arranged in pairs within each row, the officers' huts behind the men's huts in parallel rows. Both the documents and the excavated remains indicate a much greater degree of regularity of layout than at Valley Forge.

Washington had ordered that any hut that be out of line be pulled down and rebuilt in its proper alignment, and in fact, one hut in the New Jersey Brigade was torn down prior to an inspection of the unit by Washington (Rutsch and Peters 1977:24). Excavation of Stark's Brigade area at Morristown revealed 24 huts laid out in two parallel rows with huts more or less paired across and along the street (Rutsch and Peters 1977:Fig. 3b). Other excavated brigade encampments at Morristown showed a degree of regimentation varying somewhat from this, but still organized in a superior fashion than at Valley Forge, excepting Maxwell's Brigade. (The huts on the New Jersey Line at Morristown, as at Valley Forge, were highly ordered and regularly spaced) (Rutsch and Peters 1976:93).

The huts themselves at Morristown apparently all measured approximately 16 by 14 ft. Those on the hillside had been terraced into the slope on earthen platforms, and details such as log molds of the huts' base logs, and the original floors, showing usage paths from the hearths to the doorways, were well preserved (Rutsch and Peters 1977:33 and Fig. 4). Placement of doors, windows and hearths differed from brigade to brigade, even from hut to hut (Rutsch and Peters 1977:24). The practice of excavating out the floors of huts was discouraged after the Valley Forge encampment, as indicated by the general orders of December 14, 1778, when the Army was camped at Middlebrook. "Much of the sickness among the troops seems to have been occasioned by the improper method adopted in forming many of the huts last winter; some being sunk into the ground and others covered with earth" (Fitzpatrick 1936, 13:395).

Poirier points out that "the primary foci of analysis upon the unearthed hut and fireplace features [at Revolutionary War encampment sites] have been the identification of internal constructional details and the spatial alignment patterns of individual huts within a brigade line of encampment" (Poirier 1976:40). That there now exists a body of information on these aspects of camp life has been made evident. The not particularly startling conclusion that Valley Forge graphically presents a picture of an army learning how to organize itself arises from a comparison of Morristown, and perhaps also Camp Reading, with Valley Forge.

Little research has been published on artifacts from the temporary military encampments of the Revolutionary War period, which were occupied for a short duration of time. At Morristown, "artifacts and their analysis," write Rutsch and Peters, "have taken a back seat to the primary goal of site location . . . and an attempt to study them conclusively has not been a part of the present survey" (1977:35). While Rutsch and Peters quite rightly recommend that the artifacts from all the excavations in the park should be analyzed and interpreted, so far this recommendation has not been implemented, and most of this excavated material is still in store at Morristown (S. Kopczinski, pers. comm.).

The work at Camp Reading provides a contrast in that the artifacts are discussed in some detail and quantitative information is available about them (Poirier 1976: 47–49). Unfortunately the actual number of artifacts recovered is small and trends observed within the sample may be skewed by the paucity of the artifact assemblage.

We have avoided breaking down the artifacts from Valley Forge statistically for reasons noted above. We were encouraged to note, however, that 65 percent of the total artifact count from Camp Reading was made up of lead shot and sprue, nails and buttons, because we had felt that the collecting using a metal detector might have skewed the sample at Valley Forge towards those items. In fact, at Wayne's Woods, they made up only 31 percent of the total count. In the sample from Conway's Brigade area, the other site where the metal detector was used, only 15 percent of the total count consisted of articles other than lead shot, sprue, nails, and buttons, but this sample was skewed by the 331 nails (64 percent of the total count) collected from the burnt hut.

Stanley South has made an attempt to group artifacts from historic sites into classes, depending upon their function, so that for example, objects such as buttons, buckles and thimbles are attributed to a clothing group, and swords, bayonets, insignia, etc., belong to a military group (South 1977:95–96). On a purely military site it could be argued that all artifacts found should be designated as part of the military group as their presence and function are dictated by the fact that the people using them were all attached in some fashion to the military. There are other difficulties, as for instance the attribution of a button with a regimental designation;

does it belong to the clothing group with the buttons, or to the military group with the insignia? It would seem that the specialized nature of some sites negates the use of this method of classifying and quantifying artifacts, and this limitation was acknowledged by South (1977:96).

An attempt was in fact made (Parrington 1980:Table 2) to divide the artifact assemblage from the Virginia Line at Valley Forge according to South's categories in order to make a comparison with the "Frontier Artifact Pattern" as defined by South (1977:141–164). This comparison, however with four fort sites: Fort Ligonier, Pennsylvania (1758–66), Fort Prince George, South Carolina (1753–69), Fort Moultrie, South Carolina (American) (1779–94), Fort Moultrie, South Carolina (British) (1780–81), and Fort Watson, South Carolina (1780–81), merely underlines the real distinction that must be made between relatively long-term occupations in permanent military outposts and transitory camping in makeshift dwellings. Clearly, at Valley Forge and at other transient cantonments of the Revolutionary Army, we are dealing with something very different from the permanent, fortified military occupation sites of the frontier, where there appears to have been a significant presence of "luxury" objects that were culturally reinforcing.

The pattern at Valley Forge from all four brigade encampments is one of minimalism. Not only is there a general paucity of artifacts, but the vast majority are items that would have been issued by the Army for military use or subsistence. (At Camp Reading 98 percent of the total Revolutionary War cultural material is faunal [Poirier 1976:49].) The items that might be personal belongings stand out by virtue of their scarcity—a teapot, a teacup, a mug, coins and marbles, a thimble, a ring—and are likely as well to be indicators of social stratification in camp. The one item which one might have expected the private soldier to use and discard, that most ubiquitous of historical period artifacts—the clay pipe—is virtually nonexistent at Valley Forge. The only exceptions—cutlery, buttons, and buckles—reinforce this impression, since the documentation makes it clear that these are the articles which of necessity would often have been supplied from the civilian context.

Given this pattern, the predominance of such basic essentials as buttons, lead shot and sprue, gun parts and flints, and nails, as can be seen at both Camp Reading and Valley Forge, is no longer something to query. Not only was there little else to lose, but also the straitened circumstances and recurrent supply crises would presumably have dictated use and reuse of all articles. (The manipulation of musket balls and scrap lead and the adaption of barrel hoops to grills demonstrate this.)

In historical literature, the importance of the Continental Army as a force in homogenizing the culturally diverse colonies has been noted (Royster 1979), and it follows that the community of objects in use throughout the army, strictly limited by the requirements of portability, should become progressively more uniform throughout the eight years of the war. Historical and archaeological evidence, however, both strongly suggest that at Valley Forge the amalgamation of culturally diverse units into a national army was as yet incomplete, and that the irregularities of the central Continental supply system reinforced material diversity.

We had hoped, before analysis of the material from the four brigade areas, to be able to compare and contrast not only the spatial alignments but also the artifact assemblage from one to the next. The varying quality and scope of excavations and quantity of artifacts, however, militated against any fruitful comparison, except in a few instances. One of these was the discovery that Wayne's Brigade was equipped with a comparatively high proportion of the new imported French muskets, which perhaps ties in with the knowledge that Wayne was actively solicitous on his troops' behalf. Generally, however, what was most distressing was how little we were able to extract from 10 years of excavations on hut encampments at Valley Forge.

One reason for this stands out. Aside from the obvious problems of lack of records and reports, the excavation strategy that has been consistently employed at all three sites is one of sampling. More often than not (this is especially true of Landis' work at Valley Forge, and possibly of Campbell's work at both Valley Forge and Morristown), this sampling has been based on moving out "ideal" distances (based on historical documents) from a known hut fireplace and testing again. The danger of this method is readily apparent, as is the circular reasoning that can arise when "archaeologically" derived plans are used to substantiate historically documented layouts. Both the Wayne's Brigade and Camp Reading plans may be artifacts of this process. This is not to say that all the excavated plans at Morristown and Valley Forge are invalid, though it is interesting and possibly significant that the most irregular hut layout yet encountered is that at the Virginia Brigade at Valley Forge, where the whole area was stripped to subsoil. This is rather a plea for full-scale area excavation of at least one complete brigade encampment, based on a research strategy without built-in preconceptions. Poirier's research design for Camp Reading would be a good one: "an assessment of the overall settlement pattern [requiring] the identification of the function of structures, the location and definition of activity areas, and the determination of rank differentiated areas" (Poirier 1976:42). As noted above, Landis's testing in Wayne's Woods demonstrated the variety of Revolutionary War features other than huts that await discovery. Historical evidence confirms also that there was a variety of special use structures built at Valley Forge. The emphasis upon huts has resulted in provocative conclusions about the differences between brigades at a single site, and between different encampments, and these conclusions need to be tested.

All too frequently military occupation sites are seen as entities isolated from their cultural matrices. The indiscriminate sampling of such sites will not enlighten us as to some of the more important social questions involving military culture. We need to know more about the material relationship between military sites and the surrounding civilian communities, as well as more about the structure of military society itself. While these questions are certainly subject to historical, documentary research, we suggest here that archaeological investigation, carried out under thoughtfully defined research objectives, can provide important new information. The way in which the Continental Army operated as a social unit wants careful scrutiny, and in this archaeology has a crucial role to sustain.

The conclusions of this paper are speculative and hedged with uncertainties, because no effort has been made to carry out a long-term archaeological investigation of the physical and artifactual remains of the encampment. Until this is done our existing knowledge of conditions at Valley Forge during the winter of 1777–78 must remain tentative.

REFERENCES

Calver, W. L. and R. P. Bolton. 1950. *History Written with Pick and Shovel.* New York: New York Historical Society.

Campbell, J. L. 1962. Valley Forge Park, Archaeological Investigations, 30 April–1 June 1962: Preliminary Summary Report. On file at Valley Forge National Historical Park (NHP), Pennsylvania.

Cotter, J. L. 1966. Preliminary Report on Archaeological Investigations at the Pennsylvania Encampment at Valley Forge, July–October 1966. On file at Valley Forge NHP, Pennsylvania.

Cotter, J. L. 1972. Further Observations on the Hut 9 Excavation. On file at Valley Forge NHP, Pennsylvania.

Egloff, B., V. Packard, and J. DeM. Ramsey n.d. The Excavation of Four Hut Sites at the Outer Defensive Line of Valley Forge. On file at Valley Forge NHP, Pennsylvania.

Ewing, T. (ed.). 1928. *Military Journal of George Ewing (1754-1824), A Soldier at Valley Forge.* Yonkers, NY: privately printed.

Fitzpatrick, J. C., (ed.) 1931–44. *The Writings of George Washington from the Original Manuscript Sources*, 10 and 13. Washington, DC: U.S. Government Printing Office.

Hall, J. 1972a. A Brief Study of the Zooarchaeology of the Pennsylvania and Virginia Line Huts at Valley Forge. On file at Valley Forge NHP, Pennsylvania.

Hall, J. 1972b. The Excavation of Hut 9 on Outer Line Drive, Valley Forge. On file at Valley Forge NHP, Pennsylvania.

Hanson, L. and D. Ping Hsu. 1975. *Casemates and Cannonballs, Archaeological Investigations at Fort Stanwix, Rome, New York.* Washington, DC: National Park Service.

Landis, S. 1968. Valley Forge 1968. On file at Valley Forge NHP, Pennsylvania.

Landis, S. 1969. Valley Forge 1969. On file at Valley Forge NHP, Pennsylvania.

Olsen, S. J. 1964. Food Animals of the Continental Army at Valley Forge and Morristown. *American Antiquity* 29:506–509.

Parrington, M. 1979a. Report on the Excavation of Part of the Virginia Brigade Encampment, Valley Forge, Pennsylvania 1972–1973. MASCA, University Museum, Philadelphia. On file at Valley Forge NHP, Pennsylvania.

Parrington, M. 1979b. Geophysical and Aerial Prospecting Techniques at Valley Forge National Historical Park, Pennsylvania. *Journal of Field Archaeology* 6:193–201.

Parrington, M. 1980. Revolutionary War Archaeology at Valley Forge, Pennsylvania. *North American Archaeologist* 1(2):161–176.

Peterson, H. 1968. *The Book of the Continental Soldier.* New York: Promontory Press.

Poirier, D. A. 1976. Camp Reading: Logistics of a Revolutionary War Winter Encampment. *Northeast Historical Archaeology* 5(1–2):40–52.

Ralph, E. and M. Parrington (eds.). 1979. Patterns of the Past: Geophysical and Aerial Reconnaissance at Valley Forge. MASCA, University Museum, Philadelphia. On file at Valley Forge NHP, Pennsylvania.

Royster, C. 1979. *A Revolutionary People at War: The Continental Army and the American Character.* Chapel Hill: University of North Carolina Press.

Rutsch, E. S. and K. M. Peters. 1976. A Survey of Archaeological Resources at Morristown National Historical Park, Morristown, New Jersey. On file at Morristown NHP, New Jersey.

Rutsch, E. S. and K. M. Peters. 1977. Forty Years of Archaeological Research at Morristown National Historical Park, Morristown, New Jersey. *Historical Archaeology* 11:15–38.

South, S. 1964. Analysis of the Buttons from Brunswick Town and Fort Fisher. *The Florida Archaeologist* 17(2):113–133.

South. S. 1977. *Method and Theory in Historical Archaeology.* New York: Academic Press.

Thibaut, J. 1979. In the True Rustic Order: Material Aspects of the Valley Forge Encampment, 1777–1778. Part III of the Valley Forge Historical Research Report. Valley Forge NHP, Pennsylvania.

Thibaut, J. 1980. This Fatal Crisis: Logistics, Supply, and the Continental Army at Valley Forge, 1777–1778. Part II of the Valley Forge Historical Research Report. Valley Forge NHP, Pennsylvania.

Trussell, J. B. B. 1976. *Birthplace of an Army, A Study of the Valley Forge Encampment.* Harrisburg: Pennsylvania Historical and Museum Commission.

Weedon, G. 1902. *Valley Forge Orderly Book of General George Weedon of the Continental Army Under Command of General George Washington.* New York: Dodd, Mead and Co.

THERESA A. SINGLETON ■

Chapter Five

The Archaeology of Slave Life

If I could do it, I'd do no writing at all here. It would be photographs; the rest would be fragments of cloth, bits of cotton, lumps of earth, records of speech, pieces of food and iron, phials of odors, plates of food, and of excrement.[1]

Excavations of slave cabins in the late 1960s marked the beginning of a new research field known as African-American archaeology. From the careful analysis of tangible material remains—broken pottery, mortar, food bone, tools, buttons, and beads, for example—archaeologists are able to piece together information on how African-Americans spent their daily lives, built their homes, prepared their food, and crafted household equipment and personal possessions. Ultimately, archaeologists using these varied materials are seeking answers to general questions about African-American life. How, for example, was an African heritage transplanted, replaced, or reinterpreted in America? In what ways are the artifacts recovered from African-American sites reflections of ethnic patterns or of social conditions such as poverty and the unequal access to material goods? How did African-Americans survive the rigors of everyday life?

What are the material differences in the lives of slaves, free blacks, and tenant farmers, or between urban and rural communities? In the southern United States, the primary concern of African-American archaeology is the investigation of former slave quarters. Archaeologists since the 1930s have excavated sites of the plantation big house, and have thereby supplied important information for the restoration of planters' houses later opened to the public. Inspired by the growing scholarly interest in America's diverse ethnic heritage and in the poor and powerless as well, archaeologists more recently have turned to the study of slaves and other people who left few written records. Archaeologists have thus in more recent years investigated slave sites in nearly every state of the former plantation South, from

This article was originally published in *Before Freedom Came: African-American Life in the Antebellum South*, Edward D. C. Campbell, Jr. ed., with Kym S. Rice, pp. 155–191, Charlottesville: University Press of Virginia, ©1991.

141

Maryland to Texas, including the plantation homes of George Washington and Thomas Jefferson.

But the archaeology of slave sites brings both opportunities and problems to the scholarship of slavery, the most studied topic of the African-American experience. As an opportunity, archaeology recovers a primary source of information that may well provide numerous reinterpretations of certain aspects of slave life. Many of the activities represented by excavated artifacts—vestiges of food collection and preparation, craft practices, personal possessions, and details of house construction, alteration, and repair—are infrequently described in written and oral sources about slavery. The study of these objects, however, offers even more. From the studies of excavated remains come suggestions for understanding the context of everyday plantation life, the African-American response to enslavement, and processes of change and exchange between masters and slaves.

The problems presented by archaeological data are also many. The archaeologist can only interpret abandoned, discarded, or lost objects preserved in buried deposits. This leaves out any cherished objects that may have been kept and handed down from generation to generation. As for organic materials—clothing, wood, and basketry, for example—most remain preserved underground in only the most exceptional circumstances. The preservation of deposits left by a site's former occupants is also affected by subsequent activities, whether deep plowing, dredging, or construction. Thus disturbed, such materials raise questions for archaeological inquiry. Archaeology is not, however, simply the study of the recovered objects alone—it is also the study of the context in which the object is found and how it relates to other excavated materials. Moreover, all the evidence that the archaeologist studies is indirect: artifacts provide the basis for inference on particular aspects of behavior, not direct evidence of behavior. The artifacts are, instead, the by-products of behavior. Therefore, the interpretation of slavery's archaeological record requires that archaeologists also incorporate historical and ethnographic descriptions of slave behavior derived from written sources and oral tradition.

Thus reinforced, archaeological studies of slavery have made significant contributions in, first, the identification of African-American ethnic patterns and, second, in providing information on slave living conditions.[2] These themes, however, represent only two of the primary ways that archaeologists view and interpret data to study plantation society.[3] The two themes are also somewhat arbitrary, as they form only part of a larger, integrated complex of human activities anthropologists traditionally define as *culture*. A deliberate attempt is made here, however, to distinguish between two aspects of culture, between what are termed *value culture* and *reality culture*. The former, as applied to slave life, refers to customs, beliefs, and values presumably influenced by an African heritage. The latter includes those aspects of slave life largely influenced instead by external forces, especially social controls inherent within slave society.[4] Using this approach, objects can often be understood from both perspectives. For example, the study of slave foodways provides insights into African-American customs associated with food preparation and serving, an aspect of a value culture. However, the foods slaves consumed were determined to a large extent by a reality culture: slaves ate the foods supplied to them or foods they foraged for themselves.

Conclusions are, however, based upon preliminary research and thus necessarily speculative. Further, because the unit of analysis for most archaeological research is often a single site, to suggest that the archaeological findings characterize an entire southern region or the entire South is an as-yet untested assumption. That said, many of the generalizations offered here are, nevertheless, based upon findings uncovered at numerous sites and, in a few cases, at all the sites excavated to date.[5] Historical and ethnographic accounts also support many of the generalizations.

One of the initial objectives for excavating slave sites was to identify material elements of an African heritage. Several early studies in slave archaeology were undertaken on the cotton and, later, rice plantations along the coastal reaches of Georgia where a large slave population once lived in relative isolation from whites. Archaeologists became particularly interested in these coastal slave sites because scholars had discerned several cultural traditions in language, music, and material culture among modern-day descendants of the sites' slave communities.[6] What archaeologists had hoped to uncover were remnants of slave crafts that would shed light on the origin and development of material culture traditions.[7] When archaeologists failed to uncover any identifiable African or African-styled artifacts, some assumed that such objects were likely made from only perishable materials that had long ago deteriorated and disappeared.[8] As a consequence, most of the subsequent research at Georgia slave sites addressed questions concerning slave living conditions.

Since the initial studies of slave sites on the Georgia coast, the search elsewhere for archaeological evidence of African-American ethnicity has been more successful. Although interpretations are tentative, the sites have supplied empirical data for the widely held view that enslaved Africans and their descendants nurtured and sustained a few aspects of an African heritage in spite of the oppressive and dehumanizing conditions of slavery. Archaeological evidence of African-American ethnicity is indicated from several sources: objects presumably brought from Africa, recreations of African-styled or African-influenced objects, and mass-produced objects and other European-American materials reinterpreted by slaves for a special African-American meaning.

In light of the more recent archaeological evidence of African-American ethnicity recovered from other areas, reasons for the absence of ethnic objects from the Georgia sites are still unclear. Most of the artifacts recovered from Georgia slave sites date from the 1800s, when many slave owners supplied their slaves with mass-produced objects fashioned for European-American tastes rather than with slave-crafted objects. The availability of ready-made objects prompted by England's Industrial Revolution eventually resulted in the worldwide substitution of imported objects for items handcrafted locally. Therefore, handcrafted household objects preserved in the archaeological record are found more frequently at sites dating before rather than after 1800. Although fewer handmade objects are recovered from 19th-century sites, archaeologists have nevertheless been able to identify ethnic patterns from the careful study of both mass-produced and reworked European-American objects.

Although the vast majority of slaves brought few, if any, objects with them from Africa, several objects of presumed African origin have been recovered from slave sites. Cowrie shells, Indo-Pacific artifacts used widely in Africa as a medium of exchange, are one example. Only three cowrie shells have been uncovered in North America, one each at sites in Virginia, North Carolina, and Louisiana.[9] Perhaps the slaves who once owned these small objects were wearing the shells when captured in the slave trade. How slaves used these shells is unknown, although seven cowrie shells found in a slave burial site in Barbados suggest a possible answer. Along with European-made glass beads, drilled dog teeth, fish vertebrae, and a carnelian bead (a handcrafted product of Cambray in southern India), the seven shells formed part of an elaborate and striking necklace with African characteristics.[10]

Another object—an ebony-wood ring recovered from Portici plantation at Manassas National Battlefield Park, Virginia—is also believed to be African in origin. Made of a hard, heavy wood native to African and Asian tropical environments, this curious artifact was found with yet another ring, one made of animal horn. It, too, may be of African origin. Recovered from in and around the plantation's detached kitchen, both rings most likely belonged to domestic servants involved in preparing food for the main house.[11] Yet another two rings have been unearthed in Virginia: one, made of horn, at Monticello and another, made of bone, recovered from a slave pen in Alexandria.[12]

Although the origin, function, and significance of these objects remain a mystery, both the rings and cowrie shells document the presence and use of African objects by slaves. Such artifacts may have functioned as heirlooms especially as some of these objects have been found within mid-19th-century contexts, when fewer African-born slaves were still alive.

Objects made on plantations also display African influences. Such recreations of African motifs provide the most compelling archaeological evidence for the persistence of an African heritage. African influences are suggested in decorations, pottery making, foodways, building techniques, charms, and ritual objects.

The earliest manifestations of an African-American cultural expression may have been the African-influenced designs placed upon objects made in colonial Virginia. In his study of 17th-century tobacco pipes from the Chesapeake region, Matthew C. Emerson has suggested that slaves crafted the clay pipes' decorative work, especially the stamped and incised motifs highlighted in white. He has identified similar design elements within the same time period in the arts and crafts of Ghana, Nigeria, and Senegal-Mali. As the pipes are European in form and made of Chesapeake clays,

Emerson believes the pipes reflect a combination of European form, native materials, and some African art. If his theory is correct, these pipe decorations may be the earliest physical evidence of an African-American expression of cultural identity in the southern United States.[13]

Emerson's interpretation of slave-made pipes is, however, highly controversial. Early historical accounts as well as archaeological studies have provided evidence that Algonkian Indians also made clay pipes. Furthermore, British colonists apparently made clay pipes, too, particularly during periods of economic hardship when imported goods from England were scarce and expensive.[14] Yet the possibility that enslaved Africans may have influenced pipe-making practices cannot be totally discounted. Seventeenth-century Chesapeake society offered social conditions and labor relationships that permitted an exchange of ideas, technology, and information among Native Americans, Europeans, and Africans. The three groups often worked and resided together under circumstances that rarely occurred in later times. In this way, Chesapeake pipes may be an early material example of a three-way cultural exchange.

Incised decorations found on pewter spoons may be another example of enslaved Africans applying an African aesthetic to enhance a European object. Vestiges of geometric designs found on spoons from the Garrison plantation in Maryland and the Kingsmill plantations in Virginia are remarkably similar to the spoon bowls and handles decorated today by Maroons (descendants of self- emancipated slaves) living in Surinam, South America.[15]

Ceramics, though, are the most frequently recovered slave-produced artifacts. Used for preparing, serving, and storing food, slave-made ceramics are frequent finds at plantation sites in South Carolina, Virginia, and several islands in the Caribbean. Known as colono ware in the southern United States, such ceramics are a low-fired, unglazed earthenware apparently made by both Native and African-Americans.[16] Archaeologists once thought that only Native Americans produced this pottery and that its presence at colonial sites was thus an indicator of European and Native American cultural interaction. Native Americans indeed fashioned their colono ware pottery to suit the tastes of European settlers. In the British colonies, for example, they fashioned punch bowls, porringers, and drinking cups, as well as plates and bowls with the ringed feet that English settlers preferred. In Spanish Florida, their vessels sometimes replicated Spanish olive jar and majolica earthenware forms. Present-day Native Americans—such as the Catawba, near Rock Hill, South Carolina—still produce pottery similar to colono ware. But, in recent years, scholars have agreed that African slaves also produced a variety of colono ware shaped into large and small globular pots and shallow' bowls. These forms are found at sites once occupied by slaves long after the demise of Indians in the same area.

In South Carolina, several clues support the inference that slaves made pottery for their own use. Excavations at three plantations have yielded evidence of damaged vessels, lumps of fired clay, unfired pottery fragments, as well as clay pits—all signs that pottery was made on the plantation.[17] Colono ware, in fact, often comprises 80 to 90 percent of the ceramics found at sites occupied by slaves in the 1700s. Further research by Leland Ferguson, an historical archaeologist at the University of South Carolina, has suggested that some of the forms resemble pottery still made in parts of West Africa today. More recently, he has from a small sample of pottery identified markings similar to the cosmograms used in traditional rituals of the Kongo people from Africa's Congo-Angolan region.[18] To the Kongo, the icon—a cross enclosed within a circle—symbolizes the daily course of the sun and the continuity of life through birth, death, and rebirth.

Many archaeologists agree that slaves produced some colono ware, but the extent to which this pottery exhibits African origins is still uncertain. Matthew Hill, an archaeologist working in Africa at historic sites along the middle Gambia River, has identified vessel forms similar in shape to South Carolina examples. He observed, though, that African ceramics were far from plain, that they were in fact elaborately decorated, even ostentatious, whereas the South Carolina colono ware was in contrast undecorated. Hill's findings raise the possibility that while colono ware is a form of pottery from a distinctly non-European tradition, Africans produced the vessels under newly established conditions rather than in recreated and traditional African forms.[19]

Unlike in South Carolina, no direct evidence for slave-made pottery has been recovered from plantations in Virginia, although rounded vessels similar to those found in South Carolina have been identified at the Mount Vernon and Portici plantations. At Portici, the pottery fragments recovered from areas occupied by slaves date from the period between 1806 and 1863, several generations after the last indigenous Native Americans resided in the area. This finding suggests that slaves made the pots.[20] Some archaeologists believe that slaves also produced colono ware that copied European forms. James Deetz, an archaeologist at the University of California, Berkeley, believes that on tidewater plantations along the James River slaves began making colono ware in English forms as a consequence of their contact with whites. Based on his work at Flowerdew Hundred, Deetz found that on sites dating prior to 1680, when black slaves and white indentured servants shared their living space with planters, no colono ware ceramics were present. After that date, planters increasingly turned to African slaves for labor and housed them separately from whites. Colono ware is found at such later sites. Deetz reasoned that enslaved blacks, when settled in segregated quarters without household utensils, produced pottery in forms they had previously used in the planter's household.[21]

Why is evidence of pottery making among enslaved African-Americans so important? The archaeological data on slave-made ceramics provides information on an African-American craft practice that was virtually unknown from other sources. More important, the use of this pottery suggests that enslaved African-Americans prepared food to suit their own tastes, perhaps incorporating aspects of traditional African cuisines. Thus, some African customs associated with preparing and serving food may have been maintained during slavery. Slaves also used these slave-made ceramics to prepare food for their masters. Colono ware accounts for a significant portion—sometimes more than half—of the ceramics used in planter households, thus suggesting that culinary techniques used by slaves influenced the local cuisine of southern whites as well. Gumbos, pilaus, and pilafs—all southern meals prepared in a single pot—are but a few examples of the present-day legacy of the African influence in culinary practices.[22]

Excavated food remains also point to the general practice of cooking one-pot meals. Carcasses cut into small portions, highly fragmented bones, or bones from which the meat has apparently been sliced all suggest that meats were boiled, in stews or soups for example, rather than roasted.[23] The making of stews was perhaps a culinary preference, but it may also have been a creative way of using pieces of meat considered undesirable by slaveholders.[24]

The best documented evidence of enslaved Africans' influencing their material world is seen in numerous examples of architecture.[25] Excavations at the sites of Curriboo and Yaughan, two former indigo plantations in Berkeley County, South Carolina, have revealed the earliest archaeological evidence of African-styled slave housing identified on a southern plantation. These slave quarters made of mud walls and presumably covered with thatched palmetto leaves are similar to the thatch-roof houses found in many parts of Africa. Although no standing walls survive, archaeologists have found wall trenches containing a mortar-like clay. Presumably the entire structure was made of this material. The importance of clay as a primary material for both construction and pottery making is further suggested by the presence of numerous nearby clay pits.[26]

Slaves built the mud-wall houses at Curriboo and Yaughan plantations in approximately 1740 and lived in them until about 1790 when the houses were razed and replaced with frame structures occupied until the plantations closed in 1820. The change from mud-wall to frame dwellings also coincided with a decreasing use of colono ware ceramics at both plantations. These changes may well indicate that the slaves' opportunity to fashion domestic material as they desired was rapidly disappearing.

Nearly every slave site has at least one or two unexplained objects. Archaeologists in all subject areas have a tendency, however, to interpret such unexplained objects as charms or ritual items. Many of these interpretations are supported by historical and ethnographic documentation, whereas others are more speculative. Unfortunately, the purpose and meaning of some objects may always remain a mystery.

Two charms recovered from slave cabins at the Hermitage, the plantation home of Andrew Jackson outside Nashville, Tennessee, may be akin to charms used by slaves in both the antebellum South and in Latin America. Although stylistically different, both charms, made of stamped brass or another copper alloy, depict the same image—a clenched human hand. The image is believed to be quite similar to certain Latin American amulets, or *figas*, associated with African-oriented spiritualist cults and in widespread use since at least the mid-1800s.[27] The charm may also be what was referred to as a "hand" to "keep de witches away." An ex-slave in Florida recollected that an

> Old witch doctor, he want ten dollars for a piece o' string, what he say some kinda charm words over. . . . I didn't have no ten dollar, so he say ifen I git up five dollar he make me a hand—you know, what collored folks calls a jack. Dat be a charm what will keep de witches away. I knowns how to make em, but day doan do no good thout de magic words, and I doan know dem.[28]

The best evidence of ritual paraphernalia comes from the Jordan plantation in Brazoria County, south of Houston, Texas. There, archaeologist Kenneth Brown uncovered an assemblage of artifacts from a cabin apparently used in healing and divination rituals. The Jordan plantation operated with slave laborers from 1848 until emancipation and with wage laborers, most of whom were former slaves, until 1890 or 1891. Until forced to leave, the workers continuously occupied the now-excavated cabins and both written and archaeological records suggest that they maintained a cultural continuity from slavery to freedom. Brown believes that because of their forced abandonment of the site, the occupants hastily left behind objects not customarily found in the archaeological record. Excavations of the remains of several individual cabins revealed vestiges of specialized activities: the community evidently included a carpenter, seamstress, a cattle herder, or cowboy, and a shaman, or healer.

Ritual materials recovered from a restricted area of the shaman's cabin included several bases from cast-iron kettles, pieces of much-used chalk, bird skulls, fragments of a small weighing scale, an animal's paw, samples of medicine, seashells, bottles, parts of one or more dolls, spoons, nails, knives, and scrapers made from chert, a flintlike rock. Many of these objects were no doubt once used for a number of other purposes, but when taken together the artifacts suggest some form of ritual use. Support for Brown's interpretation comes from abundant ethnographic studies conducted in the Caribbean and parts of Africa that describe the use of wooden or metal trays, white chalk or powder, metal staffs, bird symbols, and other objects used in healing rituals.[29]

The assemblage of artifacts from the Jordan plantation presents an excellent example of how African-Americans reworked mass-produced and other objects to achieve a special African-American meaning. Colored glass beads, particularly blue beads found in slave sites from Virginia to Texas, provide another example of the slaves' reinterpretation of manufactured objects to meet their own cultural uses. William H. Adams, an archaeologist at Oregon State University, has recently suggested that the predominance of blue beads in the antebellum South may well be a vestige of the widespread belief within the Muslim world, including many parts of Africa, that a single blue bead worn or sown on clothing protected the bearer against "the evil eye."[30] Blue beads, in fact, often comprise as much as a third of all the beads found at slave sites.

Still other artifacts might have held a special meaning for slaves. Although archaeologists have yet to decipher what the objects meant to the people who used them, they have recovered coins, frequently of Spanish origin and pierced for hanging, from both Monticello and Harmony Hall plantation in Georgia as well as the smoothed and polished penis bone of a raccoon, unearthed at Mount Vernon. An incised line encircles one end of the bone, suggesting that the object was worn suspended from a string or thin chain. The type of bone suggests its use as a fertility symbol. Polygonal objects, resembling gaming pieces, and made primarily from pottery as well as glass and reworked wood, have been recovered from several plantations, including Thomas Jefferson's Poplar Forest and Monticello and the Portici plantation, all in Virginia, as well as the Garrison plantation near Baltimore, Maryland, and the Drax Hall plantation in Jamaica.[31]

It is possible that these artifacts may not be expressions of African-American ethnicity at all, but instead simply attempts by slaves to make adornments, gaming pieces, and other objects from what was available to them. The material poverty of slaves—the concept of "making do"—should not be overlooked as a potential explanation for the slaves' reworking of discarded materials to create something else.[32] Yet the African-American community's selection of certain objects, such as coins, as suggested by the testimony of ex-slaves, may indeed reflect some aspect of ethnic conjuring practices.[33] But because most of what became African-American is an amalgam of reinterpreted African culture and adopted European materials, identifying the excavated evidence of African-American ethnic patterns thus poses a continuing challenge to archaeologists.

Every archaeological study of a slave site contributes information on living conditions, whether or not the topic is an expressed goal of the research. The study of the slaves' material life also sheds light on how a particular plantation operated, especially how certain plantation resources were distributed, utilized, and recycled. Archaeology thereby supplies detailed information that can amplify other sources. For example, provision records, when available, are often incomplete and contain information on objects not generally found in the archaeological record, objects such as clothing, blankets, boneless meats, cornmeal, and vegetables, items long since disappeared. On the other hand, some items that do find their way into the arch-aeological record—purchased housewares, personal possessions, or the remains of wild foods collected by slaves—are virtually absent from these written records. The interpretation of these otherwise undocumented records of the slaves' material culture has often become the subject of archaeological debate.[34] Other archaeological resources supplement existing narrative descriptions of slave life and together reveal much of the slaves' housing, household equipment, personal possessions, diet, nutrition, and health.

Most archaeological studies of slave settlements are generally undertaken in and around slave dwellings and consequently yield information on the dwellings themselves. Slave housing varied over time and from place to place and was often dictated by the slaveholders' preferences. Studies conducted by architectural historians and folklorists have shown the development, regional styles, and variations in slave housing from the colonial to the antebellum period.[35] These studies utilize verbal descriptions, sketches, photographs, and standing structures to provide a wealth of information on the above-ground appearance of slave dwellings. In turn, archaeology contributes to the study of slave housing by providing structural details and evidence of how slaves lived in their cabins. Excavations yield information on materials and methods used to lay foundations and to make repairs and modifications, while the artifacts recovered from building trenches provide an approximate date of construction. Those artifacts found in and around houses also suggest the period of occupation and an approximate date for abandonment.

Colonial slave housing is, however, poorly understood from both historical and archaeological resources. Most scholars agree that early slave housing was makeshift and flimsy—with many slaves living in lofts, barns, kitchens, sheds, and in houses with communal arrangements. For the most part, the quartering of slaves in separate cabins became a widespread practice only in the 19th century. Thus, archaeology can in time make a major contribution by providing details of early slave housing. Unfortunately, with few notable exceptions, most archaeological studies have furnished more data on the well-documented housing of the 1800s. Traces of earlier slave houses were likely destroyed as slave owners expanded, rebuilt, and reorganized their plantations.

A few colonial slave quarters have, though, been excavated. At the Kingsmill plantations near Williamsburg, Virginia, archaeologists uncovered several buildings dating from 1705 to 1789 that presumably housed slaves. The structures included brick dependencies flanking the mansion and housing the kitchen, plantation office, and probably quarters for a number of slaves as well; a 40-by-18-ft and a 28-by-20-ft communal slave quarter; and earth-bound wooden houses of varying sizes.[36] At George Washington's Mount Vernon the cellar of a frame slave quarter built upon a brick foundation has recently been excavated. Based upon a slave census compiled in 1786, this communal slave quarter known as the "House for Families" may have housed as many as 50 to 60 slaves from 1760 to 1793.[37] In the Lower South, the earliest excavated slave dwellings are the ca. 1740–1790 mud-wall structures at Yaughan and Curriboo. The African-styled houses functioned as individual cabins, each housing 3 to 4 slaves.[38] The practice of placing slaves in individual cabins apparently came early to the South Carolina low country.

Excavations of 18th-century slave quarters in Virginia have uncovered a distinctive but curious feature—earthen root-cellars. Ranging in size from 2 by 3 ft to 5 by 8 ft and from 2 to 4 ft deep, the cellars were either unlined or, if lined, fashioned with brick, stone, or wood, and usually contained tools, locks, nails, ceramics, some glass, buttons, and discarded food remains. Archaeologist William M. Kelso excavated 18 cellars from one large communal quarter at Kingsmill and 10 more found within six cabins along Mulberry Row at Monticello.[39] Because the root cellars were slowly backfilled with artifacts and refuse, he believes that they were used not only for storing food but also for concealing pilfered goods. Kelso suggests that "hiding tools might make a workday shorter, and that leftover bones from the theft of good quality meat could hardly go out in the yard to give the thief away."[40] Kelso's interpretation is supported by narratives of both masters and slaves describing just such activities. At Thomas Jefferson's plantation, Poplar Forest, the manager wrote that there the workers had been "razing eny kind of vegetable." But "the very moment your back is turned from thee place Nace takes every thing out of the garden and carries them to his cabin and burys them in the ground."[41] The slaves sometimes had good reason to put any food remains in the cellars, too. As Charles Grandy, an ex-slave, later recalled,

> I got so hungry I stealed chickens off the roos'. Yessum, I did, chickens used roos' on de fense den, right out in de night. We would cook de chicken at night, eat him an' bu'n de feathers. Dat's what dey had dem ole paddyrollers [slave patrols] fer. Dey come roun' an' search de qua'ters fer to see what you bin stealin'. We always had a trap in de floor fo' de do' to hide dese chickens in.[42]

Apparently, the slow buildup of refuse in these root cellars eventually resulted in health hazards, which may in part explain their absence in many antebellum slave houses.

In many cases, owners prevented slaves from digging root cellars. In an analysis of antebellum housing in Virginia, Larry McKee proposes that while the stated purpose of the "reformed" or "improved" slave housing advocated in period agricultural journals was to promote healthy living conditions, the planters' implied goal was to control unauthorized behavior. The desire was most obviously expressed in the building of slave cabins upon foundation piers that raised wood plank floors 1.5 ft to 2 ft above ground. The raised floors did allow "healthy" air to circulate beneath the structure, but, more important, prevented the digging of any root cellars. The crawl space underneath the cabin was still used for storage but, unlike root cellars, could easily be checked by a plantation owner or manager. McKee further suggests that contemporary descriptions of the "filth" surrounding the slaves' cabins may have been the way African-Americans resisted the planters' desire for cleanliness, orderliness, and control of the quarters.[43] Archaeologists have excavated antebellum slave cabins raised above ground and without root cellars at the Willcox and Shirley plantations along Virginia's James River.[44] But period cabins with such cellars have also been identified, suggesting that the struggle between master and slave, over that issue at least, was not always won by the planter.

Although researchers generally believe that only a very small number of slaves ever lived in well-built housing, antebellum slave dwellings took many forms. Two distinct floor plans, however, such as identified at both Virginia plantations, seem to have predominated. At the Willcox plantation a single-family structure measured 16 by 20 ft; at Shirley a double pen, or duplex, measured 20 by 40 ft and housed two family units separated by a common wall. Slave houses of comparable dimensions and floor plans have been identified archaeologically in several localities.

There were also larger structures housing three or more slave families. Though less common, several multifamily dwellings still stand or have been investigated archaeologically. Along Horton Grove, at the Stagville plantation outside Durham, North Carolina, slaves occupied a two-story quarter divided into four units. Similar two-story slave dwellings have been excavated at the Somerset plantation in Creswell, North Carolina.[45] At the Jordan plantation in Texas yet another variation has been identified. There archaeologists have uncovered eight long, barracks-like structures built in pairs. Archaeological evidence indicates that three to four individual living units were built within each building. After emancipation, when the plantation employed wage laborers, some of the barracks were reorganized to accommodate only two families, thus allowing the recently freed laborers to double their living space.[46]

A variety of materials were used to build slave quarters. Houses were generally log or frame and occasionally all brick. Along the southeastern coast, oyster shells offered a distinctive masonry material called *tabby*, a cement-like substance made of crushed shells, sand, and lime. Tabby could be molded into bricks for chimneys and foundations, or poured like modern-day cement to form walls and floors. It was also used as mortar. Excavations have revealed that crushed oyster shells also served as footings for building foundations and in making floors and pathways.[47] Slaves apparently collected oysters and deposited the discarded shells in and around their dwellings, a practice identified archaeologically at numerous slave sites along the Georgia coast. In the late 1830s Fanny Kemble commented on the shells' common occurrence when visiting her husband's Hampton plantation on Saint Simons Island, Georgia. As the oysters "are a considerable article of the people's diet," she wrote,

> the shells are allowed to accumulate, as they are used in the composition of which their huts are built, and which is a sort of combination of mud and broken oyster shells, which forms an agglomeration of a kind very solid and durable for building purposes; but, instead of being all carried to some specified place out of the way, these great heaps of oyster shells are allowed to be piled up anywhere and everywhere, forming the most unsightly obstructions in every direction.[48]

In addition to documenting a structure's floor plan, building materials, or modifications, archaeology also provides tangible information on living conditions in the slave quarters. For example, unearthed evidence frequently indicates that houses rarely contained glass windows; that chinking, daub, and other materials were needed to insulate drafty walls; and that hearth fires were extremely hot, often causing chimneys made of mud and sticks to collapse. The heat was so intense that even brick chimneys sometimes show signs of buckling and an accompanying separation of the hearth from the outer chimney walls.[49] Other evidence indicates that rodent infestations were apparently common, and the vestiges of refuse found within and around the dwellings support some of the contemporary descriptions that cabins were dirty and unhealthy. On the other hand, archaeological evidence also shows that some dwellings were well built and regularly maintained.

Household and personal items recovered from slave quarters also provide information on the quality of life in cabins. Slaves possessed a few meager household possessions—generally coarse earthen- and stoneware vessels used to prepare and store food, cooking pots and kettles of colono ware or iron, and mismatched dishes, usually bowls and cups for consuming soups or stews. As so few spoons or forks have been recovered, either such utensils were seldom left behind or perhaps slaves used other objects or even their hands. Some evidence of furnishings—such as a drawer pull, an upholstery tack, a caster, or even a brass pulley from a clock—is occasionally recovered.[50] Recovered personal possessions vary from site to site. Some are associated with clothing and adornment—buttons, beads, jewelry, or combs—while others are related to the slaves' nonwork hours, items used in hunting and fishing, gardening, playing music and games, smoking, imbibing alcoholic beverages, perhaps even reading.

Fine china and tea sets have been uncovered from several slave cabins. Some archaeologists suggest that this may be another indicator that a few slaves, particularly artisans and drivers, occupied a higher status within the plantation community. Written records from specific plantations often refer to larger food rations and sometimes amenities such as tobacco awarded to specific slaves, usually skilled craftsmen or field laborers performing very difficult work. Nevertheless, there are no written references in plantation records to the provisioning of slaves with ceramics. Because it remains unclear how slaves received these items, archaeologists have offered three possible explanations. First, these objects were perhaps castoffs that slaves received as gifts from the planter's household. Second, slaves may have purchased them with cash they earned through "hiring out" their labor or by selling or trading produce, handicrafts, or livestock to acquire money for the items. And third, china was perhaps stolen from the big house. Although any of these possibilities may account for slaves' possessing chinaware, all three factors most likely occurred to varying degrees from time to time.

The recovery of objects associated with food preparation indicates that slaves prepared at least some of their meals in their cabins and not in a plantation's central kitchen. Although the presence of central kitchens is well documented in plantation records, no evidence of these kitchens has been recovered archaeologically. The conflicting information presented by written plantation records and archaeological discoveries raises several questions. Were some meals prepared in plantation kitchens while others were in slave cabins? Do the cooking equipment and food remains recovered from cabins represent the preparation and consumption of regular meals or occasional efforts to satisfy hunger? When did central kitchens come into use for the preparation of slave meals? And why have archaeologists as yet been unable to identify central kitchens? Only future research can reconcile the conflicting information presented by the two sources of information.

There is also contradictory written and archaeological evidence as to slave literacy and the use of firearms. Excavated artifacts suggestive of literacy among slaves include graphite pencils, writing slates (some with words and numbers etched on the surface), even eyeglasses. Evidence of firearms includes buckshot, lead shot, gun plates, trigger guards, and flints. Initially, archaeologists were surprised to find such objects associated with activities often prohibited by law in many slave states.[51] But references found in plantation records, slave testimony, and other accounts indicate that some slaves acquired reading and writing skills and some had access to firearms for hunting. However, the frequency with which these objects turn up at archaeological sites suggests that more slaves had access to firearms and possessed literacy and enumerative skills than previously thought from the study of written records alone.

The study of food remains has perhaps contributed more to the amplification of written records on slave living conditions than any other archaeological resource. Written records reveal that the plantation laborers' diet normally included preserved meats, cornmeal, and vegetables grown in provision gardens, foods that normally leave few, if any, archaeological remains. And yet extensive food traces, particularly of animal bones, have been found, indicating that slaves consumed other kinds of foods to supplement their normal plantation rations.[52]

Through *zooarchaeology*, the study of animal food-bone, many characteristics of the slaves' food habits can be determined: for example, the kinds and relative proportions of animal foods consumed, the cuts of meat, the amounts of consumable meat represented by the remains, and sometimes how these foods were prepared— whether, for example, slaves boiled or roasted the food. Most zooarchaeological studies indicate that domestic animals furnished the bulk of the animal protein in the slaves' diet. And although the remains of pork or beef are the most commonly found, at a few sites sheep and goats evidently were an important food source. Chickens, however, appear to have been a minor food item consumed only occasionally and perhaps valued more for their eggs. Slaves often received the less meaty and lower quality meat-portions of these domestic animals, likely livestock raised on the plantation. Some zooarchaeologists have interpreted the slaves' consumption of low-quality meats as an indicator of African-Americans' inferior social status within the plantation hierarchy. In fact, some skeletal elements (such as skulls, feet, and ribs) often found at slave sites may have been meat portions discarded as waste in the butchering of meat for the planter household.[53]

Evidence from several sites suggests that there were dietary variations among slaves of the same plantation. This is consistent with numerous provision records indicating that the amount of rations a slave received depended upon the worker's skill level or other factors. But the archaeological findings seem to point to differences not just in the quantity of rations but also in the quality of meat and methods of food preparation. For example, along Mulberry Row at Thomas Jefferson's Monticello, zooarchaeologist Diana Crader observed carving marks on pig-limb bones identical to the marks found on bones recovered from the plantation kitchen that serviced the mansion. Crader suggests that "the discovery of such carving marks on meaty limb bones suggests a higher quality of meat and a different method of meat preparation (roasts instead of stews) than would be expected in a slave dwelling."[54] Since the food remains recovered from the other cabins along Mulberry Row conform more to the usual patterns of slave diet, the different diet evident in building "o" (as designated in Jefferson's insurance records) is attributed to the higher status of certain African-Americans within Monticello's slave community. Similar evidence of dietary differences between house slaves and field hands has been identified at Portici plantation.[55]

Other zooarchaeologists question whether the recovery of "low-quality" meats is alone sufficient evidence of class differences either between planter and slaves or between members of the slave community.[56] In a study of 19th-century urban foodways, Joanne Bowen Gaynor found that wealthy households regularly consumed supposedly inferior parts of meat—such as heads, feet, and other forms of offal—as these foods were delicacies in many socially fashionable cuisines. She concludes that what constituted dietary variation along class lines appears to be much more complex than simply the consumption of low- versus high-quality meats. Also to be considered, she adds, are the "quantity and variety of food, the use of imported spices and specialty foods, characteristic dishes, their ingredients, and the way that they are combined, and rules guiding the presentation and consumption of food."[57]

The study of wild-food remains provides even more revealing evidence of slave food habits. At every slave site where food remains have been recovered and analyzed, there is evidence that African-Americans consumed at least some wild foods, often making use of every possible food resource within reach, taking "advantage of the woods, fields, rivers, and creeks surrounding the plantation."[58] This was particularly true on plantations located along the southeastern coast where wild-food resources abounded in the ocean, marshes, and tidal creeks as well as in the oak and hickory forests. It is estimated that wild foods may have comprised as much as 40 percent of the meat in the slaves' diet.[59] Coastal slaves apparently hunted and fished throughout the year, collecting crabs, clams, oysters, sea catfish, sting rays, sharks, mullet, turtles on both sea and land, opossum, raccoon, and rabbit. Zooarchaeologist Elizabeth Reitz and several colleagues suggest that many of these resources could be captured easily using nets or traps and with minimal expenditure of time or effort while attending to other chores.[60] Curious, though, is that deer, wild birds, and ducks were found to be insignificant food resources at these sites. But as these animals are often taken with guns, their absence may be more a sign of the slaves' restricted access to firearms or to specific game than a matter of taste preference.

At inland sites, the slaves' reliance upon wild food resources differed from plantation to plantation. Wild foods comprised less than 5 percent of the animal species represented at Monticello, located in the Virginia piedmont.[61] But at the Hermitage, near Nashville, Tennessee, wild birds and small mammals were significant food resources that made up 60 percent of the animal species represented. The use of wild birds in particular suggests more active hunting than was required to obtain fish and turtles along the coast. Designated hunters may have been responsible for provisioning slaves with these foods.[62] The preliminary analysis of food remains at Mount Vernon suggests that fish were an important source of food for those slaves living in the "House for Families." Most of the fish were presumably caught from Washington's plantation fishery. The remains of nonriverine fish species imply that the slaves may have caught still others using hook and line.[63]

Food remains provide information on the kinds of animal food slaves consumed, but the quality and quantity of foods consumed can only be estimated.[64] To determine the diet's nutritional value requires an analysis of human remains. Such studies can yield information on diet, nutrition, disease, and general health, but due to legal, religious, and moral considerations, archaeologists generally avoid, whenever possible, excavating burial sites. However, in the search for other information, researchers sometimes inadvertently unearth abandoned and forgotten slave burial sites. Such finds are usually recovered from unmarked cemeteries, though human remains are sometimes found among domestic sites and work areas.[65] Cemeteries are, though, intentionally excavated when threatened by land redevelopment or environmental damage.[66]

While archaeologists generally analyze an excavated cemetery's artifacts and mortuary patterns, the technical analysis of human remains is the field of physical or biological anthropologists. Analyses of human bones and teeth can provide a wide range of information on biological and social factors affecting a population's health. Nutrition intake, metabolism, genetics, aging, hormonal interactions, biomechanical stress, diet, type and levels of activity, as well as a subject's reproductive history all affect the human skeleton.[67]

Researchers have unearthed fewer slave cemeteries than slave dwellings, but the African-American populations studied by physical anthropologists represent a broader cross-section of slave society than archaeologists' studies of workers' quarters.[68] Archaeologists' excavations of particular settlements have been directed primarily toward the study of plantation slaves. Physical anthropologists, on the other hand, have also studied urban slaves in New Orleans and industrial slaves engaged in ironworking at the Catoctin Furnace in Maryland.[69] In spite of population differences, several general health problems were common to the three populations of rural, urban, and industrial workers. In each case slaves had diets very high in carbohydrates and sugar and low in protein; they withstood periods of malnutrition, particularly in childhood; they experienced high levels of tooth decay, tooth loss, and dental diseases; and they suffered from degenerative arthritic conditions resulting from physically strenuous lives.

Differences in health appear to be largely in the degree of occurrence. For example, some evidence of anemia—presumably both genetic (sickle cell) and acquired (iron-deficiency)—was found in all three populations. Anemia was, though, a major health problem among the industrial and plantation slave populations, only a minor condition in the urban African-American population.[70] Similarly, evidence of physical stress resulting from occupational activities was more pronounced among industrial and plantation slaves than among urban slaves. Both males and females within the industrial and plantation populations showed arthritic conditions associated with the heavy work of lifting, digging, or pounding.[71] The skeletal remains of urban slaves displayed more variation in the degree of occupational stress: only some showed signs of pronounced patterns of such stress, probably attributable to manual labor on the docks of New Orleans or work on the canals and levees. Generally, though, the urban slaves' workday was not characterized by heavy occupational stress—perhaps reflecting the diversity of slave labor in an urban setting.[72] Each population showed signs of generalized infections, but chronic infection was particularly high among the plantation slaves. Written sources repeatedly point to infection as a major health problem on southern plantations, and this finding supports that condition. The combined effects of infective organisms, diet, labor demands, and living conditions all played a role in the high infections among plantation slaves.[73]

Indications of how slaves were treated for health problems can also be discerned through archaeology. Collections of charms and other healing paraphernalia, such as uncovered at the Jordan plantation in Texas, suggest the kinds of folk medicine slaves sought. But excavations of slave quarters also provide indications of the kinds of medications slave owners administered to their workers. For example, excavations along the Georgia coast revealed that slaves regularly consumed patent medicines with high alcoholic content.[74] While some of this consumption reflects recreational imbibing, plantation records for the Butler plantation, visited by Fanny Kemble, also indicate that planters dispensed patent medicines and homemade rum to the slaves as a preventative for rheumatic diseases.[75] Future excavations of plantation infirmaries may possibly turn up medical instruments and other objects used to treat slaves.

The continuing archaeological study of slave living conditions will, therefore, provide detailed information on slave provisioning, whether slaves acquired or were given household and personal objects, what activities slaves pursued when not working, and the impact of unhealthy housing, a deficient diet, and strenuous labor upon the physical well-being of African-Americans. In short, these studies seek to document through tangible evidence the everyday lives of slaves.

Whereas slave sites have been the major focus of African-American archaeology in the South, sites occupied by antebellum free blacks and by emancipated men and women after the Civil War are receiving increased attention. Like those for slave sites, these studies have attempted to identify ethnic patterns and living conditions. But unlike the growing manifestations of ethnicity in ceramic production and use, architecture, and ritual objects found at slave sites, such archaeological evidence at sites occupied by nonslaves is considerably more subtle. For instance, no distinctly African-American crafts such as colono ware have been attributed to southern free blacks or ex-slaves.[76] On the other hand, these sites do provide information on the material world of African-Americans in other realms of southern society.

Free-black sites investigated thus far vary widely. They range from the frontier outpost of Gracia Real Santa Teresa de Mose, established just north of present-day Saint Augustine by self-emancipated slaves who fled from South Carolina to Spanish Florida in the early 1700s, to the homes of prominent individuals, such as Benjamin Banneker and Frederick Douglass. In general, few differences are found between the sites occupied by free blacks and by whites of comparable social and economic position.[77] The most extensive study of a free-black antebellum community conducted thus far examined 10 sites in two Alexandria, Virginia, neighborhoods.[78] The major ethnic difference in the material world of white middle-class artisans and merchants and free-black Alexandrians was apparent in foodways. Black Alexandrians consumed more pork than did whites and displayed a particular preference for pigs' feet. In addition, the predominance of bowls suggests that free blacks, as did slaves, may have preferred soups, stews, and other single-dish meats. At present, foodways seem to be the most sensitive indicator of an African-American value culture. Even at post-Reconstruction sites, distinctive patterns of African-American foodways have been identified.[79] But the inequalities between black and white in antebellum Alexandria are also evident in the archaeological record. For example, the white middle class had access to private wells and by the 1850s even piped water. Black Alexandrians, however, had few wells and had "to walk several blocks to procure their water in buckets."[80]

Some slave sites often contain deposits that date after emancipation and demonstrate a considerable degree of cultural continuity from slavery to freedom. Such was again the case at the Jordan plantation in Texas. Two studies of communities established for the resettlement of former slaves have also been recently undertaken, one being at Mitchelville, part of the Union army's 1862 Port Royal experiment to settle black laborers on the South Carolina Sea Islands.[81] Located on Hilton Head Island and occupied until the early 1880s, the Mitchelville site has provided detailed information on a planned community of freedmen. Compared to those found at coastal slave sites, the artifacts and food remains at Mitchelville show marked differences. The freedmen and -women, for example, purchased expensive items such as furniture, stemware, silver utensils, and other tableware, as well as fancy jewelry. They also consumed more domestic meat (pork, beef, chicken, turkey, and goose) than did slaves. Emancipation for the freedmen at Mitchelville undoubtedly meant greater access to material goods than they had ever experienced before.[82]

What does the future hold for African-American archaeology? Certainly the immediate future seems bright, with new projects far too numerous to list here. Suffice it to say that investigations have thus far been initiated in at least 30 states, Canada, several Caribbean islands, and Central America. A few sites associated with the slave trade are currently being studied in Africa so as to examine systematically the trade's impact on both sides of the Atlantic. Moreover, there is much more to be learned from African-American archaeology than a community's ethnic patterns and living conditions. The archaeological record can be used to examine other kinds of questions for which material culture can serve as a primary source of information. For instance, future studies will explore questions of cultural change, power relationships between slave and master, even slave resistance. In time, yet other questions and problems will be added to the list, making archaeology an increasingly significant field of inquiry in the study of African-American life.

Acknowledgments

Much of the data presented are from either unpublished studies or research in progress and has been graciously provided by the following colleagues: David Babson, Kenneth Brown, Pamela Cressey, Matthew Emerson, Leland Ferguson, Joanne Bowen Gaynor, Christopher Hughes, Larry McKee, Kathleen Parker, Dennis Pogue, Stephen R. Potter, and Lesley Rankin-Hill. The author assumes full responsibility for any misrepresentations of their research. Several colleagues graciously shared comments on earlier versions of this essay: Mark Bograd, Leland Ferguson, Joanne Bowen Gaynor, David R. Goldfield, Larry McKee, Charles Orser, Dennis Pogue, and Stephen R Potter.

NOTES

1. J. Agee and W. Evans, *Let Us Now Praise Famous Men: Three Tenant Families* (Boston: Houghton Mifflin, 1941; reprinted, 1969), p. 13.

2. The terms *African-American ethnicity* or *African American ethnic patterns* refer here to behavior that is frequently found among African-American communities. This does not mean that these practices are found exclusively among African-Americans. Other ethnic groups may have developed similar behavior either independently or as a consequence of their interaction with African-Americans.

3. A third and growing approach archaeologists use to study plantation life is the examination of the power relationships between slave owners and slaves. See, for example,

C. Orser, The Archaeological Analysis of Plantation Society: Replacing Status and Caste with Economics and Power, *American Antiquity* 53 (1988):735–751.

4. For a detailed discussion of both value and reality culture, see E. Wolf, Culture: Panacea or Problem, *American Antiquity* 49 (1984):393–400.

5. Approximately 30 to 35 of the plantations investigated thus far have yielded information on slave life. While this essay does not mention each individual study, it does examine general patterns applicable to those sites as well as patterns peculiar to particular sites or groups of related sites. Most of the research in slave archaeology has been undertaken in Virginia, South Carolina, and Georgia.

6. Numerous studies have examined the African-American communities in coastal Georgia and South Carolina. See, for example, Savannah Unit, Georgia Writers' Project, Work Projects Administration, *Drums and Shadows: Survival Studies Among the Georgia Coastal Negroes* (1940; reprinted, Athens, 1986); T. A. Singleton, The Archaeology of Afro-American Slavery in Coastal Georgia: A Regional Perception of Slave Household and Community Patterns (Ph.D. dissertation, University of Florida, 1980).

7. See, for example, C. H. Fairbanks, The Plantation Archaeology of the Southeastern Coast, *Historical Archaeology* 18(1) (1984):1–14.

8. See, for example, J. S. Otto, *Cannon's Point Plantation, 1794–1860: Living Conditions and Status Patterns in the Old South* (Orlando, 1984), p. 87.

9. Archaeologists have unearthed cowrie shells at Monticello in Albemarle County, Virginia, the Stagville plantation near Durham, North Carolina, and the Ashland-Belle Helene plantation in Louisiana (W. M. Kelso, Mulberry Row: Slave Life at Thomas Jefferson's Monticello, *Archaeology* 39 [September–October 1986]:30 [illustration]; J. Garlid, Stagville Field School in Historical Archaeology: A Nineteenth-Century Slave Cabin [Site Report, Historic Sites Section, North Carolina Department of Archives and History, Raleigh, 1979]; 22; D. W. Babson, *Pillars on the Levee: Archaeological Investigations at Ashland-Belle Helene Plantation, Geismar, Ascension Parish, Louisiana* [Site Report, Midwestern Archaeological Research Center, Illinois State University, Normal, IL, 1989], p. 86).

10. J. S. Handler and F. W. Lange, Plantation Slavery on Barbados, West Indies, *Archaeology* 32 (July–August 1979):45–52.

11. K. A. Parker and J. L. Hernigle, Portici, Portrait of a Middling Plantation in Piedmont Virginia, in *Occasional Reports #3, Regional Archaeology Program*, ed. National Capital Region, National Park Service (Washington, DC, forthcoming), p. 213.

12. Kelso, Mulberry Row, p. 30 (illustration); E. Artemel, E. A. Crowell, and J. Parker, *The Alexandria Slave Pen: The Archaeology of Urban Captivity* (Washington, DC, 1987), p. 121.

13. See M. C. Emerson, *Decorated Clay Tobacco Pipes from the Chesapeake* (Ann Arbor: University of Michigan Press, 1988), pp. 130–138.

14. S. R Potter (National Capital Region, National Park Service, Washington, DC), communication with author, October 1990; S. L. Henry, Terra-Cotta Tobacco Pipes in 17th Century Maryland and Virginia: A Preliminary Study, *Historical Archaeology* 13 (1979):15.

15. E. Klingelhofer, Aspects of Early Afro-American Material Culture: Artifacts from the Slave Quarters at Garrison Plantation, Maryland, *Historical Archaeology* 21(2) (1987): 112–119.

16. Colono ware refers to a very broad category of ceramics of which numerous varieties have been identified. Not all archaeologists agree that African-Americans had a role in the manufacture of these ceramics.

17. Archaeologists have uncovered evidence of colono ware manufacture at the Drayton Hall, Yaughan, and Curriboo plantations in South Carolina (L. Ferguson, pers. comm., May 1983; P. Garrow and T. Wheaton, Colonoware Ceramics: The Evidence from Yaughan and Curriboo Plantations, in *Studies in South Carolina Archaeology: Essays in Honor of Robert L. Stephenson*, A. Goodyear, III and G. T. Hanson [eds.] [Columbia, SC: South Carolina Institute of Archaeology and Anthropology, 1989], p. 176).

18. L. Ferguson, The Cross is a Magic Sign: Marks on Pottery on Eighteenth-Century Bowls from South Carolina (paper delivered at the conference Digging the Afro-American Past: Archaeology and the Black Experience, University of Mississippi, May 17–21, 1989).

19. M. H. Hill, The Ethnicity Lost? The Ethnicity Gained?: Information Functions of African Ceramics in West Africa and North America, in *Ethnicity and Culture: Proceedings of the Eighteenth Annual Chacmool Conference*, R. Auger et al. (eds.) (Calgary: Department of Anthropology, University of Calgary, 1987), pp. 137–138.

20. Parker and Hernigle, Portici, Portrait of a Middling Plantation, p. 227.

21. J. Deetz, American Historical Archaeology: Methods and Results, *Science* 22 (1988), 365–367. Deetz's interpretation has, however, been highly criticized by archaeologists knowledgeable of Chesapeake ceramics.

22. The one-pot meal is not unique to African-American cuisine, but certain southern dishes such as okra gumbo, hoppin John, red rice, or jambalaya appear to be African in origin. For a discussion of slave foodways and African origins see S. G. Moore, "Established and Well Cultivated": Afro-American Foodways in Early Virginia, *Virginia Cavalcade* 39 (1989):70–83.

23. L. McKee, Delineating Ethnicity from the Garbage of Early Virginians: Faunal Remains from the Kingsmill Plantation Slave Quarter, *American Archaeology* 6(1) (1987): 36; D. Crader, Faunal Remains from the Slave Quarter at Monticello, Charlottesville, Virginia, *Archaeozoologia* 3 (1989):3.

24. L. McKee, Plantation Food Supply in Nineteenth-Century Tidewater Virginia (Ph.D. dissertation, University of California, Berkeley, 1988), p. 131.

25. Descriptions of African-styled architecture include W. E. B. Du Bois (ed.), *The Negro American Family*, no. 13 (Atlanta: Atlanta University Publications, 1908), p. 49; G. W. McDaniel, *Hearth and Home: Preserving a People's Culture* (Philadelphia: Temple University Press, 1982), pp. 34–44; M. Sobel, *The World They Made Together: Black and White Values in Eighteenth-Century Virginia* (Princeton: Princeton University Press, 1987), pp. 119–213; J. M. Vlach, *The Afro-American Tradition in Decorative Arts* (1978; reprinted, Athens: University of Georgia Press, 1990), pp. 122–138.

26. P. Garrow and T. Wheaton, Acculturation and the Archaeological Record in the Carolinas, in *The Archaeology of Slavery and Plantation Life*, T. A. Singleton (ed.) (Orlando: Academic Press, 1985), pp. 243–248.

27. Researchers recovered the charms during separate investigations (S. O. Smith, *An Archaeological and Historical Assessment of the First Hermitage* [Nashville: Division of Archaeology, Tennessee Department of Conservation, 1976], 210–211; L. McKee [The Hermitage, Hermitage, TN], pers. comm., August 1990).

28. Quoted in J. F. Smith, *Slavery and Plantation Growth in Antebellum Florida, 1821–1861* (Gainesville: University Press of Florida, 1973), p. 199.

29. K. Brown, From Slavery to Wage Labor Tenancy: Structural Continuity in an Afro-American Community (paper delivered at the conference Digging the Afro-American Past: Archaeology and the Black Experience, University of Mississippi, May 17–21, 1989).

30. W. H. Adams, (ed.), Historical Archaeology of Plantations at Kings Bay, Camden County, Georgia, in *Reports of Investigations* 5. Department of Anthropology, University of Florida (Gainesville, 1987), p. 204.

31. Kelso, Mulberry Row, p. 30; Adams, Historical Archaeology of Plantations, p. 204; D. Pogue (Chief Archaeologist, Mount Vernon Ladies' Association of the Union, Mount Vernon, VA), pers. comm., August 1990; Klingelhofer, Aspects of Early Afro-American Material Culture, pp. 115–116; Parker and Hernigle, Portici, Portrait of a Middling Plantation, p. 202.

32. See, for example, McDaniel, *Hearth and Home*, p. 103.

33. Adams, Historical Archaeology of Plantations, p. 204.

34. Archaeologists differ in their interpretation of how slaves acquired certain possessions such as expensive ceramics and other housewares (See, for example, W. H. Adams and S. J. Boling, Status and Ceramics for Planters and Slaves on Three Georgia Coastal Plantations, *Historical Archaeology* 23(1) [1989]:69–96).

35. See, for example, McDaniel, *Hearth and Home*, pp. 45–102; E. A. Chappell, Slave Housing, *Fresh Advices: A Research Supplement*, Nov. 1982, p. iiv; Sobel, *The World They Made Together*, pp. 100–126; M. L. Walston, "Uncle Tom's Cabin" Revisited: Origins and Interpretations of Slave Housing in the American South, *Southern Studies* 24 (1985): 357–373; D. Upton, White and Black Landscapes in Eighteenth-Century Virginia, in *Material Life in America, 1600–1860*, R. B. St. George (ed.) (Boston: Northeastern University Press, 1988), pp. 357–368.

36. W. M. Kelso, *Kingsmill Plantations, 1619–1800: An Archaeology of Country Life in Colonial Virginia* (Orlando: Academic Press, 1984), pp. 104–110, 112–113, 121–123.

37. D. Pogue, Slave Lifeways at Mount Vernon, in *The Mount Vernon Ladies' Association of the Union: Annual Report 1989* (Mount Vernon: Mount Vernon Ladies Association, 1990), pp. 35–40.

38. Garrow and Wheaton, Acculturation and the Archaeological Record, p. 244.

39. Kelso, *Kingsmill Plantations*, p. 120; W. M. Kelso, The Archaeology of Slave Life at Thomas Jefferson's Monticello: A Wolf by the Ears, *Journal of New World Archaeology*, 6(4) (1986):13.

40. Kelso, The Archaeology of Slave Life, p. 14.

41. Ibid.

42. C. L. Perdue, T. E. Barden, and R. K. Phillips, (eds.), *Weevils in the Wheat: Interviews with Virginia Ex-Slaves* (1976; reprinted, Bloomington: Indiana University Press, 1980), p. 116.

43. L. McKee, The Ideals and Realities Behind the Design and Use of Nineteenth-Century Virginia Slave Cabins, in *Material Culture, World View, and Culture Change: Essays in Honor of James Deetz*, M. C. Beaudry and A. Yentsch (eds.) (Caldwell, NJ: The Telford Press, forthcoming), typescript copy, p. 24.

44. McKee, Plantation Food Supply, p. 92; G. Leavitt, Slaves and Tenant Farmers at Shirley, in *The Archaeology of Shirley Plantation*, T. R. Reinhart (ed.) (Charlottesville: University Press of Virginia., 1984), pp. 157–163.

45. C. Hughes (Stagville Plantation Center, North Carolina Department of Archives and History, Durham), pers. comm., May 1990.

46. Brown, From Slavery to Wage Labor Tenancy, p. 6.

47. Otto, *Cannon's Point Plantation*, p. 38.

48. F. A. Kemble, *Journal of a Residence on a Georgian Plantation in 1838–1839*, J. A. Scott (ed.) (1961; reprinted, Athens: University of Georgia Press, 1984), p. 257.

49. By recreating a mud-and-stick chimney, archaeologist William M. Kelso has demonstrated how slaves deliberately slanted chimneys away from the dwelling so that they could easily be pushed away in case of fire (J. Dent, *Chronicle-Digging for Slaves*, BBC Production, 1989, presented as a segment on Footsteps of Man, Arts and Entertainment Network, 12 Jan. 1990). Tabby-brick chimneys, often used on plantations along the Georgia coast, were also highly susceptible to fire (T. A. Singleton, Buried Treasure: Rice Coast Digs Reveal Details of Slave Life, *American Visions*, Apr. 1986, p. 38; Singleton, The Archaeology of Afro–American Slavery in Coastal Georgia, pp. 130–131).

50. Archaeologists found evidence of a clock, for example, at Cannon's Point plantation on Saint Simons Island, Georgia (Otto, *Cannon's Point Plantation*, p. 76).

51. See, for example, Fairbanks, The Plantation Archaeology of the Southeastern Coast, pp. 2–3.

52. The recovery of plant-food, or botanical, remains is also possible but usually requires the implementation of special field techniques and the expertise of specialists. Since few archaeologists applied these techniques to slave sites, the subject is not included here.

53. McKee, Delineating Ethnicity from the Garbage of Early Virginians, p. 35; McKee, Plantation Food Supply, p. 131.

54. Crader, Faunal Remains from the Slave Quarter at Monticello, p. 5.

55. Parker and Hernigle, Portici, Portrait of a Middling Plantation, p. 183.

56. E. Reitz, Vertebrate Fauna and Socioeconomic Status, in *Consumer Choice in Historical Archaeology*, S. Spencer-Wood (ed.) (New York: Plenum, 1987), pp. 107–116.

57. J. B. Gaynor, Faunal Remains and Urban Household Subsistence, in *Material Culture, World View, and Culture Change*, typescript copy, pp. 14, 22.

58. McKee, Plantation Food Supply, p. 111.

59. See especially E. Reitz, T. Gibbs, and T. A. Rathbun, Archaeological Subsistence on Coastal Plantations, in *The Archaeology of Slavery and Plantation Life*, T. A. Singleton (ed.) (Orlando: Academic Press, 1985), pp. 163–191.

60. Ibid., p. 184.

61. Crader, Faunal Remains from the Slave Quarter at Monticello, p. 4.

62. Reitz, Gibbs, and Rathbun, Archaeological Subsistence on Coastal Plantations, p. 185.

63. J. B. Gaynor, Preliminary Notes on House for Families Faunal Assemblage (Typescript report, Mount Vernon Ladies' Association of the Union, Mount Vernon, VA, 1989).

64. Reitz, Gibbs, and Rathbun, Archaeological Subsistence on Coastal Plantations, p. 185.

65. See, for example, Kelso, *Kingsmill Plantations*, p. 102. In the British West Indies, slaves may have been intentionally buried within slave villages (see J. Handler and F. Lange, *Plantation Slavery in Barbados: An Archaeological and Historical Investigation* [Cambridge, MA: Harvard University Press, 1978], p. 174).

66. L. M. Rankin-Hill, Afro-American Biohistory: A Theoretical and Methodological Consideration (Ph.D. dissertation, University of Massachusetts, 1990), p. 29.

67. Ibid., p. 47.

68. Other African-American populations studied by physical anthropologists include an antebellum Philadelphia community, a Union military encampment on Folly Island, South Carolina, and postemancipation communities in Atlanta and Cedar Grove, Arkansas (See, for example, Rankin-Hill, Afro-American Biohistory).

69. For analyses of such research see T. A. Rathbun, Health and Disease at a South Carolina Plantation: 1840–1870, *American Journal of Physical Anthropology* 74 (1987): 239–253; D. W. Owsley et al., Demography and Pathology of an Urban Slave Population from New Orleans, *American Journal of Physical Anthropology* 74 (1987):185–197; J. O. Kelly and J. L. Angel, Life Stresses of Slavery, *American Journal of Physical Anthropology* 74 (1987):199–211.

70. Rathbun, Health and Disease at a South Carolina Plantation, pp. 239, 246–247; Kelly and Angel, Life Stresses of Slavery, p. 209; Owsley et al., Demography and Pathology of an Urban Slave Population, p. 196.

71. Kelly and Angel, Life Stresses of Slavery, 207–208; Rathbun, Health and Disease at a South Carolina Plantation, p. 248.

72. Owsley et al., Demography and Pathology of an Urban Slave Population, pp. 195–196.

73. Rathbun, Health and Disease at a South Carolina Plantation, pp. 247–248.

74. Singleton, Buried Treasure: Rice Coast Digs, p. 38.

75. R. King, Jr., to Major P. Buder, 22 October 1803, Butler Family Papers, Box 2, Folder 12, No. 1447, Historical Society of Pennsylvania, Philadelphia.

76. North of the slave South, James Deetz tentatively identified African-influenced architecture and foodways at the Parting Ways site in Plymouth, Massachusetts, which four

free-black families occupied from 1783 to the 1840s (J. Deetz, *In Small Things Forgotten: The Archaeology of Early American Life* [New York, 1977], pp. 149–154).

77. See, for example, P. Cressey, The Archaeology of Free Blacks in Alexandria, Virginia (Typescript report, Alexandria Archaeology, Office of Historic Alexandria, 1985); R. J. Hurry, An Archaeological and Historical Perspective on Benjamin Banneker, *Maryland Historical Magazine* 84 (1989):361–369; T. Padgett, The Final Report on Test Excavations at the William Johnson House, Natchez, Mississippi (Mississippi Department of Archives and History, Jackson, 1978).

78. Cressey, The Archaeology of Free Blacks in Alexandria, p. 2.

79. See, for example, C. D. Cheek and A. Friedlander, Pottery and Pig's Feet: Space, Ethnicity, and Neighborhood in Washington, D.C., 1880–1940, *Historical Archaeology* 24(1) (1990):34–60.

80. Cressey, The Archaeology of Free Blacks in Alexandria, p. 2.

81. Among the two studies of freedmen's communities is M. Trinkley, (ed.), Indians and Freedmen: Occupation at the Fish Haul Site, Beaufort County, South Carolina, in *Research Series* 7 (Columbia, SC: Chicora Foundation, 1986). Another study, one of a James City, NC, site, is in preparation (Thomas Wheaton [New South Associates, Stone Mountain, GA], pers. comm., May 1990).

82. Trinkley, ed., Indians and Freedmen, pp. 268–278, 310–311.

Chapter Six

The Overseas Chinese in El Paso:
Changing Goals, Changing Realities

In 1983, New Mexico State University conducted archaeological investigations at locations in El Paso, Texas, about to be impacted by downtown redevelopment. A research plan was developed and preliminary archival research for three site locations was conducted (Sick et al. 1983). Subsequently, archaeological testing was carried out at all three sites (Figure 6.1), and the results led to the recommendation for mitigation, again at all three sites. Detailed reports and two lengthy monographs contain the descriptive results of these investigations (Sick, Staski, and Batcho 1983; Staski 1984a, 1984b, 1984c, 1985; Staski and Batcho 1983).

The sites in downtown El Paso contained a wealth of cultural material, and it has been possible to address such research issues as the ecological history of the area, changing patterns of refuse disposal in the growing city, and developing trade and economic conditions. Yet, the most exciting and fruitful research undertaking has been the attempt to study changing ethnic relations in this multicultural west Texas city, primarily because the recovered materials represent activities once carried out by the three largest ethnic groups ever to inhabit the area. These groups were European-Americans, Mexicans, and overseas Chinese. It is this last group of immigrants which is the focus of the present chapter.

The distinctive Chinese artifacts were recovered from the Cortez Parking Lot site, named after the adjacent and historically significant Cortez Hotel. Fieldwork resulted in the recovery of a large and diverse collection of overseas Chinese material.

This chapter begins with a consideration of certain basic concepts. Next, a brief history of the Chinese in El Paso is presented. Following is a discussion of the

This article was originally published in *Hidden Heritage: Historical Archaeology of the Overseas Chinese*, Priscilla Wegars, comp. and ed., pp. 125–149, Baywood Monographs in Archaeology Series, Robert L. Schuyler, series ed., Amityville, NY: Baywood Publishing Co., ©1993.

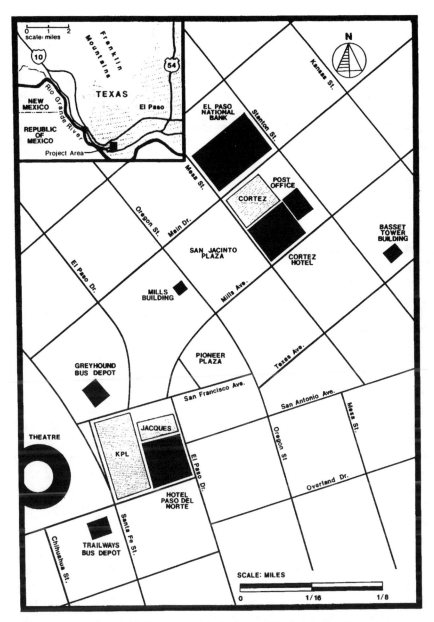

Figure 6.1. Downtown El Paso archaeological sites. Stippled areas indicate locations of excavations. "Cortez" is the Cortez Parking Lot site, from which all the Chinese material was recovered.

nature of the material recovered from the Cortez Parking Lot. Finally, these artifacts and observed artifact patterns are interpreted with reference to current research emphases among those who have studied the overseas Chinese archaeologically, focusing on questions regarding the nature and extent of assimilation that this population might have undergone. In particular, it will be shown that El Paso's Chinese community exhibited behavioral patterns that were in many ways similar to those of other Chinese groups, though in certain important ways they might have responded distinctively to unique circumstances. It is thought that the results of work in El Paso will contribute to a broader, more accurate image of the overall Chinese role in America.

Concepts and Definitions

The study of culture change by assimilation has a long history in anthropology and the other social sciences (e.g., Mead 1932; Park and Burgess 1921; SSRC Seminar 1954). Yet, substantive study of contact and assimilation is a fairly new endeavor for archaeologists, primarily because of the difficulty of recognizing ethnic or cultural groups in many prehistoric contexts. The recent and rapid growth of historical archaeology, with its ability to identify ethnic and cultural variations by reference to documentary materials, has altered this situation in dramatic fashion (Staski 1990).

A number of relevant organizational principles and general concepts have appeared in the historical archaeological literature (e.g., McGuire 1979, 1982; Schuyler 1980). For example, it is generally accepted that cultural materials can be sensitive indicators of whether ethnic groups maintained separation, or significantly assimilated with each other or into the host society. Furthermore, the most valuable archaeological measure of these processes appears to be reached by analyzing patterns of material which best correlate with ethnically distinct patterns of behavior (e.g., faunal remains indicative of diet, architectural reflections of the use of domestic space). Such an approach has proven more useful than the simple search for specific objects of obvious ethnic affiliation, which often have limited distributions in the archaeological record (Wobst 1977).

Assimilation studies in historical archaeology have developed, in fact, to a point where general theoretical models of assimilatory processes have been advanced (McGuire 1982). Nevertheless, a systematic archaeological approach to issues of ethnicity and assimilation has yet to be developed. The lack of rigor in our methods, and the absence of substance in our theories, is most obviously reflected by the inability of archaeologists to reach a consensus, or even an awareness, of just what such concepts as ethnicity and assimilation mean. The following brief discussion is meant to help correct this state of affairs. As a first step, it seems appropriate to propose an explicit definition of *ethnic group*, and by extension, *ethnicity*. Foremost, this definition must be consistent with historical and sociological facts as presently understood. Only secondary consideration can be given to the inherent strengths and weaknesses of archaeology, and to our variable ability to observe and measure a limited number of sociocultural phenomena. We cannot allow the limitations of our discipline, whatever they are perceived to be, to play a greater role in determining our concepts than does sociocultural reality.

Such a task is not as straightforward as many might believe, including numerous historical archaeologists who have uncritically used the concept of the ethnic group, along with other related concepts. Throughout the past several decades, a good number of definitions for ethnic group and ethnicity have been offered, however, stressing such diverse factors as the patterns of ecological-economic interdependencies (Barth 1969:7–38); the persistence of psychological identification and a shared sense of "peoplehood" (Gordon 1964:24–29); the quest for political and social power through exploitation of ethnic identity (McGuire 1982); and the structural composition of and interaction between various social groupings (Gordon 1964:30–53). Deciding what should be emphasized, when considering ethnic experiences in the United States specifically, is not accomplished without effort.

Following Gordon (1964), and to some extent Barth (1969), it is argued here that the most sound sociological definition of the ethnic group is one that recognizes two related functions: (1) providing individuals with an ascriptive and exclusive group with which to identify, and (2) allowing individuals to confine primary relationships to others within that group. Primary relationships are those which are personal, intimate, often informal, and face-to-face, and require the involvement of the entire personality (Gordon 1964:32). The recognition of the ethnic group thus serves to channel these relationships towards those who claim the same identification, that is, ethnicity.

These two functions appear to be the most significant contributions of ethnic groups, particularly in the modern world where economic and political systems are quite impersonal and assume global proportions. The fact that these functions might not always be directly or easily translatable into archaeological measures presents a methodological challenge to archaeologists, not a requirement for them to distort sociocultural reality.

Having thus defined ethnic group and ethnicity, it is now appropriate to consider the precise meanings of *assimilation* and *acculturation*. These meanings must be logically follow from the previous discussion. Thus, assimilation is defined here as a series of processes which, if completed, totally eliminate the need for and operation of the two most significant ethnic group functions, described above. Acculturation, in contrast, is considered merely one of these processes: the one which eliminates particular behavioral patterns which serve to identify those who are within or without the ethnic population. The balance of assimilatory processes—structural assimilation, marital assimilation, and others—involve structural changes necessary to alter patterns of primary social relations, as discussed in detail by Gordon (1964:61–81). Changes in both identifying behaviors (acculturation) and structural relations (the other types of assimilation) seem to be appropriate and manageable subjects for archaeological study.

While many archaeologists have used the term acculturation consistently in their writings, it should now be clear why reference is made to assimilation throughout this chapter. Assimilation is, after all, the more inclusive term. Nevertheless, it is recognized that those archaeologists studying the overseas Chinese should not be unfairly criticized for focusing on acculturation. It is well established that the Chinese assimilated relatively little during their first 80 years in the United States, and changes in behavioral identifiers usually are the first steps towards further assimilation. Proper research questions regarding the overseas Chinese, then, might appropriately focus on degrees of acculturation. Still, other groups, particularly those who originated from European countries, appear to have assimilated significantly in both behavioral and structural ways. The attempt to reach a unified archaeological approach to ethnic issues requires that the more inclusive term be used.

The preceding discussion makes it necessary to now briefly consider whether 19th-century Chinese immigrants to the United States did indeed represent a legitimate ethnic group. This question might at first glance seem trivial, and the answer obvious. Indeed, historical archaeologists have generally assumed the answer to be yes. Yet, other social scientists have recently raised important questions regarding two critical issues: (1) the relevance or impact of ethnicity in general, relative to other social categories such as class and status (Wilson 1980), and (2) the significance of ethnic identification for particular groups of people, given the colonial nature of their transfer to and experiences in North America (Blauner 1972). While the first issue has been raised for all observable groups, the second has focused on those with distinctive physical characteristics, including the Chinese. It is thus appropriate to ask whether these Chinese were indeed an ethnic group as defined above, before considering the degrees or types of assimilation they experienced.

The answer seems to be that the overseas Chinese were a legitimate ethnic group in all important respects. Being recognized as Chinese, or more precisely South Chinese, was to all people an ascriptive and exclusive categorization. Furthermore, the vast majority of these Chinese immigrants found it both adaptive and necessary to restrict primary relationships to others of Chinese origin: adaptive because such interactions aided in economic and social survival, and necessary because these relationships could not be shared with the non-Chinese. The limitations on primary group membership can be seen in various social practices, ranging from the economic and social separation of Chinese from non-Chinese railroad labor gangs (Mark and Chih 1982:8–11) to the widespread occurrence of segregated urban "Chinatowns" (e.g., Great Basin Foundation 1987; Lister and Lister 1989). Such limitations seem to have been in operation in the El Paso case as well, at least until the early 20th century.

Finally, the conclusion that the Chinese were a true ethnic group, as defined above, is supported by the fact that these people strongly identified with ascriptive and exclusive categories of kin while still in South China, that is, before emigration to the United States. In contrast to the Japanese, the most powerful identification for a person near Canton was with the local village, and not the nation (Lyman 1968; cf. Daniels 1988). As a result, the Chinese emphasized ethnicity long before they arrived in the New World, and most effectively transferred this primary identification when they moved.

The notion that the overseas Chinese were forced to participate in the internal colonial system of the United States, thus having experiences more similar to those of African-Americans than to those of European people, is a possibility raised by several students of contemporary race relations (e.g., Blauner 1972). As a result, it has been questioned whether the concepts of ethnicity and assimilation, originally intended to apply to European immigrant history, are valid given that the dynamics of colonialism and free immigration are not the same. This important issue is the focus of much current debate among sociologists, and cannot be addressed adequately in this chapter. It can be pointed out, nevertheless, that the Chinese appear to have come to North America by choice, if only to stay temporarily. Although many became economically dependent on other people to complete the trip, and started out unaware of the poor treatment to come, few were forced to take the journey. In all of these respects the overseas Chinese experience mirrors that of the vast majority of European immigrants.

The Chinese in El Paso

No aspect of El Paso's history can be understood without a clear appreciation of the remarkable impact of the railroad. That is certainly true for the history of the Chinese in the city, who might very well never have settled there if the railroad did not arrive. As with many other areas of the American West, the Chinese moved into west Texas initially as laborers along the railroad line (in this case, the Southern Pacific). Others followed via the railroad after the community was established.

The Southern Pacific, arriving from the west on or around May 19, 1880 (Leach 1965; Sonnichsen 1982), was only the first of five approaching rail lines to arrive. Within three years the city was connected to major trade centers to the east, north, west, and south. The impact this transportation revolution had on El Paso's demographic, economic, and social growth cannot be overstated. What in 1880 was still an insignificant point along trade routes became an "Instant City" (Barth 1975; Staski 1984c) of regional importance. Population climbed from 736 in 1880 to over 11,000 in 1888. The cattle, mining, and manufacturing industries became significant sources of national economic growth nearly overnight. Finally, the diversity of cultural and economic groups within the city expanded dramatically.

Yet it was not within El Paso, but rather some 400 miles to the east, that circumstances led to the establishment of a Chinese community there. The Southern Pacific finally met the west-moving Galveston, Harrisburg, and San Antonio near Pecos, Texas, to complete the second transcontinental railroad. As they had done numerous times before, railroad officials then summarily dismissed many of the Chinese laborers, as their efforts were no longer needed. These Chinese were left poor, without work, and without any means of returning to California, from where they originated. They settled in the nearest community of any size, El Paso, in the hope of finding any kind of employment.

Documentary evidence suggests that life was quite foreign and difficult for the Chinese in El Paso, at least at first. Dwellings were crowded, and sanitary conditions were terrible. Few Chinese women were ever present. The non-Chinese community was hostile and resisted giving the immigrants either social or economic support (Farrar 1972; Rhoads 1977). Yet, perhaps most disturbing to the residents of this small Chinatown, was the initial inability to acquire Chinese goods and live in a traditional Chinese manner.

This initial isolation of the community is foremost evidenced in various city directories and business listings. Chinese merchandise stores, carrying goods from China which were not available in other establishments, were apparently not in operation until several years after initial settlement in the city. Only three such stores are reported in 1886 (Farrar 1972:7). The number of such establishments grew to seven by 1892, however, and then to eight by 1907 (Rhoads 1977:13). Obviously, the inability to create exchange networks with China, and acquire desired Chinese goods, was only a temporary situation.

Indeed, these records are evidence for a gradual though steady increase in the degree of self-sufficiency experienced by the Chinese, brought about by the growing capability to create ties to the West Coast and the Old World. Such trends clearly occurred when it came to the availability of goods, an important point to be brought out later in this chapter by the results of the El Paso archaeological investigations. Other documents, regarding other community developments, also support these apparent trends.

As with all Chinese in the United States and elsewhere, El Paso's Chinese community found it necessary to form social alliances among its members which reflected or at least substituted for those left behind. The rigors of emigration, and particularly the absence of many women and other kin, made it impossible to maintain previous social relations. In their place, the overseas branch of the revolutionary Triad Society (the Chee Kung Tong) gradually became a central institution for the El Paso community. The importance of this ritual brotherhood cannot be overemphasized. Being one of the most influential secret societies in South China, and having had many members who fought in the Taiping Rebellion and the Red

Turban Uprisings in Guangdong, the Triad Society was the first to be formed by immigrants in the United States (Mark and Chih 1982:56). Nevertheless, it took nearly a decade for a significant portion of the Chinese population in El Paso to join (Rhoads 1977). Its influence, particularly its role in giving economic support to members, continued growing throughout the remainder of the 19th and early 20th centuries.

In yet another enterprise, the smuggling of Chinese into the United States, it is obvious that El Paso's Chinese community only gradually became more independent of the balance of the city. Illegal entry, of course, became a regular endeavor after the passage of the Exclusion Act of 1882, at nearly the same time that El Paso's Chinatown came into existence. Yet, smuggling operations in the city did not reach their well-known enormous proportions until the early 20th century (Rhoads 1977:16). From 1905 until about 1915 El Paso's Chinese ran the largest port of entry for illegal Chinese immigrants arriving via Mexico, supporting the notion that the community had developed an effective, integrated system by that time.

Finally, growing hostile attitudes within the non-Chinese community of El Paso further encouraged isolation and self-sufficiency. By the turn of the century the general perception of Chinatown was that it was a place of moral degradation, filth, and crime (Farrar 1972:12). The "opium problem," for instance, was perceived as growing increasingly worse through the late 19th century and into the 20th century, and legal penalties for selling, receiving, or smoking the drug became more severe through time. Violence and danger were, in addition, viewed as becoming more common in the streets of Chinatown, and efforts to further restrict the geographical extent of the Chinese community became more frequent. In the face of these official and unofficial anti-Chinese attitudes, the Chinese found it necessary to become increasingly independent.

This growing independence did not result in the establishment of a permanent Chinese community in El Paso. For various reasons, including a possible increase in the degree of assimilation, discussed below, this west Texas Chinatown vanished during the first half of the 20th century. The precise time of the demise of El Paso's Chinatown is a matter of debate, with dates given as early as 1917 (Farrar 1972:33) and as late as 1938 (Rhoads 1977:18). Certainly, however, a number of specific events can be held partly responsible for the decline and disappearance of the community. Included is the Mexican Revolution, which made life intolerable for Chinese immigrants in northern Mexico and thus curtailed the flow of illegal Chinese aliens through Juarez and El Paso. Also playing a significant role was the continuing enforcement of the various federal exclusion laws, which disallowed the legal arrival of additional Chinese people, particularly women. With both illegal and legal entry brought almost to a standstill, El Paso's Chinese population became static and eventually declined.

The Archaeological Record

A total of 57 feature designations were assigned during the combined efforts of archaeological testing and mitigation at the Cortez Parking Lot site, "feature" being defined broadly to denote any separate and identifiable archaeological formation that is useful in site interpretation. Twelve features contained direct material evidence of the presence of the Chinese community, including five refuse pits (purposefully dug pits most likely designed for refuse deposition), six trash concentrations (naturally or accidentally occurring concentrations of refuse), and one privy filled with Chinese material culture. Complete descriptions of all recorded features are presented elsewhere (Staski 1985:131–227).

Five of these Chinese features were relatively small, highly disturbed, or otherwise determined insignificant, and little or no additional work was conducted on them after initial testing. The remaining seven, however, were remarkable for their large size, the amount and density of material culture within them, the uniform nature of their functional associations, and the wide range of depositional dates they represented. Several hundred kilograms of material were recovered from these seven features alone. All except one (number 38) appeared to have been sealed deposits in clear association with a number of Chinese laundries and residences known to have once stood on the block. Dates of deposition can be confidently placed between ca. 1890 and ca. 1915, with intermediate dates occurring within this 25-year period. Basic data concerning this small though highly useful sample of deposits are summarized in Table 6.1.

There is one temporal pattern in these basic data requiring explicit consideration. When the estimated dates of deposition are compared with the mean bottle manufacture dates, the former are all significantly more recent than the latter, with estimated lag times ranging from ten and one-half to sixteen years. "Estimated Date of Deposition" is, in all seven cases, a strong inference based on several sources of information, including documented dates of associated structures and activities, stratigraphic relationships, and several artifact attribute relative frequencies. It is thought to be the most reliable temporal indicator of deposition. "Mean Bottle (Ceramic) Dates" are, in contrast, merely mean manufacture dates determined by following the methods of Henry and Garrow (1982:269–292), previously derived from South's mean ceramic dating formula (South 1977). Bottles were relied on more frequently than ceramics for this analysis because only two deposits (numbers 18 and 38) contained enough tightly datable ceramic material to make the technique useful.

These apparent dating discrepancies suggest that the mean dating formula might not be an accurate or sensitive indicator of actual feature formation date, especially when applied to later 19th- and early 20th-century bottles. Similar results have been obtained when applying South's original method to later 19th-century ceramics (Henry and Garrow 1982). Indeed, a systematic investigation of glass container

TABLE 6.1

Descriptive Data for Significant Chinese Features

Estimated Date of Deposition	Feature Number	Feature Type	Functional Association	Mean Bottle (Ceramic) Dates
1890–1895	17	trash pit	laundry/ residence	1884.5
1895–1900	16	trash pit	laundry/ residence	(insufficient data)
1900	3–3/ 14–14[a]	trash pit	laundry/ residence	1887.4
1900	15a	trash concentration	laundry/ residence	1887.0
1900	18	trash pit	laundry/ residence	1887.1 (1883.5)
1910–1915	26	trash concentration	laundry/ residence	(insufficient data)
1910–1915	38	trash concentration	(unclear)	1899.0 (1895.4)

[a] This single feature has three numerical designations due to the fact that it was perceived as potentially being three separate features during archaeological testing.

manufacture-deposition lag time shows that numerous social and economic factors might play a role in postponing deposition by a similar number of years as observed in El Paso (Hill 1982, especially Table 12.26). Clearly, such lag time needs to be considered in all such analyses.

In the case of the Chinese deposits, it appears that reuse and recycling of bottles by Chinese residents might have played an important role in the postponement of deposition. As discussed in detail elsewhere (Staski 1985:127–128, 229–235), the vast majority of glass containers used by the overseas Chinese was of American manufacture, primarily because the glass industry in late 19th-century China was nearly nonexistent. In addition, there is convincing evidence that the Chinese were using a number of these bottles for purposes other than those for which they were originally intended.

A number of remarkable artifacts give direct and incontrovertible evidence of reuse. One is a patent-extract bottle which contains traces of bluing, a preparation of blue dyes commonly used in laundries to counteract yellowing of white fabrics. Others include two American-made bottles upon which Chinese labels are adhered. These artifacts not only indicate reuse, but also suggest that reuse and recycling were occurring among the overseas Chinese in both a widespread and organized fashion.

The label on one American-made beer bottle advertised a "wine" considered by the Chinese to be useful in promoting male virility (Figure 6.2). The brand name,

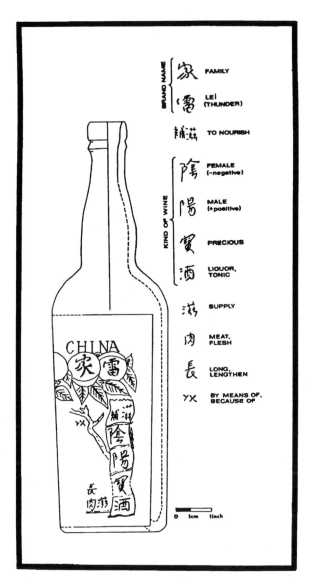

Figure 6.2. American beer bottle with Chinese label.

type, of alcohol, and supposed effects of its consumption are all described. A similar artifact consists of a familiar Dr. J. Hostetter's Stomach Bitters bottle, with a Chinese label advertising some sort of liquid useful for the cleaning of clothing (Figure 6.3).

These artifacts make it seem likely that Chinese entrepreneurs had to buy empty bottles wholesale, or at least collect them rather systematically once emptied of original contents. It was, in addition, necessary for these same or other Chinese businessmen to have access to the resources required for label production. The bottles had to be filled with a product known to be in demand among the overseas Chinese. Finally, the bottles most likely had to be shipped to various Chinese settlements across the United States. The economic capabilities of small Chinatowns like El Paso's, although quite developed by the turn of the century, were probably never adequate for a market venture of this kind. Rather, the products probably were prepared and bottled in one of the larger and more established Chinatowns (such as San Francisco), and distributed from there.

Because the Chinese use of American-made bottles was widespread and intensive, and because the systematic, organized reuse of these bottles required economic efficiency, it is likely that many bottles were used for such purposes. Although there is presently no way of determining what percent of all bottles recovered from the Cortez Parking Lot were reused, it can nevertheless be argued that a significant number of them were. Such a conclusion calls into question any interpretation of product preference and use among the overseas Chinese which has exclusive dependence on the analysis of bottle types. All such analyses were done with caution. Whenever possible, analyses were conducted with reference to artifact classes other than glass.

The two labeled bottles are also highly significant because they are part of a body of evidence suggesting that a certain amount of assimilation—more specifically, acculturation—might have been occurring among El Paso's Chinese residents.

Assimilation Among The Overseas Chinese

At the present time it appears difficult, if not impossible, to measure arch-aeologically the precise degrees and types of assimilation experienced by any minority group. Yet, it is possible to recognize in patterns of material culture whether assimilation into a dominant society was a major or insignificant factor in the lives of a group of people. Such an analysis of the El Paso material begins with consideration of the two labeled bottles described previously.

Careful observation reveals that the Chinese labels not only have Chinese characters on them, but English words as well. The beer bottle has the word "CHINA" clearly written along the top (Figure 6.2), and the Hostetter's bottle has a portion of an English statement ". . . moved to 513 Sixth . . ." written along one

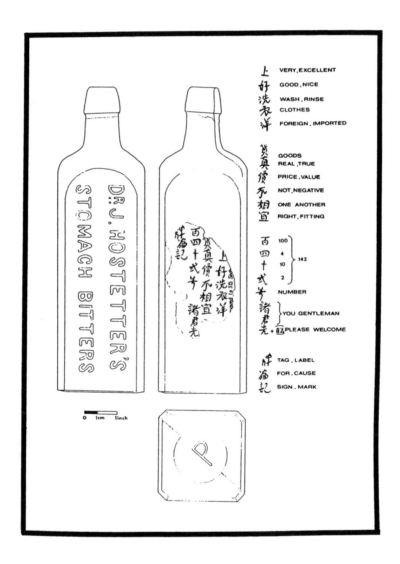

Figure 6.3. Dr. J. Hostetter's Stomach Bitters bottle with Chinese label.

side (Figure 6.3). It is intriguing to ask for whom those statements were intended. Obviously, the bottles, and the contents within them, were intended for the overseas Chinese. There is thus the possibility that the English messages were intended for these Chinese as well, suggesting some degree of literate bilingualism and thus some degree of assimilation. This suggestion, recognized as initially based on little evidence and weak inference, can nevertheless be explored in a more systematic and reliable fashion by reference to other material evidence recovered from the Cortez Parking Lot.

Artifact Relative Frequencies

Archaeological data suggesting that the Chinese experienced little assimilation include the relatively large amounts of Chinese ceramic material always recovered from overseas Chinese sites. The El Paso collection is no exception, with the majority of ceramics (measured by weight for this analysis) from most Chinese deposits being of Chinese manufacture (Table 6.2). Yet, it appears that the degree of dependence placed on either Chinese or non-Chinese ceramic items changed through time, in a way which complements the documentary history of the city's Chinese community.

As discussed earlier in this chapter, a major theme emerging from the documentary record is that it took a number of years, up to two decades, for El Paso's Chinese to gain employment and some economic stability, create internal social institutions thought necessary, effectively aid other Chinese who wanted to enter the country, and establish a reliable economic network to the West Coast so that desired Chinese merchandise could arrive in adequate quantities. The delay in this community's establishment, caused by poor economic conditions, small population size, and the great distance between El Paso and the West Coast, is suggested somewhat in the archaeological record.

The data (Table 6.2), restricted here to ceramics because of the complexities of American bottle reuse, suggest that just over half of all ceramic material available to the Chinese laundry workers was coming from China during the early 1890s (Feature 17). By the late 1890s, this figure appears to have climbed to over 60 percent (Feature 16). Then, by the turn of the century, over 85 percent of the ceramics available to, and used by, some of these same workers were manufactured in China (Features 3–3/14–14 and 15a). It seems that the gradual growth of self-sufficiency in El Paso's Chinese community, most obviously the improving economic ties to the West Coast and the increasing number and efficiency of Chinese merchandise stores, is indeed archaeologically observable.

It can be further concluded from both the documentary and archaeological records that El Paso's Chinese were going to great lengths to maintain ethnic separation from the dominant society, and becoming more successful at this

TABLE 6.2
Artifactual Data from Significant Chinese Features

Estimated Date of Deposition	Feature Number	Chinese Ceramic within Total (Percent)	Porcelain within Chinese (Percent)	Rice Bowls within Porcelain (Percent)	Serving Bowls within Porcelain (Percent)	Liquor Containers within Stonewares (Percent)	Food Storage Jars within Stonewares (Percent)	Soya Sauce Containers within Stonewares (Percent)
1890–1895	17	54.6	47.2	40.4	32.5	18.3	16.6	29.5
1895–1900	16	62.1	3.3	0.0	37.1	0.0	63.2	2.0
1900	3–3/ 14–14[a]	86.1	18.5	31.6	43.9	58.9	19.5	10.7
1900	15a	85.4	19.9	41.6	34.5	47.7	15.4	5.9
1900	18	47.4	23.0	17.3	21.5	9.6	50.0	15.4
1910–1915	26	100.0	48.9	38.5	38.0	0.0	11.9	49.0
1910–1915	38	10.4	67.1	75.4	0.0	16.5	4.5	5.4

[a] This single feature has three numerical designations due to the fact that it was perceived as potentially being three separate features during archaeological testing.

endeavor as the 19th century was coming to a close. Yet, it is possible to suggest that other forces were at work as well, and observe that only some members of the community were depending on Chinese ceramics to a greater and greater extent as availability improved. Others, apparently, began depending on these Chinese goods less and less.

Fewer than 50 percent of the ceramics from one deposit are Chinese, and this trash pit (Feature 18) is thought contemporary with Features 3–3/14–14 and 15a. In contrast, a deposit dating to the second decade of the 20th century contained nothing but ceramics of Chinese manufacture (100 percent; Feature 26). Finally, just over ten percent of the ceramics from Feature 38, contemporary with number 26, were manufactured in China. Thus, the apparent pattern is one of a growing diversity or range of dependence on Chinese goods, after an initial overall increase in such dependence. Percent of total ceramics that are Chinese is the only measure exhibiting any apparent chronological trend (Table 6.2).

Clearly, sample size might be responsible for the pattern that has been observed. It is also possible that an additional though as yet unrecognized variable led to the apparent distributions. Additionally, it must be mentioned that the inference being made concerning assimilation is fairly weak, and requires further confirmation before being accepted without question. Nevertheless, the possibility exists that a portion of El Paso's Chinese community had increasing access to Chinese ceramics (and their contents) but chose not to depend on them to as great an extent as would otherwise be expected. The factor of choice suggests that assimilation within this portion of the community was occurring, and is being observed archaeologically.

Diet

Other data sources support the notion that some assimilation, in the form of acculturation, might have been occurring. One of these is the large quantity of faunal material recovered. It is well known that dietary patterns are some of the most enduring aspects of an ethnic group's behavioral separation from the host society (Baer 1981, 1991). If important dietary changes can be observed archaeologically for any ethnic minority, it is reasonable to conclude that a high degree of acculturation was taking place. For this reason, along with the fact that traditional South Chinese dietary patterns are well documented (Anderson 1988; Chang 1977) and known to have been highly distinctive from common American foodways, archaeologists have devoted considerable time to the study of Chinese diet in America (Evans 1980; LaLande 1982; Langenwalter 1977, 1978, 1980; McEwan 1984, 1985).

The material recovered from the Cortez Parking Lot is similar to that from other overseas Chinese sites, in that the faunal assemblage can be easily distinguished from non-Chinese faunal collections. Emphasis on sea fauna, fowl, and pork stands in striking contrast to the typical non-Chinese diet of turn-of-the-century El Paso, with its almost exclusive reliance on beef. Yet, there are some intriguing differences between the data from El Paso and other overseas Chinese sites, and it does seem as if the dominant dietary regime was influencing Chinese patterns (LaLande 1982; McEwan 1984, 1985).

From the material examined—to date restricted to that recovered from Feature 3–3/14–14, one of the deposits thought to have dated to ca. 1900—the following observations can be made. Pig (*Sus scrofa*) was the predominant species recovered. Pig remains comprise nearly 20 percent of the individuals and 25 percent of the estimated biomass. Yet, fully 57 percent of the pig bone with evidence of butchering was cut with a non-Chinese saw, and not in a traditional Chinese manner. The remaining 43 percent was cut with the use of a cleaver. Thus, although pork was common in the El Paso Chinese diet, preparation techniques and cuts might often have been quite different than those of South China.

Supporting the notion that some change in dietary patterns was occurring is the fact that cow (*Bos taurus*) was the second most important contributor to the diet, based on biomass estimates. In addition, over 80 percent of the recognizably butchered beef elements (only 3 percent of the total, it should be noted) were prepared with non-Chinese implements. All recognizable cuts were identified as typically European-American, and it appears that the Chinese in west Texas were eating different quantities of food types, possibly in what was to them a foreign manner.

The analysis of the faunal material from the Cortez Parking Lot will remain incomplete until assemblages from additional features are taken into account. Further evidence that some diet-related behavioral changes might have taken place is available now, however, and can be gleaned by considering patterns of alcohol consumption among the overseas Chinese. The evidence from El Paso is neither incontrovertible nor clear in many respects, given the fact that the extent of bottle reuse remains unknown. Still, if the assumption is made that even a minority of bottles did contain originally intended contents, then it can be argued that non-Chinese alcohol was an important element in the Chinese diet. This argument is reasonable, because so many alcohol bottles were recovered.

The rate and quantity of alcohol consumption among the overseas Chinese have received some attention in the archaeological literature. Alcohol has been "an integral part of Chinese culture for several thousand years" (LaLande 1982:44), and archaeological evidence indicates that the immigrants consumed both Chinese and American alcoholic beverages. What is most fascinating is that the rate and quantity consumed, as suggested by archaeologists, appear much greater than that described in written records and reflected in popular perceptions. Much of the documentary evidence depicts the Chinese as relatively light or moderate drinkers, with a low incidence of pathological drinking behaviors. Archaeological data from El Paso, in contrast, suggest that relatively heavy drinking might have been the norm.

An explanation for this discrepancy between the documentary and archaeological records is found when the nature of both drinking behavior patterns and drunken comportment are considered (MacAndrew and Edgerton 1969). Non-Chinese culture of the western frontier prescribed drinking in public groups, and the public display of drunkenness was not considered horrible or highly immoral. In contrast, the overseas Chinese generally drank in private, hidden from the non-Chinese population. They seldom displayed the effects of consumption publicly. The apparent "sobriety" of the Chinese in the non-Chinese mind was thus the result of an effort by the immigrants to keep their drinking practices secret (LaLande 1982:44–46).

Similar contrasts between public and private drinking behaviors have been discussed for the Navajo and Hopi (Levy and Kunitz 1974), and 19th-century Irish and Jewish immigrants to the United States (Staski 1983). It has been concluded that most available measures of alcohol consumption rates are reactive to the public, social environment. Archaeological investigations, of course, are nonreactive and thus more accurate when it comes to the study of actual drinking behavior (Staski 1983).

When considering drinking in relation to assimilation, both the actual patterns of consumption and the publicly displayed patterns of use must be taken into account. The first is a measure of behavior while the second is a measure of perceptions and attitudes. Clearly, assimilation involves changes in both behaviors (acculturation) and attitudinal repertoires (primarily what Gordon [1964:71]) calls "Identificational Assimilation," though behavioral changes are involved as well). Alcohol consumption appears to be a most appropriate subject of inquiry for assimilation studies, precisely because the related actions and attitudes are quite distinctive.

Nevertheless, a number of caveats in this analysis must be pointed out immediately. First, it is at this time impossible to estimate changing rates of alcohol consumption among individuals, or even groups, since no accurate correlations between number of responsible people, actual duration of deposition, and particular trash deposit can be made. Second, it should be pointed out that no measure of ethanol consumption was attempted. Since different alcoholic beverages contain different amounts of the drug (i.e., have different "proofs"), it follows that any measure of alcohol consumption requires knowledge of these percents. It was decided that any estimation of Chinese alcohol proofs would be difficult to confirm.

Third, as already mentioned, the presence of American bottle reuse among the Chinese clearly presents a problem since glass alcohol containers comprise a large portion of the data under analysis. Finally, accurately estimating numbers of functional bottle and ceramic types from an urban setting, necessary for the analysis to be complete, is highly problematic given the complex nature of urban depositional histories.

Despite these problems, and the recognized substantial limits imposed on the analysis, it is still intriguing to note that chronological relative frequencies of estimated total alcohol containers from China and the United States exhibit a remarkably similar pattern to that displayed when the weights of all ceramics are considered (compare Tables 6.2 and 6.3). During the 1890s, it appears that a relatively large amount of the alcohol consumed by El Paso's Chinese was American made (Features 17 and 16; see Table 6.3). This dependence on American beverages most probably resulted because few Chinese goods, including liquor, were available in El Paso at the time. By the turn of the century, however, there

TABLE 6.3

Absolute Numbers and Percents of Chinese and American Alcohol Bottles

Feature Number	Number Chinese Liquor Containers	Number American Alcohol Bottles	Total	Percent Chinese of Total	Percent American of Total
17	13	27	40	32	⎰ 68
16	0	4	4	0	1 ⎱ 100
3–3/ 14–14ᵃ	117	57	174	67	33
15a	56	18	74	75	2 ⎰⎱ 25
18	20	87	107	19	81
26	0	2	2	0	3 ⎰ 100
38	1	9	10	10	⎱ 90

ᵃ This single feature has three numerical designations due to the fact that it was perceived as potentially being three separate features during archaeological testing.

1 = Evidence of nonavailability of Chinese goods.

2 = Growing availability, little or no assimilation.

3 = Growing availability, greater assimilation.

seems to have been relatively greater use of Chinese spirits, reflecting the growing self-sufficiency of the community (Features 3–3/14–14 and 15a). Finally, beginning with and continuing into the early 20th century (Features 18, 26, and 38), use of American liquor predominated once again. This time, however, the apparent overwhelming use of non-Chinese beverages was most probably the result of choice, not merely availability. Assimilation is suggested once again. It must be noted that the general pattern is similar when total ceramic weight artifact frequencies and estimated number of alcohol bottles are compared, though the particular patterns exhibited by individual features are not. For example, Feature 26 contained Chinese ceramics exclusively, yet all recovered alcohol-containing vessels are American made. The former measure indicates little or no assimilation among those responsible for feature formations, while the latter measure suggests significant behavioral changes. Clearly, the processes of culture change and assimilation are mosaic in nature, with different behaviors changing at different times and rates. Nor are they easy to reconstruct on any but a very general level of abstraction. Nevertheless, the fact that both total artifact weights and estimated numbers of alcohol bottles reveal similar general patterns lends strength to the suggestion that some significant changes were occurring among portions of the Chinese community. The observation that these patterns are similar also suggests that the distorting influences of the caveats mentioned previously might not be as significant as thought.

The other aspect of alcohol consumption needing consideration is that involved with attitudes regarding public displays and comportment. As stated earlier, the Chinese had an image of being light to moderate drinkers because they kept their drinking hidden most of the time. Yet, this proclivity to hide activities is also an ethnic or cultural marker, and changes in attitudes are as indicative of changes in ethnic identification (i.e., assimilation) as are changes in actual behavior. Unfortunately, the documentary record concerning the public display of Chinese behaviors is so distorted and incomplete that not even general conclusions can be reached at this time. Perhaps further research will suggest methods to retrieve more information from the few available documents.

Concluding Discussion

To this point, this chapter has been concerned with (1) defining such concepts as ethnicity and assimilation, and determining that the Chinese in late 19th-century America were indeed an ethnic group, (2) tracing the general history of the overseas Chinese experience in El Paso, and (3) examining the archaeological record and the patterns of behavioral changes it possibly reflects. It is now necessary to consider how these behavioral changes might have related to the processes of assimilation, and what these relations can tell us about the dynamics of both assimilation and ethnic boundary maintenance.

First, it is clearly the case that the inferred changes experienced by at least a portion of El Paso's Chinese community could not possibly have been any type of assimilation other than acculturation. No significant alterations in social structure are apparent in either the archaeological or documentary data, and the vast majority of Chinese seem to have restricted primary relationships to within their community. They did so, furthermore, during the entire time they lived in the city, even when they might have found it difficult. For example, only one marriage of a Chinese man to a non-Chinese woman (apparently legal in El Paso) is recorded over a period of approximately 35 years, despite the fact that only four Chinese women were ever reported to be present. Needless to say, and for numerous reasons, these records might be inaccurate, but certainly not to the extent necessary to distort the general pattern.

A situation of "acculturation only" (Gordon 1964:77) is not uncommon, and does not contradict the general definitions presented previously. In addition, some reflection on the dynamics leading to this situation naturally leads to a consideration of theories regarding the underlying causes of ethnic boundary maintenance. Three influential theories are discussed here.

Barth (1969), with his ecological orientation, claims that the degree of boundary maintenance is determined by the extent of overlap between each group's economic activities. The greater the overlap, he argues, the weaker the boundary. In contrast, Spicer (1971, 1972) sees boundaries strengthening among minorities as a powerful group increases its attempts to absorb the smaller groups. Opposition to such attempts is, for Spicer, the proximate cause of the persistence of ethnic diversity. Finally, McGuire (1982), one of the few archaeologists to consider the theory of ethnic group dynamics, regards degrees of disparity in the distribution of power as the critical factor determining the strength of ethnic boundaries. It is intriguing to consider the El Paso situation with each of these three theoretical views in mind.

The archaeological and documentary records regarding the Chinese in El Paso do not support the argument put forth by Barth. Ethnic boundaries between these people and others remained high, as suggested by the fact that only a certain amount of acculturation is indicated. Yet, there was a significant amount of overlap in the economic activities of the Chinese and other groups, particularly Mexicans. Records indicate that there were numerous instances of resentment, and even violence, resulting from competition for jobs in such areas as laundry service, restaurant operation, and truck farming. Only gradually did the Chinese establish monopolies within these occupations, and for most of their stay they had to struggle with others doing the same sort of work (Rhoads 1977).

Nor does the evidence support the model developed by Spicer. There is absolutely no indication that the non-Chinese population had any interest in absorbing, or assimilating, the overseas Chinese. Rather, all efforts were directed at keeping these people separated from the balance of the community. Clearly, the lack of assimilation other than some acculturation was not the result of Chinese opposition, as defined by Spicer.

McGuire's model cannot be rejected so completely. There is no question that the distribution of power was unequal in turn-of-the-century El Paso, and the Chinese had very little, if any, influence on general metropolitan policies or directions. They were always relatively few in number, never elected one of their own to political office, appear not to have contributed any leaders to the outside community, and had no means of curtailing the various discriminatory actions taken against them. Certainly, this unfair situation might have encouraged the Chinese to maintain strong ethnic boundaries.

What McGuire fails to mention, and what the El Paso material seems to suggest, is that certain amounts of acculturation can occur even when the disparity of power is great and not decreasing. Put another way, it appears as if behavioral and cultural patterns might not be very important in maintaining strong ethnic boundaries. Rather, these boundaries are maintained most effectively by avoiding structural assimilation, that is, by limiting primary social relationships to those within the group. This interpretation does not contradict the view that a disparity of power creates the need to maintain or strengthen the boundaries. Neither does it weaken the general opinion that structural assimilation is the "keystone" of all assimilation (Gordon 1964:81). Indeed, it lends support to this observation.

If this conclusion is correct, then archaeologists wishing to study ethnic group dynamics will have to look more often for patterns of social structure, rather than limiting themselves to the investigation of changing behavioral repertoires. Such an approach might help us better understand both the distribution of power and the composition of primary groups, as reflected in a number of both historical and prehistoric archaeological settings.

REFERENCES

Anderson, E. N. 1988. *The Food of China.* New Haven: Yale University Press.

Baer, R. D. 1981. The Effects of Social and Cultural Variables on Food Consumption Patterns and Dietary Adequacy. Manuscript on file, Arizona State Museum, Tucson.

Baer, R. D. 1991. Cultural Factors Affecting Relationships between Household Refuse and Household Food Consumption. In *The Ethnoarchaeology of Refuse Disposal*, E. Staski and L. D. Sutro (eds.), *Anthropological Research Papers*, No. 42, pp. 5–12. Tempe: Arizona State University.

Barth, F. 1969. Introduction. In *Ethnic Groups and Boundaries*, F. Barth (ed.), pp. 7–38. Boston: Little, Brown.

Barth, G. 1975. *Instant Cities: Urbanization and the Rise of San Francisco and Denver*. New York: Oxford University Press.

Blauner, R. 1972. *Racial Oppression in America*. New York: Harper and Row.

Chang, K. C. (ed.). 1977. *Food in Chinese Culture: Anthropological and Historical Perspectives*. New Haven: Yale University Press.

Daniels, R. 1988. *Asian America: Chinese and Japanese in the United States since 1850*. Seattle: University of Washington Press.

Evans, W. S. 1980. Food and Fantasy: Material Culture of the Chinese in California and the West circa 1850–1900. In *Archaeological Perspectives on Ethnicity in America: Afro-American and Asian American Culture History*, R. L. Schuyler (ed.), pp. 89–96. Amityville, NY: Baywood.

Farrar, N. 1972. The Chinese in El Paso. *Southwestern Studies Monograph*, No. 33, Texas Western Press, University of Texas at El Paso.

Gordon, M. M. 1964. *Assimilation in American Life: The Role of Race, Religion, and National Origins*. New York: Oxford University Press.

Great Basin Foundation. 1987. *Wong Ho Leun: An American Chinatown*. 2 vols. San Diego: Great Basin Foundation.

Henry, S. L. and P. H. Garrow. 1982. The Historic Component. In *City of Phoenix Archaeology of the Original Townsite, Blocks 1 and 2*, J. S. Cable, S. L. Henry, and D. E. Doyel (eds.), pp. 183–382. *Soil Systems Publications in Archaeology*, No. 1, Phoenix: Soil System, Inc.

Hill, S. H. 1982. An Examination of Manufacture-Deposition Lag for Glass Bottles from Late Historic Sites. In *Archaeology of Urban America: The Search for Pattern and Process*, R. S. Dickens, Jr. (ed.), pp. 291–327. New York: Academic Press.

LaLande, J. M. 1982. "Celestials" in the Oregon Siskiyous: Diet, Dress, and Drug Use of the Chinese Miners in Jackson County, ca. 1860–1900. *Northwest Anthropological Research Notes* 16(1):1–61.

Langenwalter, P. E., III. 1977. The Archaeology of 19th Century Chinese Subsistence at Lower China Crossing, Madera County, California, Unpublished manuscript, National Park Service, San Francisco.

Langenwalter, P. E., III. 1978. A Late 19th Century Chinese Store in the Sierran Foothills. Paper presented at the annual meeting of the Society for California Archaeology, Yosemite National Park, California.

Langenwalter, P. E. 1980. The Archaeology of 19th Century Chinese Subsistence at the Lower China Store, Madera County, California. In *Archaeological Perspectives on Ethnicity in America: Afro-American and Asian American Culture History*, R. L. Schuyler (ed.), pp. 102–112. Amityville, NY: Baywood.

Leach, J. 1965. Farewell to Horseback, Muleback, Footback, and Prairie Schooner: The Railroad Comes to Town. *Password*. El Paso Historical Society Publication.

Levy, J. E. and S. J. Kunitz. 1974. *Indian Drinking: Navajo Practices and Anglo-American Theories*. New York: John Wiley.

Lister, F. C. and R. H. Lister. 1989. The Chinese of Early Tucson: Historic Archaeology from the Tucson Urban Renewal Project. *Anthropological Papers of the University of Arizona*, No. 52. Tucson: University of Arizona Press.

Lyman, S. M. 1968. Contrasts in the Community Organization of Chinese and Japanese in North America. *The Canadian Review of Sociology and Anthropology* 5.

MacAndrew, C. and R. B. Edgerton. 1969. *Drunken Comportment: A Social Explanation*. Chicago: Aldine.

Mark, Diane Mei Lin and G. Chih. 1982. *A Place Called Chinese America*. Dubuque, IA: Kendall/Hunt.

McEwan, B. G. 1984. Appendix C: Faunal Analysis, in "Beneath the Border City, Volume One: Urban Archaeology in Downtown El Paso," by E. Staski, pp. 271–301. *University Museum Occasional Papers*, No. 12. Las Cruces: New Mexico State University.

McEwan, B. G. 1985. Appendix B: Faunal Analysis, in "Beneath the Border City, Volume Two: The Overseas Chinese in El Paso," by E. Staski, pp. 262–283. *University Museum Occasional Papers*, No. 13. Las Cruces: New Mexico State University.

McGuire, R. H. 1979. Rancho Punta de Agua. *Contribution to Highway Salvage Archaeology in Arizona*, No. 57. Tucson: Arizona State Museum.

McGuire, R. H. 1982. The Study of Ethnicity in Historical Archaeology. *The Journal of Anthropological Archaeology* 1:159–178.

Mead, M. 1932. *The Changing Culture of an Indian Tribe*. New York: Columbia University Press.

Park, R. E. and E. W. Burgess. 1921. *Introduction to the Science of Sociology*. Chicago: University of Chicago Press.

Rhoads, E. J. M. 1977. The Chinese in Texas. *Southwestern Historical Quarterly* 71:1–36.

Schuyler, R. L. (ed.). 1980. *Archaeological Perspectives on Ethnicity in America: Afro-American and Asian American Culture History*. Amityville, NY: Baywood.

Sick, D., M. Roberts, D. Batcho, and W. A. Timmons. 1983. *Documentary Research, Photo Documentation, the Research Design and Plan for Public Programs for the City of El Paso Downtown Revitalization Project*. Report prepared for the City of El Paso by the Cultural Resources Management Division of New Mexico State University, Las Cruces.

Sick, D., E. Staski, and D. Batcho. 1983. Archaeological Testing of 41EP2370, the Kohlberg Parking Lot Site, El Paso, Texas. Report prepared for the City of El Paso by the Cultural Resources Management Division of New Mexico State University, Las Cruces.

Sonnichsen, C. L. 1982. *Tucson: The Life and Times of an American City.* Norman: University of Oklahoma Press.

South, S. 1977. *Method and Theory in Historical Archaeology.* New York: Academic Press.

Spicer, E. H. 1971. Persistent Cultural Systems. *Science* 174:795–800.

Spicer, E. H. 1972. Plural Society in the Southwest. In *Plural Society in the Southwest,* E. H. Spicer and R. H. Thompson (eds.), pp. 21–64. New York: Interbook.

SSRC Summer Seminar on Acculturation. 1954. Acculturation: An Exploratory Formulation. *American Anthropologist* 56:973–1002.

Staski, E. 1983. Patterns of Alcohol Consumption Among Irish-Americans and Jewish Americans: Contributions from Archaeology. Ph.D. dissertation, Department of Anthropology, University of Arizona.

Staski, E. 1984a. *Archaeological Testing of the Jacque's Bar Site, El Paso, Texas.* Report prepared for the City of El Paso by the Cultural Resources Management Division of New Mexico State University, Las Cruces.

Staski, E. 1984b. *Archaeological Testing of the Cortez Parking Lot Site, El Paso, Texas.* Report prepared for the City of El Paso by the Cultural Resources Management Division of New Mexico State University, Las Cruces.

Staski. E. 1984c. Beneath the Border City, Volume One: Urban Archaeology in Downtown El Paso. *University Museum Occasional Papers*, No. 12, New Mexico State University, Las Cruces.

Staski, E. 1985. Beneath the Border City, Volume Two: The Overseas Chinese in El Paso. *University Museum Occasional Papers*, No. 13, New Mexico State University, Las Cruces.

Staski, E. 1990. Studies of Ethnicity in North American Historical Archaeology. *North American Archaeologist* 11(2):121–145.

Staski, E. and D. Batcho. 1983. *A Preliminary Report on Archaeological Testing of the Cortez Parking Lot Site, Mills Block 3, West Half.* Report prepared for the City of El Paso by the Cultural Resources Management Division, New Mexico State University, Las Cruces.

Wilson, J. W. 1980. *The Declining Significance of Race.* Chicago: University of Chicago Press.

Wobst, H. M. 1977. Stylistic Behavior and Information Exchange. In *For the Director: Research Essays in Honor of James B. Griffin. Anthropological Papers*, No. 61. C. E. Cleland (ed.), pp. 317–342. Ann Arbor: University of Michigan.

Chapter Seven

Mrs. Starr's Profession

Mrs. Starr, an established Baltimore madam, arrived in Washington, DC, in 1858. In 1862, she purchased property at No. 62 Ohio Avenue. One of her daughters, Mrs. Mary Jane Treakle (also known as Mollie Turner), moved from Norfolk, Virginia, to Washington to run the house (J. O. Hall, pers. comm. 1989). The Provost Marshal's 1865 inventory of bawdy houses lists the establishment run by Mollie Turner as a class I house with three inmates (Provost Marshal 1865; Tidwell 1988: 337). Mrs. Starr's daughter Ellen Starr (also known as Ella Turner, Nellie Starr, and Fannie Harrison) was living at No. 62 Ohio Avenue[1] when she gave her statement to the police on 15 April 1865:

> My name is Nellie Starr. My native place is Baltimore, State of Maryland. I have been in Washington City D. C. since a week before Christmas. I am about nineteen or twenty years of age. I am not married. I have known John Wilkes Booth about three years; he was in the habit of visiting the house where I live kept by Miss Eliza Thomas, No. 62 Ohio Avenue in the City of Washington. The house is one of prostitution. I have never heard him speak unfavorable of the President. I heard him speak of the President as being a good man just as other people did. I do not distinctly recollect how he was dressed, when I last saw him; I think he had on dark clothes. I think he wore a slough hat. I do not think it is the one shown me by the district attorney. I know nothing more about the case. I know not with whom he associated with, as I have not been on good terms with him for over a year. The last time I seen Mr. Booth was two weeks ago, at the said house. [signed] Nellie Starr, Ella Starr, Fannie Harrison (National Archives and Records Administration 1865).

The Starr family business was located in the Washington, DC neighborhood known as Hooker's Division. The appellation refers to the district frequented by the

This article was originally published in *Those of Little Note: Gender, Race, and Class in Historical Archaeology*, Elizabeth M. Scott, ed., pp. 149–173, Tucson and London: The University of Arizona Press, ©1994.

men of General Joseph Hooker's division, attractive to Union soldiers and officers during the Civil War because of its saloons and bawdy houses. Although prostitutes lived in the neighborhood from the 1860s until 1914, the neighborhood of the 1860s through 1880s was a working-class neighborhood that included prostitutes among the working women boarding there. During the 1890s, however, the neighborhood be came a red-light district characterized by rows of brothels. Census records, contemporary accounts, and archaeological data document the change in the neighborhood and the changes in the business of prostitution.

At Home in Hooker's Division

The neighborhood historically known as Hooker's Division is within the modern Federal Triangle in Washington, DC—the triangle formed by Fifteenth Street, Pennsylvania Avenue, and Constitution Avenue (Figure 7.1). The neighborhood, then as now, is in the capital city's center, between the White House and the Capitol and north of the Smithsonian Mall. In the mid-19th century, the neighborhood was occupied by households of working-class people, including native-born American blacks and whites as well as German, Irish, and Russian immigrants, among others. Although most households were headed by a male skilled or unskilled worker, several were headed by women. These female heads of household included Caroline Graniger (1367 Ohio Avenue), who kept a grocery, and Frances Johnson (1309 C Street), a 40-year-old, French-born woman who ran a boardinghouse occupied by a laborer, a housekeeper, a printing-office worker, a 7-year-old child, and two prostitutes. Mrs. Johnson, like Mrs. Starr, may have been running a family business: perhaps the 20-year-old prostitute Fanny Johnson was Mrs. Johnson's daughter and the child, Mary Johnson, another daughter or granddaughter. A household at 312 131/2 Street was a brothel, occupied by four African-American prostitutes, all born in Maryland or Virginia. Three were in their early twenties; the head of the household, Florence Hall, was 35 (U.S. Bureau of the Census [USBC] 1870). Working-class households and brothels continued to share the neighborhood in the 1880s: prostitutes were living in brothels and boarding in working-class households with families and boarders working in other trades (USBC 1880). "Prostitute" is one of a limited number of occupations listed for working-class women in this Washington, DC neighborhood.

A review of occupations listed in the census records from 1870 and 1880 shows that the women of the neighborhood were engaged in traditionally female occupations: domestic servant, laundress, cook, housekeeper, seamstress, dressmaker, and nurse. In the mid-19th century, the ideal woman's work was homemaking. However, even for many skilled workers, men's wages alone were inadequate to support a family, so daughters and wives often contributed to the family income. But wages for women's work were even lower and employment options were

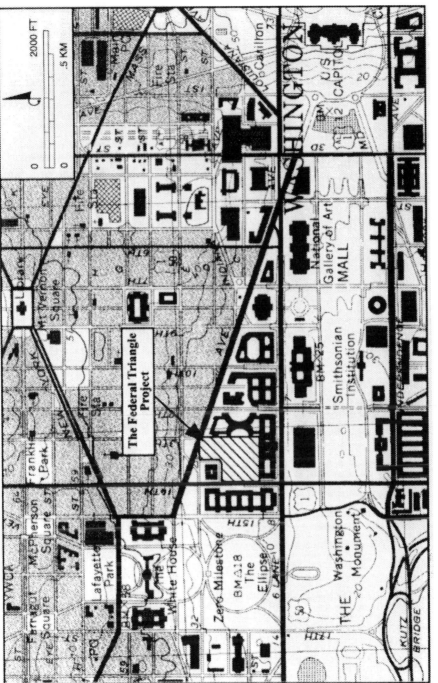

Figure 7.1. Location of the project area in the west end of the Federal Triangle (USGS 1983).

limited. There were few factory jobs in Washington, DC; most employment was in the service sector (Green 1962, 1:356).

The women of Hooker's Division—whether they were wives, heads of household, daughters, or single women—were providing homemaking services for others or working in the clothing trades. Such women's work rarely paid a living wage, much less enough to support dependents. There were two notable exceptions in the neighborhood: Caroline Graniger, a widow, was a grocer, running an inherited family business. The other exception was the prostitutes. Prostitution was the only employment generally available to working-class women that offered a chance to escape poverty. The change in the organization of work from the productive household to wage labor in capitalist businesses (with the male provider and female homemaker) increased women's dependency on men (Stansell 1986:45, 52, 218). The sudden loss of a male wage earner in a family—through death, disability, or desertion—immediately left a working-class family destitute. For a woman on her own with or without dependents, prostitution was one choice among limited, undesirable options (Stansell 1986:177–179, 191).

Prostitution may have been a choice for some working-class young women on their own after leaving the natal household and before marriage (Stansell 1986:185–186). Most prostitutes listed in census records are young women (in their teens and early twenties), and historical sources indicate that some of these young women went on to marry—rather than die horribly within a few years, as reformers argued (Hobson 1990:86–87; Stansell 1986:88; cf. Sanger 1939:453). Young working-class women often worked in wage labor during early adulthood, and prostitution may have been an option selected, particularly by women living away from family. By 1900, most of the households in Hooker's Division were brothels, headed by a female who ran the boardinghouse (the madam) and several women in their teens and early twenties for whom no occupation was listed. Some brothels included servants. Brothels were segregated by race, although some white brothels included black servants. The few family households were occupied by skilled and unskilled workers; most were native born (USBC 1900). The 1910 census shows a similar pattern of occupation (USBC 1910), although some immigrant families had moved in.

The brothels were closed in 1914, when Congress enacted legislation banning houses of prostitution in the District of Columbia (Commissioners of the District of Columbia 1914). Tax records and city directories indicate that some of the buildings housing brothels became vacant; some were reoccupied by working-class residents (Cheek et al. 1991, Appendix I).

Neighborhood, Household Type, and Material Culture

The household types that constitute a neighborhood are useful analytical units in studying the archaeology of urban life. Aggregate data from several deposits representing known household composition and function are more likely to represent the households characteristic of the neighborhood than data from any single documented household (see Cheek and Seifert 1994). In an urban setting where residents move frequently, as in Hooker's Division, correlating an archaeological deposit with a specific household is often difficult. However, where documents indicate that a lot was occupied by the same type of household over a period of time, the household type is the most useful unit of comparison. Different household types (defined by composition and function) can be compared within a period of time and over time. This approach proved successful in the analysis of the archaeological assemblage from Hooker's Division, where the character of the neighborhood and the types of household within it were known but specific residents could not always be correlated with specific deposits.

Examining household types in the context of the neighborhood is appropriate because of the importance of the neighborhood in working-class women's lives. By the middle of the 19th century, urban middle-class families carefully separated the public life of work, the milieu of men, from the private life at home, the domain of women and children (Stansell 1986:41). The public and the private, work and home, were not so clearly divided for working-class women, who spent much of their time out of the home and in the neighborhood.[2] The daily tasks of getting food, fuel, and water consumed much of the working-class homemaker's time, and these necessities were acquired in the neighborhood. Few of the goods needed for the home were produced by the urban household, so women bought goods from street vendors and neighborhood shops. With little ready cash, working-class homemakers made frequent trips and small purchases. Bartering, pawning, and scavenging were also common aspects of the domestic economy of the working poor (Stansell 1986:52). Before the advent of municipal utilities, the work of homemaking included hauling fuel and water (Stansell 1986:46, 49). Although Washington, DC had a city water system by 1863, houses in poorer neighborhoods such as Hooker's Division were still not equipped with plumbing in the 1880s and 1890s, so women and children pumped water from cisterns or carried it home from wells in public squares (Green 1962, 2:42, 45). Even houses with running water often had only one tap and one water closet.

In the crowded conditions of urban neighborhoods, the affairs of everyday life were rarely private, and neighbors involved themselves in each other's concerns, resulting in cooperation or confrontation, depending on the personalities and circumstances (Stansell 1986:56). While some of the men living in the working-class neighborhood probably worked there also, most were employed in workplaces outside the neighborhood. Men, therefore, spent more of their time away from the neighborhood, associating with men involved in the same type of work. Working-class men might be involved in labor associations, but women in wage labor were less likely to belong to such associations, and the working-class homemakers' community was the neighborhood (Stansell 1986:55).

Archaeological investigations in the neighborhood known as Hooker's Division recovered assemblages from two types of households, working-class households and brothels, for two periods, 1870 to 1890 and 1890 to 1920. The two types of households were defined on the basis of household composition as given in census records. Brothel assemblages were from households composed of a female head, resident prostitutes, and household servants. Working-class households included a family group; some also included boarders. While the census records also list households with family groups and boarders (including prostitutes), none of the archaeological deposits was from such a household.

Two time periods are represented by archaeological deposits that can be correlated with specific household types. The earlier period, 1870 to 1890, includes the post–Civil War economic and social dislocations and adjustments and the capital city's response to population growth during the war and the influx of freed slaves. The later period, 1890 to 1920, includes the depression of the 1890s, the recovery and building boom, and the closing of the brothels in 1914 (Green 1962). The year 1890 was selected as the dividing point for two reasons: archaeological deposits could be separated as earlier or later than 1890 on the basis of datable building episodes and artifacts, and, despite the lack of 1890 manuscript census records, other documents (such as Sanborn fire insurance maps from 1888 and 1903 and a newspaper article from the mid-1890s, "Within Sight of the White House" [1895]) indicate that by the early 1890s, the neighborhood had become a red-light district. While working-class women were involved in wage labor in both periods, the later period is marked by the national increase of middle-class women in commercial and industrial employment and the concomitant reformers' concern over the impact of such employment on these young women and on the next generation. Washington, DC was not an industrial city; nevertheless, the development of capitalist business changed the organization of work as the independent prostitute was replaced by the brothel inmate, who worked not for herself or the madam but for the owner of the business (Rosen 1982:70–71; Seifert 1991:88–89; U.S. Senate 1913:28–29).

Prostitution's principal attraction was negotiable compensation, but evidence from Hooker's Division gives little indication that the material conditions of life in brothels were better than those of working-class households during the period from 1870 to 1890. By the turn of the century, however, there are indications that prostitutes enjoyed some of the comforts of life not available to their working-class neighbors.

The archaeological excavations conducted in historic Hooker's Division in 1989 sampled deposits from ten house lots. Census data were collected for a larger sample of lots, including all excavated lots and several neighboring lots near the corner of 131/2 Street and Ohio Avenue (Figures 7.2 and 7.3). Four archaeological assemblages representing household types are analyzed and compared in this paper:

early working-class, early prostitute, late working-class, and late prostitute house-holds. The archaeological data for each household type from each period were aggregated from two or three deposits that had been dated and assigned to a house-hold type on the basis of census data. Combining data from two or more archaeo-logical samples was judged to produce more representative samples for comparison.[3]

To compare artifact assemblages among types of households, artifact pattern analysis developed by Stanley South (1977) was used (Table 7.1).[4] Artifacts were grouped by function, and the relative percentages of the functional groups were compared. In addition, the specific composition of artifact groups was examined, and ceramic indices (using the methods developed by George Miller [1980, 1991] and Susan Henry [1987]) were calculated as a measure of socioeconomic status. The differences between early working-class and early brothel assemblages reflect dif-ferences in household composition and function; the differences between the late working-class and late brothel assemblages also suggest differences in material comforts. The distinctive assemblage of the late brothels reflects an increase in the acquisition of consumer goods, related to changes in the business of prostitution.[5]

Hooker's Division, 1870–90

Kitchen and architecture artifacts make up about 90 percent of both assemblages (Table 7.1). Obvious construction and destruction deposits were excluded from the data base used for this study. Therefore, the higher percentage of the architecture group in the brothel is a reflection not of building activities but of different consumption patterns.

The kitchen group accounts for a higher percentage of the working-class assemblage compared to the brothel, which may reflect the importance of providing sustenance for a family household. While plate and bowl ceramic indices from the assemblages overlap, cup-and-saucer indices for the working-class assemblage are consistently higher (Table 7.2). The higher cup-and-saucer indices for the working-class assemblage may reflect families' display of status through use of more expensive tewares. However, both brothel and working-class indices are relatively low, a reflection of the limited means of working-class people (Cheek et al. 1991:47). Minor differences exist in the relative proportions and composition of the personal and clothing groups. (The only sewing tool is in the working-class assemblage, and the only bead is in the prostitute assem-blage.) Differences in the personal, tobacco, and activities groups' percentages are worth examining, however. Relatively small differences in percentages and composition in these groups may reflect important differences in household consumption patterns.

Although the percentages of the personal group are close, the composition of the group is different. The brothel assemblage includes mirror fragments, slate pencils,

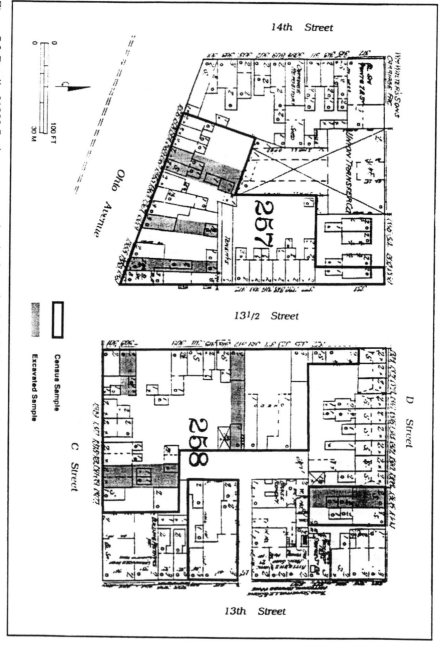

Figure 7.2. Detail of 1888 fire insurance map showing house lots included in excavated and census samples (Sanborn Map Company 1888).

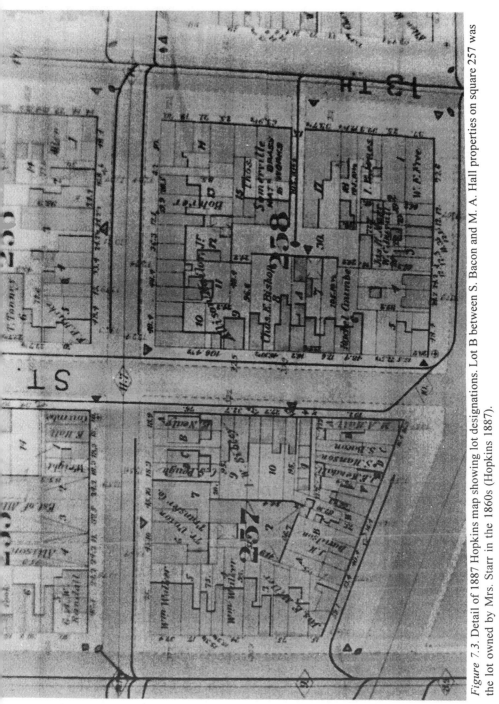

Figure 7.3. Detail of 1887 Hopkins map showing lot designations. Lot B between S. Bacon and M. A. Hall properties on square 257 was the lot owned by Mrs. Starr in the 1860s (Hopkins 1887).

TABLE 7.1
Frequency of Selected Artifact Groups by Household Type and Time Period

Artifact Group[a]	Working Class		Prostitute	
	n[b]	%	n	%
EARLY 1860–1890				
Assemblage total				
(all groups)	3181	99.99	1291	99.99
Architecture	737	23.17	557	43.14
Kitchen	2228	70.04	641	49.65
Furniture	—	—	—	—
Arms	—	—	—	—
Clothing	10	0.31	11	0.85
Personal	22	0.69	7	0.54
Tobacco	24	0.75	39	3.02
Activities	160	5.03	36	2.79
LATE 1890–1920				
Assemblage total				
(all groups)	7699	100.00	10,727	100.00
Architecture	1896	24.63	3403	31.72
Kitchen	5391	70.02	5441	50.72
Furniture	8	0.10	26	0.24
Arms	—	—	2	.02
Clothing	34	0.44	240	2.24
Personal	35	0.45	125	1.17
Tobacco	32	0.42	136	1.27
Activities	303	3.94	1354	12.62

[a] SOURCE: South 1977.

[b] Number of fragments.

TABLE 7.2
Ceramic Indices by Period and Household Type

Period/Household	Cup and Saucer[a]	Plates	Bowls	Mean Index
Early working class	2.15	1.54	1.89	1.80
Early prostitute	1.89	1.72	2.31	1.87
Late working class	1.37	1.52	1.26	1.44
Late prostitute	1.91	1.40	1.44	1.51

[a] Indices for the early-period households are based on Miller (1991); indices for the late-period households are from Henry (1987).

and hair combs. The working-class assemblage includes these types of artifacts as well as jewelry. There is a higher percentage of mirror fragments in the prostitute assemblage but a lower percentage of hair combs. The differences are small, suggesting that the prostitutes' personal effects were not much different from those of working-class women.

The activities group includes toys, tools, hardware, flowerpots, and lamp glass. Over 80 percent of the artifacts in the activities group for both working-class and brothel assemblages is lighting glass. However, there are other interesting differences in the composition of the activities group by household type. The working-class assemblage also includes toys (marbles and a toy dish), hardware, and tools (hammers), probably reflecting children and laborers in residence. The brothel assemblage includes a marble, hardware fragments, and flowerpot sherds.

The tobacco group is represented primarily by pipe stems and bowls. The higher frequency of pipes in the brothel assemblage is probably related to the frequency of visiting men, although the resident prostitutes may have smoked as well (see Cook 1989:224).

Evidence of neighborhood foodways is reflected in the faunal and floral remains recovered during excavation. Pork is well represented, but there are only three elements of beef in the early working-class assemblage. Rabbit, duck, fish, and opossum are also represented. The early prostitute assemblage has a lower frequency of pork bones and four elements of beef. Chicken, pigeon, and fish are also represented. Neither assemblage includes many expensive cuts, such as steaks or roasts (Cheek et al. 1991:53–54). Overall, the two assemblages are similar and are consistent with assemblages recovered from other working-class sites in the East (C. Holt, pers. comm.).

Household composition and related consumer patterns are probably responsible for the differences in the assemblages: family groups and boarders of both sexes and a range of ages acquired more food storage, preparation, and serving vessels, more tools, and more toys. Single women living and working together apparently did not enjoy a lavish lifestyle, but lived much as their neighbors did.

Hooker's Division, 1890–1920

While the material culture of working-class households changed only slightly, changes in the material life of prostitutes at the turn of the century were pronounced. These changes were probably related to increased purchasing power in the brothel households as the business of prostitution became more lucrative. The archaeological assemblage of the late brothel household is distinctly different from the late working-class household.

The relative percentages of architecture and kitchen groups from the early period are essentially the same in the later period (Table 7.1). Mean ceramic indices for both late working-class and brothel assemblages are lower than the indices from the earlier period, and the cup-and-saucer index for the working-class assemblage is lower than the brothel index (Table 7.2). The low mean indices, however, suggest little difference in socioeconomic status: both indices are within the range found for other working-class households in the East (Cheek et al. 1991:46–48, Table 11).

The clothing group percentage for the late working-class assemblage is slightly higher than in the earlier period. The late brothel assemblage evidences a greater increase, however. In both early-period assemblages, 90 percent of the clothing group is buttons. In the later period, a wider variety of artifacts is represented, including other fasteners, beads, shoe parts, and sewing tools (represented in both the working-class and brothel assemblages). The most important difference between the two late assemblages is in the types of buttons: the working-class assemblage is made up of simple white porcelain buttons of the kind used on undergarments and plain clothing. The brothel assemblage, however, also includes fancy black glass buttons, used on dressy outer clothing. Such buttons are probably evidence of prostitutes' "putting on style," the distinctive and flamboyant dress style affected by working-class young women at the turn of the century (Peiss 1986:66). Based on the archaeological data, prostitutes apparently had the income to dress in the style to which working-class young women aspired (Seifert 1991:99, 104).

Through time the personal group percentage increases for the brothel assemblages and decreases slightly for the working-class assemblages. In the later period, the working-class assemblage has more pencils and coins, while the brothel assemblage includes more mirror fragments, jewelry parts, and hair combs, suggesting greater expenditures by the prostitutes on personal adornment. Pharmaceutical and cosmetic bottles are not included in the personal group in the version of artifact pattern analysis used in this study. However, there are some interesting differences in the kinds of such artifacts in each assemblage. The working-class assemblage includes a Fletcher's Castoria bottle and a perfume bottle stopper. The brothel assemblage includes Putnam's White Satin Bouquet, Chesebrough Mfg. Co. Vaseline, Mrs. Winslow's Soothing Syrup, Bromo Seltzer, and Valentine's Meat Juice, which has been identified as a cure for "social diseases" (Herskovitz 1978:16).

The tobacco group percentage declines for both working-class and brothel assemblages in the later period, although the brothel percentage is still higher. The decline in both assemblages may be related to an increase in cigarette smoking (replacing pipe smoking) by the early 20th century (Cook 1989:224; Peiss 1986:99).

A dramatic change is seen in the activities group: the percentage of the group declines in the late working-class as compared to the early working-class assemblage but increases from about 3 percent to 13 percent from the early to late brothel assemblage. The composition of the late assemblages is similar to the composition of the activities group in the earlier period: both include toys (though there are more in the working-class assemblage), and there are more tools and more hardware in the working-class assemblage and more flowerpots in the brothel assemblage. While 80 percent of the late working-class activities group is made up of lighting glass, over 90 percent of the late brothel activities group is lighting glass. The high frequency of lighting glass may be related to the brothel as workplace where most of the workday was after dark (Seifert 1991:101).

Another distinctive aspect of the late brothel assemblage is the high frequency of expensive meat cuts represented in the butchered bones recovered. No beef elements were recovered from the late working-class assemblage, but pork continues to be well represented. Duck and fish are included as in the earlier period, and pigeon is added to the late working-class assemblage. Beef, pork, sheep, rabbit, chicken, duck, turkey, and fish are represented in the late brothel assemblage. While the early brothel, early working-class, and lateworking-class assemblages exhibit frequencies of steaks and roasts within the expected range for households with limited means, the late brothel had startlingly high frequencies of these expensive cuts (C. Holt, pers. comm.). The majority of these bones were from steaks, which are considered individual portions. The high frequency of steak bones suggests eating well and eating alone. The bones may represent individual meals served to clients (see Rosen 1982:94–95) or meals eaten by resident prostitutes (Cheek et al. 1991:55).

The evidence for good food, along with the archaeological evidence for personal adornment, suggests that late-period prostitutes enjoyed greater material comforts than their working-class neighbors. A major inducement to enter the profession (cited by social workers and prostitutes alike) was the high wages and amenities of middle-class life available to prostitutes (Rosen 1982:145–147; Seifert 1991:87). While higher wages were also a factor during the period from 1870 to 1890, practicing prostitution, at least in Hooker's Division, does not appear to have translated into material conditions that were dramatically different from those of their working-class neighbors. Differences in the social climate and business of prostitution may account for the differences observed in the archaeological record of the later period.

Daily Life for the Working Women of Hooker's Division, 1870–1920

Complementary data from historical sources and archaeological excavations provide the basis for a better understanding of life in Hooker's Division during the late 19th century and early 20th century. Census records and historic maps indicate that the 1870–90 neighborhood, which included industrial facilities, commercial establishments, and residences occupied by working-class households and brothels, changed in the early 1890s to a red-light district. Archaeological evidence demonstrates that both working-class households and brothels were households of limited means during the earlier period. Because of low wages for unskilled and semiskilled workers, such as those living in Hooker's Division, families were always struggling to make ends meet. Women in working-class households contributed to the household income by taking in piecework, laundry, and boarders. Adolescents worked in unskilled jobs, contributing most (for boys) or all (for girls) of their income to the household.

Household furnishings were limited, and families moved frequently—often when the rent was due (Stansell 1986:55, 247n). Homemakers were taxed with the physical hardships of cooking, washing, and cleaning for their families and boarders. Daily tasks included hauling water for cooking and laundry and fuel for stoves and lamps. Nearly all clothing was sewn by hand. Working-class households usually included boarders as well as family members. Although boarders provided extra household income, they also meant extra work for the homemaker. Modest consumer purchases were a function of low income. The working-class households of Hooker's Division reflect the limited means of the residents: little was spent on ceramics (mean ceramic indices are low), and few expensive meat cuts were purchased (few steak and roast bones).

Women living in early-period brothels in the neighborhood lived very much like their neighbors in terms of material possessions. In fact, without documentary evidence, the brothels could not have been identified on the basis of archeological evidence: the content of the assemblage is different, but the socioeconomic status the assemblage reflects is essentially working class. Although madams such as Mrs. Starr may have enjoyed the profits of the business, the prostitutes in Hooker's Division in the 1870s and 1880s were apparently women of limited means like their neighbors in working-class households.

The neighborhood changed to a red-light district during the 1890s, and the business of prostitution changed as well. The madam-owned brothels were replaced by capitalist business with nonresident owners, madam-managers, and employee-prostitutes. The material culture of the brothel changed as well. Based on the archaeological evidence, brothel residents enjoyed some material comforts that their working-class neighbors did not. Expensive meat cuts and buttons from fancy clothes suggest that prostitutes ate better and dressed better than their neighbors. The few working-class households remaining in the neighborhood at the turn of the century were households of limited means, and the residents may not have been able to afford to live in a more desirable neighborhood. On the basis of the archaeological evidence alone, the brothels were clearly unusual households: the meat cuts represented suggest expenditures more like middle-class households, but the ceramic indices are comparable to working-class households. With the aid of documentary sources, a sharper picture emerges of life in the best-known red-light district of Washington, DC.

Nineteenth-century prostitution was largely an institution of working-class young women selling sexual services to middle- and upper-class men. Women resorted to prostitution particularly in response to loss of a male wage earner to avoid destitution without seeking charity. Prostitution might be occasional (when need was urgent) or practiced for a period during young adulthood by women living away from family (either by choice or necessity) before marrying. Most prostitutes practiced for a few years, rarely past their mid-twenties. Contemporary reformers argued that this short time was a period of precipitous decline from loss of virtue to utter ruin and death. However, other documents indicate that some women left prostitution and married. Working-class people accepted a flexible definition of virtue, unlike the middle-class policymakers and reformers (see Hobson 1990:106; Rosen 1982:70; Stansell 1986:179–180).

The census data from 1870 and 1880 for Hooker's Division indicate that prostitutes lived in the neighborhood among practitioners of other professions, sometimes in the same houses. The segregation and protection of the brothel was less important than later, when pressure from reformers and police harassment accelerated. While these prostitutes may have been able to earn more than the seamstresses, laundresses, and servants in the neighborhood, there are several factors to consider in understanding the similarity of material culture. Several members of the family were contributing to the income of a working-class household; some of the other women in the neighborhood may also have been practicing occasional prostitution to supplement earnings from sewing or laundry; and all residents of this neighborhood were probably included in the growing class of the working poor whose material possessions were few (see Stansell 1986:46–50).

By the turn of the century, prostitution had changed in organization, like most other trades, from the independent practitioner or small shop (like the family brothel) to a capitalist business (Hobson 1990:103; Rosen 1982:70–71). Increasing pressure from the antiprostitution movement may have made the shelter of the brothel more attractive. The brothels in Hooker's Division were managed by women but were probably owned by businessmen who realized much of the profit (Seifert 1991:89; U.S. Senate 1913:28–29; cf. Shaw 1951:3). Mrs. Starr's family business was replaced by the organization of corporate owners that characterized the profession of George Bernard Shaw's Mrs. Warren.[6] The change in the organization of the profession may have cost practitioners some independence, but it offered greater material comfort for those living in brothels. The archaeological evidence suggests that the prostitutes in Hooker's Division enjoyed a higher standard of living by the turn of the century (and the houses may have served a wealthier clientele).

The results of the archaeological investigations in Hooker's Division demonstrate the utility of the household type as analytical unit and the neighborhood as context. In urban settings where it is not possible to correlate individuals or families with specific archaeological deposits, the household type is an appropriate unit of comparison. The working-class households and brothel households reflect the differences in material culture between households of different composition and function. Understanding the neighborhood is critical to understanding the daily life and social community of working-class women. The privacy and separate sphere of the home cultivated by middle-class women of comfortable means was not the experience of working-class women, who spent as much of their day in the street as in the home, struggling to make ends meet. Such differences in the patterns of everyday life are important to understanding the archaeological record: the use history of consumer goods recovered from middle-class deposits is likely to be simpler than the use history of the same kinds of goods in deposits in working-class neighborhoods. The simple model of purchase, use, and discard is appropriate for the middle-class consumer item. However, the use history of consumer items associated with a working-class household may also include exchange through barter, pawn, and secondhand purchase and use by more than one household before discard and deposition in an archaeological context. Analyzing data by household type (based on aggregate data) within the context of neighborhood provides more reliable results in situations where the acquisition of consumer goods is a complex process.

The historical and archaeological investigations of Hooker's Division have contributed to understanding the material conditions of those whose lives are documented in the census records, city directories, and police records and in the debris cleared from their tables and swept from their floors and thrown on the ash heap. The remains recovered through archaeological excavations reflect economic decisions that were made in the face of limited options by all of the women of Hooker's Division—seamstresses, laundresses, and servants, as well as the ruined girls and fallen women and the practitioners of Mrs. Starr's profession.

Acknowledgments

I am grateful to James O. Hall, who generously shared his information on Civil War Hooker's Division and the careers of Mrs. Starr and her daughters Ellen and Mary Jane. Mr. Hall sent me copies of documents and provided information on Mrs. Starr's purchase of the property at 62 Ohio Avenue; my research in the tax records confirmed her ownership of the property from 1862 to 1868.

Cheryl Holt shared her knowledge of meat consumption patterns in Hooker's Division in contrast to patterns she has observed in other Eastern urban contexts. Elizabeth Scott offered many useful comments on the early draft of this chapter; I am grateful to her also for her willingness to organize and introduce this collection.

The archaeological data on which this chapter is based are from the investigations at the Federal Triangle, which were undertaken in accordance with the National Historic Preservation Act of 1966. The project was sponsored by the Pennsylvania Avenue Development Corporation and conducted by John Milner Associates, Inc., in cooperation with TAMS Consultants, Inc., and in consultation with the District of Columbia Historic Preservation Office and the Advisory Council on Historic Preservation. The graphics used in this paper were prepared by Joe McCarthy and Sarah Ruch; Dana Heck assisted in the data retrieval; and support for the preparation of the manuscript was provided by John Milner Associates, Inc.

NOTES

1. Historical sources provide conflicting information concerning the location of No. 62 Ohio Avenue and the location and address of the house occupied by the younger Ellen Starr. However, most of the information supports the interpretation that No. 62 Ohio Avenue was the second lot from the corner of Ohio Avenue and 131/2 Street in Northwest Washington, DC.

Various records document Mrs. Starr's ownership of lot B, subdivision of lot 1, square 257, in Washington, DC, during the 1860s. Lot 1 of square 257 was subdivided in 1858 by Eugene Schwingerhamer, and lot B was the second lot from the corner of Ohio Avenue and 131/2 Street West (Faehtz and Pratt 1874). Ellen Starr bought lot B on 18 August 1862 (Hall, pers. comm.,

1989). She began paying tax on the improved property in 1862. From 1864 through 1866, taxes were paid by Thomas D. Donn, in trust for Mary Jane Tauch, who may be Mrs. Starr's daughter Mary Jane Treakle. In 1867 and 1868, Ellen Starr is again listed in the tax books as the owner, but she sold the property in 1868. Between 1864 and 1867, Mrs. Starr was also paying taxes on several other properties in the city (District of Columbia Tax Books 1862–69).

The evidence suggests that the address in the provost marshal's list for the house run by Mollie Turner (62 C Street) is incorrect. The entry for Mollie Turner is probably the house at 62 Ohio Avenue, on square 257, facing Ohio Avenue, not C Street. The address may have been mistakenly recorded as C Street because of the way Ohio Avenue, a diagonal street, crosses C Street (which runs east-west) at 131/2 street (which runs north-south). The 1864 city directory lists Mrs. Mary Turner at 62 Ohio Avenue (Boyd 1864). A contemporary newspaper account places the house of Mollie Turner, where Ellen Starr (identified as Ella Turner, Booth's mistress) lived, at the corner of 13th Street and Ohio Avenue (*Evening Star* April 17, 1865, 2). The 1865 city directory includes a street directory that indicates that 62 Ohio Avenue is at the corner of Ohio Avenue and 131/2 Street (Boyd 1865); however, in the 1860s, the corner lot (lot A) may have been vacant, so No. 62 was the house closest to the corner.

The house numbering system in Washington, DC changed after the Civil War. The new address of the house at 62 Ohio Avenue was 1353 Ohio Avenue, N.W.

2. The home as workplace is discussed in another study based on data from Hooker's Division (Seifert 1991). Many working-class women contributed to the household income by taking in piecework and providing services for boarders.

3. Archaeological deposits were dated by using stratigraphic position, type of deposit (such as fill, construction or destruction debris, or midden), and datable artifacts in conjunction with documentary records such as building permits, Baist (1903) and Hopkins (1887) real estate maps, Sanborn (1888, 1903) fire insurance maps, city directories, and general assessments, which document building construction and modifications. Census records and city directories were used to correlate specific, dated deposits with household occupants. The deposits from the lot at 62 Ohio Avenue/1353 Ohio Avenue, which was owned by Mrs. Starr in the 1860s and occupied by Ellen Starr in 1865, were included in the early prostitute assemblage. However, based on datable artifacts, these deposits are probably related to the brothel household listed in the 1880 census (USBC 1880). No deposits that could be clearly associated with the 1865 occupation of the lot were identified.

4. Pattern analysis is designed to identify patterns in the percentages of the artifact groups that reflect patterns in cultural and historical processes (South 1988: 27). The artifact pattern analysis used in this study is based on Garrow's (1982) version, used in his analysis of the archaeological investigations at the Washington, DC Civic Center. This version was selected because it has been used in the analysis of several Washington, DC sites, including Howard Road (Louis Berger and Associates 1985, 1986) and N Street/Quander Place (Cheek et al. 1983). The following functional groups are used in this analysis: architecture, kitchen, furniture, clothing, personal, tobacco, and activities. Artifacts of several materials and types are included in each group. For example, the kitchen group includes ceramic and glass tableware, glass bottles, and metal utensils. The clothing group includes clothing parts as well as sewing tools. The personal group includes coins, keys, mirrors, and jewelry. The activities group includes tools associated with traditionally male activities, such as hammers and hardware, as well as lamp glass, toys, and marbles. Note that in this version

of pattern analysis lighting glass is included with the activities group and pharmaceutical bottles are included with the kitchen group. Artifact pattern analysis is most useful for broad comparisons. Careful analysis of specific artifacts is necessary to evaluate the differences between assemblages. For example, artifacts representing men's work are primarily placed in the activities group, while those reflecting women's work are placed in the kitchen, clothing, personal, and activities groups.

5. Consumer goods refer to the material items purchased for use by the occupants of the household. In the context of late 19th-century Washington, DC, most of the goods consumed in the household were market purchases; an increasing amount of such goods were mass produced. Ceramic tablewares and meat cuts are generally thought to be the most sensitive of the common consumer purchases reflected in the archaeological record (Cheek et al. 1991:5). Selection of housing is a consumer decision, but architectural artifacts are not useful in addressing consumer behavior, although selection of a neighborhood is important in understanding the socioeconomic status of a household (Cheek and Seifert 1994: 3). Since household purchases vary according to several factors, including market access, availability, household income, social status, and ethnicity, analysis of archaeological remains of consumer goods indicates consumer behavior. Evidence from the archaeological investigations in Hooker's Division shed light on differences in consumer behavior among the four household types considered in this paper.

6. Mrs. Warren is partner and managing director of several high-class brothels on the Continent in Shaw's 1894 play about the business of prostitution. During the course of the play, Mrs. Warren's daughter learns of the source of her mother's wealth from her business partner. In response to her daughter's disapproval, Mrs. Warren argues that hers is the only business in which she could accumulate capital; therefore, she chose prostitution—rather than earn nine shillings a day in a mill and die of lead poisoning, as her sister did (Shaw 1951, 66–67, 82–83). In his preface, Shaw describes his objectives in writing the play:

> Mrs. Warren's profession was written in 1894 to draw attention to the truth that prostitution is caused, not by female depravity and male licentiousness, but simply by underpaying, undervaluing, and overworking women so shamefully that the poorest of them are forced to resort to prostitution to keep body and soul together. Indeed, all attractive unpropertied women lose money by being infallibly virtuous or contracting marriages that are not more or less venal. If on the large social scale we get what we call vice instead of what we call virtue it is simply because we are paying more for it. No normal woman would be a professional prostitute if she could better herself by being respectable, nor marry for money if she could afford to marry for love.
>
> Also, I desire to expose the fact that prostitution is not only carried on without organization by individual enterprise in the lodgings of solitary women, each her own mistress as well as every customer's mistress, but organized and exploited as a big international commerce for the profit of capitalists like any other commerce, and very lucrative to great city estates, including Church estates, through the rents of the houses in which it is practiced.

REFERENCES

Baist, G. W. 1903. *Baist's Real Estate Atlas of Surveys of Washington, District of Columbia.* G. W. Baist, Philadelphia. Map on file, Geography and Map Division, Library of Congress, Washington, DC.

Boyd, A. 1864. *Boyd's Directory of Washington and Georgetown.* Boyd's Directory Company, Washington. Washingtoniana Room, Martin Luther King, Jr., Branch, District of Columbia Public Library, Washington, DC.

Boyd, A. 1865. *Boyd's Directory of Washington and Georgetown.* Boyd's Directory Company, Washington. Washingtoniana Room, Martin Luther King, Jr., Branch, District of Columbia Public Library, Washington, DC.

Cheek, C. D., A. Friedlander, C. A. Holt, C. H. LeeDecker, and T. E. Ossim. 1983. *Archaeological Investigations at the National Photographic Interpretation Center Addition, Washington, D.C.,* Navy Yard Annex. Prepared for Soils Systems, Inc., Alexandria, VA.

Cheek, C. D. and D. J. Seifert. 1994. Neighborhoods and Household Types in Nineteenth-Century Washington, D. C.: Fannie Hill and Mary McNamara in Hooker's Division. In *The Historical Archaeology of the Chesapeake,* P. A. Shackel and B. J. Little (eds.), pp. 267–281. Washington, DC: Smithsonian Institution Press.

Cheek, C. D., D. J. Seifert, P. W. O'Bannon, C. A. Holt, B. R. Roulette, Jr., J. Balicki, G. Ceponis, and D. B. Heck. 1991. *Phase II and Phase III Archeological Investigations at the Site of the Proposed International Cultural and Trade Center/Federal Office Building Complex, Federal Triangle, Washington, D.C.* Prepared by John Milner Associates, Inc., West Chester, PA.

Commissioners of the District of Columbia. 1914. *Acts of Congress Affecting the District of Columbia.* Commissioners of the District of Columbia, Washington, DC.

Cook, L. J. 1989. Descriptive Analysis of Tobacco-Related Material from Boott Mill Boardinghouses. In *The Boarding House System as a Way of Life,* M. C. Beaudry and S. A. Mrozowski (eds.), pp. 187–208. Interdisciplinary Investigations of the Boott Mills, Lowell, Massachusetts, 3. Cultural Resources Management Studies, 21. Division of Cultural Resources, Boston.

District of Columbia Tax Books. 1862–69. District of Columbia Tax Books. National Archives and Records Administration, Washington, DC.

Evening Star [Washington]. 1865. 17 April 1865, page 2, col. 2.

Faehtz, E. F. M., and F. W. Pratt. 1874. Real Estate Directory of the City of Washington, D.C. Washington, D.C. Map on file, Geography and Map Division, Library of Congress, Washington, DC.

Garrow, P. H. (ed.). 1982. *Archeological Investigations at the Washington, D. C., Civic Center.* Prepared by Soil Systems, Inc., Marietta, GA.

Green, C. M. 1962. *Washington: A History of the Capital, 1800–1950.* 2 vols. Princeton: Princeton University Press.

Henry, S. L. 1987. Factors Influencing Consumer Behavior in Turn-of-the-Century Phoenix, Arizona. In *Consumer Choice in Historical Archaeology*, S. M. Spencer-Wood (ed.), pp. 359–382. New York: Plenum Press.

Herskovitz, R. M. 1978. *Fort Bowie Material Culture*. Anthropological Papers of the University of Arizona, 31. Tucson: University of Arizona Press.

Hobson, B. M. 1990. *Uneasy Virtue: The Politics of Prostitution and the American Reform Tradition*. Reprint, with new preface. Chicago: University of Chicago Press.

Hopkins, G. M. 1887. *A Complete Set of Surveys and Plats of Properties in the City of Washington, District of Columbia*. G. M. Hopkins, Philadelphia. Map on file, Martin Luther King Memorial Library, Washington, DC.

Louis Berger and Associates, Inc. 1985. *Archaeological, Architectural, and Historical Investigations at the Howard Road Historic District, Washington, D.C.* Vol. 2, Technical Appendices. Prepared by the Cultural Resources Group, Louis Berger and Associates, Inc., East Orange, NJ.

Louis Berger and Associates, Inc. 1986. *Archaeological, Architectural, and Historical Investigations at the Howard Road Historic District, Washington, D.C.* Vol. I, Final Report. Prepared by the Cultural Resources Group, Louis Berger and Associates, Inc., East Orange, NJ.

Miller, G. L. 1980. Classification and Economic Scaling in Historical Archaeology. *Historical Archaeology* 14:1–40.

Miller, G. L. 1991. A Revised Set of CC Index Values for Classification and Economic Scaling of English Ceramics from 1787 to 1880. *Historical Archaeology* 25(1):1–25.

National Archives and Records Administration. 1865. Deposition of Nellie Starr, United States vs. J. Wilkes Booth, Preliminary Examination. Investigation and Trial Papers Relating to the Assassination of President Lincoln, M-599, reel 6, frame 0258. National Archives and Records Administration, Washington, DC.

Peiss, K. 1986. *Cheap Amusements: Working Women and Leisure in Turn-of-the-Century New York*. Philadelphia: Temple University Press.

Provost Marshal. 1865. List of Bawdy Houses in Washington, D.C. Provost Marshal's Department of Washington, 22nd Army Corps, 1864–1865. Vol. 289, RG 393. National Archives and Records Administration, Washington, DC.

Rosen, R. 1982. *The Lost Sisterhood: Prostitution in America, 1900–1918*. Baltimore: Johns Hopkins University Press.

Sanborn Map Company 1888. *Fire Insurance Map of Washington, D.C.* Sanborn Map Company, New York. Map on file, Geography and Map Division, Library of Congress, Washington, DC.

Sanborn Map Company. 1903. *Fire Insurance Map of Washington, D.C.* Sanborn Map Company, New York. Map on file, Geography and Map Division, Library of Congress, Washington, DC.

Sanger, W. W. 1939. *The History of Prostitution, Its Extent, Causes, and Effects Throughout the World*. Reprint of 1858 edition. New York: Eugenics Publishing Company.

Seifert, D. J. 1991. Within Sight of the White House: The Archaeology of Working Women. *Historical Archaeology* 25(4):82–108.

Shaw, G. 1951. Mrs.Warren's Profession. In *Seven Plays by Bernard Shaw*, pp. 1–122. Originally published 1898. New York: Dodd, Mead.

South, S. 1977. *Method and Theory in Historical Archeology.* New York: Academic Press.

South, S. 1988. Whither Pattern. *Historical Archaeology* 22(1):25–28.

Stansell, C. 1986. *City of Women: Sex and Class in New York, 1789–1860.* New York: Alfred A. Knopf.

Tidwell, W. A. 1988. *Come Retribution: The Confederate Secret Service and the Assassination of Lincoln.* Jackson: University Press of Mississippi.

United States Bureau of the Census (USBC). 1870. Manuscript Population Census of the United States, 1870. Government Printing Office, Washington. National Archives and Records Administration, Washington, DC.

United States Bureau of the Census (USBC). 1880. Manuscript Population Census of the United States, 1880. Government Printing Office, Washington. Microfilm copy on file, National Archives and Records Administration, Washington, DC.

United States Bureau of the Census (USBC). 1900. Manuscript Population Census of the United States, 1900. Government Printing Office, Washington. Microfilm copy on file, National Archives and Records Administration, Washington, DC.

United States Bureau of the Census (USBC). 1910. Manuscript Population Census of the United States, 1910. Government Printing Office, Washington. Microfilm copy on file, National Archives and Records Administration, Washington, DC.

United States Geological Survey (USGS). 1983. Washington, District of Columbia-Maryland-Virginia, Quadrangle Map. 7.5 minute series. U. S. Geological Survey, Reston, VA.

U.S. Senate. 1913. *Abatement of Houses of Ill Fame: Hearings Before a Subcommittee of the Committee of the District of Columbia, United States Senate 62nd Congress, Third Session on S. 5861.* Washington, DC: U.S. Government Printing Office.

Weiner, L. Y. 1985. *From Working Girl to Working Mother: The Female Labor Force in the United States, 1820–1980.* Chapel Hill: University of North Carolina Press.

Within Sight of the White House [1895]. Newspaper clipping on file, Geography and Map Division, Library of Congress, Washington, DC.

PART III

Historic Artifacts:
A Focus on Ceramics

Historical archaeologists, like all archaeologists, excavate a broad variety of artifacts in the course of their fieldwork. In a technical sense, an artifact is anything that is made or modified by conscious human action. Historical archaeologists probably excavate a greater variety of artifacts than prehistorians because of the rise of large-scale industrialism and mass consumption in the post-Columbian world. Just thumbing quickly through an old Sears catalog will give you some idea of the vast variety of items available during the historic period.

Historical archaeologists study glass bottles, iron nails, clay smoking pipes, and a plethora of other items, many of which you will read about in this book. Within this vast collection of physical things, ceramics are always some of the most popular. There are many reasons for the historical archaeologists' interest in ceramics. Not only do post-Columbian ceramics generally preserve well in many kinds of soil, they can often be dated fairly tightly. The companies that produced them often kept accurate records of their styles and patterns. In addition, many of the ways of manufacturing ceramics were technological breakthroughs that have been well documented. Historical archaeologists rely on these technological advancements as well as on the record books of potteries to help date ceramics. They also use sophisticated mathematical methods designed to yield a mean date of manufacture for ceramic collections. At the same time, historical archaeologists know that ceramics carry powerful messages about the people who bought them for their dinner tables. They wonder why people in the past selected certain patterns, colors, and styles of dishes over others. Was it because of cost or because of their ethnic affiliation or professional attitudes? Or, was there some complex combination of social, economic, and even ideological factors that could explain ceramic selection?

Today's historical archaeologists do not always agree about the reasons behind ceramic purchasing habits, and much exciting research is still under way. From the growing literature on historic-period ceramics, I have compiled just four studies. These articles do not cover all the lines of investigation currently being pursued, but they will give you a good idea of the ways in which historical archaeologists approach the study of an important class of artifact. By extension, these articles can be used as a guide to understand the approaches historical archaeologists use to make sense of all artifacts.

In the first chapter in this section, Sarah Peabody Turnbaugh, an archaeologist at the Museum of Primitive Culture in Rhode Island, examines a class of ceramics that are poorly represented in historical records: 17th- and 18th-century redwares. Faced with a lack of supporting documentation, Turnbaugh falls back on the time-honored type-variety method pioneered by prehistoric archaeologists. Her article is instructive because it demonstrates a good way in which to describe and to analyze a collection of artifacts that are otherwise virtually undocumented. Her use of the type-variety method also shows how historical archaeologists can adopt methods from prehistoric archaeology when they are needed. Turnbaugh uses the type-variety method as a tool for helping her to interpret the redwares found at the Salem Village Parsonage site, in Danvers, Massachusetts, the birthplace of the infamous witchcraft hysteria of the 1690s. In doing this, she hints at the broader use of ceramics in the archaeological interpretation of past society. She shows, first, that the people at the Parsonage site obtained their redware vessels, not from England, but from local potters, and second, that the ministers who once lived at the site were quite well off financially.

The relationship between economic position and ceramic purchase is explored fully by Susan L. Henry in the next chapter. Studying archaeological deposits in Phoenix, Arizona, Henry, now with the National Park Service in Washington, DC, first investigates the nature of consumer behavior in general and then examines it closely with deposits dating from the late 19th to the early 20th centuries. In the best tradition of historical archaeology, she combines archaeological and historical sources, and uses an economic scaling technique invented by archaeologist George Miller to study ceramics and the remains of butchered food bone. Her investigation reveals that consumer behavior is more than just a mirror reflection of socio-economic status. Instead, factors such as the fluctuation in a household's economic condition, the availability of goods in the market place, the durability of a particular product, and several other factors influence why people buy the things they do.

In the next chapter we travel from turn-of-the-century Phoenix back in time to the slave plantations of colonial South Carolina. Leland Ferguson, from the University of South Carolina, examines an unglazed ceramic called colono ware pottery. Archaeologists across much of the American South and the Caribbean have found colono ware for years in both urban and rural settings. Though they first mis-identified these sherds as the sole product of Native American potters, they now consider them illustrative of a pottery tradition that combines Native American and West African elements. Ferguson describes the pottery as representing an unconscious form of resistance to the harsh plantation system. When compared to the glazed ceramics studied by Henry, colono wares show no evidence of representing social inequality. Vessel shape and decoration alone do not appear to have carried messages about social hierarchies that may have existed among slaves. On the contrary, the homogeneity of the colono wares appears to portray the social uniformity of most New World slaves. Ferguson sees in the pottery a message of unity, a togetherness that stood in stark contrast to the social hierarchy that structured antebellum plantation society.

In the final chapter in this section, archaeologists Mary C. Beaudry, from Boston University, and Lauren J. Cook and Stephen A. Mrozowski, examine ceramics (and glass bottles) as part of a discourse carried on by members of different social classes. They see artifacts as texts that carry unique, symbolic messages about the discourse. These messages are typically not the same ones that are reported in historical documents. The historical silence that surrounds the discourse makes the approach presented in this chapter assume monumental importance because it opens a way for historical archaeologists to examine human relations that are otherwise lost forever. To show the strength of their approach, Beaudry and her colleagues focus on the archaeological deposits in the backlots of a tenement and a boarding house associated with the 19th- and 20th-century Boott Mills, in Lowell, Massachusetts. The corporate executives who owned the mill worked unceasingly to control both the work and the leisure hours of their labor force through a system of unbending corporate paternalism. At the same time, the workers attempted to control as much of their daily lives as possible. For Beaudry, Cook, and Mrozowski, the artifacts found at the Boott Mills worker's quarters are symbols of the discourse between workers and owners. As a result, the artifacts are not perceived as passive products of consumer behavior but as potent instruments of symbolic action.

Taken together, the four studies in this section illustrate the breadth of the approaches historical archaeologists can use when they attempt to make sense of the artifacts they excavate. In some cases, they have recourse to abundant historical records and the knowledge they contain. In other cases, they work almost like prehistorians in total absence of supporting documentation. In both cases, they forge new paths through the past, creating knowledge as they go. As historical archaeologists follow the approaches outlined here, and a great many others, they will make exciting new discoveries about the relationships between historic artifacts and the men and women who made, purchased, and used them.

Chapter Eight

17th and 18th Century Lead-Glazed Redwares in the Massachusetts Bay Colony

Historical archaeologists working with ceramic assemblages frequently are blessed with good historical documentation of artifact types and their periods of manufacture. Yet, despite the comprehensive information so often available, occasionally a topic of research is only sparsely documented. Even ceramics—with the wealth of information provided by bills of lading, probate inventories, and other types of primary documentation, as well as ceramic encyclopedias and descriptive and interpretive studies—have their poorly described class, the plain earthenwares.

Coarse earthenwares of both European and domestic origins proliferate on many 17th- and 18th-century household sites in New England. In the Massachusetts Bay Colony, this artifact class often comprises more than 85 percent of the total ceramic assemblage for a 17th- or 18th-century site (cf. Deetz 1973:Fig. 1; Robbins 1969; Turnbaugh 1977:Fig. 8). At the Salem Village Parsonage site (1681–1784) in Danvers, Massachusetts, where the witchcraft delusion of 1692 began, for example, wheel-thrown plain earthenwares comprise 89.6 percent of the total ceramic assemblage (Turnbaugh 1976:68). Only 4 percent of these wares (i.e., Class I, Types B–D: lead plus tin-glazed earthenware, tin-glazed earthenware, and dotted and combed slipwares) could be identified with the aid of historical documentation or the traditional classificatory approaches of historical archaeology. The remaining 85.6 percent could be identified only as one general type of plain earthenware, lead-glazed redwares (Class I, Type A), since little specific information as to these sherds' origins, their ages, or their periods of manufacture could be gleaned from existing primary and secondary historical records.

This article was originally published in *Historical Archaeology* (1983) 17(1):3–17.

This substantial body of unidentified redware material promised to reveal a lot about this early household, its occupants, and the region, if only the information it represented could be described and interpreted. This dilemma eventually led to a partial solution. First, a system was devised for classifying the Salem Village Parsonage site's total ceramic assemblage, including the redwares (Turnbaugh 1976:43–73). As a result of using this approach, 100 percent of the Parsonage site's redwares could be classified. 44.7 percent of the lead-glazed redwares were badly broken and could be classified only into "groups." But 55.3 percent of the redwares, or almost half of the Salem Village Parsonage site's total ceramic assemblage, could be more specifically described, thus increasing the data available for precise interpretation of the site.

Second, the significance of the variation inherent in this redware subassemblage needed to be identified and interpreted. In the absence of sufficient primary historical documentation, this need was met archaeologically with determination of probable vessel forms and functions and with intrasite and intersite analyses of both 17th- and 18th-century Bay Colony domestic sites and 10 Massachusetts Bay Colony potters' kilns and waster dumps. Quantitative analysis of the ceramic types, forms, and functions within this single site's assemblage shed light on intrasite dynamics of ceramic continuity and change through time. Comparison of ceramic analyses between contemporary Bay Colony domestic sites as well as between kiln assemblages constituted the spatial, intersite analytical dimension (cf. Turnbaugh 1976, 1977:201–213). Once the domestic sites' and kilns' assemblages had been considered, it was then possible to interpret patterning in the archaeological record by comparing these data with the Salem Village Parsonage site's redware data.

Since this approach should have more general application, the classification of redwares will be presented below, as will some of the interpretations made on the basis of using this method. It should soon become evident that historical archaeologists' interpretations can only benefit by including precise considerations of redwares when analyzing ceramic assemblages. The method provided below should help to make more precise description and interpretation possible.

Classification of Redwares

Most redware types that appear in colonial assemblages are not historically documented. Perhaps these lead-glazed wares are only sparsely referenced because domestically produced redware, in particular, was a comparatively inexpensive commodity. As George Corwin's Essex County shop-probate inventory for 1684 attests (cf. Watkins 1950:14), individual vessels sold for only a few pence. These vessels tended to have shorter life spans than other wares, due to more frequent and harder usage in dairy/kitchen/food preparation categories, relative inexpensiveness, and lower firing temperatures (Brose 1968; David 1972; Foster 1960; Turnbaugh

1977:215). For these reasons, redware types and forms are seldom as specifically itemized in probate inventories or bills of lading as are other categories of material goods that were in use.

Various deductive approaches that attempt to identify redware types by using the available historical documentation have not yet provided a consistent, thorough, and objective means of classifying lead-glazed redware types and varieties that may be found at any given site. Some redware varieties, such as "mottled ware," may be identified in this way, but most redware sherds continue to be ignored, for lack of an equivalent descriptive label. Instead, a useful solution to the classificatory problem may be found with an inductive approach more usually associated with prehistoric archaeology, i.e., the combined use of type and attribute analysis (Rouse 1960; Wright 1967) and the type-variety method (Gifford 1960; Phillips 1958; Wheat, Gifford, and Wasley 1958).

The type-variety method was initially presented by Wheat, Gifford, and Wasley (1958) and successfully applied by Phillips (1958). The advantages of this technique are that it is inductive, and its use can be very precise. The type-variety method encourages consistent analysis of *all* types within one assemblage. In addition, the typology can be adapted and expanded simply by adding new classes, types, and varieties as the data base increases and new categories are needed. The approach is consistent, when properly applied, and may be used for any number of sites that may represent a variety of contexts and ecosystems (e.g., Brain 1972; Beaudry et al. 1980; Fairbanks 1962; Marwitt 1967; Sabloff and Smith 1969; Smith, Willey, and Gifford 1960; Stone 1974; Willey et al. 1980).

The theoretical justification for using typological classification in historical archaeological inquiries, as well as its complementarity to crucial considerations of vessel style, form, and function, is treated more fully elsewhere (Turnbaugh 1976:43–73), but will be discussed briefly here. A detailed, descriptive classificatory system for lead-glazed red earthenwares that is both consistent and empirical has been absent in considerations of 17th- and 18th-century redwares. If historical archaeologists had the luxury of working with assemblages of whole redware vessels, then a fuller consideration of technology, as well as details of form and function, would be possible. But in the absence of such ideal assemblages, the Type-Variety Approach, described subsequently, permits consideration of a previously ignored set of archaeological data. The Type-Variety Approach facilitates the precise definition of significant technological attributes comprising each type and variety within the lead-glazed redware set. It also establishes a common methodological basis for subsequent formal and functional considerations and intersite comparisons and regional studies.

As any names for specific redware varieties are later determined by using historical records, the typological units of this Type-Variety Approach may be integrated with the historically named varieties that are found in classic historical archaeological treatments (e.g., Cotter 1968; Deetz 1973; Noël Hume 1970; South 1972, 1977). In the meantime, descriptive nomenclature, based on Munsell designations for glaze color plus notation of decorative technique(s), is recommended in a later section of this paper to simplify terminology and provide the greatest possible usefulness for intersite comparisons.

The classification system used in the present study isolates *cognitive types* which are formed when purely descriptive or *morphological types* are ordered to produce groupings corresponding to mental templates (Thomas 1974:11–14). Historical documentation of culturally important attributes such as mottled black glaze or kaolin slip decoration, when combined with Type-Variety Approach data and with reconstructions of probable vessel forms and functions, has made it possible to define probable cognitive types for these colonial redwares.

The five taxonomic categories used in this redware classification are class, type, variety, subvariety, and group (Turnbaugh 1976:47–49). Divisions within each category are defined by using mutually exclusive attributes or combinations of attributes (see Table 8.1).

TABLE 8.1

Type-Variety Approach to Bay Colony Redware Classification

CLASS—descriptive nomenclature; sample size (*n*); general paste color (e.g., red, etc.); paste hardness (Moh scale); technique of manufacture (wheel-thrown, molded, etc.)

TYPE—sample size (*n*); specific paste color (Munsell designation and descriptive nomenclature); paste texture and inclusions; type of glaze (lead, tin, salt, etc.)

VARIETY—sample size (*n*); glaze color (Munsell designation and descriptive nomenclature); glaze application (none, inside only, outside only, both sides, etc.); decoration (slip, tooling, etc.)

SUBVARIETY—wares that can be identified archaeologically and historically as made in the manner of a specific potter and that share consistent attributes for the appropriate class-type-variety sequence to which they belong; sample size (*n*)

GROUP—sample size (*n*); paste, glaze, and decoration characteristics (see above) when identifiable.

In addition to method of manufacture (i.e., wheel-thrown, molded, etc.) and general paste color (e.g., red), body permeability and degree of vitrification as determined by hardness of paste defines each general "class" of ware. Hardness of red earthenware is Moh 3–5. Only one ceramic class, wheel-thrown red earthenware, is discussed here. Other classes of ceramics that were excavated at the Salem Village Parsonage site included: molded red earthenware, wheel-thrown improved earthenware (i.e., creamware and pearlware), wheel-thrown stoneware, molded stoneware, wheel-thrown vitreous china, and wheel-thrown porcelain. These classes have been treated elsewhere (Turnbaugh 1976:54–73).

More specific attributes associated with paste composition and surface finish of each "class" include such qualities as paste color, texture and inclusions and glaze composition. These attributes have been used to define each "type." Paste color has been described by using the Munsell Color Charts and the associated descriptive definitions of each color's hue, value, and chroma (Munsell 1942, 1949). Paste color was always determined for clean, weathered breaks on dry specimens to ensure analytical consistency. General glaze composition may be described as lead, salt, tin, etc.

Significant differences in variation within a "type" are distinguished in the more specific category "variety." Each "variety" may be defined by seemingly purposeful, rather than accidental or unintentional, variation in glaze color or application and by the presence or absence of slip, tooling, or other ornamentation.

The "subvariety" is a special category that, as used for these redwares, has been reserved for those sherds that can be assigned to a particular provenience or manufacturer, such as the potter James Kettle of Salem Village. This category relies upon specific attributes *plus* historical documentation (i.e., both documentary and kiln assemblages) to identify subvarieties within redware varieties.

"Group" is essentially a residual category for all small, broken, or badly weathered fragments of indeterminable type that demonstrate consistency within the range of color and/or form of a particular class (cf. Sabloff and Smith 1969). In the Type-Variety Approach, a "group" falls between a "type" and a "variety." A sherd in which breakage or weathering has hampered the determination of the exact nature of glaze application or decoration is classified into a "group" rather than a "variety." In the Salem Village Parsonage site assemblage, for example, lead-glazed red earthenware's Group B (cf. Turnbaugh 1976:53) is comprised of 942 sherds with clear yellow-red glaze color identical to that of Variety 1 (see Table 8.2). In Variety 1, the glaze is applied on the sherd's inner surface only, and the sherd is not decorated in any way. But with sherds in Group B, no determination can be made as to whether glaze is applied on only one or on both surfaces and whether the sherds originally had been undecorated, slip decorated, and/or tooled. Since these sherds could not be positively placed into Variety 1, but might actually belong with one of the similar varieties 5, 6, 7, 8, 9, 13, 17, 20, or 24 (see Table 8.2), they are placed in Group B.

The value of including the "group" category in analysis is two-fold. First, on the theoretical level, its consideration maintains the consistency of the Type-Variety Approach by ensuring treatment of each and every sherd, despite condition. Second, on the methodological level, the inclusion of "groups" is useful at the analytical level of sherd counts. At the Parsonage site, a consideration of "groups" in addition to "types" and "varieties" has permitted treatment of the total percentage of lead-glazed earthenware sherds present in the ceramic assemblage, thus significantly affecting final sherd counts and percentages derived for this assemblage. In the

TABLE 8.2

Application of the Type-Variety Approach to Redwares
from the Salem Village Parsonage Site
Total Ceramic Assemblage: *n = 5981*

Variety	*n*	Glaze Color	Glaze Application	Decoration
1	797	2.5YR3/6 to 5YR4/8–5/8 to 7.5YR5/6–5/8 (dark red to yellow red to strong yellow brown)	inside only	none
2	41	2.5Y5/4–4/4 to 5Y7/6–5/6 (olive brown to olive yellow)	inside only	none
3	80	5YR2/1–2/2 to 7.5YR 2/0–2/1 (black to very dark reddish gray)	inside only	none
4	14	10YR5/1–3/1 (reddish gray to dark reddish brown)	inside only	none
5	151	Same as variety 1	inside only	slip (kaolin)
6	6	Same as variety 1	inside only	tooling
7	11	Same as variety 1	inside only	slip and tooling
8	3	Same as variety 1	outside only	none
9	2	Same as variety 1	outside only	slip
10	4	Same as variety 3	outside only	none
11	3	2.5YR4/6–2/0 (average 3/4–2/2) (mottled—red to dark reddish brown to dusky red to black)	outside only	none
12	34	Same as variety 4	outside only	none
13	581	Same as variety 1	both sides	none
14	95	Same as variety 2	both sides	none
15	267	Same as variety 3	both sides	none
16	50	Same as variety 4	both sides	none
17	291	Same as variety 1	both sides	slip
18	33	2.5Y4/4–5/4 (olive brown to light olive brown)	both sides	slip
19	22	Same as variety 3	both sides	slip
20	66	Same as variety 1	both sides	tooling
21	12	Same as variety 2	both sides	tooling
22	52	Same as variety 3	both sides	tooling
23	15	1OYR3/1–3/2 (very dark gray to very dark grayish brown)	both sides	tooling

TABLE 8.2 continued

24	7	Same as variety 1	both sides	slip and tooling
25	4	Same as variety 3	both sides	slip and tooling
26	74	outer=2.5/5YR2/2– 2/0; inner=2.5/10YR 4/4 (black outer, clear inner)	both sides	none
27	87	Same as variety 11	both sides	none
28	3	Same as variety 26	both sides	tooling
29	10	Same as variety 11	both sides	tooling
30	16	2.5Y4/6–7/6 (average 5/6–6/6) (light olive brown to yellow)	both sides	sgraffito (variety of slip and tooling)
31	4	10GY5/4–4/4 (yellowish green)	inside only	all-over slip outside (2.5Y9/3; (yellowish white)

SUBTOTAL	2835 sherds
PLUS	2286 sherds in Groups A–F (see Turnbaugh 1976:53)
TOTAL	5121 Type A sherds

Class I—Red earthenware; n = 5360; Moh 3–5; wheel-thrown

Type A—n = 5121; paste = Munsell 2.5YR5/4–6/4 to 5YR6/8–7/8, reddish brown to reddish yellow; lead-glaze

present treatment, "group" data generally are not useful in finer formal and functional analyses of sherds.

When the Type-Variety Approach was applied to the ceramic assemblage of the Salem Village Parsonage site, 2835 of the 5121 wheel-thrown, lead-glazed redware sherds could be classified into 31 varieties. The remaining 2286 redware sherds were classified into six groups (Turnbaugh 1976:53) that will receive little further consideration here. The 31 varieties and their characteristics are of primary interest and are listed in Table 8.2. These varieties of Type A redware (n = 2835) comprised almost 50 percent of the total ceramic assemblage. Without using the Type-Variety Approach, these sherds could not have been considered in subsequent analysis and interpretation of the assemblage.

Forms and Functions of Redwares

Despite the fragmented condition of much of the Salem Village Parsonage site's ceramic assemblage, it has been possible to reconstruct the probable forms of the vessels to which many of the sherds belonged. The Type-Variety Approach was first used to order the ceramic data. Then, consideration of criteria such as vessel circumference, body wall thickness, construction of bases and rims, base and rim diameters, body composition and surface finish, and the restricted or unrestricted angle of vessel walls facilitated this analysis (cf. Turnbaugh 1977:194–201). For fragmented vessels and sherds in the Parsonage site assemblage, consideration of particular attributes such as body wall thickness and rim and base diameter was especially helpful. The forms of more than 21 percent of all of the ceramic sherds, including 15 percent (n = 763) of the lead-glazed redware sherds, could be determined in this way. The ranges of several attributes for red earthenware forms are presented in Table 8.3; the entire assemblage has been treated elsewhere (Turnbaugh 1977:194–201).

TABLE 8.3

*Attributes of Redware Forms Represented in the
Salem Village Parsonage Site Assemblage*

Redware Form	No.	%	Body Wall Thickness (mm)	Diameter (base) (cm)
Pots	143	18.9	8–15	19–21
Pans	92	12.0	7–8	24–28
Strainers	2	0.25	5	?
Jars	4	0.5	8	12–14
Jugs/Pitchers	58	7.6	6	12
Platters/Plates	10	1.25	4–8	?
Bowls/Chamberpots[a]	116	15.2	4–6	8–12
Mugs[a]	322	42.3	3–6	7–10
Teapots	16	2.0	4–6	?
TOTAL	763	100.0		

[a] Interpolated vessel circumference is a major distinguishing attribute between bowls and mugs; bowls = 34.6–50.3 cm, mugs = 22–33.0 cm.

These attributes were determined through precise sherd measurements and interpolations and through subsequent comparison with vessel attributes of Bay Colony potters' archaeological kiln specimens and historical reconstructions of typical redware forms (cf. Turnbaugh 1977:Fig. 11; Watkins 1950). When combined with the Type-Variety Approach, these attributes aided the delineation of "cognitive" types based on the morphology of the empirical data.

This consideration of attributes of form necessarily precedes identification of probable vessel styles and analyses of their functions and their temporal and spatial significance. The relations between vessel form and function have been detailed elsewhere (Turnbaugh 1977: 197–203). In sum, the premise that form implies cultural function has been adopted. Documentary and archaeological data have been integrated to establish the probable general cultural functions of the ceramic forms represented in the Parsonage site's assemblage. Inferences pertaining to function have been restricted to the general use of a vessel, such as food storage/preparation and social and hygienic functions. This functional analysis for redwares from the Salem Village Parsonage site is presented in Table 8.4; most forms functioned in contexts of food preparation and dining.

TABLE **8.4**

Functional Analysis of Parsonage Site Redware Forms

Function	Redware Form	No.	Category Total	%
Food Storage/	Pots	143		
Preparation	Pans	92		
	Strainers	2		
	Jars	4		
			241	31.6
Serving/	Jugs/Pitchers	58		
Dining	Platters/Plates	10		
	Bowls	5		
	Bowls/Chamberpots	96		
	Mugs	322		
			491	64.3
Decorative	Figurines	0		
			0	0.0
Social	Teapots	16		
	Teabowls/Saucers	0		
			16	2.1
Hygienic	Chamberpots	15		
	Ointment jars	0		
			15	2.0
TOTAL			763	100.0

Interpretation of Bay Colony Redwares

After the types, forms, and functions of redwares from the Parsonage site had been described, some way of delineating significant patterning and interpreting the inherent meaning of these redwares had to be found. The use of probate inventories, newspaper ads, bills of lading, and other appropriate documentary sources had been helpful for analyzing vessel forms and dynamics of ceramic change through time and variation over space (cf. Turnbaugh 1976, 1977), but this approach proved to be inadequate. However, redware assemblages excavated from a number of domestic potters' kilns and waster dumps were available for study (L. Watkins, pers. comm.). Assemblages of data from ten 17th–18th-century Massachusetts Bay Colony potters were examined (Turnbaugh 1977:189–193) in order to define the range of redware varieties produced in Essex County and the Bay Colony and to establish the manufacture periods for as many of these varieties as was possible. This approach also led to the definition of several European-derived, locally produced redware traditions.

This analytical method, which is summarized below, facilitated identification of subvarieties of redwares—subvarieties that were made in the manner of a specific, identifiable domestic potter (Turnbaugh 1976:61–64). About one-fourth of the sherds (*n* = 646) in the Salem Village Parsonage site's redware subassemblage (*n* = 2815) could be classified into these subvarieties. And this 23 percent represents only the minimal number of sherds that most probably were made in the manner of a local potter; some locally produced redwares undoubtedly went unidentified, so the real percentage present in this assemblage may be substantially higher. Table 8.5 lists the names, locations, and dates of operation of the potteries being considered here. Specific description of sherds from these potters' kilns is available elsewhere (Turnbaugh 1977:189–193).

TABLE 8.5

Late 17th- and 18th-Century Bay Colony Potters

(Kiln Sherds Described in Turnbaugh 1977:189–193)

Name	Location	Dates of Operation
William Vinson	Gloucester, MA	1649–1690
James Kettle	Danvers, MA	ca. 1687–1709/10
Joseph Gardner	East Gloucester, MA	1693–1749
Joseph Bayley	Rowley, MA	1722–1735
Daniel Bayley (early)	Gloucester, MA	1749–1753
Daniel Bayley (later)	Newburyport, MA	1763–1799
William Southwick	Peabody, MA	late 18th c.
Joseph Osborn	Danvers, MA	ca. 1725–1780
John Henry Benner	Abington, MA	1765–1795
Clark Purinton	Somerset, MA	1781–1817

Approximately 175 potters are known to have lived and worked in Massachusetts between 1650 and 1770 (Watkins 1950:253). Judging from the wealth of archaeological evidence, the Bay Colony redware tradition appears to have been strong and was at least as, and usually more, highly developed as were other early domestic pottery-manufacturing centers on the eastern seaboard (cf. Barber 1893; Hudson and Watkins 1957; Jelks 1958; Kindig 1935; Spargo 1974). The varied forms and varieties of the numerous sherds from Bay Colony potters' kiln sites (Turnbaugh 1977:Fig. 9) support this historically documented indication of the strength of the local industry. Similarly, the percentage of redware sherds, made in the manner of local potters, that were excavated at the Salem Village Parsonage site suggests the success of this industry.

Chronological Development

The development of self-conscious schools or traditions of early Bay Colony production can be inferred from these kiln assemblages. These schools appear to have been conservatively rooted in British ceramic traditions (cf. Turnbaugh 1977: 217–220). Though not traced further here, these roots may have gone back still further into other European ceramic traditions. The English traditions and the corresponding domestic types and varieties are listed in Table 8.6. As illustrated in this table, the imitative domestic traditions generally seem to lag behind and change more slowly through time than do their British counterparts.

TABLE **8.6**

Corresponding Domestic and British Traditions

Domestic Traditions (Varieties and Potters)	British Traditions (Common Names and References)
1. Ferruginous gray-black-glazed redwares. Class I,Type A, Varieties 4, 12, 16 (23). Produced in Bay Colony ca. 1685–1735 (Kettle, J. Bayley)	1. Cistercian ware. Wheel-thrown redware with shiny, ferruginous brown-black lead glaze; dates prior to 1650 on Plymouth/Bay Colony sites (Deetz 1973: Fig.1)
2. Olive-glazed redwares. Class I, Type A, Varieties 2, 14, 21, (18). Produced in Bay Colony ca. 1650–1800 (Vinson, Gardner, J. Bayley, D. Bayley)	2. Tudor Green; Sandywares. Red or buff bodied with bright green lead glaze; dates prior to ca. 1675 on Plymouth/Bay Colony sites (Deetz 1973: Fig.1)
3. Mottled-glazed redwares. Class I, Type, A, Varieties 11, 27, 29. Produced in Bay Colony ca. 1725–1815 (J. Bayley, Osborn, D. Bayley, Southwick, Benner, Purinton)	3. English manganese mottled ware. Buff bodied with dark mottled glaze, it was made ca. 1680–1750 (cf. Kelly and Greaves 1974:3); dates to ca. 1705–1730 on Massachusetts sites (Deetz 1974, pers. comm.)
4. Black-glazed redwares. Class I, Type A, Varieties 3, 10, 15, 22, 26, 28, (19), (25). Produced in Bay Colony ca. 1725–1815 (J. Bayley, Osborn, D. Bayley, Southwick, Purinton)	4. Jackfield/Whieldon-type and English black-glazed tea service prototypes. Red or purplish bodied ware with shiny black lead-glaze; dates to ca. 1715 and later in Bay Colony (Watkins 1950)

Table 8.6 lists four domestic traditions, all of which include varieties found in the Salem Village Parsonage site assemblage (see Table 8.2). To facilitate easy reference to these four probable traditions, in terms of simpler terminology and usefulness for intersite comparisons, descriptive word labels have been given to these four traditions, plus to a fifth category of Type-Variety Approach varieties not included in Table 8.6. These labels incorporate Munsell descriptive nomenclature for glaze color of varieties, plus notation of decorative techniques, provided in Table

8.2. Each category includes tooled and untooled varieties. Approximate date ranges for periods of manufacture of these categories have been estimated by examining Bay Colony potters' kiln assemblages.

Twenty-nine of the 31 varieties in Table 8.2 may be incorporated into these five categories of varieties. (Variety 30 is sgraffito; variety 31 is green glazed majolica.) These five descriptive categories, their probable manufacturing dates, and the associated Type-Variety Approach nomenclature are as follow:

1. a) Yellow-red-glazed redware   ca.   1650–1800
      (Varieties 1, 6, 8, 13, 20)
   b) Yellow-red-glazed slipware   ca.   1685–1800
      (Varieties 5, 7, 9, 17, 24)
2. a) Olive-glazed redware   ca.   1650–1800
      (Varieties 2, 14, 21)
   b) Olive-glazed slipware   ca.   1685–1800
      (Variety 18)
3. a) Ferruginous gray-black-glazed redware ca.   1685–1735
      (Varieties 4, 12, 16, 23)
4. a) Black-glazed redware   ca.   1725–1815
      (Varieties 3, 10, 15, 22, 26, 28)
   b) Black-glazed slipware   ca.   1685–1735
      (Varieties 19, 25)
5. a) Mottled-glazed redware   ca.   1725–1815
      (Varieties 11, 27, 29)

Both typological analysis of locally produced ceramics represented in Massachusetts Bay Colony kiln assemblages and study of possible English derivations of these redwares may help to reveal the early stylistic orientations of 17th- and 18th-century Bay Colony potters (see Table 8.7). Daniel Bayley, for example, learned the redware trade from his father, Joseph. Yet, their wares differ considerably (Turnbaugh 1977:189–191). Table 8.7 summarizes these differences. Joseph's wares are earlier and appear to have been more restricted to British models. Tradition, not fashion, may have dictated vessel form, design, and execution.

Joseph's son Daniel operated two kilns, the first in Gloucester (1749–1753) and the second in Newburyport (1763–1799). Based on the study of a limited number of existing sherds from his earlier kiln, Daniel's early wares are also traditional in form, design, and execution and are reminiscent of his father's wares. Some of the many sherds from Daniel's later kiln also are traditional. But the majority are creative as well as fashionably imitative of innovative British styles and varieties. Daniel's later wares exhibit a much greater range of forms and methods of decorating and glazing redwares than do either his father's or his own earlier wares.

TABLE **8.7**

Comparison of Joseph Bayley and Daniel Bayley Kiln Sherds
(cf. Turnbaugh 1977:190–191)

Joseph Bayley Sherds (1722–1735)	Daniel Bayley Sherds (1763–1799)
1. Narrow range of glaze colors (clear yellow-red, ferruginous gray-black, black, olive green)	1. Many varied glaze colors (clear yellow-red, black, olive green, greenish and orangish mottling in clear glaze, mottled black, mottled and speckled clear and green glazes)
2. Brush-applied kaolin slip decoration consisting of restrained, simple elements (straight lines and U-shaped lunettes)	2. Brush- and quill-applied kaolin slip decoration consisting of creative, free elements (flourishes, squiggles, straight lines, lunettes)
3. Forms of vessels, rims, and handles are traditional; limited repertory (e.g., little variation from one or two basic styles for rims on sherds from utilitarian vessels)	3. Considerable variation in vessel forms and in styles of rims and handles (e.g., at least six rim styles are used on sherds from utilitarian vessels)
4. Little innovation or experimentation in general (e.g., no sponge decoration, quill-applied slip decoration, or tooling; produced fewer forms of redware vessels)	4. Comparatively greater innovation and experimentation, as well as possibly self-conscious imitation of British manufacture methods (e.g., quill-applied slip decoration and mottling of glazes)

More generally, stylistic characteristics of the earliest domestic redwares, such as type of ornamentation, decoration technique, rim and base form, and vessel size, also seem to be rooted in traditional British models (cf. Turnbaugh 1977:217–220). The existence of late 17th- and 18th-century traditions of domestic pottery production that exhibit direct English influence suggests that the early domestic styles were imitative, perhaps in an attempt to fulfill the settlers' traditional concept of an exact transplantation of English society to the Massachusetts Bay Colony. This early concept of "transplantation" is documented historically (Bradford 1952; Morgan 1958) and may now be demonstrated archaeologically for the Bay Colony, with the aid of potters' kiln sherds.

By 1740, a widespread religious revival, known as the "Great Awakening," was producing profound changes in New England and the Bay Colony. From this period on, domestic imitation of English styles became freer and less restricted, as demonstrated archaeologically by progressive changes in the earlier and later ceramic products of Daniel Bayley (Table 8.7), for example, among other potters. Daniel Bayley's break from strict imitation may indicate a desire to follow more creative English trends, as has been suggested for other colonies (cf. Noël Hume 1973), as the Bay Colony settlers shed their isolationism and regionalism and became more worldly and cosmopolitan. This shift in emphasis may be associated with more general ideo-cultural change, marked historically by the "Great Awakening" in New England and the Enlightenment in Europe. This trend also has been explored more generally in intrasite analyses and intersite comparisons of Bay Colony domestic sites' archaeological assemblages and probate inventory analyses (Brown 1973; Deetz 1973; Turnbaugh 1976, 1977; Turnbaugh et al. 1979).

Later in the 18th century, as both changing ceramic varieties and forms and declining domestic redware sherd frequencies in the archaeological record attest (Deetz 1973; Turnbaugh 1977:207), the inhabitants of the Bay Colony gradually forsook some domestic redwares and readopted increasingly available, inexpensive British varieties. Through time, a shift in formal and functional groups of redwares is demonstrable for the Parsonage site (see Table 8.8). This trend is currently being explored further for the archaeological record of the Massachusetts Bay Colony.

TABLE 8.8

Temporal Change in Redware Form and Function

(cf. Turnbaugh 1977: Fig. 16)

Redware Functions/Forms		Pre-1731/1733[a]		Post-1731/1733[a]	
		No.	%	No.	%
Food storage/	Pots	30		2	
Preparation	Pans	5		9	
SUBTOTALS		35	56.5	11	5.5
Serving/	Jugs/				
Dining	Pitchers	22		0	
	Plates/				
	Platters	0		3	
	Bowls	0		5	
	Bowls/				
	Chamberpots	3		46	
	Mugs	2		105	
SUBTOTALS		27	43.5	159	80.3
Decorative	Figurines	0	0.0	0	0.0
Social	Teapots	0		13	
	Teabowls	0		0	
SUBTOTALS		0	0.0	13	6.6
Hygienic	Chamberpots	0		15	
	Ointment jar	0		0	
		0	0.0	15	7.6
PERIOD TOTALS		62	100.0	198	100.0

[a] The conjunction of the median site occupation date, the mean pipestem date, and the mean ceramic date (cf. Turnbaugh 1977:201)

It is the present author's contention that the readoption of European wares may have been a result of the 18th-century settler's perseverance in following new English styles and adopting such wares when domestic imitation could no longer compete with Wedgwood and other innovative British potters. This point is important and cannot be overstressed. The 18th-century Bay Colony potters could no longer compete successfully because they did not have quantities of raw materials, such as fine kaolin clays, flint, and manganese, necessary for making the popular 18th-century buff-bodied wares. Furthermore, unlike Wedgwood who could import some of these raw materials (Barber 1893:59–63; Watkins 1950:72–73), the Bay Colony potters had neither the sociopolitical organization, the economic resources, nor the authority for such importation. To do so might have directly threatened the English policy of mercantilism, which under the Navigation Acts regulated trade and commerce of the colonies for the benefit of the home country.

Spatial Variation

Analysis of kiln sherds from domestic potteries also suggests that temporal change and spatial variation in types and functions of redwares (Turnbaugh 1977:189–193, 201–208, 219) from the Bay Colony kiln assemblages and from the Salem Village Parsonage site may be indicative of differential rates of cultural change and variation within the Bay Colony. This cultural variation possibly resulted from the relative degree of isolation of inland versus coastal communities (Turnbaugh 1977:208–213). Analyses of vessel style, forms, and functions (Turnbaugh 1977:194–208), as well as typological considerations, have contributed to these interpretations. English black-glazed teapots, for example, were first imported to Massachusetts in 1715 (Watkins 1950:58). As summarized in Table 8.6, potters in communities close to the cosmopolitan ports of Salem, Charlestown, and Boston began creating wares that were similar in form as well as type and variety by ca. 1725. Analyses of kiln assemblages suggest that potters in more distant, isolated communities such as Abington were not manufacturing such wares at this time (see Table 8.6; see also Turnbaugh 1977:Figs. 9, 21).

Similarly, English mottled ware, which is well represented in assemblages from Bay Colony sites, was produced between ca. 1680 and 1750 (Kelly and Greaves 1974:3). Domestic potters near the major port of Salem in Essex County appear to have begun producing a local version probably as early as 1709/10, though the earliest fine imitations of English mottled ware are first found in the Daniel Bayley and the Osborn kiln assemblages (post 1725). About 40 years later, after 1765, this ware first appears in the kiln assemblage of John Henry Benner from the more isolated inland community of Abington (cf. Turnbaugh 1977:189–193).

Variation in form, function, and manufacturing technique of domestically produced redwares implies differential popularity of and/or accessibility to specific wares over space, as well as through time, within the Bay Colony. Variation in the colony's redware products may be interpreted as at least partly dependent upon the geographic location, isolation, and relative distances between the early pottery-manufacturing communities and more cosmopolitan towns and commercial ports (Turnbaugh 1977:221). Sometimes, not always, potters' kilns were situated in these more cosmopolitan communities. The interpretations presented above have resulted from comparisons of assemblages from kilns located in contemporary but differing types of communities.

Interpretation of Parsonage Site Redwares

The redwares present in the Salem Village Parsonage site assemblage are of many varieties and subvarieties and comprise almost 90 percent of the total ceramic assemblage. At least 23 percent of these redwares can be identified as probably made by a local domestic potter, as was discussed above. Furthermore, substantial quantities of the historically documented popular varieties such as "mottled ware" are present. Almost the full range of varieties and forms found in contemporary potters' kiln assemblages are represented in the Parsonage site assemblage. Finally, some of the remaining redwares have slip application and footed, glazed vessel bases that indicate probable British origins (cf. Watkins 1950). However, not more than 50 sherds from the Parsonage site, or less than 1 percent of the total redware assemblage, could be assigned a probable British origin on the basis of these attributes.

These data suggest that the occupants of the Parsonage relied heavily on the domestic redware industry while making only insignificant use of English redwares. In addition, the range and quantity of ceramic varieties suggest archaeologically that the ministers were comfortable in a material sense. For example, the fanciest domestic redware types available, such as tooled "mottled ware" mugs and kaolin slip decorated bowls and chamberpots, are represented in the Salem Village Parsonage site's assemblage (Turnbaugh 1977:Figs. 14, 16). Probate inventory data, in fact, indicate that some of these ministers actually were quite well off for their day (Turnbaugh 1977:180–182; Fig. 5), which corroborates these interpretations of the archaeological data. Finally, the Salem Village Parsonage site's redwares (at least 23 percent) that were made in the manner of a number of local potters suggest that a strong, successful regional distribution network was operative during the late 17th and 18th centuries between communities in Essex County, on the north shore of Massachusetts.

Discussion

Wider application of the type-variety classificatory outline proposed here, to redwares from other historical household and kiln sites in various regions, should serve to increase the historical archaeologist's ability to describe and interpret ceramic data precisely. In the present study, the type-variety classification of the ceramic assemblage of the Salem Village Parsonage site, combined with formal and functional analysis, has provided a solution to the problem of how to describe the 17th- and 18th-century redwares. Using this approach, the total ceramic assemblage could be classified consistently. Then, vessel forms and functions and dynamics of temporal change and spatial variation could be studied precisely, within this typological context (Turnbaugh 1976, 1977). When considered in relation to sherds from contemporary domestic kiln assemblages, patterning in the assemblage could be delineated and the Parsonage site's redwares could be interpreted as representative of an upper-middle-class household of its period. Evidence of an efficient regional distribution network for domestic potters' wares also was identified. Historical documentation corroborates these interpretations.

When the assemblage of the Salem Village Parsonage site is considered in a broader context, in relation to domestic Bay Colony potters' wares, some general temporal and spatial trends emerge. Both the existence and development of Bay Colony redware manufacturing traditions may be delineated, and differential rates of cultural change and variation appear to be linked to communities' spatial locations and relative degree of isolation from more cosmopolitan ports and towns. By using this Type-Variety Approach in combination with analyses of redware style, form, and function to describe and interpret the ceramic data, the early colonists' acceptance of the potters' redware styles emerges, and the more general ideological development of 17th- and 18th-century Bay Colony settlers seems to be demonstrable archaeologically. Again, quantitative data such as sherd counts have been combined with inferred vessel forms and functions to provide an empirical database necessary to support these interpretations of patterning in the archaeological record.

Classification of colonial redwares by using the Type-Variety Approach described herein, complemented by considerations of vessel form and function, provides a strong, consistent means of tackling problems of redware classification, identification, and description. Eventually, paste compositional analysis—through instrumental neutron activation and petrographic analyses—may be used in conjunction with similar analyses of redware types and forms to further substantiate inferred trends. When temporal and spatial patterning have been defined for colonial period redwares and ceramic assemblages, these patterns in material culture can be interpreted in relation to historically documented socioeconomic and ideocultural trends. These linkages between the archaeological record and historical documentation are only as strong as the analytical methods used to support interpretations; in historical archaeology, ceramic analyses that make use of the Type-Variety Approach, among other precise and comprehensive analytical methods, should be indispensable.

REFERENCES

Barber, E. A. 1893. *The Pottery and Porcelain of the United States.* New York: G. P. Putnam's Sons.

Beaudry, M. P., R. L. Bishop, R. M. Leventhal, and R. J. Sharer. 1980. Typological and Compositional Analysis of Classic Painted Ceramics in the Southeast Maya Area. Paper presented at the annual meeting of the Society for American Archaeology, Philadelphia.

Bradford, W. 1952. *Of Plymouth Plantation, 1620–1647.* S. E. Morison (ed.). New York: Alfred A. Knopf.

Brain, J. P., A. Toth, and A. Rodriguez-Buckingham. 1972. Ethnohistoric Archaeology and the DeSoto Entrada Into the Lower Mississippi Valley. *Conference on Historic Site Archaeology Papers* 7:232–289.

Brose, D. S.1968. On the Relationship Between History and Archaeology. *Conference on Historic Site Archaeology Papers* 3(2):112–115.

Brown, M. R., III. 1973. Ceramics from Plymouth, 1621–1800: The Documentary Record. In *Ceramics in America,* I. M. G. Quimby (ed.), pp. 41–74. Charlottesville: University Press of Virginia.

Cotter, J. L. 1968. *A Handbook for Historical Archaeology, Parts I and II.* John L. Cotter, 8125 Heacock Lane, Wyncote, PA.

David, N. 1972. On the Life Span of Pottery, Type Frequencies and Archaeological Inference. *American Antiquity* 37(1):141–142.

Deetz, J. J. F. 1973. Ceramics from Plymouth, 1620–1835: The Archaeological Evidence. In *Ceramics in America,* I. M. G. Quimby (ed.), pp. 15–40. Charlottesville: University Press of Virginia.

Fairbanks, C. H. 1962. Excavations at Horseshoe Bend, Alabama. *Florida Anthropologist* 15(2):41–56.

Foster, G. M. 1960. Life-Expectancy of Utilitarian Pottery in Tzintzuntzan, Michoacan, Mexico. *American Antiquity* 25(4):606–609.

Gifford, J. C. 1960. The Type-Variety Method of Ceramic Classification as an Indicator of Cultural Phenomena. *American Antiquity* 25(3):341–347.

Hudson, J. P. and C. M. Watkins. 1957. The Earliest Known English Colonial Pottery in America. *Antiques* 71(1):51–54.

Jelks, E. B. 1958. Ceramics from Jamestown. In *Archaeological Excavations at Jamestown,* by J. L. Cotter, Appendix A, pp. 201–212. Archaeological Research Series 4. National Park Service, Washington, DC.

Kelly, J. H. and S. J. Greaves. 1974. The Excavation of a Kiln Base in Old Hall Street, Hanley, Stoke-on-Trent, Staffs. SJ 885475. *City of Stoke-on-Trent Museum Archaeological Society Report 6.*

Kindig, J., Jr. 1935. A Note on Early North Carolina Pottery. *Antiques* 27(1):14–15.

Marwitt, R. H. 1967. A Preliminary Study of Seven Coarse Earthenwares from the Fortress of Louisbourg. *Conference on Historic Site Archaeology Papers* 1:53–59.

Morgan, E. S. 1958. *The Puritan Dilemma, The Story of John Winthrop.* Boston: Little, Brown.

Munsell Color Company, Inc. 1942. *Munsell Book of Color.* Baltimore: Munsell Color Company.

Munsell Color Company, Inc. 1949. *Munsell Soil Color Charts, Hues 7.5 R through 5.0 Y.* Baltimore: Munsell Color Company.

Noël Hume, I. 1970. *A Guide to the Artifacts of Colonial America.* New York: Alfred A. Knopf.

Noël Hume, I. 1973. Creamware to Pearlware. In *Ceramics in America,* I. M. G. Quimby (ed.), pp. 217–254. Charlottesville: University Press of Virginia.

Phillips, P. 1958. Application of the Wheat-Gifford-Wasley Taxonomy to Eastern Ceramics. *American Antiquity* 24:117–125.

Robbins, R. W. 1969. *Pilgrim John Alden's Progress, Archaeological Excavations in Duxbury.* Plymouth, MA: The Pilgrim Society.

Rouse, I. 1960. Classification of Artifacts in Archaeology. *American Antiquity* 25(3): 313–323.

Sabloff, J. A. and R. E. Smith 1969. The Importance of Both Analytic and Taxonomic Classification in the Type Variety System. *American Antiquity* 34(3):278–285.

Smith, R. E., G. R. Willey, and J. C. Gifford. 1960. The Type-Variety Concept as a Basis for the Analysis of Maya Pottery. *American Antiquity* 25(3):330–340.

South, S. A. 1972. Evolution and Horizon as Revealed in Ceramic Analysis in Historical Archaeology. *Conference on Historic Site Archaeology Papers* 6(2):71–116.

South, S. A. 1977. *Method and Theory in Historical Archaeology.* New York: Academic Press.

Spargo, J. 1974. *Early American Pottery and China.* Reprint of 1926 edition. Rutland, VT: Charles E. Tuttle.

Stone, L. M. 1974. Fort Michilimackinac 1715–1781: An Archaeological Perspective on the Revolutionary Frontier. *Michigan State University Anthropological Series* 2. East Lansing.

Thomas, D. H. 1974. *Predicting the Past: An Introduction to Anthropological Archaeology.* New York: Holt, Rinehart, and Winston.

Turnbaugh, S. P. 1976. An Anthropological Historical Archaeology Inquiry into Cultural Variation and Change Based on Ceramic Assemblages from the Massachusetts Bay Colony. Unpublished B.A. thesis, Harvard University, Cambridge.

Turnbaugh, S. P. 1977. Ideo-Cultural Variation and Change in the Massachusetts Bay Colony. *Conference on Historic Site Archaeology Papers* 11:169–235.

Turnbaugh, W. A. and S. P. Turnbaugh. 1979. Alternative Applications of the Mean Ceramic Date Concept for Interpreting Human Behavior. *Historical Archaeology* 11:90–104.

Turnbaugh, W. A., S. P. Turnbaugh, and A. P. Davis, Jr. 1979. Life Aboard HMS Orpheus. *Archaeology* 32(3):43–49.

Watkins, L. W. 1950. *Early New England Potters and Their Wares.* Cambridge: Harvard University Press.

Wheat, J. B., J. C. Gifford, and W. W. Wasley 1958. Ceramic Variety, Type Cluster, and Ceramic System in Southwestern Pottery Analysis. *American Antiquity* 24:34–47.

Willey, G. R., R. J. Sharer, R. Viel, A. Demarest, R. Leventhal, and E. Shortman. 1980. A Study of Ceramic Interaction in the Southeast Maya Periphery. Paper presented at the annual meeting of the Society for American Archaeology, Philadelphia.

Wright, J. V. 1967. Type and Attribute Analysis: Their Application to Iroquoian Culture History. In *Iroquoian Culture, History, and Prehistory: Proceedings of the 1965 Conference on Iroquoian Research*, E. Tooker (ed.), pp. 99–100. Albany.

Chapter Nine

Factors Influencing Consumer Behavior in Turn-of-the-Century Phoenix, Arizona

Introduction

Socioeconomic status has been put forth as an explanation for some of the variability in the archaeological record: People buy what they do because of their status position in society. This should not come as much of a surprise since it is quite apparent, in the world around us today, that less affluent, "lower-class" people possess different kinds of things than do more affluent, "upper-class" people (consider cars, houses, and clothes, for example). In fact, successful advertising firms and market analysts depend upon this phenomenon to develop advertising campaigns for manufacturers that sell a bewildering array of consumer goods (see Kassarjian and Robertson 1973a; Levy 1973; Martineau 1958). The valuable contribution made by historical archaeological research has been to verify empirically that this phenomenon did in fact occur in the past, and to suggest the degrees to which patterns of material culture varied according to socioeconomic status. While valid as a general explanation, it does not go quite far enough. How does socioeconomic status account for this variability—what are the processes? By looking at a particular kind of human behavior—consumer behavior—and the factors that influence that behavior, we can come closer to understanding why and how the variability covaries with status. If a sufficient database has been developed, research can focus on analytical units larger than the single site, making comparisons within and between social groups (socioeconomic as well as ethnic). This kind of research could lead toward an understanding of the nature of cultural and

This article was originally published in *Consumer Choice in Historical Archaeology*, Suzanne M. Spencer-Wood, ed., pp. 359–395, New York and London: Plenum Press, ©1987.

social systems in the historic past, the goal toward which we, as anthropologists, are striving to reach.

It is hoped that the research reported here will be a step in that direction. For three years, Soil Systems, Inc. (SSI), under contract to the City of Phoenix, investigated several downtown areas that were undergoing urban redevelopment. Archival and artifactual data from two residential areas are used in the analyses in this study. As a laboratory for the study of urban growth and human behavior in urban settings, the situation in Phoenix was extremely advantageous. Archival data were readily available and fairly complete; the identification of function and chronology was possible for the majority of artifacts recovered; and in some cases, project area residents were able to provide valuable first-hand information. Yet a major problem remained. Phoenix represents American urban culture of the late 19th and early 20th centuries, a period and site type that has received relatively little intensive attention, even in the West. This has meant that standard analytical techniques used in other urban areas of other time periods were not generally applicable to Phoenix data. Since one major goal of the Phoenix research was to be able to compare its results with those obtained in other urban research projects, several of these analytical techniques were modified slightly (Henry and Garrow 1982). The primary analytical techniques used in addressing questions of consumer behavior are: (1) a hierarchical ranking of occupational titles derived from the work of urban historians studying mid- to late-19th-century Philadelphia (Hershberg and Dockhorn 1976); and (2) an economic scaling of ceramics and butchered food bone developed from Miller's (1980) economic scaling technique. While certain problems have yet to be resolved, these techniques appear to have some use in studying late 19th- and early 20th-century urban consumer behavior.

Factors Influencing Consumer Behavior

The primary cultural unit of archaeological analysis is the household (Deetz 1982:717), except in those cases of nondomestic sites such as commercial or industrial complexes and public institutions. A household is a domestic residential group, consisting of the inhabitants of a dwelling or a set of premises and who appear as a discrete group in the documents (e.g., census or tax records) (Laslett and Wall 1972:86). The household is usually coterminous with the family (extended, nuclear, fraternal, etc.), but it may also include nonrelated members, such as boarders and servants. The importance of the household-family in archaeological analysis derives from the fact that the family "functions as the context wherein individuals are brought to an awareness of their culture's rules, and conversely, where those rules are frequently expressed in physical form" (Deetz 1982:718). The patterns of "artifacts and structures that formed the physical focus of family or household activity . . . are reflective of the shared beliefs and behavior of their owners and users, a minimal and understandable level of cultural behavior which nonetheless embodies the world view of the society at large" (Deetz 1982:719).

Not only does the household reflect the society at large, but also various subgroups within that society. A group is defined as a collectivity whose members share common beliefs, values, attitudes, standards of behavior, as well as symbols that represent the group (Kassarjian and Robertson 1973b:292; Vivello 1978:107–108). There are a number of groups to which an individual belongs, such as family, church, school, job, recreation, hobby, neighborhood, ethnic group, and social class. By extension, the household can generally be seen as a member of the groups to which its members belong (particularly neighborhood, ethnic group, and social class).

Some groups have more meaning, for, or exert a greater level of influence on, an individual. These are "reference groups," used by an individual as a "point of reference in determining his judgments, beliefs, and behavior" (Kassarjian and Robertson 1973b:292–293). The individual does not need to be a member of a group to use it as a point of reference (e.g., when an upwardly mobile person aspires to become a member of another group), nor must the reference group function in a positive way (as in the avoidance of the values and behavior standards of a negative reference group) (Kassarjian and Robertson 1973b:293). Nearly every household is a member of two powerful reference groups: social class and ethnic group. This commonality of group membership has important ramifications for archaeological analyses since it permits comparisons of large numbers of households based on consistent measures.

A characteristic of technologically complex industrial societies, such as that in the United States, is social stratification, which is a "system of classifying persons in a hierarchically arranged series of social strata (classes or castes) having differential access to the resources, goods, and skills . . . available to the society as a whole" (Vivello 1978:121). Class systems are open-ended and fluid, permitting movement upward or downward in the hierarchy (Kassarjian and Robertson 1973a:390; Vivello 1978:122). Since the term "class" (as in upper class, middle class, lower class) tends to be defined in many different ways, by different people (researchers, lay public), and in different situations, it lacks a certain precision of meaning. The term "socioeconomic status," as used here, is defined as the position in society occupied by an individual, and, by extension, by a household, based primarily on social and economic factors. Researchers (Coleman and Rainwater 1978; Kassarjian and Robertson 1973a; Warner and Lunt 1941; Willigan and Lynch 1982) note that occupation, income, aggregate wealth, level of education, and religious affiliation are factors that are important in determining socioeconomic status. While income and wealth appear to be the most significant factors in determining status (Coleman and Rainwater 1978:278–283; Warner 1973:404), economic factors are not sufficient to predict where a particular family or individual will be [in the status hierarchy] or to explain completely the phenomena of social class. . . . *Money must be translated into socially approved behavior and possessions*, and they [behavior and possessions] in turn must be translated into intimate participation with, and acceptance by, members of a . . . class (Warner 1973:404; my emphasis).

Each socioeconomic status level, then, constitutes a group, members of which share common beliefs, values, and standards of behavior, including consumption behavior.

A rich man is not simply a poor man with more money (Martineau 1958:122). The consumer behavior of each reflects the values, attitudes, and life-styles of the socioeconomic group to which each belongs, since "consuming is ultimately one of the ways in which people implement their values" (Levy 1973:410). In fact, "consumption patterns operate as prestige symbols to define class membership, which is a more significant determination of economic behavior than income" (Martineau 1958:130). Additionally, upwardly mobile individuals tend to purchase external symbols of the status to which they aspire (Martineau 1958:123–124). An individual's style of consumption—what he or she purchases—is a "primary means of asserting and/or validating social status and identity" (Laumann and House 1973:430). Studies have also shown (Kassarjian and Robertson 1973a) that within each status group there is variability in income earned by its members, and those who earn considerably more or considerably less than the average exhibit different consumer behavior than typical members of the group.

Ethnic groups are also influential points of reference for their members, who share a common traditional heritage, which differs from that of the society at large. An ethnic group is therefore a subculture, a minority in the dominant national culture, and may be differentiated on the basis of race, religion, language, or national origin (e.g., blacks, Jews, Italians) (Gordon 1978; Kassarjian and Robertson 1973c; Schuyler 1980). From a review of the literature on class and ethnicity, Gordon (1978:261, 262) notes that "the ethnic factor plays a large role in restricting intimate social relationships not only to members of one's own status level or social class, but to members of one's own ethnic group," and that "the behavioral similarities of social class are more pronounced than those of ethnic group." Thus, it appears that while ethnic group affiliation is a major influence on an individual's behavior, class or socioeconomic status exerts a greater influence.

Other factors also influence consumer behavior. One of these is age, since as the head of the household grows older, there is a general increase in earning power due to accumulated seniority and experience, and a corresponding increase in household income (Wells and Gubar 1970:513–514). Studies have shown, however, that the life cycle of a household is a more accurate indicator of consumption patterns than is age alone (Wells and Gubar 1970). As households pass through the stages in the life cycle, from single unmarried, to newlywed, to a family with children, to older couples whose children have set up their own households, to the elderly single, needs for consumer goods change in quantity and quality (Schiffer et al. 1981; Wells and Gubar 1970).

Another factor influencing consumer behavior is the market availability of consumer goods. If a particular item, or type of item, is not to be found in the marketplace, it cannot be purchased (see Gaw 1975). Usually, however, especially in urban areas, there is a variety of consumer goods on the market, differing in type, style, brand name, quality, size, or some other dimension, and the consumer must make choices. In addition to those factors already considered, price of the item influences consumer choice, since if the item is priced beyond the consumer's ability to pay, it will not be purchased. In fact, Miller (1980:3) noted that the "social status of any commodity is related to how much the object costs." The nature of some consumer goods also influences consumer behavior. Studies have shown (Howard and Sheth 1973; Levy 1973; Wells and Gubar 1970) that consumption patterns for durable goods (objects purchased infrequently, such as furniture) are different than those for nondurable goods (items purchased repeatedly and often, such as food).

The artifacts recovered from the excavations in Phoenix represent choices made by Phoenix consumers. It is hypothesized, based on the foregoing discussion, that those choices were influenced primarily by the socioeconomic status position(s) held by those consumers, but that other factors played a role in consumer decision making as well. It is expected that the relative value of durable and nondurable goods, as measured by economic scaling of ceramics and butchered food bone, will vary according to status level, as measured by occupational ranking, and that variability will be due to the influence of other factors. Two separate, but equal, data sets are used to investigate this research problem: archival data and artifactual data.

Data From Phoenix

Overview of Phoenix History

Pioneers coming into the desert environment of the Salt River Valley of the 1860s encountered the ruins of adobe towns and irrigation canals built by the prehistoric Hohokam (Mawn 1979). Foresighted settlers reexcavated these old canals and successfully grew crops to provision the series of Indian forts then being established in the Arizona Territory. The success of this venture encouraged increased settlement in the valley, which led to the founding of Phoenix in 1870. Named for the mythical bird that was reborn from its own ashes, Phoenix grew rapidly upon the ruins of the Hohokam civilization. The arrival of the railroad in the late 1880s and early 1890s expanded Phoenix's influence as a marketing center. The young city was no longer an isolated, dusty desert town, but was linked efficiently with the rest of the nation by rail. A wider variety of manufactured goods became available to Phoenix consumers, and large numbers of visitors and immigrants came in response to publicity campaigns waged by the Phoenix Chamber of Commerce. The area's agricultural base expanded beyond grain crops to include citrus and fruit orchards, vegetable farms, dairy and livestock herds, and even lucrative ostrich ranches which marketed ostrich feathers to adorn turn-of-the-century ladies' hats. Phoenix quickly grew beyond the boundaries of its Original Townsite, encouraged in part by the construction and expansion of the street-car system after the 1880s.

On the eve of the 20th century, Phoenix was as modern a city as any of its contemporaries, and could boast multistoried office and commercial buildings; residential suburbs; municipal refuse collection; sewer, water, electric, and gas systems; police and fire departments; mail delivery; telephone service; schools; churches, libraries; and many other social and cultural attractions (Mawn 1979). The completion of the Roosevelt Dam in 1911 guaranteed a dependable, year-round water supply to Phoenix and the surrounding agricultural communities, and the granting of Arizona statehood engendered considerable optimism in the future of Phoenix and the Salt River Valley. The years of World War I were prosperous for the valley in general, as agricultural output was intensified and new industries were established to aid in the war effort. The first 50 years of Phoenix's development saw the city develop into a major southwestern urban center.

Project Area Descriptions

Soil Systems, Inc., investigated four spatially discrete areas in downtown Phoenix. Data from two of these project areas are used in the analyses here.

The first project area consisted of Blocks 1 and 2 of the Original Townsite, which were initially settled in the 1870s (Henry and Garrow 1982). Intensive settlement occurred during the 1880s and 1890s, influenced by the construction of large homes by the Phoenix elite nearby on the edges of the central business district. Homes in the project area were, however, more modest. In general, residents were shop proprietors, office workers, and tradesmen with European-American, Mexican-American, French-Canadian, and Italian surnames. During the 1920s, expansion of the central business district reached Blocks 1 and 2, and some houses were replaced by commercial structures. This pattern of increased commercialization continued until used car lots and gas stations characterized the area in the 1960s.

The second project area was a 9-acre portion of the Murphy Addition to Phoenix, located just outside the eastern boundary of the Original Townsite, and one block southeast of Blocks 1 and 2 (Henry et al. 1983). The Murphy Addition was platted in 1884, specifically for residential subdivision, although development occurred gradually over the next 20 to 25 years. Until the 1930s, the area was predominantly a European-American neighborhood of single-family homes. During the 1930s, the neighborhood changed in character as the older houses were subdivided and new multifamily residences were built. By the late 1940s, the neighborhood was a high-density residential district.

Nature of the Phoenix Data

Two sets of data were used in the Phoenix investigations: archival and artifactual. Primary documentary sources were particularly rich in information on the project areas. Real estate title records, municipal tax assessment records, city directories, federal manuscript census, photographs, and the Sanborn-Perris Fire Insurance maps provided information on the physical nature of each property lot (location, size, function, construction material, structural alterations) and on the residents of each lot (names of household members, occupations, household composition, and property value). Tax assessment records were, however, of marginal use for wealth data since they are not available after 1912. The federal manuscript censuses are not available after 1910. The city directories were therefore relied upon to provide most of the information for 20th-century residents of the project areas. City directories provided information on name, occupation, and address of residence (and sometimes place of work), and were available yearly from 1892 to the present, with only nine missing directories, scattered throughout the series. The level of reporting in the directories is somewhat inconsistent—for example, some individuals or their occupation titles may be omitted from one directory, although present in the directory for a preceding or subsequent year. This is a relatively minor problem, given the fact that this information is available for specific years, while feature depositions can be dated only to a general time period. The problem arises, however, from the very detailed nature of the temporal information provided by the directories. Since each property lot was perceived as a behavioral unit separate from its neighbor, features located within the boundaries of a lot were associated with the household(s) residing on that lot during the period of deposition. Thus, the temporal specificity in the directories permits several households to be associated with one deposit during a short period of time. Unfortunately, it was often not possible to associate only one household with a particular deposit, since none of the features examined here was stratified, either stratigraphically or artifactually. This problem could not be eliminated entirely, and it is doubtful that it ever will be, especially in cases of high tenant turnover; in cases of residential longevity, the problem rarely arises.

The artifactual data used in this study of consumer behavior were recovered from 12 privy pits and 3 trash deposits. All materials were associated with domestic activities and were discarded between ca. 1880 and 1940 (Henry and

Garrow 1982; Henry et al. 1983). Deposition of trash in unused privy shafts tended to correspond with the opening of new privy vaults, the construction of septic tanks in some cases (ca. 1910–1915), and linking with the municipal sewer system, which was mandatory after 1915 (Mawn 1979:204, 442). Pits specifically dug to receive trash were not common in the project areas, and the three trash pits which yielded some of the data used here were originally dug for other purposes (in one case, to extract clay for use in making adobe bricks—Henry and Garrow 1982:237, 239). There is little information on municipal trash collection, so its impact on the archaeological record is not clearly understood.

Materials from each feature were treated as a single assemblage, since little stratigraphy was visually evident in the field, and stratigraphic segregation was not observed during ceramic cross-mend analyses. The data from each feature are assumed to be representatives of all the materials originally discarded. A 100 percent recovery rate was not achieved for two reasons: two features (F309 and F2–2) had been partially looted, and nearly all features experienced some minor damage from the backhoe trenching used to locate features during the testing phases of the projects. The impact of these actions on analysis was relatively minor, however, since looters sought only specific, intact items (such as bottles) and disregarded broken materials, and since materials were recovered when the backhoe located features. (Seriously damaged features are not included in this analysis.) In addition, the sizes of the assemblages were large enough in most cases (ranging from 880 to 16,768 in the features used here) to offset the effects of missing materials.

Two types of artifacts are used in this analysis: ceramics and butchered food bone. Ceramics are particularly suitable for this kind of analysis since, as Miller (1980) and other researchers (see Klein and Garrow 1984) have shown, price, and therefore status, are associated with observable ceramic attributes (decoration and ware). The ceramics recovered were in good condition; many had identifiable maker's marks that provided excellent date ranges, decorative techniques were easily distinguished, and vessel types could be identified for the majority of the sherds in the collection. Butchered food bone is also suitable for this analysis, since other researchers (Davidson 1982; Mudar 1978; Reitz and Cumbaa 1983; Schulz and Gust 1983) have shown that differential access to food resources is identifiable archaeologically. Two-thirds of the faunal remains recovered from the two project areas were identifiable (Henry and Garrow 1982; Henry et al. 1983). Not all food bone would have survived, however, primarily due to cooking processes, which act to break down the structural properties of the bone (Chaplin 1971). Additionally, since some meat is retailed without the bone, a household's use of these cuts would leave no evidence in the archaeological record. Therefore, bone data used in this study represents only a part of the total household diet.

Analytical Techniques

Two analytical techniques are used in this study of consumer behavior: hierarchical ranking of occupations held by residents, and economic scaling of ceramics and butchered bone.

Occupational Ranking

Occupational titles for individual residents were obtained from city directory listings and assigned to a hierarchical ranking scale based on that developed and tested on 19th-century data by the Philadelphia Social History Project (PSHP) (Hershberg and Dockhorn 1976). The PSHP occupational scale was "neither purely intuitive" (based on status, prestige, or skill), nor entirely empirically derived from wealth, income, or wages (Hershberg and Dockhorn 1976:60). The scale was tested on a portion of the large, computerized data base that PSHP researchers had compiled from mid- to late-19th-century documents, resulting in close correlation between the different rank categories and measurable variables such as level of education, wages, and property owned (Hershberg and Dockhorn 1976:60, 68). This scale is a general one, and does not segregate known variability within rank categories, since PSHP's goal (as well as that of this research) was to understand the behavior of the group rather than that of any individual member of the group (Hershberg and Dockhorn 1976:68).

The ranking scale used here is not inconsistent with that used in analyzing socioeconomic status in Wilmington, Delaware (Klein and Garrow 1984), nor with the scales developed by Katz (1972:85, 87) in studying 19th-century Hamilton, Ontario, Canada. Seven occupational categories are used: (1) professional, high white-collar (e.g., banker, lawyer, physician); (2) proprietary and low white-collar (e.g., storekeeper, clerk, teacher); (3) skilled trades (e.g., carpenter, tinsmith, engineer); (4) semiskilled and unskilled (e.g., waiter, teamster, laborer); (5) unclassifiable (job title is unclear or only the work place is listed); (6) unemployed (includes the jobless, as well as students, widows, housewives, and the retired); (7) occupation not recorded. The focus of analysis is upon the first four categories, since the last three yield less information on economic ranking in the absence of more detailed research of other kinds of documents (which was outside the scope of SSI's contract). Within each occupational category, different occupations may have been associated with varying amounts of income and prestige, and individuals holding the occupations ranked here may have perceived status to have been arrayed somewhat differently. These factors are not specifically addressed here, since they are difficult to measure in the present, and even more so in the past.

Economic Scaling

Although many researchers had suggested that variations in ceramic assemblages are associated with socioeconomic status (Miller 1974; Otto 1977; Rathje and McCarthy 1977; Shephard 1980), it was not until Miller (1980) developed his economic scaling technique that archaeologists have been able to measure the nature of the relationship between material culture and socioeconomic level. With this technique, the relative economic value of a ceramic assemblage can be determined, which then provides a means with which to discuss the relative economic level of the households that purchased, used, and discarded the ceramics.

Based on an extensive study of 19th-century ceramic price lists, Miller (1980) developed an economic scaling of ceramics based on the cost relationships of variously decorated wares to the cheapest undecorated ware (cream-colored, or CC ware). The values of decorated wares are expressed in relation to a fixed index value of 1.00 for CC ware at specific points in time. For example, transfer-printed teacups and saucers with an 1860 index value of 4.00 cost four times as much as contemporary undecorated CC teacups and saucers with an index value of 1.00 (Miller 1980:30). Results obtained from calculating the formula are expressed in terms of average relative economic values for cups, plates, and bowls in an assemblage. By summing the products for cups, plates, and bowls, and dividing by the total number of these vessels, a mean economic value for the assemblage is obtained (Klein and Garrow 1984). These mean values can be used to compare the value of one assemblage with that of another.

Miller's (1980) price indices, however, are incomplete for the period after 1870, and nonexistent after 1881. This presented a major problem in applying the technique to the ceramic collections from Phoenix, the majority of which were purchased and discarded after 1880. There appeared to be a solution to this dilemma: a study of ceramic prices listed in seven mail-order catalogues from 1895 through 1927 (Montgomery Ward and Company 1895, 1922; Sears, Roebuck and Company 1897, 1900, 1902, 1909, 1927) indicated that ceramic prices continued to be linked to various decorative techniques, and that open-stock prices for individual ceramic vessel forms were available on the majority, if not all, of the decorative and ware types offered by these mail-order firms.

Given the availability of ceramic prices for the period during which the two project areas were occupied, a series of price indices were developed for use in discussing the relative economic level of the project area residents. Prices of open-stock cups and saucers, plates, and bowls were collected from the seven mail-order catalogues. From these data, index values were generated based on the price relationships of decorated wares to the cheapest undecorated ware (Miller 1980:11). Miller's cheapest undecorated ware was CC, which was not a ware type identified by name in the catalogues. Therefore, the role filled by CC in Miller's study was filled in this analysis by undecorated "semiporcelain," which was in all cases the least costly. The catalogues also exhibited some variability of prices within each decorative category. Since variability among, rather than within, decorative categories is the sensitive element of this analytical technique, prices within each category were averaged to obtain a single figure, which was used to generate the indices. A combined index value was used for tea- and coffee cups since the distinction between them in archaeological collections is not often clear. Likewise, since plate diameters often cannot be determined from sherds, index values for all plate sizes were averaged. Since none of the catalogues included all ranges of, or open-stock prices for, all decorative techniques, data from several catalogues were combined to create indices for a time period, rather than for specific years, as Miller has. A set of mid-1890s indices was generated from data in the 1895 Montgomery Ward and 1897 Sears, Roebuck catalogues, while data from the 1900, 1902, and 1909 Sears catalogues were combined to create indices for the period 1900–1910, and the 1922 Montgomery Ward and 1927 Sears catalogues provided data for a set of indices for the 1920s (Table 9.1).

TABLE 9.1
Ceramic Price Indices

| Decoration | n | Average Price per Dozen | | | Indices | | |
		Cups and Saucers	Plates	Bowls	Cups and Saucers	Plates	Bowls
1895–1897							
Undecorated	1	$1.10	$0.68	$1.00	1.00	1.00	1.00
Molded	2	1.26	0.75	1.15	1.15	1.10	1.15
Transfer	5	1.49	1.00	1.37	1.35	1.47	1.37
Transfer, gilt	10	1.73	1.32	1.94	1.57	1.94	1.94
Porcelain	4	4.12	2.71	2.80	3.75	3.99	2.80
1900–1902–1909							
Undecorated	2	$0.68	$0.50	$0.72	1.00	1.00	1.00
Molded	2	1.07	0.73	0.97	1.57	1.46	1.35
Color, gilt	4	1.70	1.27	1.71	2.50	2.54	2.38
Porcelain	1	2.82	2.01	—	4.15	4.02	4.00[a]
1922–1927							
Undecorated	2	$2.21	$1.50	$1.51	1.00	1.00	1.00
Molded	1	2.52	1.63	1.93	1.14	1.09	1.28
Gilt band	5	3.41	1.70	2.16	1.54	1.13	1.43
Decal	12	4.69	2.36	2.77	2.12	1.57	1.83
Porcelain	7	6.10	4.31	4.02	2.76	2.87	2.66

[a] Estimated value based on the relationship of porcelain to other categories (no bowl prices available).

The 1890s indices reflect the decoration-price relationships identified by Miller (1980). A new decorative technique appears in the catalogues for the first decade of the 20th century: Wares decorated by the decalcomania process were offered by the 1902 Sears catalogue. Although only two of the 13 sets offered were decorated with the new technique, prices for these sets were not inconsistent with those for transfer-printed sets. Not commonly available except on imported European porcelains prior to 1900, decal became the prevalent decorative technique by 1909 (see Sears, Roebuck and Company 1909; Wegars and Carley 1982:7). Given the coexistence of transfer-print and decal designs on ceramics, and since there was little price differentiation between them, these two decorative categories are combined under the term "color" in the listing of index values for the first decade of the 20th century (Table 9.1).

By the 1920s, shifts in the price relationships among the various decorative and ware categories have occurred. The most startling of these changes is that, in the 1927 Sears catalogue, German porcelain was cheaper than English semiporcelain decorated with decal designs. While German porcelain advertised by Sears over the preceding years had always been less expensive than French (Haviland) porcelain, it had never before been cheaper than semiporcelain. In the 1922 Montgomery Ward catalogue, however, the only porcelain offered was German made. Three of the sets were less costly than four semiporcelain sets, and two of the three sets were two to six times as expensive as the French porcelain offered by Sears. This shift in cost relationships may have been associated with post–World War I conditions in Germany, which may have either affected the quality of the ware or influenced its status abroad. Another shift in price relationships was a marked range of prices within each decorative category. For example, a dozen teacups and saucers decorated with decal and gilt highlights could have been purchased for as little as $1.48 or as much as $8.35. Additionally, within the decorative category of gilt band, there are two separate cost levels, apparently associated with the quality of the gilt applied. In order to mitigate some of the effects of these shifts on the analysis, and so that results would be comparable to earlier periods, several categories were combined in developing the 1920s index values. Prices for decal-decorated ceramics of English and American manufacture were combined, as were those of ceramics with gilt banding, in addition to combining prices for German and French porcelains. The resulting index values (Table 9.1) are more conducive for use with archaeological collections, in which distinctions are not easily made on gilt quality or on origin of manufacture in the absence of maker's marks.

Data requirements for conducting economic scaling analysis of ceramic collections are an accurate minimum vessel count, an accurate identification of vessel form and decorative-ware type, and an adequate sample. The ceramic collections from 14 features fulfilled these requirements. The mean ceramic date obtained from each feature guided the selection of which set of indices was appropriate, since the MCD more closely approximated time of purchase than did deposition period. In calculating the values for cups, the minimum number of cups and saucers was used because, with few exceptions, a cup and saucer were sold as a unit. The exception was in the occasional catalogue reference for institutional ("hotel ware") ceramics, which are not included in this analysis.

This economic scaling technique was also adapted for use in analyzing the butchered food bone recovered from the two project areas. Traditional faunal analyses rely upon calculations of minimum number of individual animals, age of animals at death, or weight of edible meat represented by the bones in an assemblage (Jolley 1983). While these kinds of analyses may be appropriate for certain kinds of dietary studies, they provide little useful information in under-standing dietary consumer behavior in an urban setting, where most meat was obtained through retail purchase. Since professional butchering techniques have been relatively standard for the past 100 years (see Schulz and Gust 1983:48), an analysis of the cuts of meat purchased provides results that are more culturally relevant to understanding urban behavior (Henry and Garrow 1982; Henry et al. 1983; Klein and Garrow 1984; Mudar 1978; Schulz and Gust 1983).

The unit of analysis used is the "butchering unit" identified through a study of professional butchering references (Bull 1951; Romans and Ziegler 1977), that indicated the manner in which carcasses were initially divided into wholesale cuts, here termed "butchering units." The wholesale cuts were subsequently butchered into smaller retail cuts, such as steaks and roasts, for household consumption (see Davidson 1982 for a discussion and illustration of the procedures with specific reference to archaeological collections). Bones retrieved from archaeological sites are more readily associated with wholesale units than with the smaller retail cuts.

Studies of late 19th- and early 20th-century butchering guides and meat value relationships (Davidson 1982; Mudar 1978; Schulz and Gust 1983), compared with current relative values and prices (Bayhem et al. 1982; Henry and Garrow 1982; Roberson and Roberson 1966), indicate that the relative values of different butchering units have remained fairly constant over the past 100 years. It was thus possible to generate a scale of economic indices based on prices of retail meat cuts obtained from five Phoenix markets (Bayhem et al. 1982; Henry and Garrow 1982). These indices were developed in the same way as those for ceramics. Indices for the different butchering units for beef, mutton, and pork are presented in Table 9.2. Meat values for each meat type in a feature, and a mean value for each feature, were calculated in the same way as for ceramics.

A comparison of the meat index values in Table 9.2 with the ceramic index values in Table 9.1 indicates a considerable range in the intervals between the upper and lower ends of the scales. This variability is reflected in the results of the index calculations, where, for example, one assemblage yielded a mean meat value of 3.45 and a mean ceramic value of 2.08. In order to be able to determine whether these two values reflect similar or dissimilar levels of expenditures for the two types

TABLE 9.2

Average Prices and Index Values for Beef, Mutton, and Pork Butchering Units[a]

Butchering Unit	n	Average Price per Pound	Economic Index
Beef			
Hindshank	1	$0.59	1.00
Feet	1	0.69	1.17
Neck	5	0.88	1.49
Plate	5	1.51	2.56
Frontshank	1	1.57	2.66
Chuck	23	1.81	3.07
Tail	3	1.82	3.08
Rump	4	2.32	3.93
Round	14	2.67	4.53
Ribs	7	3.33	5.64
Full loin	18	3.69	6.25
Mutton			
Neck/head	1	$0.69	1.00
Breast	2	1.28	1.86
Leg	5	2.17	3.14
Chuck	4	2.28	3.30
Rack	2	4.17	6.04
Loin	2	4.99	7.23
Pork			
Head/neck	1	$0.49	1.00
Feet	3	0.71	1.45
Picnic shoulder	2	1.49	3.04
Boston butt	9	1.54	3.14
Ribs	3	1.55	3.16
Ham/leg	6	2.14	4.37
Loin	14	2.20	4.49

[a] From Henry and Garrow 1982:347.

of consumer goods, the variability evident in the scales had to be mitigated. This was accomplished by subdividing the range for each scale into 10 equal parts, creating a decile ranking scale. Preliminary comparisons using the precision of this scale resulted in little evident patterning, so pairs of decile ranks were used, with "1" indicating the highest two-tenths of a scale, and "5" indicating the lowest two-tenths. These slightly more general scales are more conducive for use with the general scale used in ranking occupational titles.

Results

Occupational titles held by members of the households associated with the 15 features analyzed were assigned to their appropriate ranking, and economic values were calculated for the ceramic vessels and butchered food bone from those features. The results obtained are presented in Table 9.3.

At first glance, the mean economic values for ceramics and meat appear quite variable and seem to bear little relationship to occupational ranking. When the decile-pair ranks for the ceramic and meat values are compared, however, the results seem fairly consistent. In order to measure the strength of the relationships among the ceramic values, the meat values, and the occupational ranking, Kendall's *tau* statistics for rank-order correlation (Thomas 1976) was calculated. With Kendall's *tau*, a score of ± 1.0 indicates perfect correlation, and a score of 0.0 indicates no correlation. Since some features were associated with multiple households (Table 9.3), the occupational rank used was that of the household residing on the lot the longest during feature deposition. Results indicate a weak correlation between mean ceramic value and occupational rank (*tau* = 0.256), a somewhat stronger, but still weak, correlation between mean meat value and occupational rank (*tau* = 0.389), and a very weak correlation between mean value rankings for ceramics and meat (*tau* = 0.167). Since cups tend to represent social ritual and status display and therefore should reflect social status, and since the common denominator in all faunal assemblages was beef, economic value ranks of these two subsets of the ceramic and bone assemblage were compared to occupational rank using the Kendall's *tau* statistic. Results show a moderately strong correlation between cup value rank and occupational rank (*tau* = 0.4871, a slightly stronger correlation between beef value rank and occupational rank (*tau* = 0.556), but a very weak correlation between the rankings of beef values and ceramic values (*tau* = 0.111). These data suggest that, as expected, there is a correlation between socioeconomic status (as measured by occupation) and consumer choices for ceramics and meat. However, consumer behavior associated with ceramic purchase bears little relationship to that associated with meat purchase. This suggests that, although expenditures for both are influenced to some degree by socioeconomic status, that influence affects consumer choices in different ways. This may be due to the fact that different kinds of commodities—durable versus nondurable goods—influence different kinds of consumer choices.

The relationship between status and the values for ceramics and meat is not, however, an overly strong one. The sample size (14 features for ceramics and 9 for meat) has, no doubt, affected the results. Additionally, households at the very upper and very lower ends of the status scale are not represented in the Phoenix data, and all occupational ranks are not equally represented. Eight of the 15 features are associated with households at the relatively high rank of 2. It is possible that, in dealing on the specific level of individual households, the hierarchical ranking scale is not effective. In fact, historical demographers have recognized that "information on occupation . . . is insufficient by itself for understanding the individual or group experience of occupation" (Willigan and Lynch 1982:100). In other words, just

TABLE 9.3

Summary of Analysis Results

Feature Number	Deposition		Ceramic Values (Rank)[a]				Meat Values (Rank)[a]				Occupation Rank
	MCD	Date	Cups	Plates	Bowls	Mean	Beef	Mutton	Pork	Mean	
331	1877.5	1880–1890	1.94(4)	1.00	1.00	1.59(4)	3.29(3)	3.53	2.52	3.22(4)	3
321	1904.1	ca. 1912	2.04(4)	2.20	1.61	2.02(4)	2.63(4)	0	2.53	2.62(4)	2
327	1920.7	ca. 1924	1.51(4)	1.70	1.00	1.40(4)	—	—	—	—	2
69/328	1895.0	1903–1910	1.55(5)	2.36	1.00	1.74(4)	—	—	—	—	7
305	1897.2	1907–1915	2.26(3)	1.35	1.76	1.76(4)	3.19(3)	2.38	2.92	3.07(4)	1, 2, 3, 4
310	1916.9	1915–1925	2.08(4)	1.85	2.30	2.05(4)	3.68(3)	2.75	3.31	3.45(4)	2, 4
309	1910.7	1911–1915	2.85(3)	2.76	1.89	2.64(3)	—	—	—	—	1, 2, 3
2-2	1896.1	1902–1927	1.82(4)	1.28	1.05	1.62(4)	—	—	—	—	2
2-3	—	1905–1927	—	—	—	—	4.45(2)[b]	4.05	0	4.25(3)	2
2-4	1898.1	1915–1927	2.00(4)	1.31	1.29	1.73(4)	3.79(3)	3.25	2.26	3.37(4)	2
1-15	1927.3	1913+	2.06(2)	1.75	1.56	1.93(3)	3.71(3)	3.58	3.36	3.48(4)	4
1-132	1924.2	1929+	1.64(4)	1.34	1.65	1.54(4)	3.71(3)	3.58	1.30	3.58(3)	2, 7
3-13	1909.4	1930+	2.12(2)	1.84	2.09	2.04(3)	3.87(3)[b]	3.38			2,7
3-14	1919.1	1930+	1.62(4)	1.23	1.66	1.53(4)					
4-5	1915.8	1928–1930	3.82(1)	2.46	3.19	3.17(2)	4.35(2)	2.98	3.59	4.09(3)	3, 4, 7

[a] Numbers in parentheses refer to rank.

[b] Faunal analysis was conducted on remains from combined features associated with the same household(s).

aspirations, or life-style. Furthermore, there is considerable variability in the economic scaling results that may be due to other factor(s) influencing consumer behavior.

Ethnic group membership may account for some of this variation. It is possible that the Mexican heritage of at least two of the households associated with four features (331, 321, 327, 310) influenced differential consumption patterns reflected in the faunal variability. Since foodways are often the most durable of ethnic traditions (Glassie 1968:206–207, 216, 237), a comparison was made of the extent to which Mexican-American and European-American households purchased different kinds of meat. To test the equality of the proportions of beef, mutton, pork, chicken, and wild game consumed by the two groups, the Z statistic was calculated, using the null hypothesis that there is no difference between the frequencies of different meat types associated with both groups (Freund 1973:275–278, 317–320). Table 9.4 presents the data and results. At the 0.005 level of confidence, results exceed ± 1.96, except for chicken, indicating that for beef, mutton, pork, and wild game, proportions between the two groups are different. Since beef is a major component in all assemblages, the calculations were done again after eliminating the figures for beef (Table 9.4). Results for mutton and pork again exceed the ± 1.96 range for the 0.005 level of confidence, indicating that proportions of these kinds of meat are different between the groups. There is, however, no significant difference between the groups in the proportions of chicken and wild game. These results suggest that, at least in the case of some meat types, ethnic group membership influences consumer choices.

Changes in household life cycle may account for some of the variability observed in the ceramic and meat values. On Block 1, the Donofrio household increased as five children were born and grew to adulthood, their mother died, and the head of the household experienced financial difficulties with his confectionery business (interview with the youngest son, the late Judge Francis Donofrio). These factors—changes in the family life cycle and business reversals—may explain the decrease in ceramic values over time (F 321 and F 327 in Table 9.3). In the Murphy Addition, the Shott household was also passing through stages in the family life cycle as the daughters grew up and married, and their husbands joined the household. The head of the household held positions of respect in the community as city councilman and manager of the Pioneer Band. Additionally, the household experienced an increase in status as Mr. Shott was promoted from department store salesman to manager of the hardware department in that store. It is likely that household income increased due to the promotion (although both occupations are ranked the same) and due to the contribution of wages of the sons-in-law; the ceramic

TABLE 9.4
Comparison between Ethnicity and Frequencies of Meat Types

	Mexican-American[a]			European-American[b]			Z scores	
	Number	Percentage	Percentage w/o Beef	Number	Percentage	Percentage w/o Beef	Z	Z w/o Beef
Beef	616	64.1	—	1235	68.2	—	-2.18	—
Mutton	121	12.6	35.1	290	16.0	53.2	-2.39	-5.28
Pork	98	10.2	28.4	70	3.9	12.8	6.58	5.80
Chicken	89	9.3	25.8	172	9.5	31.6	0.17	-1.85
Wild[c]	37	3.9	10.7	73	2.4	7.9	2.24	1.42
TOTAL	961			1810				
TOTAL w/o beef	345			545				

[a] Features 310, 321, 327, 331 (Henry and Garrow 1982).
[b] Features 1–132, 2–2, 2–3, 2–4, 3–13, 3–14, 4–5, 305 (Henry and Garrow 1982; Henry et al. 1983).
[c] Includes duck, quail, dove, pigeon, rabbit, and fish.

values indicate an increase in ceramic expenditures over time (F 2–2 and F 2–4 in Table 9.3).

External economic conditions and market availability may also explain some of the variability observed in the ceramic values. Figure 9.1 shows the ceramic cup values from 14 features arrayed in chronological order by mean ceramic date. The decrease in values during the mid-1890s may have been influenced by the economic depression of the early 1890s (Mawn 1979). The general increase during the next decade and a half may represent the increased level of prosperity and business activity in Phoenix despite the drought during the early years of 1900 and the economic Panic of 1907 (Mawn 1979). It is appropriate to note that, during this period, Phoenix was enjoying full communication with the rest of the nation via the railroad, and that the Murphy Addition was being actively settled. The decrease in values during and immediately following World War I reflects the presence of fewer French and German porcelains in the archaeological record. European porcelain production was considerably curtailed during the war, and the lower cup values from the mid-teens through the mid-1920s may be due more to availability of supply than to decreasing household expenditures.

Beef values do not reflect a similar chronological trend, although the lowest value occurs during the first decade of the 20th century, which may reflect the impact of the drought on the area's livestock industry. Several factors may explain why beef (and mean meat) values do not reflect these economic conditions, as do ceramics. Meat was grown and processed locally, so the impact of economic conditions on the manufacture and transport of merchandise was not much of a factor in meat supply. As a durable consumer good, ceramics are purchased infrequently, and in times of economic difficulty these expenditures can be deferred; food is a nondurable commodity that must be purchased frequently, therefore expenditures cannot be easily deferred. Due to this difference, consumer choices associated with food may also be influenced to a greater degree by individual preferences, by variability in the means of acquisition (retail purchase, poultry raising, hunting), by diversity in culinary practices, and by changes in food storage technology.

The observed values for ceramics from Feature 4–5 are at variance with the rest of the collection. This feature was primarily associated with a widow who owned a fair amount of property elsewhere in the city, according to the latest tax records available (Henry et al. 1983). Her status and corresponding level of consumption would have been related to the status of her late husband, about whom no data were available. Additionally, a meatcutter is known to have resided on the property for a period of time during and after 1925. If his household contributed to the deposits in Feature 4–5, this may be reflected in the meat values and frequencies obtained. The meat values for this feature, although high, are not the highest observed, however, except for pork.

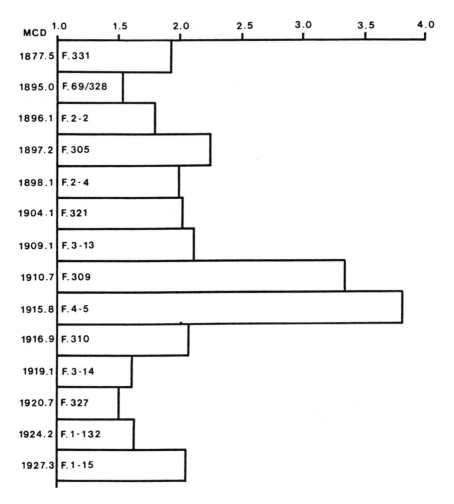

Figure 9.1. Chronological trends in ceramic cup values.

Conclusions

The results of these analyses illustrate that many factors, not merely socioeconomic status, influenced consumer behavior in turn-of-the-century Phoenix. Although the household sample size is small, these results indicate that household life cycle, the economic fortunes (or misfortunes) of individual households, external economic conditions, market themselves affect the decisions consumers had to make. While material culture patterns reflecting consumer behavior are observable in the archaeological record, these patterns are best understood when integrated with data from primary documents and results from research conducted by market analysts, historians, and sociologists.

In conducting these analyses, several problem areas were identified that should be resolved if we are to fully understand urban consumer behavior and the processes involved in consumer decision making. The paramount difficulty is that of defining and measuring socioeconomic status with confidence. Historians, sociologists, and market analysts who study social stratification (see Coleman and Rainwater 1978; Hershberg and Dockhorn 1976; Levy 1973; Warner 1973; Willigan and Lynch 1982) define "class" in terms that are difficult and time consuming to measure quantifiably. These researchers all point out that occupation alone is an insufficient measure of status position. This situation was reflected in using an occupational ranking scale in these analyses. It is possible that such a scale is useful for certain studies specifically related to the job experience, but it should not be used in the absence of other measures of social stratification. In fact, such a measure does not appear to be a valid technique in comparing individual households, although it may be useful when comparisons of large groups of households are to be made (i.e., when comparing neighborhoods). Additionally, diagnostic characteristics of different social strata and social groups have not been sufficiently identified for archaeologists to determine which patterns of material culture represent which strata or groups (excepting perhaps the social extremes of the very wealthy and the very disadvantaged; see Otto 1977), or why such patterns reflect the strata or groups that they do. Archaeological techniques that address differential social strata, such as economic scaling, should be evaluated in terms of more precise definitions of those strata. The economic scaling of ceramics technique used here needs to be refined, taking into consideration different systems of ceramic pricing and marketing (e.g., discounting; mail order versus retail store).

Since the household is the appropriate unit of archaeological analysis (Deetz 1982), future research should focus on an identification of the various types of household, on defining household life cycle stages, and on how patterns of material culture vary during the life of a household. The differences between durable and nondurable consumer goods, and the corresponding variations in consumer behavior, are not often recognized by archaeologists, although an 8-year life cycle of the ceramic set postulated by one researcher (Garrow 1982) seems to reflect consumption and use behavior associated with a durable good. Additionally, the effects of commodity supply need to be investigated in more depth.

Given the number of factors that influence consumer behavior, not to mention the effects of individual household idiosyncracies, there is considerable variability in the data, not only in Phoenix, but from other urban areas as well. To offset this so that patterns and processes of consumer behavior can be understood, very large, synchronous samples of households need to be amassed. The quantity of urban areas that have been studied (see Staski 1982) represent a potentially valuable data base of American urban culture that could be used to resolve some of these problems. If the data from all of these urban research projects could be gathered together and analyzed using consistent procedures, we should be able to identify, with a higher level of confidence, material culture patterns associated with consumer behavior and the processes involved in consumer decision making.

REFERENCES

Bayhem, F. E., P. C. Hatch, and J. Balsom. 1982. Interpretation of Faunal Remains from the Original Phoenix Townsite, Blocks 1 and 2, manuscript on file, Soil Systems, Inc., Phoenix.

Bull, S. 1951. *Meat for the Table*. New York: McGraw-Hill.

Chaplin, R. 1971. *The Study of Animal Bones from Archaeological Sites*. New York: Seminar Press.

Coleman, R. P. and L. Rainwater. 1978. *Social Standing in America: New Dimensions of Class*. New York: Basic Books.

Davidson, P. E. 1982. Patterns in Urban Food Ways: An Example from Twentieth-Century Atlanta, In *Archaeology of Urban America: The Search for Pattern and Process*, R. S. Dickens (ed.), pp. 381–388. New York: Academic Press.

Deetz, J. F. 1982. Households: A Structural Key to Archaeological Explanation. In *Archaeology of the Household: Building a Prehistory of Domestic Life*, Richard R. Wilk and William L. Rathje (eds.), *American Behavioral Scientist* 25:717–724.

Freund, J. E. 1973. *Modern Elementary Statistics*. 4th ed. Englewood Cliffs, NJ: Prentice-Hall.

Garrow, P. H. (ed.). 1982. *Archaeological Investigations at the Washington, D.C. Civic Center Site*. Report prepared for the Historic Preservation Office, Department of Housing and Community Development, Government of the District of Columbia, by Soil Systems, Inc., Marietta, GA.

Gaw, L. P. 1975. The Availability and Selection of Ceramics in Silcott, Washington, 1900–1930. *Northwest Anthropological Research Notes* 9:166–179.

Glassie, H. 1968. *Pattern in Material Folk Culture of the Eastern United States*. Philadelphia: University of Pennsylvania Press.

Gordon, M. M. 1978. *Human Nature, Class, and Ethnicity*. New York: Oxford University Press.

Henry, S. L. and P. H. Garrow. 1982. The Historic Component, Part II. In *The City of Phoenix: Archaeology of the Original Phoenix Townsite, Blocks 1 and 2*, J. S. Cable, S. L. Henry, and D. E. Doyel (eds.). *Soil Systems Publications in Archaeology 1*. Professional Service Industries, Inc., Phoenix.

Henry, S. L., K. S. Hoffman, F. Ritz, and J. A. McKenna. 1983. The Archaeology of an Early 20th-Century Residential Neighborhood in the Murphy Addition. Draft report, Soil Systems, Inc., Professional Service Industries, Phoenix.

Hershberg, T. and R. Dockhorn. 1976. Occupational Classification. *Historical Methods Newsletter* 9(2–3):59–98.

Howard, J. A., and J. N. Sheth. 1973. A Theory of Buyer Behavior. In *Perspectives in Consumer Behavior*, H. H. Kassarjian and T. S. Robertson (eds.), pp. 519–540. Glenview, IL: Scott, Foresman.

Jolley, R. L. 1983. North American Historic Sites Zooarchaeology. *Historical Archaeology* 17(2):64–79.

Kassarjian, H. H. and T. S. Roberts. 1973a. Social Class. In *Perspectives in Consumer Behavior*, H. H. Kassarjian and T. S. Robertson (eds.), pp. 390–400. Glenview, IL: Scott, Foresman.

Kassarjian, H. H. and T. S. Roberts. 1973b. Social Processes. In *Perspectives in Consumer Behavior*, H. H. Kassarjian and T. S. Robertson (eds.), pp. 292–299. Glenview, IL: Scott, Foresman,

Kassarjian, H. H. and T. S. Roberts. 1973c Culture and Subcultures. In *Perspectives in Consumer Behavior*, H. H. Kassarjian and T. S. Robertson (eds.), pp. 450–465. Glenview, IL: Scott, Foresman.

Katz, M. B. 1972. Occupational Classification in History. *Journal of Interdisciplinary History* 3:63–88.

Klein, T. H. and P. H. Garrow (eds.), 1984. *Final Archaeological Excavations at the Wilmington Boulevard, Monroe Street to King Street, Wilmington, New Castle County, Delaware.* (DELDOT Archaeological Series, Number 29), Delaware Department of Transportation, Dover.

Laslett, P. and R. Wall (eds.). 1972. *Household and Family in Past Time.* Cambridge: Cambridge University Press.

Laumann, E. O. and J. S. House. 1973. Living Room Styles and Social Attributes: The Patterning of Material Artifacts in a Modern Urban Community. In *Perspectives in Consumer Behavior*, H. H. Kassarjian and T. S. Robertson (eds.), pp. 430–440. Glenview, IL: Scott, Foresman.

Levy, S. J. 1973. Social Class and Consumer Behavior. In *Perspectives in Consumer Behavior*, H. H. Kassarjian and T. S. Robertson (eds.), pp. 409–420. Glenview, IL: Scott, Foresman.

Martineau, P. 1958. Social Classes and Spending Behavior. *Journal of Marketing* 23:121–130.

Mawn, G. P. 1979. Phoenix Arizona: Central City of the Southwest, 1870-1920. Unpublished Ph.D. dissertation, Arizona State University.

Miller, G. L. 1974. A Tenant Farmer's Tableware: Nineteenth Century Ceramics from Tabb's Purchase. *Maryland Historical Magazine* 69:197–210.

Miller, G. L. 1980. Classification and Economic Scaling of 19th Century Ceramics. *Historical Archaeology* 14:1–40.

Montgomery Ward and Company. 1895. *Montgomery Ward and Co. 1894-95 Catalogue and Buyers Guide No. 57.* Reprinted in 1969. New York: Dover.

Montgomery Ward and Company. 1922. *Montgomery Ward and Co. Catalogue No. 97, Fall & Winter, 1922–23.* Reprinted in 1969. New York: H. C. Publishers.

Mudar, K. 1978. The Effects of Socio-cultural Variables on Food Preferences in Early 19th Century Detroit. *The Conference on Historic Sites Archaeology Papers* 12:322–391.

Otto, J. S. 1977. Artifact and Status Differences—A Comparison of Ceramics from Planter, Overseer, and Slave Sites on an Antebellum Plantation. In *Research Strategies in Historical Archaeology*, S. South (ed.), pp. 91–118. New York: Academic Press.

Rathje, W. L. and M. McCarthy. 1977. Regularity and Variability in Contemporary Garbage. In *Research Strategies in Historical Archaeology*, S. South (ed.), pp. 261–286. New York: Academic Press, New York.

Reitz, E. J. and S. L. Cumbaa. 1983. Diet and Foodways of Eighteenth-Century Spanish St. Augustine. In *Spanish St. Augustine: The Archaeology of a Colonial Creole Community*, K. Deagan, pp. 151–185. New York: Academic Press.

Roberson, J. and M. Roberson. 1966. *The Meat Cookbook.* New York: Collier Books.

Romans, J. R. and P. T. Zeigler. 1977. *The Meat We Eat.* Danville: Interstate Printers and Publishers.

Schiffer, M. B., T. E. Downing, and M. McCarthy. 1981. Waste Not, Want Not: An Ethno-archaeological Study of Re-use in Tucson, Arizona. In *Modern Material Culture: The Archaeology of Us*, R. A. Gould and M. B. Schiffer (eds.), pp. 67–86. New York: Academic Press.

Schulz, P. D. and S. M. Gust. 1983. Faunal Remains and Social Status in 19th-Century Sacramento. *Historical Archaeology* 17(1):44–53.

Schuyler, R. L. 1980. Preface. In *Archaeological Perspectives on Ethnicity in America: Afro-American and Asian American Culture History*, R. L. Schuyler (ed.), pp. vii–viii. New York: Baywood, New York.

Sears, Roebuck and Company. 1897. *Sears, Roebuck and Company Consumer Guide, Catalogue No. 104.* Reprinted in 1976. New York: Chelsea House.

Sears, Roebuck and Company. 1900. *Sears, Roebuck and Co. Consumers Guide Catalogue No. 110, Fall 1900*, J. J. Schroeder, Jr. (ed.). Reprinted in 1970. Northfield, IL: DBI Books.

Sears, Roebuck and Company. 1902. *Sears, Roebuck and Company Catalogue No. 111.* Reprinted in 1969. New York: Bounty Books.

Sears, Roebuck and Company. 1909. *Sears, Roebuck and Company Consumers Guide, Catalogue No. 118.* Reprinted in 1979. New York: Ventura Books.

Sears, Roebuck and Company. 1927. *Sears, Roebuck and Company Catalogue.* Reprinted in 1970. New York: Bounty Books.

Shephard, S. J. 1980. An Archaeological Model: Change in the Nineteenth Century Middle Class. Paper presented at the annual meeting of the Society for American Archaeology, Philadelphia.

Staski, E. 1982. Advances in Urban Archaeology. In *Advances in Archaeological Method and Theory, Vol. 5*, M. B. Schiffer (ed.), pp. 97–149. New York: Academic Press.

Thomas, D. H. 1976. *Figuring Anthropology: First Principles of Probability and Statistics.* New York: Holt, Rinehart and Winston.

Vivello, F. R. 1978. *Cultural Anthropology Handbook: A Basic Introduction.* New York: McGraw-Hill.

Warner, W. L. 1973. Social Class in America. In *Perspectives in Consumer Behavior*, H. H. Kassarjian and T. S. Robertson (eds.), pp. 400–409. Glenview, IL: Scott, Foresman.

Warner, W. L. and P. S. Lunt. 1941. The Social Life of a Modern Community. *Yankee City Series, Vol. 1.* New Haven: Yale University Press.

Wegars, P. and C. E. Carley. 1982. "The Very Latest Rage": Design Trends in Twentieth Century Ceramics. Paper presented at the annual meeting of the Society for Historical Archaeology, Philadelphia.

Wells, W. D., and G. Gubar. 1970. Life Cycle Concept in Marketing Research. In *Research in Consumer Behavior*, D. T. Kollat, R. D. Blackwell, and J. F. Engel, (eds.), pp. 512–527. New York: Holt, Rinehart and Winston.

Willigan, J. D. and K. A. Lynch 1982. *Sources and Methods of Historical Demography.* New York: Academic Press.

Chapter Ten

Struggling with Pots in Colonial South Carolina

In this paper I use the folk pottery of colonial South Carolina in presenting a fundamental aspect of the resistance of slaves to the European-American ideology that justified slavery. My goal is not only to report on the "archaeology of resistance," that is illustrating the material remains of past people we know to have overtly resisted the conditions of slavery but also to use pottery and foodways to demonstrate how parts of the material culture of slaves were actively creating resistance. My general thesis is that the cultural differences between slaves and elites in colonial South Carolina were so great that they can be seen as an ever-present impediment to the plantation system; and I am looking for evidence of these differences in the foodways of the two groups.

Most writers (e.g., Aptheker 1974; Genovese 1974:585–660; Wood 1974: 285–326) have dealt with resistance as conscious, covert, or overt acts of defiance such as slowing down work, feigning ignorance, stealing, burning barns, murdering, running away, and openly rebelling. I propose that another *unconscious* resistance must have been manifest in the content and structure of daily activities such as foodways that were controlled by slaves. That is, by striving to build and live their own subculture (see Stuckey 1987), different in kind as well as material quality from that of their white owners, African-Americans unconsciously distanced themselves from the kinds of rationalizations that would have helped make slavery work. They resisted slavery by being themselves.

The slave population of colonial Carolina was so large and rice plantations so remote that many slaves lived and died in a world apart from their masters and, in some cases, even from white overseers. In 1737 a Swiss visitor commented that

This article was originally published in *The Archaeology of Inequality*, Randall H. McGuire and Robert Paynter, eds., pp. 28–39, Oxford: Blackwell Publishers, ©1991.

Carolina was "more like a negro country than a country settled by white people" (Wood 1974:132). In this "negro country" a few enslaved Native Americans and a very large number of enslaved Africans were struggling to build lives for themselves and their families within the harsh constraints of plantation slavery. They were building what would become African-American culture. Economic, social, demographic, and environmental factors resulted in the slaves of colonial South Carolina having significant control over their domestic lives, including foodways and the use of pottery.[1]

Following the notion of Ian Hodder (1982:10) that "the daily use of material items within different contexts recreates from moment to moment the framework of meaning within which people act," I think that the separate patterns of foodways including the different ceramic wares in planters' houses and slave villages were part of a larger, dual symbolic system that established contrasting and conflicting meaning on southern plantations. Moreover, I believe that differences in the symbolic systems of the two groups, including the material symbols, created a schism between white and black understanding which countered, or more probably doomed from the beginning, the development of a consistent ideology for both owner and slave. Due to the dramatic cultural differences there could be no ideology allowing slavery to operate as efficiently as the planters envisioned. Aspects of this "resistance of incongruity" may have been unconscious on the part of the enslaved practitioners and apparently benign to the domineering elite. Yet where the system of meaning and posture of attitude of slaves were at odds with the ideology of the planters, there was an endemic, cultural resistance.

In his review of "Some Opinions About Recovering Mind," Mark Leone (1982) has restated Karl Marx's view of ideology as that class of "givens" and "taken-for-granteds" held unawares by society and functioning to mask contradictions and conflicts and to suppress resistance. According to Marx, in a class-structured society with a well-integrated ideology, production without parity of profit would proceed without the necessity of physical coercion by the elite. "Common understanding" would provide an acceptable rationale for the differences. For slaves such a common understanding would have meant that they accepted the planter's view of their place in plantation society and believed that anything benefiting and pleasing to their masters was ultimately best for them. On the other hand, without this common understanding slaves would not have worked because it was their accepted role; they would have worked only to avoid punishment.

In the British empire of the 18th century, including colonial South Carolina, an elite ideology was established that effectively separated heaven and earth, souls and bodies, religion and science, and man and nature. White men, knowledgeable in science, were taken to occupy the pinnacle of a well ordered, earthly hierarchy—a position represented symbolically by the Georgian style (Deetz 1977), wherein material things were structured such that the hierarchy and the position of the elite was "obvious" (Isaac 1982; Leone 1984). In general, part of the power of such an elite resides in their access to material things that are valued by, and inaccessible to, the nonelite. These items serve as evidence of elite superiority, and their arrangement may be used to reinforce the relative status of elite and nonelite—to create and recreate the "obvious" hierarchy (Gero 1983). Moreover, with a consistent ideology the elite are in a position to manipulate subordinates through rewards consistent with the style and following the ideology. Carried to the absurd, the Georgian style and the ideology it represented had the aim of maintaining the British empire, and the component institution of slavery, without violence. If slaves recognized and accepted their place in the obvious order, they would serve without resistance, with some saying they would receive a more equitable reward in another realm—heaven.

Through exposition by Deetz and explanation by Leone we know the archaeological features of Georgian style and the relationship of this style to 18th-century ideology. Another important consideration of this style and underlying ideology concerns the social relations of production it was designed to rationalize, direct, and drive. Was the symbolic system successful in transmitting the ideology and thus effecting a more efficient agrarian capitalism based on slave labor? We know that the answer to this question is negative. Major aspects of the ideology disappeared, Georgian style became antiquated, and the institution of slavery was abolished. "Obvious" as the Georgian symbols may have been to the crafters, such distinctions, which were not fully accepted by British society, must have been of little import to slaves who suffered the violence required to maintain slavery.[2] I suppose that when most slaves looked upon Georgian mansions, elegant gardens and imported finery, they may have been impressed with the power of their oppressors to secure such items. Slaves, however, were from a different culture with a significantly different history from that of western Europeans and European-Americans. Despite the demands on their labor, in colonial Carolina they created a domestic environment based on their history and experience. Perhaps if they contemplated Georgian structures with separate kitchens and bedrooms, individualized place settings, and rigid, formal gardens, they reacted as runaway slave Charles Ball described in 1854 (Lester 1968:87) when he wrote that "the native Africans . . . generally place little, or even no value upon the fine houses and superb furniture of their masters . . . They are universally of the opinion . . . that after death they shall return to their own country." I believe Carolina slaves must have thought their oppressors had some fine things and some peculiar ways. The obvious question is: As European-Americans were building mansions and formal gardens, what symbolic world were slaves creating? A look at foodways gives us a start in answering this question.

Slave foodways were significantly different from those of European-Americans. The Georgian foodways of European-Americans drew from urban centers, used anonymously manufactured European utensils, and promoted individualism and hierarchy through differences in the quality and design of the items. Slave foodways, like the rest of slave culture, were concentrated and strongest in rural areas, primarily used locally made folk ceramics and displayed little evidence of individualism, group segmentation or hierarchy.

Archaeologists working on slave quarters in South Carolina have recovered various material effects of slave foodways including folk-produced ceramics—so-called colono ware with West African and Native American antecedents (Ferguson 1980)—as well as imported European ceramics, iron pots and kettles, and glass bottles. In addition to these well-preserved items we know from written and oral sources, as well as a few archaeological specimens, that slaves also used dried gourds for bowls and dippers, they carved wooden bowls and buckets, and they wove mats and baskets for use in their homes.

While the entire assemblage of containers and other utensils is important in analyzing the foodways of slaves, colono ware is especially significant. This ware is the major artifactual component of archaeological collections from slave quarters, comprising an average of 70 percent of all ceramics recovered.[3] Forty-eight percent of all ceramics from rural sites in the Colony is colono ware, while the ware comprises only 2.2 percent of the ceramics recovered from urban sites. Thus, the data indicate that colono ware was primarily a rural phenomenon associated with slaves, and that this domestically produced ceramic (Wheaton et al. 1983:225–250) was a major material component of the slave food system.

Combining these wares with unpreserved wooden, basketry, and gourd utensils suggests a "container environment" that was dominated by handmade items similar to those of the African motherland of the majority of slaves. From birth, slave children were surrounded at mealtimes, not by the few pieces of slipware and stoneware bought for them by planters, but by traditionally styled earthenware made by their mothers or other African-American women. Although planters could buy exotic items, slave children could see the collective "mothers" of their lives making the things that nourished them every day.

In crafting colono ware, slave women produced artifacts that show little evidence of individual or group segmentation or hierarchy. From site to site the pottery is quite similar—plain and undecorated. Ceramic decoration implying segmentation appears only during the influx of Indian slaves resulting from raids on Spanish missions early in the 18th century. The evidence suggests that, except for the time when Indians were being brought into slavery, the ceramic ware emphasized the similarities of slaves and reinforced their common heritage and their differences from whites.

Not only were the artifacts of black foodways domestically produced and homogeneous, but the pattern of those foodways including the shape of the vessels, the foods prepared, the manner of preparation, and the etiquette of eating were different from the Georgian style and most similar to a generalized West African pattern. Small unrestricted bowls that average close to a liter in volume comprise about two-thirds of the entire collection of 67 reconstructed colono ware shapes recently inventoried from South Carolina sites (Ferguson 1992) (Figure 10.1). Most of the remaining vessels are small jars that were charred in fires (Figure 10.2). The high frequency of bowls in South Carolina is consistent with a pattern discovered by archaeologist John Otto (1984:67) from a 19th-century slave quarter in coastal Georgia. Although there was no colono ware in this primarily 19th-century assemblage, Otto's conclusion was that the imported British manufactured bowls used by slaves were part of a system of foodways similar to those of West Africa (Otto 1984:59–69, 85). My conclusions concur with and extend those of Otto.

Figure 10.1. Colono ware bowl from Bluff Plantation, Combahee River, South Carolina. 7.8 cm tall.

Two of the most commonly occurring vessel forms in Africa in colonial as well as in recent times are cooking jars and serving bowls (Leith-Ross 1970; David and Hennig 1972:7–16; MacGaffey 1975:29). The jars commonly have rounded bases and flaring rims, occasionally with handles. Bowls are usually unrestricted and commonly used for drinking as well as for serving food. West Africans use these vessels for preparing and serving their general fare, which may be soup but is more commonly starch, such as millet, rice, or maize. These starches are often served with a vegetable relish to which meat or fish in small quantities is sometimes added. Cooks usually boil the starchy main dish in a large jar, while the sauce or sauces are cooked in smaller ones. This main dish is most often served in a large wooden, gourd, or ceramic bowl and smaller bowls filled with the sauces are placed near the central serving. Sitting on the ground, people eat the meal with their hands, taking a ball of the starchy main dish and dipping it into the relish.[4]

The handmade cookwares from colonial Carolina are generally consistent with this pattern. The volume distribution of jars is bimodal with a large size of approximately 5 l appropriate for cooking the starchy main dish, and a smaller size

Figure 10.2. Colono ware jar from West Branch of Cooper River, South Carolina. 12 cm tall.

averaging almost 1.75 l appropriate for cooking sauces.[5] In one case a perforated sherd has been recovered (Wheaton et al. 1983:233) that appears to me to be the basal portion of a type of perforated jar similar to those used in the northern portion of West Africa to steam couscous, although it might also be for drying meat or other purposes (David and Hennig 1972:13; Dieterlen 1951:168; Leith-Ross 1970:28, 98, 176, 183; Park 1954:8).

Nine of the whole jars from South Carolina show evidence of having been used in fires, and many of these have thick encrustations of charring showing heavy use (Figure 10.3). The shape of the jars, with generally rounded bases rather than the flat and tripodal bases of European vessels, is consistent with African and American Indian domestic technology rather than that of Europeans. This shape is well suited for use on three-stone hearths or hearths of three lumps of clay commonly found in West Africa.

Figure 10.3. Fragment of charred colono ware jar, Berkeley County, South Carolina. Approximately 5.5 cm tall.

Earthenware pots generally cook slower and cooler than those of metal, and Blakely reports (1978:104) from the contemporary Hemba of the Congo that earthenware pots are preferred to metal ones for cooking manioc leaves because they cook more slowly. White Southerners, creolized through contact with their African and Indian slaves, showed a similar preference. In an 1828 cookbook, Virginia cook Mary Randolph (Randolph 1984:34–35) included a recipe for okra soup that called for cooking in an earthenware pipkin and serving over rice; and William Gilmore Simms (1970:361) wrote that many of the "old [white] ladies" insisted that okra soup "was always inferior if cooked in any but an Indian pot" and that an "iron vessel is one of the last which should be employed in the preparation of this truly southern dish." Importantly, both okra and rice were brought to the South from Africa, and both African and Indian slaves came from traditions of using handmade earthenware. Simms refers to earthenware as an Indian pot because by the mid-19th century most African-American slaves had stopped making earthenware, and unglazed earthenware cooking jars and bowls were commonly acquired from itinerant Catawba Indians.

With rounded bases and unrestricted shapes the majority of colono ware bowls are similar in shape as well as size to those used in West Africa for warming and serving food (David and Hennig 1972:13; MacGaffey 1975:29; Prazan 1977:97). And the evidence for use is consistent with generalized West African practices— charring from cooking fires is rare and there is little evidence of cuts and wear from utensils. Native Africans would have eaten from bowls like these with their hands, and while there is no direct evidence that Carolina slaves ate from these bowls in this way, there is little evidence of utensil marks or wear.

Of the 45 bowls in the collection of whole vessels, only one shows evidence of cutlery marks, and evidence of other utensil wear in the soft fabric is evident on the interior bottom and rim of only three vessels—two of them from urban and cosmo-politan Charleston. The colono ware data show that on the rural plantations, colonial slaves were not eating like their European masters but like their African ancestors. Most colonial slaves probably ate similarly to Shadwick Hall's African grandmother who came to live on a Georgia plantation near the end of the slave trade. Hall said she "use tuh set down in the middle of the flo of uh house when she go tuh eat and she alluz eat out of a wooden bowl. Sometimes she use a spoon, but most of the time she jis eat with uh fingers" (WPA 1986:193–194).

Colono ware vessels with similarity to European shapes are definitely in the minority in collections from South Carolina, and they are found where we might expect them—in urban centers and in rural areas where European influence was the greatest, such as near the kitchens of plantation houses. Two of the three plates in the collection are from Charleston; there is clear evidence of utensil wear on one of these plates. There is also a bowl from Charleston shaped like the pewter bowls of the 18th century. Vessels from the kitchen at Drayton Hall near Charleston are different from the majority of the ware in that there are shallow flat-bottomed pans similar to European pie pans. Archaeologist Lynne Lewis, who excavated this site, notes that Drayton Hall was not a working plantation but served "as a business management and country seat for the Drayton holdings" (Lewis 1978:11). It seems clear that in areas where there were European demands, pieces of colono ware were manufactured in European forms, but in the isolated communities of rural slaves, wares continued in the African form.

My conclusion is that the foodways of 18th-century African-American slaves in South Carolina were quite similar to those of West Africa and significantly different from those of European-Americans of the same time period. The pattern appears strong in the eighteenth century; Otto's evidence as well as some of the oral history of ex-slaves indicates that the pattern continued in some areas to the middle of the 19th century.

Thus, while the Georgian style prescribed using knives, spoons, and forks together with individual place settings of industrially manufactured flatware, African-American slaves appear to have been eating one-dish meals with their hands from cookware and dishes that had been domestically manufactured. The differences were not simply qualitative, they were differences of kind, indicating significantly different foodways in a different domestic environment. To the elite, this difference in kind was probably quite understandable; it emphasized the "obvious" dichotomy between European and "Negro" and exemplified the barbaric nature of Africans. The pressing question, however, is "What did this environment symbolize to African and African-American slaves?"

Looking at this faintly reconstructed environment, we may first recognize that the symbols are obviously not Georgian; and, at least to the degree that material symbols create ideology, we cannot expect African-American ideology to have been consistent with that of their Georgian-inspired owners. A striking feature of the collection of colono ware is *sameness*. Although there are differences in the quality of manufacture of vessels, there are few shapes and very little decoration. From the evidence, it seems that there was little difference in colono ware from plantation to plantation throughout the Low Country. There is no evidence of social segmentation or hierarchy being represented in the ceramics manufactured by slaves. The only evidence of similarity to European forms is in urban areas and near the kitchens of main houses. In general, it seems that neither shape nor decoration was used extensively to define individual or group boundaries or status within the slave community. Colono ware emphasizes similarity, not difference. The pottery is folk —traditional and regionally homogeneous.

In their foodways, slaves of South Carolina were not surrounded by an everyday symbolic environment that reinforced and explained their position in a hierarchy. They were within an ethnic environment that must have emphasized reciprocal relationships with one another, resourcefulness, competence and traditional ties to ancestral culture. This example of their symbolic world suggests no illusion to mask the contradictions. To the majority of slaves, the white elite must have been part of an alien world for which there may have been no well-developed explanation, and without a generally accepted explanation of the social and economic differences between blacks and whites there must have been inefficiency in production. Thus, the building of an African-American culture, different in kind from that of southern whites, maintained an unconscious resistance to slavery and the plantation system.

The result, I believe, was that southern culture, including African-American culture, developed not at the direction of the elite but through a process of quasi-political negotiation—a conclusion similar to that presented by several historians (e.g., Blassingame 1979; Genovese 1974; Sobel 1987; Stuckey 1987). The exciting prospect of archaeology is that through an examination of the material record, such as the initial study presented here, we shall be able to look at the early stages of this negotiation from both sides.

Acknowledgments

My thanks to colleagues Joan Gero and Theodore Rosengarten for critically reviewing this paper, and to Carol Speight for her editorial assistance. Part of my research on colonial Carolina pottery was supported by a grant from the National Endowment for the Humanities.

NOTES

1. See Wood 1974; Littlefield 1981; and Morgan and Terry 1982 for a discussion of the demography, isolation, and relative autonomy of slaves in colonial South Carolina.

2. See Wood 1974:271–284 for examples of the violence of slavery in colonial South Carolina.

3. These percentages are an average from 23 South Carolina sites (Ferguson 1992).

4. For examples showing this pattern and its persistence through time, see: for the Kingdom of Mali, AD 1352, Oliver and Oliver 1965:13; the Gambia River, AD 1623, Jobson 1968:48–49; the Coast of Guinea, AD 1704, Bosman 1967:392; Sierra Leone, AD 1803, Winterbottom 1969:64–66; Angola, AD 1865, Monteiro 1968:288–289; Mossi, contemporary, Hammond 1966:57; Dukkawa of Northeast Nigeria, contemporary, Prazan 1977.

5. For African examples of similar vessels, see Blakely 1978:25; David and Hennig 1972:11; Leith-Ross 1970; Mangin 1921:70.

REFERENCES

Aptheker, H. 1974. *American Negro Slave Revolts*. New York: International.

Blakely, P. 1978. Material Culture in a Hemba Village. Unpublished M.A. thesis, Department of Folklore, Indiana University.

Blassingame, J. W. 1979. *The Slave Community: Plantation Life in the Antebellum South*. New York: Oxford University Press.

Bosman, W. 1967. *A New and Accurate Description of the Coast of Guinea: Divided into the Gold, the Slave, and the Ivory Coasts*. London: Frank Cass.

David, N. and H. Hennig. 1972. The Ethnography of Pottery: A Fulani Case Seen in Archaeological Perspective. *McCaleb Module in Anthropology* 21:1–29. Reading, MA: Addison Wesley.

Deetz, J. 1977. *In Small Things Forgotten*. New York: Doubleday.

Dieterlen, G. 1951. *Essai sur la Religion Bambara*. Paris: Presses Universitaires de France.

Ferguson, L. 1980. Looking for the 'Afro' in Colono-Indian Pottery. In *Archaeological Perspectives on Ethnicity in America*, R. L. Schuyler (ed.), pp. 14–28. Farmingdale, NY: Baywood.

Ferguson, L. 1992. *Uncommon Ground: Archaeology and Colonial African-America*. Washington, DC: Smithsonian Institution Press.

Genovese, E. D. 1974. *Roll, Jordan, Roll: The World the Slaves Made*. New York: Pantheon Books.

Gero, J. M. 1983. Material Culture and the Reproduction of Social Complexity: A Lithic Example from the Peruvian Formative. Unpublished Ph.D. dissertation, University of Massachusetts. Ann Arbor: University Microfilms.

Hammond, P. B. 1966. *Yatenga: Technology in the Culture of a West African Kingdom*. New York: Free Press.

Hodder, I. 1982. Theoretical Archaeology: A Reactionary View. In *Symbolic and Structural Archaeology*, I. Hodder (ed.), pp. 1–16. Cambridge: Cambridge University Press.

Isaac, R. 1982. *The Transformation of Virginia, 1740–1790*. Chapel Hill: University of North Carolina Press.

Jobson, R. 1968. *The Golden Trade or a Discovery of the River Gambra, and the Golden Trade of the Aeothiopians*. London: Dawsons of Pall Mall.

Leith-Ross, S. 1970. *Nigerian Pottery*. Ibadan: Ibadan University Press.

Leone, M. 1982. Some Opinions About Recovering Mind. *American Antiquity* 47:742–760.

Leone, M. 1984. Interpreting Ideology in Historical Archaeology: The William Paca Garden in Annapolis, Maryland. In *Ideology, Power and Prehistory*, D. Miller and C. Tilley (eds.), pp. 26–35. Cambridge: Cambridge University Press.

Lester, J. 1968. *To Be a Slave*. New York: Dell.

Lewis, L. G. 1978. *Drayton Hall: Preliminary Archaeological Investigation at a Low Country Plantation*. Charlottesville, VA: National Trust for Historic Preservation.

Littlefield, D. C. 1981. *Rice and Slaves: Ethnicity and the Slave Trade in Colonial South Carolina*. Baton Rouge: Louisiana State University Press.

McGaffey, J. 1975. Two Kongo Potters. *African Arts* 9(1):29–31, 92.

Mangin, E. 1921. *Les Mossi: Essai sur les us et coutumes du peuple Mossi au Soudan Occidental*. Paris: Augustin Challamel.

Monteiro, J. J. 1968. *Angola and the River Congo, Vol. I*. London: Frank Cass.

Morgan, P. D. and G. D. Terry. 1982. Slavery in Microcosm: A Conspiracy Scare in Colonial South Carolina. *Southern Studies: An Interdisciplinary Journal of the South* 21(2): 121–145.

Oliver, R. and C. Oliver (eds.). 1965. *Africa in the Days of Exploration*. Englewood Cliffs, NJ: Prentice-Hall.

Otto, J. S. 1984. *Cannon's Point Plantation, 1794–1860: Living Conditions and Status Patterns in the Old South*. New York: Academic Press.

Park, M. 1954. *Travels of Mungo Park*. New York: E. P. Dutton.

Prazan, C. 1977. *The Dukkawa of Northwest Nigeria*. Pittsburgh: Duquesne University Press.

Randolph, M. 1984. *The Virginia House-Wife*. Columbia: University of South Carolina Press.

Simms, W. G. 1970. *The Wigwam and the Cabin*. New York: AMS Press.

Sobel, M. 1987. *The World They Made Together: Black and White Values in Eighteenth-Century Virginia*. Princeton: Princeton University Press.

Stuckey, S. 1987. *Slave Culture: Nationalist Theory and the Foundations of Black America*. New York: Oxford University Press.

Wheaton, T. R., A. Friedlander and P. H. Garrow. 1983. *Yaughan and Curriboo Plantations: Studies in Afro-American Archaeology*. Atlanta: Soil Systems, Inc.

Winterbottom, T. 1969. *An Account of the Native Africans in the Neighborhood of Sierra Leone, Vol. I*. London: Frank Cass.

Wood, P. 1974. *Black Majority*. New York: Alfred A. Knopf.

Works Projects Administration. 1986. *Drums and Shadows*. Athens: The University of Georgia Press.

MARY C. BEAUDRY ■
LAUREN J. COOK
STEPHEN A. MROZOWSKI

Chapter Eleven

Artifacts and Active Voices:
Material Culture as Social Discourse

The only way to preserve the fantasy of the inarticulate masses is never to listen to members of the masses when they are articulate.

> Henry Glassie *Passing the Time in Ballymenone* (1982).

The anthropological mode of history . . . begins from the premise that individual expression takes place within a general idiom.

> Robert Darnton *The Great Cat Massacre and Other Episodes in French Cultural History* (1984).

Transformation and *mediation*: the two most essential characteristics of human social life.

> Anthony Giddens *A Contemporary Critique of Historical Materialism* (1981).

Material Expressions of Culture

A common theme connecting interpretations of the material record of the past is how people engage the material world in cultural expression in the negotiation of everyday life. The relationship of behavior to the material world is far from passive; artifacts are tangible incarnations of social relationships embodying the attitudes and behaviors of the past. "The underlying premise [of material culture study] is that objects made or modified by man reflect, consciously or unconsciously, directly or indirectly, the beliefs of the individuals who made, commissioned, purchased, or used them and, by extension, the beliefs of the larger society to which they belonged" (Prown 1988:19).

Historical archaeologists have long acknowledged the pivotal role material culture studies play in their research (see Ferguson 1977); James Deetz, perhaps

This article was originally published in *The Archaeology of Inequality*, Randall H. McGuire and Robert Paynter, eds., pp. 150–191, Oxford: Blackwell Publishers, ©1991.

the field's most creative exponent of artifacts as cultural message-carriers,[1] has even proposed that historical archaeology is best thought of as "the science of material culture" (Deetz 1977a:12). Few historical archaeologists have heeded his call; meanwhile, the past decade has witnessed the emergence and growth of material culture studies as a strongly interdisciplinary field in its own right.[2]

Material culture studies in historical archaeology have for the most part been conducted within the research paradigm that until recently dominated the field—logical positivism/logical empiricism (see Gibbon 1989)—and researchers have purposely avoided the issue of meaning while criticizing the few who grappled with understanding the cognitive aspects of artifact use in the past. Hence we are burdened with a positivist legacy that produced a literature replete with descriptive studies providing details on artifact identification, typology, and chronology[3] linked either to constructing often quite colorful culture histories or "explanatory models" that were unstintingly empiricist in nature. The recent surge of interest in "the recovery of meaning" stems both from dissatisfaction with the old paradigm as well as from the inexorable penetration of new intellectual trends from literary theory, history, and anthropology past the barriers of a lingeringly intransigent positivism into the mainstream of archaeological thought.

Those who look for meaning in the archaeological record approach it from a variety of theoretical perspectives, including structuralism, cognitive semiotics, economic theory, Marxism, and critical theory. For many historical archaeologists, new, post-positivist[4] approaches offer an opportunity for interpretation and explanation of social differentiation that was impossible under the generalizing mode of the old paradigm, with its overriding concern for statistical regularities. A new concern for intensive, often prosopographic detail in carefully framed case studies does not signal the emergence of a new particularism. This move, according to Hodder (1987a:2), has come about because many have recognized that "historical explanation . . . involves an attempt at particular and total description, and it does not oppose such description to explanation and general theory. Rather, our generalizing anthropological concerns can progress only through an adequate description, and hence understanding, in our terms, of the particular."

While Hodder's statement seems to fly in the face of much of what has been dogma in historical archaeology, attention to recent intellectual trends reveals that once again archaeologists have fallen victim to what Leone (1972) once referred to as "paradigm lag."[5] Paynter (1984) has noted that positivist epistemology has been largely discredited by prehistorians and others (cf. Hodder 1986; Leone et al. 1987; Shanks and Tilley 1987; Wylie 1989; but see also Earle and Preucel 1987), yet far too many historical archaeologists seem to be operating within a paradigm that others have forsaken. Only the most extreme and reductionist of pattern-seekers could find any merit in the bizarre lengths to which South's pattern analysis (South 1977, 1978)[6] and Miller's economic scaling (Miller 1980) have been taken. This sort of objectification lies outside of the realm of a truly anthropological investigation and in fact reduces historical archaeology to a most dry and impersonal sort of economic history.

Recent trends in anthropological thought and in the social and human sciences as a whole involve a shift away from "totalizing frameworks" (Marcus and Fischer 1986:9):

> social thought in the years since [the 1960s] has grown more suspicious of the ability of encompassing paradigms to ask the right questions, let alone provide answers, about the variety of local responses to the operation of global systems, which are not understood as certainly as they were once thought to be under the regime of "grand theory" styles. Consequently, the most interesting theoretical debates in a number of fields have shifted to the level of method, to problems of epistemology, interpretation, and discursive forms of representation themselves.

Social theorists have become more and more concerned with appropriate and adequate levels of description as well as with problems of representation; much of the intellectual content of recent thought in anthropology, archaeology, and the human sciences in general is derived from theories of interpretation developed in the fields of philosophy and literary criticism (cf. Hunt 1989; Rabinow and Sullivan 1979, 1987). A self-critical mode and careful consideration of "such issues as contextuality, the meaning of social life to those who enact it, and the explanation of exceptions and indeterminants rather than regularities in phenomena observed" (Marcus and Fischer 1986:8) characterize the new "experimental" trend in both anthropology and archaeology.

In this essay we advocate blending an interpretive approach, normally applied to "symbolic" aspects of culture, with the archaeologist's necessary focus on things material and particular. Geertz (1980:135) points out that part of our intellectual legacy from the 19th century is a notion that "'symbolic' opposes to 'real' as fanciful to sober, figurative to literal, obscure to plain, aesthetic to practical, mystical to mundane, and decorative to substantial." Our approach attends both to the materiality of the data—their substantive and functional roles—as well as to the ideological roles. Our concern for the "situatedness" of the data prompts us to focus on context—archaeological, historical, institutional, and behavioral context—while avoiding the tendency to treat meaning and context as static, suspended in time. The archaeological record encodes time and encodes change over time; hence we can derive from it evidence of historical process and cultural change.

Interpretive approaches in anthropology are characterized by attention to belief systems or world views and by a concern for meaning within its cultural and historical contexts; culture is seen as meaningfully constituted, cultural facts as observations subject to multiple interpretations.[7] Yentsch (n.d.:7) notes that in interpretive studies

> the focus is on historical moments and repetitive events that convey information about a specific culture. The emphasis is on small-scaled and detailed examinations of

specific, varied expressions of cultural meaning, on a small range of human activity that tells of ordinary social action, on the day-to-day behavior that in its particularity and complex texture reveals the meaning that gave form to peoples' lives in a given time and place.

Attention to historical and cultural context allows human beings an active role in creating meaning and in shaping the world around them; they are seen to interact with their environment rather than simply react to it. Material culture is viewed as a medium of communication and expression that can condition and at times control social action. Our version of an interpretive approach involves combining several recent trends in the human sciences: semiotics and the study of symbolism; sociological and anthropological theories of social action and social discourse; and detailed construction of the historical and cultural context of artifact use through a critical reading of cultural texts.

Artifact as Text and Symbol

In semiotic terms, meaning is said to be signified by a particular signifier (a word, a written character, an image, or an object).[8] This relationship between representation and meaning, signifier and signified, is known as a sign. For example, red roses signify passion, and when used intentionally to do so, they constitute a sign of passion (Barthes 1957:197–198). A symbol is an arbitrary sign, such as a red traffic signal—there is no particular reason that a red traffic signal should be a sign to stop, except that that meaning has been assigned to it by society (Hawkes 1977:129). The function of the symbol is one of linkage in the process of communicating about the unknown by means of the known (the symbol itself). That is, properties assigned to the symbol by consensus may be transferred by the observer to the situation in which the symbol is employed. The symbol and the symbolized are not seen as being in a static cognitive relationship, but rather articulate with one another as components of a shifting and dynamic relationship (Turner 1974:25–30). Symbols are signs used in a communicative, semiotic process. Objects often function as symbols and have been approached semiotically by scholars (Krampen 1979).

While particular objects and their symbolism vary among cultures, the use of objects as symbols is pancultural. Attempts on the part of prehistorians to identify symbols and symbolic domains in the material culture of preliterate populations (e.g., Hodder 1987b; Shanks and Tilley 1982; Shennan 1982) are predicated on the universal role that the relationship between symbolic action and object-symbols plays in social interaction. Csiksentmihalyi and Rochberg-Halton argue quite persuasively that our interaction with certain categories of objects as material entities is inextricable from our interaction with them as symbols. The domestic objects that clutter our living space may be viewed as "meaningful only as part of a communicative sign process and are active ingredients of that process" (Csiksentmihalyi and Rochberg-Halton 1981:173). As symbols, artifacts fix on their owners and users certain culture-specific attributes—in effect, they serve as "the visible part of culture," by "making firm and visible a particular set of judgments in the fluid processes of classifying persons and events" (Douglas and Isherwood 1979:66–67). Through an analysis of the use of material items in facilitating judgment, classification, and self-expression we can begin to understand the ways in which individuals constructed their cultural identity.

Construction of cultural identity is first and foremost a public act of mediation between self and other; often workers and members of subordinated groups (e.g., slaves, Native Americans, women) find room for self-expression not so much in work as during off-work hours. The role of leisure activities, or those activities that are not considered work, is important to self-definition and self-expression. While the importance of work in the process of self-definition is undeniable, there is a considerable support for the contention that it is through leisure, or at least nonwork, activities that the greater part of self-definition and self-expression takes place (Godbey 1981:98, 123–125; Huizinga 1970; Pieper 1952)—people "create strong and complex selves by investing their psychic energy in activities that are usually called 'leisure'" (Csiksentmihalyi and Rochberg-Halton 1981:48). In a capitalist, industrialized society the working class will not control the means of production, but its members will express themselves individually and as a subculture through other components of what Csiksentmihalyi and Rochberg-Halton (1981:49) call "the means of action." They define the means of action as "any object or sign that allows a person to 'make his self manifest'" (including, where applicable, the means of production).[9]

Social psychologists tell us that the process of classifying others and assessing their intentions and motives is a transitory, swift, and necessary component of public interaction. Through a staggering variety of signs (including objects), gestures and postures, we communicate to those with whom we interact, telling them who we are and what we are doing: "Everyone knows of course, that the individual necessarily provides a reading of himself when he is in the presence of others. Gender, age class, state of health, ethnicity will all be conveyed, in the main unwittingly" (Goffman 1971:127). Those social psychologists specializing in urban interaction emphasize that these presentations of self occur in the arena of the street (cf. Sennett 1978:164–166). Lyn Lofland refers to this process of classification of others as "appearential ordering," a term that stresses both the classificatory function of the activity and its reliance on appearance as the criterion of judgment. In such a "problematic world of strangers" as the city, "all the city dweller had to go on, to know anything at all about these other people, was the information he could glean by looking at them. . . . City life was made possible by an 'ordering' of the urban populace in terms of appearance and spatial location such that those within the city could know a great deal about one another by simply looking" (Lofland 1973:22).

The process of "decoding" the appearance of others is based on the interpretation of visible symbols encoded primarily in forms of dress and other bodily adornments (jewelry, hair styles, etc.) as well as in behavior (Praetzellis et al. 1987). The Victorian context was marked by a "miniaturization" of visible symbols, in which appearential ordering turned on the smallest details of dress or appearance (Sennett 1978:165–168).

The power of material symbols to communicate often lies in their use "out of context"—that is in contexts other than those in which the dominant cultural tradition would apply them. An extreme example would be the "punk" usage of safety pins as earrings rather than as fasteners. Such recycling of the mundane in a symbolic context is informative to the initiated (cf. Barthes 1981:58).

> The tensions between dominant and subordinate groups can be found reflected in the surfaces of subculture—in the styles of mundane objects which have a double meaning. On the one hand, they warn the "straight" world in advance of a sinister presence—the presence of difference—and draw down upon themselves vague suspicions, uneasy laughter, "white and dumb rages." On the other hand, for those who erect them into icons, who use them as words or curses, these objects become signs of forbidden identity, sources of value (Hebdige 1979:2–3).

Style, then, communicates subculture, and is instrumental in group definition and boundary maintenance. Ethnic and class subcultures wield style as a tool to identify those who "belong" and occasionally as a weapon to annoy those who do not.

Belonging—group identity, group membership—is inevitably linked to relations of power and to social differentiation. Too often historical archaeologists interested in the relations of power have failed to heed E. P. Thompson's (1978:157) call to examine class from the bottom up, or Henry Glassie's (1978:86) exhortation to study people "from the inside out." Hence in part the method we employ arises from a reaction against what we perceive as the limitations of an approach to artifact use in relations of power that seems to permit only the powerful to make statements with artifacts.[10] This has come about through the application of Marxist-derived critical theory employing Althusser's dominant ideology thesis to case studies in historical archaeology. It is an approach that has found an ever-growing body of critics.

From the Artifacts of Hegemony to Artifacts in Hegemonic Discourse

In a particularly well-published example of class analysis of material culture outside the workplace, Mark Leone and others at Historic Annapolis, Inc., have explored the ideological function of William Paca's garden (Leone 1984, 1986, 1987, 1988a, 1988b; Leone et al. 1989).[11] Paca was a lawyer and jurist, a signer of the Declaration of Independence, and the governor of Maryland from 1782 to 1785—by any standard, he was a member of that colony's economic and cultural elite (Malone 1946:123–124). Analysis of Paca's reconstructed formal garden has centered around the symbolism of power over nature, as a metaphor for power relations in society. In a critique of the role of ideology in the work of Marxian archaeologists, Ian Hodder (1986:61–70) uses Leone's research on the Paca Garden to illustrate four problems in the treatment of ideology:

1. "There is no indication anywhere that the same material culture may have different meanings and different ideological effects for different social groups" (Hodder 1986:65). The assumption is that all of Annapolis shared Paca's view of the garden.
2. There is a tendency to oppose social reality and ideology, with the latter falsifying, "naturalizing or masking inequalities in the social order" (Hodder 1986:65). Rather than obscuring Paca's elite status, his garden would appear instead to emphasize it.
3. Insufficient attention is paid to the specific historical context in which the garden is supposed to have served its ideological function.
4. The linkage between the functions of ideologies and their purported products is not well drawn. "One is left with the question, where does the particular ideology . . . come from?" (Hodder 1986:69). For example, the principles of perspective that Leone sees as serving the social function of legitimating Paca's dominant position in society are within a historical tradition of landscape construction that can ultimately be traced back to the Classical world. These concepts of order may have played a role in creating Paca's aspirations, as much as they were a tool for realizing them.

These problems with the treatment of ideology have important implications for an archaeology of social class. In regard to the first problem, one of the most disconcerting features of analyses of Paca's garden is their treatment of the role of ideology in class relations. They rely on the "Dominant Ideology Thesis," drawn from Louis Althusser's (1971) essay on the function of ideology on the state level, which holds that the ideologies of the dominant groups in society are imposed on submissive groups. This thesis denies subordinate groups the ability to formulate their own ideologies and has been found to be subject to many exceptions when measured against historical situations (Abercrombie et al. 1980; Miller 1987: 162–163; McGuire 1988:439–440; Rojek 1989:100–101). The result is a "trickle down" model of relationships between the classes, a model that tends to deny the very existence of a working-class culture.[12]

The problem seems to be that Leone's analyses have examined only Paca and his activities and motivations, ignoring those of the "ruled." But we must be careful not to equate the powers of artifacts with the power of their owners or users; further, there is no reason to assume that gardens, or other artifacts, are capable of serving only one symbolic function, and a good deal of reason to assume that they can mediate a variety of meanings, often simultaneously.[13] It is clear that the "dominant ideology thesis" implies a degree of social control on the part of elites that makes it particularly unsuitable as a model for class relationships in developed, industrialized societies—even less so in preindustrial societies or ones still strongly enmeshed in an economic system characterized by barter rather than exchange of cash (cf. Giddens 1981:55).

Other critiques of the dominant ideology thesis in historical archaeology draw on a wide range of scholarship in other fields that likewise find the approach unsatisfactory. Martin Hall (n.d.:11) critiques both the structuralist program employed by Deetz as well as Leone's use of the dominant ideology thesis, noting that Abercrombie et al. (1980) "have tracked the notion of dominant ideology through feudalism, early capitalism, and advanced capitalism, and have found it wanting." Those authors found that dominant ideologies were often inconsistent and seldom had great effect on subordinate classes; in medieval times the peasantry was "kept in order by brute force rather than ideological subtlety" (Hall n.d.:11), while under early capitalism, domination was achieved through economic forces (ibid.). Hall suggests that Annapolis gardens can be reinterpreted without the notion of false consciousness or masking ideologies; instrumentation, garden design, and fashion in dishes and other material goods can be seen as "a means whereby the elite incorporated themselves as a class" (ibid.:12). He points out that if we elect to view "ideology, vested in material culture . . . as a way in which the large planters of the Tidewater convinced themselves of their position in life" (ibid.:13), we approach James Scott's (1985) concept of ideology as a bridge channeling the material world into ongoing social discourse, "constituting and reconstituting existence with the semiotic power of 'texts without words', with the reading of artifacts as ideology, expressing actors' views of their relationships between themselves and others" (ibid.:14). Hall uses Scott's concept of ideology and his notion of "everyday resistance" to reinterpret the material culture of slave life in the plantation South and to offer insight into the archaeological record of slave dwellings at the Cape of Good Hope in South Africa.[14] He does so by incorporating into the paradigm the concept of discourse, drawn from Foucault (1972), with its emphasis on the importance of the sign.[15] When the material world and the actions of those who create it, come into contact with it, and use it for whatever ends, are all seen as statements in a discourse, it is the ambiguity arising out of the multiple meanings material objects carry—the polysemic status of artifacts—that provides the point of entry for explanation. Hall's complementary use of "the varied texts of official records, kitchen refuse, and literary impression" illustrates a way of approaching "artifacts as integral parts of the statements through which people create and re-create themselves, and these statements as integral parts of discourses that create and re-create one another" (Hall n.d.:26).

What we seek, then, is a class-based model of relationships within and between subcultures that is flexible enough to account for the accommodations of interest that in fact occur among and between social classes and ethnic groups (and that can be demonstrated to have occurred in the historical past). One framework that appears to have the potential to subsume complex processes of cultural change involving class, ethnic, and gender groups has been used extensively by British students of popular culture (e.g., Bennett et al. 1981, 1986; Hargreaves 1989). This is the notion of "cultural hegemony," adapted from the work of the Italian Marxist, Antonio Gramsci. Gramsci was expressly concerned with the tendency of "scientific" Marxism to view ideology as a passive reflection of an economic substructure, rather than as a "real" entity, active in its own right. According to Gramsci, members of social classes put forth competing ideologies, centered around what they perceive to be their own interests. Class relationships consist of the negotiation of these ideologies in the cultural arena. Symbols may be adopted and manipulated by the members of different groups, in a process through which each group "seeks to negotiate opposing class cultures onto a cultural and ideological terrain which wins for it a position of leadership" (Bennett 1986:xv).

"Hegemony," then, is an ever-shifting "prevailing consciousness," negotiated among interest groups, that is internalized or accepted to varying degrees by members of those groups (Boggs 1976:39). Raymond Williams (1977:110) sees hegemony as transcending what is traditionally defined as ideology, to include experience as well:

> It [hegemony] is a whole body of practices and expectations, over the whole of living: our senses and assignments of energy, our shaping perceptions of ourselves and our world. It is a lived system of meanings and values constitutive and constituting—which as they are experienced as practices appear as reciprocally confirming. It thus constitutes a sense of reality for most people in the society, a sense of absolute because experienced reality beyond which it is very difficult for most members of the society to move, in most areas of their lives. It is, that is to say, a "culture," but a culture which has also to be seen as the lived dominance and subordination of particular classes.

Discussions of "lived" hegemonies, then, must involve detailed examination of the historical contexts in which they arose and operated.

Constructing Historical and Ethnographic Context

To suggest, as do Leone and Potter (1988a:12–13), that it is possible to confuse the documentary record with the ethnographic record is to confuse etic and emic perspectives (cf. Schuyler 1978; see also Melas 1989). The ethnographic record is the product of the ethnographer and as such is an etic document. Yentsch (1988b:152–153) notes that the documentary record can be approached from both etic and emic perspectives; this is possible because documents are created with words. Hence we can analyze them as reflective of past semantic systems: "the way pre-modern people used and structured their language, or the words they used in [documents], reveals more about the [past] than appears if the words are taken at face value. . . . The words in the [documents] are residual pieces of a bygone world-in-action in which they played a major role" (Yentsch 1988b:153). To use documents to generate archaeological expectations or to attach functions to artifacts is certainly akin to the use of ethnographic data by prehistorians. But is this all historical archaeologists do with documents? The answer is no; the use of the written word in historical archaeology in the construction of context and history is far more developed than Leone and Potter (1988a:11–12) suggest (cf. Beaudry 1988a; Schmidt and Mrozowski 1983).

Leone and Potter subscribe to the erroneous view that the archaeological record and documentary record were produced by "people who usually had no direct connection with one another" (1988b:14). Making direct, one-to-one match-ups between producers of documents and excavated artifacts is of limited utility under any circumstances; documents do, in point of fact, encode connections among people at many levels: face-to-face relations of kin, family, household, neighborhood, and community; impersonal relations of power between factory owners and workers, and so forth. For instance, documents that record commercial connections provide an emic window on the social relations of production (cf. Paynter 1988). It goes without saying that documentary analysis (in addition to and in distinction to "historical research") is integral to the study of material life in historical times, and we contend that it is in fact a vital element in all historical archaeological research. It is vital for constructing context.

Context is where meaning is located and constituted and provides the key to its interpretation. Recovery of meaning is predicated on recovery of context because context not only frames meaning by tying it to actual situations and events, but it is inextricably bound up with meaning. The existence of a context implies the presence of meanings functioning within it, and, conversely, meanings cannot exist in the absence of context. While we can talk about meaning taking place "out of context," we are not implying the absence of context, but rather that the context of use is not the usual or expected context. Often it is in unusual or unexpected contexts that meaning is renegotiated or redefined.

Analysis of cultural texts gives us insight into peoples' attitudes toward the world around them—an integral component of the recovery of meaning as well as of explanation of the archaeological record. Historical archaeologists have the means at hand to inject into their etic, objective studies of the past an emic, culturally sensitive perspective; interpretive analysis, with its concern for meaning and for folk classification and perception, offers a framework for textual analysis aimed at recovering folk meaning. It does so by taking an analytical and ethnographic approach to documents, an approach labeled variously "historical ethnography" (cf. Beaudry n.d.; Schuyler 1988; Yentsch 1975) and "documentary archaeology" (cf. Beaudry 1988a).

In essence, what we seek is the "full and inclusive context" which Taylor indicated should be our primary interest (Taylor 1948:32). As Schmidt and Mrozowski note, the construction of cultural context is the way in which cultural meaning may be added to archaeology and to any patterns that may be deduced from archaeological evidence: "We must carefully research different historical documents and the literature of history to derive constructs that can be synthesized to build a complex cultural context for our archaeological excavation, be it a shipwreck, an Iron Age factory site in Tanzania, or a colonial privy. . . . If we fail to do this, then we overlook cultural contexts that tell us most about behavior" (Schmidt and Mrozowski 1983:146–147). Despite claims to the contrary (i.e., Leone 1988a; Leone and Potter 1988a:14–18), this sort of approach *does not* confuse the documentary record with the ethnographic record or render the one equivalent to the other; rather, it permits a critical, interpretive, and culturally sensitive approach to historical documents with the aim of avoiding overobjectification of its subject matter. And while some perhaps are tempted to extend to such an approach the dismissive label "eclecticism" (e.g., Orser 1988:314–315), it can be said in its favor that an interpretive approach, because it is receptive to differing perspectives, manages to avoid the pitfalls of the doctrinaire application of modern radical political thought inherent in what Orser and others propose as a more "unified" (we would say *rigid*) theoretical perspective tied to the dominant ideology thesis.

There is a persistent "fear of the emic" that is likely a residue of positivism. Many historical archaeologists retain the bias toward documents acquired during their training in prehistory, and some researchers remain oblivious to the possibilities for sophisticated and sensitive analysis of both the material and documentary records. South quite clearly continues to consider archival sources as no more than straightforward documentation, as historical background or as verification: "historical archaeology offers tremendous potential for controlling archaeological variables against the background of historical documentation" (South 1988:38–39). Leone and Potter's (1988b:12–14) suggestion that we treat the documentary and archaeological records as wholly distinct bodies of data, testing one against the other, offers a perspective not very different from South's partitive approach.[16]

Others remain so suspicious of documents as to recommend they be relegated to a minor role in interpretation. Rubertone (1989:32), for example, claims that "the archaeology of 17th-century Native America serves as a source of information on Indian history that exists independent of written accounts produced by European observers." Preferring the "unwritten record" for what it reveals about Native American resistance to European domination, Rubertone dismisses documents because "partisan observers wrote to serve their own best interests and in doing so have omitted from the written evidence how the Narragansett Indians struggled to preserve their independence."[17] This suspicion of documents, this notion that the biases of those who recorded them cannot be analyzed and interpreted but in fact will inevitably taint the researcher, is as naive as it is counterintuitive and unproductive. In another instance, Ashmore and Wilk (1988:5) impute strange power to documents, dreading that the increased sophistication in deciphering ancient texts will lure Mesoamerican archaeologists away from material evidence and hence bias their conclusions. They feel that each source has "special uses" (and presumably, in the case of texts, these are limited) but do acknowledge that if material and textual sources are examined critically, they "can even be employed together as complements" (ibid.) Ashmore and Wilk nevertheless state uncategorically that "archaeologists should continue to *rely* on the more direct material evidence" (emphasis added).[18]

Analyzing written sources from both etic and emic perspectives (or, as some students of material culture put it, from both producer and user perspectives) can resolve this dilemma over what to do with documents. For, as Michael Ann Williams (1990; see also Williams 1986) asks, should we refuse to study women's roles in households and women's use of household space just because we "know" that in historical times houses were "male" artifacts because men built them? Can we assume that a producer controls how users perceive and employ the artifact? Certainly not in the case of texts, unless one assumes that reading merely constitutes "a submission to textual machinery" (Chartier 1989:156). To a certain extent our critical reading of documents is an "appropriation," an interpretation "outside of the text" (ibid.:157) that incorporates attention to the motivation of the producer, to the actions or response of the intended audience, and to our intentional use of the text in constructing our own narrative of interpretation. The synthesis we seek cannot be accomplished through a partitive and reductionist scheme whereby the documentary record is ignored, treated uncritically, or set wholly apart from other sources of evidence.

To move away from the attitude that the use of documents is a literal exercise in obtaining only the information intentionally conveyed by those who recorded them, we need to approach the documentary record as a body of texts (as anthropologists and folklorists do with tales, myths, etc.) and be mindful that our reading is in fact an interpretation of someone else's perceptions. Even our own perceptions cannot be taken at face value (cf. Beaudry 1980b:5). For linguists, a text is any record of a language event. This can be recalled, sound-recorded, written, or printed; it is both a physical thing and a semantic unit. The crucial aspects of texts are *content, form,* and *situation.* Situation, the "environment in which texts comes to life" (Gregory and Carroll 1978:3–4), has constant features that allow us to look for variations in the formal or substantial aspects of texts. Assuming, for instance, a reasonable degree of shared language used among a given body of, say, Anglo-American records, we may examine how information recorded varied either in its internal meaningful structure in a synchronic fashion, or how differences over time and space reflect changes in attitudes, availability of consumer goods, or contact between people of differing social, economic, or cultural backgrounds.

E. P. Thompson (1963:9–10) points out that research into social relations of class "must always be embodied in real people and in a real context" and advocates that documents be "scrutinized upside-down" (Thompson 1978:157) The implication is that documents, even those produced by members of the superordinate class, can be unintentionally revealing about otherwise disenfranchised or inarticulate members of society.[19] Such ethnographically and contextually sensitive data can be extracted through critical analysis of documentary texts in combination with material culture analysis. But looking at history from the "bottom up" or from the "top down" is insufficient, and an emic perspective aims to study meaning "from the inside out." Henry Glassie conveys this with eloquence and power in his stunning work *Passing the Time in Ballymenone*, and we quote him at length.

> In the ceili, makers of tea and chat create the community. In the street, cattle mart, and public house, they buy and sell, watch and march, listen and sing and form the crowd, the population of their region. . . . And beyond that . . . you have seen them, a little lost, standing alone in wordless confusion, country people, dressed neatly, poorly, on the streets of big cities.
>
> That is where the politicians and their agents, the false scholars, want them: weak, bewildered, and, above all, silent. The man who is a learned educator at the fireside, a sparkling wit in the ceili, a bold singer in the pub, becomes, in the gigantic milieu of the nation, silent, nearly nothing, a follower for a politician's doctrine, a statistic for a scientist's scheme, a member of the inarticulate masses. The idea is evil. . . . [T]o support a frantic equation of power and wealth with intelligence and verbal skill, the false scholar contrives a pyramidal picture of society with kings and madmen at its peak, a silent majority at its spreading base. Then reality is ordered to trickle down from top to bottom, from power to weakness, wealth to poverty, intelligence to stupidity, invention to imitation, light to obscurity, texts to silence. Even scholars who strive to be democratic sometimes accept the ugly metaphor and propose to study things from the bottom up. Society is not peaked like a pyramid or layered like a cake. It is composed of communities simultaneously occupying space and time at the same human level. . . . All seem reasonable from within, strange from without, silent at a distance. The way to study people is not from the top down or the bottom up, but from the inside out, from the place where people are articulate to the place where they are not, from the place where they are in control of their destinies to the place where they are not (Glassie 1982:85–86).

Carmel Schrire, a prehistorian who has turned to historical archaeology to examine issues of contact between native South Africans and Dutch colonialists, came quickly to the realization that archival sources interact with archaeological data; she points out that the success of an archaeological study of the impact of colonialism on indigenous people "hinges on its ability to dig as deeply into the archives as into the sands of an abandoned settlement by analyzing words and artifacts that encode a day's meal, a month's shipment of meat to an outpost, and a century's colonial policy enacted by the servants of the great Dutch East India Company" (Schrire n.d.:2). We argue that this is as true for any other endeavor in historical archaeology as it is of Schrire's work at a 17th-century Dutch outpost in South Africa.

Archaeological Context

We have discussed at length the importance of context in assigning meaning to material culture, but the archaeological record as context requires corresponding attention. Especially in urban communities, archaeological deposits often result from rapid depositional episodes (see, e.g., Beaudry 1986; Carver 1987; Mrozowski 1984; Praetzellis et al. 1980). In cities, these rapid depositional events can be the consequence of household-level transitions (Mrozowski 1984; Beaudry and Mrozowski 1987b) or communitywide changes in waste and water management facilities (Beaudry 1986; Honerkamp and Council 1984; Praetzellis et al. 1988). The very structure of the archaeological record can also reveal past behavioral dynamics.

Historical archaeology cannot really be a "science of material culture" in the sense Deetz implied, nor can it be merely "material culture with dirt on it." Archaeological sites are complex matrices: understanding their internal structure, formation, and the relationships among site sediments, depositional processes, and artifacts in the matrix is a vital component of archaeological research (cf. Binford 1976, 1979, 1981; Schiffer 1987). Just as documents are not best used as background context to test against artifacts, artifacts are not best used when considered independent of the contexts from which they were recovered. The historical archaeologist must perform contextual analysis in its most comprehensive and inclusive form. Even a fairly straightforward example helps illustrate the power of contextual analysis arising from merging complementary control of both archaeological and historical contexts.

The presence of beverage alcohol containers at the Lowell boardinghouses is undeniable evidence of liquor consumption, but the discovery of empty bottles in a cache beneath a privy floor is evidence of deliberate concealment—of clandestine disposal presumably following upon clandestine drinking. Situating this archaeological observation in a historical context constructed with the aid of company documents dealing with restrictions on alcohol consumption in the boardinghouses (Bond 1989a), we create a behavioral link whereby the ordinary fragments of backyard refuse begin to speak for the seemingly inarticulate. The close contextual analysis of artifacts provides a counterpoint or subtext to writings of middle- and upper-class observers and reformers, subtly raising the volume of workers' voices so they can be heard above those who speak to us in such loud chorus through written texts.

Artifacts and Multiple Voices:[20]
Examples of Artifact Discourse Analysis

As noted above, a model based on cultural hegemony rather than dominant ideology has several advantages. First, it does not equate economic or political domination with social or cultural domination. For example, while elites may control much of the economic and political structures, it may be the bourgeoisie that has the most influence on the prevailing consciousness. Second, cultural hegemony is seen as based on control through consensus rather than coercion; this requires consideration of the *accommodations* reached by parallel, or even opposing, interests, as well as the equally important areas of conflict that are more easily and more often studied (Stedman Jones 1977:163). Third, and most important, hegemony is not seen as ever being complete (Boggs 1976:40). Initiatives and contributions emerge that are alternative and oppositional to existing hegemonies, although usually framed in the same terms of discourse, and some of these may be negotiated into hegemonic positions (Williams 1977:114). Thus, contributions from the working classes may find acceptance, or at least toleration, by the bourgeoisie and elites. This allows working-class ideology and working-class culture creative, active roles in the social process, rather than viewing them as dictated by and distilled from the ideologies and cultures of politically or economically dominant groups.

The idea of cultural hegemony is fully compatible with the communication-centered model for material culture that was outlined above, and therein lies its usefulness to archaeology. An important dimension of material culture is its communicative function, and much of that function takes place in the day-to-day negotiation of hegemony. The 18th-century merchant with his matching dishes and symmetrical house and grounds, and the 20th-century "punk" with his safety pins and engineer's boots are equally involved in those negotiations, and much of what is recovered archaeologically may be seen as the product of hegemonic discourse, intentional or otherwise. In fact we may see the range of items available at any given time, with their varying moral and symbolic values, as extensions of contemporary hegemony—or even as a "material hegemony" that is every bit as shifting and fluid through time as is cultural hegemony.

A class-based archaeology based on cultural hegemony permits us to interpret our material in its communicative and symbolic aspects, and opens up new avenues for inquiry. For example, if Georgianization was the cultural contribution of the merchant class during the 18th century, as several archaeologists have recently proposed (Harrington 1989; Leone 1988b), then it may be viewed as an element in hegemonic discourse. While we could simply note that Georgianization occurs fairly universally across that class, it would be much more interesting and informative to go beyond this normative viewpoint to examine the ways in which other classes and cultural groups adopted, changed, or rejected the Georgian world-view and its associated material culture—to examine where Georgianization came from, how it became hegemonic in the 18th century, what it meant and how those meanings changed over time, how and by what it was superseded in the hegemony, when and why it reentered the hegemony in "revivals," and what remains of it today.

The examples of material culture analysis we offer here are drawn from our recent collaborative research into the Boott Mills boardinghouses of 19th- and 20th-century Lowell, Massachusetts (Beaudry and Mrozowski 1987a, 1987b, 1988, 1989). Excavation focused on the rear yards of Boott units No. 45, a "typical" boardinghouse where workers dwelt, and No. 48, a tenement for supervisory personnel. The residents of the boardinghouse constituted a corporate household; the tenement was in effect an apartment lived in by a single, usually quite small, nuclear family who at times may have taken in boarders. From the backlots we recovered impressive quantities of everyday objects—buttons, beads, clay pipe fragments, bottle glass, costume jewelry, ceramics, hair combs, marbles, animal bones—left behind by the hundreds of mill employees who inhabited these houses during their operation. Perhaps it is ironic that so many who spent hour upon hour laboring in the mills producing fortunes for others would leave such a humble legacy of buttons, glass "gems," and liquor bottles. For while the archaeological and documentary record provide testimony to the power of corporate paternalism and of the boardinghouse system, those same data evoke expression, if not of resistance, of personal aspirations and self-expression. Despite the fact that limited economic means placed genuine impediments in the way of the material wants of Lowell's mill workers, evidence of adaptive behavior—of the creation of subculture—is visible. It is visible in the use of medicines more desirable for their alcohol content than their efficacy in curing illness (Bond 1989b), in humble aspirations to middle-class status reflected in the selection and use of household ceramics by tenement dwellers (Dutton 1989), and in the deliberate choices made by working women in buying and wearing less costly imitations of expensive jewelry and hair ornaments (Ziesing 1989). It is also expressed in the use of white clay pipes as expressions of class affiliation and even of class pride.

Discourse Through Tobacco-Related Material Culture

An important element of the Lowell study sought to view tobacco use as an element of hegemonic discourse between classes and ethnic groups, as well as between men and women. The focus was on the 19th and early 20th centuries (Cooke 1989). While tobacco use may seem a minor area in which to approach major issues of class relations, those relations penetrated daily life and were interwoven with its threads. Class provided, and provides, contours for the surfaces of everyday activities and interactions, such that its operation may be seen in the most mundane and trivial actions.[21]

The episodes of tobacco use found in the historical record were analyzed along three major dimensions (after Mercer 1986:54, who modified the procedure from Foucault 1972:50–55). The first of these is the *site* of use—the position, in space, in time, and in social context, in which the episode occurs. The second dimension considered is that of the *status* of the event—who the actors are, and their relative positions in structures of authority. Finally, the *subjectivities* of the behavior—the meanings that are conveyed—are considered wherever they are accessible.

Analysis of documentary sources written during the 19th and early 20th centuries indicates an increasing association of short-stemmed white clay pipes with working-class men. Irish immigrants, African-Americans, and other ethnic groups were also associated with their use to varying degrees. Women, at least middle- and upper-class women, were not supposed to smoke at all in the Northeast, particularly in public.

Nineteenth-century smoking emerges from contemporary documents as an activity devoid of overtones of class conflict—unlike the consumption of alcohol—until one looks at the role that smoking played in class-based conflicts over the use of public space. Smoking, like drinking, some team sports, and displays of sexuality, was not politely carried on in public places—streets, parks, restaurants, etc.[22] While smoking itself could be seen, and was seen, as a behavior that united classes, its indulgence by members of certain classes, ethnic groups, and genders in the social context of public space imbued it with subversive meanings and discomforting overtones when viewed by middle- and upper-class writers. Smoking thus found expression in the negotiation of both class- and gender-linked hegemonies, often by serving as an expression of identity and intrusive presence.

The materials used were crucial to the context of the smoking act, signaling the class, ethnic background, or perception of gender relations on the part of the smoker. The combined use of documents and excavated artifacts allows us to recover past contexts and actions, and the meanings that linked them. The pipe collection from the Boott Mills tenements and boardinghouses shows evidence that the working-class smokers who lived there broke the stems of certain types of white clay pipes to shorten them before use. Within the context of contemporary behavior, such actions were clear expressions of membership in the working classes. Ethnic identity is clearly manifest in the presence in the collection of pipes bearing Irish political slogans, such as "Home Rule," and the names of such Irish martyrs as Wolfe Tone. Documents produced for the most part by middle- and upper-class writers can be combined with material evidence for working-class actions to reveal worklng-class meanings.

Discourses of Control and Defiance

Kathleen H. Bond's (1989a) detailed analysis of Boott Company correspondence brought into focus a number of areas of conflict between workers and management;

many of the problems arose over worker behaviors the company officials found unacceptable because they eroded profitability or because certain public behaviors were destructive of the image the corporation wished to project. In a number of instances boardinghouse keepers found themselves rebuked for trying to eke out extra profits for themselves by circumventing company rules about who to board and how to collect rents, or for permitting drinking on the premises. Aberrant worker behavior, especially public drinking and rowdiness, were, however, the prime target of supervisory wrath. Bond notes that the internally consistent themes of the correspondence reveal that company attempts at control of the work force were consistently ineffectual; she links this with evidence from the archaeological excavations to illustrate the contradictory nature of company "concern" for workers (Bond 1989a:35):

> The information gleaned from the letters—that the boardinghouse yards were messy, that the overall condition of the backlots was poor, and that workers consumed alcohol in the units—concurs with the archeological evidence. In some instances the letters were even written to or about individuals who lived in the units investigated archeologically. The neat, orderly image of the mills that the owners took pains to present, however, is made all the more hollow by the archaeological evidence. The archeology helps to strip off the façade of neatness and order; in so doing, it exposes management's attempts to regulate workers' behavior without taking equal responsibility for workers' lives. Managers, however, could not completely eliminate certain behavior. They could only "purify our corporation by discharging the offenders" and remain vulnerable, at least in a small way, to workers' attempts to retain control of their lives.

Much of the evidence to which Bond refers exists in the form of beverage alcohol containers in the backlots (Bond 1989b); apart from these, however, there were large numbers of patent medicine bottles, purported remedies for a wide variety of ailments, all with extremely high alcohol content. It is clear that drinking was prevalent despite unremitting efforts of the corporation to eliminate and prevent it. Bond (1989a:29) observes that "workers drank for a variety of reasons—ethnic customs, as means to promote working-class solidarity, and to temporarily escape from the realities of poverty—it was behavior the workers chose for themselves. If a worker wished to drink whiskey, no amount of 'moral' lecturing would change that fact." The archaeological record is testimony to the fact that the discourse between workers and managers about who controlled workers' leisure behavior in the boardinghouses was played out endlessly in small acts of everyday resistance in ways over which management ultimately had very little control indeed.

Discourse Through Household Ceramic Use

The management policy of the Lowell corporation involved paternalism, but it was a paternalism without rights. It was in leisure behavior and off-work time, as well as personal dress and comportment, that individual workers expressed themselves and signaled the affiliations of ethnicity, subculture, and class.

Quite intriguing to consider in this regard is the use of tea wares and comparatively elaborate table settings by tenement residents. Dutton (1989) found that this contrasted with the patterning of the boardinghouse ceramic assemblage and can be linked to household composition—corporate versus nuclear household—as well as to cultural values. Aside from tea- and coffeeware, the two ceramic assemblages were remarkably similar (Tables 11.1–11.3). Undecorated whitewares dominated both collections with smaller percentages of transfer printed and handpainted ware present. The increased availability of ceramic tableware types and forms in the late 19th century lessens the number of observed differences between ceramic assemblages of households with similar financial means.

TABLE 11.1
Summary of Ceramics by Ware Type

Ware Type	Tenement		Boardinghouse	
	No.	%	No.	%
Bennington	0	0.00	1	0.52
Creamware	1	1.16	5	2.61
Earthenware	0	0.00	1	0.52
Pearlware	2	2.32	1	0.52
Porcelain	11	12.79	8	4.18
Redware	12	13.95	12	6.28
Stoneware	3	3.48	11	5.75
Whiteware	56	65.11	149	78.01
Yellowware	1	1.16	3	1.57
TOTAL	86	100.00	191	100.00

The ceramic assemblages recovered from the boardinghouse and tenement backlots at Lowell reflect two late 19th-century working-class households in similar economic circumstances but with different household composition. Ceramic purchasing patterns reflect attempts at economy while providing the necessary forms for food service and consumption. The tenement residents sought to emulate middle-class dining habits by including more vessels in a table setting per person even though these were unspecialized in function. This suggests that for the tenement, vessel function was versatile and that particular forms served in capacities other than their intended use. At the boardinghouse, however, the keeper provided only the basics for food service and consumption. Complete meals were served to individuals on a single plate with little in the way of accessories (e.g., vegetable dishes, bread plates, and salad plates). Hence the tenement household emulated mainstream middle-class dining rituals by adapting its limited ceramic assemblage to reproduce as closely as possible a middle-class table service, while the boarding

TABLE 11.2
Summary of Ceramics by Vessel Type

Vessel Form	Tenement		Boardinghouse	
	No.	%	No.	%
Ale bottle	1	1.16	0	0.00
Bowl	18	20.93	50	26.17
Chamber pot	1	1.16	0	0.00
Crock	1	1.16	2	1.04
Cup	13	15.11	22	11.51
Flowerpot	3	3.48	5	2.61
Gravy boat	0	0.00	1	0.52
Jar	4	4.65	4	2.09
Jug	0	0.00	1	0.52
Plate	10	11.62	30	15.70
Platter	3	3.48	10	5.23
Pot	4	4.65	1	0.52
Saucer	18	20.93	36	18.84
Teapot	0	0.00	1	0.52
Washbasin	0	0.00	1	0.52
Unidentified	11	12.79	26	13.61
TOTAL	87	100.00	190	100.00

TABLE 11.3
Summary of Ceramics by Decoration

Decoration	Tenement		Boardinghouse	
	No.	%	No.	%
Decal	1	1.16	4	2.09
Dipped	0	0.00	3	1.57
Edged	6	6.97	11	5.75
Gilded	9	10.46	8	4.18
Handpainted	9	10.46	8	4.18
Lead glazed	6	6.97	10	5.23
Molded	9	10.46	29	15.18
Overglazed	1	1.16	0	0.00
Salt glazed	1	1.16	5	2.61
Sponge	3	3.48	6	3.14
Transfer print	12	13.95	32	16.75
Undecorated	28	32.55	74	38.74
Wash	1	1.16	1	0.52
TOTAL	86	100.00	191	100.00

housekeeper, concerned with providing a service for her boarders, eschewed such refinements in vessel function.

Recent work of other historical archaeologists provides us with the means for understanding the nature of these differences and the reasons for them. Wall (1987) was able to demonstrate through the analysis of a series of ceramic assemblages from 18th- and 19th-century New York City that such tablewares closely reflect a new set of values that emerged as urbanization and industrialization took place (see also Mrozowski 1988, who ties the widespread values of the 19th century to developments in 18th-century American cities). Ceramic assemblages from late in the second quarter of the 19th century tend to reflect a set of ideals that developed more or less as a response to changing social conditions brought about by industrialization and the emergence of the middle class. Chief among these values was the notion of separation of the home and the workplace, with woman's sphere being at home and proper work for women being running a household (but not necessarily physically engaging in housework). This notion of striving for refinement and middle-class status through adoption of middle-class standards for polite entertaining and social display, especially through tea drinking, is of interest in that it adds a dimension to ceramic analysis beyond economic considerations. It is obvious that ceramics were often symbols as much as they were everyday objects; historical archaeologists are increasingly willing to interpret their ceramic assemblages in light of the multiple functions they served in order to place their use in its proper cultural context: Burley (1989) and Yentsch (1991) are especially fine examples of such analyses. Such studies bring women into focus, revealing how, especially in 19th-century homes, women influenced the nature of the household. An example from Fort Independence in Boston, Massachusetts, makes this clear and provides insight into the Lowell case.

Clements (1989) found that critical differences occurred between the ceramic and glassware not so much in the assemblages of officers versus enlisted men but between married and bachelor officers. Deposits from households of married officers had by far the greater proportion of serving/entertaining vessels (e.g., fine dinnerwares of blue-and-white transfer-printed pearlware or of Canton porcelain, in forms such as tureens, platters, vegetable nappies, tea wares, etc.). Both assemblages had drinking vessels—stemware and tumblers—but deposits from the bachelors' quarters had significantly more vessels related to alcohol consumption than to tea and coffee drinking or even to food consumption (probably because bachelor officers ate in the mess hall). In deposits from married officers' quarters other, nonfood-related artifacts, most notably toys, enhance the image of families and the activities families carry out. The presence of women and children hence had an unmistakable effect on the archaeological record; the stabilizing influence of women was not lost on the U.S. Army, which encouraged its officers to marry. This afforded them respectability as well as stability, something the military valued highly in its early years when it was faced with public opposition to a standing army and fear—especially in major urban centers—of the possible ill effects of bringing large numbers of unattached, transient males into the community.

The Fort Independence example comes to life when we read the lament of the fort's unmarried physician, who complained of the instability of his life as well as remarking on the favor with which his superiors viewed the married state. Marriage, married life, and the need to maintain a social life in keeping with middle-class values would have been an important part of daily life for officers at an early 19th-century military post. Yet not all members of the garrison would adhere to such views; at a highly stratified military post it is far from surprising to find differences of rank reinforced materially. Solidarity among ranks was promoted through material culture use just as it was used to differentiate between ranks, yet much of the material difference perceived archaeologically reflects the fact that married officers maintained conventional households while unmarried officers and enlisted men did not.

It seems likely that the differences between ceramic assemblages at the Lowell Boott Mills boardinghouse and tenement can similarly be attributed to the differences in household makeup. While women were present and perhaps out-numbered males in both households, married women whose families rented Boott tenements could aspire to stable family life and could put into practice the values linked to the domestic ideology of the 19th century through the structure of meals and entertaining in the home, especially through the ritual of tea-time. While many of the same values found expression in the "professional" management of the boardinghouses by their keepers (Landon and Beaudry 1988; Landon 1989), purchase and use of ceramics was contextually quite different in the two households—boardinghouse residents, be they mill girls or immigrants, did not participate in discourse through ceramic selection and use, though they regularly ate off dishes provided by the keeper.[23] Tenement dwellers, because they were responsible for their own purchases, could and did make active use of ceramic items, not only in self-expression, but also in attempting to create new identities. Viewed in this way, ceramics from historical sites can be interpreted as elements in social discourse and their purchasers as active participants in such discourse. Here the discourse is embedded in the household and in family life and hence functions in a different social context than expression of working-class values through pipe smoking or drinking in public.

Conclusion

The material record, or at least that portion of it that came from the backlots of what were once the Boott Mills boardinghouses, can be viewed as part of a hegemonic discourse that has much to tell us that is not illuminated by the documentary record, as well as much that is. The material adds a texture, a *reality*, to the surfaces of the past that are revealed in print, filling out what Raymond Williams (1977:110) called "the whole substance of lived identities and relationships." Material is not seen here as just a passive product of economic behavior, but as an instrumental component of symbolic actions. The fact that symbolic behaviors are ephemeral makes their material traces that much more important.

At Lowell, our aim has been to go beyond economics, chronology, and spatial distribution in the analysis of ordinary residues of daily life such as bottle glass, clay pipe fragments, and pottery sherds. Blessed with rich documentary sources and a data-laden archaeological record, we have been able to delve deeply into the interpretation of meaning in material culture while maintaining a strong connection with the empirical. This combination enables us to construct context in its most comprehensive form. As Mary Douglas (1973:11–12) noted in commenting on Bourdieu's (1973) analysis of the "complexity and richness" of the rules organizing space in and around the Berber house, "if the author had limited himself to one system of signs, say furniture, or the house without the outside, or the whole material culture without the supporting rites and proverbs which he cites, he would have missed these meanings." Attention to cultural and historical contexts as well as to archaeological contexts from both etic and emic perspectives attunes us to the multiple meanings artifacts have for their users. By analyzing cultural texts, written or otherwise, from "the inside out," we can begin to reconstruct meaning in the active voice, in the multiple voices of the "silent majority" whose past discourse through artifacts reveals they were not so inarticulate after all.

NOTES

1. As early as 1967, Deetz proposed in his monograph *Invitation to Archaeology* that we conceive of artifacts as akin to elements of language, offering a formulation of *factemes* and *formemes* as the material culture equivalents of morphemes (words) and phonemes (meaningful sounds). While few, Deetz among them, have made explicit use of his scheme, a number of scholars have used linguistic models as the basis for material culture analysis (e.g., Beaudry 1978, 1980a, 1980b, 1980c, 1988b; Glassie 1976; Yentsch 1988b), and many more have applied the structuralist paradigm derived from linguistics (e.g., Deetz 1977b; Yentsch n.d., 1988a, 1988c, 1990). See Tilley 1989 for a recent discussion of language theory and material culture analysis in archaeology.

2. For discussions of the growth and direction of material culture studies, see Prown 1988; Roberts 1985; St. George 1988a; Upton 1983; Wells 1986. Anthologies of material culture studies include Bronner 1985; Quimby 1978; St. George 1988b; Schlereth 1980, 1982, 1985; see also the journal *Material Culture*.

3. For instance, Noël Hume (1969) provides a comprehensive descriptive guide to identifying artifacts of the colonial period; Stone (1974) employs the type-variety method to

establish a typology for the thousands of artifacts recovered from the site of Fort Michilimackinac in Michigan; Harrington (1954), Binford (1962), and Walker (1965, 1967, 1977, 1983) all provide ways of dating sites and their levels by the clay pipes in them—Binford's use of a straight-line regression formula is in keeping with the best efforts of the New Archaeology to derive laws through quantification and formulaic approaches to data analysis; South (1977, 1978, 1979) pays homage to Binford, building on the comprehensive descriptive groundwork laid by Noël Hume, by offering a formula for ceramic dating, a discussion of site structure in historical archaeology, and a battery of ahistorical, statistically derived patterns based on "neutral" artifact groupings that in the long run have proved to be devoid of ethnographic import (cf. Yentsch 1989).

4. While most refer to recent trends as "postprocessual" (cf. Leone 1986; Hodder 1989b), we find the appellation misleading and inaccurate. Self-styled postprocessualists claiming to do "archaeology as long-term history" (e.g., Hodder 1987a) or "historical anthropology" (e.g., Little and Shackel 1989) are for all intents and purposes looking at process; post-processualism, as we understand it, rejects the strictly empiricist paradigm of the New Archaeology (cf. Courbin 1988; Gibbon 1989) in order to pursue a concern for ideology, symbolism, and meaning, and for power in society. Hodder (1989b:70) explains that the term denotes a general postmodernist/poststructuralist trend in archaeology to break down the old dichotomy between "on the one hand, normative, culture-historical, idealist archaeology and, on the other hand, processual, cultural ecological, and materialist archaeology." Our own interest in the negotiation of meaning with and through artifacts is a processual approach of sorts; we suggest that archaeologists do themselves a disservice by seeming to eschew an interest in cultural and historical process when in fact what they are rejecting is not process but an unhealthy positivism. These remarks may seem mere cavilling, but concern with the interpretation of cultural texts ought inevitably to spark an awareness of the significance and power of language, especially of labels.

5. Not all of our most influential thinkers in historical archaeology would agree. In a recent publication (1988a) Deetz indicates that his interest in broad patterns of cognitive structure reflected in material culture has been influenced to a certain extent by critical theory (a perspective Deetz notes was presaged by Walter Taylor in *A Study of Archeology*, first published in 1948). Deetz states that archaeologists use "material culture as the primary data base for the construction of context" (1988a:18). This is decidedly something of a departure, for attention to context has never been a strong point of structuralist analysis; what is more, the statement points to the prehistorian's preference for material over documentary context (see note 18). (Sahlins's (1981, 1985) revised structuralism, which incorporates structure with a concern for historical time depth, has regrettably had very little influence in archaeology to date; a recent volume (Hodder 1989a) concerned with meaning, symbolism, and material culture contains a total of 25 essays, only one of which cites Sahlins.) Deetz denies that there is any need for concern over paradigm lag in the field of archaeology (for which he prefers the neologism *archaeography*—this after castigating certain of his colleagues for committing a similar offense by introducing the term *ethnoarchaeology* (1988a:18): "Why invent a new term, when two older ones do the job? Once combined, the terms cannot help but run together in ways that are not productive."). Deetz's new term is a lexical buttress for his opinion that theory resides only in ethnology, which is arguable given the fact that many of the theories employed in archaeology are borrowed from disciplines outside of

anthropology and that some theory does in fact arise from the practice of archaeology itself. It would also seem that the denial of paradigm lag is at least an implicit denial of the relevance or validity of any other than Deetz's "culture as mental construct" paradigm (1988a:22; see also Deetz 1989). But, lip service to recent trends notwithstanding, Deetz has not given up interest in the search for broad cultural patterns; his recent interpretation of patterning in the distribution of colono ware in the American South (1988b) is a particularly elegant and provocative example of his use of the "pure" structuralist paradigm. Martin Hall (n.d.:3) rightly notes, however, that "the results of this synchronic, decontextualized method of structuralism seem often to be brilliant descriptions awaiting explanations."

6. Peña and Peña (1988) provide an especially apt exposé of the shortcomings of pattern analysis.

7. See, for example, Geertz 1982, 1983; Leach 1982; Taylor 1979; Wagner 1975; Yentsch n.d., 1988a, 1988b, 1988c, 1989, 1990; Yentsch et al. 1987; Beaudry and Mrozowski 1989 is an example of a full-scale, monograph-length interpretive case study.

8. As William Sturtevant (1964:107) noted, "material culture resembles language in some important aspects: some artifacts—for example, clothing—serve as arbitrary symbols for meanings." This means that material culture can be conceptualized within the semiotic notion of signs: "semiology aims to take in any system of signs, whatever their substances and limits, images, gestures, musical sounds, objects, and the complex associations of all of these, which form the context of ritual, convention or public entertainment: these constitute, if not language, at least systems of signification" (Barthes 1964:9). Hence semiotics is characterized by the conscious treatment of all aspects of human life, verbal and nonverbal, written or otherwise as texts amenable to critical analysis (cf. Coward and Ellis 1977; Heath 1974). For a seminal discussion of "object language" and nonverbal communication, see Kruesch and Kees (1956:96–159).

9. According to Giddens (1981:51), this involves a measure of control over resources of "allocation" rather than resources of "authorization"; workers seldom control the means of production, but they do maintain a high degree of control over produced goods: "Allocation refers to man's capabilities of controlling not just 'objects' but the *object-world*. Domination from this aspect refers to human domination over nature. Authorization refers to man's capabilities of controlling the humanly created world of *society itself*. "What is critical to understanding the use of material culture—produced goods—in the definition of self and in the creation of subculture, ethnic identity, or in "everyday resistance" is the recognition that people transform the meaning of goods through their actions: "At the heart of both domination and power lies the *transformative capacity* of human action, the origin of all that is liberating and productive in social life as well as all that is repressive and destructive" (Giddens 1981:51).

10. Much of what we see today in the study of social inequality, of meaning conveyed through artifact production and use, or of artifacts in social discourse, superimposes new concepts onto old ways of doing things. In their practice of material culture analysis, some historical archaeologists (and others: cf. the essays in Hodder 1989a) continue to seek out the "one right way," and not a few evangelists preach the narrow path of theoretical righteousness. Our discussion of the construction of context, below addresses the consequences of this continued insistence on "paradigmatic purity" (cf. Deetz 1983).

11. It should be noted that other principals (i.e., Dent and Yentsch) in the Annapolis research have quite different analytical and theoretical approaches. See, for example, Yentsch n.d., 1988c, 1990; Yentsch and McKee 1987.

12. This largely negative perspective on power relations is criticized by Giddens (1981:51), who notes that "the tendency to regard domination as inherently negative, and as intrinsically inimical to freedom of action on the part of those subject to it, is closely related politically to the idea that power is inherently *coercive,* and that its use inevitably implies the existence of *conflict.* Neither of these ideas withstands close scrutiny; each usually reflects the assumption that power is not an integral and primary aspect of social life." He further points out that the basic premise of an alternative theory of power set forth by Foucault, although it "does not see power as inherently coercive and conflictful," views social life as essentially formed by struggles for power. Such a perspective renders inarticulate those not in power except in terms of resistance and conflict, as reactive rather than active. If we consider E. P. Thompson's (1963, 1978) observation that class (ethnicity as well) exists only when it is articulated, we begin to understand why the dominant ideology thesis makes it impossible to examine artifacts as elements in social discourse. Martin Hall (n.d.:13) comments that Leone's interpretation of the adoption of individual place settings by Annapolitans comes across "almost as if the possession of matching tableware turned the worker into an automaton, as if the capitalist had won the struggle for ideological control as soon as he had persuaded his laborer to adopt good table manners."

13. Meaning is "negotiable, interpenetrating, and fluid" (Beeman 1976:575); when objects are used as a way of creating meaning, of communicating on a nonverbal level, meaning is not embedded in artifacts themselves but is assigned or attributed to objects by individuals operating in group-specific cultural contexts (see, e.g., Hodder 1989a, 1989b; Wobst 1977).

14. Larry McKee's work on slave life on 19th-century Virginia plantations similarly explores the manipulation of material culture as a form of discourse between planter and slave (1987,1988, n.d.); see also Upton 1985.

15. O'Brien (1989) provides a cogent discussion of Foucault's contributions to historical method as well as an evaluation of his critics.

16. South's (1979) article on site structure was his last major push forward with an extrapolation of one of Binford's ideas into historical archaeology. His long silence opened the door for Leone to appropriate the same formula for success by rushing in with an adaptation of Binford's middle-range theory set forth initially in Leone and Crosby (1987) and further developed in Leone (1989) and Leone and Potter (1988b). The proposal is "disingenuously reductionist" (cf. Yentsch 1989), for it involves treating documentary and archaeological data as analytically and epistemologically separate. Rather than critically analyzing both as elements of discourse, we are enjoined to test one against the other to flush out and resolve ambiguities. There is certainly merit in this procedure, but it fails as a method for documentary analysis because it does not move beyond the etic or descriptive grid derived from superficial treatment of documents. What is more, and this is truly insidious, this version of middle-range theory has very little to do with Binford's emphasis on using middle-range theory as a medium for understanding the structure of the archaeological record by developing inferences, usually through ethnographic analogy, "aimed at the isolation of organizational variables characteristic of past systems" (Binford 1987:449). In essence, what

Leone and his colleagues propose is a method that fails to treat either the documentary or the archaeological record with the analytical thoroughness both richly deserve and that the recovery of meaning requires.

17. This cannot be interpreted as anything other than a rationalization for not using documents critically, for it is far from an accurate representation of what can he gleaned from the primary sources. It is not in fact altogether clear that Rubertone has consulted primary sources, although much of the recent literature on the archaeology of Native American–European interaction makes excellent use of documents and material evidence in combination to examine not just resistance but deliberate construction of cultural identity by Native Americans (e.g., Bradley 1987; Bragdon 1988; Brenner 1988; Crosby 1988; Hamell 1983, 1987; Merrell 1988, 1989).

18. Perhaps the strong urge to remain a prehistorian in the face of textual evidence stems from what seems to be an underlying worry that adding documents into the equation calls for a critical approach not otherwise necessary because material evidence is somehow more direct than texts and hence more reliable, less in need of critical analysis.

19. Beaudry (1980a, 1980b) proposes that documents such as probate inventories can be treated as "eliciting contexts" from which the researcher can recover information on non-literate or "semiliterate" segments of society. In a study of "heated" speech (profanity, slander, and insults), St. George (1984) analyzed court records to reconstruct speech performances; his interpretations bring to light many aspects of social relations in 17th-century Massachusetts that recorders never intended to reveal. Rhys Isaac's (1988) discussion of the manipulative behavior of Landon Carter's slaves through a critical reading of Carter's own diary is a particularly splendid example of textual analysis. Isaac turns the intentions of the "partisan observer" literally "inside out" to reveal the nature of Carter's less-than-successful efforts to control his slaves and to command respect from them.

20. The concept of "multiple voices" is drawn from Mascia-Lees et al. in the Autumn 1989 issue of *Signs*; we are grateful to Anne Yentsch and Suzanne Spencer-Wood for bringing this article to our attention.

21. Social and cultural historians have increasingly focused on everyday life and on private and public ritual as the nexus of social action (e.g., Darnton 1984; Davis 1983; de Certeau 1984; Larkin 1988). In great measure this outgrowth of Marxist and Annales schools of social history is a result of the increasingly strong influence of anthropological thought within history as well as cross-fertilization between the two disciplines. We argue here that historical archaeologists need to follow the lead of material culture specialists (e.g., Mackiewicz 1990) by becoming aware of and receptive to these trends. Perhaps we can look forward to a "reanthropologicization" of historical archaeology.

22. Class conflict over leisure behavior in public places was pervasive in the urban Northeast, and remains so today. Roy Rosenzweig (1983) uses holiday celebrations, public park policy, and legislative control of saloons to trace the course of this conflict in Worcester, Massachusetts, during the late 19th and early 20th centuries.

23. We found this to be true as well of ceramic use by residents of the Kirk Street Agents' House, who were near the top of the economic and social hierarchy in Lowell. The vessel forms did not differ greatly from those found at the boardinghouses, nor did the cuts

of meat represented by faunal remains (see Beaudry and Mrozowski 1987b), yet we infer from the cultural context that mealtimes at the two sorts of households were vastly different in quality, character, and symbolic import.

REFERENCES

Abercrombie, N., S. Hill, and B. S. Turner. 1980. *The Dominant Ideology Thesis.* London: George Allen and Unwin.

Althusser, L. 1971. Ideology and Ideological State Apparatuses (Notes Towards an Investigation). In *Lenin and Philosophy and other Essays*, L. Althusser (ed.), pp. 127–186. New York: Monthly Review Press.

Ashmore, W. and R. R. Wilk 1988. Household and Community in the Mesoamerican Past. In *Household and Community in the Mesoamerican Past*, R. R. Wilk and W. Ashmore (eds.), pp. 1–27. Albuquerque: University of New Mexico Press.

Barthes, R. 1957. Le mythe, aujourd'hui. In *Mythologies*, R. Barthes (ed.), pp. 191–247. Paris: Editions du Seuil.

Barthes, R. 1964. *Elements of Semiology.* 1967 ed. New York: Hill and Wang.

Barthes, R. 1981. *Le grain de la voix, entretiens 1962–1980.* Paris: Editions du Seuil.

Beaudry, M. C. 1978. Worth its Weight in Iron: Categories of Material Culture in Early Virginia Probate Inventories. *Quarterly Bulletin of the Archeological Society of Virginia* 33(1):19–26.

Beaudry, M. C. 1980a. "Or What Else You Please to Call It": Folk Semantic Domains in Early Virginia Probate Inventories. Ph.D. dissertation, Brown University. Ann Arbor: University Microfilms.

Beaudry, M. C. 1980b. Analysis of Semi-Literate Text. Paper presented at the annual meeting of the Society for Historical Archaeology, Albuquerque.

Beaudry, M. C. 1980c. Pot-Shot, Jug-Bitten, Cup-Shaken: Object Language and Double Meanings. Paper presented at the annual meeting of the American Anthropological Association, Washington, DC.

Beaudry, M. C. 1986. The Archaeology of Historical Land Use in Massachusetts. *Historical Archaeology* 20(2):38–46.

Beaudry, M. C. (ed.). 1988a. *Documentary Archaeology in the New World.* Cambridge: Cambridge University Press.

Beaudry, M. C. 1988b. Words for Things: Linguistic Analysis of Probate Inventories. In *Documentary Archaeology in the New World*, M. C. Beaudry (ed.), pp. 43–50. Cambridge: Cambridge University Press.

Baudry, M. C. n.d. Ethnography in Retrospect: The Archaeology of Everyday Life in Historical Times (A Review Essay). In *Material Culture, World View, and Culture Change*, M. C. Beaudry and A. E. Yentsch (eds.). Caldwell, NJ: The Telford Press, forthcoming.

Beaudry, M. C. and S. A. Mrozowski (eds.). 1987a. *Interdisciplinary Investigations of the Boott Mills, Lowell, Massachusetts. Vol. 1: Life at the Boarding Houses. A Preliminary*

Report. Cultural Resources Management Study 18. Boston: National Park Service, North Atlantic Regional Office.

Beaudry, M. C. and S. A. Mrozowski (eds.). 1987b. *Interdisciplinary Investigations of the Boott Mills, Lowell, Massachusetts. Vol. 2: The Kirk Street Agents' House.* Cultural Resources Management Study 19. Boston: National Park Service, North Atlantic Regional Office.

Beaudry, M. C. and S. A. Mrozowski. 1988. The Archeology of Work and Home Life in Lowell, Massachusetts: An Interdisciplinary Study of the Boott Cotton Mills Corporation. *IA: The Journal of the Society for Industrial Archeology* 14(2):1–22.

Beaudry, M. C. and S. A. Mrozowski (eds.). 1989. *Interdisciplinary Investigations of the Boott Mills, Lowell, Massachusetts. Vol. 3: The Boarding House System as a Way of Life.* Cultural Resources Management Study 21. Boston: National Park Service, North Atlantic Regional Office.

Beeman, W. O. 1976. The Meaning of Stylistic Variation in Iranian Verbal Interaction. Unpublished Ph.D. dissertation, University of Chicago.

Bennett, T. 1986. Introduction: Popular Culture and 'The Turn to Gramsci.' In *Popular Culture and Social Relations,* T. Bennett, C. Mercer, and J. Woolacott (eds.), pp. xi–xix. Milton Keynes, England: Open University Press.

Bennett, T., C. Mercer, and J. Woolacott (eds.). 1981. *Culture, Ideology, and Social Process.* London: Batsford Academic and Educational.

Bennett, T., C. Mercer, and J. Woolacott. 1986. *Popular Culture and Social Relations.* Milton Keynes, England: Open University Press.

Binford, L. R. 1962. A New Method for Calculating Dates from Kaolin Pipe Stem Fragments. *Southeastern Archaeological Conference Newsletter* 9(1):19–21.

Binford, L. R. 1976. Forty-seven Trips: A Case Study in the Character of Some Formation Processes of the Archaeological Record. In *The Interior Peoples of Northern Alaska,* Mercury Series 49. E. S. Hall, Jr. (ed.), pp. 299–381. Ottawa: National Museum of Man.

Binford, L. R. 1979. Organization and Formation Processes: Looking at Curated Technologies. *Journal of Anthropological Research* 35:195–208.

Binford, L. R. 1981. Behavioral Archaeology and the 'Pompeii Premise.' *Journal of Anthropological Research* 37:255–273.

Binford, L. R. 1987. Researching Ambiguity: Frames of Reference and Site Structure. In *Method and Theory for Activity Area Research: An Ethnoarchaeological Approach,* S. Kent (ed.), pp. 449–512. New York: Columbia University Press.

Boggs, C. 1976. *Gramsci's Marxism.* London: Pluto Press.

Bond, K. H. 1989a. 'That we may purity our corporation by discharging the offenders': The Documentary Record of Social Control in the Boott Boardinghouses. In *Interdisciplinary Investigations of the Boott Mills, Lowell, Massachusetts. Vol. 3: The Boarding House System as a Way of Life,* Cultural Resources Management Study 21, M. C. Beaudry and S. A. Mrozowski, (eds.), pp. 23–36. Boston: National Park Service.

Bond, K. H. 1989b. The Medicine, Alcohol, and Soda Vessels from the Boott Mills. In *Interdisciplinary Investigations of the Boott Mills, Lowell, Massachusetts. Vol. 3: The Boarding House System as a Way of Life*, Cultural Resources Management Study 21, M. C. Beaudry and S. A. Mrozowski, (eds.), pp. 121–140. Boston: National Park Service.

Bourdieu, P. 1973. The Berber House. In *Rules and Meanings: The Anthropology of Everyday Knowledge*, M. Douglas (ed.), pp. 98–110. Harmondsworth, England: Penguin.

Bradley, J. W. 1987. *Evolution of the Onandoga Iroquois: Accommodating Change, 1500–1655*. Syracuse: Syracuse University Press.

Bragdon, K. 1988. Material Culture of the Christian Indians of New England. In *Documentary Archaeology in the New World*, M. C. Beaudry (ed.), pp. 126–131. Cambridge: Cambridge University Press.

Brenner, E. M. 1988. Sociopolitical Implications of Mortuary Ritual Remains in 17th-Century Native Southern New England." In *The Recovery of Meaning: Historical Archaeology in the Eastern United States*, M. P. Leone and P. B. Potter, Jr. (eds.), pp. 147–181. Washington, DC: Smithsonian Institution Press.

Bronner, S. J. 1985. *American Material Culture and Folklife: A Prologue and Dialogue*. Ann Arbor: UMI Research Press.

Burley, D. V. 1989. Function, Meaning and Context: Ambiguities in Ceramic Use by the Hivernant Métis of the Northwestern Plains. *Historical Archaeology* 23(1): 97–106.

Carver, M. O. H. 1987. The Nature of Urban Deposits. In *Urban Archaeology in Britain*, Council for British Archaeology Report No. 61, J. Schofield and R. Leach (ed.), pp. 9–26.

de Certeau, M. 1984. *The Practice of Everyday Life*. Berkeley: University of California Press.

Chartier, R. 1989. Texts, Printings, Readings. In *The New Cultural History*, L. Hunt (ed.), pp. 154–175. Berkeley: University of California Press.

Clements, J. 1989. The Maturation of the American Military: A Case Study from Fort Independence, Boston, 1800–1820. Unpublished M.A. thesis, Department of Anthropology, University of Massachusetts, Boston.

Cook, L. J. 1989. Tobacco-Related Material Culture and the Construction of Working-Class Culture. In *Interdisciplinary Investigations of the Boott Mills, Lowell, Massachusetts. Vol. 3: The Boarding House System as a Way of Life*, M. C. Beaudry and S. A. Mrozowski (eds.), pp. 209–230. Cultural Resources Management Study 21. Boston: National Park Service.

Courbin, P. 1988. *What is Archaeology? An Essay on the Nature of Archaeological Research*, P. Bahn (trans.). Chicago: University of Chicago Press.

Coward, R. and J. Ellis. 1977. *Language and Materialism: Developments in Semiology and the Theory of the Subject*. London: Routledge and Kegan Paul.

Crosby, C. A. 1988. From Myth to History, or Why King Philip's Ghost Walks Abroad. In *The Recovery of Meaning: Historical Archaeology in the Eastern United States*, M. P. Leone and P. B. Potter, Jr. (eds.), pp. 183–209. Washington, DC: Smithsonian Institution Press.

Csiksentmihalyi, M. and E. Rochberg-Halton. 1981. *The Meaning of Things: Domestic Symbols and the Self.* Cambridge: Cambridge University Press.

Darnton, R. 1984. *The Great Cat Massacre and Other Episodes in French Cultural History.* New York: Basic Books.

Davis, N. Z. 1983. *The Return of Martin Geurre.* Cambridge, MA: Harvard University Press.

Deetz, J. 1967. *Invitation to Archaeology.* New York: Natural History Press.

Deetz, J. 1977a. Historical Archaeology as the Science of Material Culture. In *Historical Archaeology and the Importance of Material Things*, L. G. Ferguson (ed.), pp. 9–12. Special Publication Series 2. Tucson: Society for Historical Archaeology.

Deetz, J. 1977b. *In Small Things Forgotten: The Archaeology of Everyday Life in Early America.* New York: Anchor Books.

Deetz, J. 1983. Scientific Humanism and Humanistic Science: A Plea for Paradigmatic Pluralism in Historical Archaeology. *Geoscience and Man* 22:27–34.

Deetz. J. 1988a. History and Archaeological Theory: Walter Taylor Revisited. *American Antiquity* 53(1):13–22.

Deetz, J. 1988b. American Historical Archeology: Methods and Results. *Science* 239: 362–367.

Deetz, J. 1989. Archaeography, Archaeology, or Archeology? *American Journal of Archaeology* 93:429–435.

Douglas, M. 1973. Introduction. In *Rules and Meanings: The Anthropology of Everyday Knowledge*, M. Douglas (ed.), pp. 9–13. Harmondsworth, England: Penguin.

Douglas, M. and B. Isherwood. 1979. *The World of Goods.* New York: W. W. Norton.

Dutton, D. H. 1989. Thrasher's China or Colored Porcelain: Ceramics from a Boott Mills Boardinghouse and Tenement. In *Interdisciplinary Investigations of the Boott Mills, Lowell, Massachusetts. Vol. 3: The Boarding House System as a Way of Life*, Cultural Resources Management Study 21, M. C. Beaudry and S. A. Mrozowski (eds.), pp. 83–120. Boston: National Park Service.

Earle, T. K. and R. W. Preucel. 1987. Processual Archaeology and the Radical Critique. *Current Anthropology* 28:501–538.

Ferguson, L. G. (ed.). 1977. *Historical Archaeology and the Importance of Material Things.* Special Publication Series 2. Tucson: Society for Historical Archaeology.

Foucault, M. 1972. *The Archaeology of Knowledge and the Discourse on Language.* London: Tavistock.

Geertz, C. 1980. *Negara: The Theatre State in Nineteenth-Century Bali.* Princeton: Princeton University Press.

Geertz, C. 1982. *The Interpretation of Culture.* New York: Basic Books.

Geertz, C. 1983. *Local Knowledge: Further Essays in Interpretive Anthropology.* New York: Basic Books.

Gibbon, G. 1989. *Explanation in Archaeology.* Oxford: Basil Blackwell.

Giddens, A. 1981. *A Contemporary Critique of Historical Materials. Vol. 1: Power, Property and the State.* 1987 ed. Berkeley: University of California Press.

Glassie, H. 1976. *Folk Housing in Middle Virginia: A Structural Study of Folk Artifacts.* Knoxville: University of Tennessee Press.

Glassie, H. 1982. *Passing the Time in Ballymenone: Culture and History in an Ulster Community.* Philadelphia: University of Pennsylvania Press.

Godbey, G. 1981. *Leisure in Your Life: An Exploration.* Philadelphia: Saunders College Publishing.

Goffman, E. 1971. *Relations in Public: Microstudies of the Public Order.* New York: Harper and Row.

Gregory, M. and S. Carroll. 1978. *Language and Situation: Language Varieties and Their Social Contexts.* London: Routledge and Kegan Paul.

Hall, M. n.d.. Small Things and The Mobile, Conflictual Fusion of Power, Fear and Desire. In *Material Culture, World View, and Culture Change*, M. C. Beaudry and A. E. Yentsch. Caldwell, NJ: The Telford Press, forthcoming.

Hamell, G. R. 1983. Trading in Metaphors: The Magic of Beads. In *Proceedings of the 1982 Glass Trade Bead Conference*, Research Records 16, C. F. Hayes, III (ed.), pp. 5–28. Rochester, NY: Rochester Museum and Science Center.

Hamell, G. R. 1987. Mythical Realities and European Contact in the Northeast during the Sixteenth and Seventeenth Centuries. *Man in the Northeast* 33:63–87.

Hargreaves, J. 1989. The Promise and Problems of Women's Leisure and Sport. In *Leisure for Leisure: Critical Essays*, C. Rojek (ed.), pp. 130–149. New York: Routledge.

Harrington, F. 1989. The Emergent Elite in Early 18th-Century Portsmouth: The Archaeology of the Joseph Sherburne Houselot. *Historical Archaeology* 23(1):2–18.

Harrington, J. C. 1954. Dating Stem Fragments of Seventeenth- and Eighteenth-Century Clay Tobacco Pipes. *Quarterly Bulletin, Archaeological Society of Virginia* 9(1):10–14.

Hawkes, T. 1977. *Structuralism and Semiotics.* Berkeley: University of California Press.

Heath, S. 1974. *Vertige du deplacement.* Paris: Fayard.

Hebdige, D. 1979. *Subculture: The Meaning of Style.* London: Methuen.

Hodder, I. 1986. *Reading the Past: Current Approaches to Interpretation in Archaeology.* Cambridge: Cambridge University Press.

Hodder, I. 1987a. The Contribution of the Long Term. In *Archaeology as Long-Term History*, I. Hodder (ed.), pp. 1–8. Cambridge: Cambridge University Press.

Hodder, I. 1987b. The Contextual Analysis of Symbolic Meanings. In *The Archaeology of Contextual Meanings*, I. Hodder (ed.), pp. 1–10. Cambridge: Cambridge University Press.

Hodder, I. 1989a (ed.). *The Meanings of Things: Material Culture and Symbolic Expression.* London: Unwin Hyman.

Hodder, I. 1989b. Post-Modernism, Post-Structuralism, and Post-Processual Archaeology. In *The Meaning of Things: Material Culture and Symbolic Expression*, I. Hodder (ed.), pp. 64–78. London: Unwin Hyman.

Honerkamp, N. and R. B. Council. 1984. Individual Versus Corporate Adaptations in Urban Contexts. *Tennessee Anthropologist* 9:22–31.

Huizinga, J. 1970. *Homo ludens: A Study of the Play Element in Culture.* New York: J. and J. Harper.

Hunt, L. (ed.). 1989. *The New Cultural History.* Berkeley: University of California Press.

Isaac, R. 1988. Ethnographic Method in History: An Action Approach. In *Material Life in America, 1600–1860,* R. B. St. George (ed.), pp. 39–61. Boston: Northeastern University Press.

Krampen, M. 1979. Survey of Current Work on the Semiology of Objects. In *A Semiotic Landscape: Proceedings of the First Congress of the International Association for Semiotic Studies, Milan, June 1974/Panorama semiotique: Actes du premier congres de l'Association Internationale de Semiotique, Milan, juin 1974,* S. Chatman, U. Eco, and J. M. Klinkenburg (eds.), pp. 158–168. The Hague: Mouton.

Kruesch, J. and W. Kees. 1956. *Nonverbal Communication: Notes on the Visual Perception of Human Relations.* 1972 ed. Berkeley: University of California Press.

Landon, D. B. 1989. Domestic Ideology and the Economics of Boardinghouse Keeping. In *Interdisciplinary Investigations of the Boott Mills, Lowell, Massachusetts. Vol. 3: The Boarding House System as a Way of Life,* Cultural Resources Management Study 21, M. C. Beaudry and S. A. Mrozowski (eds.), pp. 37–48. Boston: National Park Service.

Landon, D. B. and M. C. Beaudry. 1988. Domestic Ideology and the Boardinghouse System in Lowell, Massachusetts. Paper presented to the annual meeting of the Dublin Seminar on New England Folklife, Durham, NH.

Larkin, J. 1988. *The Reshaping of Everyday Life, 1790–1840.* New York: Harper and Row.

Leach, E. 1982. *Social Anthropology.* New York: Oxford University Press.

Leone, M. P. 1972. Issues in Anthropological Archaeology. In *Contemporary Archaeology: A Guide to Theory and Contributions,* M. P. Leone (ed.), pp. 14–27. Carbondale: Southern Illinois University Press.

Leone, M. P. 1984. Interpreting Ideology in Historical Archaeology: Using the Rules of Perspective in the William Paca Garden in Annapolis, Maryland. In *Ideology, Power, and Prehistory,* D. Miller and C. Tilley (eds.), pp. 25–35. Cambridge: Cambridge University Press.

Leone, M. P. 1986. Symbolic, Structural and Critical Archaeology. In *American Archaeology Past and Future: A Celebration of the Society for American Archaeology, 1935–1985,* D. J. Meltzer, D. D. Fowler, and J. Sabloff (eds.), pp. 413–438. Washington, DC: Smithsonian Institution Press.

Leone, M. P. 1987. Rule by Ostentation: The Relationship Between Space and Sight in Eighteenth-Century Landscape Architecture in the Chesapeake Region of Maryland. In *Method and Theory for Activity Area Research: An Ethnoarchaeological Approach,* S. Kent (ed.), pp. 604–633. New York: Columbia University Press.

Leone, M. P. 1988a. The Relationship Between Archaeological Data and the Documentary Record: 18th-Century Gardens in Annapolis, Maryland. *Historical Archaeology* 22(1): 29–35.

Leone, M. P. 1988b. The Georgian Order as the Order of Merchant Capitalism in Annapolis, Maryland. In *The Recovery of Meaning: Historical Archaeology in the Eastern United States*, M. P. Leone and P. B. Potter, Jr. (eds.), pp. 235–261. Washington, DC: Smithsonian Institution Press.

Leone, M. P. 1989. Issues in Historic Landscapes and Gardens. *Historical Archaeology* 23(1):45–47.

Leone, M. P. and C. A. Crosby. 1987. Epilogue: Middle-Range Theory in Historical Archaeology. In *Consumer Choice in Historical Archaeology*, S. M. Spencer-Wood (ed.), pp. 397–411. New York: Plenum Press.

Leone, M. P., E. Kryder-Reid, J. H. Ernstein, and P. A. Shackel. 1989. Power Gardens of Annapolis. *Archaeology* 42(2):35–39, 74–75.

Leone, M. P. and P. B. Potter, Jr. (eds.). 1988a. *The Recovery of Meaning: Historical Archaeology in the Eastern United States*. Washington, DC: Smithsonian Institution Press.

Leone, M. P. and P. B. Potter, Jr. (eds.). 1988b. Introduction: Issues in Historical Archaeology. In *The Recovery of Meaning: Historical Archaeology in the Eastern United States*, M. P. Leone and P. B. Potter, Jr. (eds.), pp. 1–22. Washington, DC: Smithsonian Institution Press.

Leone, M. P., P. B. Potter, Jr., and P. A. Shackel. 1987. Toward a Critical Archaeology. *Current Anthropology* 28(3):283–302.

Little, B. and P. A. Shackel. 1989. Scales of Historical Anthropology: An Archaeology of Colonial Anglo-America. *Antiquity* 63:495–509.

Lofland, L. H. 1973. *A World of Strangers: Order and Action in Public Space*. New York: Basic Books.

McGuire, R. H. 1988. Dialogues with the Dead: Ideology and the Cemetery. In *The Recovery of Meaning: Historical Archaeology in the Eastern United States*, M. P. Leone and P. B. Potter, Jr. (eds.), pp. 435–480. Washington, DC: Smithsonian Institution Press.

McKee, L. 1987. Delineating Ethnicity from the Garbage of Early Virginians: The Faunal Remains from the Kingsmill Plantation Slave Quarter. *American Archeology* 6(1):31–39.

McKee, L. 1988. Plantation Food Supply in Nineteenth-Century Tidewater Virginia. Ph.D. dissertation, University of California, Berkeley.

McKee, L. n.d. The Ideals and Realities Behind the Design and Use of Nineteenth-Century Virginia Slave Cabins. In *Material Culture, World View, and Culture Change*, M. C. Beaudry and A. E. Yentsch (eds.). Caldwell, NJ: The Telford Press, forthcoming.

Mackiewicz, S. 1990. Philadelphia Flourishing: The Material World of Philadelphians, 1682–1760. Unpublished Ph.D. dissertation, University of Delaware.

Malone, D. (ed.). 1946. *Dictionary of American Biography*. New York: Charles Scribner's Sons.

Marcus, G. E. and M. M. J. Fischer. 1986. *Anthropology as Cultural Critique: An Experimental Moment in the Human Sciences*. Chicago: University of Chicago Press.

Mascia-Lees, F. E., P. Sharpe, and C. B. Cohen. 1989. The Postmodernist Turn in Anthropology: Cautions from a Feminist Perspective. *Signs* 15(1):7–33.

Melas, E. M. 1989. Emics, Etics, and Empathy in Archaeological Theory. In *The Meanings of Things: Material Culture and Symbolic Expression*, I. Hodder (ed.), pp. 137–155. London: Unwin Hyman.

Mercer, C. 1986. Complicit Pleasures. In *Popular Culture and Social Relations*, T. Bennett, C. Mercer, and J. Woolacott (eds.), pp. 50–68. Milton Keynes, England: Open University Press.

Merrell, J. H. 1988. The Indians' New World: The Catawba Experience. In *Material Life in America, 1600–1860*, R. B. St. George (ed.), pp. 95–112. Boston: Northeastern University Press.

Merrell, J. H. 1989. Some Thoughts on Colonial Historians and American Indians. *The William and Mary Quarterly* 46:94–119.

Miller, D. 1987. *Material Culture and Mass Consumption*. Oxford: Basil Blackwell.

Miller, G. L. 1980. Classification and Economic Scaling of Nineteenth-Century Ceramics. *Historical Archaeology* 14:1–40.

Mrozowski, S. A. 1984. Prospect and Perspective on an Archaeology of the Household. *Man in the Northeast* 27:31–49.

Mrozowski, S. A. 1988. 'For Gentlemen of Capacity and Leisure': The Archaeology of Colonial Newspapers. In *Documentary Archaeology in the New World*, M. C. Beaudry (ed.), pp. 184–191. Cambridge: Cambridge University Press.

Noël Hume, I. 1969. *A Guide to Artifacts of Colonial America*. New York: Alfred A. Knopf.

O'Brien, P. 1989. Michel Foucault's History of Culture. In *The New Cultural History*, L. Hunt (ed.), pp. 25–46. Berkeley: University of California Press.

Orser, C. E. Jr., 1988. Toward a Theory of Power for Historical Archaeology: Plantations and Space. In *The Recovery of Meaning: Historical Archaeology in the Eastern United States*, M. P. Leone and P. B. Potter, Jr. (eds.), pp. 313–343. Washington, DC: Smithsonian Institution Press.

Paynter, R. 1984. Social Dynamics and New England Archaeology. *Man in the Northeast* 27:1–11.

Paynter, R. 1988. Steps to an Archaeology of Capitalism: Material Change and Class Analysis. In *The Recovery of Meaning: Historical Archaeology in the Eastern United States*, M. P. Leone and P. B. Potter, Jr. (eds.), pp. 407–433. Washington, DC: Smithsonian Institution Press.

Peña, J. T. and E. S. Peña. 1988. Review of *The Archaeology of Slavery and Plantation Life* (T. Singleton, ed.). *American Journal of Archaeology* 92:153–155.

Pieper, J. 1952. *Leisure, The Basis of Culture*. New York: Pantheon.

Praetzellis, A., M. Praetzellis, and M. Brown, III (eds.). 1980. *The Archaeology of the Golden Eagle Site*. Anthropological Studies Center, Sonoma State University, Rohnert Park, CA.

Praetzellis, A., M. Praetzellis, and M. Brown, III. 1987. Artifacts as Symbols of Identity: An Example from Sacramento's Gold Rush Era Chinese Community. In *Living in Cities: Current Research in Urban Archaeology*, E. Staski (ed.), pp. 38–47. Special Publication Series 5. Pleasant Hill, CA: Society for Historical Archaeology.

Praetzellis, A., M. Praetzellis, and M. Brown, III. 1988. What Happened to the Silent Majority? Research Strategies for Studying Dominant Group Material Culture in Late Nineteenth-Century California. In *Documentary Archaeology in the New World*, M. C. Beaudry (ed.), pp. 192–202. Cambridge: Cambridge University Press.

Prown, J. D. 1988. Mind in Matter: An Introduction to Material Culture Theory and Method. In *Material Life in America, 1600–1860*, R. B. St. George (ed.), pp. 17–37. Boston: Northeastern University Press.

Quimby, I. M. G. (ed.). 1978. *Material Culture and the Study of American Life*. New York: W. W. Norton.

Rabinow, P. and W. M. Sullivan (eds.). 1979. *Interpretive Social Science: A Reader*. Berkeley: University of California Press.

Rabinow, P. and W. M. Sullivan. 1987. *Interpretive Social Science: A Second Look*. Berkeley: University of California Press.

Roberts, W. E. 1985. Untitled essay on material culture studies. *Material Culture* 17: 89–93.

Rojek, C. 1989. Leisure and 'The Ruins of the Bourgeois World.' In *Leisure for Leisure: Critical Essays*, C. Rojek (ed.), pp. 92–112. New York: Routledge.

Rosenzweig, R. 1983. *Eight Hours for What We Will: Workers and Leisure in an Industrial City, 1870–1920*. Cambridge: Cambridge University Press.

Rubertone, P. E. 1989. Archaeology, Colonialism and 17th-century Native America: Towards an Alternative Interpretation. In *Conflict in the Archaeology of Living Traditions*, R. Layton (ed.), pp. 32–45. London: Unwin Hyman.

Sahlins, M. D. 1981. *Historical Metaphors and Mythical Realities: Structure in the Mythology of the Sandwich Island Kingdom*. Ann Arbor: University of Michigan Press.

Sahlins, M. D. 1985. *Islands of History*. Chicago: University of Chicago Press

Schiffer, M. B. 1987. *Formation Processes of the Archaeological Record*. Albuquerque: University of New Mexico Press.

Schlereth, T. (ed.). 1980. *Artifacts and the American Past*. Nashville: American Association for State and Local History, Nashville, Tennessee.

Schlereth, T. 1982. *Material Culture Studies in America*. Nashville: American Association for State and Local History.

Schlereth, T. (ed.). 1985. *Material Culture: A Research Guide*. Lawrence: University Press of Kansas.

Schmidt, P. R. and S. A. Mrozowski. 1983. History, Smugglers, Change, and Shipwrecks. In *Shipwreck Anthropology*, R. A. Gould (ed.), pp. 143–171. Albuquerque: University of New Mexico Press.

Schrire, C. n.d.. Digging Archives at Oudepost I, Cape, South Africa. In *Material Culture, World View, and Culture Change*, M. C. Beaudry and A. E. Yentsch (eds.). Caldwell, NJ: The Telford Press, forthcoming.

Schuyler, R. L. 1978. The Spoken Word, the Written Word, Observed Behavior, and Preserved Behavior: The Contexts Available to the Archaeologist. In *Historical Archaeology: A Guide to Substantive and Theoretical Contributions*, R. L. Schuyler (ed.), pp. 267–777. Farmingdale, NY: Baywood Press.

Schuyler, R. L. 1988. Archaeological Remains, Documents, and Anthropology: A Call for a New Culture History. *Historical Archaeology* 22(1):36–42.

Scott, J. 1985. *Weapons of the Weak: Everyday Forms of Peasant Resistance.* New Haven: Yale University Press.

Sennett, R. 1978. *The Fall of Public Man.* New York: Vintage Books.

Shanks, M. and C. Tilley. 1982. Ideology, Symbolic Power and Ritual Communication: A Reinterpretation of Neolithic Mortuary Practices. In *Symbolic and Structural Archaeology*, I. Hodder (ed.), pp. 129–154. Cambridge: Cambridge University Press.

Shanks, M. and C. Tilley. 1987. *Social Theory and Archaeology.* Albuquerque: University of New Mexico Press.

Shennan, S. 1982. Ideology, Change, and the European Early Bronze Age. In *Symbolic and Structural Archaeology*, I. Hodder (ed.), pp. 155–161. Cambridge: Cambridge University Press.

South, S. 1977. *Method and Theory in Historical Archaeology.* New York: Academic Press.

South, S. 1978. Pattern Recognition in Historical Archaeology. *American Antiquity* 43(2): 223–230.

South, S. 1979. Historic Site Content, Structure, and Function. *American Antiquity* 44: 213–237.

South S. 1988. Santa Elena: Threshold of Conquest. In *The Recovery of Meaning: Historical Archaeology in the Eastern United States*, M. P. Leone and P. B. Potter, Jr. (eds.), pp. 27–71. Washington, DC: Smithsonian Institution Press.

St. George, R. B. 1984. Heated Speech and Literacy in Seventeenth-Century New England. In *Seventeenth-Century New England*, D. D. Hall and D. G. Allen (eds.), pp. 275–309. Charlottesville: University Press of Virginia.

St. George, R. B. 1988a. Introduction. In *Material Life in America, 1600–1860*, R. B. St. George (ed.), pp. 3–13. Boston: Northeastern University Press.

St. George, R. B. (ed.). 1988b. *Material Life in America, 1600–1860.* Boston: Northeastern University Press.

Stedman Jones, G. 1977. Class Expression versus Social Control? A Critique of Recent Trends in the Social History of 'Leisure.' *History Workshop* 4:162–170.

Stone, L. M. 1974. *Fort Michilimackinac, 1715-1781: An Archaeological Perspective on the Revolutionary Frontier.* East Lansing: Michigan State University Press.

Sturtevant, W. C. 1964. Studies in Ethnoscience. *American Anthropologist* 66:99–131.

Taylor, C. 1979. Interpretation and the Sciences of Man. In *Interpretive Social Science*, P. Rabinow and W. M. Sullivan (eds.). Berkeley: University of California Press.

Taylor, W. W. 1948. *A Study of Archeology*. 1967 ed. Carbondale: Southern Illinois University Press.

Thompson, E. P. 1963. *The Making of the English Working Class*. 1966 ed. New York: Vintage.

Thompson, E. P. 1978. Eighteenth-century English Society: Class Struggle Without Class? *Social History* 3(2):133–165.

Tilley, C. 1989. Interpreting Material Culture. In *The Meanings of Things: Material Culture and Symbolic Expression*, I. Hodder (ed.), pp. 185–194. London: Unwin Hyman.

Turner, V. 1974. *Dramas, Fields, and Metaphors: Symbolic Action in Human Society*. Ithaca: Cornell University Press.

Upton, D. 1983. The Power of Things: Recent Studies in American Vernacular Architecture. *American Quarterly* 35:262–279.

Upton, D. 1985. White and Black Landscapes in Eighteenth-Century Virginia. *Places* 2(2): 59–72.

Wagner, R. 1975. *The Invention of Culture*. 1981 ed. Chicago: University of Chicago Press.

Walker, I. C. 1965. Some Thoughts on the Harrington and Binford Systems for Statistically Dating Clay Pipes. *Quarterly Bulletin, Archeological Society of Virginia* 20(2): 60–64.

Walker, I. C. 1967. Statistical Methods for Dating Clay Pipe Fragments. *Post-Medieval Archaeology* 1:90–101.

Walker, I. C. 1977. Clay Tobacco-Pipes, with Particular Reference to the Bristol Industry. *History and Archaeology*. Ottawa: Parks Canada.

Walker, I. C. 1983. Nineteenth-Century Clay Tobacco Pipes in Canada. In *The Archaeology of the Clay Tobacco Pipe. Vol. 3: America*, P. Davey (ed.). Oxford: BAR International Series 175.

Wall, D. di Z. 1987. At Home in New York: Changing Family Life Among the Propertied in the Late Eighteenth and Early Nineteenth Centuries. Unpublished Ph.D dissertation, New York University.

Wells, C. 1986. Old Claims and New Demands: Vernacular Architecture Studies Today. In *Perspectives in Vernacular Architecture*, C. Wells (ed.), pp. 1–10. Columbia: University of Missouri Press.

Williams M. A. 1986. The Little 'Big House': The Use and Meaning of the Single-Pen Dwelling. In *Perspectives in Vernacular Architecture*, C. Wells (ed.), pp. 130–136. Columbia: University of Missouri Press.

Williams, M. A. 1990. Pride and Prejudice: Understanding the Appalachian Boxed House. Lecture to the Boston University American Studies Program, Boston.

Williams, R. 1977. *Marxism and Literature*. Oxford: Oxford University Press.

Wobst, H. M. 1977. Stylistic Behavior and Information Exchange. In *For the Director: Research Essays in Honor of James B. Griffin*, Anthropological Papers of the Museum of Anthropology 61, C. E. Cleland (ed.), pp. 317–342. Ann Arbor: University of Michigan.

Wylie, A. 1989. Gender Theory and the Archaeological Record: Why Is There No Archaeology of Gender? Paper presented at the annual meeting of the Society for American Archaeology, Atlanta.

Yentsch, A. E. 1975. Understanding Seventeenth- and Eighteenth-Century Families—An Experiment in Historical Ethnography. Unpublished M.A. thesis, Brown University.

Yentsch, A. E. 1988a. Legends, Houses, Families, and Myths: Relationships between Material Culture and American Ideology. In *Documentary Archaeology in the New World*, M. C. Beaudry (ed.), pp. 5–19. Cambridge: Cambridge University Press.

Yentsch, A. E. 1988b. Farming, Fishing, Whaling, Trading: Land and Sea as Resource on 18th-Century Cape Cod. In *Documentary Archaeology in the New World*, M. C. Beaudry (ed.), pp. 138–160. Cambridge: Cambridge University Press.

Yentsch, A. E. 1988c. Some Opinions on the Importance of Context. Paper presented at the annual meeting of the Council for Northeast Historical Archaeology, Québec.

Yentsch, A. E. 1989. Access and Space, Symbolic and Material, in Historical Archaeology. Paper presented at the Annual Chacmool Conference, Calgary, Alberta.

Yentsch, A. E. 1990. The Calvert Orangery in Annapolis, Maryland: A Horticultural Symbol of Power and Prestige in an Early 18th-Century Community." In *Earth Patterns: Essays in Landscape Archaeology*, W. M. Kelso (ed.), pp. 169–187. Charlottesville: University Press of Virginia.

Yentsch, A. E. 1991. The Symbolic Divisions of Pottery: Sex-Related Attributes of English and Anglo-American Household Pots. In *The Archaeology of Inequality*, R. H. McGuire and R. Paynter (eds.), pp. 192–230. Oxford: Basil Blackwell.

Yentsch, A. E. n.d. The Use of Land and Space on Lot 83, Annapolis, Maryland. In *New Perspectives on Maryland Archaeology*, R. J. Dent and B. J. Little (eds.). Special Publication of the Maryland Archaeology Society, forthcoming.

Yentsch, A. E. and L. McKee. 1987. Footprints of Buildings in Eighteenth-Century Annapolis. *American Archeology* 6(1):40–50.

Yentsch, A. E., N. Miller, B. Paca, and D. Piperno. 1987. Archaeologically Defining the Earlier Garden Landscapes at Morven: Preliminary Results. *Northeast Historical Archaeology* 16:1–30.

Ziesing, G. H. 1989. Analysis of Personal Effects from Excavations of the Boott Mills Boardinghouse Backlots in Lowell. In *Interdisciplinary Investigations of the Boott Mills, Lowell, Massachusetts. Vol. 3: The Boarding House System as a Way of Life*, Cultural Resources Management Study 21, M. C. Beaudry and S. A. Mrozowski (eds.), pp. 141–168. Boston: National Park Service.

PART IV

Interdisciplinary Studies

Most people who know even a little bit about archaeology are aware that archaeologists use abandoned sites and old artifacts to reconstruct the histories and cultures of ancient men and women. Not many realize, however, the significant role that other kinds of information plays in furthering the archaeologist's ability to probe the mysteries of the past. It is not unusual, for example, to find archaeologists in close collaboration with geographers, geologists, botanists, chemists, zoologists, geophysicists, and other specialists who are not generally associated with archaeological research. But modern archaeology is at its heart a multidisciplinary endeavor, and most excavators eagerly seek the aid of colleagues in other fields. The insights and methods of these specialists can often put a new spin on an old archaeological problem, and by opening new lines of inquiry, these scholars' ideas can deepen the archaeologist's understanding of the past.

For this section, I have selected three papers that demonstrate the power that can be brought to bear on archaeological topics when methods and techniques from other fields are intertwined with archaeological research. The number of fields from which to draw is vast, but I have selected three that are used frequently in historical archaeology: pollen analysis, faunal analysis, and physical anthropology.

In the first chapter, Gerald Kelso, from Cultural Ecology Laboratories, and archaeologist Faith Harrington, analyze pollen samples from the William Pepperrell site, located on an island off the coast of Maine and occupied continuously since 1623. It would be easy to ignore the microscopic remains from this site, but Kelso and Harrington show how such information can be put to good use. They demonstrate, for instance, that pollen studies can be used to provide a natural history of the island and to show the effects of forest clearing and destruction of the chestnut. They also explain the relationship between soil disturbance and the rise of the resort industry on the island. In an interesting twist of archaeological fate, they show that the buildings on the island actually preserved, rather than destroyed, the island's pollen record. Kelso and Harrington's stated purpose for the study was to obtain data on plant use by the island's colonial inhabitants, and this article shows how pollen specialists work to provide this kind of information. At the same time, though, the technical aspects of the article aptly demonstrate the years of specialized training and experience that are needed to provide such highly sophisticated studies.

In the next chapter we turn from the microscopic to the visible, from pollen samples to animal bones, as archaeologist Christine Szuter, of the University of Arizona, analyzes the animal bones from the Hubbell Trading Post in northeast Arizona. Szuter's article is useful because she demonstrates precisely how animal bone specialists—called zooarchaeologists—approach a collection of bones. Szuter explains how zooarchaeologists identify the species present, both wild and domestic, determine the age of the animals at the times of their deaths, and examine the bones for signs of weathering and gnawing that have occurred after the bones were discarded. More importantly, perhaps, zooarchaeologists also examine animal bones to determine what species people in the past preferred to eat, how they butchered their animals, and which cuts of meat they preferred. In making these detailed examinations, Szuter shows that zooarchaeologists provide a human face to our understanding of past archaeological sites because the zooarchaeologists present information about eating, one of the most basic of human activities. In this study, Szuter finds that the Hubbell family ate much more beef, sheep, and goats than pig, a much rarer animal in Arizona. This finding, in turn, provides concrete proof that pork was not a large part of the overall economic system in this part of the American West.

Next we turn from animal bones to human remains, from a site that is new to you to one that is world famous: the site of the Battle of the Little Bighorn. In this study, National Park Service archaeologist Douglas Scott teams up with world-renowned forensic anthropologist Clyde Snow to examine a skull, a humerus (upper arm bone), and a clavicle (collar bone) that were found eroding out of a river bank in the vicinity of the 1876 battle. After carefully examining these remains, Scott and Snow determined that they belonged to a white male who died between the ages of 30 and 45. As the remains were found in this historic locale, Scott and Snow quickly realized that they belonged to a member of Major Reno's ill-fated command at the battle. Scott and Snow then set out like archaeological detectives to determine whose bones they had. Based on the information available to them at the time this article was first published in 1991, they pared the list of possible candidates down to two. In the years since this article appeared, however, Scott and Snow continued their research, and in an addendum first published here they reveal the actual identity of the dead soldier. Studies such as this one are important for showing the close relationship that often exists between historical archaeology and physical anthropology. In most cases, archaeologists and physical anthropologists work together at cemetery sites to reconstruct the health and dietary patterns of past populations, but sometimes, as in this case, the remains can be examined in a much more focused way.

I could present many other studies that show the collaboration of historical archaeologists with other scientists. But in this brief section I have sought to give you just a peek at the kinds of interdisciplinary studies that are possible. As you continue to learn about modern historical archaeology, you undoubtedly will encounter many more such studies, from an ever-expanding cadre of nonarchaeological scholars.

GERALD K. KELSO ■
FAITH HARRINGTON

Chapter Twelve

Pollen Record Formation Processes at the Isles of Shoals:

Botanical Records of Human Behavior

Introduction

This article reports the results of an exploratory pollen study of soil samples recovered from the alleged William Pepperrell site (ME 226–62) on Appledore at the Isles of Shoals an archipelago located approximately 8 miles south of Portsmouth New Hampshire in the Atlantic Ocean. This group of nine islands was occupied by 1623 on a seasonal basis to exploit the nearby cod fishing grounds and was inhabited year-round by the 1640s. The fishing here continued to be viable until the first few decades of the 14th century. By the 1850s the building of hotels. On the two largest islands of Appledore and Star ushered in the resort era and saw a general decline in the fishing industry. The resorts prospered until after the 1890s when competition stiffened as a result of the building of new retreats on the mainland more accessible by motorcar. In 1914 a fire destroyed most of the buildings, including a major hotel, on Appledore and ended intensive occupation of the island (Bardwell 1989:113). Today the Shoals Marine Laboratory operates a marine field station on Appledore Island, and the Star Island Corporation hosts religious conferences throughout the summer on nearby Star Island.

Archaeological Research at the Isles of Shoals

Archaeological investigations at the Isles of Shoals have been conducted as part of a long term interdisciplinary research project by Harrington since 1986 (Harrington 1987, 1988, 1989, 1990, 1992; Harrington and Kenyon 1987) These investigations indicated that cultural resources at the Shoals are extensive, intact, and date from as early as the colonial period. During the 1988 and 1990 field seasons on

This article was originally published in *Northeast Historical Archaeology,* Volume 18 (1989):70–84.

Appledore Island, teams of participants from Earthwatch, Boston University, and the University of Southern Maine inventoried 51 historical sites for the Maine Historic Preservation Commission, one of the continuing project sponsors. Subsurface testing has been conducted at three stone foundation sites on the southwest end of Appledore. All three structures proved to be domestic sites that were occupied initially in the second or third quarters of the 17th century and abandoned prior to, or during, the Revolutionary War Period. The archaeological evidence thus corroborates secondary historical sources that suggest that the islands were evacuated by the British during the Revolutionary War, partly for the protection of the Shoalers and partly because the British were unsure of their loyalty (Rutledge 1971:44).

Site ME 226–62 is alleged to have been the home of William Pepperrell, father of the victor at Louisbourg, William Pepperrell, Jr. The site became the focus of intensive excavation during the 1990 season, after the discovery of a rich kitchen midden deposit that provided our first detailed look at material life at the Isles of Shoals in the last decades of the 17th century and the first few decades of the 18th century. The archaeological record of the site begins about 1675, and the *terminus post quem* for site abandonment is approximately 1760, based on the presence of several types of English white salt-glazed stonewares and the absence of later creamwares and pearlwares. There is no evidence of any later occupation at the Pepperrell site. Eighteenth-century materials were recovered within 3 cm of the surface in some units and a scattering of 19th- and 20th-century artifacts was found on the surface.

Subsistence and the Environment at the Isles of Shoals

Since many major research questions focus on the subsistence base of the early fishing community at the Shoals, several different approaches are being employed to study the plant materials on these sites. The topic of this paper is pollen analysis at the Pepperrell site, but this is only one of several avenues being explored to gain a greater understanding of the cultural uses of plants at the Shoals, the success or failure of certain crops, and the reconstruction of the historic environment.

A feasibility study was performed in 1989 to determine the presence or absence of phytoliths at the Pepperrell site. Dr Lawrence Kaplan of the University of Massachusetts at Boston reported the presence of phytoliths in deeply stratified deposits at the Pepperrell site (pers. comm.). These samples contained no evidence for maize, beans nor squash, but the presence of phytoliths deep in the profile is encouraging. Phytolith analysis will remain an integral part of interdisciplinary research at the Shoals.

Macrofloral remains are also being studied at the Shoals. Approximately 200 soil samples representing soils from all strata, levels, and zones encountered during excavations at the Pepperrell site, were processed in a flotation tank. Preliminary results indicate excellent recovery of seeds, nuts, pits, and seed casings (as well as numerous small fish and bird bones, gun shot, sewing pins, and even a human baby tooth). Analysis is in process.

The present flora of Appledore Island was surveyed during 1988 to determine species composition, dates for species introduction and cultural uses of plants (Sweeney 1988). Contemporary plant materials (including seeds) were collected and preserved as part of a comparative collection for macrofloral analysis. Dendro-chronological cores were taken from apple trees in the vicinity of the three colonial sites on the southwest end of Appledore in 1990. All of the apple trees are growing within enclosed stone walls that may represent early gardens or orchards The tree rings, however, indicated that none of the trees were older than approximately 70 years. It is possible that apple trees were planted early in the island's history and that the extant trees are the result of natural revegetative processes.

Historical Landscape Analysis: The Pollen Record

Historical landscape analysis is a critical element in any archaeological investigation of the European-American era. Each generation has modified its environment characteristically, and the ways in which the environments were modified can reveal much about economics, life-styles, and values of the period. Structures and gross geographical features may remain from particular historical periods, but the accompanying flora, a few specimens of long-lived taxa excepted, has been modified beyond recognition by the activities of succeeding generations and by natural processes of vegetational succession. Paleobotanical research methods must be employed in concert with archival and archaeological studies to effectively reconstruct the floral elements of historic environments.

The majority of archaeologists and palynologists consider pollen to be too poorly preserved in most temperate zone soils to warrant analysis (King, Klipple, and Duffield 1975), and it has been demonstrated that pollen is moved postdepositionally by natural processes (Dimbleby 1985). The rate of pollen movement and degradation varies with the nature of the matrix and changing human activities (Kelso 1991:5). Before pollen analysis could be applied to questions about the 17th- and 18th-century fishing communities on Appledore, it was necessary to determine whether pollen was preserved in this unique island environment and whether the archaeological and pollen records could be correlated. There were, consequently, three objectives to this exploratory pollen study on Appledore:

1. to ascertain whether pollen preservation at the Isles of Shoals is adequate to permit meaningful interpretation of the pollen spectra;

2. to ascertain whether land-use data may be recovered by pollen analysis on Appledore Island; and

3. to ascertain the age of the pollen record that may be recovered from exposed profiles on the island.

Methods

A pollen column of 14 contiguous 3-cm samples (Figure 12.1) was collected from the north wall of excavation unit N2W6 adjacent to the foundation of the structure. Three natural stratigraphic deposits were evident in this excavation unit (Figure 12.1). Stratum I (samples 1–7a) consisted of black silty sand with ash (7.5YR 2/0) and Stratum II (samples 8–11) consisted of a black sandy loam with gravel (7.5YR 2/0). Stratum I and Stratum II contained diagnostic artifacts dating to ca. 1720– 1760, based on the presence of English white salt-glazed stonewares, Astbury wares, Nottingham stonewares, Iberian wares, and mottled wares. Although some of these ceramic types postdate 1760, the absence of creamwares and pearlwares suggests a date prior to about 1770. Stratum III (samples 12–14), on the other hand, contained no imported ceramics. Stratum III dates of ca. 1675 to 1720 are suggested by pipe fragments and redwares and are corroborated by archival sources. Pollen sample 2 (-3 to -6 cm) was inadvertently not collected and is not represented on the pollen diagram. The deepest 1.5 cm of sample 7 was originally thought to be a feature and was collected as a separate sample, 7a. The total interval of samples 7 and 7a is 3 cm.

Mehringer's (1967) mechanical/chemical pollen extraction method was employed, but was modified by eliminating the HNO_3 step and reducing the NaOH strength to 1 percent to minimize oxidization of the already degraded and fragile pollen characteristic of the deeper portion of temperate zone soil profiles. Pollen residues were mounted in glycerol for viewing. Counting was done at 430¥, with problematical pollen grains examined under oil immersion at 970¥. Four hundred pollen grains were tabulated per sample. The greatest diameter of all intact grass pollen grains in all samples was measured in microns.

Five lycopodium tablets containing 11,300 ± 400 spores were added to each sample to permit computation of pollen concentrations per gram of sample with Benninghoff's (1962) exotic pollen addition method. Pollen concentration figures were not calculated for individual taxa, because these would not be meaningful where pollen has moved postdepositionally in soil deposits.

All pollen grains too degraded to be identified were tabulated to provide further control over corrosion factors. These unidentifiable pollen grains were not incorporated in any sum from which the frequencies of other types were computed, but the data for this pollen group, as a percentage of total identifiable and unidentifiable pollen, are presented for each profile. Corroded oak pollen grains, a prominent type that retains its identity while readily degrading (van Zeist 1967:49), were also tabulated. The terms "corroded" and "degraded" are used interchangeably and refer to any kind of pollen deterioration other than tearing. They are not intended as references to the specific classes of deterioration defined under these terms by Cushing (1964) and Havinga (1984).

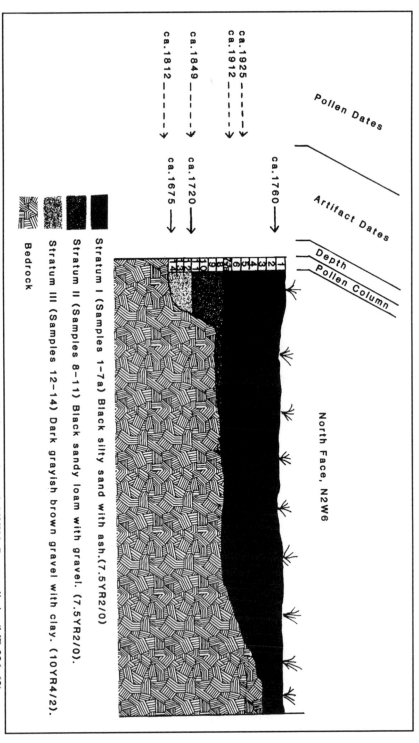

Figure 12.1. Stratigraphy, sample location, and chronometric dates, north wall of excavation unit N2W6, Pepperrell site (ME 226—62).

Percentages based on two kinds of sums are presented in the pollen diagram (Figure 12.2). The open line bars are based on relative frequencies (percentages) computed from separate sums for arboreal and nonarboreal pollen types, while the solid colored portion of the diagram reflects percentages computed from the total sum of all pollen types (AP, NAP, and undetermined) present. This separation serves to differentiate regional and local pollen sources to some extent and makes it possible to recognize the statistical distortions that the contributions of pollen types reflecting different phenomena induce in each other. By comparing the two kinds of sums for the same pollen type it is often possible to determine whether a shift in the representation of the type records real change in the pollen contribution of the parent taxon or statistical response to a change in some other pollen type within the fixed numerical sum upon which the percentages are based.

Plants are most frequently encountered under English names in historical documentary sources; to maintain perspective for historical archaeologists, the common New England names for plant taxa are employed in both the text and the diagrams. A conversion table (Table 12.1) of Latin and vernacular names is provided.

Results

The results of pollen analysis at the William Pepperrell House site are presented in Figure 12.2. Pollen preservation was very good throughout the profile, and pollen concentrations were high at the bottom of the profile relative to most pollen sequences from dry soil in New England (Kelso 1989:Fig. B–4; Kelso, Mrozowski, and Fisher 1987:Figs. 6–2, 6–3, 6–4; Kelso et al. 1989:Figs. 12–9, 12–10). The presence of a few grains of European cereal pollen in the profile indicates that the upper half of the deposit, at least, postdates European colonization of the island. Four trends are evident among the pollen spectra of this diagram. One of these trends reflects natural postdeposition pollen record formation processes in the deposit at the site. A second trend registers the effect of an alien pathogen on mainland vegetation, while the third trend reflects land-use patterns on the mainland. The fourth trend records vegetation response to changes in local land use.

Pollen Record Formation Processes

The most basic trend in the Pepperrell site pollen spectrum is the steady decline in pollen concentrations, and the regular increase in the quantities of pollen that was too degraded to recognize and corroded oak pollen from the top of the profile to the bottom. These patterns are the product of normal pollen record formation processes. Pollen is annually deposited on the surface of the ground. This pollen is carried down into the profile by percolating rainwater. This percolation produces a pattern in which most of the oldest pollen is at the bottom, the majority of the intermediate

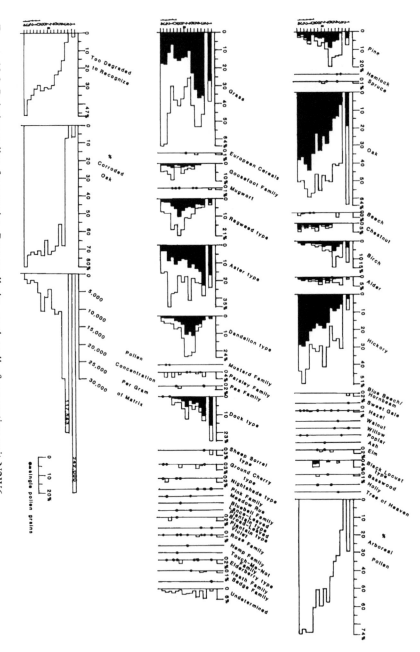

Figure 12.2. Relative pollen frequencies, Pepperrell site, north wall of excavation unit N2W6.

TABLE 12.1

Latin and Vernacular Names of Plants Discussed in the Text

Arboreal Vernacular—Latin	Nonarboreal Vernacular—Latin
Pine—*Pinus*	Grass—Gramineae
Hemlock—*Tsuga*	European cereal grass—Cerealia
Spruce—*Picea*	Goodfoot family—Chenopodiaceae
Oak—*Quercus*	
Beech—*Fagus*	Ragweed family—Compositae
Chestnut—*Castanea*	Mugwort—*Artemisia*
Birch—*Betula*	Ragweed-type: *Ambrosia*-type
Alder—*Alnus*	(wind-pollinated Compositae)
Hazel—*Corylus*	Aster/sunflower/goldenrod-type:
Hornbeam—*Ostrya*	*Aster*-type (insect-pollinated Compositae)
Blue beech—*Carpinus*	Dandelion-type Compositae:
Hickory—*Carya*	Liguliflorae
Walnut—*Juglans*	Mustard Family—Cruciferae
Willow—*Salix*	Parsley family—Umbelliferae
Sweet gale—*Myrica*	Pea family—Leguminoseae
Poplar/cottenwood—*Populus*	Sheep-sorrel-type: *Rumex acetosella*-type
Ash—*Fraxinus*	Dock-type: *Rumex mexicanus*-type
Holly—*Ilex*	Rose family—Rosaceae
Black locust—*Robinia*	Nightshade family—Solanaceae
Elm—*Ulmus*	Groundcherry-type: *Physalis*-type
Tree-of-heaven—*Ailanthus*	Meadow rue—*Talictrum*
	Bluebell family—Campanulaceae
	Hemp family—Cannabinaceae
	Touch-Me-Not family—Balsaminaceae
	Honeysuckle family—Caprifoliaceae
	Elderberry-type: *Sambucus*-type
	Lance-leaved plantain-type:
	Plantago landeolata-type
	Broad-leaved plantain-type:
	Plantago major-type
	Viole—*Viola*
	Heath family—Ericaceae
	Sedge family—Cyperaceae

age pollen grains are in the middle of the profile, and most of the recent pollen grains are at the top (Dimbleby 1985:5). Dimbleby's (1985:Fig. 3) schematic diagram of this distribution is presented in Figure 12.3.

As pollen moves downward, it is attacked and progressively destroyed by aerobic fungi (Goldstein 1960) and by free oxygen in the percolating groundwater (Tschudy

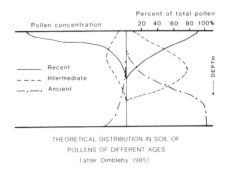

THEORETICAL DISTRIBUTION IN SOIL OF
POLLENS OF DIFFERENT AGES
(after Dimbleby 1985)

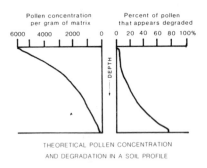

THEORETICAL POLLEN CONCENTRATION
AND DEGRADATION IN A SOIL PROFILE

Figure 12.3. Theoretical distributions of percolated pollen, pollen concentrations, and degraded pollen in a soil profile.

1969). This produces patterns of pollen concentration and degradation in which the highest pollen concentrations are located near the surface and the largest proportion of pollen grains that are too degraded to recognize are situated near the bottom of the profile. A schematic of this sequence is presented in Figure 12.3. Very similar pollen concentration and pollen degradation patterns have been seen in 15 profiles from 10 European-American period archaeological sites in the northeastern United States (Kelso 1989, 1990a, 1990b, 1990c, 1990d; Kelso, Mrozowski, and Fisher 1987; Kelso, Stone, and Karish 1990; Kelso et al. 1989), and there is no doubt that pollen percolation and degradation are normal postdepositional soil processes affecting pollen spectra. These pollen concentration and preservation measures are important in the interpretation of pollen spectra because the presence of these characteristic concentration and degradation patterns indicate that the profile has developed naturally (i.e., soil processes have not been interrupted or disrupted) and that the succession of pollen spectra visible in the profile have leached down to their present positions from the surface. Where human activity was intense, as in urban situations, rapid profile aggradation and soil compression often prevent pollen leaching and oxygen penetration, and these characteristic patterns are not found (Kelso 1991:5).

The presence of these normal pollen concentration and degradation patterns in the Pepperrell House excavation unit N2W6 profile indicates that the sediment has not been disturbed and that human activity on the site was not intense during the period of pollen deposition. The pollen sequence is a normal pollen profile developed by pollen percolation into the soil from the ground surface. This normal percolation pattern will permit dating various parts of the spectrum when the pollen percolation rate is established.

Mainland Pathogenic Vegetation Changes

Chestnut (*Castanea*) pollen was not found in level 5 or above in the Pepperrell House profile (Figure 12.2), despite several hours spent scanning slides in search of the type in samples 1–5. Chestnut trees are not now present on the island (Borror 1988:8–13) and may never have been (Gross 1988:3). These trees are wind pollinated, and the chestnut pollen in samples 6 and below probably originated on the adjacent mainland. The disappearance of the type in the pollen record appears to register the virtual extermination of the native American chestnuts (*Castanea dentata*) by a foreign pathogen during the first half of the 20th century.

The blight was introduced in the New York City area around 1904. It had destroyed most of the chestnuts south and west of New Hampshire by 1920 (Anderson 1974:679, Fig. 1) and was deep into Maine by 1930 (Davis 1967:144). It should have reached the coast opposite the Isles of Shoals by about 1925. This can be used to establish the leaching rate for the Pepperrell House profile.

The absence of chestnut pollen in sample 5 suggests that its pollen spectra dates to ca. 1925. The bottom of sample 5 was 15 cm down in the profile (allowing for missing sample 2). The samples were taken in 1988, and the elapsed time since the deposition of the 5 sample sediment in ca. 1925 is 63 years. The pollen percolation rate in the upper portion of the profile, at least, is ca. 4.2 years per cm or 10 cm every 42 years.

The Mainland Land-Use Record

None of the primary trees contributing to the pollen diagram are currently present on Appledore Island (Borror 1988:8–13). The absence of timber from the islands was noted early in the occupation (Rutledge 1971:9), and the soil has probably always been too shallow to support tall growth (Gross 1988:3). Most of the arboreal pollen in the sampled deposit was wind transported from the mainland. The

Pepperrell House arboreal pollen spectrum is part of the regional rather than the local pollen rain.

The third significant trend among the Pepperrell House pollen spectra in the William Pepperrell House profile is the steady decline in pollen percentages of oak (*Quercus*) and hickory (*Carya*), the two most prominent arboreal pollen types in the spectrum, and in the combined arboreal pollen sum from the bottom of the profile up through sample 3. This pattern is interrupted in samples 10 and 11 by a brief peak of oak that also raised the total percentage of arboreal pollen, but it can only reflect the forest clearance on a regional scale that characterized European-American land use from the third decade of the 17th century into the late 19th century (Carrol 1973:51; Russell 1976:460). Pine (*Pinus*) and birch (*Betula*) pollen percentages increase in samples 7 and 7a, respectively. Both of these taxa are recognized secondary succession trees in New England (Barrett 1980:52; Fowells 1965:99-333), and the increase in their pollen contribution records the beginning of secondary forest succession in the area. The Appledore pollen percolation rate of 4.2 years per cm that was computed from the chestnut decline suggests that this reforestation began ca. 1900. If a few years are allowed for trees to reach the age of anthesis, this date is consistent with Russell's (1976:460) statement that Maine reached its highest point of land clearance in 1880.

The Local Land-Use Record

The fourth significant trend in the Pepperrell House pollen sequence is registered among the nonarboreal pollen spectra. Nonarboreal pollen originates close to the ground where wind velocities are relatively low and the possibility of loss through impact with vegetation is relatively high. Little herb pollen is lifted high enough into the atmosphere to be incorporated in the regional pollen rain (Janssen 1973:33), and most, if not all, of the William Pepperrell House nonarboreal pollen is local in origin. A comparison of the arboreal and nonarboreal sums will provide some information about the relative density of the local ground cover producing the nonarboreal pollen spectrum.

The concentration of airborne arboreal pollen incorporated in the regional pollen rain thins out as it is drawn into the upper atmosphere (Raynor, Ogden, and Hayes 1974), and the regional pollen rain on soils is usually masked by the larger pollen contributions of the local flora. On large bare spaces or in large lakes, where the pollen contribution from local vegetation is much smaller, the regional pollen rain is more visible and may even dominate the spectrum (Martin 1963:Fig. 2; Tauber 1965:33). This is significant because the majority of the pollen grains in the deepest 9 samples of the William Pepperrell House profile are from trees, and tree pollen clearly dominates samples 11 through 14 (Figure 12.2). It is probable that the ground cover in the vicinity of the

Pepperrell House during deposition of samples 11 and below was less dense than in later times.

Grass pollen dominates this nonarboreal spectrum throughout the occupation and is particularly prominent at the bottom of the profile (Figure 12.2). The proportion of grass pollen decreases above sample 13, and the size of the grass pollen grains in the samples is reduced from a mean of 23 microns to 20 microns (Figure 12.4). This last trend either suggests a phenotypic response to physical stress of some sort, or the replacement of one kind of grass by another. As grass declines in importance in samples 12 and 11, the insect-pollinated Compositae (Aster type), goosefoot-type, dock-type, ragweed-type and dandelion-type contributions to the counts begin to increase. This trend is partially reversed above sample 7. The grass pollen contribution grass increases markedly above sample 7, as grass pollen grains get larger. Goosefoot, ragweed and dandelion-types drop off fairly abruptly in sample 5, but the aster and dock type pollen percentages continue to increase to the top of the profile, and sheep-sorrel pollen (*Rumex acetosella*-type) pollen appears in the spectrum. A local land-use episode appears to be recorded in these changes in the spectra.

Perennial grasses are intolerant of soil disturbance because it destroys their perennating organs (Behre 1983:229). Higher grass pollen frequencies in historical profiles correlate with relatively stable soil (Kelso and Schoss 1983:74; Kelso, Stone, and Karish 1990:10; Solomon and Kroener 1971:Figs. 8, 9). Ragweed pollen, on the other hand, is the premier soil disturbance indicator in North American historical period pollen spectra. Plants producing this kind of pollen are better able to endure the harsh moisture and temperature regimen of bare ground (Bazzaz 1974:112) and peaks of ragweed-type pollen have frequently been used as a horizon marker for the advent of European-style agriculture in pollen profiles (Solomon and Kroener 1971:33). The ragweed-type pollen frequencies on Appledore are, however, low relative to those of known agricultural sites (Kelso 1985:Fig. 43; Kelso, Stone, and Karish 1990:Fig. 2), and the plants shedding aster-type pollen, dandelion-type pollen, dock-type pollen and the members of the goosefoot family are more prominent on inactive farmland, on pastures, and on waste ground than on tilled soil (Fernald 1970:1357–1567; Muenscher 1955:422–505). Goosefoot has a definite preference for rich soil (Behre 1983:236). Sheep sorrel prefers poor soil to such an extent that it is best controlled by fertilization (Fernald 1970:571; Muenscher 1955: 174). Modest soil disturbance, but not cultivation, in the vicinity of the Pepperrell House is indicated in samples 6–11. A more stable, less fertile soil condition is recorded in samples 1–6, but the ground cover did not entirely revert to the predisturbance situation. A thicker cover of, possibly, a new variety of grass is indicated by the pollen data, while dock and asters were entrenched in waste ground near the site.

The decline in grass and the increase in aster-type marking the beginning of this trend occurred in sample 12, the initial increase in ragweed-type and chenopodium

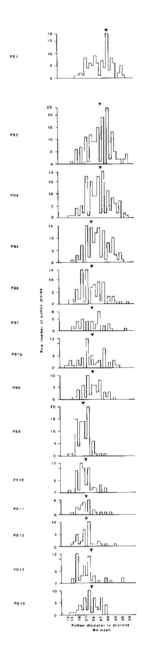

Figure 12.4. Grass pollen grain size in microns at the William Pepperrill House site.

occurred in sample 11, and dandelion-type counts really started to increase in sample 10. If the Appledore pollen percolation rate of 42 years per cm calculated rom the chestnut blight data is applied to these data, grass began its decline and aster-type populations in creased sometime between 1837 and 1849, ragweed and dock populations expanded after 1849, and dandelions became prominent after 1862. Construction of the first bay of the hotel on Appledore Island was started in 1848. Two additional hotel bays followed in 1852 (Bardwell 1989:113). The soil disturbance trend appearing in the mid-19th century (samples 12–10) reflects the inception and development of the resort hotel industry on Appledore Island.

The shifts in the ragweed-type, dandelion-type, and goosefoot family pollen frequencies at the sample 6/5 boundary overlap the change in the grass pollen counts at the sample 7/6 boundary, suggesting that the recorded change in land use occurred sometime early in the deposition of the 3-cm-deep sample 6 pollen spectrum. When the pollen percolation rate of 4.2 years per cm is applied to the increase in grass frequencies at the lower boundary of sample 6, the change in soil stability suggested by these counts occurred after 1912–1913. The goosefoot, ragweed and dandelion frequencies imply that the shift actually occurred slightly later, some time during deposition of the 3-cm interval of sample 6. The event recorded is undoubtedly the virtual abandonment of the island following the 1914 fire that destroyed the hotel. The decrease in soil fertility indicated by the decline in the goosefoot frequencies and the appearance of sheep sorrel on the island can reasonably be attributed to a reduction in the amount of organic garbage generated on the island with the closing of the hotel era.

Summary and Conclusions

Three cultural and natural events are recorded among the William Pepperrell House site pollen spectra. One of these is the clearance of the New England forest during the European-American era. The second event is the blight that destroyed the chestnut population on the adjacent mainland ca. 1925. The third event is the increase and subsequent decrease in soil disturbance associated with the development of the resort hotel industry on the island in the second half of the 19th century and the abrupt end of the resort era with the fire that destroyed the hotel in 1914.

The sedimentation rate for the William Pepperrell House site was calibrated from the pollen record of the early 20th-century chestnut blight at 10 cm per 42 years (1 cm per 4.2 years). The mid-19th-century development of the hotel industry and the abandonment of the island following the fire of 1914 occur at depths in the profile that suggest that this rate is fairly accurate. When this sedimentation rate is applied to the total length of the profile it suggests that the pollen in the deepest sediment was deposited ca. 1812.

There are major conflicts between the dates for portions of the profile derived from artifacts and dates indicated by the pollen spectra. The material culture recovered from the William Pepperrell House indicates that samples 14, 13, and 12, were deposited between 1675 and 1720, and that samples 11 through 2 were deposited between 1720 and 1760 (Figure 12.1). The associated pollen spectrum originated considerably later. When the known age of the pollen spectra of the stratigraphic excavation levels are plotted against the known age of the artifacts recovered in the same levels (Figure 12.1, right), the ca. 1925 and 1912–1914 pollen spectra are seen to occur in sediment that accumulated during the early to mid-18th century, while the pollen deposited on the surface ca. 1849 was recovered from sediment dating to the early 18th century. The oldest pollen in our profile should date to ca. 1812, but it was found in sediments that accumulated during the last quarter of the 17th century. There is only one explanation for this phenomenon. More recent pollen deposited on the surface has percolated down through the undisturbed earlier archaeological deposit.

This finding has significant methodological implications. Some North American palynologists have questioned the validity of the Dimbleby model (1985:5, Fig. 3) presented in Figure 12.3. The essence of these criticisms, as expressed by Schoenwetter (1987:205), is that palynologists working in southwestern and Mesoamerican sites normally assume that items (including pollen) embedded in a deposit were trapped as the deposit was formed and that Dimbleby's evidence that pollen spectra are altered by postdepositional processes is too limited to be convincing. The association between undisturbed 19th- and 20th-century pollen spectra and undisturbed 17th- and 18th-century artifact deposits at the Pepperrell site cannot be doubted. Earthworms move pollen up and down, tending to homogenize the spectra of deposits, and pollen only moves down in their absence (Walch, Rowley, and Norton 1970). Bioturbation did not produce the Pepperrell site pollen distribution. It can only be the product of pollen percolation. Dimbleby's (1985:5) model works in temperate zone settings, like Appledore Island, where cultural activities do not interfere with natural soil processes. Given the amount of time that has passed since the demise of most southwestern and Mesoamerican archaeological cultures, it is probable that pollen percolation has biased the pollen spectra of exposed sites in those regions as well.

The William Pepperrell House pollen study has established that pollen can be well preserved in the exposed environment of Appledore Island, that normal pollen percolation processes prevail there, and that the in tensity, at least, of land use by the inhabitants of the island is recorded among the spectra of the nonarboreal pollen types. This study indicates, however, that 17th- or 18th-century land-use pollen records will probably not be recovered from exposed soil profiles on Appledore Island. The island soils are highly permeable and deposits are too shallow to contain a record of much more than 175 years duration. This does not mean that older land-use data cannot be preserved on Appledore.

The remains of structures spanning the occupation of the island have been recognized on Appledore. These range from stone house foundations through stone animal enclosure pens to stone retaining walls for garden soil (Harrington 1990). Soil deposits on the island are shallow, and the foundations of structures were not normally laid in builder's trenches. In most structures the bottom stones appear to have been laid directly on the ground surface at the time of construction. Pollen under large flat stones is protected from percolation (Dimbleby 1985:57). Our pollen leaching data suggest that a pollen record of ca. 175 years preceding construction will be preserved under the foundation stones of each edifice. The same principle should apply to the pollen records under wall stones placed on the ground during the dismantling of a structure. By arranging such records chronologically into a profile and comparing the preoccupation (subfoundation) record with the occupation period record preserved under stones thrown down at dismantling, we should be able to ascertain the nature of the land use during the occupation from changes in the vegetation and in the pollen percolation and degradation records.

Acknowledgments

Many individuals have contributed to this research effort. We particularly wish to thank Roger Larochelle for the use of his maps, Leslie Mead for drafting support, and Elisa McClennan for photographing the illustrations. Funding for the ME 226–62 pollen study was provided by the Maine Historic Preservation Commission, and laboratory space was provided by the Boston University Department of Archaeology. Pollen laboratory equipment was procured under National Science Foundation grant No. BNS-7924470 to Boston University.

REFERENCES

Anderson, T. W. 1974. The Chestnut Pollen Decline as a Time Horizon in Lake Sediments in Eastern North America. *Canadian Journal of Botany* 11:678–685.

Bardwell, J. D. 1989. *The Isles of Shoals: A Visual History.* Portsmouth, NH: The Portsmouth Marine Society.

Barrett, J. W. 1980. The Northeastern Region. In *Regional Silviculture of the United States*, J. W. Barrett (ed.), pp. 25–66. New York: Wiley Interscience.

Bazzaz, F. A. 1974. Ecophysiology of *Ambrosia artemisiifolia*: A Successional Dominant. *Ecology* 55:112–119.

Behre, K-E. 1983. The Interpretation of Anthropogenic Indicators in Pollen Diagrams. *Pollen et Spores* 23(2):225–245.

Benninghoff, W. S. 1962. Calculation of Pollen and Spore Density in Sediments by Addition of Exotic Pollen in Known Amounts. *Pollen et Spores* 6(2):332–333.

Borror, A. C. 1988. Checklist of the Marine Flora and Fauna, Including the Birds of the Isles of Shoals and the Vascular Plants of Appledore Island. Manuscript on file, Shoals Marine Laboratory, Appledore Island, Isles of Shoals, Kittery, ME.

Carrol, C. F. 1973. *The Timber Economy of Puritan New England.* Providence: Brown University Press.

Cushing, E. J. 1964. Redeposited Pollen in Late Wisconsin Pollen Spectra from East-Central Minnesota. *American Journal of Science* 262:1075–1088.

Davis, R. B. 1967. Pollen Studies of Near Surface Sediments in Maine Lakes. In *Quaternary Paleoecology*, E. J. Cushing and R. B. Webb (eds.), pp. 143–173. New Haven: Yale University Press.

Dimbleby, G. W. 1985. *The Palynology of Archaeological Sites.* New York: Academic Press.

Fernald, M. L. 1970. *Gray's Manual of Botany.* 8th ed. New York: Van Nostrand Reinhold.

Fowells, H. A. 1965. *The Silvics of Forest Trees.* USDA Forest Service Handbook 271. Washington, DC: United States Department of Agriculture.

Goldstein, S. 1960. Degradation of Pollen by Phycomycetes. *Ecology* 41:543–545.

Gross, L. B. 1988. Geologic Contributions to the Field Report, Isles of Shoals Archaeology Project. Manuscript on file at the New England Studies Program, University of Southern Maine, Portland.

Harrington, F. 1987. Field Report, Isles of Shoals Archaeological Project, Summer 1987. Manuscript on file, New England Studies Program, University of Southern Maine, Portland.

Harrington, F. 1988. Archaeology at the Isles of Shoals. *Context* 6(3–4):13–16.

Harrington, F. 1989. New England's First Settlers. Preliminary Report of the 1988 Field Season of Earthwatch, New England's Settlers Archaeological Project. Report on file at the New England Studies Program. University of Southern Maine, Portland.

Harrington, F. 1990. Preliminary Report on the 1990 Field Season of the Isles of Shoals Archaeology Project. Report on file at the Maine Historic Preservation Commission, Augusta.

Harrington, F. 1992. The Dynamics of the Fishing Community at the Isles of Shoals. In *The Art and Mystery of Historical Archaeology: Essays in Honor of James Deetz*, A. Yentsch and M. C. Beaudry (eds.). Boca Raton, FL: CRC Press.

Harrington, F., and V. Kenyon. 1987. New Hampshire Coastal Sites Survey, Summer 1986. *The New Hampshire Archaeologist* 28(1):52–62.

Havinga, A. J. 1984. A 20-Year Investigation into Differential Corrosion Susceptibility of Pollen and Spores in Various Soil Types. *Pollen et Spores* 26(3–4):541–558.

Janssen, C. R. 1973. Local and Regional Pollen Deposition. In *Quaternary Plant Ecology*, H. B. J. Birks and R. G. West (eds.), pp. 31–42. London: Blackwell Scientific.

Kelso, G. K. 1985. Palynology and Historic Land Use in Central New England: The Record from Shattuck Farm. In *The Camp at the Bend of the River*, B. E. Luedtke (ed.), pp. 360–399. Occasional Publications in Archaeology and History 4. Boston: Massachusetts Historical Commission.

Kelso, G. K. 1989. Exploratory Pollen Analysis of Central Artery Sites. In *Phase 11 Archaeological Investigations of the Central Artery/Third Harbor Tunnel Project in Boston, Massachusetts, Volume One: Text and Illustrations*, R. J. Elia (ed.), pp. 101–105. Boston: Office of Public Archaeology, Boston University.

Kelso, G. K. 1990a. Report of Exploratory Pollen Analysis in the Pequot Refuge, Ledyard, Connecticut. Manuscript on file, Division of Cultural Resources, North Atlantic Regional Office, National Park Service, Boston.

Kelso, G. K. 1990b. Report of Exploratory Pollen Analysis in the "British Woods," Saratoga National Historical Park. Manuscript on file, Division of Cultural Resources, North Atlantic Regional Office, National Park Service. Boston.

Kelso, G. K. 1990c. Exploratory Pollen Analysis of Historical Matrices at the David Brown Homestead. In *Archeological Investigations of Minute Man National Historical Park. Vol. 1: Farmers and Artisans of the Historical Period*, A. T. Synenki (ed.), pp. 85–106. Cultural Resources Management Study 22. Division of Cultural Resources, North Atlantic Regional Office. Boston: National Park Service.

Kelso, G. K. 1990d. Report of Exploratory Pollen Analysis on Two Profiles from the Carns Site, Coast Guard Beach, Cape Cod National Seashore. Manuscript on file, Division of Cultural Resources, North Atlantic Regional Office, National Park Service, Boston.

Kelso, G. K. 1991. Interdisciplinary Research in Historic Landscape Management. *CRM* 14(6) Technical Supplement: 1–11.

Kelso, G. K, and J. Schoss. 1983. Exploratory Pollen Analysis of the Bostonian Hotel Site Sediments. In *Archaeology of the Bostonian Hotel Site*, J. W. Bradley, N. DePaoli, N. Seasholes, P. McDowell, G. Kelso and J. Schoss (eds.), pp. 67–76. Occasional Publications in Archaeology and History 2. Boston: Massachusetts Historical Commission.

Kelso, G. K., S. A. Mrozowski, and W. F. Fisher. 1987. Contextual Archeology at the Kirk Street Agent's House Site. In *Interdisciplinary Investigations of the Boott Mills, Lowell, Massachusetts. Vol. 2: The Kirk Street Agents' House*, M. C. Beaudry and S. A. Mrozowski (eds.), pp. 97–130. Cultural Resources Management Study 19. Division of Cultural Resources, North Atlantic Regional Office. Boston: National Park Service.

Kelso, G. K., S. A. Mrozowski, W. F. Fisher, and K. J. Reinhard. 1989. Contextual Archeology at the Boott Mill Boardinghouse Backlots. In *Interdisciplinary Investigations of the Boott Mills, Lowell, Massachusetts. Vol. 3: The Boarding House System as a Way of Life*, M. C. Beaudry and S. A. Mrozowski, (ed.), pp. 231–278. Cultural Resources Management Study 21. Division of Cultural Resources. North Atlantic Regional Office. Boston: National Park Service.

Kelso, G. K., R. Stone, and J. F. Karish. 1990. Pollen Analysis in Historic Landscape Studies at Fort Necessity National Battlefield. *Park Science* 10(2):10–11.

King, J. E., W. E. Klipple, and R. Duffield. 1975. Pollen Preservation and Archaeology in Eastern North America. *American Antiquity* 40(2):180–190.

Martin, P. S. 1963. Geochronology of Pluvial Lake Cochise, Southern Arizona II, Pollen Analysis of a 42 Meter Core. *Ecology* 44:436–444.

Mehringer, P. J., Jr. 1967. Pollen Analysis of the Tule Springs Area, Nevada. In *Pleistocene Studies in Southern Nevada*, H. M. Wormington and D. Ellis (eds.), pp. 120–200. Carson City: Nevada State Museum Anthropological Papers 13.

Muenscher, W. C. 1955. *Weeds*. 2nd ed. New York: MacMillan.

Raynor, G. S., E. C. Ogden, and J. V. Hayes. 1974. Mesoscale Transport and Dispersion of Airborne Pollens. *Journal of Applied Meteorology* 3(1):87–95.

Russell, H. S. 1976. *A Long, Deep Furrow: Three Centuries of Farming in New England*. Hanover, NH: University Press of New England.

Rutledge, L. V. 1971. *The Isles of Shoals in Lore and Legend*. Boston: Star Island Corporation.

Schoenwetter, J. 1987. Review of *The Palynology of Archaeological Sites* (1985) by G. W. Dimbleby. *American Antiquity* 25:204–206.

Solomon, A. M., and D. F. Kroener. 1971. Suburban Replacement of Rural Land Uses Reflected in the Pollen Rain of Northeastern New Jersey. *Bulletin of the New Jersey Academy of Science* 16(1–2):30–44.

Sweeney, M. A. 1988. Plant Inventory, Appledore Island. Manuscript on file at the New England Studies Program, University of Southern Maine, Portland.

Tauber, H. 1965. *Differential Pollen Dispersion and the Interpretation of Pollen Diagrams*. Geological Survey of Denmark Series II, No. 89. Copenhagen.

Tschudy, R. H. 1969. Relationship of Palynomorphs to Sedimentation. In *Aspects of Palynology*, R. S. Tschudy and R. S. Scott (eds.), pp. 79–96. New York: John Wiley.

Van Zeist, W. 1967. Archaeology and Palynology in the Netherlands. *Review of Palaeobotany and Palynology* 4:45–65.

Walch, K. M., J. R. Rowley, and N. J. Norton. 1970. Displacement of Pollen Grains by Earthworms. *Pollen et Spores* 12:39–44.

CHRISTINE R. SZUTER ∎

Chapter Thirteen

A Faunal Analysis of Home Butchering and Meat Consumption at the Hubbell Trading Post, Ganado, Arizona

Introduction

Faunal remains from historic sites have increasingly been used to answer questions relating to the types of animals used in the diet, the methods used to butcher animals, seasonality of the occupation, and the ethnic or cultural affiliation and socioeconomic status of the site's inhabitants. Many of the recent studies have focused on an urban setting where the occupants of the site have bought their meat from the local market in town (Baham et al. 1982; Davidson 1982; Hamblin 1981). The inhabitants' choice in the purchase of different cuts of meat was argued to reflect either their socioeconomic or ethnic background.

The faunal remains from the Hubbell Trading Post reflect a completely different set of circumstances than these urban, historic sites. Animals were known to be butchered and their meat consumed at the trading post. Home butchering and home consumption meant that all portions of the animal would potentially be found in trash deposits. The Hubbell family members were not choosing and buying meat from their local butcher; they _were_ the local butcher as well as the local consumer. This site, though, did not just represent a rural ranch—it was also a trading post and way station for visitors. The Hubbell Trading Post is located in northeastern Arizona near the town of Ganado. As a trading post it was not only involved in the selling of Indian arts and crafts. Early records show an assortment of food, including

This article was originally published in _MASCA Research Papers in Science and Archaeology_, Supplement to Vol. 8, _Animal Use and Culture Change_, Pam J. Cabtree and Kathleen Ryan, eds., pp. 78–89, ©1991.

meat, was sold at the store. If bones were retained in meat that was sold, that is, if the meat was not deboned, then the faunal trash would be lacking in particular cuts of meat.

Because Hubbell was a trading post, numerous visitors passed through the doors. John Lorenzo Hubbell was known to be quite a host to the many people who came through Ganado (McNitt 1962). He entertained many guests, including artists, scientists, and writers, and at one event he fed 300 Indians at his home (Utley 1957: 87). With this level of entertaining occurring, the trash is not only representative of the household, but also includes all the material trash remains that friends and guests brought to the site. An examination of the socioeconomic or ethnic status would be fruitless at such a 19th–20th-century rural outpost of the American West.

The focus of this study is to provide a description of the species utilized by all the occupants, permanent or transient, of Hubbell, to discuss the home butchering of domestic animal, and to examine the cuts of meat recovered from different spatial and temporal contexts.

Methods

Sampling Strategy

A total of 4229 faunal remains was recovered from excavations undertaken in 1982 and 1983 at the Hubbell Trading Post with James Bradford, archaeologist for the Southwest Region National Park Service, as principal investigator. Excavations of the porch, trash area, and alley were part of the preservation and rehabilitation efforts conducted at the Hubbell Trading Post. Porch floor boards needed to be replaced and a drainage system had to be installed near the trash area. Table 13.1 lists the five different provenience areas and the quantity of bone recovered from each. Figure 13.1 is a plan map of the site showing the location of the units excavated.

A total of 992 of these remains from two provenience areas—the porch area and Trash Area 1—was analyzed. The porch area was chosen because of its proximity to the house and its generally undisturbed nature (J. Bradford, pers. comm.). All the bone from the porch subfloor of the Hubbell Trading Post, dating from approximately 1910 up through 1966 (145 fragments after analysis), was analyzed. Three test units in Trash Area 1—Nos. 12, 23, and 83—were chosen because of their complete stratigraphic sequence. Units 23 and 83 date to as early as the 1880s with deposits extending to a depth of 4 ft (J. Bradford, pers. comm.). While a beginning date is not known for Test Unit 12, the entire trash area was used until the mid-1960s when Mr. Hubbell turned over his property to the National Park Service. All of the remains from Levels 1 through 6 of Test Unit 12 (230 fragments) and Levels 1 through 7 of Test Unit 23 (312 fragments) were analyzed. This included

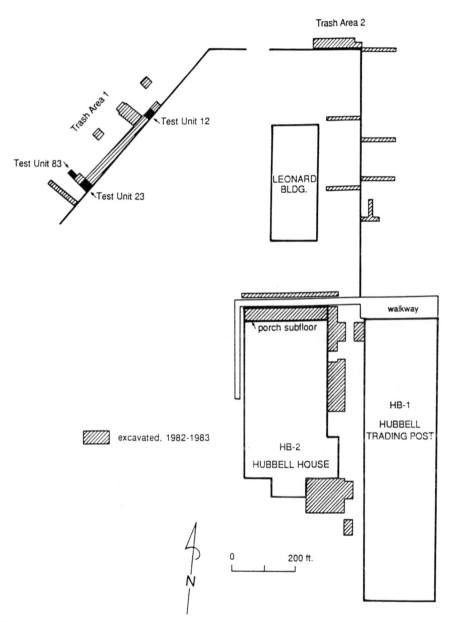

Figure 13.1. Plan of Hubbell Trading Post site, showing areas excavated.

the bones from Pit 1 in Test Unit 23. However, the faunal remains from variable levels of the overall grid in Test Unit 23 were not analyzed. Test Unit 83 contained 577 faunal fragments. Slightly over 50 percent of this total was randomly drawn from each level (1–8) within this test unit (305 fragments).

TABLE 13.1

Total Quantity of Bone Recovered from the 1982 and 1983 Excavations at the Hubbell Trading Post by Provenience Area

Provenience Area	No. of Fragments[a]
HB-2 porch subfloor	137
Trash Area 1	3278
Alley between HB-1 and HB-2	155
Trash Area 2	479
Leonard Building testing	180
TOTAL	4229

[a] Quantity of bone are totals counted by the laboratory before the faunal analysis was completed. These quantities may differ slightly from the actual totals reported in this paper. These totals were used to determine the sampling strategy.

Identification

Identifications were made to the lowest possible taxonomic level. Domestic animals—goats, sheep, cattle, horse, chickens—comprised the majority of identified animals. Morphological characters were used to separate different species. Often it was not possible to distinguish sheep and goat—the fragments were too small and the comparative collection did not have a large number of specimens from any one species in order to examine interspecific variability. Due to the small quantity of positively identified sheep and goat bones, all analysis of sheep and goat is subsumed under the category "sheep/goat." These species are separated in tables that give the quantity of different taxon by provenience, however.

Many of the fragments recovered were classified as unidentified mammals. Distinctions in these cases were made on the basis of the size of mammal represented by the fragment. "Small" unidentified fragments were rabbit-sized or smaller, "medium" unidentified fragments were dog-sized. "Medium-large" unidentified remains were sheep/goat-sized, while "large" unidentified fragments were cattle/horse-sized. "General large" mammalian unidentified fragments ranged from sheep/goat to cattle/horse size—the exact size range could not be determined.

Information Recorded

Each skeletal element was identified and information on symmetry, portion, fusion, burning, weathering, breakage pattern, and quantity were recorded. A few comments on some of these variables need to be made.

Symmetry, or the side of the skeletal element was recorded in order to compute the minimum number of individuals (MNIs). Fusion was recorded as fused, unfused, or epiphyseal lines present. Aging of the animals was based on epiphyseal fusion or eruption of teeth when these could be observed. Burned bone was either classified as scorched (black/brown in color) or calcined (blue/grey/white in color). Bone with an intact cortical surface was in good condition; heavily weathered bone had a flaking cortical surface; slightly weathered bone was intermediate between these two categories. Breakage patterns described if the bone was freshly broken during or after excavation or had an old break prior to excavation. Measurements as proposed by von den Driesch (1976) were overwhelmingly not possible to make because the measuring points proposed by her were not present on the fragments.

The above information was recorded for all faunal fragments. In addition, bone that was butchered was further described. Lyman (1977) describes a method for recording butchering marks, including saw and cut marks, that was used in this analysis. The description of the saw cuts included a description of the striations left by sawing, the number of saw cuts, the direction of the saw cut, and the maximum and minimum width of the cut. The description of cut marks included the number of cut marks, their location, and whether they were incomplete saw cut marks or knife cut marks.

Results

Taxonomic Identification and Distribution of the Faunal Remains

Table 13.2 is a taxonomic list of the animals recovered from the porch subfloor and Trash Area 1 of the Hubbell Trading Post. Wild species only include one fragment from a rock squirrel (*Spermophilus variegatus*). Domestic animals, which were far more plentiful, include goat (*Capra hircus*), sheep (*Ovis aries*), pig (*Sus scrofa*), cattle (*Bos taurus*), and horse/ass (*Equus* sp.). Two taxa, *Canis* sp. and *Anas* sp. could be either coyote/domestic dog or teal/domestic duck, respectively. The table presents the quantity of butchered and nonbutchered bone for each taxonomic group from the porch subfloor and Trash Area 1. The percent and minimum number of individuals for each taxonomic group is also given. Only 25 percent of the bone from the porch subfloor was unidentifiable (36 out of 145 fragments), whereas 61 percent of the bone (520 out of 847 fragments) from Trash Area 1 was unidentifiable.

Chicken, cattle, and combined sheep, goat, and sheep/goat (20.7, 24.1, 25.5 percent, respectively) were fairly evenly represented among the remains in the porch subfloor. In Trash Area 1, in contrast, chicken and turkey bones only made up 1.0

TABLE 13.2

Quantity of Butchered (B) and Nonbutchered (N-B) Bone for Each Taxon
from Trash Area 1 and the Porch Subfloor of the Hubbell Trading Post

Taxon	Common Name	Trash Area 1				Porch Subfloor			
		N-B	B	%[a]	MNI[b]	N-B	B	%	MNI
Aves	Unidentified bird	5	0	0.6	—				
Galliformes	Guinea fowl, chicken	4	0	0.5	—				
Gallus gallus	Domestic chicken	8	0	0.9	1	29	1	20.7	2
Meleagris gallopavo	Domestic turkey	1	0	0.1	1				
Anas sp.	Domestic duck or teal	9	0	1.1	2				
Spermophilus variegatus	Rock squirrel	1	0	0.1	1				
Canis sp.	Domestic coyote or dog	5	0	0.6	1				
Artiodactyla	Artiodactyl	1	0	0.1	—				
Capra hircus	Domestic goat	1	0	0.1	1	0	1	0.7	1
Ovis aries	Domestic sheep	4	0	0.5	1	2	0	1.4	1
Ovis/Capra	Sheep or goat	87	90	20.9	—	23	11	23.4	—
Sus scrofa	Domestic pig	2	4	0.7	1	1	0	0.7	1
Bos taurus	Domestic cattle	24	69	11.0	3	7	28	24.1	1
Equus sp.	Horse or ass					2	0	1.4	1
Bos/Equus	Cattle or horse	3	9	1.4	—	0	4	2.8	—
Medium mammal		12	0	1.4	—	1	0	0.7	—
Med.–Lg. mammal		137	22	18.8	—	0	12	8.3	—
Lg. mammal		71	38	12.9	—	0	8	5.5	—
General Lg. mammal		187	52	28.2	—	6	9	10.3	—
Unidentified bone		0	1	0.1	—				
TOTAL		562	285	100.0		71	74	100.0	

[a] Percentage of each taxonomic group.
[b] Minimal number of individuals.

percent of the assemblage. This same area had 21.5 percent sheep, goat, and sheep/goat remains and 11.0 percent cattle. Both areas have small quantities of pig (0.7 percent for each area).

Material from Test Units 23 and 83 in Trash Area 1 dates to as early as the 1880s. In the lowest levels of each test unit no chicken or turkey bones were recovered. Sheep/goat, however, was ubiquitous. Every level of each test unit contained sheep and goat. Cattle was nearly as common. Only two levels of Test Unit 23 and one level of Test Unit 12 did not include any cattle remains. Pig was less common overall and was concentrated in Levels 3, 4, and 6 of Test Unit 23 and Levels 3 and 4 in Test Unit 12.

Aging of Specimens

The determination of the age at death of the domestic ungulates was made on the basis of epiphyseal fusion of the bones following Silver (1963).

With the exception of one cervical and one thoracic vertebra, all of the cattle vertebrae with observable ossification were unfused. The centrum fuses to the body of the vertebra at 5 years, therefore the majority of cattle butchered were less than 5 years old. Other cattle elements suggest even younger ages at death. Both the distal ulna and radius and proximal ulna fuse at 3–3.5 years. These cattle elements were all unfused, indicating an age of less than 3–3.5 years for some of the specimens. Finally, the lower third premolar had not erupted in one mandible, giving an age for that individual of less than 2.5 years. Since there is no way of knowing whether these individual bones came from one or more individuals, only general statements on the age at which cattle were butchered can be made. First, the majority of cattle were less than 5 years old and some were even younger than 2.5 years. Second, the fusion of the two vertebrae suggests an older age, at least 5 years, for some butchered cattle.

Only five pig elements could be used for aging and only one of these is unfused. The proximal ulna, being unfused, indicates an age of less than 3–3.5 years. The fused proximal humerus and fused proximal ulna represent an age of at least 3.5 years, while a fused proximal and distal radius indicates an age of at least 1 year. With only one unfused pig bone, an age structure of butchered pigs cannot be determined.

The aging of the sheep/goat remains is based on the assumption that most of the remains are sheep. This assumption is supported by the overwhelming identification of sheep in an earlier faunal report of a previous excavation at the Hubbell Trading Post in which a *matanza* pit was excavated (Olsen and Beezly 1975).[1] The remains were primarily identified as sheep based on morphological differences in sheep and goat metapodials and phalanges. (Metapodials and phalanges are rare in the present sample, hence identifications below the level of sheep/goat were not easily made.)

Sheep are classified as lamb, yearling mutton, or mutton. Lambs are 0–13 months, yearling mutton are 13–24 months and have unfused distal metapodials (or spool joints), and mutton are older than 24 months with fused distal metapodials. The relative abundance of sheep/goat remains with ossification centers demonstrates that at least lambs and yearling mutton were butchered. Both fused and unfused distal humeri were recovered. Fusion of this element occurs at 10 months, therefore some sheep/goat were "lambs" while others were "yearlings" or "mutton." With the exception of the proximal ulna (fuses at 2.5–3 years), all the late fusing long bones, such as the proximal femur (fuses from 2.5–3 years), proximal humerus (3–3.5 years), distal radius (3 years), and proximal tibia (3–3.5 years), were not fused indicating the butchering of these animals before they were 3.5 years old. The distal tibiae, which fuse at 1–1.5 years, were sometimes fused and sometimes unfused. This evidence again suggests a range in ages of slaughtered sheep from lambs to mutton (Table 13.3).

TABLE 13.3
Age of Epiphyseal Fusion of Sheep Skeletal Elements and Their Presence in the Hubbell Trading Post

Skeletal element	Fuses by	Observed
Distal humerus	10 mos.	F & UNF
Distal tibia	1.5 yrs.	F & UNF
Proximal femur	2.5–3 yrs.	UNF
Proximal ulna	2.5–3 yrs.	F & UNF
Distal radius	3 yrs.	UNF
Proximal humerus	3–3.5 yrs.	UNF
Proximal tibia	3–3.5 yrs.	UNF

F = fused.
UNF = unfused.

Modifications of the Bone: Weathering and Gnawing

The greater degree of identifiable taxa from the porch area may relate to the overall better condition of the bone from this provenience. All the bone from the porch area was in good or slightly weathered condition, while 18.9 percent (160 out of 847 fragments) of the Trash Area 1 bones were heavily weathered. The porch area, though, did have a small quantity (4 fragments) of bone that were carnivore or rodent gnawed. No bone from the trash area was gnawed and in fact the only possible intrusive bones found in the trash area was one element of a rock squirrel. The porch subfloor was a known living area for the local cats and therefore the bone in this context may have been more likely to be gnawed.

The porch subfloor and Trash Area 1 also differed in the quantity of butchered bone. Fifty-one percent of the porch subfloor bones were butchered (74 out of 145 fragments), while only 33.6 percent (285 out of 847 fragments) of the Trash Area 1 bones had butchering marks. The presence of either saw cuts or knife marks was used to define a bone as being butchered.

Butchering Methods

The butchering of ungulates is completed in two steps—the slaughter of the animal and the processing of the carcass. This latter step involves the further partitioning of the carcass into wholesale and retail cuts. While overall similarities exist in the butchering of cattle, sheep/goat, and pig, the wholesale and retail cuts differ both in terms of what they are called and the types of bones associated with each cut. For the purpose of this analysis additional skeletal elements recovered from an archaeological context—such as those associated with the head, neck, feet, and hindshank—need to be considered along with the wholesale cuts. Table 13.4 presents the cuts of meat used in this analysis and the skeletal elements associated with each cut.[2]

The first stage of butchering—the slaughter of the animal—was described by Olsen and Beezley (1975) in their analysis of the animal remains from the *matanza* pit at the Hubbell Trading Post. The second stage—the processing of the carcass—is examined through the analysis of the bones from the trash of the Hubbell Trading Post residents. As will be demonstrated throughout this analysis, the types of bones associated with each of these two stages of butchering an animal are dramatically different.

Figures 13.2 and 13.3 show the carcasses of cattle and sheep, after the animal is slaughtered and dressed out. The major wholesale cuts and the bones associated with each cut are also shown. Figure 13.4 gives the anatomical and butchering names for each of the bones in a beef carcass. Figure 13.5 is a cutting diagram for beef that shows each wholesale cut and the procedure used for separating each cut.[3]

As has been noted by previous authors, commercial butchering has remained standard for some time (Bayham et al. 1982; Davidson 1982). Although the butchering at the Hubbell Trading Post was done at the household level, the procedure was fairly standardized. It must be noted, though, that not all household butchering conforms to one standard. The level of technology employed, membership in different cultural and ethnic groups, and individual variation all play a part in the patterns of butchering (Szuter 1984a, 1984b). Butchering at a household level also involves the entire animal, therefore remains of all body parts are retrieved and need to be considered in any analysis. The following is a description of the butchering of cattle and sheep/goat at the Hubbell Trading Post as reflected in the bone recovered from trash deposits.

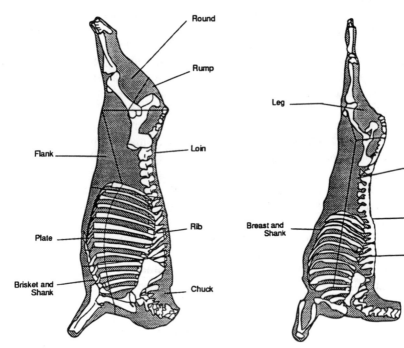

Figure 13.2. Cow carcass, slaughtered and dressed out.

Figure 13.3. Sheep carcass, slaughtered and dressed out.

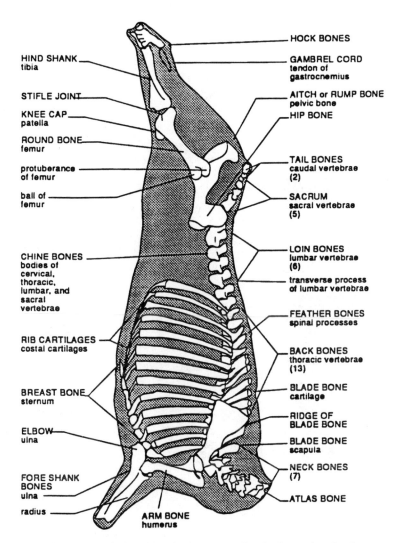

Figure 13.4. Anatomical and butchering names for the bones in a beef carcass.

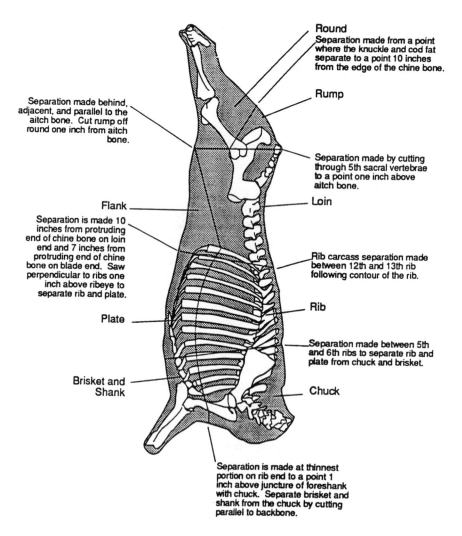

Round
Separation made from a point
where the knuckle and cod fat
separate to a point 10 inches
from the edge of the chine bone.

Rump

Separation made behind,
adjacent, and parallel to the
aitch bone. Cut rump off
round one inch from aitch
bone.

Separation made by cutting
through 5th sacral vertebrae
to a point one inch above
aitch bone.

Flank

Loin

Separation is made 10
inches from protruding
end of chine bone on loin
end and 7 inches from
protruding end of chine
bone on blade end. Saw
perpendicular to ribs one
inch above ribeye to
separate rib and plate.

Rib carcass separation made
between 12th and 13th rib
following contour of the rib.

Rib

Plate

Separation made between 5th
and 6th ribs to separate rib and
plate from chuck and brisket.

Brisket and
Shank

Chuck

Separation is made at thinnest
portion on rib end to a point 1
inch above juncture of foreshank
with chuck. Separate brisket and
shank from the chuck by cutting
parallel to backbone.

Figure 13.5. Cutting diagram for beef showing each wholesale cut and the procedure used
to separate each cut.

TABLE 13.4

Cuts of Cattle and Sheep/Goat,
and Skeletal Elements Associated with Each Cut,
for the Hubbell Trading Postfaunal Analysis

Cut	Cattle—Associated Bones
Head	Cranium, mandible, hyoid
Neck	Atlas, axis, and other cervical vertebrae
Chuck[a]	Scapula, proximal humerus and shaft, thoracic vertebrae 1–5
Rib[a]	Rib with head and shaft, thoracic vertebrae 6–12
Foreshank[a]	Radius, ulna, distal humerus
Brisket[a]	Ribs 1–5 with sternal end and shaft
Short loin[a]	Lumbar vertebrae
Full loin[a]	Ilium, sacrum
Round[a]	Femur shaft
Rump[a]	Ischium, proximal femur, pubis, caudal vertebrae
Hindshank	Tibia

Cut	Sheep/Goat—Associated Bones
Neck	Atlas, axis, cervical vertibrae
Shoulder[a]	Scapula, proximal humerus and shaft, thoracic vertebrae 1–5, ribs 1–5 with head and shaft
Foreshank[a]	Radius, ulna, distal humerus
Breast[a]	Ribs 1–12 with sternal end and shaft
Rack[a]	Ribs 6–12 with proximal head and shaft, thoracic vertebrae 6–12
Loin[a]	Lumbar vertebrae
Leg[a]	Femur, innominate
Hindshank	Tibia
Head	Cranium, mandible
Feet	Matepodials, tarsals, carpals, phalanges

[a] Wholesale cuts.

Two tools, knives and saws, were readily identifiable as the instruments used in butchering from the marks that were left on the bone. The frequency of their use varied with the animal butchered. Few knife cuts were observed on cattle bone (Table 13.5), while these marks were far more frequent on sheep/goat bone (Table 13.6).

With the exception of the cattle hyoid, all butchered cattle bones had at least one saw cut. Knife cuts were only observed in conjunction with saw cuts and only on 9 fragments. The hyoid was the only bone with knife cuts and no accompanying saw cuts. More sheep/goat bones had knife cuts without any saw cuts (16 fragments) than did the cattle bones. Nine sheep/goat fragments also had both knife and saw cuts.

TABLE 13.5

The Quantity of Each Skeletal Element of Cattle with Saw Cuts
and/or Knife Cuts Recovered from Trash Area 1 and the Porch Subfloor
at the Hubbell Trading Post

Skeletal Element	Trash Area 1			Porch Subfloor		
	Saw	Knife	Both	Saw	Knife	Both
Hyoid	—	—	—	—	1	—
Mandible	3	—	—	—	—	—
Vertebrae, type indet.	4	—	2	—	—	—
Atlas	—	—	1	—	—	—
Axis	—	—	—	1	—	—
Cervical	4	—	—	2	—	1
Thoracic	8	—	1	5	—	1
Lumbar	7	—	—	1	—	—
Sacrum	1	—	—	—	—	—
Caudal	1	—	—	—	—	—
Ribs: head and shaft	1	—	—	1	—	1
Ribs: shaft	22	—	1	—	—	—
Scapula: glenoid fossa	1	—	—	1	—	—
Scapula: body	2	—	—	3	—	1
Humerus: shaft	1	—	—	1	—	—
Radius and ulna: articulated	—	—	—	1	—	—
Radius: shaft	—	—	—	2	—	—
Ulna: shaft	—	—	—	1	—	—
Ulna: distal and shaft	—	—	—	1	—	—
Ischium	3	—	—	—	—	—
Ilium	2	—	—	—	—	—
Femur: shaft	2	—	—	—	—	—
Tibia: shaft	2	—	—	2	—	—
Tibia: distal and articulated tarsals	—	—	—	1	—	—
TOTAL	64	0	5	23	1	4

By examining the types of butchering marks, the angle and direction of the marks, and the frequency of the marks left on each skeletal element the procedure used to butcher cattle and sheep/goat can be described.

The separation of the skull from the atlas was done with the use of a knife for both cattle and sheep/goat. Cut marks were found on both the occipital condyles of the skull and the articular surfaces of the atlas of sheep/goat and cattle. In addition to this method, a second means of separation was observed for sheep/goat. An axis and atlas that remained articulated exhibited a transverse saw cut on the axis, suggesting that the head was sawed rather than cut off.

While no butchered sheep/goat mandibles or hyoids were found, the recovered ones from cattle were butchered in a consistent pattern. The hyoid, as has been mentioned, had numerous knife cuts on it consistent with removal of the tongue.

Three mandibles were sawn along the posterior portion, removing the angle of the ramus and ascending ramus. While the meat value of the mandible would be rather low, its grease content would be high.

TABLE 13.6

The Quantity of Each Skeletal Element of Sheep, Goat, and Sheep/Goat with Saw Cuts and/or Knife Cuts Recovered from Trash Area 1 and the Porch Subfloor at the Hubbell Trading Post

Skeletal Element	Trash Area 1			Porch Subfloor		
	Saw	Knife	Both	Saw	Knife	Both
Skull	—	—	—	—	1	—
Atlas	—	1	—	—	—	—
Axis	1	—	—	2	—	—
Cervical	5	—	—	3	—	—
Thoracic	16	—	3	1	—	—
Lumbar	14	1	1	—	—	—
Sacrum	—	1	—	—	—	—
Ribs: head and shaft	2	2	—	—	—	—
Ribs: shaft	12	4	2	2	—	—
Scapula: glenoid fossa	—	—	—	1	—	—
Scapula: body	6	—	1	—	—	—
Humerus: shaft	2	—	1	—	—	—
Humerus: distal	1	1	—	—	—	—
Radius: shaft	1	—	—	—	—	—
Radius: distal	1	—	—	—	—	—
Ilium	3	—	—	—	—	—
Acetabulum	1	—	—	—	—	—
Femur: proximal	1	2	—	—	—	—
Femur: shaft	1	1	1	—	—	—
Tibia: proximal and shaft	—	—	—	1	—	—
Tibia: distal and shaft	—	—	—	—	1	—
Calcaneum	—	1	—	—	—	—
TOTAL	67	14	9	10	2	0

The carcass of ungulates is generally split by sawing down the vertebral column, or backbone, splitting the animal into two halves. This procedure was overwhelmingly observable from the cattle cervical, thoracic, lumbar, sacral, and caudal vertebrae. Most vertebrae had both sagittal and transverse cuts. This contrasts with the sheep/goat vertebrae that rarely (six fragments) had sagittal cuts. Transverse cuts across the centrum area, rather than through it, were most prevalent. Sheep/goat were not regularly halved. This difference between cattle and sheep/goat is probably due to the difference in size of these ungulates. Halving a cattle carcass makes it more manageable, whereas the relatively small size of a sheep/goat carcass is easily handled without splitting it in two.

Differences observed in the halving of the ungulates is further reflected in how the ribs of these animals are butchered. For sheep/goat, ribs were either sawed off from the vertebral column below the rib head or kept fairly complete with only knife cuts along the shaft. Only one cattle rib (also sawn) had a knife cut; otherwise all butchered cattle ribs were sawn. Those cattle rib fragments with an intact head also had portions of the shaft of the ribs present. The remaining portions of cattle ribs were cut into small riblets that ranged from 39 to 78 mm in length. Few sheep/goat ribs (three fragments) were processed in this manner. No ribs with the sternal end intact were recovered from either cattle or sheep/goat. As mentioned before, the size difference between cattle and sheep/goat is probably the reason for differences in the halving of the carcass and butchering of the ribs.

The cuts from the scapula were fairly similar for cattle and sheep/goat. The glenoid fossa was removed along the neck of the scapula by sawing. On one cattle bone the glenoid fossa had two perpendicular saw cuts through it. The body of the scapula was cut across its width into cuts 15–21 mm thick for sheep/goat and 15–32 mm thick for cattle.

While the scapulae of both sheep/goat and cattle were butchered similarly, long bones of these two animals were treated differently. More variation in butchering existed among sheep/goat than among cattle long bones. The humerus, femur, and tibia shafts of cattle were cut across into sections that measured 20–26 mm for the humerus, 15–85 mm for the femur, and 30–66 mm for the tibia. The humeri cuts are steak cuts while the cuts from the femorae and the tibiae are both steaks and roasts. The humerus, femur, and tibia of sheep/goat were also sawn into these cuts, but in addition, some of these two elements only had knife cuts along the shaft while others had both saw and knife cuts. Cattle bones were uniformly butchered into retail cuts of steaks and roasts, whereas sheep/goat long bones were butchered in a greater variety of ways.

The radius of sheep/goat was sawn through the shaft. The distal end of the radius was removed by sawing just above the distal epiphysis. The separation of the foot from the radius and ulna of cattle was done either by sawing off the distal end of these elements or by using a knife to separate the carpals from the distal end of the radius.

Innominate bones were most frequently the ilia for both cattle and sheep/goat. Both parallel and perpendicular saw cuts were present on cattle ilia. Sheep/goat ilia generally had only one saw cut and the other edge was broken off. No pubis fragments were recovered from either species.

The preceding discussion presents the butchering of cattle and sheep/goat from the butchering marks observed on each fragment of bone. These skeletal elements were then classified into different cuts of meat (Table 13.4) which are used in the following discussion.

Skeletal Representation

Not all bone fragments can be readily identified as coming from a particular cut of meat. For example, four wholesale cuts of cattle—the short plate, the chuck, brisket, and rib—all contain portions of rib bones. Two wholesale cuts—the chuck and rib—contain thoracic vertebrae. Since neither the rib fragments nor the thoracic vertebrae were identified as to position the classification of these fragments as coming from a particular wholesale cut is more difficult. Rib fragments with the proximal head are either rib or chuck, rib fragments with the sternal end are brisket or short plate. Rib shafts are simply classified as being from any one of the four cuts mentioned. Thoracic vertebrae have been classified as rib and this is noted in the tables that refer to specific cuts of meat. Table 13.7 presents the quantity and percent of each cut of meat for cattle and for the combined category of goat, sheep, and sheep/goat.

Rib fragments, whether coming from the short plate, chuck, brisket, or rib, are the most common cut of meat for both cattle (51.5 percent) and sheep/goat (43.1 percent). The head and neck account for 12.8 percent and 13.4 percent of sheep/goat and cattle, respectively. The leg of sheep/goat and the comparable rump and round of cattle represent 11.8 percent and 13.4 percent of the remains, respectively. Similarities are also observed for the sheep/goat shoulder cut (10.8 percent) and the cattle chuck (10.3 percent), the foreshank and hindshank (sheep/goat = 5.9 percent; cattle = 6.2 percent). The major differences in percentages of different cuts are between the ribs (mentioned above) and the loin (sheep/goat = 15.7 percent; cattle = 8.2 percent). Proportionately more cattle ribs to loin cuts were consumed than sheep/goat ribs to loin cuts.

Overall, when considering both butchered and nonbutchered bone, foot elements —metapodials, carpals, tarsals, and phalanges—were infrequently found in either Trash Area 1 or the porch subfloor. Only 7.3 percent of the sheep/goat bones and 4.7 percent of the cattle bones were from the fore or hind feet. Previous excavations in the *matanza* pit yielded completely different proportions in the elements (Bayham 1975; Olsen and Beezley 1975). Approximately 80 percent of the sheep/goat and 95 percent of the sheep remains were foot elements. Nearly 10 percent of the cattle bones were fore and hind feet elements. The dramatic difference, particularly among the sheep/goat elements, reinforces the known functions of each area excavated. The *matanza* area represents the first stage of butchering —the slaughtering, skinning, and dressing out of the animal. The trash deposits are the remains from animals eaten for a meal.

While not all of the trash recovered from the present excavations could be separated into discrete time periods, the fill of Test Units 23 and 83 contained material in the deeper levels from the 1880s. An examination of the cuts of meat recovered from different stratigraphic levels, however, indicated that temporal differences in the use of various animal parts did not exist.

TABLE 13.7

Quantity and Percent of Different Cuts of Cattle and Sheep,
Goat, and Sheep/Goat from Trash Area 1 and the Porch Subfloor
at the Hubbell Trading Post

| | Cattle | |
Cut	*n*	%
Head	4	4.1
Neck	9	9.3
Rib	15	15.5
Loin	8	8.2
Rump	7	7.2
Round	6	6.2
Chuck	10	10.3
Foreshank	5	5.2
Hindshank	1	1.0
Rib, loin, or chuck	6	6.2
Rib, chuck, plate, or brisket	23	23.7
Rib or chuck	3	3.1
TOTAL	97	100.0

| | Sheep, Goat, and Sheep/Goat | |
Cut	*n*	%
Head	1	0.9
Neck	12	11.8
Rack	24	23.5
Loin	16	15.7
Leg	12	11.8
Breast or Rack	20	19.6
Shoulder	11	10.8
Foreshank	4	3.9
Hindshank	2	2.0
TOTAL	102	100.0

Comparison with the Frijole Ranch Site Faunal Remains

Comparisons in animal butchering and meat consumption were made between the Hubbell Trading Post and the Frijole Ranch site. Both were occupied through portions of the 19th–20th centuries, but were quite different occupations. The Frijole Ranch site, located in the Guadalupe Mountains National Park in west Texas, was occupied successively by three separate families who each made their living by different types of ranching and farming. The Hubbell Trading Post, as well as being occupied by the Hubbell family, also served as a commercial establishment. The faunal assemblages at the two sites therefore are the result of different, though at times overlapping, functions. Both similarities and differences are observed in the assemblages.

The Frijole Ranch site was a considerably smaller assemblage than that from the Hubbell Trading Post. Even with a small bone sample, the domesticated animals included chicken, turkey, goat, sheep/goat, pig, and cattle. Few chicken or turkey remains were identified at Hubbell. At the Frijole Ranch site numerous bones from intrusive animals,which were not common at Hubbell, were present, such as mice, raccoons, and skunks. No bone from the Frijole Ranch site was burned.

A marked contrast between the two sites exists in the quantity of butchered bone. Only 13 percent of the Frijole Ranch site was butchered compared to 36 percent of the Hubbell Trading Post remains. Though the quantity of butchered bone varied, the methods used in butchering the animals were quite similar. A knife was used more frequently on sheep and goat than on cattle. Cattle were split down the vertebral column by sawing the animal in half. Sheep and goat were not halved. The ribs of sheep and goat were cut below the head, whereas cattle ribs were cut further down the rib shaft. The quantity of pig remains was so small that inferences on butchering methods could not be made.

The age at which animals were butchered varied according to taxon. Some of the pig remains at both sites indicate an age of at least 3.5 years. At Hubbell some of the pig remains were from animals less than 3.5 years. Cattle remains from the Frijole Ranch site indicate an age of at least 5 years while at Hubbell the cattle bones suggest an age of less than 5 years. Sheep and goat at Hubbell were less than 3.5 years or in the range of lamb and mutton. At the Frijole Ranch site, the sheep/goat were 6–10 months or lambs. The Frijole Ranch site sample was so small that the age designations of any taxon were only based on a few elements. More variation in the age structure of butchered animals may have existed.

Although somewhat different in the economic activities carried out at each of these sites, the faunal assemblages show some similarities in the types of animals butchered and how they were butchered. Cattle and sheep/goat are most commonly recovered. Pig remains make up a small portion of each assemblage. Cattle are halved and butchered primarily with a saw, while sheep/goat are not halved and the elements frequently butchered with a knife.

Conclusions

An examination of the Hubbell Trading Post fauna has provided information on the types of animals used by the occupants, the home butchering methods used on sheep/goat and cattle, and the different cuts of meat eaten by the Hubbell family and their visitors. It has also provided detailed information on the faunal remains that includes natural and cultural modifications of the bone and the age of the slaughtered animals.

When the bones from the *matanza* pit excavated earlier were analyzed pig remains were not identified. However, excavations at the trash area and porch subfloor located a small amount of pig remains. Pig, though butchered and eaten at the trading post, was a rare taxon. In a study among Mexican ranchers, pigs were found to be raised by individuals for home consumption (Szuter 1984a, 1984b). They were not a large part of the overall economic system which emphasized cattle ranching and small-scale husbandry of goats. The individual raising and consumption of pigs in this community also may relate to the lack of refrigeration for preserving the meat. Beef can easily be dried, goats are small enough to eat in one evening, but pork is fatty and is not considered suitable to jerk. A pattern of low pork consumption was also the case at Hubbell. Few fragments have been recovered from the trash contents examined. Sheep/goat, however, were found in every level of every test unit and provenience examined. Cattle were just as common though not as abundant.

Home butchering of sheep/goat and cattle followed fairly conventional standards with two noted exceptions. First, since the butchering was done at home, all body parts could be retrieved. The mandible of cattle, which would generally not be a butchered cut bought at a market, was found butchered at Hubbell. This element was consistently butchered in the same manner, suggesting the removal of grease from it. Second, generally cattle and sheep/goat carcasses were split or halved. The sagittal cuts of vertebrae indicate this method was employed for cattle but was not the primary procedure used to butcher sheep/goat. More sheep/goat vertebrae were only cut transversely.

The cuts of meat eaten by all at Hubbell during all time periods were those associated with ribs. Ribs of either sheep/goat or cattle were found in the porch subfloor and in every level of Trash Area 1. Certainly the most common elements in the carcass, ribs form a part of four major wholesale cuts of meat—the chuck, rib, brisket, and short plate. The further partitioning of a rib into retail cuts of riblets further adds to the multitude of remains. An average of approximately 50 percent of the sheep/goat and cattle bones from Test Units 23 and 83 of Trash Area 1 were ribs. All other body parts made up a far lesser percent of the total number of bones.

The Hubbell Trading Post is a unique type of historic site for the analysis of faunal remains. As a trading post it not only served as living quarters for a family and their multitude of guests, but it also was a store where the sale of meat occurred. In addition, the faunal remains represent home butchering as opposed to the commercial butchering of animals. This faunal analysis suggests many questions concerning the use of meat at a trading post on the American western frontier. Sheep and goat were the primary animals butchered at the trading post. Not all of this meat was used for personal consumption as some mutton was sold at the trading post. The next step in the analysis of the Hubbell faunal remains, which was not completed for this study, would be to correlate the analysis with the documentary information in the Hubbell Trading Post Papers,[4] to answer questions such as who bought meat, what types of meat were sold, what was the cost of meat, and if certain types of meat were only sold during particular seasons. With the examination of both the archaeological and ethnohistorical record, a clearer picture of the social and economic factors of life during the 19th and 20th centuries at a trading post in northern Arizona can be known.

Acknowledgments

A version of this article was submitted in 1985 to the Southwest Region, National Park Service, in fulfillment of Contract No. PX7029–4–0175. I would like to thank Professor Stanley J. Olsen, Zooarchaeologist, Arizona State Museum, University of Arizona, Tucson, for his kindness and encouragement throughout this project. He provided space in the zooarchaeology laboratory to conduct the identification of the faunal remains. He also provided access to his own personal faunal collection. The National Park Service faunal collection that is housed at the Arizona State Museum was also used as a comparative collection.

Elliott Lax and Keiko Yoshikawa worked with me on the identification of the Hubbell Trading Post faunal remains. Their dedication and skill were greatly appreciated. A special thanks to the two anonymous reviewers and to Helen Schenck, whose advice was appreciated.

NOTES

1. A *matanza* pit contained discarded butchering refuse. It was located beneath a butchering rack or *matanza* used to hoist the animal up. During the butchering the *matanza* pit would be covered with wood planks (Gates 1973:28–29, photographs 2–12).

2. The small quantity of pig bone recovered makes any description of the butchering of these bones tenuous; therefore discussion of butchery marks on the pig bones is omitted.

3. The drawings are based on handouts used in a course entitled "The Science of Meat and Meat Production," given through the Department of Animal Sciences at the University of Arizona by Dr. John Marchello. Similar drawings can be found in Ashbrook (1955) as well as any major cookbook that discusses cuts of meat or in charts prepared by the National Livestock and Meat Board.

4. The Hubbell Trading Post Papers are housed in Special Collections, University Library, University of Arizona, Tucson.

REFERENCES

Ashbrook, F. G. 1955. *Butchering, Processing and Preservation of Meat*. New York: Van Nostrand Reinhold.

Bayham, F. E. 1975. *Final Report Faunal Analysis of Material Collected at the Hubbell Trading Post during May and June 1973*. Submitted to Western Archaeological Center, National Park Service, Tucson.

Bayham, F. E., P. C. Hatch, and J. Balsom. 1982. *Interpretation of Faunal Remains from the Original Phoenix Townsite, Block 1 and 2*. On file at Soil Systems, Inc., Phoenix.

Davidson, P. E. 1982. Patterns in Urban Foodways: An Example from Early Twentieth-Century Atlanta. In *Archaeology of Urban America*, R.S. Dickens, Jr. (ed.), pp. 381–397. New York: Academic Press.

Driesch, A. von den 1976. *A Guide to the Measurement of Animal Bones from Archaeological Sites*. Peabody Museum of Archaeology and Ethnology Bulletin No. 1. Cambridge, MA: Harvard University.

Gates, G. R. 1973. *Hubbell Trading Post National Historic Site Archaeological Project—Grade Testing*. On file at Southwest Region National Park Service, Santa Fe.

Hamblin, N. 1981. Faunal Analysis. In *The Lewis-Weber Site: A Tucson Homestead*, N. Curriden (ed.), pp. 242–291. Publications in Anthropology No. 14. Western Archaeological Center, National Park Service, Tucson.

Lyman, R. L. 1977. Analysis of Historical Faunal Remains. *Historical Archaeology* 11:67–73.

McNitt, F. 1962. *The Indian Traders*. Norman: University of Oklahoma Press.

Olsen, S. O. and J. Beezley 1975. Domestic Food Animals from Hubbell Trading Post. *The Kiva* 41(2):201–206.

Silver, I. A. 1963. The Ageing of Domestic Animals. In *Science in Archaeology*, D. Brothwell and E. Higgs (eds.), pp. 250–268. New York: Basic Books.

Szuter, C. R. 1984a. From the Hoof to Garbage: An Ethnoarchaeological Study of Animal Butchering, Products, Distribution and Garbage Disposal in Cucurpe, Sonora. Paper presented at the annual Ethnobiology Conference, Seattle.

Szuter, C. R. 1984b. *Come Carne*: The Social Dimensions of Meat Distribution in a Mexican Village. Paper presented at the annual meeting of the American Anthropological Association, Denver.

Utley, R. M. 1959. Special Report on Hubbell Trading Post, Ganado, Arizona. On file at Southwest Region National Park Service, Santa Fe.

DOUGLAS D. SCOTT ■
CLYDE COLLINS SNOW

Chapter Fourteen

Archaeology and Forensic Anthropology of the Human Remains from the Reno Retreat Crossing, Battle of the Little Bighorn, Montana

Introduction

Inclement weather forced suspension of the 1989 archeological work at Custer Battlefield National Monument on May 25. Volunteer crew members chose to disperse and find their own means to pass the time until the weather cleared and work could resume at the Reno-Benteen equipment disposal site. Four volunteers decided to explore the west side of the Reno Retreat Crossing which is situated on lands outside the National Monument boundary. They drove to the area and obtained permission from the adjacent landowner for access to the crossing area, which is owned by the Custer Battlefield Preservation Committee. Mr. Monte Kloberdanz found human remains eroding from the left or west bank of the river at approximately 11:30 A.M. as the group was preparing to leave the crossing area.

The remains consisted of a human skull, a left humerus, and a right clavicle. Mr. Kloberdanz collected the specimens, as he feared they were in imminent danger of falling into the river. He and his companions returned to Custer Battlefield National Monument and contacted the archeological project director. Acting Superintendent Douglas McChristian was immediately informed of the find and proceeded to telephone the land owner of record, the Big Horn county attorney, and the county

This article was originally published in *Papers on the Little Bighorn Battlefield Archaeology: The Equipment Dump, Marker 7, and the Reno Crossing*, Douglas D. Scott, ed., pp. 207–236, Lincoln: NE: J & E Reprint Co. ©1991.

coroner to notify them of the discovery. The county attorney and coroner determined that adequate expertise was available, with the archaeologists on site at
Custer Battlefield National Monument, for investigation of the find. A preliminary
assessment of the remains suggested the site to be the last resting place of one of
Reno's command. Representatives of the Crow Tribe were also contacted; since the
remains appeared to be those of a white soldier, the tribe indicated no concern with
the remains.

Investigation of the Discovery Site

Verbal authorization (written authorization was received) to conduct an
examination on behalf of the Big Horn County Coroner, Mr. Terry Bullis, was
received at approximately 3:30 P.M. The project director drove to the location
accompanied by Acting Park Superintendent Douglas McChristian and archaeologists Melissa Connor, Colleen Winchell, Patrick Phillips, and Dick Harmon.
Mr. Kloberdanz, his two brothers Murray and Mike, and Mr. John Craig (who
were nearby, but not present, when the find was made) also accompanied the
investigative team to the location.

The discovery site was identified by the negative cast of the skull in the soil
matrix of the river bank. The skull impression was located between 40 and 50 cm
below the lip of the west bank of the Little Bighorn River, and approximately 3 m
north of a large cottonwood tree. The specific site is in the SE quarter of the SW
quarter of the SW quarter of the SW quarter of Section 34, Township 3 South and
Range 35 East. A white marble marker indicating where Lt. Benjamin Hodgson was
killed is across the river and approximately 30 m upstream.

Mr. Kloberdanz also identified the spot where the other two bones were found.
They were in a section of bank slump about 30 cm below the skull impression.
This area was carefully scoured for other bones and cultural material, but none
were observed.

The bank area was examined for about 100 m in either direction. The only other
bones observed were those of a recently dead deer. The area below the skull
impression was troweled downward about 50 cm and into the bank soil
approximately 25 cm. No bones were found, but a relatively recent tree limb or
snag was found embedded in the bank behind the location where the bones were
originally situated. Next the impression of the skull cast was troweled down and a
similar situation was encountered.

It appears the bones were dislodged from their primary context and fell or were
in some manner deposited (lodged), against the snag. According to Mr. Kloberdanz
the skull was upside down with the maxilla and foramen magnum exposed when
discovered. The skull exhibits some bleaching on the maxilla, foramen magnum,
and the occipital condyles are bleached and eroded. The evidence is consistent

with Mr. Kloberdanz's statements, and the bleaching is suggestive of several months exposure.

The skull and other bones appear to be a recent secondary deposit. It is possible there was a more complete burial at or near this location and that it was lost to the river as the bank collapsed due to high water eroding the bank.

The entire area was metal detected for 25 m in either direction along the bank and 10 m to the landward side to determine if any buttons, bullets, or other metallic debris were present. None was encountered.

Description of the Remains

The detailed analysis of the human remains follows. Osteometric measurements and observations on these bones are provided in the tables.

1. Cranium

This is an intact human cranium (Figure 14.1). It is medium tan in color except in the basilar area of the occipital which shows some bleaching due to exposure. Aside from some cortical erosion of the occipital condyles and tip of the left mastoid process, fracture of the right styloid, damage to the delicate bone of the medial orbital walls, and several teeth missing postmortem, the specimen is intact. The bone is well mineralized.

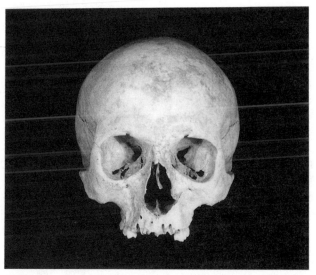

Figure 14.1. Frontal view of the Reno Crossing skull. Note the evulsed teeth and the fracture of the right maxilla.

Age at Death: 30–45 years

The basisphenoidal synchondrosis is fused. Cranial vault suture closure is advanced. Dentition is fully adult and there is moderate dental attrition with minimal dentine exposure on premolar and molar cusps. These findings indicate an age at death in the range of about 30–45 years.

Sex: Male

Morphological sex indicators are predominately male. These include large mastoid processes, well-developed nuchal ridges, medium-sized supraorbital brow-ridges, dull orbital margins and robust dentition. Cranial discriminate function analysis confirms the morphological diagnosis (Tables 14.1, 14.2, and 14.3).

TABLE 14.1

Sex and Race Discriminant Function Analysis of Reno Crossing Cranium

Case: Reno Crossing			Male		Female	
	mm	Sex	Black	Indian	Black	Indian
1. Maximum L	185	1.16	1.60	−0.25	1.28	−1.04
2. Maximum B	148		−1.90	−1.56	−1.18	−5.41
3. Basibregmatic H	133		−1.79	0.73	−0.14	4.29
4. Basion-Nasion L	98	1.66	−4.41	−0.29	−2.34	−4.02
5. Bizygomatic B	133	3.98	−0.10	1.75	0.38	5.62
6. Basion-Nasion L	90	−1.00	3.06	0.10	1.74	3.05
7. Nasion-Prosthion H	70	1.54	2.59	−0.16	−0.01	−1.00
8. Nasal B	22		10.56	−0.88	2.45	−2.19
DF Score:		924.42	20.27	2.73	74.56	87.31
Section point:		891.12	89.27	22.28	92.20	130.10
DF—SP:		33.30	−69.20	−19.55	−17.64	−42.79
Sex: Male				Race: White		

Race: White

Morphological race indicators are Caucasoid. These include relatively high and broad cranial vault, moderate nasion depression, high and salient nasal bridge, narrow nasal aperture with raised nasal ridges, and orthognathous lower facial profile. Cranial discriminate function analysis confirms the morphological diagnosis (Tables 14.1, 14.2, and 14.3).

Perimortem Trauma: Blunt force trauma to lower face

The specimen displays several signs of perimortem blunt force trauma:

a. The inferior one-third of the right nasal bone is missing.

b. A transverse linear fracture extends laterally from the lower right nasal margin to the midpoint of the inframaxillary fossa.

c. On the left nasal margin there is a triangular fracture defect extending laterally and superiorly to end just medial to the infraorbital foramen.

d. The right lateral incisor, canine, and first premolar are fractured transversely at or just above the alveolar margins.

TABLE 14.2
Craniometrics of Reno Crossing Cranium

Measurement	Value
1. Cranial length	185
2. Cranial breadth	148
3. Basibregmatic height	133
4. Basion-nasion length	98
5. Bizygomatic breadth	133
6. Basion-prosthion length	90
7. Nasion-prosthion height	70
8. Nasal breadth	22
9. Nasal height	54
10. Nasion-gnathion height	(mandible missing)
11. Biorbital breadth	96
12. Orbitale-nasion breadth	51
13. Orbital breadth	40
14. Orbital height	33
15. Maximul frontal breadth	26
16. Minimum frontal breadth	99
17. Alveolar breadth	62
18. Alveolar length	48
19. Tooth row length	(3rd molars unerupted)
20. Foramen magnum length	40
21. Foramen magnum breadth	33
22. Mastoid length	32
23. Frontal chord	120
24. Frontal arc	138
25. Cranial circumference	528

The complex of injuries observed above is consistent with an episode of blunt force trauma sustained at or around the time of death. Such trauma could have resulted from one or more blows inflicted transversely across the lower face. These injuries alone would not have been sufficient to have caused death.

2. Dentition

The adult dentition is fully erupted except for the left third maxillary molar. That this tooth was impacted is shown by its position and its closed root apices. The right third molar is missing antemortem. The lack of signs of periapical infection and the defect of the lateral alveolar wall of this tooth make it more likely that it was extracted than simply lost. The minimal socket resorption indicates that the extraction was fairly recent—probably no more than a few weeks prior to death. Periodontal disease is moderately advanced. The absence of tar stains suggests that this individual was not a smoker. Both central incisors, the left lateral incisor, and the left canine are missing postmortem. As noted above, there are perimortem fractures of the lateral incisor, canine, and first premolar on the right.

TABLE 14.3

Cranial Indices and Obervations on Reno Crossing Cranium

Index	Value	Class
Cranial	80.0	Brachycranic
Height/Length	71.9	Orthocranic
Height/Breadth	89.9	Tapeinocranic
Mean height	79.9	Low
Frontoparietal	78.6	Eurymetopic
Transver. frontal	78.6	Divergent
Sagittal frontal	87.0	Chamaemetopic
Cranofacial	89.9	Cryptozygic
Total facial	NA	(Mandible missing)
Upper facial	52.6	Mesene
Nasion projection	18.0	Medium
Orbital	82.5	Mesoconchic
Nasal	40.7	Leptorhinic
Prognathic	91.8	Orthognathic
Alveolar	129.2	Brachyranic
Dental	NA	(3rd molars unerupted)
Foramen Magnum	82.5	Medium
Cranial Modulus	155.3	Medium
Cranial capacity	1542 cc	Megacranic

Observations	(Scored 1–5)		
Cranial size	3	Orbital margins	3
Supraorbital torus	3	Zygomatic size	3
Forehead angle	3	Nasal profile	2
Frontal ridge	1	Nasal elevation	3
Sagittal contour	3	Nasal breadth	2
Postbregmatic dep.	1	Nasal gutter	1
Inion	4	Prognathism	1
Nuchal ridge	4		
Mastoid size	3		
Pterion type	H		

3. Clavicle: Young adult white male

This right clavicle is well mineralized and medium tan in color except for a bleached area indicating exposure on the anterior medial surface. There is no evidence of antemortem or perimortem pathology. The epiphyses are closed with no sign of recent union, a finding suggesting that the individual was beyond 23 years of age at death. On the other hand, there are no signs of joint degenerative changes that would suggest an age over 40. Metrical and morphological criteria diagnose the specimen as male (Table 14.4). The degree of sinuosity, moderately developed conoid tubercle, and broad lateral end are traits more typical of Caucasoids.

TABLE 14.4
Postcranial Measurements and Indices of Reno Crossing Cranium

Clavicle			(mm)
Maximum length			156
Lateral breadth			29
Circumference			35
	Lateral breadth index	18.6	Broad
	Robusticity index	22.4	Gracile
	Claviculo-humeral index	46.8	Medium

Humerus			(mm)
Maximum length			333
Physiological length			325
Vertical head diameter			48
Diaphysial diameter, maximum			22
Diaphysial diameter, minimum			19
Bicondylar breadth			63
Circumference			67
Suptrochlear Foramen			absent
	Diaphysial index	86.4	Eurybrachic
	Robusticity index	20.1	Medium

4. Humerus: Young adult male

This is a left humerus. The bone is well mineralized. Signs of exposure are limited to a small area around the lateral condyle. There is no evidence of antemortem disease or perimortem trauma. All epiphyses are closed. There are no signs of degenerative joint disease. The findings are consistent with an age at death between 18 and 40 years. Morphological and metric sex indicators are male. Antemortem stature, derived from the Trotter-Glesser equation for U.S. males is estimated at 173.0 cm (68.1 in) within a 95 percent probability range from 164.9 to 181.1 cm (64.9–71.3 in).

Summary:

In age at death, sex, and preservation characteristics, these three bones are consistent with belonging to a single individual. Age at death was between 30 and 40 years. Craniological features yield a diagnosis of white male. Antemortem stature is estimated at about 5 ft 8 in. The cranium displays perimortem blunt force trauma resulting in minor fractures. These injuries were not sufficient to have caused death.

The human bone was radiographed and examined by Dr. John Fitzpatrick, chairman of the Trauma Radiology Department, Cook County Hospital, Chicago, Illinois. Dr. Fitzpatrick observed the impacted wisdom tooth in the radiographs. No other pathologies, anomalies, or trauma were noted in his analysis (J. Fitzpatrick, pers. comm.).

In all probability, the remains found at the Reno Retreat Crossing are those of one of Maj. Reno's dead. The age and height are consistent with that of other members of the Seventh Cavalry who participated in the battle. The wear to the teeth is consistent with a coarse diet of the type soldiers of the 19th century endured, and the mineralization of the bones indicates they had been buried for many years. There is no evidence to suggest the bones are other than that of one of Reno's soldiers. The lack of other cranial and postcranial bones may be the result of bank cutting, or the combination of bank cutting action and a previous disturbance. If an earlier disturbance occurred it may have been a result of a disinterment by a reburial party, a nonmilitary collection of the remains, or disturbance due to agricultural practices.

History of the Area and Possible Identities of the Remains

Before attacking the Indian village, Custer divided his troops (Gray 1976; Stewart 1955). Three companies were assigned to Maj. Marcus Reno. Reno was to follow the west side of the Little Bighorn River and attack the village from the south. Custer would follow the east side of the river, cross, and attack at the north end of the village with the remaining five companies. Between them, they would encircle and capture the Indians. Capt. Frederick Benteen would be to the south and west to capture any who attempted to escape. Reno and Custer paralleled each other on the opposite sides of the river until Reno encountered the village and began the attack. As Reno's men began fighting Custer was seen on the bluffs on the opposite side of the river, riding north.

After initial confusion in the Indian village, Reno's men encountered heavy opposition. Their position was outflanked by the warriors, and Reno's command retreated to the woods near the river, and then across the river and up the bluffs on the river's east side. The retreat was confused and disorderly, at best. When fording the river, skirmishers were not deployed as a defensive measure, and the men crossing the river became easy targets for the Indians. Some men did not hear the retreat call, or were not able to move from their position, and were left in the woods in the valley. They straggled in over the next 48 hours to rejoin the command on the bluffs on the east side of the river where a defensive position was established.

Maj. Reno suffered 52 dead in his command during the Battle of the Little Bighorn. Six additional wounded died later bring the total to 58. Of the 52 killed and buried on the field, 47 are identified in various historic records as to location either killed or buried. The valley fight including the skirmish line and timber fights accounted for 25 of the identified dead (Hardorff 1990). The retreat across the river and up the bluffs adds another 7 to the list. The rest were killed in the defensive positions or in the case of 5 individuals their place of death or burial is not recorded in the oral history of the fight.

Disregarding the locations of known Reno dead a search of the casualty list was made. Those men between 30 and 40 years of age and between 5 ft 6 in and 5 ft 10 in in height were included in a list of possible candidates for the identity of the Reno Crossing remains. Seven possible candidates were identified (Table 14.5).

TABLE 14.5
Possible Identities of the Reno Crossing Remains

Company	Rank	Name	Age	Height
A	Pvt.	J. Armstrong	34	5'8.75"
G	Sgt.	E. Botzer	30	5'6.5"
A	Pvt.	W. Moodie	35	5'8"
G	Pvt.	H. Seafermann	36	5'7.5"
G	Saddler	C. Selby	31	5'5.5"
G	Farrier	B. Wells	32	5'6.5"
	Guide	C. Reynolds	34	unknown

Two individuals, Charlie Reynolds and Henry Seafermann, are known to have been photographed. The photograph purported to be Seafermann (Hart 1986:14) was only recently published. Since the configuration of the Reno Crossing skull is similar to Reynolds' head shape, a facial reconstruction was made in an attempt to identify the remains.

Greg Brown of the Nebraska State Museum made a microscopically exact cast of the skull. Betty Pat Gatliff of SKULLpture laboratory, created a facial reconstruction.

Gatliff took the cast of the Reno skull and fashioned a wire framework bust for it from hardware cloth. She also had to fashion a mandible, since none was recovered. She took a series of precise measurements on the skull and through a mathematical modeling procedure was able to shape a mandible that fit the skull (Krogman 1962). Tissue markers were placed at critical locations on the skull and mandible. Each piece was the thickness of the muscle and tissue at that point on the skull. These measurements have been averaged from hundreds of similar measurements obtained in earlier studies (Gatliff 1984, 1986; Krogman 1962).

Using these markers as guides a facial reproduction was sculpted. The position of the ears was matched by the position of the auditory meatus in the skull. The actual shape of the ear cannot be determined by the skull, but the ear and nose are roughly the same length, and Gatliff created an "average" ear, one that will not detract from other facial details.

The shape of the mouth is determined from the jaw and the location of the canine teeth, but not the thickness of the lips, so these were again made "average."

The position, width, thickness, and length of the nose is determined from the skull's nasal opening. A nose was created using these measurements.

At this point, she dealt with the hair and clothing. A typical male hair style for a 19th-century military man was sculpted, avoiding color and texture choices. For clothing, she used a shirt of the style worn by the cavalrymen. She also added a mustache for a touch of realism (Figure 14.2).

Figure 14.2. Facial approximation of the skull found at Reno Crossing.

A comparison of the facial reconstruction with the photographic likenesses of Charlie Reynolds and Henry Seafermann clearly ruled out a match. The reconstruction was then individually compared to all the known photographs of others killed in the Battle of the Little Bighorn. No possible matches were observed.

The five remaining individuals, drawn from the casualty list (Table 14.5) are the possible candidates. Historical evidence in the form of oral history accounts of where these men were killed or buried provides some additional information on possible identities. Hammer (1976:134) notes that Sgt. Edward Botzer was killed near the river on the retreat to the bluffs. Pvt. William Moodie was buried on the west bank of the river near the retreat crossing (Walter M. Camp interview with William G. Hardy, box 2, folder 10, page 78, Camp Notes, Brigham Young University Library). Camp also mentions in his notes of the Seventh Cavalry muster roll that Moodie was formerly an English Dragoon.

Of the other four possible candidates Pvt. William Armstrong's head was purported to have been identified in the Indian village, Pvt. Benjamin Wells' horse bolted with him into the Indian village and his body was not reported as found for burial (Carroll 1974:41; Everett 1930:5), although Hardorff (1990:146) indicates that Pvt. Theodore Goldin identified Wells' body south of the column's line of retreat from the timber. Pvt. James Boyle stated he found Wells in the river north or northwest of Lt. McIntosh's body. It is not known where Pvt. Seafermann nor Saddler Selby were killed. The historical evidence, while not ruling out any of the candidates, does point to Sgt. Botzer and Pvt. Moodie as highly probable candidates.

Hollywood producer Bill Armstrong's video production *Custer's Last Trooper* (Bill Armstrong Productions, copyright 1989) features the facial reconstruction. Members of the Batzer family, while viewing the Arts and Entertainment network presentation, were struck by a strong resemblance between the facial reconstruction and a family scion, Rudolph Batzer. Batzer immigrated from Germany prior to 1875 (S. B. Cobb, pers. comm.) as had Sgt. Edward Botzer. A photograph of Rudolph Batzer, provided by the family, does exhibit a striking similarity to the facial reconstruction. Dr. Charles Strom attempted to extract human DNA from a molar from the skull. Unfortunately only nonhuman bacterial DNA was recovered (C. Strom, pers. comm.) so no cross match could be made with the Batzer family. As yet the Batzer family cannot prove a definite link between Rudolph Batzer and Edward Botzer, but the available data are, at least, intriguing.

Conclusions

The human remains recovered on the west side of the Reno Retreat Crossing are those of a 30- to 40-year-old white male who was approximately 5 ft 8 in tall. Near the time of death he suffered blunt instrument trauma across the upper lip of the face that caused the bone to fracture below the nose evulsing three teeth. The blow would not have been sufficient to have caused death. Other than a recently removed wisdom tooth and an impacted wisdom tooth the individual appeared to be in good health. Tooth wear indicates a coarse diet that is consistent with that of a soldier of the 19th century. The mineralized nature of the bones indicates burial for a lengthy period of time. In all probability the remains represent one of Maj. Reno's soldiers who was killed during the retreat from the woods to the bluff on the afternoon of June 25, 1876. No definite identity can be assigned to the remains. However, age and stature compared to battle casualty records suggest that the remains may be one of six candidates. Two of those candidates, Sgt. Edward Botzer and Pvt. William Moodie, are considered to be the most likely individuals based on historic accounts that place their bodies at the retreat crossing. A strong resemblance between the facial reconstruction and members of the Batzer family is intriguing but not corroborative evidence of a possible identity.

Addendum

Since the initial publication of the Reno Crossing skeletal analysis and the airing of Mr. Armstrong's television special, additional developments have occurred that aided in probable identification of the remains. In the spring of 1995, a private collector of historic photographs came forward stating that he owned a 19th-century photograph of a soldier purported to be Sgt. Edward Botzer (Figure 14.3). An analysis of the photograph by then Little Bighorn Battlefield historian Douglas McChristian indicated that it could indeed be Sgt. Botzer. McChristian's analysis of the uniform and equipment depicted in the photograph suggested that the image was taken sometime between 1869 and 1871.

Figure 14.3. A period photograph of Sgt. Edward Botzer. Video superimposition of the skull with the photograph indicates a match. The skull can be reasonably assumed to be Sgt. Botzer.

The age of the individual depicted in the photograph can be estimated in the twenties, consistent with Botzer's age at that time (Barnard 1995). The skull was compared with the photograph by video superimposition. The skull and photograph matched (Barnard 1995). Without DNA analysis, a final determination of identity cannot be positively confirmed, but all internal evidence and the photographic superimposition match strongly indicate that the Reno Crossing remains are those of Sgt. Edward Botzer. The remains were reburied in the Custer National Cemetery located on the grounds of the Little Bighorn Battlefield National Monument, in the same grave as other human remains recovered during the various archaeological investigations.

REFERENCES

Barnard, S. 1995. Edward Botzer: Was He Custer's "Lost Trooper"? *Greasy Grass* 11:2–4.

Carroll, J. (ed.). 1974. *The Benteen-Goldin Letters on Custer and His Last Battle*. Bryan, TX: John M. Carroll.

Everett, J. 1930. Battles, Boots, and Saddles. *Sunshine Magazine* 11 (1):1–10.

Gatliff, B. P. 1984. Facial Sculpture on the Skull for Identification. *American Journal of Forensic Medicine and Pathology* 5(4):327–332.

Gatliff, B. P. 1986. Forensic Sculpture Adapts to Museum Use. *Scientific Illustration, Selected Papers from the 7th Annual Conference of the Guild of Natural Science Illustrators*, pp. 13–17. Washington, DC.

Gray, J. 1976. *Centennial Campaign: The Sioux War of 1876*. Fort Collins, CO: Old Army Press.

Hammer, K. 1976. *Men with Custer*. Fort Collins, Co: Old Army Press.

Hardorff, R. 1990 . *The Custer Battle Casualties*. El Segundo, CA: Upton and Sons.

Hart, G. 1986. Pvt. Henry Seafermann. *Military Images* 8(2):14.

Krogman, W. M. 1962. *The Human Skeleton in Forensic Medicine*. Springfield, IL: Charles C. Thomas.

Stewart, E. I. 1955. *Custer's Luck*. Norman: University of Oklahoma Press.

PART V

Landscape Studies

When engaged in scientific fieldwork, archaeologists usually focus intently on one particular site at a time. Even while conducting this kind of intensive research, however, archaeologists realize that the sites they study did not exist in a vacuum. They know that people in the past, just like people today, were surrounded by vast cultural and natural landscapes that were as many and as varied as the world's cultures themselves. Archaeologists, anthropologists, and geographers do not always agree on what constitutes a landscape, or where one landscape ends and another begins. For our purposes, it is sufficient to think of a landscape as encompassing all of the natural and cultural features that exist both inside and outside human settlements: houses, bridges, waterways, trees, grass, mountains, and other settlements.

Because the features of a landscape may be as vast as all outdoors, a complete catalog of archaeological landscape studies would fill several library shelves. To introduce you briefly to what landscape studies entail in historical archaeology, I have selected three articles.

The first article is Mark Leone's intriguing study of the geometric, formal garden planted behind William Paca's Georgian mansion in Annapolis, Maryland. Leone, an archaeologist at the University of Maryland, argues that Paca's garden was more than we may think at first: simply a passive collection of trees, shrubs, and flowers. Using the notion of ideology, Leone proposes that Paca's garden was actually intended as an active, symbolic statement of Paca's lofty position in Chesapeake society. Leone shows how Paca, signer of the Declaration of Independence and slaveowner—though an ardent defender of individual liberty—used the garden to manipulate nature in a way that made it appear natural. In doing so, says Leone, Paca employed the garden to help symbolize and stress social continuity at a time of great social change. The garden was important because it was the landscape within which elite men like Paca sat and thought about the way things should be in the new United States of America. In manipulating this small plot of ground, the framers of the new nation, men like Paca, could imagine that they could successfully manipulate the social order in ways they found comforting. Paca's garden, as explained by Leone, was much more than a collection of greenery; it was a statement about society as a whole.

Since it was first published in 1984, Leone's article has generated abundant discussion. Readers will remember that we first read about this article in Chapter 11, in the critique of Beaudry, Cook, and Mrozowski. When taken together, these two articles illustrate something central to scholarship in historical archaeology: that intelligent, highly competent men and women can disagree not only about how to analyze the past but also about what the evidence means. These differences of opinion and perspective, rather than being troubling, actually help historical archaeology to advance as a serious discipline. Controversies such as that generated by Leone's study allow individual archaeologists to discuss and to debate the complexities of the past with an eye toward creating better understanding.

The next chapter represents a different kind of landscape, this one peopled not with trees and shrubs, but with men and women in transition. I conducted this study with Annette Nekola at Millwood Plantation, a cotton-producing estate in the South Carolina upcountry. Because Millwood was organized in 1832 and continued to operate until the 1930s, it was a perfect place to study plantation settlement both before and after the American Civil War (1861–65). In making this study, we sought to understand how African-American men and women, once freed from the confines of slavery, decided where to settle on their old plantation estates. Though slavery was horrible by any standard, many emancipated slaves stayed on the estates on which they lived as slaves because these places were their homes. Human bondage and the subsequent rise of African-American tenant farming constitutes one of the most dramatic stories in American history. We learned in this study that before the war African-American slaves were housed in tightly spaced cabins in spots that were selected by the plantation owner because they were close to places of work. In the immediate postwar period, newly freed farmers moved into nucleated settlements where they took up a kind of communal farming under the direction of a leader. The final evolution of the postbellum plantation was completed a few years later, as African-American tenant farmers established their own homesites in places of their own choosing. Analyzing 17 environmental and distance variables, we learned that the tenant farmers made conscious and careful choices when situating their homes, choosing to group them together on the estate's highlands.

In the final chapter in this section, our spatial focus moves to an entire region. In this article, Scott Hamilton, an archaeologist at Lakehead University in Ontario, analyzes a central aspect of Canadian history: the 18th- and 19th-century fur trade. Hamilton notes that most scholars who have examined this commercial empire have concentrated on the fur-bearing animals themselves as the single most important feature on the landscape. This emphasis is not unreasonable since the animals were the reason fur traders were in the region in the first place, but Hamilton looks at something else: food. The fur traders were overwhelmingly interested in obtaining furs from their native trading partners, to be sure, but they also had an understandable concern for the food they would need to stay alive. Taking this innovative tack, Hamilton first explores the ecological implications of large-scale fur extraction from Canada, and then considers the relationship between the social system of the fur trade and shortages in foodstuffs. In his analysis, we can see the tensions that were created by the strain of being snowbound in a tiny trading post in northern Canada during the height of the fur-trading season. Food became an important tool for asserting authority and for reinforcing the social hierarchies of the European fur trade. In taking this unique approach to the fur trade—a subject historians have considered for many years—Hamilton forces us to see the implications of the trade, from natural and social perspectives, in a new and intriguing way.

These three articles show that historical archaeologists, like all archaeologists, conduct their analyses along a number of spatial scales. Here we see Leone focusing on one particular garden in Annapolis and using the site to extrapolate larger social and political issues. Orser and Nekola use the changes in settlement pattern across the landscape of a single cotton-producing estate to demonstrate changes in the physical arrangement of farmers through the American South. Hamilton examines an even larger landscape to address significant issues of environmental exploitation and animal extinction to illustrate the relationship between foodstuffs and the social arrangement of people engaged in fur trading.

Collectively, these studies make an important point: though archaeologists must excavate single sites, it does not mean that they cannot investigate places larger than single sites. Archaeologists must focus their activities at specific spots on a landscape because that is the nature of their fieldwork. Logistics, shrinking budgets, and time constraints mean that archaeologists cannot excavate several sites at once. Practical restrictions, however, do not represent real limitations. Archaeologists regularly excavate several sites over many years and then compile the information into large-scale studies. They also use information from other sites in a comparative way to gain an understanding of an entire landscape. Archaeology, though focused on individual sites, is more than just a collection of site studies. As a kind of historical anthropology, modern archaeology is a disciplinary that studies both small- and large-scale issues.

MARK P. LEONE ■

Chapter Fifteen

Interpreting Ideology in Historical Archaeology:

Using the Rules of Perspective in the William Paca Garden in Annapolis, Maryland

The 18th century in Tidewater Virginia and Maryland is today the subject of intensive, rigorous, and multidisciplinary research. There are few areas in the United States where there is more work done by creative people using materials from the past. Historians, architectural historians, folklorists, and historical archaeologists are all producing studies which offer the first new ideas on Chesapeake society since the turn of the century and which are giving the area an historical importance rivalling that long claimed for New England. The Chesapeake is being endowed with a deeper historical identity.

Understanding of the founding and growth of American civilization in the Chesapeake has been furthered by social historians, through the application of basic concepts of anthropology (Breen 1976; Tate and Ammerman 1979). Architectural historians and folklorists have used social history and structuralism from Chomsky's linguistic theory to analyze Chesapeake buildings (Glassie 1975). Historical archaeologists have drawn from the fields of cultural ecology and settlement-pattern theory, to study the region's colonial remains. There has been some use of critical theory, but by far the greatest combination of ideas used to comprehend Chesapeake society in the 17th and 18th centuries is the quantitative, genealogically precise social history which takes the anthropological concept of culture and describes the anonymous, the statistical, the customary, and the vernacular

This article was originally published in *Ideology, Power and Prehistory*, Daniel Miller and Christopher Tilley, eds., pp. 25–35, Cambridge: Cambridge University Press, ©1984.

in order to produce a more comprehensive view of a past society than has hitherto been available.

Virtually all of these studies (with full citations) have been used in the most recent and powerful synthesis of the Chesapeake, *The Transformation of Virginia 1740–1790* (1982a) by Rhys Isaac. He uses symbolic analysis of the kind most closely associated with Clifford Geertz to interpret a tightly controlled and widely inspected body of archival, archaeological, and decorative arts data. Isaac's analysis is important here because it allows us to pinpoint the theme of this essay. Using Isaac as a foil, I hope to show the contribution which may follow the application of critical theory to data from material culture, including historical archaeology. This may prove useful both because Isaac makes little use of archaeology (despite his familiarity with the basic materials) and because historical archaeologists, whose data often come from societies in which capitalism was evolving, rarely employ any of the variants of Marxist theory which could contribute to an interpretation of archaeological data.

The critical approach used here concentrates on the concept of ideology put forward by Shanks and Tilley (1982:129–154) and derived largely from their critique of Althusser (1971:127–186). I derive my understanding of the concept also from my reading of Lukács (1971:82-222). The concept of ideology used throughout this essay therefore contains two points. The first is that ideology, being neither worldview nor belief, is ideas about nature, cause, time, and person, or those things that are taken by a society as given. Second, these ideas serve to naturalize and thus mask inequalities in the social order; ideas, such as a notion of person, when accepted uncritically, serve to reproduce the social order. Ideology's function is to disguise the arbitrariness of the social order, including the uneven distribution of resources, and it reproduces rather than transforms society.

Ideology takes social relations and makes them appear to be resident in nature or history, which makes them apparently inevitable. So that the way space is divided and described, including the way architecture, alignments, and street plans are made to abide by astronomical rules, or the way gardens, paths, rows of trees, and vistas make a part of the earth's surface appear to be trained and under the management of individuals or classes with certain ability or learning, is ideology. Ideology is the ordering of time as well, and the mechanical measures of time, whether these be prehistoric henges, premodern sundials, or clocks. They are the material culture of the ideology of time. The ideology of time in capitalism cuts up daily activity into fragments which appear more rational and which thus become more controllable. Similarly, when time past is cut up and called precedent, it may be easier to control the present, for in the kind of society which looks to history as a guide for actions taken in the present, a continuum with the past may be made to appear inevitable when it is actually arbitrary. Thus, the class or interest group which controls the use of precedent does so to insure its own interests. It is in this sense that the classic Marxist writers have said that history tends to be written for class purposes.

Forms of ideological representation may be found in discussions of nature, or cause, or of matters considered obvious and inevitable. Ideology has been discovered in archaeological contexts through analyses of prehistoric astronomical markers and observatories (Thorpe 1981), and European Neolithic tombs (Shanks and Tilley 1982:129–154), and may very likely be found amid all those items archaeologists have for so long lumped under labels like ceremonial objects or style. Such objects and configurations of objects often appear to have little or no adaptive and utilitarian function but, when taken as manifestations of ideology, may be shown to function in such a way that they reproduce unequal distribution of resources, while masking this process in actions taken as given. This is as likely to be true in ranked precapitalist societies as in the later and more familiar capitalist societies.

Rhys Isaac presents a bountiful amount of material on 18th-century Virginia. My own interpretation of his work, mediated by the concept of ideology and using archaeological and archival data from 18th-century Annapolis, Maryland, is stimulated by Isaac's work and is intended to complement it.

Rhys Isaac argues that between 1740 and 1790 in Tidewater Virginia, the social hierarchy became more and more rigid with the planter-gentry isolating itself on the top of a pyramid which was becoming ever more shaky. With wealth and the sources of its prosperity becoming ever more constricted as a result of English control over the colonial economy and the continued long-term decline of tobacco prices, those with wealth constructed, with an undetermined degree of consciousness, a local order which acted to maintain control over what they possessed. The result was a tight hierarchy with little access to the premier places from below or from outside. Since the top of the hierarchy had little or no support from the English crown, there was no defense from Britain for the erosion of their economic position. And since the underpinning of the society from within was based on a large number of slaves and an ever larger number of impoverished whites, the base of the society was shaky indeed. Isaac comes to two conclusions as a result of this position. The one of general interest is that the planter-gentry made common cause with the poorer whites of the colony to claim independence from the English crown, which of course resulted in a new government, the United States, which was controlled by property-holders. Isaac argues that such a coalition of property-owners, from largest to least, acted to preserve the standing social order for the short run. All this was done in the name of liberty, in places like Virginia and Maryland. Isaac's second conclusion, and the one of interest here, is that as the hierarchy in Virginia became more and more threatened, it sought greater and greater control, which was expressed as the Georgian order. The Georgian order or style included behavior as well as material culture. Indeed, it was a cohesive way of thought. The operative principle within Georgian thought has been expressed by James Deetz (1977). It is organized around the bilateral symmetry or the segmentary dividing of life, its functions and things, into parts arrayed into a hierarchy of isolated elements. This segmentation was expressed throughout the material environment, as in houses, windows, doors, and place-settings. But when it was imposed on nature, as in gardens, vistas, systematic observations of the stars, winds, tides, and native peoples, the segmentation quickly became confused with nature itself. And the system of segmentation, ordering, and even grading toward hierarchy was mistaken as itself being natural and discovered within nature. This segmentation and its confusion with nature, as in gardens and astronomical observations, had the impact of making the social world, which was similarly arrayed, appear to be unquestionable.

Isaac argues that in the presence of colonial Virginia's incomplete institutions, the Georgian order was an attempt at creating a set, controlled, rational-appearing, and unemotional mentality which gave planters control over all society in an era of increasing disorder. Incompleteness included the absence of precedent as a form of reasoning when making decisions. frequent use of expediency to govern, and the emotional emptiness of Anglicanism, as well as the weakness coming from this combination.

Isaac interprets Virginian taste and style as including the use of architecture, interior design, furniture, decoration, silverware, dress, dance, as well as manners as Georgian space, Georgian distance (Isaac 1982b). Georgian refinement is the compartmentalization necessary to preserve the economic and political hierarchy which was being so steadily compromised by the rise and the close interaction of formerly distant classes, now newly threatening the established classes through religious revivalism and revolutionary sentiment (1982:303, 305, note 7).

Isaac is not saying that Georgian ideas are manifested in architecture, silverware, and manners; nor is he saying that Georgian style passively reflects the breakdown of a creaky economic and political order. He is saying, though, that the material culture—place-settings, table manners, etiquette, individualization and privatization achieved through doors, distance, chairs, hyphens, wings, place-settings, and gardens—all created the inhibitions, withdrawal, and isolation needed to prevent any attack on the established order (1982a:308). The concept of ideology adds to his discussion the question of the naturalization of the Georgian style, through its shrouding by contemporary discussions of natural philosophy, astronomy, Isaac Newton's theories, observations of the weather, plants and soil conditions. These all served to remove the arbitrary Georgian conventions from challenge by making them appear to be derived from nature or antiquity. With this construction it is possible to ask: who could fail to believe that those who systematically observed nature were not also those who should define and discuss a more natural or God-given political order? The same inevitability was created when the elite recited history, for who could fail to believe that those who knew the stars and plants and the ancient deities from Jupiter to Mars should not also be in charge of handling the historical precedents of their own society in the form of law. Those who knew how the natural order worked and those familiar with the long gone and esteemed ancient political orders should surely be the same to head the current order. Thus the scientific equipment, books, observations, the ancient history, the classical and Biblical allusions are not the product of the idle time of the rich, or of arcane interests, or of cultivated and rare intellect; rather these activities placed hierarchy and control in nature and history, making hierarchy and distance appear inevitable. When this logic, which is the ideology of class in Virginia and Maryland, was believed, society was reproduced intact. This logic was most likely to appear when the existing hierarchy could be most easily challenged. Thus, Georgian style in Virginia, and most likely in other places, not only expresses hierarchy but also disguises it. The disguise is composed of the ability to make aspects of nature and the human past look as though they are organized into commensurable orders and units with those of the observer. The disguise hides the arbitrariness of the social order and, when believed and acted on, perpetuates that order.

Isaac points out that the Georgian order grew more definite as the challenges to it grew in strength. As the American Revolution approached, the Georgian order came to its fullest expression. When the Revolution was over, and its effects on the mobility and growth of American society were fully felt in the early 19th century, and when those planters who had controlled the American Revolution died, the Georgian world—anything but mobile and expansive, or in ideological terms, libertarian and democratic—died also. The ideology of permanent hierarchy ended with the old planter gentry as did its Georgian style. The coincidence of their demise is indicative of the importance of Georgian style within the culture. Isaac correctly sees the Georgian order as a behavioral effort to control economics and politics. My addition has been to suggest that the effort to control worked by placing the order in nature and history in order to remove the effort from challenge. When the order died and the Georgian style ceased, its material culture and referents ceased too.

An extension of this example of the operation of ideology, when it creates equivalent divisions in natural realms, also involves the use of citations from the past. When the past is used as precedent for action taken now or to meet current conditions, it may be appropriated for current use. As the 18th century wore on, the past became a more pressing concern and a subject of ever more precise description in Virginia and Maryland. This was true of plants, plantations, native peoples, individuals, and political units. Isaac does not explore this development but it is an extension of his idea and may be explained using the notion of ideology. In making regular and divisible observations on nature, like wind or the movement of the planets, these, once compiled, became a guide to knowledge for the present and future of these same phenomena. The behavior of plants observed regularly and precisely, when published, formed a compendium predicting regular behavior. Precise and uniform observations created an even, unbroken flow from past to present thus making the two seem continuous. Earlier observations had been qualitative and irregular, often regarding nature in America as freakish or inferior

376   MARK P. LEONE

to what was then known. The new factor which appeared by the mid-18th century was the regular collection of data, made by systematic observations, with pre-determined comparability, uniformity of recording, often on charts and tables, having even flow over intervals. Whether these observations were on heat, rainfall, yield of fields, plants, seasons, sizes, or shadows and light, they composed an even set of lapses, which once observed, provided what appeared to be a rational basis in nature for current and future practice. Such behavior became ever more current in America as the 18th century wore on.

When applied to mid-18th-century human affairs, the compilation of even observations occurred through the building of precedent, and there are three or four important developments in analogous uses of the human past. Philip Vickers Fithian, a young Presbyterian minister from Princeton, New Jersey, kept a diary (1773–74) in Tidewater Virginia where he was tutor for a year to Robert Carter's children. He observed himself as well as his surroundings. He deliberately recorded his own spiritual development; he used his diary to watch himself change. His own self-observations were intended to form a precedent for and measure of his change. He created his own history out of regular, even, comparable units of observation on himself and his society.

"I shall collect together and write down what I have been doing in the last year. But will my life bear the review? Can I look upon my actions and not blush? And shall I be no less careful, or have no better success, in the prosecution of my duty the year to come . . . ?" (Farish 1943:61). We do not know how Fithian actually used his careful observations, but with his diary we can see the beginning of a natural history of self-observation.

A second example of interest in data from the past that developed in the 18th century involved classical history. Many writers and diarists cited classical Greek and Roman authors and frequently read both. Eighteenth-century diarists were familiar with the ancient texts and with the Renaissance uses of the ancient world and employed these as adornments to their own world. But even so, the classical texts were not so much understood as they were recited, and they were not compared to each other, nor were used to understand classical society. Antiquity was not as precisely observed, described, compared, or subjected to activities like those imposed on the natural world. Virginia and Maryland may have differed from Italy or England in this way, for the American elite did not handle antiquity nearly as rigorously as it handled observations on nature. Thus, the citations to the classical world, whether they were in diaries or in gardens expressed as urns, statues, or terraces, are likely to be best seen as an early and undeveloped appearance of universal history and its potential for use as precedent. In 1709, William Byrd notes: "I rose at 5 o'clock and read in Homer and a chapter in Hebrew" (Wright and Tingling 1963:16–17). And on another day in 1739, "I rose about 6, and read Hebrew and Greek" (Woodfin 1942:121). The entries referring to the classics are all episodic and virtually never mention why he read them, what he thought of them, or how he connected them with his own life. If such reading was to be used as precedent, we do not have ready access to the process nor do we have enough information to tell whether he understood the ancient writers' meaning. All we know is that he was familiar with the texts.

By the 1750s and 1760s in Maryland, there may be a greater understanding of the context of classical citations than there had been earlier in Virginia, and here we may see the development of precedent. *New Principles of Gardening* by Batty Langley was published in 1726 and was found in Annapolis, Maryland in several libraries. It was probably used in the construction of several of the formal gardens found there which feature classical citations (Charles Carroll letterbook). The following quote dates from the 1720s, but if used at all in Annapolis, would have had meaning in the 1760s and 1770s.

> Principle XXVII. There is nothing adds so much to the beauty and grandeur of gardens, as fine statues; and nothing more disagreeable, than when wrongly plac'd; as Neptune on a terrace-walk, mount, etc. or Pan, the god of sheep, in a large basin, canal, or fountain. But to prevent such absurdities, take the following directions.
>
> For open lawns and large centers:
> Mars, god of battle, with the goddess Fame; Jupiter, god of thunder, with Venus, the goddess of love and beauty; and the Graces Aglaio, Thalia, and Euphrosyne; Apollo, god of wisdom, with the nine Muses . . .
>
> For woods and groves:
> Ceres and Flora; Sylvanus, . . . and Ferona, goddess of the woods; Actaeon, a hunter, whom Diana turn'd into a hart, and was devoured by his own dogs; Eccho, a virgin rejected of her lover, pined away in the woods, for sorrow, where her voice still remains, answering the outcries of every complaint . . .
>
> For fruit-gardens and orchards:
> Pomona, goddess of fruit, and the three Hesperides, Eagle, Aretusa, and Hisperetusa, who were three sisters that had an orchard of golden apples kept by a dragon, which Hercules slew when he took them away . . .
>
> For small paddocks of sheep, etc. in a wilderness[garden]: Morpheus and Pan, gods of sheep; Pates, the shepherd's goddess; Bubona, the goddess of oxen; and Nillo, a famous glutton, who used himself to carry a calf every morning, until it became a large bull, at which time he slew it with his fist, and eat him all in one day . . . (Langley 1726:204–206).

Some of the original attributes of the gods and *dii minores* are understood, although there is no information to show how they might have been used as precedent for modern conditions.

A third area which shows how material from the past was beginning to be handled as precedent, and thus provide a guide for the present, is law. Isaac described early 18th-century Virginian law as an *ad hoc* mixture of provincial enactments and uncertain applications of English law (1982a:199) which led to confusion and continual but useless appeals to England. No such conditions prevailed later in the 18th century in either Virginia or Maryland. The use of precedent, including familiarity with English law, and the capacity to use these to win a case, all developed. Some Americans even received training at the Inns of Court. The units of the past, in this case law and its logic, were codified, compared, situated in different contexts, and given different meaning depending on use. This part of the past, whose origins and earlier cases had no direct tie to the world of the colonial experience, was handled in the same way as the natural world; it was given regularity and compared in even units so that it could be used to meet undefined but pressing circumstances.

The citation of precedent became important in Maryland because the use of English law became a means of containing the proprietary government (L. Carr, pers. comm.). English law and citation of precedent may have been one way in which Marylanders created a past for their own use. Marylanders defended living situations by placing them in history, using legal precedent as the vehicle, thus making the origins of current practice difficult to question. This practice may have been a different form of naturalizing the condition of those in control, including whatever inequalities composed their condition, but it is analogous to the even subdivisions seen in the creation of natural philosophies and a natural order.

I would now like to turn to Annapolis, Maryland, and to a famous, re-created 18th-century garden there, in order to explore further the rationalization of the past. The hypothesis offered is that the garden represents the use of the past as a set of precedents which appear so natural and convincing that they eliminate doubts about the extant social order, thus perpetuating it at a time of its own weakness. The garden, then, may be an expression of ideology in which the ordering of plants and historical objects in space may provide a key to the beginning of the use of past as precedent. Precedent in nature and precedent in law would serve to make its owner's place at the top of the hierarchy appear fixed and deserved.

The garden under consideration (Figure 15.1) was built, along with the house, in the 1760s by William Paca, one of the Signers of the Declaration of Independence. The house is a large, five-part Georgian mansion with a two-and-a-half-story central block separated by hyphens from one-and-a-half-story dependencies on either side. The house was altered in the 19th and 20th centuries, when it was turned into a hotel, but it was never destroyed completely. The house and its immediate grounds were excavated and fully reported by Stanley South (1967). The 2-acre garden, which is at the back of the house, was buried and partially destroyed when the house was turned into a hotel. It was excavated by Bruce Powell (1966), Glenn Little (1967), and Kenneth and Ronald Orr (1975).

On his marriage William Paca became a wealthy man and shortly afterwards he had his house and garden designed and laid out professionally. The garden as it stands now is a reconstruction and is the product of documentary research and

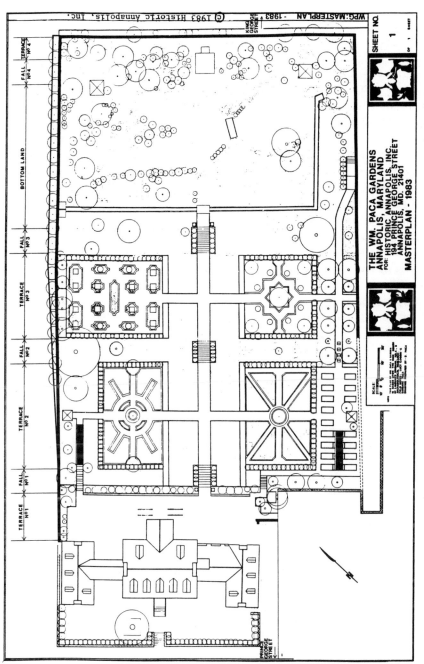

Figure 15.1. The William Paca garden, Annapolis, Maryland, as now reconstructed. The outlines of the garden, including basic subdivisions, are archaeologically derived. The parterres are conjectural, as are the positions of most of the plantings. The pond's shape is archaeologically valid. The garden slopes from left to right 16.5 ft. Drawing prepared by Barbara Paca, courtesy of Historic Annapolis, Inc.

archaeological excavation. A fraction of the garden, including two outbuildings, are portrayed in a coeval painting. In addition there are some references to it by people who noted some of its features when they visited it before it disappeared. In addition, there are similar gardens in Annapolis and surrounding states to facilitate comparison. Such gardens exist at the Ridout and Carroll houses in Annapolis, the Mount Clare Mansion in Baltimore, Mulberry Fields on the Potomac River, and Middleton Plantation in South Carolina. In other words there are enough known, dated, and surviving examples to provide extant proof of a genre of landscape. There are also garden books which were used in Annapolis and in the colonies generally to guide in the construction and maintenance of all aspects of making a great garden. Such gardens were largely ornamental, but probably also contained a kitchen garden. The gardens were symmetrical, were walled either with built or planted materials, often contained exotic and imported plants, and had built terraces —frequently five—descending in an even series to some natural or constructed focal point, thus controlling the view. The descending terraces and controlled lines of sight indicate that the garden was thought of as a volume, not as a flat space.

The Paca House is a Georgian mansion and its façade and floor plan are bilaterally symmetrical, although not perfectly so. If bisected, the two halves of the façade or floor plan look alike even though in the case of this floor plan they are not mirror images of each other. It is likely that the characteristics which Deetz suggested (1977) are associated with this style, namely ideas of the person as individual, the afterlife as a specific reward for personal behavior in this one, privacy, segregation of everyday life's different activities from each other, and segregation of the members of the family, also apply to this example of Georgian style and life.

The Paca House garden is also Georgian in style. It has a central axis dividing it into two parts using a straight, broad path which descends through four sets of steps as it goes away from the house. Even though in this case the axis is not down the exact middle of the garden, the visual effect is one of equal division. The steps lead a person physically and visually down over five brief slopes or terraces which fall away from the house. The terraces are similar to each other and create the same effect as when looking at a Georgian façade, Georgian window, or floor plan: bilaterally balanced symmetry. The reconstruction shows formal plats or parterres on each terrace, balanced sets of urns on pedestals, and in general, the complete predictability of one side given a look at the other. This is so despite the fact that the halves and compartments created by the axis are not of equal dimensions. There is certainly enough archaeological and comparative evidence to justify the balanced symmetry.

Authors like Miller (1733), Langley (1726), and Le Blond (1728) prescribed the kind of careful measurements and geometrical forms, plants, ponds, fountains, mazes, grass plots, groves, arbors, and the general dispositions of all items needed in gardens. They described the precedents which should be observed in order to maintain a successful and ongoing garden, including knowledge of local soil, wind, and flora. It is this knowledge which is common to Landon Carter, George Washington, and Thomas Jefferson. It is knowledge based on the past behavior of plants and winds, animals and clouds, which have been uniformly and continuously divided, labeled, and recorded. The theory and practice of gardening are based on closely controlled past performance and may demonstrate elements of Georgian segmentation imposed on nature, and on nature's past. Consequently, the garden may be a clue to how events from the past could be ordered; this marks the arrival of universal chronology or universal history.

The systematic use of past plant and weather behavior to plan and predict is made up of minute observation of many small items like past plant and weather performance and is the same process that is used in the creation of a systematic law. This process may be comparable to subdividing the human past when it is made into precedent. The building of legal precedent occurred in the later 18th century at a time when those who depended on the law in Maryland were most vulnerable from the crown, the proprietary government, and from the classes below. The tie to the garden may be as follows: just as precedent inserted into law allowed the established order to protect its own position by making that position appear historically valid, so that same social position seemed to be more fixed when it appeared to be served by optical, astronomical, and geometrical phenomena displayed in the garden's *allées* and vistas.

It is useful at this point to look at the rules for building pleasure gardens in order to see how perspective, which is the link to precedent, was developed. The rules may support the hypothesis that the garden is ideology, and includes at least the beginnings of the modern ideological constitution of the past. There are two areas in which it is possible to see garden building as naturalizing a specific attitude to the past. The first involves the initial rules for planning a garden's future. The planning is based on observations of wind and weather, shade and soil, and is often then set out as principles.

> Before the design of a garden be put in execution, it ought to be considered what it will be like in twenty or thirty years time, when the palisades are grown up, and the trees are spread: for it often happens, that a design, which looks handsome when it is first planted, and in good proportion, becomes so small and ridiculous in process of time, that there is a necessity either to alter it, or destroy it entirely, and so plant anew (Miller 1733, "Garden").

To follow this advice, Miller relays an experiment in natural history carried out by Dr. Stephen Hales who modeled his work on Isaac Newton's scientific methods. Miller goes on:

> the incomparable Sir Isaac Newton has not only shortened the geometrician's work, by his wonderful discoveries in abstract mathematics, but has also taught us, by his own practice, how to make and judge of experiments and observations with the utmost accuracy. . . .

"The author [Reverend Dr Hales] having covered, with milled land, a garden plot, in which a sunflower was growing, so as to leave only one passage for air to communicate, and another to pour in water to water the plant, made several curious experiments upon it.

"1. That the plants which weighed about 3 pounds, perspired about 30 ounces in a 12 hour day, in the month of July, 1724, but in a warm night it perspired only 3 ounces, and nothing in a cold night . . .

"2. That as the area of the surface of the leaves was equal to 5616 square inches; and the area of roots only to 2286 square inches, the water or moisture imbibed by the roots to supply the perspiration at the leaves, must move faster in the roots than through the leaves, in the proportion of 5 to 2. But in the stem, whose transverse section was one square inch, faster than in the leaves, in the proportion of 5616 to one" (Miller 1733, "Vegetable Staticks").

We know that Washington and Jefferson made and recorded regular observations on a wide variety of phenomena in their respective gardens (Klapthor and Morrison 1982:156–160). We do not know whether William Paca did the same, since most of his papers have been lost, but it would not be out of character since he built two large and varied landscape gardens in his lifetime. But whether he did or not is immaterial, for the age dictated careful observations like these, and Paca and his peers saw gardens as a way of thinking concretely about natural philosophy. They experimented with nature by grouping, segmenting, grafting, breeding, and trans-planting, and they linked these activities with similar observations on sunlight, fire, soil, weather, and water. They ordered nature and built a past for it.

The second area in which it is possible to see garden building as naturalizing a specific attitude to the past by using the idea of perspective is in garden geometry. Hedges tall and short, clipped trees, geometric patterns in the parterres which enclose flowers, and exotic plants imported from their native areas, rows of evenly planted trees, the regularly cut-back edge of the forest, all define the treatment of plants by shaping or moving them in conformity with geometrical definitions.

If we take the whole garden, it may be seen as an exercise in optics, or in the regular study of vision and light. The terraces in the Paca garden descend evenly downward to a pond and then beyond to a focal point which is a mount with a miniature temple topped with a winged Mercury. The terraces carry the axis downward toward the distant point. If one stands at the door of the main house or at the head of the path, or somewhere lower on the median, one realizes the garden is not flat but a volume attempting to operate like a Renaissance painting: to create a different distance from what actually exists between viewer and object. There are explicit directions for this. First:

In a fine garden, the first thing that should present itself to the sight should be an open level piece of grass. . . . There ought always to be a descent from the house to the garden. . . . On the opposite side of the gravel walks may be borders four feet wide for flowers, which will sufficiently answer the purpose of parterres; and if from the back of these borders there are evergreens planted in such a manner, as to rise from the borders gradually, so as to form an evergreen slope, it will bound the prospect very agreeably; and where there are any objects worthy of sight, or distant prospects to be obtained, there should be the vistas left. 'The principal walk must be in the front of the house, and should extend from the grass-plat next the house, to the end of the garden: if they be very wide, the sides should be turfed next the borders, and at the ends they may be terminated by a fosse [ditch] to continue the view' (Miller 1733, "Garden").

To build a terrace the gardener might employ principle "XXVII. The proportion that the base of a slope ought to have to its perpendicular, is a three to one, that is, if that perpendicular height be ten feet, its base must be thirty feet; and the like of all others" (Langley 1726:201).

The manipulation of space in order to create perspective is made precise in principle:

> XV. That all walks whose lengths are short, and lead away from any point of view, be made narrower at their further ends than at the hither part; for by the inclination of their sides, they appear to be of a much greater length than they really are; and the further end of every long walk, avenue, etc. appears to be much narrower than the end where you stand.
>
> And the reason is, that notwithstanding the sides of such walk are parallel to each other, yet as the breadth of the further end is seen under a lesser angle than the breadth of that part where you stand, it will therefore appear as if contracted, altho' the sides are actually parallel; for equal objects always appear under equal angles, Q.E.D. (Langley 1726:196).

The garden is therefore a three-dimensional setting, manipulated to create illusions of distance through the use of perspective. The basic pattern used to create perspective in the Paca garden is terracing; this is made to descend to a distant place, which is in turn made to appear more distant through the illusion created by the systematic lowering of the bottom plane. Rows of evergreens are planted along the line of sight, and although they are parallel, assist in making the distant views appear further away. At Mulberry Fields (constructed 1755, gardens predate 1814) the fence lines of the field below the terraces are opened out as one goes away from the house. This has the effect of bringing the Potomac River much closer than the mile away it actually is. The illusion created by the application of the rules of perspective corresponds to that involved in Renaissance painting, where mathematical rules were used to create distances between objects which were not in reality distant. These mislead the eye through their creation of an image of reality. Depending on how the rules were used, objects could appear further away or closer as the artist desired, or "in perspective." These are the rules, used with a degree of precision in 18th-century gardens, that made objects like a river, pond, or temple appear further away or closer than they actually were.

The gardener deals explicitly with geometry and with optics. Slightly less explicitly, he deals with the rules for creating illusions using space, so he is concerned with fooling the eye or with misrepresentation. Now, if ideology is also a misrepresentation of reality and serves to misrepresent the conditions of existence, what unequal human relationships are naturalized through the garden? Since the garden is manipulated space, is there some cultural practice represented in it which is, as a consequence, placed in nature so that it seems inevitable and beyond question? Just as the citation of precedent grew to protect the established social order, so also gardens took optical, astronomical, or meteorological phenomena and ordered them in such a way that they appeared to naturalize the social hierarchy. They displayed their principles in the *allées*, vistas, and parterres of their gardens.

The link between the optical illusions using garden space and the development of precedent in law is best explained by John Rowe, who correctly placed the origin of the idea, which he referred to as "perspective distance," in the Renaissance. Rowe defined perspective distance as an understanding about time as well as space, not just about painting (1965:1–20). Rowe placed the origin of seeing things in the perspective of both space and time inside the assumption that other peoples on the globe and other eras of history were separate, had their own integrity, and were worth knowing as such. This idea Rowe called perspective distance, and placed its origins in the Italian Renaissance. With its advent in the 13th century, classical antiquity was acknowledged to be dead, not continuous with the present, and other cultures to be quite different and not necessarily versions of those living. Knowledge of the distant eras in space and time was possible through direct observation of the foreigners or the remains of the dead societies. Both were acknowledged to be apart from the viewer; separate but internally consistent. Just as mathematical rules used in painting could make what was close appear more distant, so the assumption that other spaces and other times were not continuous with one's own but were separate and internally consistent, allowed them to be brought closer and to appear to be seen as wholes.

The Paca garden probably attempted to control sight by using the optical illusion of perspective. The garden handled distance in space and it may also have handled distance in time because there are references to antiquity at the ends of some vistas. And of course the garden was very likely built out of handbooks, themselves based on compilations of past behaviors of plants, etc.

Given that the Paca garden may illustrate growing control over the notion of perspective, applied to time as well as space, then one of the end points of such a development is the emergence of universal history and evenly segmented time. This did not appear fully developed in America until the 19th century, but the development of an ability to use perspective in gardens and precedent in law were probably its beginnings. They are part of the regular use of events set in uniform time. Describing universal time is not my goal here. Rather my concern is a fragment of it; the construction of events from the past in an orderly, segmented pattern as both chronology and precedent. This includes the practice of placing evenly segmented units backward to include all past events, which is what perspective looks like when applied to the past.

If this development can be seen in the Paca garden, then why would it be there? We know that William Paca was descended from planters, was tied to merchants, and was a successful, and later, a famous lawyer. He came to teach law in later life. William Paca's surviving records show his involvement in an urban, mercantile, profit-oriented economy, which used some wage labor, rent, and interest on lent capital. They also reveal a society preoccupied with law and its basis in precedent (Stiverson and Jacobsen 1976). Paca was a lawyer by training and continual practice; it was his profession and he handled many cases early in his career, attended the Continental Congress, was governor of Maryland three times and a federal judge. His skill in law and ability to influence others through its practice was a matter of note. "Paca's contributions to the *Maryland Gazette* [the chief newspaper in Annapolis] during the controversy [over state support for the established church] were brilliantly conceived and argued, and they established him in the judgment of one historian as the ablest constitutional lawyer of the province at the time . . . Paca [showed] brilliant insights and remarkable powers of logic." Further, "Paca preferred fighting injustice and oppression by constructing finely argued newspaper essays that traced constitutional precedents and appealed to man's natural rights . . . " (Stiverson and Jacobsen 1976:62).

The environment in which Paca practiced as lawyer, writer, representative, governor, and judge was, moreover, one of economic and political change. Annapolis was a merchant town, Maryland a maritime colony with an extensive trade with Europe and the Caribbean. It was an area which was in rebellion over taxation and tariff; it was an economy based on massive use of credit, struggling to calculate interest, with finding efficient ways of bookkeeping and accounting, and with periods of staggering devaluation and inflation. The whole problem of tying money and profit to time lapsed and space traveled was faced in the later 18th century and saw, among other economic changes, several experiments with printing new monies (Papenfuse 1975:62, 67, 95, 131–134, 207, 232, 234). Paca was not born to wealth; he married into substantial amounts of it. He grew up and lived in economic circumstances where everyone around him was faced with serious economic fluctuation and political change.

Then, to add conflict to instability, there was the problem of slavery. Paca owned over 100 slaves himself (Stiverson and Jacobsen 1976:92). Yet he argued so strongly for freedom that he "quarrel[ed] with the Constitution . . . [which] he felt . . . did not adequately safeguard individual rights, and many of the guarantees he sought—particularly freedom of religion, freedom of the press, and legal protection for those accused of crimes . . . " (Stiverson and Jacobsen

1976:91). This argument occurred before the Bill of Rights was written and added to the U.S. Constitution.

The major contradiction we see in Paca's life, and which arose at the time of the Revolution, was between a slave-holding society and one proclaiming independence in order to promote personal freedom and individual liberty. The contradiction has been highlighted and analyzed often. It is of some significance here because it reveals the internal pressures building within the society which helped to provoke the alliances behind the Revolution and the later social upheaval in the American Civil War. Paca lived in a time in which fundamental social contradiction—slavery and individual freedom, in principle for all—was dealt with temporarily and the tensions were well enough disguised that society remained stable for at least Paca's generation.

The contradiction hidden by the quest for a fixed natural order, whether in law or nature (i.e. formal gardens, astronomy, or natural philosophy) is that between slavery for others and freedom for themselves. Slavery involved

> fratricidal conflict, prisoners of war [in Africa], the horrors of oceanic travel, landlords, overseers, and taskmasters . . . undeserved suffering, imbrutement, lawless domination, patrollers and spies, sexual assault, kangaroo courts . . . branding irons and chained feet . . . insults . . . the auction block . . . The freedom sought and won by white Americans for themselves was intended to prevent slavery for themselves since they saw themselves becoming at the hands of Great Britain no better than 'hewers of wood, and drawers of water.' The plight of the colonials between 1704 and 1770 bore a striking resemblance to that of the Afro-Americans during the heyday of the Transatlantic traffic in human beings (Okoye 1980:20–21).

Given this, Isaac argues that the growing economic and political closeness of slaves and owners provoked the Revolution, which had the impact of temporarily preserving the sought-for distance between the classes. Thus the Revolution and all its natural philosophy and Georgian style, some of whose physical manifestations have been treated here, acted to gloss over the growing double contradiction: liberty was won to prevent conditions which seemed like enslavement to whites, but was not to be extended to blacks who were essential in preserving hierarchy, economic as well as racial. These are the conditions of the time of the garden and are behind the contradictions it was very likely built—although not necessarily consciously—to mask. That is why the garden, and the Georgian order in general, are ideology.

In the Paca garden we can see that space was manipulated to create a perspective, and the rules embodied in creating true perspective provide a clue to Paca's and his era's perception of time. The material references to classical antiquity compose an index to some notion of the past in the garden, while the use of garden books shows clear use of precedent. Given the link between the use of perspective in Paca's garden and his deep and successful immersion in law, the garden may naturalize perspective which is the principle that ties them together, and thus the garden may have substantiated the cultural segmentation of space and time. Perspective allows one to view space and time in measurable interchangeable segments; and this is how universal space and time link Mr. Paca's garden to his law, Annapolis's workers to their hours, capital to interest, ships at sea to weeks traveled and thus to profit and loss (Gurevich 1976:240–241).

The division into equal units of space, work, travel time, lending time, the turning of past into precedent, all preface a full development in the next decades, 1790–1870, of quantified treatments of virtually all of society. From nature, precision moved to the past, and then into the workplace and credit house, and then into all the divisions of industrializing society. Indeed such universalization helped to create the divisions into which society was stratified. The divisions and the statistics bringing them to life may be seen fruitfully as part of ideology.

> In the 1790s, inventories of descriptive facts about society were touted as providing an authentic, objective basis for ascertaining the common good. Complete possession of the facts, it was hoped, would eliminate factionalism and allow government to rule in the best interest of the public. Further, collections of social data were thought to constitute the proper scientific proof that the new experiment in republicanism did indeed benefit all citizens. By 1820 . . . avid collectors of statistics had come to recognize that distinctions and divisions in American society legitimately existed and had to be reckoned with. The particular distinctions they made—for example, between agriculture, commerce, and manufacturing—they regarded as inherent in the social order; empiricism, they insisted, was objective and value free. But of course their empiricism was freighted with unacknowledged values. The kinds of things they did not count and calculate in 1820—for instance, the number of slave-owners, black mortality, the incidence of crime, female illiteracy . . .

are an illustration of how segmentation, quantification, and precision can create society and hold it intact (Cohen 1981:55). All this is ideology and is seen in an early way in the 1760s garden and its associated activity—the division and subdivision of cultural space and time and making it appear as though the divisions were actually derived from nature or antiquity through the use of the idea of perspective.

As American society evolved in the later 18th century, or was transformed, as Isaac puts it, substantial stress appeared in the social order, and if the hypothesis in this paper is an appropriate vehicle for organizing the data, then we might expect ideological activity to intensify throughout the 18th century. Certainly that is what happened by extending precision into all aspects of the social order, as seen above. But we would also expect to find elements of this ideological activity in material culture. And we do.

The specific version of the hypothesis in this paper acknowledges the contradiction of Paca's substantial inherited wealth, based in part on slavery, and his passionate defense of liberty. It can be argued that if liberty were realized, his position was likely to be compromised. To mask this contradiction, to make it appear to disappear, to prevent its becoming a conflict, his position of power was placed in law and nature. This was done both in practicing law and in gardening, through the citation of precedents, which is a segmentary view of space and time made available through the use of the laws or rules of perspective. One would predict then that the more the contradictions of the social order became manifest, the more intense the ideological activity would be. This is plainly seen in the back third of the Paca garden.

The far one-third of the Paca garden is a so-called wilderness garden, the only one known to have existed in prerevolutionary America. As opposed to rectangular symmetry, the far third consists of a pond with curved edges looking like a fish, crossed at an odd angle by a Chinese style bridge, and contains meandering paths, scattered clumps of bushes, trees, and small half-hidden buildings. The wilderness garden, sometimes called a Romantic garden in Victorian times, is thought to represent a freer and more spontaneous approach to nature, but the Paca garden appears by the 1760s and probably represents neither freedom nor spontaneity. My hypothesis would be that the introduction of the arcane geometry of a wilderness garden should serve as an index to greater mystification of the roots of the social order.

Lévi-Strauss, following B. Karlgren, a Sinologist, has pointed out that elaborated curvilinear designs and arabesques "represent the formal survival of a decadent or terminated social order. [They] constitute, on the esthetic level, its dying echo" (Lévi-Strauss 1963:265). Curvilinear designs may occur in a wide range of art forms, from painting, architecture, to rugs and gardens. Such design is not usually associated with the Georgian style, but when it is, it should not appear as mysterious as Lévi-Strauss has left it. Curves are composed of segments made up of arcs, circles, eggs, hyperbolas and other regular, segmented, strict geometrical forms. They are no less regular than lines and angles. They order nature in a different way but they order it nonetheless. The key is that they create the illusion of openness, flow, motion, and continuity, not predictable end.

> The usual method of contriving wildernesses is to divide the whole compass of ground, either into squares, angles, circles, or other figures, making the walks correspond to them; planting . . . trees [so as to seem] promiscuously without order . . .; for as these parts of a garden should, in a great measure, be designed from nature, so whatever has the stiff appearance of art, does by no means correspond therewith. . . . Walks [should] have the appearance of meanders and labyrinths, where the eye cannot discover more than twenty or thirty yards in length; and the more the walks are turned, the greater pleasure they will afford (Miller 1733, "Wilderness").

This is from one of the gardening books used in Annapolis.

Such design uses the geometrical organization of plants which naturalizes the changes in the social order to maintain a continuity. The order of Tidewater society faced a fundamental dilemma in the 1760s and 1770s of upholding traditional authority and supporting popular sovereignty. The wilderness garden may be an intensified effort to implant in nature and arithmetic the twists and turns of the ideology which was so constructed that the order of traditional society was maintained in the presence of substantial pressures to open the hierarchy and promote mobility. Even though it was probably built with the rest of the garden, it serves like the mazes in other American formal gardens: it creates the illusion of flow and movement but is in fact the rigid control over spontaneous movement.

The formal garden was not an adornment, the product of spare time; it was not for food and still less for idle fashion. It was a place for thinking and for making the observations which were essential to economic and social life. It was not passive; it was very active, for by walking in it, building it, looking at it, admiring and discussing it, and using it in any way, its contemporaries could take themselves and their position as granted and convince others that the way things are is the way they always had been and should remain. For the order was natural and had always been so.

Acknowledgments

An earlier version of this paper was presented in a symposium "Is Structuralism Possible in Historical Archaeology?" organized by Anne E. Yentsch at the 1982 annual meeting of the Society for Historical Archaeology.

I am grateful for the long, patient, and generous help in describing landscape restoration, and the William Paca Garden in particular, given me by Mrs. J. M. P. Wright, chairman of the Board of Historic Annapolis, Inc. and chairman of the William Paca Garden Committee. Barbara Paca provided many of the references to and much of the information on 18th-century gardening. Dr. Lois Green Carr provided helpful information and Jean Russo gave the paper a careful, sympathetic reading. Lisa Morton patiently and carefully guided me through the files on the garden at the William Paca Garden Visitors' Center in Annapolis, Maryland. Jacquelyn Winter did all the typing. Historic Annapolis, Inc. generously provided complete access to its files and resources for this essay and without its help and permission the research would not have been possible. Any errors of fact or interpretation are my responsibility alone.

Rhys Isaac's essay (1982b), "Terrain, Landscape, Architecture, and Furnishings: Social Space and Control in Old Virginia" was read at a symposium "History and Anthropology in the Colonial Chesapeake" organized by this author, and much of the inspiration for this essay comes from his. Ann M. Palkovich explained much of the material on perspective, depth of field, and their geometry. Elaine G. Breslaw introduced me to the Tuesday Club papers and the world view of 18th-century Annapolis. Garry Wheeler Stone clarified Mulberry Fields.

REFERENCES

Althusser, L. 1971. Ideology and Ideological State Apparatuses. In *Lenin and Philosophy and Other Essays*, L. Althusser (ed.), pp. 127–186. New York: Monthly Review Press.

Breen, T. H. (ed.). 1976. *Shaping Southern Society*. New York: Oxford University Press.

Charles Carroll Letterbook. 1760. September. Hall of Records, Annapolis, Maryland.

Cohen, P. C. 1981. Statistics and the State: Changing Social Thought and the Emergence of a Quantitative Mentality in America, 1790–1820. *William and Mary Quarterly* 38:35–55.

Deetz, J. F. 1977. *In Small Things Forgotten*. Garden City, NY: Doubleday.

Farish, H. D. (ed.). 1943. *Journal and Letters of Philip Vickers Fithian, 1773–1774, Plantation Tutor of the Old Dominion*. Williamsburg: Colonial Williamsburg Inc.

Glassie, H. 1975. *Folk Housing in Middle Virginia*. Knoxville: University of Tennessee Press.

Greene, J. P. (ed.). 1965. *The Diary of Colonel Landon Carter of Sabine Hall, 1752–1778, Vol. 1*. Charlottesville: The University of Virginia Press.

Gurevich. A. J. 1976. Time As a Problem of Cultural History. In *Cultures and Time*, P. Ricocur (ed.), pp. 229–245. Paris: The Unesco Press.

Isaac, R. 1982a. *The Transformation of Virginia, 1740–1790*. Chapel Hill: University of North Carolina Press.

Isaac, R. 1982b. Terrain, Landscape, Architecture, and Furnishings: Social Space and Control in Old Virginia. Paper read at the annual meeting of the Northeastern Anthropological Association. Princeton, NJ.

Klapthor, M. B. and H. A. Morrison. 1982. *G. Washington: A Figure Upon the Stage*. Washington, DC: Smithsonian Institution Press.

Langley, B. 1726. *New Principles of Gardening*. London: Bettsworth and Batley.

Le Blond, A. 1728. *The Theory and Practice of Gardening*. London: Bernard Lintot.

Lévi-Strauss, C. 1963. Split Representation in the Art of Asia and America. In *Structural Anthropology*, pp. 245–268. New York: Basic Books.

Little, J. G. 1967–68. Re: Archaeological Research on Paca Garden. November 8,1967, May 24, 1968. Letters on file, William Paca Garden Visitors' Center, Annapolis, MD.

Lukács, G. 1971. Reification and the Consciousness of the Proletariat. In *History and Class Consciousness*. Cambridge: M.I.T. Press.

Miller, P. 1733. *The Gardener's Dictionary*. London: Printed for the author.

Okoye, F. N. 1980. Chattel Slavery as the Nightmare of the American Revolutionaries. *William and Mary Quarterly* 37:3–28.

Orr, K. G. and R. G. Orr. 1975. The Archaeological Situation at the William Paca Garden, Annapolis, Maryland: The Spring House and the Presumed Pavilion House Site, April. Typescript on file, William Paca Garden Visitors' Center, Annapolis, MD.

Papenfuse, E. C. 1975. *In Pursuit of Profit: The Annapolis Merchants in the Era of the American Revolution, 1763–1805*. Baltimore: Johns Hopkins University Press.

Powell, B. B. 1966. Archaeological Investigation of the Paca House Garden, Annapolis, Maryland, November 16, 1966. Typescript on file, William Paca Garden Visitors' Center, Annapolis, Maryland.

Rowe, J. H. 1965. The Renaissance Foundations of Anthropology. *American Anthropologist* 67:1–20.

Shanks, M. and C. Tilley. 1982. Ideology, Symbolic Power and Ritual Communication: A Reinterpretation of Neolithic Mortuary Practices. In *Symbolic and Structural Archaeology*, I. Hodder (ed.). Cambridge: Cambridge University Press.

South, S. 1967. The Paca House, Annapolis, Maryland. Unpublished manuscript. Historic Annapolis, Inc., Annapolis, MD.

Stiverson, G. A. and P. R. Jacobsen. 1976. *William Paca: A Biography*. Baltimore: Maryland Historical Society.

Tate, T. W. and D. L. Ammerman. 1979. *The Chesapeake in the Seventeenth Century*. New York: Norton.

Thorpe, I. J. 1981. Anthropological Orientations on Astronomy in Complex Societies. Paper read at the Third Theoretical Archaeology Conference, Reading, England.

Woodfin, M. H. (ed.). 1942. *Another Secret Diary of William Byrd of Westover, 1739–1741*. Richmond, VA: The Dietz Press.

Wright, L. B. and M. Tingling (eds.). 1963. *The Great American Gentleman William Byrd of Westover in Virginia: His Secret Diary for the Years 1709–1712*. New York: Putnam's Sons.

Yentsch, A. E. 1982. Letter on Spring House Excavations, William Paca Garden. 15 March, on file, William Paca Garden Visitors' Center, Annapolis, MD.

CHARLES E. ORSER, JR. ■
ANNETTE M. NEKOLA

Chapter Sixteen

Plantation Settlement from Slavery to Tenancy:
An Example from a Piedmont Plantation in South Carolina

Introduction

Archaeologists have understood the value of studying the spatial arrangement of settlement locales since the 19th century, but it has only been within the last three decades that archaeologists have begun to view the study of past settlement systems as a respectable and fruitful area of research (Chang 1972:1; Clarke 1977:3). Since the 1950s archaeologists in North America and Europe have sought to understand settlement systems better and have adopted a number of geographical and statistical techniques for use with their archaeological data sets (Hodder 1977; Hodder and Orton 1976; Zimmerman 1978). While many different types of spatial analyses have been conducted by archaeologists, perhaps the greatest potential is in the area of settlement dynamics (Crumley 1979). It is in this area of study that plantation archaeology can make the greatest contribution to our knowledge of past settlement practices.

Although the development of a slave-based system of plantation agriculture in the American South has received considerable attention, less notice has been paid to the plantation as a physical entity. The plantation, because of its special economic purpose and social configuration, had a particular spatial organization that was designed to maximize its economic profitability. Even the social relationships that developed at plantations had clear spatial correlates (Blassingame 1979:223; Thompson 1975:32; Wolf 1959:136–137). With the Civil War and emancipation, the settlement system of the plantation underwent a radical change as the social

This article was originally published in *The Archaeology of Slavery and Plantation Life*, Theresa A. Singleton, ed., pp. 67–94, Orlando: Academic Press, ©1985.

relationships and economic composition of the plantation was altered. The purpose of this chapter is to present a model of plantation spatial organization in the North American Southeast and to evaluate how the spatial organization of one 19th-century South Carolina piedmont plantation conforms to the model.

Modeling Plantation Settlement Systems

While it is true that there has not been a concentrated effort to study the spatial organization of southern plantations, there have been at least two notable exceptions. These studies, by David Crenshaw Barrow and Merle Prunty, Jr., provide the basis for the following model of plantation settlement organization and change.

In 1881 David C. Barrow published an article in *Scribner's Monthly* in which he attempted to explain to skeptical Southerners—who could remember the Civil War and who believed that southern agriculture would come to total ruin once slavery was abolished—that the "labor-relations of the two races are adjusting themselves and working out a solution of the dreaded 'negro problem' in a practical way" (Barrow 1881:830). Even though a subtle strain of racism runs through the article, Barrow makes a number of interesting observations on the social life of the postwar plantation and his comments on plantation spatial organization are particularly interesting.

Speaking of antebellum plantation settlement, Barrow (1881:831–832) noted that the houses of the planter and overseer were located near the linearly arranged slave dwellings, or "quarters," in order to provide the maximum in slave control and surveillance. With formal emancipation this spatial pattern changed as the houses of the former slaves, now small farmers, became dispersed throughout the plantation lands as the freedmen attempted to acquire "more elbow-room." According to Barrow, "the transformation has been so gradual that almost imperceptibly a radical change has been effected" (1881:831).

The settlement pattern shift observed by Barrow was later expanded upon by geographer Merle Prunty, Jr., who used the works of Barrow and others in conjunction with his own empirical data to define what he termed the "Ante Bellum Plantation Occupance Form" and the "Post Bellum 'Fragmented' Occupance Form" (Prunty 1955). (Prunty also identified a third form, the "Neoplantation Occupance Form" which was developing at the time of his study. This third settlement form is not considered here because it is characterized by the agricultural mechanization of the 1950s.) The postbellum form evolved, not through the destruction of the antebellum form, but rather through its modification. For Prunty (1955:460) the plantation continued to exist after 1865 as a discrete physical unit with a distinctive spatial form.

Prunty (1955:465) observed, as had Barrow earlier, that the antebellum plantation settlement pattern was distinctive in that the owner's house was usually "situated near a cluster of service buildings and slave quarters" which were "grouped compactly in rows along short roads." The agricultural fields were arranged on the lands surrounding the buildings in ways that would permit the slaves quick access to the fields with a minimal loss of work time.

Prunty reinforced Barrow's observation that after 1865 the clustered settlement pattern was abandoned in favor of a more dispersed system. Within this fragmented form, Prunty distinguished between the "cropper type" and the "tenant-renter type" based on the arrangement each small farmer had made with the plantation owner and landlord. In the cropper type, the owner supplied everything used in production except the labor and one-half of the seed and fertilizer, while in the tenant-renter type, the tenant supplied everything necessary for cultivation including two-thirds of the seed and fertilizer costs (Prunty 1955:474–475). According to Prunty (ibid.: 467), the cropper type was the most common form of postbellum settlement with approximately 60 percent of all southern plantations organized in this manner in 1936. There is no compelling evidence to suggest that the type of tenancy practiced had any racial basis (Higgs 1974).

For the purposes of this discussion, the differences between Prunty's fragmented settlement subtypes are of minor importance because the dispersed settlement pattern after 1865 is characteristic of both systems. The only significant spatial differences between the settlement subtypes do not concern the actual dwellings themselves, but rather the outbuildings associated with the dwellings. Barns and sheds tended to be more centralized in the cropper subtype because they belonged to the plantation owner who was responsible for their maintenance. On the other hand, each tenant-renter was required to maintain his own barns and sheds, which in turn were located on his land. In a tenant-renter system, then, there were many more outbuildings associated with each dwelling rather than more dwellings. The differences exhibited between the cropper and tenant-renter subtypes are important only if a between-structure, or micro, settlement analysis (after Clarke 1977:11–14) is conducted; such differences are not important when studying the general shift in settlement patterns from the antebellum to postbellum periods on the macro, or between-site, level. In this discussion, the settlement change from slavery to tenancy noted by Prunty can be considered, in Chang's (1968:3) terms, "significant and meaningful" because the configuration and structure of the plantation community was altered to such a degree that a new spatial organization resulted.

The observations of both Barrow and Prunty are consistent in that two distinct forms of plantation spatial organization, according to the time of occupancy, were recognized. On antebellum plantations, the racial basis of slavery was reflected in living arrangements, in that whites lived separately from blacks. In reality, however, division of labor actually determined settlement location; it was just that all slaves were black. The spatial separation between blacks and whites was largely a function of the size of the plantation. Spatial divisions in housing were clear on large plantations, but on smaller plantations it was not uncommon for the owner to labor alongside his slaves (Stampp 1956:35). In some cases, slaves on larger plantations resided in the owner's house in order to render special services such as tending the fire or emptying the chamber pot at night (Genovese 1974:327–441). Field slaves generally resided in the "quarters" located perhaps as much as several hundred yards from the owner's home, or as one contemporary writer observed, "neither too near nor too far from the [owner's] house" (Durr n.d.). Owners did not want to be too close to the slave quarters for fear of contracting the terrible diseases which were rampant in the quarters (Savitt 1978:57).

Spatial Organization Based on the Division of Labor

The idea that antebellum plantation settlement was organized around divisions of labor rather than strict divisions of race must be reinforced. The groups formed by this organization produced what Wolf (1959:136) has termed the "class structure" of a plantation. Important qualifications exist to demonstrate that plantation groups were not necessarily spatially organized strictly on the basis of race. First of all, there were those slaves mentioned previously who performed special tasks within the planter's home, and who often resided in or very near this structure. Secondly, there were also white overseers who lived in spatial proximity to the slave quarters. While many overseers were sons or relatives of planters, the largest number of overseers came from the semiprofessional class of itinerant overseers who expected to oversee until they had enough money to buy their own land (Bonner 1944:677; Genovese 1974:12–13). These simple qualifications suggest that the spatial organization of the plantation was one based on the division of labor rather than one based strictly and solely on race. However, because all slaves were black, racial characteristics did seem to determine plantation settlement to some observers.

Even though exceptions and qualifications to this simple view of antebellum plantation settlement do exist, the antebellum plantation was usually characterized by a fairly nucleated settlement pattern that contained a cluster of dwellings and service buildings surrounded by agricultural fields. This nucleation is the distinctive element of antebellum plantation settlement.

Barrow's (1881:831) observation that the change in plantation spatial organization was a subtle one must be reiterated. Confronted with emancipation, blacks and whites faced a host of problems, none more severe than those involving agriculture. Labor shortages were common as black women and children withdrew from the labor pool and as black families migrated out of the rural South (Ransom and Sutch 1977:44–47). Immediately after the Civil War and often until the end of Reconstruction, planters employed wage laborers as field hands. Except for the receipt of wages in return for labor, this system did not result in the significant spatial reorganization of most plantations (Wright 1978:161). Under the wage labor system, blacks continued to labor in groups under the supervision of either white or black foremen (Shlomowitz 1979a, 1979b). The wage system did not cause the complete breakup of the nucleated plantation settlement system because the planter continued to own and house the agricultural tools and animals necessary for cultivation. The development of the "squad system" of agriculture after 1865, however, did cause some modification in the plantation settlement system as former slaves and wage laborers were divided into semiautonomous groups of peer workers. According to Shlomowitz (1979b:571, 1982), each squad was composed of an extended family core and usually contained from 2 to 10 workers. Each group would conceivably occupy its own settlement cluster close to its fields. The nucleated settlement form disappeared gradually as freedmen acquired freedom from constant supervision and the control of agricultural lands and animals (Prunty 1955:470). During the 1880s and 1890s, the owner's home was no longer "the center of a busy life revolving around a great social and economic establishment" (Coulter 1929:159).

In summary, a general shift in settlement form from nucleation during antebellum times to full dispersion during postbellum times occurred at some plantations (Figure 16.1). Such a shift has been observed both by contemporary writers (Barrow 1881) and by modern scholars (Prunty 1955). What is not known is how widespread this settlement shift was or whether it can be used as a general model that has recognizable archaeological correlates. The applicability of this simple model of settlement dynamics, however, can be evaluated with empirical archaeological and historical data from Millwood Plantation in Abbeville County, South Carolina, and Elbert County, Georgia.

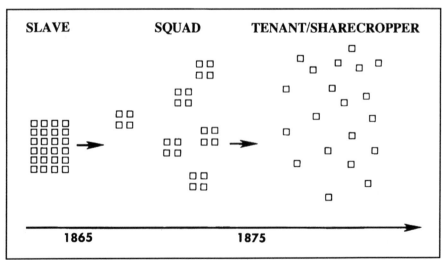

Figure 16.1. Idealized model of plantation settlement dynamics from clustered slave quarters to dispersed tenant farmer and sharecropper homes with a "squad" arrangement intermediary.

Data Set

Millwood Plantation, located on both sides of the Savannah River in northwestern South Carolina and northeastern Georgia, was owned and inhabited by James Edward Calhoun from 1832 until his death in 1889. Calhoun was the brother-in-law and cousin of the famous southern statesman, John C. Calhoun. James Edward was a well-educated gentleman who had served as the "young astronomer" with the Stephen H. Long Expedition of 1823 through Minnesota (Blegen 1963:111; Kane and Holmquist 1978). Even though Millwood was located in a rugged portion of the piedmont region, by 1860 Calhoun had transformed the plantation into a large enterprise that included 194 slaves and over 15,000 acres (U.S. Census 1850, 1860a, 1860b). Calhoun was an eccentric man who left a lasting impression on the Abbeville area long after his death, and his Millwood Plantation is still remembered by local residents (Dundas 1949; Perrin 1933).

The site of Millwood Plantation (38AB9) was excavated in 1980 and 1981 under the direction of Charles E. Orser, Jr. (Orser et al. 1981, 1982). The site was located within the floodpool of the future Richard B. Russell Reservoir and contained 33 building foundation ruins within the main site area and many others at smaller sites throughout the estate lands. Two of these small sites (38AB12 and 9EB253) and 28 of the foundations at the main site (38AB9) were archaeologically tested. A number of the yard areas, which were devoid of archaeological remains, were also tested. The extensive research was funded by the U.S. Army Corps of Engineers, Savannah District, and was monitored and administered by the Southeast Office of the Archaeological Services Division of the National Park Service. This research effort provided the data for this chapter.

Documenting Settlement Pattern Dynamics at Millwood Plantation

The Antebellum Period (1832–1865)

The site of Millwood Plantation was occupied until the 1930s, and much of the evidence for the antebellum plantation has been removed or drastically altered by natural forces such as severe erosion (see, for example, Bennett 1943:164–167 and Trimble 1974), and by cultural processes such as yard sweeping (see Bonner 1977:3). As a result, much of our archaeological perception of Millwood's antebellum spatial form stems from historical information and inferences based on the present condition of the site.

Even though the majority of the material culture collected from the Millwood foundations was clearly of postbellum age (Orser et al. 1982:674–736), the spatial characteristics of the foundations conformed to the antebellum settlement model proposed by Prunty (1955). While the entire Calhoun estate included over 15,000 acres, the main plantation area was located within only 32 acres (Figure 16.2). Spatial clusters are apparent within the complex of structural remains that comprise the Millwood archaeological site. The first of these clusters contains nine foundations (Figure 16.3). This cluster includes Calhoun's home (Structure 1), a brick smokehouse (Structure 9), three possible storage sheds (Structures 3, 4, and 5), the home of Calhoun's long-time black servant, Caroline Calhoun Walker (Structure 2), two other probable dwellings (Structures 6 and 7), the home of an overseer/manager (Structure 8), and a well.

At a distance of about 350 ft east of Structure 1 is a small complex of structures in physical proximity to the millrace. Three structures are located within this cluster. One of them is identified as a dwelling and the possible home of the plantation's millwright (Structure 27), one as an unidentified dwelling (Structure 25), and the third was probably the main millhouse (Structure 26).

The third distinct spatial cluster of Structures contains four structural ruins, three of which were probably residential (Structures 21, 23, and 24); the fourth was a dependent, nonresidential outbuilding (Structure 22). One possible structure was designated Structure G. There are eight more structures immediately north of the first cluster. This area includes five small structures which are identified as dwellings because they contain fireplace hearths (Structures 10, 11, 13, 17, and E). Two dependent outbuildings (Structures 12 and 15), and a sorghum-processing structure (Structure 16) occur within this complex (Orser 1985). Two possible structures of unknown function were designated structures C and D. Another cluster of foundations on the far northeastern side of the main plantation area contains one dwelling (Structure 19), one possible support structure (Structure 20), and two possible structures (Structures 18 and F) (Figure 16.3). The main residential portion of the site occurs within the first and fourth clusters.

The available historical documentation states that by 1834 Calhoun occupied an overseer's house at Millwood while awaiting the time when he could build something better (Calhoun 1834). This evidence is unclear and confusing with regard to the number, location, and nature of the homes Calhoun eventually occupied at Millwood, but it is certain that with his marriage to Maria Simpkins in 1839 he started the construction of a better house. However, local legend claims that Calhoun abandoned this new house upon the death of Mrs. Calhoun in childbirth in 1844, moved back to the overseer's cabin, and allowed the new house to fall into disuse and ruin (Dundas 1949; Perrin 1933).

While the actual design of Calhoun's antebellum home is not known, the large, grand homes often associated with southern plantations were infrequent in the rural South (Bonner 1945), and he probably lived in a simple home. Those classic homes that did occur on plantations evolved slowly from simple "dog-trot" log cabins that contained only two rooms and a central open breezeway (Eaton 1961:121–122). These breezeways were later developed into the great central hallways in many

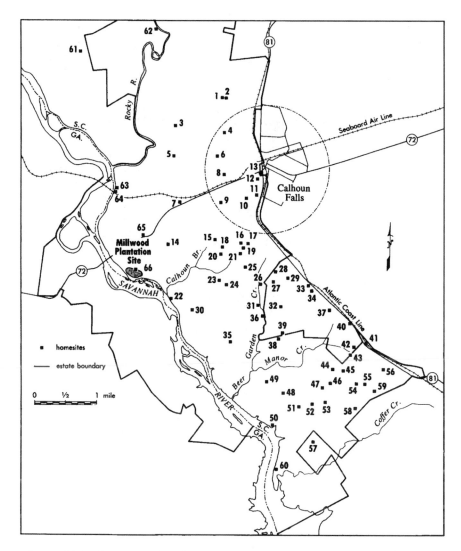

Figure 16.2. The James Edward Calhoun estate, showing the location of Millwood Plantation (38AB9), the estate boundaries, and the location of houses according to the 1932 soil survey.

plantation "big houses" (Bonner 1945:388). Nonetheless, planters' homes, while often not grand, did frequently contain porches and special use areas, and were constructed from durable materials (Otto 1975:123). Even though the exact appearance of Calhoun's antebellum home is a mystery, one description of his house as it looked in 1879 may provide some clues about its antebellum form: [it was] a long and very comfortable one story building. At the west end were two rooms, one used as a living room and an office, and one as a bedroom. Extending east was a long hall, with shelves on each side and filled with a very valuable collection of books. . . . At the east end of the hall was the dining room (Dundas 1949:7).

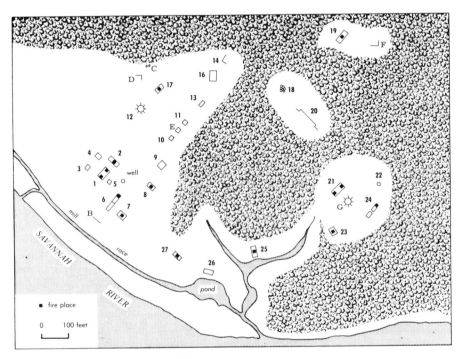

Figure 16.3. Simplified plan of Millwood Plantation showing the location of the various foundation ruins.

Both the archaeological remains located at Structure 1 and the historical documentation for Calhoun's Millwood residence strongly support the contention that Structure 1 was indeed Calhoun's home (Orser et al. 1982:140–172). Having established this spatial reference point, it was next necessary to establish the location of the slave quarters. As noted earlier, slave houses were commonly located in tight clusters near the planter's home. In Calhoun's case, however, this arrangement may have presented problems. As a common practice, planters wanted their slaves housed within easy walking distance of the agricultural fields to which they were assigned the northernmost fields. Some would have even had to cross the Savannah River to reach those fields in Georgia. As a result, some of Calhoun's slaves probably lived away from his home area outside the nucleated settlement. In addition, Calhoun also operated a number of mills along the Savannah, and he probably had slave mill-wrights housed in these locales. For economic reasons, then, Calhoun probably had slave quarters located throughout his sprawling estate. It is equally likely that he also retained a resident overseer at each locale as was common practice (Stampp 1956:292). Even though it is possible and even quite likely that in 1860 Calhoun housed his 194 slaves at various locations around the plantation, it is also possible that some field slaves lived near Calhoun in order to work those fields around the plantation nucleus. The small structures that appeared in a row north of Structure 1 (Structures 10, E, 11, and 13) may represent the remains of slave quarters that were inhabited by some of Calhoun's field slaves. These are small structures of simple construction with simple fireplace hearths. It is also quite possible, as the local oral tradition suggests, that Calhoun's slaves lived at the base of a hill north of Structure 1. At least two informants questioned stated that slaves had lived in this area; another knowledgeable and reliable informant stated that slaves lived on the other side of a slough that ran north of Calhoun's house in the approximate area of the hill (Orser et al. 1982:559, 563, 570–571). The location of this slough has been identified by Clemson University botanist, Dr. John E. Fairey III, during his survey north of Structure 1 (Orser et al. 1982:585–610).

If it can be assumed that Structure 1 was the planter's home and that the slaves were housed north of this structure, either around the base of a hill or in Structures 10, 11, 13, and E, Structure 8, which is intermediate between the two, may have been an overseer's house. Structure 8 contained at least two rooms and a central brick chimney and included a small porch on its northwest side and probably a small shed or addition on its northeast side. Based on this design, the inhabitants of Structure 8 enjoyed at least some specialized space and probably a separation between living and sleeping areas.

An analysis of the living space available in the structures attributed to the planter, overseer, and slaves supports the conclusion that such groups inhabited these structures. Since the historical data states that Calhoun lived alone throughout most of his life, it is assumed that he had all of the 773 ft^2 in Structure 1 available to him (Table 16.1). In the absence of knowing the exact composition of the Millwood overseer's household, an arbitrary figure of four persons has been adopted. Using this number, almost 135 ft^2 of living space per person is obtained for Structure 8. The size and simple construction of the structures north of Structure 1 suggest that they were probably intended for slave use, with Structure 11 being representative of them. With interior dimensions of 13 by 17 ft, the size of Structure 11 is consistent with the size of slave cabins reported at other archaeologically investigated plantations. For example, the slave cabins at the Stafford Plantation on Cumberland Island, Georgia, were found to measure 18 by 18 ft (Ascher and Fairbanks 1971:8) and 16 by 21 ft (Ehrenhard and Bullard 1981:33), while those at the Kingsley Plantation in northeastern Florida ranged in size from 5 by 7 ft to 18.6 by 24.5 ft (Fairbanks 1974:67, 76). Using the figure of 5.2 slaves per dwelling, as suggested by Fogel and Engerman (1974:115–116), the available space per person for Structure 11 was 43 ft^2. These figures correlate well with the findings at Cannon's Point Plantation where between 45.3 and 53.3 ft^2 per slave was the living space norm (Otto 1975:134).

TABLE 16.1

Available Living Space per Dwelling

Structure/Resident	Family Size	Square Ft	Square Ft per Person
1 (planter/owner)	1.0	773.0	773.0
8 (overseer)	4.0	539.0	134.7
11 (slave)	5.2[a]	224.0	43.1
11 (slave)	5.7[b]	224.0	39.3

[a] Mean size of slave family as suggested by Fogel and Engerman (1974:115–116).
[b] Mean size of slave family at Millwood Plantation as suggested by the 1860 slave schedule (U.S. Census 1860b).

An 1860 listing of the 194 Millwood slaves suggests that they were housed according to family groupings in 29 dwellings (U.S. Census 1860b). Adult males and females appear first in these lists followed by a series of minors. A figure of 5.7 persons per dwelling was obtained by averaging the number of people contained in each of these "families." This figure is within the range of from 3.7 to 8.8 slaves per dwelling noted at other plantations (Blassingame 1979:254–255). A figure of 39.3 ft^2 results when 5.7 persons per dwelling is used to compute the available living space in Structure 11.

Similarly, an analysis of the structural elements present at Structures 1, 8, and 11 also supports their association with the antebellum planter, overseer, and slave if it is assumed that planters and overseers were accorded more elaborate living spaces than slaves. Structure 1, the largest and most massively constructed building, contained the most architecturally related items (nails, flat glass, tile, brick, slate, and mortar) and the most furnishings (hinges, screws, latches, hooks, stove parts, furniture fittings, fireplace hardware, and decorative fasteners). Structure 8 contained less such materials, and Structure 11 even less (Table 16.2). While these simple frequencies are undoubtedly affected by sample size and excavation strategy, the differences between the structures and their contents appear striking. In summary, all of the available evidence—archaeological, historical, oral, and comparative—supports the conclusion that during the antebellum period Millwood Plantation conformed to the antebellum nucleated settlement pattern identified by Prunty (1955). The planter's home was located near the center of the plantation, at least some of the slave force was housed north of the planter's home within the plantation nucleus, and at least one overseer was probably housed between the two.

TABLE 16.2
Presence of Structural Items at Structures

Structure/Resident	Architectural		Furnishings		Total	
	No.	%	No.	%	No.	%
1 (planter/owner)	8387	86.6	104	81.9	8491	86.5
8 (overseer)	1147	11.8	18	14.2	1165	11.9
11 (slave)	153	1.6	5	3.9	158	1.6
TOTAL	9687	100.0	127	100.0	9814	100.0

The Immediate Postwar Period (1865–1875)

After emancipation, Calhoun, like all southern planters, was forced to confront new social and economic conditions (Gallman and Anderson 1977:41–42; Roark 1977). While some planters in the Abbeville District adopted a modified wage system to conduct their agricultural businesses (see, for example, Freedman's Bureau 1867a), Calhoun organized around another system. On January 1, 1867, Calhoun entered into an agreement with seven freedmen (three of whom had the last name Calhoun, suggesting that they were former slaves) who were to "cultivate carefully and industriously" on seven different large field plots. Each of the seven was required to pay Calhoun a rent of one-half of their total production (Freedmen's Bureau 1867b). So, rather than organizing a unified plantation on the basis of either cash or share wages, Calhoun subdivided his estate into seven parts and organized around a share tenancy system.

This system, however, was not the simple family sharecropping system that later became prevalent throughout the South. In the Millwood case, each of the seven freedmen was required to hire a crew of laborers to cultivate their fields. In effect, these freedmen were subcontractors who were responsible not only for the labor but also for the behavior of their employees. The distribution of this system within Abbeville District is uncertain, but this system was popular elsewhere in South Carolina. This system, called the "squad system," has been identified as an important stage in the transition from slave to tenant agriculture (Shlomowitz 1979a, 1979b).

The spatial ramifications of the squad system, as represented in Figure 16.1, are that the slave quarters were disassembled in favor of a number of small "hamlets" of agricultural squad laborers. In Calhoun's case, these squads may have been composed of the various slave populations that were undoubtedly dispersed throughout the 15,000-acre plantation during the antebellum period. If such an organization did occur, then it is possible that the squad labor arrangement would not have clear spatial correlates at Millwood Plantation because of the possible location of different slave quarters throughout the estate (Orser 1983, 1986).

The Postbellum Period (1875–1930s)

Both the available historical evidence and the oral data gathered from local informants indicate that by the 1880s Millwood Plantation had evolved into a full tenant system that included both share and cash renting (Orser 1981). In 1880 Millwood Plantation housed 33 tenants, one-third of whom rented their land on shares while the remainder paid fixed rents (U.S. Census 1880). By 1890 the estate had 94 tenants, and as late as 1928 Millwood supported 98 tenants (Abbeville County Court of Probate 1890; Orser et al. 1982:771). Just how many of these tenants rented for set crop amounts, shares of their produce (called "working on halves" by the informants), or variations of the two, is unclear. Of the eight informants who discussed tenant farming arrangements, five reported both "standing" crop rentals and sharecropping, four reported sharecropping exclusively, and one renting exclusively. It is possible, therefore, that many variations in rent arrangements existed at Millwood as they did at other southern plantations (Orser and Holland 1984). Nonetheless, the ramifications of the development of a tenancy system, regardless of form, are obvious in terms of settlement. The dispersed settlement system, or the "fragmented occupance form" of Prunty (1955), was adopted as the tenants began to farm their own plots of rented land at a ratio of about 1 to every 30 or 40 acres (The History Group 1981:187).

While the informants questioned stated that there were many tenants spread throughout the Calhoun estate in the early 20th century, the only evidence for the actual house locations derives from a 1932 map of Abbeville County soils. In addition to showing the distribution of soil types within the county, this map also shows many house sites. This map was used to provide the data for the postbellum settlement pattern of Millwood Plantation under the assumptions that this map shows the locations of all standing structures on the estate in 1932, that all structures shown are located accurately, and that all of the structures represent tenant or sharecropper home sites (Figure 16.2).

An examination of Figure 16.2 shows the degree to which the plantation settlement pattern was altered after the antebellum period. The site of the main complex of Millwood Plantation occurs at house location 66 near the left center of the map. The other 65 houses are distributed throughout the estate in what can clearly be considered a "fragmented" form of occupation.

Analyzing the Data

In order to understand the distribution of these house sites in more detail, 17 variables were selected for further study. These variables were: soil association (SOILASSC), agricultural, pasturage, and woodland potential of the land (AGPOTEN, PASPOTEN, and WDPOTEN), current vegetation (CURRVEG), elevation above mean sea level (ELEV), direction or aspect of land slope (SLOPEASP), distance to Savannah River (DISSAVR), distance and direction to nearest stream (DISNRST and DIRNRST), rank order and type of nearest stream (STORDER and STRTYPE), proximity to confluence of nearest stream (STPROX), and distance to the nearest road, railroad, neighbor, and Calhoun Falls—the closest town (DISROAD, DISRROAD, DISNEIG, and DISCFALS). Distance measurements, slope aspect, current vegetation, elevation, and stream order data were gathered from modern (1964) topographic maps, while the environmental data were taken from the 1980 Abbeville County soil survey (Herron 1980). The environmental variables were selected for study because of the suspected importance of environmental factors to small farmers, and the distance variables were included in order to account for cultural choice in settlement location. We hoped that the combined study of both types of variables would yield the most information about the choice of house locales for tenants and sharecroppers.

Once values for each variable were collected for each of the 66 sites in the sample, descriptive statistics were generated using the SPSS (Statistical Package for the Social Sciences) subprogram entitled FREQUENCIES (Nie et al. 1975:181–202). The frequencies for the environmental variables appear in Table 16.3, and the frequencies for the distance variables appear in Table 16.4xx. Using these data as a guide, a profile of the "typical" Millwood Plantation tenant/sharecropper farm was compiled.

The typical farm was located above 475 ft mean sea level on Cataula sandy loam B horizon soil. The land of this idealized farm presently has medium agricultural and woodland potential, a high pasture potential, and is forested. This farm was located near a slope that faced either southwest, west, or southeast, 1.5 miles from the Savannah River with the nearest stream being a fourth-order, intermittent stream located less than .3 mile in a southeastern direction. The proximity of the stream confluence was less than .5 mile away. This farm was also from .5 to 1.5 miles from the nearest road and railroad, less than .3 mile from its nearest neighbor, and over 1.5 miles from Calhoun Falls. Information gathered from local informants supports the picture of Millwood's tenant homes as "dilapidated, unpainted, weatherbeaten frame cabin[s] leaning out of plumb on rock or brick pilings" (Tindall 1967:411). (For similar comments on tenant housing, see Agee and Evans 1941:127–253; Hagood 1977:93–99; Vance 1936.)

In order to determine whether there are significant interrelationships between the variables, pairs of variables were statistically compared. The nominal-level (environmental) variables compared by employing the SPSS subprogram CROSSTABS, while the ratio-level (distance) variables were compared using the SPSS subprogram SCATTERGRAM (Nie et al. 1975:218–248, 293–300). Once the contingency tables were generated by the CROSSTABS subprogram, the nominal-level variables were compared using the symmetric uncertainty

TABLE 16.3

Frequencies and Percentages of Environmental Variables

Variable Label	No.	%	Variable Label	No.	%
SOILASSC			ELEV		
Cataula SL B	15	22.7	Above 475 ft	14	21.2
Cataula SL C	6	9.1	Below 475 ft	52	78.8
Cataula SCL	4	6.1			
Cecil SL B	10	15.2	SLOPEASP		
Cecil SL C	3	4.5	North	6	9.1
Cecil SL D	2	3.0	Northeast	7	10.6
Cecil SCL	2	3.0	East	4	6.1
Chewacla L	1	1.5	Southeast	10	15.2
Davidson L B	6	9.1	South	8	12.1
Davidson L C	1	1.5	Southwest	11	16.7
Enon SL	1	1.5	West	11	16.7
Madison SL	1	1.5	Northwest	9	13.6
Mecklenburg SL	1	1.5			
Pacolet SL	7	10.6	DIRNRST		
Pacolet CL	1	1.5	North	10	12.5
Toccoa SL	2	3.0	Northeast	5	7.6
Wilkes SL	3	4.5	East	10	15.2
			Southeast	12	18.2
AGPOTEN			South	8	12.1
Low	19	28.8	Southwest	7	10.6
Medium	30	45.5	West	8	12.1
High	17	25.8	Northwest	6	9.1
PASPOTEN			STORDER		
Low	11	16.7	First	6	9.1
Medium	9	13.6	Second	1	1.5
High	45	69.7	Third	4	6.1
			Fourth	55	83.3
WDPOTEN					
Low	4	6.1	STRTYPE		
Medium	59	89.4	Intermittent	56	84.8
High	3	4.5	Permanent	10	15.2
CURRVEG					
Open	22	33.3			
Forested	44	66.7			

coefficient (*U*). The derived coefficients appear in Table 16.5. The uncertainty coefficient is a measure of association between two nominal-level variables that computes the amount of certainty for predicting the dependent variable once the independent variable is known (Nie et al. 1975:226–227). The symmetric version of this statistic measures the proportional reduction of uncertainty that is gained by knowing the joint distribution of cases rather than by knowing the combined uncertainty of the row and column totals as in the asymmetric version. A value of 1.000 denotes the complete reduction of uncertainty, while a value of 0.000 indicates that there has been no improvement in predictive power.

TABLE 16.4

Frequencies and Percentages of Distance Variables

| | Distance (in miles) | | | | | |
| | <0.30 | | 0.30–0.50 | | >0.50 | |
Variable	No.	%	No.	%	No.	%
DISNRST	65	98.5	1	1.5	0	0.0
DISNNEIG	37	56.1	13	19.7	16	24.2

| | <0.50 | | 0.50–1.50 | | >1.50 | |
	No.	%	No.	%	No.	%
DISSAVR	9	13.6	33	50.0	24	36.3
STPROX	45	68.2	20	30.0	1	1.5
DISROAD	22	33.3	34	51.5	10	15.2
DISRROAD	26	39.4	31	47.0	9	13.6
DISCFALS	2	3.0	7	10.6	57	86.4

An examination of Table 16.5 reveals that the vast majority of environmental variables are not strongly associated or, in terms of the uncertainty coefficient, that our ability to predict one value from knowledge of the other is not great. The largest coefficients occur where they would be expected. For example, the coefficient of 0.607 between soil association and agricultural potential is one that is reasonable because there is a known relationship between a soil type and its agricultural potential. Similarly, the strong association between stream order and stream type ($U = 0.761$) is to be expected because such variables are known to be interrelated; first- and second-order streams are permanent, while third- and fourth-order streams are intermittent. The low values throughout the remainder of the matrix suggest that little covariation exists between the variables.

The distance variables were compared using the Pearson product-moment correlation coefficient (r). This statistic is a widely used measure that is employed to assess the relationship between two variables. Values of 1.000, -1.000, and 0.000 denote a perfect positive linear relationship, a perfect negative linear relationship, and no relationship between the variables respectively (Roscoe 1975:97–99). The Pearson coefficients generated for the distance variables appear in Table 16.6.

It will be observed that stronger correlations occur between the distance variables than among the environmental variables. Some of these correlations are predictable. For example, the relatively high correlation between elevation and distance to the

TABLE 16.5
Symmetric Uncertainty Coefficients for Environmental Variables

	PHYZONE	SOILASSC	AGPOTEN	PASPOTEN	WDPOTEN	CURRVEG	SLOPEASP	DIRNRST	STORDER	STRTYPE
PHYZONE	1.000									
SOILASSC	0.236	1.000								
AGPOTEN	0.066	0.607	1.000							
PASPOTEN	0.078	0.503	0.434	1.000						
WDPOTEN	0.274	0.287	0.145	0.242	1.000					
CURRVEG	0.040	0.126	0.025	0.057	0.007	1.000				
SLOPEASP	0.081	0.359	0.094	0.093	0.110	0.048	1.000			
DIRNRST	0.116	0.310	0.043	0.043	0.087	0.011	0.267	1.000		
STORDER	0.273	0.271	0.135	0.100	0.267	0.091	0.126	0.125	1.000	
STRTYPE	0.188	0.164	0.054	0.016	0.239	0.014	0.043	0.045	0.761	1.000

TABLE 16.6
Pearson Product-Moment Correlation Coefficients for Distance Variables

	ELEV	DISSAVR	DISNRST	STRPROX	DISROAD	DISRROAD	DISNNEIG	DISCFALS
ELEV	1.000							
DISSAVR	0.641	1.000						
DISNRST	0.448	0.089	1.000					
STRPROX	0.588	0.492	0.591	1.000				
DISROAD	−0.490	−0.581	−0.098	−0.267	1.000			
DISRROAD	−0.436	−0.564	−0.061	−0.194	0.794	1.000		
DISNNEIG	−0.436	−0.299	0.001	−0.196	0.553	0.578	1.000	
DISCFALS	−0.199	−0.374	−0.103	−0.479	0.483	0.562	0.254	1.000

Savannah River ($r = 0.641$) is understandable because the elevation of the land increases naturally as the distance from the Savannah increases. Nonetheless, meaningful correlations do occur within this data set.

The highest correlation occurs between the distance to nearest road and distance to nearest railroad variables ($r = 0.794$). This high correlation is perhaps partially due to the fact that the two railroads in the area, the Atlantic Coast Line and the Seaboard Air Line, parallel South Carolina highways 81 and 72, respectively. However, this explanation does not account for all of the association between the variables because the original measurements for this study were made to the nearest road regardless of size. The network of minor two-track roads throughout the Calhoun estate, on which many of the sites were situated, serves to lessen the effect of the physical correlation between the railroads and the current major highways near the estate.

These analyses suggest that little real correlation exists within the environmental variables and the distance variables for the 66 suspected tenant sites located within the boundaries of the Calhoun estate. Even though the sites appear roughly clustered when inspected visually, it would seem that no standard criteria of settlement were selected by the tenant or sharecropper who first settled there. The apparent site randomness, of course, is only related to the variables selected for study here. It remains possible that the locations were not at all random in terms of social, familial, economic, and political factors which were not measured by the variables chosen for analysis.

In order to make the determination of site clustering in an unbiased manner, the nearest-neighbor statistic was used. Many strengths and weaknesses are inherent in this statistical method. Perhaps the most serious limitation is the problem faced when determining the universe boundaries and the dangers of excluding sites that were within the network under study but outside the created boundaries. Others have demonstrated that the presence of artificial boundaries has a marked effect on the results of nearest-neighbor analysis (Hodder and Orton 1976:41–42), and the boundaries used in this study are those of the original Calhoun estate.

Those sites that were closer to the Calhoun estate boundary than to a neighbor were dropped from the sample in order to reduce and hopefully eliminate the edge effect in the data set. This process resulted in the exclusion of 13 sites. Another three sites were dropped from the sample because they were located within Calhoun Falls, and their nearest neighbors could not be accurately calculated. The total sample for the nearest-neighbor sample consisted of 50 sites.

The computation of the nearest-neighbor statistic demonstrated that the sites were indeed clustered ($R = 0.76$, where $R = 1.000$ represents a random distribution). These clusters may be the remnants of the squad spatial arrangement that occurred in the 1865–1875 period. In this case, the "randomness" of the tenant locations probably relates to this earlier squad system. This clustering may also be a function of location near poor roads that have since disappeared. A fairly even distribution of tenant houses along poor roads was common in the rural South during the 1920s (Hart 1980:518–519; Hart and Chestang 1978:454).

The lack of association between the different environmental variables may merely represent the problem of using environmental data from 1964 and 1980 in conjunction with locational data from 1932. This over 48-year difference may be too great given the destructive nature of severe soil erosion in the Piedmont region. Nonetheless, it would seem that meaningful correlations in the distance variables should have occurred if the house locations were chosen along similar distance criteria.

Conclusions

Based on the preceding analysis, Millwood Plantation can be considered to have developed along the lines consistent with the model presented by Prunty (1955). The nucleated antebellum settlement that once existed at the center of the plantation largely disintegrated as the plantation labor burden shifted from slaves to tenant farmers and sharecroppers. The study of the spatial organization of Millwood Plantation, however, suggests the following qualifications to Prunty's model:

1. While the general models of settlement nucleation during the antebellum period and settlement fragmentation during the postbellum period appear valid, Prunty failed to recognize the apparent continued use of the settlement nucleus following emancipation. For example, at Millwood Plantation the late 19th-century mean dates derived from the artifact samples (Orser et al. 1982:736) imply a continued use of most of the structures within the nucleus until at least 1900. After 1865 a resident manager probably occupied Structure 8 and wage hands probably lived in Structures 10, 11, 13, and E. These houses probably served as overseer and slave residences, respectively, before 1865. Structure 1 was inhabited by Calhoun until his death and may have been inhabited by someone else thereafter. The spatial proximity of wage laborers' and employers' homes has been documented in the postbellum rural South (Woofter et al. 1936), and the presence of resident managers at Millwood has been affirmed by local informants, including the wife of one such manager (Orser et al. 1982:559–584). It would appear, then, that the plantation nucleus retained its form, if not its function, through time.

2. The plantation nucleus itself has meaningful internal spatial divisions which appear on the microlevel (or between structures). These divisions are functional ones that relate to the maintenance of plantation production. Internal spatial organization is characterized by task-specific structures, but moreover by the orientation of dwellings to specific site areas. Certain elements of this organization should be common to all plantations, varying only with plantation size, prosperity, and economic diversification.

3. The spatial separation of living quarters of different ethnic groups on the plantation is primarily a function of the division of labor rather than race. The physical separation of resident plantation groups is racial only insofar as one's role in plantation production is

racially ascribed. In addition, the dwellings inhabited by each resident group will be recognizable by their structural elements and associated artifacts (Otto 1975, 1977, 1984).

4. The possible presence of the squad labor arrangement as an intermediate step between slave and tenant settlement must be considered. Such labor arrangements have a particular settlement organization that may affect the settlement pattern of the full tenancy system.

The archaeological and historical record for Millwood Plantation is sufficient in revealing the general settlement pattern change that occurred throughout the 19th- and early 20th-century plantation South. Millwood Plantation continued to exist as an entity after 1865 and generally developed along the lines suggested by Barrow (1881) and Prunty (1955). The settlement nucleus, however, was not abandoned but was only functionally reorganized. Nonetheless, it must be kept in mind that the spatial evolution of Millwood Plantation may be particular only to this one Piedmont plantation. While this possibility does not seem too likely, the settlement dynamics observed at Millwood deserve further study at other plantation sites.

Acknowledgments

We would like to acknowledge the great assistance given us by our valued colleague and fine southern historian, James L. Roark, who conducted the original historical research for our bigger research effort at Millwood Plantation. We are also grateful to Edwin A. Hession of the National Park Service, Atlanta, who showed great professional and personal interest in the Millwood project, and to Janice L. Orser who read, commented upon, and typed this essay. We also wish to acknowledge Dr. Milton Newton and the cartography laboratory of the Department of Geography and Anthropology Louisiana State University, who prepared the maps.

REFERENCES

Abbeville County Court of Probate. 1890. Return on Estate of James Edward Calhoun, Deceased. Abbeville County Courthouse, Abbeville, South Carolina.

Agee, J. and W. Evans. 1941. *Let Us Now Praise Famous Men: Three Tenant Families.* Boston: Houghton, Mifflin.

Ascher, R. and C. H. Fairbanks. 1971. Excavation of a Slave Cabin: Georgia, U.S.A. *Historical Archaeology* 5:3–17.

Barrow, D. C. 1881. A Georgia plantation. *Scribner's Monthly* 21:830–836.

Bennett, H. H. 1943. Adjustment of Agriculture to Its Environment. *Annals of the Association of American Geographers* 33:163–198.

Blassingame, J. W. 1979. *The Slave Community: Plantation Life in the Antebellum South.* Revised ed. New York: Oxford University Press.

Blegen, T. C. 1963. *Minnesota: A History of the State.* Minneapolis: University of Minnesota Press.

Bonner, J. C. 1944. Profile of a Late Ante-bellum Community. *The American Historical Review* 49:663–680.

Bonner, J. C. 1945. Plantation Architecture of the Lower South on the Eve of the Civil War. *Journal of Southern History* 11:370–388.

Bonner, J. C. 1977. House and Landscape Design in the Antebellum South. *Landscape* 21 (Spring–Summer):2–8.

Calhoun, J. E. 1834. Diary entry, March 13. John Ewing Calhoun Papers, Southern Historical Collections, University of North Carolina, Chapel Hill.

Chang, K. C. 1968. Toward a Science of Prehistoric Society. In *Settlement Archaeology*. K. C. Chang (ed.), pp. 1–9. Palo Alto: National Press.

Chang, K. C. 1972. *Settlement Patterns in Archaeology.* Addison-Wesley Module in Anthropology 24. Reading, MA: Addison-Wesley.

Clarke, D. L. 1977. Spatial Information in Archaeology. In *Spatial Archaeology*, D. L. Clarke (ed.), pp. 1–32. London: Academic Press.

Coulter, E. M. 1929. A Century of a Georgia Plantation. *Agricultural History* 3: 147–159.

Crumley, C. L. 1979. Three Locational Models: An Epistemological Assessment for Anthropology and Archaeology. In *Advances in Archaeological Method and Theory, Vol. 2*, M. B. Schiffer (ed.), pp. 141–173. New York: Academic Press.

Dundas, F. de S. 1949. *The Calhoun Settlement District of Abbeville, South Carolina.* Stauton, VA: Francis de Sales Dundas.

Durr, L. J. n.d.. Brazilian Recollections. Judkins-Durr Papers, Alabama Department of Archives and History, Montgomery.

Eaton, C. 1961. *The Growth of Southern Civilization, 1790–1860.* New York: Harper and Row.

Ehrenhard, J. E., and M. R. Bullard. 1981. *Stafford Plantation, Cumberland Island National Seashore, Georgia: Archaeological Investigations of a Slave Cabin.* Southeast Archaeological Center, National Park Service, Tallahassee.

Fairbanks, C. H. 1974. The Kingsley Slave Cabins in Duval County, Florida, 1968. *The Conference on Historic Site Archaeology Papers* 7:62–93.

Fogel, R. W. and S. L. Engerman. 1974. *Time on the Cross: The Economics of American Negro Slavery.* Boston: Little, Brown.

Freedmen's Bureau. 1867a. Contract Between W. V. Clinkscales and Freedmen, January 1. Bureau of Refugees, Freedmen, and Abandoned Lands. National Archives, Washington, DC.

Freedmen's Bureau. 1867b. Contract Between James Edward Calhoun and Freedmen, February 5. Bureau of Refugees, Freedmen, and Abandoned Lands. National Archives, Washington, DC.

Gallman, R. E. and R. V. Anderson. 1977. Slaves as Fixed Capital: Slave Labor and Southern Economic Development. *The Journal of American History* 64:24–46.

Genovese, E. D. 1974. *Roll, Jordan, Roll: The World the Slaves Made.* New York: Pantheon.

Hagood, M. J. 1977. *Mothers of the South: Portraiture of the White Tenant Farm Woman.* Originally published in 1939. New York: Norton.

Hart, J. F. 1980. Land Use Change in a Piedmont County. *Annals of the Association of American Geographers* 70:492–527.

Hart, J. F. and E. L. Chestang. 1978. Rural Revolution in East Carolina. *Geographical Review* 68:435–458.

Herron, E. C. (comp.). 1980. *Soil Survey of Abbeville County, South Carolina.* Soil Conservation Service, U.S. Department of Agriculture, Washington, DC.

Higgs, R. 1974. Patterns of Farm Rental in the Georgia Cotton Belt, 1880–1900. *Journal of Economic History* 34:468–482.

History Group, The. 1981. *Historical Investigations of the Richard B. Russell Multiple Resource Area.* Report submitted to the Interagency Archaeological Services, Atlanta.

Hodder, I. 1977. Some New Directions in the Spatial Analysis of Archaeological Data at the Regional Scale. In *Spatial Archaeology,* D. L. Clarke (ed.), pp. 223–351. London: Academic Press.

Hodder, I. and C. Orton. 1976. *Spatial Analysis in Archaeology.* Cambridge: Cambridge University Press.

Kane, L. M. and J. D. Holmquist (eds.). 1978. *The Northern Expedition of Stephen H. Long: The Journals of 1817 and 1823 and Related Documents.* Minneapolis: Minnesota Historical Society.

Nie, N. H., C. H. Hull, J. G. Jenkins, K. Steinbrenner, and D. H. Bent. 1975. *Statistical Package for the Social Sciences.* 2nd ed. New York: McGraw-Hill.

Orser, C. E., Jr. 1981. Uniting Public History and Historical Archaeology. *The Public Historian* 3: 75-83.

Orser, C. E., Jr. 1983. The Spatial Organization of a Postbellum Plantation. Paper presented at the 40th Southeastern Archaeological Conference, Columbia, SC.

Orser, C. E., Jr. 1985. The Sorghum Processing Industry of a Nineteenth-Century Cotton Plantation in South Carolina. *Historical Archaeology* 19(1):51–64.

Orser, C. E., Jr. 1986. The Archaeological Recognition of the Squad System on Postbellum Cotton Plantations. *Southeastern Archaeology* 5:11–20.

Orser, C. E., Jr. and C. C. Holland. 1984. Let Us Praise Famous Men, Accurately: Toward a More Complete Understanding of Postbellum Southern Agricultural Practices. *Southeastern Archaeology* 3:111–120.

Orser, C. E., Jr., A. M. Nekola, and J. L. Roark. 1981. Summary Report of Phase I Testing and Evaluation at Millwood Plantation (38AB9), Abbeville County, South Carolina. Report submitted to the Interagency Archaeological Services, Atlanta.

Orser, C. E., Jr., A. M. Nekola, and J. L. Roark. 1982. Exploring the Rustic Life: Multidisciplinary Research at Millwood Plantation, A Large Piedmont Plantation in Abbeville County, South Carolina, and Elbert County, Georgia. Report submitted to the Archaeological Services Division, National Park Service, Atlanta.

Otto, J. S. 1975. Status Differences and the Archaeological Record: A Comparison of Planter, Overseer, and Slave Sites from Cannon's Point Plantation (1794–1861), St. Simon's Island, Georgia. Unpublished Ph.D. dissertation, University of Florida. Ann Arbor: University Microfilms.

Otto, J. S. 1977. Artifact and Status Differences—A Comparison of Ceramics from Planter, Overseer, and Slave Sites on an Antebellum Plantation. In *Research Strategies in Historical Archaeology*, S. South (ed.), pp. 91–118. New York: Academic Press.

Otto, J. S. 1984. *Cannon's Point Plantation, 1794–1860: Living Conditions and Status Patterns in the Old South*. Orlando: Academic Press.

Perrin, L. 1933. The Hermit of Millwood: An Account of the Life of Mr. James Edward Calhoun. *The Press and Banner and Abbeville Medium*, June 29. Abbeville, SC.

Prunty, Merle, Jr. 1955. The Renaissance of the Southern Plantation. *The Geographical Review* 45:459–491.

Ransom, R. L. and R. Sutch. 1977. *One Kind of Freedom: The Economic Consequences of Emancipation*. Cambridge: Cambridge University Press.

Roark, J. L. 1977. *Masters Without Slaves: Southern Planters in the Civil War and Reconstruction*. New York: Norton.

Roscoe, J. T. 1975. *Fundamental Research Statistics for the Behavioral Sciences*. 2nd ed. New York: Holt, Rinehart, and Winston.

Savitt, T. L. 1978. *Medicine and Slavery: The Diseases and Health Care of Blacks in Antebellum Virginia*. Urbana: University of Illinois Press.

Shlomowitz, R. 1979a. The Transition from Slave to Freedman Labor Arrangements in Southern Agriculture, 1865–1870. Unpublished Ph.D. dissertation, University of Chicago.

Schlomowitz, R. 1979b. The Origins of Southern Sharecropping. *Agricultural History* 53:557–575.

Schlomowitz, R. 1982. The Squad System on Postbellum Cotton Plantations. In *Toward a New South? Studies in Post-Civil War Southern Communities*, O. V. Burton and R. C. McMath, Jr. (eds.), pp. 265–280. Westport, CT: Greenwood.

Stampp, K. M. 1956. *The Peculiar Institution: Slavery in the Ante-Bellum South*. New York: Random House.

Thompson, E. T. 1975. *Plantation Societies, Race Relations, and the South: The Regimentation of Populations*. Durham: Duke University Press.

Tindall, G. B. 1967. The Emergence of the New South, 1913–1945. In *A History of the South, Vol. 10*, W. H. Stephenson and E. M. Coulter (eds.). Baton Rouge: Louisiana State University Press.

Trimble, S. W. 1974. *Man-Induced Soil Erosion on the Southern Piedmont, 1700–1970*. Ankeny, IA: Soil Conservation Society of America.

U.S. Census. 1850. Agricultural Schedule for Abbeville District, South Carolina. South Carolina Department of Archives and History, Columbia.

U.S. Census. 1860a. Agricultural Schedule for Abbeville District, South Carolina. South Carolina Department of Archives and History, Columbia.

U.S. Census. 1860b. Slave Schedule for Abbeville District, South Carolina. South Carolina Department of Archives and History, Columbia.

U.S. Census. 1880. Agricultural Schedule for Abbeville County, South Carolina. South Carolina Department of Archives and History, Columbia.

Vance, R. B. 1936. *How the Other Half is Housed: A Pictorial Record of Sub-Minimum Farm Housing in the South.* Southern Policy Paper 4. Chapel Hill: The University of North Carolina Press.

Wolf, E. 1959. Specific Aspects of Plantation Systems in the New World: Community Sub-cultures and Social Class. In *Plantation Systems of the New World*, V. Rubin (ed.), pp. 136–146. Washington, DC: Pan American Union.

Woofter, T. J., Jr., G. Blackwell, H. Hoffsommer, J. G. Maddox, J. M. Massell, B. O. Williams, and W. Wynne, Jr. 1936. *Landlord and Tenant on the Cotton Plantation.* Washington, DC: Works Progress Administration.

Wright, G. 1978. *The Political Economy of the Cotton South: Households, Markets, and Wealth in the Nineteenth Century.* New York: Norton.

Zimmerman, L. J. 1978. Simulating Prehistoric Locational Behavior. In *Simulation Studies in Archaeology*, I. Hodder (ed.), pp. 27–37. Cambridge: Cambridge University Press.

Chapter Seventeen

Over-Hunting and Local Extinctions:

Socio-Economic Implications of Fur Trade Subsistence

Introduction

The central element of the British North American fur trade was the intensive exploitation of animals for both furs and food. However, the importance of food in the fur trade is generally underestimated in the literature in favor of primary fur-bearing animals. Food was a preoccupation with all individuals residing within the trading posts. These concerns involved day-to-day subsistence needs, and supplying the labor-intensive canoe transportation system. It also involved assuring access to preferred food types. This paper briefly reviews the environmental implications of this large-scale exploitation system, and then turns to aspects of the fur trade social system affected by shortages of preferred foodstuffs.

The 18th- and early 19th-century fur trade was an economic system with an insatiable demand for raw materials. In contrast to the comparatively finite needs of aboriginal populations, the European and Asian mercantile system stimulated a virtually unlimited demand for furs. With the expansion of fur trade hinterlands, food acquisition to supply the increasingly overextended transportation system led to a flourishing provisioning industry. Also important for this discussion was the European settlement strategy of establishing semipermanent posts to which animal products were transported for consumption and export. This exaggerated the

This article was originally published in *Culture and Environment: A Fragile Coexistence. Proceedings of the Twenty-Fourth Annual Conference of the Archaeological Association of the University of Calgary*, R. W. Jamieson, S. Abonyi, and N. A. Mirau, eds., pp. 43–59, The University of Calgary Archaeological Association, ©1993.

ecological damage caused by the fur trade since the immediate hinterland of each post was heavily and continuously utilized. Consequently animal populations could not recover from the continued intense predation. This European "central place" settlement strategy forms a marked contrast to indigenous hunting and gathering strategies that almost always involved people moving regularly and strategically to locate themselves near seasonally available food resources. This aboriginal mobility, in light of finite levels of need, assured sustained food yields over the long term even in areas, such as the boreal forest, which are generally characterized by relative resource scarcity.

Fur Trade Provisioning: Economic Significance and Environmental Implications

The only economically viable means of providing food to inland fur trade posts was by acquiring it in the hinterland. These so-called "country foods" consisted of fresh meat, fat, fish and birds, plus a range of plant foods such as berries and wild rice. Sometimes agricultural produce such as corn, potatoes, cereal grains and other vegetables were grown to supplement wild foods. These materials, particularly red meat and fish, were often processed for long-term storage by drying, smoking, or salting. Animal fat was also highly valued, particularly in situations of limited availability of plant carbohydrates. The most important of these provisions was pemmican, a mixture of dried and pulverized meat mixed with rendered fat (and sometime berries), that was stored in skin bags. Pemmican was highly valued as a food staple for the transportation system due to its high nutritional value per unit of weight, and its long-term preservation capacity.

As the shape and nature of the fur trade hinterland developed in the late 1700s, the northern Plains area grew in economic importance in spite of a comparatively minor fur resource potential. This importance lay primarily in the abundance of bison, and secondarily, in the wolf hide trade. While the fur and meat resources traded at these plains-edge posts had a negligible value in Europe, the foodstuffs were essential for the transportation system. Given that this transportation system was very labor intensive, the fur trade was dependent upon locally derived provisions being available at resupply depots at strategic locations along the canoe transportation routes (Figure 17.1). Provisioning was an important function for most plains fringe posts along the Saskatchewan and Assiniboine River drainage basins.

Provisioning was also essential at posts located in the boreal forest. Given the ecological structure of the forests, there was no equivalent to the plains bison in terms of large volumes of highly valued red meat and fat. Instead, fish and sometimes migratory waterfowl and caribou were virtually the only "clumped" and reasonably reliable food resources available. These staples were supplemented with more diffuse game such as moose and small terrestrial mammals. However, these

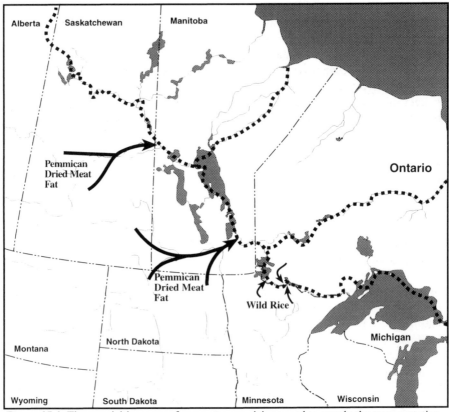

Figure 17.1. The acquisition zones for country provisions used to supply the transportation routes. The heavy dashed lines represent the primary transportation corridors (after Ray 1974:129).

latter animals were seldom either concentrated or predictable in their distribution. This lack of food prey density and predictability made it difficult to accumulate surpluses of easily preserved fat-rich animal protein. These problems became increasingly severe as time passed, and individual trading post hinterlands became depleted. As a result traders established in the boreal forest faced difficulties in satisfying winter subsistence needs, and in accumulating surpluses of preserved provisions to supply the summer canoe brigades. These chronic food supply problems were alleviated only by transporting pemmican, fat and dried meat from plain-fringe posts into the forest regions.

As the amount of fur and food needed to support the trade grew with the scale of operations, it is not surprising that regional ecosystems grew increasingly stressed. The comparatively rapid collapse of beaver populations in northern Ontario serves to illustrate the rapidity of this resource destruction (Lytwyn 1987) (Figure 17.2). By 1820, only the most remote headwaters regions in northern Ontario retained significant beaver populations. While reflecting the rapid degradation of the primary fur resource, this map also serves as a useful analog for the collapse of terrestrial food resources such as moose and caribou.

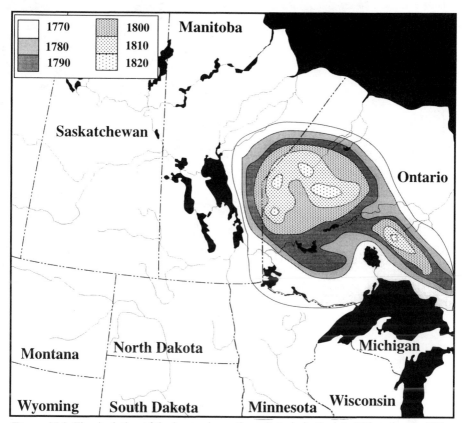

Figure 17.2. The depletion of the beaver in northern Ontario in the late 18th and early 19th centuries (after Lytwyn 1987). Shaded areas plot the regions where beaver were still reported as being plentiful.

Archaeological analyses of faunal materials from two trading posts in northeastern British Columbia also attest to the rapidity of resource collapse in face of intensive exploitation (Figure 17.3). The rapidity of this resource collapse is particularly dramatic in light of initial reports of enormous numbers of large ungulates in the upper Peace River valley when it was first explored by Europeans in 1793 (Mackenzie 1967:60–61). The first trading post established in the upper Peace River

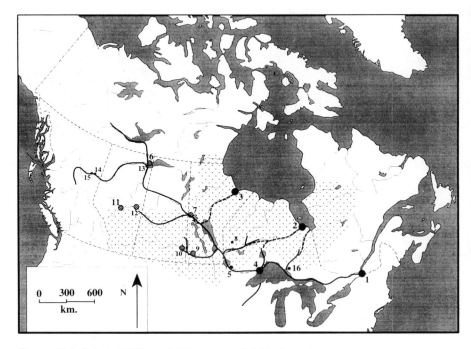

Figure 17.3. Selected 18th- and 19th-century British fur trade posts.

1. Montreal	9. Brandon House
2. Albany Factory	10. Ft. Esperance
3. York Factory	11. Ft. Edmonton
4. Ft. William/Grand Portage	12. Ft. George/Buckingham House
5. Lac la Pluie	13. Nottingham House
6. Ft. Chippewyan	14. Ft. St. John
7. Cumberland House	15. Rocky Mnt. Fort
8. Red Lake	16. Michipicotan

● Administrative headquarters

• Wintering outpost

⋮ Approximate extent of Rupert's land

Major transportation corridors are indicated by heavy solid or dashed lines.
Regional headquarters are indicated by medium-sized gray circles.

valley was Rocky Mountain Fort. It was established one year after Alexander Mackenzie's 1793 exploratory trip up the Peace River, and remained in operation for 10 years, closing in 1804 (Burley and Hamilton 1990; Burley, Hamilton, and Fladmark 1996). One of the trading posts built to replace this establishment was Fort St. John, dating between 1806 and 1823 (Fladmark 1985). Both of these posts were operated by the North West Company, which maintained a virtual monopoly over the rich Athabasca region, including the Peace River valley, until the second decade of the 19th century (Burley, Hamilton, and Fladmark 1996).

The faunal recoveries and the sole surviving journal from Rocky Mountain Fort are indicative of the relative richness of the region in terms of fur and food (Burley, Hamilton, and Fladmark 1996; Hamilton 1987; Hamilton, Burley, and Moon 1988; O'Neil 1928). Both of these information sources indicate that bison and wapiti were the primary food resources, with beaver being the most valued fur bearer. The intensity of the provisioning effort is apparent with the enormous quantities of fresh meat reported in the winter of 1799–1800 (Table 17.1), and in the density of food bone waste recovered archaeologically (Figure 17.4). These provisions served to satisfy winter subsistence needs, and to supplement the food requirements of the Lake Athabasca canoe brigades. In fact, during the occupation of Rocky Mountain Fort, surplus foodstuffs produced along the Peace River were exported to Lake Athabasca to supplement the food supplies needed to support the Fort Chippewyan (Burley, Hamilton, and Fladmark 1996). This dramatic transition is apparent in the faunal materials recovered from both sites, and is expressed by the shifting proportions of bones of each individual species (Figure 17.5). These provisioning difficulties likely led to the rapid expansion of the Fort St. John catchment area, and sharp increases in the time and effort involved in provisioning (Burley, Hamilton, and Fladmark 1996). This was because the hunters were forced to travel much further afield in search of elusive large game animals such as moose, and feed themselves from the kill while transporting the meat back to the post. The abrupt increase in the relative importance of small game, such as hare, likely reflects the dietary shortfalls experienced by the post occupants (see Figure 17.5). The financial records indicate that beaver pelts remained comparatively important in the annual fur returns (Burley and Hamilton 1990 citing Ray 1988). However, the archaeological data indicates that beaver carcasses no longer arrived at Fort St. John for consumption by the trading post personnel. Presumably, local beaver populations had been trapped out, and more distant Indians consumed the fat-rich carcasses in their camps rather than transporting them to the post for trade along with the furs. While it is a truism to say that fur trade resource exploitation resulted in widespread ecological transformation, what is remarkable is the comparative rapidity with which these collapses occurred. The social implications of these collapses remains to be explored. The remainder of this chapter will address an element of this by examining the social role of food in fur trade posts, and how shortages affected interpersonal relationships within the trading post community.

TABLE 17.1

*Furs, Hides, and Provisions Reported in the 1799–1800
Season at Rocky Mountain Fort* (after Hamilton 1987:139)[a]

	Made Beaver[b]	Lbs.	No. of Animals
Provisions			
Meat	456.5	738	
Wapiti		5154	18
Bison		9694	21
Rabbits			14
Beaver	30.5		7
Beaver tails	41.5		
Grease	3		
Castorum	13.5		
Meat and skins	2.5		
Dried meat		886	
Grease	16	215	
Pounded meat	13	129	
Tongues	2		15
Furs and Hides			
Beaver skins	4079.5		
Furs	4		
Moose hides			3
Bison hides			22
Elk hides			1
Fox			1
Green skins	633.5		19
Pack cords	2		
Dressed skins	5		3
Nets	7		
Cords and nets	5		

[a]   See journal transcription in Burley, Hamilton, and Fladmark (1996).

[b]   Made Beaver is a unit of measure based upon the barter value of one beaver skin.

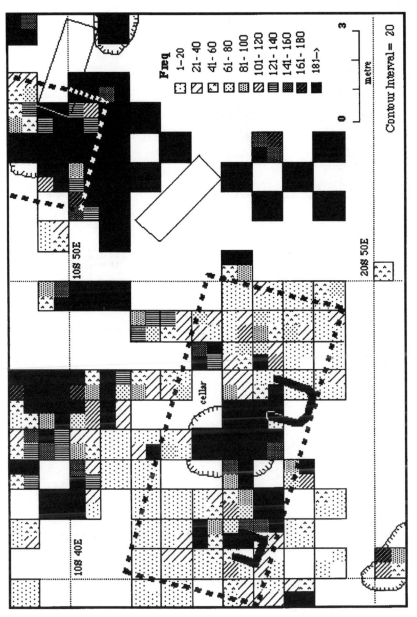

Freq
1-20
21-40
41-60
61-80
81-100
101-120
121-140
141-160
161-180
181->

Contour interval = 20

10S 50E

20S 50E

cellar

10S 40E

0   metre   3

Figure 17.4. Faunal refuse at Rocky Mountain Fort.

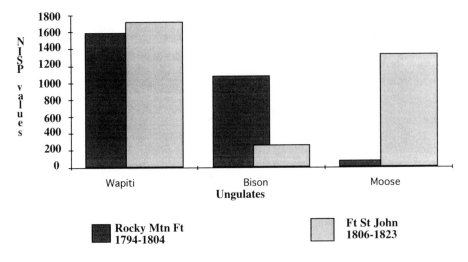

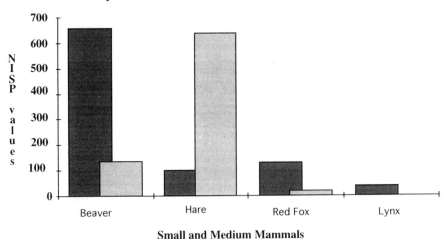

Figure 17.5. Shifts in NISP values between Rocky Mountain Fort and Fort St. John.

The Role of Food in the Social Fabric
of the Trading Post

In general, food preferences formed a continuum, with fat-rich bison or moose meat being the most preferred, and fish being the least favored (Hamilton 1990a; Hurlburt 1977). These preferences involved the fat content, palatability, and texture of the meat. Of additional concern to occupants of cold climates, a flesh-dominated diet requires fat to efficiently metabolize the animal protein (Speth 1983). Indeed, these food preferences were so strongly held that they were sometimes the cause of contention between the officers and laborers. For example, in 1804 the officer in charge of Brandon House, a HBC trading post along the Assiniboine River (see Figure 17.3), reported acquiring large quantities of fish from weirs during the spring spawn (HBC Archives, PAM, B.22/a/12/3). However, he also noted that the laborers refused to eat fish so long as bison meat and fat remained on hand in the ice house (Hamilton 1985b:95). The laborers at Brandon House also consistently used threats of work slowdowns to assure that meat and fat were not rationed (Hamilton 1985a; 1985b). In the situation of provisioning stations such as Brandon House, it appears that unlimited access to preferred foods was considered to be a right, and in no way a privilege. I maintain that the Brandon House situation represents one aspect of a very complex issue. To appreciate the social dynamics of access to food, we also have to examine the situation at posts in "older" or "impoverished" trade hinterlands that were experiencing chronic and systemic food shortages.

To understand the dynamic social role played by food, we first have to briefly address the work-related social hierarchy of the two major trade companies. Both the Hudson's Bay Company (HBC) and the North West Company (NWC) were characterized by pyramidal chains of command (Hamilton 1985a, 1990b; Prager 1985). Unlike most postmedieval corporate command structures, the isolation of the fur trade posts led to the work-related hierarchy becoming the basis of all social relationships within the post communities. Space does not permit the description of either these social systems, nor the dynamics of interpersonal relations. Suffice it to say that varying levels of social tension characterized the relationships between officers and laborers. This was particularly the case within the NWC in light of financial inequities and ethnic tensions (Hamilton 1990b).

These interrank tensions were most severe during the period of intensive competition between the trade companies (ca. 1790 to 1821). During this period, a common strategy was to establish as many small wintering outposts as possible in order to force the competition to follow suit, and thereby overextend themselves to the point of economic collapse. This resulted in numerous small competing outposts, each of which was occupied by a literate clerk and a small complement of experienced laborers to assist in trading, transporting goods, collecting firewood, hunting, and fishing. This competitive strategy sharply inflated the costs of conducting the trade, and required the maintenance of large payrolls. In the case of the NWC wintering outposts, this often resulted in young and inexperienced English-speaking clerks and apprentices being placed in nominal charge of outposts with a small group of highly experienced French-speaking engagés. When this occurred, the inexperienced officers were socially isolated, and often were unable to communicate with either their subordinates or customers. Several reminiscences written by these clerks attest to the personal and managerial difficulties experienced (see Brown and Brightman 1988; Hamilton 1990b; Harmon 1957; Van Kirk 1984).

In my doctoral dissertation, I proposed that the senior management of the trade companies helped reinforce the authority and prestige of these junior officers, clerks and apprentices in the eyes of both the native customers and the laborers (Hamilton 1990b). Some techniques of nonverbally reinforcing the hierarchical chain of command included separate officers' quarters, differential dress, and conspicuous consumption of exotic and expensive material culture. In spite of the considerable costs involved, even junior clerks were offered equipment allowances, and preferential prices for goods to enable them to purchase clothing and equipment befitting their rank. These "corporate perks" were essential since, in spite of their rank and authority, junior clerks and apprentices were poorly paid; often considerably less than the laborers that they supervised. Officers were also expected to maintain a proper social distance in their dealings with the laborers who were to be their "companions" throughout the winter season (Hamilton 1985a, 1990b). This rather militaristic code of behavior was deemed necessary in order to support the sometimes uncertain authority of the junior clerks in charge of the wintering outposts. While this behavior is apparent with both the major trade companies, it is more visible with the NWC.

The observation that valued material culture was used to symbolize social position is hardly surprising given the hierarchical nature of the command structure of these companies. However, it is interesting to note how this behavior was affected by the very high transportation costs into the interior. All goods transported inland, whether trade goods, provisions, or employees' personal property, were moved by canoes or flat-bottomed boats along often difficult water systems (see Figure 17.3). The costs of this transportation system were staggering, and was reflected in the NWC price markups as goods as they moved inland (Figure 17.6). Despite these costs, laborers and officers were provided with a sliding scale of goods that reflected their relative work-role and seniority within the company service (Hamilton 1990b). The officers' clothing and equipment allowances even included "canteens" containing European tableware, exotic alcohol, and foodstuffs. As a cost-saving measure, laborers also frequently made large purchases of personal goods from better supplied "rendezvous" posts such as York Factory, Albany Factory, Fort William, or Grand Portage (Hamilton 1990b) (see Figure 17.3). Clearly, this private property likely represented a substantial cost to the companies both in terms of the cost of the "equipment allowances," plus the loss of cargo space for trade goods in the canoes. These costs also increased sharply with the distance traveled. Thus, the cost of transporting goods into remote hinterlands such as the Athabasca district often exceeded the invoiced value of the cargo (see Figure 17.6).

While the NWC was prepared to absorb a substantial portion of the expense involved in acquiring, distributing, and transporting the physical symbols of rank used by the clerks, care was taken to keep these expenses in check (Hamilton 1990b). Given the large number and dispersed distribution of the many temporary wintering outposts, it would have been unrealistically costly to equip each junior clerk with a wide range of European icons of prestige and authority. Instead, these men seem to have identified and negotiated new materials and techniques of communicating and reinforcing their social position. These informal techniques of social posturing were characteristically local in their derivation, and therefore were inexpensive in terms of European purchase value and transportation costs (Hamilton 1990b). However, they remained valued scarce commodities in the hinterland, and could be "socially negotiated" into prestige symbols that were useful to reinforce authority.

Given the importance of "country foods" to all post occupants, we may assume that differential access to food could potentially serve as an important means of asserting social position and reinforcing authority. To a certain extent this was the case. However, the ecological situation of the posts in question was an important factor in determining whether food could be translated from a staple into a scarce and valued luxury commodity.

Trading posts characterized by comparative resource richness will be considered first. Two such posts include Brandon House and Rocky Mountain Fort. Both of these posts had access to large amounts of premium foods such as bison and wapiti meat and fat. The Rocky Mountain Fort journal makes little or no mention of fish or hare as food sources (see Table 17.1). The archaeological data also indicates that these foods were a minor component of the diet (Table 17.2). Indeed, the faunal assemblage is dominated by bone fragments from large and medium ungulates such as bison and wapiti (Hamilton, Burley, and Moon 1988). At Brandon House, bison and wapiti faunal remains also dominate the archaeological assemblage, and are by far the most important prey species reported in 18 years of continuous journals (Hamilton 1990a) (Table 17.3). These journals indicate that it was only when the winter bison hunt occasionally failed that the post occupants resorted to secondary food sources such as grouse, hare, and fish.

With the exception of the occasional failures of the large game hunt, preferred animal foods were plentiful at both Rocky Mountain Fort and Brandon House. Given this plenty, premium foods do not appear to have been a particularly useful icon of social position. This is to be expected since even highly valued food was readily available in quantities sufficient to feed all occupants through the winter trade season, and to build up a surplus for the summer canoe brigades. In such situations, premium food was not scarce and could not be considered a luxury. The

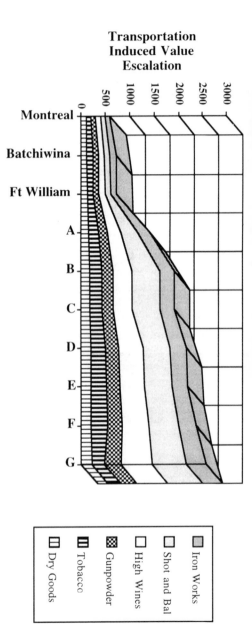

Transportation Induced Value Escalation

Legend: Iron Works, Shot and Bal, High Wines, Gunpowder, Tobacco, Dry Goods

The figure graphically represents the North West Company 1804 Tariff Structure. To illustrate transportation costs upon cargo value, imagine that the six categories of goods were each valued at £100 in Montreal. The cargo was indiscriminately marked up by 20% for posts along the north shore of Lake Superior (Batchiwina, Michipicoten and Pic). The markup upon all goods arriving at Fort William was 23% above the Montreal price. Markups upon goods travelling beyond Fort William were calculated upon the Fort William value rather than the Montreal one. Also of interest is that goods transported beyond Fort William were valued at variable rates depending upon weight and bulk.

A Fond du Lac and its dependencies

B Nipigon Department

C Lac la Pluie, Lac Ouinipigue (Lake Winnipeg), Upper and Lower Red Rivers (Assiniboine and Red Rivers) and Fort Dauphin Departments.

D Forts des Prairies (Saskatchewan) or the Riviere Opas Departments.

E English River and dependencies (Churchill River)

F Upper Athabasca River

G Athabasca and dependencies

Dry Goods include clothing, textiles, cassettes, cased guns, knives, hats & baskets of kettles

Figure 17.6. Transportation-related cost markups of some classes of North West Company goods (after Davidson 1918).

TABLE 17.2

Identifiable Faunal Material Recovered from Rocky Mountain Fort
(after Hamilton, Burley, and Moon 1988:126)

	Total ID Bone (NISP)		Total ID Bone (NISP)
Large ungulate[a]	770	Small mammal[a]	107
Bison	174	Lepus sp.	101
Moose	12	Microtus sp.	6
Med./Large ungulate[a]	879	Red squirrel	6
Med. ungulate[a]	292	Mustelid	5
Wapiti	622	Mink	2
Small ungulate[a]	0	Peromyscus sp.	2
Deer sp.	2	Martin/Mink	1
Large mammal[a]	1003	Med. rodent	1
Bear	12	Mustelid, large	1
Black bear	6	Mustelid, martin size	1
Grizzly bear	1	Martin	1
Mammal?[a]	5	Avian[a]	24
Med. mammal[a]	539	Large bird	7
Beaver	656	Med. bird	18
Red fox	133	Small bird	16
Lynx	39	Duck	48
Canis sp.	16	Duck, small	6
Porcupine	12	Mallard	6
Wolverine	12	Goose	22
Beaver/Porcupine	10	Swan	17
Large rodent	2	Grouse	11
Fisher	1	Crow	1
Large carnivore[a]	1	Passenger pigeon	1
Med. carnivore[a]	16	Woodpecker	1
Small carnivore[a]	4	Raven	2
		Coot	1
		Swan/Goose	1
		Fish[a]	144
		Catostomidae	52
		P. oregonensis	299
		Cyprinidae	6
		Burbot	3

[a] These entries represent fragments that could not be speciated, but could be classsed to a size/family category.

Brandon House laborers demonstrated this attitude when they successfully resisted efforts to replace bison meat with fish, or to ration their intake of fresh meat (Hamilton 1985b). In these situations of resource richness, differential access to food could not be enforced and was not an effective mechanism for symbolization of social position.

TABLE 17.3

Identifiable Faunal Material Recovered from Brandon House
(after Hamilton 1990b)

	Total ID Bone (NISP)		Total ID Bone (NISP)
Large Artiodactyla[a]		Avian[a]	762
Horse	1	Alcid/Gull/Shorebird	16
Bison/Domestic cow	79	Owl	6
Bison	164	Magpie/Jay	1
Domestic cow	1	Grouse	47
Moose	5	Hawk	3
Wapiti	28	Passenger pigeon	28
Sheep/Goat	3	Pigeon	2
Deer sp.	19	Swan/Goose/Duck	14
Bison/Moose/Wapiti/Deer	53	Trumpeter swan	5
Bison/Cow/Moose/Wapiti	51	Trumpeter/Whistling swan	11
Moose/Elk/Deer	9	Canada goose	19
Moose/Wapiti	25	Goose	16
Large mammal[a]	7017	Duck, large	74
Med. mammal[a]	184	Duck, small[a]	19
Small/Med. mammal[a]	115	Duck[a]	6
Bear	1	Large bird[a]	190
Carnivore[a]	6	Med./Large bird	183
Wolf	1	Med. bird[a]	153
Wolf/Coyote/Dog/Fox	20	Small/Med. bird	38
Wolf/Coyote/Dog	3	Small bird	1
Fox	1	Fish[a]	4040
Lynx	5	Sucker sp.	187
Beaver	307	Catfish sp.	12
Beaver/Porcupine	1	Sturgeon sp.	71
Badger	1	Mooneye/Goldeye	24
Skunk	3	Northern pike	9
Small mammal[a]	58	Walleye/Sauger	27
Rabbit/Hare	352	Freshwater drum	7
Muskrat	47	Amphibia[a]	4
Microtinae	6	Turtle	44
Cricetinae	10	Mollusca[a]	714
Rich. ground squirrel	1		
Squirrel	2		
Pocket gopher	14		
Mouse	3		
Small rodent	26		

[a] These entries represent fragments that could not be speciated, but could be classsed to a size/family category.

The situation in the boreal forest trading posts was quite different. In such situations there were no concentrated and reliable sources of fat-rich animal protein. The only reliable resource was fish; a food that was least valued in part because of its low fat content. One well-documented and excavated boreal forest trading post will be reviewed by way of example. Nottingham House was the HBC's first establishment in the Lake Athabasca region (see Figure 17.3), and was in operation between 1802 and 1806 (Karklins 1983). The officers and men stationed at this site were particularly unsuccessful, primarily because of the aggressive measures taken by the NWC in preventing natives from trading furs and food to the "Englishmen" (Karklins 1983, citing HBC Archives, PAM, B.39/a/1 to 5b). In addition to being located in the austere boreal forest, the HBC men also faced a blockade which assured that their tenure at the site was notable for its misery, fear, and hunger. In this situation we have the reverse of the phenomenon noted at Rocky Mountain Fort and Brandon House. That is, food of all sorts was hard to come by, and the more preferred avian and mammalian flesh was rare. In this situation preferred food types were rare luxury commodities, and the day-to-day staple was fish.

While the post journals are mute regarding the allocation of rations to post occupants, the archaeologically derived features and faunal recoveries are very illuminating. While in charge at Nottingham House, Peter Fidler described what he considered to be a good prototype plan for wintering outposts (Figure 17.7). He illustrated a rectangular building divided into four compartments. These compartments provided a communal residence for the laborers, a private room and office for the officer and his family, a combined kitchen, mess hall and trade room, and a warehouse. This spatial reinforcement of the social division of labor appears in several forms in a number of trading posts of the period (Hamilton 1990b). Excavation of Nottingham House reveals that it is essentially a mirror image of Fidler's plan, enabling identification of the residences of the two ranks (Figure 17.8).

While the European material culture from the various rooms at Nottingham House is not particularly illuminating regarding differential access to goods, the positioning of refuse pits and faunal recoveries from the rooms is very instructive. The officer's quarters are notable for the lack of food refuse disposal features within the structure. This stands in sharp contrast to disposal patterns in the laborers' quarters. Interestingly, this distinction in disposal strategy appears common in several trading posts (Hamilton 1990b). There was a conspicuous effort to collect and remove biodegradable refuse from the officer's quarters, and dispose of it in middens away from the structure. The laborers do not appear to have been nearly so concerned with refuse disposal. Small refuse pits are frequently found within the men's structures, and faunal refuse is much more densely and randomly distributed in and immediately around the laborer's quarters (Hamilton 1990b). Despite this different disposal behavior, the Nottingham House officer's quarters yields a much higher relative frequency of avian and mammalian bone fragments compared to fish (Figure 17.9). This stands in sharp contrast to the laborers' quarters which yielded a faunal assemblage dominated by fish remains. These distinctions suggest that the officer at Nottingham House appropriated a large proportion of the available

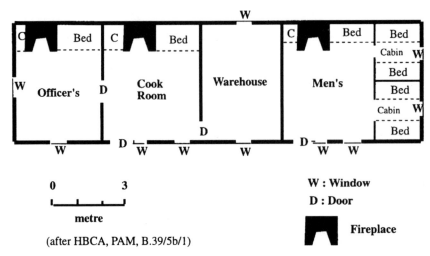

Figure 17.7. Peter Fidler's 1804 plan of a wintering post likely modeled after Nottingham House (after HBCA, PAM, B.39/a/5b/1).

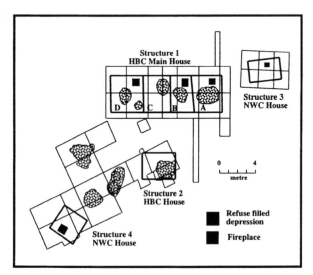

Figure 17.8. An archaeological plan of Nottingham House (after Karlins 1983:22).

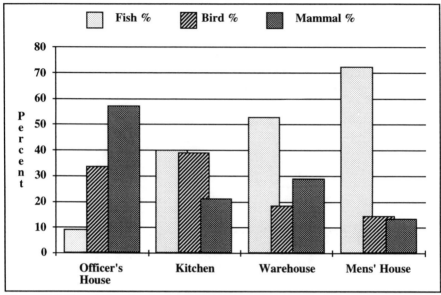

Figure 17.9. The relative abundance of faunal material in various rooms at Nottingham House (from Karlins 1983).

preferred food types for the exclusive use of his family. By contrast, the low-valued fish formed the primary staple for the laborers.

Conclusion

In the case of Nottingham House, the relative scarcity of preferred foods permitted the creation of a new kind of luxury good that was unaffected by the difficulties of transporting more conventional status items inland. Ironically, it was only in situations of food shortages or rather, scarcity of preferred foods, that officers were able to use differential access to food to symbolize and reinforce their authority. These observations, if borne out at other such trading posts, offer somewhat unexpected insight into human behavioral responses to food shortages. Given the rapid collapse of boreal forest ecological systems in the face of relentless fur trade overexploitation, the renegotiation of food from a staple into an icon of superior social position can be archaeologically measured.

If confirmed, this European response to food shortages forms an interesting contrast to aboriginal behavior in light of the same ecological collapses. These native responses, in the context of egalitarian values of mutual expectations of sharing, were more focused upon establishing new settlement systems utilizing

SCOTT HAMILTON

formerly secondary food prey, development of new patterns of land tenure (see Bishop 1970, 1974; Hickerson 1956; Rogers 1963), and sometimes even flight from the forest into the prairies (Hlady 1960; Howard 1977; Mandelbaum 1940; Milloy 1988; Ray 1974). Observation and further exploration of these varying responses to the same environmental phenomenon help us understand the dynamism of the fur trade as a social system. These observations also serve as yet another cautionary tale warning against environmental determinism, and other inappropriate uses of the environmental variable in the analysis of human culture.

REFERENCES

Bishop, C A. 1970. The Emergence of Hunting Territories Among the Northern Ojibwa *Ethnology* 9:1–15.

Bishop. C. A. 1974. *The Northern Ojibwa and the Fur Trade*. Toronto: Holt, Rinehart and Winston.

Brown, J. S. H. and R. Brightman. 1988. *The Orders of the Dreamed: George Nelson on Cree and Northern Ojibwa Religion and Myth, 1823*. Winnipeg: University of Manitoba Press.

Burley, D. V. and S. Hamilton. 1990. Rocky Mountain Fort: Archaeological Research and the Late 18th Century North West Company Expansion in British Columbia. *BC Studies* 88 (Winter):3–20.

Burley, D. V., J. S. Hamilton, and K. R. Fladmark. 1996. *Prophecy of the Swan: The Upper Peace River Fur Trade of 1794–1823*. Vancouver: University of British Columbia Press.

Davidson, G. 1918. *The North West Company*. Los Angeles: University of California Publications in History.

Fladmark, K. 1985. Early Fur Trade Forts of the Peace River Area of British Columbia *BC Studies* 65 (Spring):48–65.

Hamilton S. 1985a. The Social Organization of the Hudson's Bay Company: The Brandon House Case. In *Status, Structure and Stratification: Current Archaeological Reconstructions*, M. Thompson, M. Garcia, and F. J. Kense (eds.). Proceedings of the 16th Annual Chacmool Conference of the Archaeological Association, University of Calgary.

Hamilton, S. 1985b. The Social Organization of the Hudson's Bay Company: Formal and Informal Social Relations in the Context of the Inland Fur Trade. Unpublished M. A. thesis, Department of Anthropology, University of Alberta.

Hamilton, S. 1987. The End of Season Report of the 1986 Excavations at Rocky Mountain Fort HbRf-31. Unpublished report on file, B. C. Heritage Trust, Victoria.

Hamilton, S. 1990a. Western Canadian Fur Trade History and Archaeology: The Illumination of the Invisible in Fur Trade Society. *Saskatchewan Archaeology* 11/12:3–24

Hamilton, S. 1990b. Fur Trade Social Inequality and the Role of Nonverbal Communication. Unpublished Ph.D. dissertation, Department of Anthropology, Simon Fraser University.

Hamilton, S., D. V. Burley, and H. Moon. 1988. Rocky Mountain Fort and the Land-based Fur Trade Research Project: The 1987 End of Season Report. Unpublished report on file, B. C. Heritage Trust, Victoria.

Harmon, D. 1957. *Sixteen Years in the Indian Country*. W. Kaye (ed.). Toronto: Lamb Macmillan.

Hickerson, H. A. 1956. Genesis of a Trading Post Band: The Pembina Chippewa. *Ethnohistory* 3:289–345.

Hlady, W. 1960. Indian Migrations in Manitoba and the West. *Papers of the Manitoba Historical and Scientific Society, Series III* 17:25–33.

Howard, J. H. 1977. *The Plains Ojibwa or Bungi*. Lincoln, NE: J. and L. Reprint.

Hudson's Bay Company Archives. n. d. HBCA, PAM,B.39/a/1 to 5b, Nottingham House journals 1802–03 to 1803–05. HBCA. PAM, B.22/a/1 to 20, Brandon House journals 1793–94 to 1818. Provincial Archives of Manitoba.

Hurlburt, I. 1977. *Faunal Remains from Fort White Earth, NWCo. (1810–1813)*. Human History Occasional Paper No. 1. Edmonton: Provincial Museum of Alberta.

Karklins, K. 1983. *Nottingham House: The Hudson's Bay Company in Athabasca 1802–1806*. History and Archaeology No. 69, National Historic Parks and Sites Branch, Parks Canada, Ottawa.

Lytwyn, V. 1987. Transportation in the Petit Nord. In *Historical Atlas of Canada, Vol. 1*, R. Cole Harris (ed.). Toronto: University of Toronto Press.

Mackenzie, A. 1963. *First Man West: Alexander Mackenzie's Journal of his Voyage to the Pacific Coast of Canada in 1793*, W. Sheppe (ed.). Los Angeles: University of California Press.

Mandelbaum, D. H. 1940. *The Plains Cree*. Seattle: Publications of the American Museum of Washington Press.

Milloy, J. S. 1988. *The Plains Cree: Trade, Diplomacy and War, 1790 to 1870*. Winnipeg: University of Manitoba Press.

O'Neil, M. 1928. Journal of the Rocky Mountain Fort, Fall 1799. *Washington Historical Quarterly* 19(4):250–270.

Prager G. 1985. A Comparison of Social Structure in the North-West Company and the Hudson's Bay Company. In *Status, Structure and Stratification: Current Archeological Reconstructions*, M. Thompson, M. Garcia, and F. J. Kense (eds.). Proceedings of the 16th Annual Chacmool Conference of the Archaeological Association. Calgary: University of Calgary.

Ray, A. 1974. *Indians in the Fur Trade*. Toronto: University of Toronto Press.

Ray, A. 1988. The Place of the Athabasca and New Caledonia Districts in the Hudson's Bay Company Fur Trade 1820–24: An Overview from the District Accounts. Unpublished Ms. on file, University of British Columbia, Vancouver.

Rogers, E. S. 1963. Changing Settlement Pattern of the Cree-Ojibwa of Northern Ontario. *Southwestern Journal of Anthropology* 19:64–88.

Speth, J. D. 1983. *Bison Kills and Bone Counts: Decision Making by Ancient Hunters.* Chicago: University of Chicago Press.

Tyrrell, J. B. (ed.). 1935. *The Journals of Samuel Hearne and Philip Turner Between the Years 1774 and 1792.* Toronto: Champlain Society.

Van Kirk, S. 1984. George Nelson's "Wretched" Career, 1802–1823. In *Rendezvous: Selected Papers of the Fourth North American Fur Trade Conference, 1981*, T. C. Buckley (ed.). St. Paul: Minnesota Historical Society.

Williams, J. J. 1978. Fort D'Epinette: A Description of Faunal Remains from an Early Fur Trade Site in Northern British Columbia. Unpublished M.A. thesis, Simon Fraser University.

PART VI

International Historical Archaeology

In compiling this reader, it would be easy to give the impression that historical archaeology is restricted to North America, or even more so, just to the United States. Part of the reason for this impression is purely practical. As an American-trained archaeologist living in the United States, I have greater access to the works of my American colleagues than to the works of those living in other countries. This remains true even though I now conduct my own research largely outside the United States, in the Republic of Ireland and in Brazil. It is simply easier for me to obtain the studies of archaeologists in my home country. But this is not only an American phenomenon. Archaeologists around the world generally complain of the difficulties inherent in obtaining the writings of archaeologists in other countries. One of the goals of many professional archaeological societies—like the World Archaeological Congress—is to promote a truly international exchange of ideas and findings. A truly global archaeology will be a better archaeology.

Another reason why it may appear that historical archaeology is uniquely North American is because historical archaeology as I define it here was largely an American creation. The Society for Historical Archaeology was created in 1967 by American archaeologists. Though the society has worked diligently to foster an international historical archaeology, many scholars outside America still think of the organization as uniquely North American.

Part of the reason for this perception may occur because in Europe, historical archaeology is called postmedieval archaeology. Postmedieval archaeology mirrors historical archaeology in most ways, except that postmedievalists seldom conduct research on sites dating after 1750. The years after 1750 are typically viewed as falling within the purview of industrial archaeologists, those scholars primarily interested in the history of technology and industrial works. One of the future challenges facing historical archaeology is to link historical archaeology and postmedieval archaeology.

It would be completely incorrect, however, to imagine that historical archaeology is conducted only in North America. To the contrary, some of the most exciting historical archaeology is being conducted on the other continents, in places that are both famous—like El Mina, the fortified, colonial castle in West Africa dedicated to the international slave trade—and relatively unknown—like the tiny outposts of colonialism that dot the world's coastlines. Historical archaeologists throughout South America, Africa, Asia, and Australia are probing sites and retrieving important new information about past human cultures. The number of archaeologists engaged in this research increases every year, and many countries are beginning to sponsor whole conferences dedicated solely to historical archaeology. In addition, universities around the world are developing courses and entire programs in historical archaeology. It is truly an exciting time of growth and development in global historical archaeology.

As with the other sections of this book, it is impossible to provide the full range of research being undertaken across the globe. As done throughout, I have selected representative articles that will give you a small glimpse of historical archaeology in three places outside North America.

The first article was written by two Mexican historical archaeologists, Patricia Fournier-García and Fernando A. Miranda-Flores. In this overview, Fournier-García and Miranda-Flores chart the history of historical archaeology in their country, showing how the discipline first developed. As elsewhere in the world, Mexican historical archaeology began as a way to provide architectural details for reconstruction projects. When archaeology in general started to become more anthropological in orientation, Mexican historical archaeology followed suit. As a result, today's historical archaeology in Mexico includes a growing number of studies that focus on socioeconomic processes. But Fournier-García and Miranda-Flores stress that the future of Mexican historical archaeology has several hurdles to overcome. Two of the most significant problems concern the lack of widespread governmental support for historical archaeology and the need for protecting underwater sites from unnecessary destruction. These problems are not limited to Mexico, however, for historical archaeologists around the world must work continually to educate both public officials and the public in general to the significance of their discipline. As the growth of projects involving restoration and reconstruction in Mexico demonstrates, tourism is one important venue in which large numbers of people can be educated about the protection and preservation of archaeological sites.

The second chapter in this section focuses on historical archaeology in South Africa. In this article, Martin Hall, an archaeologist with the University of Cape Town, and Ann Markell, provide an overview of the archaeology of colonialism in South Africa. The impact caused by the contact of Europeans and indigenous peoples around the globe is one of the most important and dramatic stories in world history. As Hall and Markell point out, archaeology has a critical role to play in bringing to light the physical realities of these contacts. Beginning in the late 1970s, several South African archaeologists have taken up the challenge and are working diligently to provide detailed, culture contact studies. These investigations, many of which are long term by design, promise to change our current perspectives of the realities of culture contact as it was lived every day by real men and women from diverse cultures. Within the vast array of research being undertaken, Hall and Markell highlight two important themes that are receiving great attention: the archaeology of frontiers and the archaeology of the invisible men and women of the past, those who we often describe today as the underclass. The historical archaeology currently being pursued in South Africa is important because it helps to link the past with the present, to show that archaeology is never completely detached from the world around it. In South Africa, as elsewhere, the social problems of the present did not arise from thin air. On the contrary, they came from a past that is at least linked partly to the intercultural contacts that followed on the heels of European exploration. This is certainly the case in the Western Cape. It is exciting to think that archaeology can play a part in helping us to understand the differences and similarities of diverse peoples who have been in contact with one another for generations and who today are forging new national identities.

In the final chapter in this section we travel to another place frequently in today's news: the Middle East. Our guide is Neil Asher Silberman, a professional author who has written several important books on archaeology and who is an expert on Middle Eastern archaeology. In this article, Silberman reminds us that the past and the present are inexorably linked. While the archaeology of Early Islamic and Crusader periods have attracted great attention in the Middle East, the archaeology of the powerful Ottoman Empire has attracted very little. Only today, in the 1990s, is a new generation of young archaeologists beginning to investigate the cultures and histories of the region. Why is this so? Though the explanation is undoubtedly complex, Silberman identifies Ottoman domination as one important reason. Most people in the Middle East today see the Ottoman conquest as a low point in their cultural histories. Most men and women, including most archaeologists, prefer to think about the glorious times in their past, to concentrate on those times that can be used to construct a sense of national pride. Though these attitudes undeniably exist, Silberman gives an eloquent justification for the archaeology of the Ottoman period, using tobacco pipes as a starting point. From him we learn how the historical archaeology of the Middle East fits into the larger chronology of life in the region.

Historical archaeology undoubtedly will continue to develop around the world. Part of its growth probably will be related to tourism; other growth will stem from the intellectual curiosities of professional archaeologists. Either way, increased interest in the post-Columbian world by archaeologists will benefit us all, as we learn to understand and better appreciate the world around us.

PATRICIA FOURNIER-GARCÍA ■
FERNANDO A. MIRANDA-FLORES

Chapter Eighteen

Historic Sites Archaeology in Mexico

Introduction

From the beginning, archaeology in Mexico has been linked to the interests of the State. The government manipulates knowledge produced by historians and archaeology to reaffirm the national ideology. Indian heritage is seen as the proper subject matter of archaeology, which is limited as a discipline to the pre-Hispanic period. The description of this period is elevated in order to insure the glorification of a grandiose native past. Archaeological sites are protected by federal laws as part of the national cultural heritage. The State legally assumes control of the remains of the pre-Hispanic past, which makes the national government the ultimate force responsible for its protection. The agency with the mission of protecting archaeological sites, preserving national ideology, and generating elements to reproduce it is the National Institute of Anthropology and History (INAH).

The INAH is faced with an abundance and variety of pre-Hispanic sites. At the same time, resources available for research are limited. These factors have also contributed to the idea that archaeology's subject matter is the material remains of the cultures which developed before contact with the Western world. Most archaeologists usually restrict their studies to societies predating the Spanish arrival. They leave the study of later periods to other specialists such as ethnohistorians and historians.

It is also important to note that many Mexican archaeologists have only recently begun to seek recognition as social scientists. Most projects undertaken in the past did not have explicit research goals. Few researchers showed any

This article was originally published in *The Archaeology of the Spanish and Mexican Republican Periods*, Paul Farnsworth and Jack S. Williams, eds., *Historical Archaeology* (1992) 26(1):75-83.

concern for a theoretical orientation that could serve as a basis for inferences about past social processes.

Historical Archaeology in Mexico

Workers laboring in the field of historical archaeology in Mexico during the last three decades have included many Mexican as well as foreign investigators. Among the research conducted by foreign researchers can be counted the projects carried out by Charlton (1972, 1979a, 1979b) and his collaborators in the Otumba Valley (e.g., Borg 1975; Jones 1980; Seifert 1975, 1977), Di Peso (1959; Di Peso et al. 1974) and Barnes (1978) in northern Mexico, Andrews (1981) in Yucatán, Stark (1981) in the Papaloapan region, Gasco (1987) in Chiapas, as well as Florence and Robert Lister (1974, 1975, 1976, 1978, 1982, 1984, 1987) in central Mexico. The Listers' efforts were inspired by the pioneering studies of Goggin (1968).

A general lack of knowledge persists about the discoveries made by Mexican investigators among researchers living in the United States. This lack is due to the peculiarities of Mexican archaeology and the manner in which research results are disseminated. Few northern scholars are aware of the theoretical and methodological tendencies that have prevailed in the country. Yet North American and Mexican archaeologists have collaborated closely in a number of major historical archaeology studies (Andrews and Benavides 1985; Charlton et al. 1987).

The Development of Historical Archaeology in Mexico

The first attempt to study archaeological contexts of the Spanish colonial period was undertaken by Noguera (1934). Noguera conducted a preliminary study of historic-era ceramics with the goal of understanding processes of technical and stylistic change. He hoped that the evolution he observed would help explain the transition between pre-Hispanic and colonial traditions. His work emphasized the remains of the Contact period. The resulting study was a harbinger of the future direction of historical archaeology in Mexico, which would be closely linked to analyses of ceramics and changes resulting from European contact. Unfortunately for the field of historical archaeology, Noguera's work stood as an isolated effort during the decades that followed.

It was not until after 1964 that historic sites archaeology began to assume a more general importance in Mexico. The studies conducted in this new era can be grouped into three categories on the basis of major trends. These groups are: (1) studies where the historic past is treated as an archaeological topic in the same manner as the pre-Hispanic past; (2) studies where historic sites have been analyzed as part of larger programs of architectural restoration; and (3) studies where investigators have shown interest in the development of a scientific form of historical archaeology focused on the analysis of socio-economic processes.

The Historic Past as an Archaeological Topic

The view that historic sites should be treated as part of a broader approach to archaeology becomes apparent after 1963. This belief has had the most obvious effect on studies devoted to areas inside present-day Mexico City. Examples of projects undertaken with this orientation include those conducted at Tlatelolco (González Rul 1988); Metro Lines One, Two, Three (Arana and Cepeda 1969; Gussinyer 1969; López Cervantes 1974, 1976a, 1976b, 1977, 1979, 1982b), Four (López Wario and Ortuño 1984), Five (Carballal and Flores 1984), and Seven (Miranda and Manzanilla 1984); Chapultepec (Cabrera et al. 1975); the Molino del Rey Monument (Salas 1988); the ex-Convent of San Jerónimo (Ochoa 1980; Pompa 1980); the National Palace (Besso Oberto 1975; Zaldivar 1976, 1987); the Metropolitan Cathedral (Lister and Lister 1982); the old Cathedral (Rodríguez Díez and Sánchez Olvera 1983); the Templo Mayor (López Cervantes 1982a); the Plaza de la Banca Nacionalizada (*Boletín Oficial del INAH* [*BOI*] 1988); the Complejo Hidalgo (González Rul et al. 1984); and several houses located in Mexico City (Cano and Valencia 1989; Carvajal and Valencia 1989; Reina 1989). A few cases of projects that have shared this approach are also found in the southeastern part of Mexico in Chiapas (Beristain 1982, 1985; Gussinyer 1977) and Campeche (Luna 1984, 1985).

The characteristics this group of investigations share include: (I) the recovery of data through salvage projects; (2) the use of archaeological data to corroborate or complement documentary information; (3) databases derived from archaeological excavations which, in a few cases, include survey data and also have been conducted on surface and/or underwater sites; (4) historical archaeological data that have been collected as part of a larger effort to recover and record all archaeological evidence regardless of the period it represents; (5) a focus on the transition from pre-Hispanic to colonial eras, with the major classes of remains consisting of ceramics and burials; (6) an emphasis on the analysis of technological reuse and integration of Indian forms of work during the Spanish colonial period; and (7) the development of innovative classification techniques for archaeological materials. Particular emphasis has been placed on historic ceramics, and studies often have included vessels made in New Spain and those imported from other regions.

Archaeology and Architectural Restoration

Priorities have been set by the State for the protection of buildings dating from the Spanish colonial (1519-1821) and Post-Independence (nationalist) periods (1821–present). Since 1970 a form of restoration-related historical archaeology has enjoyed growing importance in Mexico. Such investigations have followed the example of the explorations of the Palace of Cortés in Cuernavaca, Morelos (Angulo 1979; *BOI* 1974; Charlton et al. 1987).

As with the previous group of investigations, examples of restoration-related archaeological projects are abundant in Mexico City. Examples include: the ex-Convent of San Jerónimo (Carrasco 1979, 1981; Fournier 1985a, 1985b; García Moll and Juárez 1985; Juárez 1987, 1989; Juárez and García Moll 1984; Pérez Castro 1981), the Acequia Real (M. Pérez Campa 1982, pers. comm.), the Church of Santa Teresa La Antigua (Hernández 1982), the Academy of San Carlos (Hernández and López 1987), the House of the Counts of Heras Soto, the House of the Marquises of Aguayo, the ex-College of Christ, the Tobacco Factory of the Ciudadela, the ex-Archbishop's Palace, the ex-College of San Joaquín (Martínez Muriel 1988), the House of the Apartado (Hernández 1987), the Chapel of San Antonio, the ex-Convent of Capuchinas, other houses of the central historic district as well as those found in nearby towns, such as Milpa Alta (*BOI* 1988). Investigations also include the recent work at the ex-College of Tepotzotlán (Martínez Muriel 1988).

Similar projects have been undertaken in other states within the Republic, including those focused on the ex-Convent of Huejotzingo (Merlo 1980–81) and the ex-Convent of Tecamachalco, Puebla (Chico et al. 1982). There are also investigations that have taken place at Mitla, Oaxaca (Robles García et al. 1987); the House of Montejo, Yucatán (Siller 1985); the ex-Convent of Oxolotán, Tabasco (Bueno et al. 1987); the ex-Convent of San Agustín (Ruiz 1985); and the old Hermitage of Rosario (Ferreira 1985). The last two sites are found in Veracruz. The characteristics shared by these investigations include at least six traits.

First, archaeological investigations have been subordinated to the needs and interests of restoration professionals, which has been true in projects whose principal goals have been the rehabilitation of buildings, as well as programs aimed at salvaging data from a building, or portion of a building, that was to be destroyed.

Second, in each case documentary evidence has served as the justification for the restoration of the building. It has also been used to provide technical information for the project archaeologists. Archaeological data serve to complement the historic information about building characteristics.

Third, the studies are limited to a single site component (that is to say, a single building). Investigations have all employed excavation.

Fourth, the descriptive reports on building construction phases emphasize the historic-era deposits, so that the study of buried pre-Hispanic features becomes a goal of secondary importance. The excavations are limited in scope to detecting architectural evidence, to the detriment of complete recovery and the careful study of all aspects of the archaeological record.

Fifth, emphasis has been placed on the study of architectural transformations and the identification of activity areas in buildings. Only limited interest has been shown in socioeconomic forces that led to the construction of the structures. The object of study is the edifice itself, not the society which built it. The study of architectural evidence and the general organization of space has been used to identify activity areas. Little consideration has been given to other archaeological evidence such as artifact distributions.

Finally, the broader study of archaeological material generally has become secondary to the analysis of architectural data. This trend is particularly notable in the incomplete or deficient recording given to information about nonarchitectural features of an archaeological context and the elements forming it. In a few cases studies of recovered artifacts have been used to make inferences about socioeconomic processes independent of the initial restoration objectives of this group of archaeological projects (Charlton et al. 1987; Fournier 1985a, 1985b).

Study of Socioeconomic Processes

After 1970 a third group of historical archaeological investigations is apparent in Mexico. This alternative approach is still emerging but has already established itself as an integral part of scientific archaeology. The major research goal of this approach has been to explain socioeconomic processes that have occurred since the time of European contact. Projects have considered sites and data dating from the Spanish colonial period to the present.

Unfortunately these new-style investigations have received little institutional support. Instead they have been instigated and perpetuated as a result of the particular interest of individual archaeologists. The methodological complexity of the broader study of socioeconomic contexts has made these research efforts more difficult and has delayed the general progress of this kind of social science project. Such studies have had to generate a database to describe, interpret, and explain the archaeological evidence.

The new-style investigations have taken place throughout Mexico. Examples of the approach include work conducted in Puebla and Tlaxcala (Muller 1970, 1973a, 1973b, 1978, 1981); Mixquic, Distrito Federal (Besso Oberto 1977); Sonora (Braniff 1986; Fournier and Fournier 1989); Villarrica and Antigua, Veracruz (J. Hernández, pers. comm.); Mezquital Valley, Hidalgo (Fournier and Pérez Campa n.d.; López Aguilar and Trinidad 1987; López Aguilar et al. 1988; Restrepo 1988); Las Trincheras (Barrera Rubio 1985); and the Hacienda Tabí, Yucatán (Benavides 1985).

The investigations found in this group are characterized by the following additional traits. First, most projects represent formal archaeological enterprises with an initial emphasis on the pre-Hispanic era. Historical archaeological investigations are undertaken as an adjunct to pre-Hispanic studies. In some cases the projects begin as independent inquiries devoted to sites dating from the Historic period, or as an aspect of an integrated interdisciplinary research approach that includes the historic era. Second, documentary data are used to set up working hypotheses. The dialectical relationship between material and documentary evidence is used to explain socioeconomic processes. Third, most investigations have been regional studies. A few have been restricted to a single site. Projects generally combine survey, surface collecting, and excavation. Fourth, the projects have led to the creation of systematic descriptions of historic sites and overall settlement pattern. Fifth, emphasis has been placed on the explanation of ethnic social interaction, as well as processes related to production, distribution, exchange, and consumption. Last, the projects have produced classification techniques suited to all types of historical materials, including modern-day objects.

Conclusions

From the analysis of cases presented here it can be seen that the goals of the overwhelming majority of projects carried out in historic sites in Mexico have been limited. Most have involved the study of colonial architecture and, in the best of cases, the limited analysis of recovered artifacts. The material culture investigations have emphasized ceramics. Although a scientific interest has emerged in connection with historical archaeology, many forces have insured that such an approach would remain on the fringes of the field's principal advances.

The above description of the present state of Mexican historical archaeology also indicates that several different approaches are being used by researchers in their investigation of sites. Few have arrived at a clear idea of the content and the essence of a scientific historical archaeology. Such an approach would include archaeological projects that involve the analysis of broad sociocultural processes and the use of supporting data drawn from the documentary record. It would combine techniques of historical and archaeological research. To date, a true bond between archaeological and historical data has not been achieved.

The authors consider it indispensable that in the future researchers define historical archaeology not as an obscure subfield, but as an integral part of the broader discipline of archaeology as a social science. The only difference between the study of historic sites and other archaeological research is the additional information provided by documentary data. Therefore the goals of historical archaeology must be conceived of in terms of the study of social processes associated with the rise and consolidation of the capitalist mode of production and the development of socioeconomic forms under this framework. The focus of this research remains the surviving material evidence.

Finally, it is essential that a new policy insure the participation of historical archaeologists in research institutions, which will be required to create adequate conditions for the development of appropriate programs and projects, as well as to break the isolation imposed on those archaeologists interested in historical archaeology.

Perspectives of Historical Archaeology in Mexico

Although the panorama of the state of Mexican historical archaeology presented here seems somewhat bleak, there are contributions that have, and could be, significant for the overall development of scientific historical archaeology. These include: (1) the completion of systematic descriptions of the material culture of the Spanish colonial and Post-Independence periods; (2) the explanation of distribution patterns of archaeological material in terms of socioeconomic transformations that are not always evident in historical data; and (3) the identification of material correlates of the impact of the Spanish conquest and the imposition of foreign ways of life on Indian societies.

In regards to the support that could be given by the State to the development of scientific research projects in historical archaeology, it is unlikely that the government will increase its present limited subsidies. This policy seems to be linked to the fact that inferences obtained from historical archaeology studies might produce an objective view of current social and political problems. If this happened then the official version of history might be brought into question. The support of such projects could work against the program of ideological manipulation that the State promotes through official programs devoted to archaeology and history.

An exception to the above limitations for government support can be seen in cases that involve underwater sites. As a result of recent conflicts over the salvaging of shipwrecks from the Gulf of Mexico, many people are conscious of the need to protect underwater resources as part of the national cultural heritage. They have demanded that government officials insure their safekeeping. Unfortunately this change in attitude does not necessarily guarantee support for the scientific investigation of underwater sites.

Finally, historical archaeology undertaken as part of restoration and salvage projects *could* adopt more scientific characteristics. To accomplish this aim, investigators will have to do away with the idea that buildings should be studied as isolated cases. Instead they must adopt goals linked to understanding structures as part of a broad spectrum of material remains that reflect past socioeconomic systems.

Acknowledgments

We are indebted to Anita Cohen-Williams, Paul Farnsworth, Jack Williams, Laurel Cooper, and an anonymous reviewer for their valuable comments. We particularly appreciate the editorial efforts and encouragement of Paul Farnsworth and Jack Williams.

REFERENCES

Andrews, A. P. 1981. Historical Archaeology in Yucatan: A Preliminary Framework. *Historical Archaeology* 15(1):1–18.

Andrews, A. P. and A. Benavides. 1985. Introducción. *Revista Mexicana de Estudios Antropológicos* 31:5–8.

Angulo, J. 1979. *Una visión del Museo Cuahunahuac, Palacio de Cortés: Recompilación Histórico Arqueológica del Proceso de Cambio en el Estado de Morelos.* Mexico City: INAH.

Arana, R. M. and G. Cepeda. 1969. Rescate arqueológico de la Ciudad de México. *Boletín del INAH*, Época 1(30):3–11.

Barnes, M. R. 1978. Mexican Lead-Glazed Earthenwares. In *Spanish Colonial Frontier Research*, H. F. Dobyns (ed.), pp. 92–110. Spanish Borderlands Research No. 1. Albuquerque: Center for Anthropological Studies.

Barrera Rubio, A. 1985. Arquitectura militar en un sitio del Yucatán colonial. *Revista Mexicana de Estudios Antropológicos* 31:29–36.

Benavides, A. 1985. Notas sobre la arqueología histórica de la Hacienda Tabí, Yucatán. *Revista Mexicana de Estudios Antropológicos* 31:43–58.

Beristain, F. 1982. La iglesia colonial del pueblo de Osumacinta, Chiapas. Unpublished B.A. thesis, ENAH, Mexico City.

Beristain, F. 1985. La iglesia colonial de Osumacinta, Chiapas. *Revista Mexicana de Estudios Antropológicos* 31:101–120.

Besso Oberto, H. 1975. Excavaciónes arqueológicas en el Palacio Nacional. *Boletín del INAH*, Época 2(14):3–24.

Besso Oberto, H. 1977. Arqueología histórica (un paradigma de investigación). Unpublished B.A. thesis, ENAH, Mexico City.

Boletín del INAH. 1974. *Boletín del INAH*, Época 2(8):41–50.

Boletín Oficial del INAH (BOI). 1988. *Antropología, Boletín Oficial del INAH*, Nueva Época, 20.

Borg, B. 1975. Archaeological Whitewares of the Teotihuacan Valley, Mexico. Unpublished M.A. thesis, Department of Anthropology, University of Iowa.

Braniff, B. 1986. La frontera protohistórica Pima-Opata en Sonora, México: Proposiciónes arqueológicas preliminares. Unpublished Ph.D. dissertation, UNAM, Mexico City.

Bueno, R., L. Ledesma, and R. Cruz. 1987. Proyecto Oxolotán. Manuscript in the Archivo Técnico de la Dirección de Monumentos Prehispánicos del INAH, Mexico City.

Cabrera, R., M. A. Cervantes, and F. Solís. 1975. Excavaciónes en Chapultepec, México, D.F. *Boletín del INAH*, Época 2(15):35–46.

Cano, G. and D. Valencia. 1989. Colegio de Cristo y los materiales detectados que se interrelacionan con la nómina de loceros poblanos. *Notas Mesoamericanas* 11: 207–219.

Carballal, M. and M. Flores 1984. Proyecto Metro: Linea 5. *Boletín del Consejo de Arqueología, 1984.* INAH, Mexico City.

Carrasco, R. 1979. Arqueología Colonial en el ex-Convento de San Jerónimo. *Boletín de Monumentos Históricos* 1:55–64.

Carrasco, R. 1981. Arqueología y arquitectura en el ex-Convento de San Jerónimo. Unpublished B.A. thesis, ENAH, Mexico City.

Carvajal, A. and D. Valencia. 1989. La casa de talavera. *Notas Mesoamericanas* 11: 229–245.

Charlton, T. H. 1972. *Post-Conquest Developments in the Teotihuacan Valley, Mexico. Part 1, Excavations.* Iowa City: Office of the State Archaeologist.

Charlton, T. H. 1979a. Historical Archaeology in the Valley of Mexico. *Actes du XLII Congrès International des Américanistes* 8:21–33. Paris.

Charlton, T. H. 1979b. An Archaeological Perspective on Culture Contact and Culture Change: The Basin of Mexico, 1521–1821. *Memorias de la XV Mesa Redonda de la Sociedad Mexicana de Antropología, Guanajuato*, pp. 247–254. Mexico City.

Charlton, T. H., P. Fournier, J. Hernández, and C. Otis-Charlton. 1987. Estudios de materiales arqueológicos del período histórico, El Palacio de Cortés, Cuernavaca, Morelos. Manuscript in the Archivo Técnico de la Dirección de Monumentos Prehispánicos del INAH, Mexico City.

Chico, P. A., J. A. Siller, G.A. Huslz, J. González, and J. Zavala. 1982. *Teoría y práctica en la conservación de un monumento: El-convento de Tecamachalco, Puebla.* Mexico City: INAH.

Di Peso, C. 1959. El enfoque arqueohistórico. *El Esplendor del México Antiguo* 2:671–689.

Di Peso, C., J. B. Rinaldo, and G. J. Fenner. 1974. *Casas Grandes: A Fallen Trading Center of the Gran Chichimeca, Vol. 8.* Dragoon and Flagstaff, AZ: The Amerind Foundation.

Ferreira, F. 1985. La reivindicación del tiempo: Antecedentes para una investigación en la antigua Ermita del Rosario. *Trabajos de investigación en Monumentos Históricos*, pp. 55–69. Mexico City: INAH.

Fournier, P. 1985a. Evidencias arqueológicas de la importación de cerámica en México con base en los materiales del ex-Convento de San Jerónimo. Unpublished B.A. thesis, ENAH, Mexico City.

Fournier, P. 1985b. Arqueología histórica en la Ciudad de México. *Boletín de Antropología Americana* 11:27–31.

Fournier, P. and M. L. Fournier. 1989. Materiales históricos de misiónes, presidios, reales, rancherías y haciendas de la región Pima-Opata de Sonora. *Cuaderno de Trabajo 7.* Dirección de Monumentos Prehispánicos del INAH, Mexico City.

Fournier, P. and M. Pérez Campa. n.d. Fuentes e indicadores históricos acerca de los Otomíes. On file with the authors.

García Moll, R. and D. Juárez 1985. San Jerónimo: Un ejemplo de arqueología histórica. *Antropología, Boletín Oficial del INAH,* Nueva Época, 6:18.

Gasco, J. 1987. Cacao and the Economic Integration of Native Society in Colonial Soconusco, New Spain. Unpublished Ph.D. dissertation, Department of Anthropology, University of California, Santa Barbara.

Goggin, J. M. 1968. Spanish Majolica in the New World. *Yale Publications in Anthropology,* No. 72. New Haven: Yale University.

González Rul, 1988. *La cerámica de Tlatelolco.* Mexico City: INAH.

González Rul, F., J. A. Pérez, J. M. Hernández, and M. L. Moreno. 1984. Exploraciónes arqueológicas en el Nuevo Edificio del Banco de México. *Boletín del Consejo de Arqueología, 1984.* Mexico City: INAH.

Gussinyer, J. 1969. El salvamento arqueológico en las excavaciones del "Metro" en la Ciudad de México. *Boletín Bibliográfico de Antropología Americana* 32:89–96.

Gussinyer, J. 1977. Influencias precolombinas en la distribución y desarrollo de la primera arquitectura colonial en el centro de Chiapas. *Anales del INAH,* Época 8a, 1(55):5–34.

Hernández, E. 1982. Excavaciónes en el ex-Convento de Sta. Teresa la Antigua. In *El Templo Mayor: Excavaciónes y estudios,* E. Matos (ed.), pp. 283–292. Mexico City: INAH.

Hernández, E. 1987. Una escultura azteca encontrada en el centro de la Ciudad de México. *Antropología, Boletín Oficial del INAH,* Nueva Época 13:15–19.

Hernández, E. and J. A. López. 1987. La capilla del Hospital del Amor de Dios, datos arqueológicos. *Revista Mexicana de Estudios Antropológicos* 33(2):391–408.

Jones, D. M. 1980. *The Archaeology of Nineteenth Century Haciendas and Ranchos of Otumba and Apan, Basin of Mexico.* Research Report No. 2. Mesoamerican Research Colloquium, Department of Anthropology, University of Iowa, Iowa City.

Júarez, D. 1987. Los templos del ex-Convento de San Jerónimo. *Revista Mexicana de Estudios Antropológicos* 32(2):387–392.

Júarez, D. 1989. *San Jerónimo: Un ejemplo de arqueología histórica.* Colección Científica del INAH, Mexico City.

Júarez, D. and R. García Moll. 1984. *Ex-Convento de San Jerónimo, México, D.F. Planos, cortes, alzados, detalles arquitectónicos y constructivos.* Mexico City: INAH.

Lister, F. C. and R. H. Lister. 1974. Majolica in Colonial Spanish America. *Historical Archaeology* 8:17–52.

Lister, F. C. and R. H. Lister. 1975. Non-Indian Ceramics from the Mexico City Subway. *El Palacio* 81(2):24–48.

Lister, F. C. and R. H. Lister. 1976. Distribution of Mexican Majolica along the Northern Borderlands. *Collected Papers in Honor of Marjorie Ferguson Lambert, Papers of the Archaeological Society of New Mexico* 3:113–140.

Lister, F. C. and R. H. Lister. 1978. The First Mexican Majolicas: Imported and Locally Produced. *Historical Archaeology* 12:1–24.

Lister, F. C. and R. H. Lister. 1982. Sixteenth-Century Majolica Pottery in the Valley of Mexico. *Anthropological Papers of the University of Arizona*, No. 39. Tucson: University of Arizona Press.

Lister, F. C. and R. H. Lister. 1984. The Potter's Quarter of Colonial Puebla, Mexico. *Historical Archaeology* 18:87–102.

Lister, F. C. and R. H. Lister. 1987. *Andalusian Ceramics in Spain and New Spain*. Tucson: University of Arizona Press.

López Aguilar, F., P. Fournier, and C. Paz. 1988. Contexto arqueológico y contexto momento: El caso de la alfarería Otomí del Valle del Mezquital. *Boletín de Antropología Americana* 17:99–131.

López Aguilar, F. and M. A. Trinidad 1987. Proyecto Valle del Mezquital: Informe de la primera temporada 1985–1986. Manuscript in the Archivo Técnico de la Dirección de Monumentos Prehispánicos del INAH, Mexico City.

López Cervantes, G. 1974. Porcelana Europea en México. *Boletín del INAH*, Época 2(9): 49–52.

López Cervantes, G. 1976a *Cerámica colonial en la Ciudad de México*. Mexico City: INAH.

López Cervantes, G. 1976b. Cerámica española en la Ciudad de México. *Boletín del INAH, Época* 2(18):33–38.

López Cervantes, G. 1977. Porcelana oriental en la Nueva España. *Anales del INAH*, Época 8a, 1(55):65–82.

López Cervantes, G. 1979. Notas para el estudio del vidrio en la nueva españa. *Cuadernos de Trabajo del Departamento de Prehistoria*, No. 19. Mexico City: INAH.

López Cervantes, G. 1982a. Informe preliminar sobre materiales coloniales. In *El Templo Mayor: Excavációnes y estudios*, E. Matos (ed.), pp. 255–282. Mexico City: INAH.

López Cervantes, G. 1982b. Algunos motivos decorativos de la Mayólica Azul sobre blanco novohispana. *Notas de la Ceramoteca*, No. 8. Museo Nacional de Antropología, INAH, Mexico City.

López Wario, A. and F. Ortuño. 1984. Proyecto Metro: Línea 4. *Boletín del Consejo de Arqueología*.

Luna, P. 1984. Resumen del Proyecto Cayo Nuevo en la Sonda de Campeche, México. *Boletín del Consejo de Arqueología 1984*.

Luna P. 1985. El arrecife Cayo Nuevo, Campeche, y la recuperación del cañón de bronce más antiguo de América. *Revista Mexicana de Estudios Antropológicos* 31:59–72.

Martínez Muriel, A. 1988. La arqueología histórica del INAH. *Antropología, Boletín Oficial del INAH, Nueva Época*, 22:5.

Merlo, E. 1980–81. Informe de los trabajos arqueológicos en el Proyecto Huejotzingo, Centro Regional de Puebla, INAH, Mexico. Manuscript in the Archivo Técnico de la Dirección de Monumentos Prehispánicos, Mexico City.

Miranda, F. A. and R. Manzanilla. 1984. Proyecto Metro: Línea 7. *Boletín del Consejo de Arqueología.*

Muller, F. 1970. La cerámica de Cholula. In *Proyecto Cholula,* I. Marquina (ed.), pp. 129–142. Mexico City: INAH.

Muller, F. 1973a. El origen de los barrios de Cholula. *Boletín del INAH,* Época 2(5):35–42.

Muller, F. 1973b. Efectos de la conquista española sobre la cerámica prehispánica de Cholula. *Anales del INAH,* Época 7, 3(51):97–110.

Muller, F. 1978. *La alfarería de Cholula.* Mexico City: INAH.

Muller, F. 1981. *Estudio de la cerámica hispánica y moderna de Tlaxcala-Puebla.* Mexico City: INAH.

Noguera, E. 1934. Estudio de la cerámica encontrada en el sitio donde estaba el Templo Mayor de México. *Anales del Museo Nacional de Arqueología, Historia y Etnografía,* Época 5, 2:267–282.

Ochoa, P. 1980. Materiales arqueológicos recuperados en las excavaciónes de la iglesia de San Jerónimo, D.F., Temporada 1976. *Sociedad Mexicana de Antropología, XVI Mesa Redonda* 2:31–40.

Olvera, J. 1978. The Ceramics of the Conquerors. Paper presented at the 9th annual meeting of the Society for Historical Archaeology, San Antonio, TX.

Pérez Castro, G. 1981. "Arqueología Monacal": Un caso en la Ciudad de México, ex-Convento de San Jerónimo de los siglos XVI al XIX. Unpublished B.A. thesis, ENAH, Mexico City.

Pompa, J. A. 1980. La eglesia del ex-Convento de San Jerónimo, D.F.: Aspectos de la exploración 1976. *Sociedad Mexicana de Antropología, XVI Mesa Redonda* 2:15–23.

Reina, M. 1989. Estudio de materiales de terrados de una de las casas de barrio, localizados en la nómina de loceros poblanos. *Notas Mesoamericanas* 11:220–228.

Restrepo, C. 1988. *La evangelización a través del convento de Ixmiquilpan: Un caso de arqueología de sitios coloniales.* (Tesis de Licenciatura), ENAH, Mexico City.

Robles García, N., M. L. Magadán, and A. Moreira. 1987. *Reconstrucción colonial de Mitla, Oaxaca.* Mexico City: INAH.

Rodríguez Díez, A. and L. I. Sánchez Olvera. 1983. Avance del proyecto arqueológico de la Catedral Metropolitana. Manuscript at the Archivo de la Subcomisión de Admisión del INAH, Mexico City.

Ruiz, J. O. 1985. Rescate arqueológico en el ex-Convento de San Agustín. In *Trabajos de investigación en Monumentos Históricos,* pp. 71–77. Mexico City: INAH.

Salas, M. E. 1988. *Molino del Rey: Historia de un monumento.* Mexico City: INAH.

Seifert, D. J. 1975. Archaeological Majolicas of the Teotihuacán Valley. *Actas del XLI Congreso Internacional de Americanistas* 1:238–251.

Seifert, D. J. 1977. Archaeological Majolicas of the Rural Teotihuacán Valley, Mexico. Unpublished Ph.D. dissertation, Department of Anthropology, University of Iowa.

Siller, J. A. 1985. Casa Montejo, Yucatán. *Cuadernos de Arquitectura Virreinal* 1:25–45.

Stark, B. L. 1981. Habitation Sites in the Papaloapan Estuarine Delta: Locational Characteristics. Historical Archaeology 15(1):49–65.

Zaldivar, S. 1976. Palacio Virreynal antes de 1692; Excavaciónes arqueológicas. *Actas del XLI Congreso Internacional de Americanistas* 2:560–570.

Zaldivar. S. 1987. La restauración del Palacio Nacional. Antropología, *Boletín Oficial del INAH*, Nueva Época, 12:3–15.

MARTIN HALL ■
ANN MARKELL

Chapter Nineteen

Historical Archaeology in the Western Cape

The volume from which this article comes is concerned with the archaeology of European colonial expansion into southern Africa and the archaeology of the impact of this expansion on the communities long established here. The contributions in the volume are more particularly focused on the Western Cape, although the issues raised certainly have broader regional implications. Archaeology—as the study of material culture—provides a crucial dimension in understanding colonialism. It is a way of studying both aspects of economy not evident in the documentary record, and the manner in which social relations were mapped out in tangible forms (Hall 1992). The contributions in the volume illustrate and identify some of the major areas of research in the Western Cape.

The Archaeology of Colonialism

The cape was first rounded by Portuguese ships at the end of the 15th century—part of the scramble for the legendary riches of the east. The Portuguese showed little interest in the subcontinent, making occasional landfalls, engaging in desultory conflicts and suffering inevitable shipwrecks (Axelson 1960, 1973; Schoeman 1987; Smith 1986). The east African coastline was more attractive, as Islamic city states indicated the possibilities of wealth from the interior and their harbors were suitable as bases for the final push to the spice islands of Indonesia (Axelson 1973). Later there was the lure of profits from slavery (Alphers 1975; Lovejoy 1983). The English and Dutch were similarly drawn by the immense profits of successful occidental trade (Boxer 1965; Israel 1989). Table Bay was used fairly frequently as

---

This article was originally published in the *South African Archaeological Society Goodwin Series* (1993) 7:3–7.

an anchorage in the 16th and early 17th centuries, and in 1615 a small colony was established in the name of King James on Robben Island (Penn 1992).

In 1647 the Dutch East India ship the *Haarlem* was wrecked on the shores of the bay. Its crew survived by growing vegetables and trading for cattle from the Khoikhoi, and on the basis of the favorable report of this experience, the Council of the Company was persuaded that a small garrison should be provided to look after the needs of their outward bound and return fleets. This was the nucleus of the colonial city of Cape Town (Guelke 1989; Hall 1992; Ross 1985).

At first, there was not much to the cape settlement. However, in 1657 the company decided that some of its employees should be allowed to farm to their own account, and the first lands were granted along the Liesbeeck River (Guelke 1989; Schutte 1989). In the years that followed the new frontier of farmland was pushed back, first to the mountain chain that marked off the hinterland of Table Bay from the rest of the subcontinent, and then on, hundreds of kilometers into the interior.

It is evident that this is deep and fertile ground for archaeological research (Abrahams 1984; Hall and Malan 1991), particularly as modern southern Africa lacks the degree of suburban sprawl and urban renewal characteristic of the sites of early colonial settlement in many other parts of the world. There is a growing appreciation of the potential of this archaeology of colonial settlement, as well as an increasing willingness on the part of architects and developers to employ archaeologists at an early stage in new projects. Cultural Resource Management (CRM) has begun to allow mitigative work ahead of development, providing important information for research projects. Given the diminishing financial support for research at South African universities and museums, it seems likely that CRM will be the growth area for archaeology in the future.

The foundations for contemporary work were laid in the late 1970s and early 1980s. At the University of Cape Town, staff and students began to get involved in projects such as the excavation of fortifications, outposts, and industrial sites (Heckroodt and Saitowitz 1985; Saitowitz 1982; Smith 1980, 1981). The South African Cultural History Museum employed a qualified archaeologist on its staff, leading to a survey of the archaeological potential of Cape Town and specialized studies of particular categories of artifacts (Abrahams 1985, 1987, 1989). The Stellenbosch Museum began a long-term excavation program in Stellenbosch itself (Vos 1980, 1988, 1993).

Later work has been a strengthening and diversification from this early base. An important connection has been with the University of California, Berkeley, initiated by an invitation from the University of Cape Town to James Deetz to lecture in 1984. Through this and subsequent visits Deetz has established a research direction in the eastern cape focusing on the architecture and material culture of British settlers in the 19th century, and on their contact with indigenous communities (Jeppson 1990, 1991; Scott and Deetz 1990; Winer and Deetz 1990, 1991). In parallel with this the Historical Archaeology Research Group was established at UCT, concentrating for the most part on the archaeology of 18th-century Cape Town and its hinterland. This group has excavated a number of major sites (including the Castle—the regional headquarters of the VOC), and has also looked at probate records, architecture and contemporary vernacular styles of building (Behrens 1991; Brink 1990, 1992; Graf 1992; Gribble 1989; Hall 1989, 1991b, 1991c; Hall et al. 1988, 1990, 1993; Irvine 1990; Malan 1990; Seemann 1989, 1992a, 199b; Shepherd 1989; Taylor 1990).

Closely linked with the University of Cape Town have been two projects investigating outlying Dutch period settlements. The first—under the direction of Carmel Schrire from Rutgers University—has led to the excavation of a VOC outpost, now known as Oudepost, founded on the Cape west coast in 1669. The archaeology of this small, often forgotten garrison has opened up the possibility of understanding more of the daily life of ordinary VOC soldiers, as well as the archaeology of their interaction with Khoikhoi herdsmen (Cruz-Uribe and Schrire 1991; Schrire 1987, 1988, 1990; Schrire and Deacon 1989). The second project has been an investigation of Vergelegen—a substantial estate built by a governor of the Cape at the very beginning of the 18th century. Vergelegen held a particular lure for the archaeologist of colonial settlement—a documented, dated, and apparently undisturbed slave lodge (Markell 1991, 1992; Markell et al. 1992). Vergelegen's builder may have been responsible for architectural innovations elsewhere in the early colonial Cape (Brink 1993).

Colonies are, by definition, outliers, connected to metropolitan centers. Europe's discovery of southern Africa was by sea, and throughout the 17th and 18th centuries all contact was via ships that put in to either Cape Town or the east African ports and, later, to Durban. In this situation, maritime archaeology is an important part of establishing a comprehensive archaeology of colonial settlement. Southern Africa's often dangerous shoreline has culled a rich collection of wrecks, although these have been considerably damaged through the years by treasure hunters and salvors who have paid scant respect to context or historical research. In the past few years, this situation has begun to change. A major archaeological study has begun of the *Oosterland*, a Dutch East India Company ship wrecked in Table Bay in 1697, and there have been several surveys to locate underwater sites (Werz 1989, 1990a, 1990b, 1992a, 1992b, 1993; Werz et al. 1991; Werz and Deacon 1992).

Themes

Perhaps because of its comparatively late start as an established subdiscipline, the archaeology of colonial settlement in southern Africa has the unmistakable stamp of the later 20th century; an emphasis on essentially modern themes such as vernacular building, food patterns, everyday material culture, and the lives of ordinary people. But despite the undoubted power of this "democratic archaeology" there are still many challenges to interpretations and a number of different approaches, often overlapping and not always entirely compatible.

One theme has been the study of the archaeology of impact. This approach is based on the concept of frontiers; complex, volatile zones of interaction (Lamar and Thompson 1981). In some cases, colonial vanguards had an impact well ahead of established colonial settlement—for example, sporadic European landfalls in Table Bay before 1652, or missionaries and traders pushing deep into the interior of the subcontinent, or colonial pastoralists with only the most tenuous links with colonial settlements many weeks journey behind them. In other cases, the impact of the frontier was played out long after the main thrust of colonial settlement had passed on by.

Carmel Schrire's excavations have had a major impact on our understanding of the early phases of Dutch East India Company settlement at the Cape. The unpromising heaps of collapsed stone have proved to cover the foundations of rough defensive works and a lodge for the garrison. Excavations have resulted in substantial assemblages of food debris, ceramics and other cultural debris that have survived the passage of time (Cruz-Uribe and Schrire 1991; Schrire and Deacon 1989; Schrire and Meltzer 1992).

Schrire's work, as well as other projects, has also sought evidence of new ways of life from the perspective of indigenous communities. The uppermost levels of occupation sites, sometimes containing artifacts of colonial origin, have often been designated as "disturbed" and not afforded serious study. Rock art sites sometimes have clear representations of hunter-gatherer interactions with European settlers, but again there has been little systematic study of these images (Yates et al. 1993).

Further archaeological research into impact will be vital if the full dimensionality of southern African colonialism is to be developed. However, the texture of colonial impact seems elusive. This may be a function of the nature of archaeological evidence. Material culture understood in conjunction with documentary evidence has a different quality than artefactual assemblages standing alone. At Oudepost, for instance, Carmel Schrire has been able to evoke the spirit of an individual company soldier, represented by mementos such as an ostrich egg engraved with an eastern scene (Schrire 1988). In contrast, the Khoikhoi who visited the outpost— as much individuals as company soldiers—have to be evoked through statistical profiles of formal tools, debitage and Minimum Number of Individual counts for faunal assemblages.

The problem, then, is an unequal distribution of information. For colonial societies, artifacts can often be traced with great precision and may often have been used by people whose names are known. But while leaving us documents that allow us to understand their own behavior in considerable detail, these early colonial settlers more often than not broke the threads that could have connected us with the indigenous communities of southern Africa. Both displacement and incorporation severed the continuity of oral traditions, while derogatory and inaccurate collective descriptions compromised the value of contemporary ethnographic descriptions. Until the archaeology of colonialism can develop ways to counter this methodological inheritance, frontiers will remain unevenly understood.

A second theme is the archaeology of the underclass—a natural consequence of that clarion call of modern historical archaeology—"in small things forgotten" (Deetz 1977). Colonial southern Africa was a slave society from its earliest years until well into the 19th century. The first two boatloads of slaves arrived in Table Bay in 1656, and the subsequent and massive expansion of wheat and vine cultivation depended on slave labor (Armstrong and Worden 1989). By the end of the period of Dutch East India Company control at the Cape, two-thirds of the population of Cape Town were classified as slaves (Ross 1985).

At the same time, people of different legal statuses contributed to the melange that was the bottom end of southern African colonial society. VOC soldiers were drawn from the European peasantry, often vagrant before boarding ship as a last resort. On the farms, overseers (often VOC soldiers hired out from the castle) were almost beneath the notice of estate owners, while the frontier often attracted those with no resources, and no place in town life (Guelke 1989). As a seaport used, at least sporadically, by all European fleets trading with the east, Cape Town attracted a wide variety of transients, deserters and refugees from European poverty. Given this history and diversity, the concept of an "underclass" is more flexible and appropriate than a more specific categorization.

Nevertheless, an archaeological understanding of slavery is a major goal of southern African colonial studies, both for its potential contribution to national history, and because of the opportunities for valuable comparative work with the Americas, Caribbean, and other parts of the colonial world. One project from the volume this chapter originally introduced reported on excavations at the estate of Vergelegen near modern-day Somerset West. This project was specifically designed to search for evidence of slave lifeways.

One unexpected piece of evidence from the Vergelegen slave lodge was a burial of a middle-aged woman beneath the floor (Sealy et al. 1993). The location of the burial, coupled with the rough construction of the coffin, is strong circumstantial evidence that she was a slave. Innovative isotopic analysis of tooth enamel and bone collagen has opened up the possibility of tracing life trajectories in new ways when more burials in sound archaeological contexts are discovered.

At the beginning of the 18th century Cape Town was still a small settlement and Stellenbosch was no more than a cluster of houses around a mill. As the century progressed and the distinction between town and country increased, a set of differences emerged, clearly marked in inventories of household contents, which reflect divergences in room layouts as well as taste (Malan 1990; Woodward 1981, 1982). At some stage—probably in the third decade of the century—a new tradition of elite architecture began to develop. Status was indicated by rigid symmetry in house plan and façade, and owners began to vie with one another for the latest fashion in gable design (Brink 1990, 1992). At present, though, there is little archaeological evidence for this "middle period" in Dutch East India Company rule—a function of sampling that will undoubtedly be corrected by future work. But for the last two decades of the century, by which time Cape Town was a substantial town, there is again rich archaeological evidence for the nature of underclass life.

Examples of this are the backyard areas of houses in central Cape Town—places where servants and slaves were housed, and where small shacks were rented out, often at exorbitant rates. One such backyard was in Bree Street (Hall 1991c). The debris left from the occupation of this site includes the fragments of many hundreds of ceramics and one of the largest faunal assemblages from any archaeological site in southern Africa. It is valuable testimony to the nature of underclass life in the early years of the 19th century.

Less is known about underclass life in rural areas of the 18th- and 19th-century cape. Excavations at *Paradys* in the forests that backed Table Mountain, have resulted in a sequence that covers much of the 18th century, and artifact assemblages left by woodcutters and slaves (Avery 1989; Hall et al. 1993; Smith 1980). Current work by the University of Stellenbosch in rural areas on both sides of the Hottentots Holland Mountains may provide information on rural hierarchies though the study of farm layouts, but the results of this research are not yet available (C. Rademeyer-De Kock, pers. comm.). Antonia Malan's research on material culture as revealed in household inventories strongly suggests a distinction between town and country (Malan 1990); a divergence borne out by historians of slavery at the Cape (Ross 1985; Worden 1985). It seems likely that the archaeology of the colonial countryside will have many interesting stories to tell. But, despite the abundance of most of those sites that have been excavated, there remain problems in seeing the evidence for underclass life in colonial southern Africa through the archaeological lense. There are very few traces of ethnic identity in those "small things forgotten" in places like the backyard of Bree Street or the outbuildings of Vergelegen; a few unusual potsherds, a handful of cowrie shells, a few alien coins. Overwhelmingly, the material culture used by the underclass was the material culture of their masters, passed down when no longer fashionable, bought in cheap job lots or, perhaps, stolen when the opportunity arose (Hall 1991b, 1991c, 1992). Where are the "transcripts of resistance" anticipated in the work of James Scott (1990)? Certainly, slave owners, company officials, merchants, and other members of the affluent colonial elite were scared to the point of paranoia about the possibility of rebellion against their domination. But where is the evidence that factions in the underclass organized their identities around shared tastes and categories of possession? An optimistic implication is that archaeologists need a more sophisticated set of methodologies to trace the outlines of identity and resistance; a pessimistic reading of work so far could be that such outlines are not preserved to be found.

REFERENCES

Abrahams, G. 1984. The Development of Historical Archaeology at the Cape, South Africa. *Bulletin of the South African Cultural History Museum* 5:20–23.

Abrahams, G. 1985. The Archaeological Potential of Central Cape Town. *Munger Africana Library Notes* 1–114.

Abrahams, G. 1987. Seventeenth and Eighteenth Century Glass Bottles Excavated from Fort de Goede Hoop, Cape Town. *Annals of the South African Cultural History Museum* 1(1):1–38.

Abrahams, G. 1989. The Excavated Underground Channel at Bertram House. *Bulletin of the South African Cultural History Museum* 10:17–27.

Alphers, E. 1975. *Ivory and Slaves in East Central Africa: Changing Patterns of International Trade in the Later Nineteenth Century.* London: Heinemann.

Armstrong, J. and N. Worden. 1989. The Slaves, 1652–1834. In *The Shaping of South African Society, 1652–1840*, R. Elphick and H. Giliomee, H. (eds.), pp. 109–183. Cape Town: Maskew Miller Longman.

Avery, D. 1989. Remarks Concerning Vertebrate Faunal Remains from the Main House at Paradise. *South African Archaeological Bulletin* 44:114–116.

Axelson, E. 1960. *Portuguese in Southeast Africa, 1600–1700.* Johannesburg: Witwatersrand University Press.

Axelson, E. 1973. *Portuguese in Southeast Africa, 1488–1600.* Cape Town: Struik.

Behrens, J. 1991. Bo-Kaap Architecture: A Critique of Structuralist Theory. Unpublished B.A. thesis, University of Cape Town.

Boxer, C. R. 1965. *The Dutch Seaborne Empire, 1600–1800.* London: Hutchinson.

Brink, L. Y. 1990. The Voorhuis as a Central Element in Early Cape Houses. *Social Dynamics* 16(1):38–54.

Brink, L. Y. 1992. Places of Discourse and Dialogue: A Study in the Material Culture of the Cape during the Rule of the Dutch East India Company, 1652–1795. Unpublished Ph.D. dissertation, University of Cape Town.

Brink, L. Y. 1993. The Octagon: An Icon of Willem Adriaan van der Stel's Aspirations? *South African Archaeological Society Goodwin Series* 7:92–97.

Cruz-Uribe, K. and C. Schrire. 1991. Analysis of Faunal Remains from Oudepost 1, An Early Outpost of the Dutch East India Company, Cape Province. *South African Archaeological Bulletin* 46:92–106.

Deetz, J. 1977. *In Small Things Forgotten: The Archaeology of Early American Life*. Garden City, NY: Anchor Press.

Graf, O.H.T. 1992. Clay Tobacco Pipes from Archaeological Sites from the Cape Province, South Africa. Unpublished B.A. thesis, University of Cape Town.

Gribble, J. 1989. Verlorenvlei Vernacular: A Structuralist Analysis of Sandveld Folk Architecture. Unpublished M.A. thesis, University of Cape Town.

Guelke, L. 1989. Freehold Farmers and Frontier Settlers, 1657–1780. In *The Shaping of South African Society, 1652-1840*, R. Elphick and H. Giliomee (eds.), pp. 66–108. Cape Town: Maskew Miller Longman.

Hall, M. 1989. *Block 11 Cape Town. An Archaeological Assessment*. Archaeological Contracts Office, University of Cape Town,

Hall, M. 1991a. High and Low in the Townscapes of Dutch South America and South Africa: The Dialectics of Material Culture. *Social Dynamics* 17(2):41–75.

Hall, M. 1991b. *Archaeological Work at Sea Street, Cape Town*. Cape Town: Archaeological Contracts Office, University of Cape Town.

Hall, M. 1991c. A Study in the Archaeology of Early Colonial Settlement: Cape Town in the Seventeenth, Eighteenth and Early Nineteenth Centuries. Unpublished report to the Human Sciences Research Council.

Hall, M. 1992. People in a Changing Urban Landscape: Excavating Cape Town. Inaugural Lecture, University of Cape Town.

Hall, M., L. Y. Brink, and A. Malan. 1988. Onrust 87/1: An Early Colonial Farm Complex in the Western Cape. *South African Archaeological Bulletin* 43:91–99.

Hall, M., D. Halkett, P. Huigen van Beek, and J. Klose. 1990. 'A Stone Wall Out of the Earth that Thundering Cannon Cannot Destroy'? Bastion and Moat at the Castle, Cape Town. *Social Dynamics* 16(1):22–37.

Hall, M. and A. Malan. 1991. Archaeology and Conservation in the Urban Environment: The Example of Cape Town. In *Proceedings of the National Urban Conservation Symposium*, D. Japha and V. Japha (eds.), pp. 130–133. Cape Town: Oakville Press.

Hall, M., D. Miller, and J. Moore. 1993. Provenance Studies for Stone from the Castle Gateway, Cape Town. *South African Journal of Science*. Forthcoming.

Hall, M., A. Malan, S. Amann, L. Honeyman, T. Kiser, and G. Ritchie. 1993. The Archaeology of Paradise. *South African Archeological Society Goodwin Series* 7:40–58.

Heckroodt, R. and S. Saitowitz. 1985. Characterization of Bottles Manufactured at the Cape Glass Company, Glencairn, circa 1904. *South African Archaeological Bulletin* 142:94–95.

Irvine, M. 1990. Scratching the Surface: The Archaeology of 56 Dorp Street, BoKaap. Unpublished B.A. thesis, University of Cape Town.

Israel, J. 1989. *Dutch Primacy in World Trade, 1585-1740*. Oxford: Clarendon Press, Oxford.

Jeppson, P. 1990. "The way we see it": Images of Eastern Cape History: The History Behind, Within, and Outside a New Culture History Display. Paper presented at the meeting of the Southern African Museums Association, Pietermaritzburg, South Africa.

Jeppson, P. 1991. Colonial Systems and Indigenous Responses: Material Expressions at Farmerfield Mission. Paper presented at annual meeting of the Society for Historical Archaeology, Richmond, Virginia.

Lamar, H. and L. Thompson (eds.). 1981. *The Frontier in History: North America and Southern Africa Compared.* New Haven: Yale University Press.

Lovejoy, P. 1983. *Transformations in Slavery: A History of Slavery in Africa.* Cambridge: Cambridge University Press.

Malan, A. 1990. The Archaeology of Probate Inventories. *Social Dynamics* 16(1):1–10.

Markell, A. 1991. Walls of Isolation: The Garden Fortress of Governor Willem Adriaan van der Stel. Paper presented at the annual meeting of the Society for Historical Archaeology, Richmond, Virginia.

Markell, A. 1992. Excavations at Vergelegen: The Rural Cape in the Eighteenth and Nineteenth Centuries. Paper presented at the Conference of the Southern African Association of Archaeologists, Cape Town.

Markell, A., M. Hall, and C. Schrire. 1992. The Historical Archaeology of Vergelegen, An Early Farmstead at the Cape of Good Hope. Unpublished manuscript.

Penn, N. 1992. *From Penguins to Prisoners: Robben Island, 1488–1805.* University of Cape Town, Department of Adult Education and ExtraMural Studies, Cape Town.

Ross, R. 1985. Cape Town (1750–1850): Synthesis in the Dialectic of Continents. In *Colonial Cities: Essays on Urbanism in a Colonial Context,* R. Ross and G. Telkamp (eds.), pp. 105–122. Dordrecht, South Africa: Martinus Nijhoff.

Saitowitz, S. 1982. Excavations at De Posthuys. Department of Archaeology, University of Cape Town.

Schoeman, S. 1987. Argeologiese & kultuurbestuursverslag. Die Posboom museumkompleks, Mosselbaai. Department of Archaeology, University of Stellenbosch, South Africa.

Schrire, C. 1987. The Historical Archaeology of Colonial-Indigenous Interactions in South Africa: Proposed Research at Oudepost 1, Cape. In *Papers in the Prehistory of the Western Cape, South Africa,* J. Parkington and M. Hall (eds.), pp. 424–461. Oxford: British Archaeological Reports.

Schrire, C. 1988. The Historical Archaeology of the Impact of Colonialism in 17th-century South Africa. *Antiquity* 62:214–225.

Schrire, C. 1990. Excavating Archives at Oudepost 1, Cape. *Social Dynamics* 16(1): 11–21.

Schrire, C. and J. Deacon. 1989. The Indigenous Artifacts from Oudepost 1, A Colonial Outpost of the VOC at Saldahna Bay, Cape. *South African Archaeological Bulletin* 150:105–113.

Schrire, C. and L. Meltzer. 1992. Coins, Gaming Counters and a Bale Seal from Oudepost, Cape. *South African Archaeological Bulletin* 156:104–107.

Schutte, G. 1989. Company and Colonists at the Cape, 1652–1795. In *The Shaping of South African Society, 1652–1840,* R. Elphick and H. Giliomee (eds.), pp. 283–323. Cape Town: Maskew Miller Longman.

Scott, J. 1990. *Domination and the Arts of Resistance: Hidden Transcripts.* New Haven: Yale University Press.

Scott, P. and J. Deetz. 1990. Building, Furnishing and Social Change in Early Victorian Grahamstown. *Social Dynamics* 16(1):76–89.

Sealy, J. C., A. G. Morris, R. Armstrong, A. Markell, and C. Schrire. 1993. An Historic Skeleton from the Slave Lodge at Vergelegen. *South African Archeological Society Goodwin Series* 7:84–91.

Seemann, U. 1989. The Amsterdam Battery: A Short History of the Amsterdam Battery during the Dutch and English Periods and An Account of its Excavation. Unpublished B.Sc. thesis, University of Cape Town.

Seemann, U. 1992a. The Hout Bay Forts, 1781–1829. A Report prepared for the Hout Bay Museum. Department of Archaeology, University of Cape Town.

Seemann, U. 1992b. The Amsterdam Battery: A Late 18th century Dutch Military Installation in Table Bay. *South African Field Archaeology* 1(2):72–79.

Shepherd, N. 1989. Reading the Past: Archaeology and the Residency, Simon's Town. Unpublished B.A. thesis, University of Cape Town.

Smith, A. B. 1980. Paradise: Report on Excavations, 1980. Department of Archaeology, University of Cape Town.

Smith, A. B. 1981. The French Period at the Cape, 1781–1783: A Report on Excavations at Conway Redoubt, Constantia Nek. *Military History Journal* 5(3):107–113.

Smith, A. B. 1986. Excavations at Plettenberg Bay, South Africa, of the Camp Site of the Survivors of the Wreck of the São Goncalo, 1630. *International Journal of Nautical Archaeology and Underwater Exploration* 15:53–63.

Taylor, M. 1990. The Historical Archaeology of the Verlorenvlei: The Site of Verlorenvlei Midden. Unpublished B.A. thesis, University of Cape Town.

Vos, H. 1980. Excavating our Colonial Past. *South African Museums Association Bulletin* 14(1–2):354–356.

Vos, H. 1988. Schreuderhuis: An Historical-Archaeological Reevaluation. Paper presented at the Conference of the Southern African Association of Archaeologists.

Vos, H. 1993. An Historical Archaeological Perspective of Colonial Stellenbosch, 1680–1860. Unpublished M.A. thesis, University of Stellenbosch.

Werz, B. E. J. S. 1989. Saving a Fragment of the Underwater Heritage: A Multi-faceted Approach. *Cabo: Yearbook of the Historical Society of Cape Town* 4:13–18.

Werz, B. E. J. S. 1990a. A Maritime Archaeological Project in Table Bay. *South African Archaeological Bulletin* 45:121.

Werz, B. E. J. S. 1990b. A Preliminary Step to Protect South Africa's Undersea Heritage. *International Journal of Nautical Archaeology* 19(4):335–337.

Werz, B. E. J. S. 1992a. The Excavation of the Oosterland in Table Bay: The First Systematic Exercise in Maritime Archaeology in Southern Africa. *South African Journal of Science* 88:85–90.

Werz, B. E. J. S. 1992b. Tafelbaai gee sy geheime prys. 'n histories argeologiese ondersoek van die VOC-skip *Oosterland. Huguenot Society of South Africa Bulletin* 29:54–61.

Werz, B. E. J. S. 1993. Maritime Archaeological Project Table Bay: Aspects of the First Field Season. *South African Archaeological Society Goodwin Series* 7:33–39.

Werz, B. and J. Deacon. 1992. *Operation Sea Eagle: Final Report on a Survey of Shipwrecks around Robben Island.* Cape Town: National Monuments Council.

Werz, B., J. Lee-Thorp, and D. Miller. 1991. Amber Finds from Table Bay. *International Journal of Nautical Archaeology* 20(3):247–249.

Winer, M. and J. Deetz. 1990. The Transformation of British Culture in the Eastern Cape, 1820–1860. *Social Dynamics* 16(1):55–75.

Woodward, C. 1981. Domestic Arrangements at the Cape as Recorded in the Inventories for 1709–1712. *Restorica* 10:12–14.

Woodward, C. 1982. The Interior of the Cape House, 1670–1714. Unpublished M.A. thesis, University of Pretoria.

Worden, N. 1985. *Slavery in Dutch South Africa.* Cambridge: Cambridge University Press.

Yates, R., A. Manhire, and J. Parkington. 1993. Colonial Era Paintings in the Rock Art of the South-Western Cape: Some Preliminary Observations. *South African Archaeological Society Goodwin Series* 7:59–70.

Chapter Twenty

Tobacco Pipes, Cotton Prices, and Progress

There had never been any excavations in the palace at Deir Hanna, even though its archaeological remains were among the most impressive I had seen in the Galilee. Few ancient sites in the region were so suggestive of the vast gulf between the past and the present, between an era of political power and an era of powerlessness. Situated at the top of a steep hill overlooking the green Sakhnin Valley with the modern village houses clustered in and around, the ruins of the once-ornate palace were surrounded by crumbling gates and fortification walls. Its main courtyard, though now used as a common backyard by the residents of the adjoining houses, still bore unmistakable evidence of the luxurious tastes of its builders—men who had suddenly gained enormous fortunes and sought to legitimate their newfound political power by clothing it in the trappings of royalty.

Today, Deir Hanna is one of many small Arab villages nestled on the hilltops of the central Galilee. Since 1948, with the establishment of the State of Israel, the Muslim and Christian inhabitants of this remote, rural area had lived in quiet, if sometimes tense, coexistence with the neighboring Israeli towns and agricultural settlements. Like the people of the other Arab villages of the region, the people of Deir Hanna made their living by farming the fields at the foot of the village and by working at nearby construction sites and factory jobs. The cars and pickups parked along the main street of the village and the television aerials bristling from the roofs of its houses bespoke at least a certain measure of prosperity. But few tourists ever stopped at Deir Hanna, for it was situated on a winding back road far from the popular biblical attractions of the Jezreel Valley, Nazareth, Mount Tabor, and the Sea

This article was originally published in *Between Past and Present: Archaeology, Ideology, and Nationalism in the Modern Middle East*, pp. 228–243, New York: Henry Holt, ©1989 by Neil Asher Silberman.

of Galilee. This was a part of Israel that few foreign visitors even knew existed, despite the apparent impressiveness of its archaeological remains.

For a few decades in the 18th century, the situation was quite different. The village of Deir Hanna became one of the main foci of dramatic economic and political changes in the life of the country, changes felt as far away as the commercial counting houses of Europe and the Topkapi Palace in Istanbul. Beginning in the 1720s, the Zaydani family of the Galilee made Deir Hanna one of its most important strongholds in a nearly successful attempt to establish the economic and political independence of the Galilee—and, eventually, much of the territory that would later become the State of Israel—from the country's Ottoman overlords. Taking advantage of new economic opportunities and skillfully adapting themselves to new social influences and technological innovations, the various members of the Zaydani clan amassed tremendous personal fortunes and began to change the face of the country before the combined land and sea forces of a newly appointed Ottoman governor put a premature end to their plans.

In July 1776, just a few weeks after other imperial subjects—in faraway North America—had officially begun their own struggle for independence, the autonomy of the Zaydani leaders of the Galilee was finally crushed. An army led by the new governor of the province, Ahmad al-Jazzar Pasha, accompanied by a contingent of 200 sailors and a heavy cannon removed from an Ottoman warship, made its way overland from the Mediterranean coast into the Galilee and laid siege to the palace at Deir Hanna. The village was surrounded and the palace fortifications were slowly shattered by the pounding; on July 22, Deir Hanna's defenders surrendered and the Ottoman forces razed its buildings. Local farmers later returned to reoccupy the ruins, but their small village was never again a threat to the ruling powers. Only those ruins stood as a memorial to the vanished splendor of Deir Hanna, a short-lived splendor recalled in vague local legends and folktales about the power and prestige of the Zaydani family.

After more than 200 years, a sense of sad, faded glory clung to the crumbling ruins at the summit of the village's main hill. Just beyond a covered arch that was once part of a fortified entrance to the palace, an 18th-century mosque still served as a spiritual center for the community. As I entered and stood at the back of the prayer hall, a few elderly men knelt in their afternoon devotions on thin rugs laid over the cold stone floor; the original, ornate stonework of its walls had been painted over and repaired here and there with cement.

Leaving the mosque, I followed a path over large, weed-covered mounds of dirt and fallen masonry into the roofless palace ruins. In an area once occupied by the main courtyard and reception area, goats now grazed and chickens pecked for seeds. Above them rose the heavy, square columns of a once-elegant colonnade, whose alternating courses of grey and orange limestone were mirrored in the smooth masonry of the enclosing walls. A neat perforation of small, rectangular holes extended around the main hall—above a line of intricately carved windows and niches—and marked the positions of the now-vanished beams of the palace's second floor. Another covered entrance to the palace, spanned by a pointed arch, was now blocked by lines of drying laundry, but its onetime magnificence was evident. The palace at Deir Hanna was similar in style and design to the famous Mamluk mosques and fortresses of Egypt, and even as a crumbling ruin, it evoked vivid images of mounted warriors, rising twists of smoke from Turkish pipes, and the romance of medieval Middle Eastern chivalry.

Excavations here would certainly yield a wealth of finds from the era of Deir Hanna's short-lived glory. They would shed light on the economics and political life of the country during an important historical period. The standing walls and col-onnades of the palace were substantial enough to serve as the foundation of a detailed architectural restoration—perhaps even as a tourist attraction and a memorial to the village's heritage. It would be hard to ask more of a potential site for excavation. Unfortunately, no excavation at Deir Hanna was imminent or even likely. For despite the occasional interest of historians and geographers in the surviving monuments of the Galilee's Ottoman history, the remains of the palace at Deir Hanna—and dozens of ruins from the same period—lay well beyond the expertise and even the professional interest of Israel's archaeologists.

In Israel, as in every country of the Middle East and the eastern Mediterranean that I had visited, archaeology was, in strict accordance with its dictionary definition, the study of *ancient* peoples and cultures; the historical development of the modern people and cultures of the region had never been seen as an appropriate subject for archaeological research. From its beginnings in the 18th century, Near Eastern archaeology's raison d'être was, after all, the exploration of those remote historical periods seen as the "foundations" of a particular national history or chapter in Western cultural development: the early empires of Egypt and Meso-potamia, the biblical periods, and the later empires of the Romans and the Greeks.

There had, of course, been occasional excavations of sites from the Early Islamic and Crusader periods, where impressive architecture or elaborate decorative work could be found. But the Ottoman period—except in its most lavish expression in the mosques, palaces, and bazaars of Istanbul and northwestern Turkey—attracted virtually no archaeological attention, either as an important chapter in the history of Western civilization or as a source of national pride. The centuries of Ottoman domination were, to the people of virtually every modern nation in the region, regarded as one of the low points in an otherwise glorious past. Even in Turkey, the modernizing, republican tendencies of the Atatürk era had looked to the ancient Hittites as a national example and had discouraged excessive interest in the corrupt and decadent regime of sultans and viziers overthrown in 1909 by the "Young Turks."

In the countries that were the less favored, outlying provinces of the Ottoman Empire, the memories were even more bitter. In Greece, Cyprus, and in other nations of the modern Middle East where the sultans' governors, tax collectors, and soldiers exerted their unchecked authority over the local population for centuries, the Ottoman period evoked disturbing memories of oppression and poverty—in sharp contrast to the various "golden ages" of their more remote history. So it was not hard to understand why the remains of the Ottoman period attracted little romantic attention. They represented an historical period that was antithetical to the political independence of the 20th century.

Antiquities laws in the various countries of the region helped to maintain a legal boundary between the historical periods most highly valued and those that could be safely ignored. In Israel, as in virtually every country of the region, the jurisdiction of the Department of Antiquities did not, except in the most unusual of circumstances, apply to architecture or artifacts that postdated A.D. 1700. Archaeology was, according to the conventional wisdom, not needed in the study of the Ottoman period, for its historical records were abundant and its main political events well known. As a result, the remains of the Ottoman period were seen by most archaeologists as being of little or no archaeological value. And all too often—at sites throughout the region—excavators regularly took advantage of loopholes in the antiquities legislation, using bulldozers or unsupervised work crews to clear away the uppermost levels in order to get to the more intellectually interesting layers below.

The result—however justified by popular feeling, governmental regulation, or conventional widsom—was a glaring gap in archaeological knowledge, strangely severing the modern cultures and peoples of the region from their roots in the immediate poast. No other period in the long history of the eastern Mediterranean and the Middle East was as poorly understood as the Ottoman one—from an archaeological standpoint at least. Extensive, continuing surveys and excavations had enabled archaeologists to trace alternating rhythms of prosperity and decline in the region from the appearance of the earliest *Homo sapiens sapiens*, through the rise of agriculture and the Bronze Age and Iron Age cities, through the spread of Hellenistic culture in the region, to the pagan, then Christian, splendor of the Roman and Byzantine periods. But the massive medieval fortifications and ornate religious structures of the early Muslim caliphs and the European Crusaders were the last major points of interest. Just as the story as beginning to get interesting—when the modern cultures of the region were in the process of formation—the archaeological picture went blank.

In recent years, the developing techniques of "historical archaeology" in Europe and America had underlined the potential importance of *all* archaeological remains —even in places and historical periods that were extensively documented by contemporary records and official histories. Excavations such as those undertaken at the sites of 17th-century city dwellings in London, 18th-century iron foundries in Sweden, 19th-century slave quarters in Mississippi, and early 20th-century century workers' tenements in Paterson, New Yersey, had demonstrated that the official records of an era did not necessarily tell the whole story. Even in the most familiar of historical periods, the discarded debris of daily life and regtional culture often revealed surprising insights in demographic and economic trends.

While aspects of the material culture of earlier eras had been detailined in hundreds of doctoral dissertations, while there were hundred of specialists in the pottery of the Bronze Age who could accurately date an excavacated structure to within a half-century from the characteristic pottery types found in it, there was only a handful of archaeologists who had even the most basic knowledge of Ottoman pottery. Few experts could, with absolute confidence, distinguish a simple cooking pot or flask made in the time of Sultan Suleiman the Magnificent in the 16th century from a cooking pot or flask made in the last days of Sultan Abdul Hamid, at the beginning of the 20th century. And as long as the material culture of the Ottoman period lay beyond the interest and expertise of most archaeologists working in the Middle East and the eastern Mediterranean, its ruins would remain shrouded in painful memories.

On the counter in the gift shop in the Jerusalem Citadel, a basket of broken clay pipes immediately caught my attention. Placed conveniently close to the cash register in the midst of the more usual posters and postcards at this popular tourist attraction, the shiny red and dull grey pottery fragments were offered for sale to visitors with specially printed display cards that read: "Smoking pipe sherd found in the Citadel excavations—Turkish period."

These broken pipe fragments offered tourists a chance to take home an authentic piece of history from a place where archaeologists had uncovered the superimposed ruins of the fortresses and fortifications of Jerusalem's many conquerors throughout its long history. Yet unlike the characteristic pottery sherds from the biblical, Hellenistic, Roman, and Crusader levels of the Jerusalem Citadel—which the excavators had registered and studied carefully—the pipe bowls had become a clever merchandising gimmick. One might even doubt that these artifacts had any archaeological value at all.

They certainly weren't rare or uncommon. In the uppermost rubble of many ancient sites throughout the Middle East and the eastern Mediterranean, archaeologists had found tens of thousands of similar red and grey smoking-pipe bowls that had been mass produced and sold all over the region during the last few centuries. Useful only as providing evidence of late, and therefore rather unimportant, occupation levels, they had been routinely discarded, rarely photographed, and almost never studied seriously. It seemed impossible to date them with any precision; at the excavated sites of Hama in Syria and Baalbek in Lebanon—where the excavators *had*, in fact, paid them some attention—they were dated to the Mamluk period, around A.D. 1400. But since similar pipes were depicted as late as the 19th century in drawings and portraits of Ottoman notables, their period of use seemed far too long for archaeologists to utilize them as effective chronological tools.

In a region like the Middle East, where impressive archaeological remains of the Bronze and Iron ages and the classical periods were plentiful, excavators had little hesitation in ignoring or discarding late smoking-pipe fragments. But in other parts of the world, where more recent periods were the main focus of interest, archaeologists could not afford such a luxury. As early as the 1930s, in the excavations of the first permanent British colony in North America at Jamestown, Virginia, the archaeological value of smoking pipes was clear. In examining the thousands of fragments of white clay pipes found at the site, one of the excavators, J. Summerfield Day, had suggested that the gradual transformation of the bowl size and shape—from small and narrow to large and rounded—might reflect the growing popularity and affordability of tobacco at Jamestown and provide a means of dating the levels in which certain bowl forms were found.

Archaeologists working along the banks of the Thames in London soon recognized a similar phenomenon in the thousands of pipe fragments that they found. And as analysis of 17th-, 18th-, and 19th-century pipes continued at excavations on both sides of the Atlantic, other factors such as stem length and the diameter of the stem holes were found to have sufficient dependable chronological significance to make pipes one of the most important classes of artifacts in "historical" archaeology. It was only a matter of time until this understanding spread eastward—although as it turned out, it took nearly 50 years. The heavy red and grey Middle Eastern pipe bowls were, after all, quite different from the long-stemmed white clay pipes found in England and America. But if a pioneering American scholar is correct, they may possess the same degree of cultural and chronological significance.

In a 1984 article in *Hesperia,* the journal of the American School of Classical Studies in Athens, Rebecca Robinson published one of the first detailed studies of this class of artifacts, based on the hundreds of examples found by the American excavators at Corinth and at the Athenian agora. Because both these sites were occupied at least as late as the 19th century, and the uppermost layers could be dated, at least approximately, by coins and historical records, Robinson found that she could arrange the pipe-bowl fragments chronologically. On the basis of their form, decoration, and size, she concluded that the pipes of Athens and Corinth—like the similar examples from Turkey, Syria, Lebanon, Egypt, and Israel—underwent a continuous process of development from the early 17th to the 19th centuries, and—more important—they could be used to trace the diffusion of new cultural ideas from the West to the Middle East.

Those ideas were carried on the smoke of burning tobacco, the various species of the plant genus *Nicotiana,* native to North America and, as archaeologists there had determined, widely smoked by the inhabitants of that continent from around 500 B.C. Although the seeds of *Nicotiana rustica* were first carried to Europe in 1558 by the Spanish explorer Francisco Fernández, and were subsequently popularized as a wonder cure for migraine headaches by the French ambassador to Portugal, Jean Nicot (in whose honor the genus was named), it apparently was not until a few years later, around 1562, that the early French explorers of Florida took their first drag. Although the precise place and date of that momentous event is uncertain, tobacco's addictive attractions soon became well known. Not long afterward, the British and Dutch explorers farther up the eastern seaboard were also contentedly puffing, and the popularity of tobacco then spread through Europe like wildfire. Quickly becoming the latest word in modern fashion, the habit rapidly gained acceptance in the taverns and drawing rooms of Europe—reaching, by around 1600, the divans, garrisons, and caravanserais of the Ottoman Empire.

The forms of the pipes in which the tobacco was smoked, Robinson suggested, may reveal the routes of diffusion. As earlier scholars had noted, two distinct types of pipes crossed the Atlantic with the dried tobacco leaves. The familiar, one-piece, white clay pipe of the Dutch and the English was adapted from the pipes used by the Indians of Virginia and the Middle Atlantic coastline, with whom the English and the Dutch came into closest contact. And the *chibouk* or small clay bowl, attached to a separate reed or wooden stem—the type that was to become so common throughout the Ottoman Empire—was derived from the traditional types of the native American tribes of Florida and the lower Mississippi Valley, and spread through the agency of French and Portuguese traders to Africa and ultimately to the Near East.

The uncanny similarity of the polished red pipes of the tribes of southeastern North America to the pipes found in the Middle East and the eastern Mediterranean provided a convincing disproof of their Mamluk (and pre-Columbian) date. It seemed clear that they could not have been dropped or discarded at sites such as Athens, Corinth, Hama, Baalbek, or Jerusalem before the tobacco habit reached the Middle East from its birthplace in the New World sometime in the early 17th century. And Robinson noted that the pipes might have an additional chronological significance in the tracing of subsequent developments. She observed, just as American and English excavators had discovered in their own areas, that the Turkish version of the "southern" American pipe gradually became larger as tobacco became cheaper and more readily available. And in the examples from Corinth and Athens that she studied, there seemed to be specific decorative patterns characteristic of the 17th, 18th, and 19th centuries.

Serious archaeological study of Ottoman-period pipes was just beginning, but Robinson's initial theories about the date of their appearance and the development of their decoration seemed already to have been confirmed by the study of additional pipes at ongoing excavations of Ottoman sites in Turkey and on the Balkan peninsula. Pipes could, in fact, soon prove to be the key to an archaeological breakthrough. For once the chronological ranges of specific types are established, it might be possible to date the pottery and other artifacts found with them, and the

Ottoman period might become a proper field for archaeological research at last. The appearance—or absence—of the dated pipes of the late 17th, 18th, and 19th centuries would provide an indication of the speed with which the new fashion of smoking spread throughout the region. And the study of the distribution throughout the Ottoman Empire of the products from various pipe-making centers might provide an indication of previously unsuspected cultural connections and economic ties.

If the excavators at the Jerusalem Citadel had taken the time to analyze their samples, they might have been able to date many of the pipes they uncovered and might even have used this evidence to break up the "Turkish period" into a more sophisticated chronology—one more in line with their understanding of far more remote historical periods. But the tobacco pipes tossed in the basket at the Citadel gift shop—and in the dumps of far too many excavations in the region—were yet to be generally recognized as true archaeological artifacts. And every time a pipe was either sold as a souvenir to tourists or thrown away without being studied seriously, its potential significance was lost forever. Only the image of the Ottoman period as a long, monotonous period of desolation remained.

Tobacco pipes were not the only tools that could be used to begin an archaeological exploration of the Ottoman period in Israel. The records of taxation, warfare, and political rivalry preserved in archives at the Topkapi Palace and various government offices in Istanbul offered a story as stirring as those of any of its earlier periods. Although there was virtually no archaeological interest in remains of this period, several Israeli and Palestinian historians had examined the *daftars*, or detailed Ottoman tax records, which provided indirect testimony to the country's settlement patterns, population, and economy. And other sources of information —the account books, journals, and correspondence of the French commercial agents resident in the country in this period—were still preserved in the Chambre de Commerce in Marseilles. They suggest that far from being a neglected backwater in which little of note happened, the Palestinian provinces of the Ottoman Empire were profoundly affected by the changes in life-style and economic patterns that were, by the early 18th century, sweeping over the entire Western world.

Tobacco was, as the evidence of the pipes seemed to suggest, one of the changes. Another was more directly linked to Europe's Industrial Revolution, just then picking up steam. With innovations such as John Kay's "flying shuttle" (1733) and James Hargreaves's "spinning jenny" (1764), European spinning and weaving were transformed from handicrafts to mass production, and with the greatly increased potential for output came a corresponding rise in the European demand for raw materials. Wool could be obtained from the herders of Europe, but cotton—needing a drier climate and plenty of sunshine—could not. And since European traders discovered that in all of the Ottoman Empire, the best-quality cotton for spinning and weaving was raised in the foothills of the Galilee and southern Lebanon, it was not long before they took full advantage of that natural resource.

In the early 18th century, when the Industrial Revolution was just beginning in Europe, the cotton-growing areas of the Galilee and Lebanon fell under the jurisdiction of the Ottoman governor of Sidon, whose main preoccupation was personal profit, not economic development. In accordance with the elaborate system of "tax-farming" that had developed throughout the Ottoman Empire, he had gained his position by submitting a high estimate of the taxes he thought *could* be collected from the province. Any sum he collected above that estimate was his to keep. The result was predictably destructive; the Ottoman administration in the province of Sidon, as elsewhere, concentrated on exacting the greatest possible amount of taxes from the region's farmers, whose yearly payments often were in arrears.

But in this system of tax-farming lay the seeds of its own destruction, since high-quality cotton was becoming such a valuable commodity in Europe. The French traders permanently stationed in the coastal towns of Sidon and Acre quickly recognized the value of Galilee cotton, and their growing profits encouraged the commercial representatives of other European nations to challenge the French monopoly. And in 1704, a Dutch trader named Paul Maashook came up with an ingenious strategy. Directly contacting the sheikhs of the villages in the cotton-growing regions, he agreed to advance funds for the yearly tax payments of the region's farmers—in exchange for the right to purchase their entire cotton crops at an attractive, predetermined price.

The French traders soon joined in the bidding, raising the going price of cotton, and this unofficial "futures market" effected some far-reaching changes in the economic life of the Galilee. Larger crops brought advances that exceeded even the exorbitant tax levies, and before long, the extent of cotton cultivation in the region was dramatically increased. The European demand was increasing even faster, however, and the prices for cotton steadily rose. And since the local farmers were not only fulfilling their tax obligations but also making greater profits, the forces of economic self-interest slowly transformed the agricultural pattern of the province of Sidon from its traditional mix of crops for subsistence to dependence on cotton as a major cash crop.

In the earliest stages of this process, the European traders had established separate arrangements with the sheikhs of each of the Galilee villages, but it did not take long for the highly profitable economic system to become centralized. And that development came as the result of Galilean, rather than European, initiative: Dahir al-Umar, the ambitious younger son of the prominent Zaydani family, gradually extended his power over the entire region to become the unofficial ruler of a cotton principality. And here the story takes on an ominous modern aspect, for Dahir al-Umar knew how to make the most of the Europeans' demand for cotton of the Galilee. He had the foresight to demand that at least a part of his advance payments from the traders be made in the form of European ammunition and guns.

If the worried tone of the Ottoman dispatches of the period is any indication, Dahir's control of the entire Galilee and his contempt for the authority of the governor of Sidon were seen by the sultan and his ministers as a serious threat to the empire's integrity. The influences from the West, once assimilated and manipulated by a local leader, had effects that were hard to anticipate. With firm control over the region's cotton crop and its export, Dahir changed the face of the land. The ancient port of Acre was rebuilt and a new port at Haifa was established, making the links between the Galilee and the Mediterranean closer than ever before. And throughout the villages of the hill country, Dahir's relatives and allies ensured efficient internal administration and security by the construction of palaces, fortresses, warehouses, watchtowers, and caravanserais.

This chapter in the history of Israel is largely forgotten; the most recent biography of Dahir al-Umar was published in 1942. Although many of the public buildings that he and his family erected during their period of power in the 18th century are still standing, they are like the palace at Deir Hanna, crumbling, beyond the protection of the country's antiquities laws. Of course, archaeology and archaeological legislation don't have to be static; the sharp differentiation between the periods that are considered interesting and the periods that are not could be erased.

The architecture, artifacts, and settlement patterns of the country in the 18th century could be used to trace the initial stages of a process that is still going on throughout the Middle East today. For even after Dahir's death in 1775, the country's economic connection with the West grew stronger and its economic centralization continued to intensify. And in that perspective, a serious examination of the Ottoman period would do more than fill a glaring gap in our knowledge of Israel's history. It might be possible to recognize in the buried remains of the last few centuries the first signs of modernity.

There's an unhappy ending to Dahir al-Umar's story. In 1775, the Ottoman government, which for decades had been displeased with the independence and wealth of this upstart Galilean leader, finally succeeded in destroying his power once and for all. After encouraging the governor of Egypt to launch a direct attack on Dahir's territory, Sultan Abdul Hamid dispatched his fleet to the port town of Acre, one of the main centers of the Galilean export trade. Dahir's army proved helpless in the face of combined Ottoman land and sea forces, and in August 1775, the port of Acre was conquered and Dahir was killed. His neatly severed head, proudly sent back to Istanbul by the Ottoman admiral, was displayed briefly at the gates of the Topkapi Palace as a grim warning to other would-be rebels.

Dahir's sons managed to hold out for a while in their Galilean fortresses, but with the successful siege of the family stronghold at Deir Hanna, the new Ottoman governor, Ahmad al-Jazzar Pasha—a Bosnian by birth and a tyrant by disposition— quickly consolidated his control over Dahir's cotton principality. Yet even though the Galilee and the rest of the province of Sidon were now safely returned to the

Ottoman administration, the economic changes initiated there by Dahir al-Umar remained. Jazzar soon reestablished the long-standing commercial agreements with the European traders, and even after Jazzar's death in 1804, the Ottoman governors of Sidon remained dependent on cotton as one of their primary economic supports. And therein lay the danger. With the European demand for Palestinian cotton continuing for more than a century, the region's economy had become increasingly inflexible. When the European demand for Galilean cotton suddenly dropped a few decades later, a painless economic reorientation was impossible.

An end to the Galilean cotton trade came, finally, from the same part of North America in which the pipes and tobacco of the Ottoman Empire originated. The expansion of cotton cultivation throughout the American South in the early 19th century eventually created a glut on the world commodities markets, driving down prices to a point where the farmers of the Galilee simply couldn't compete. By 1852, the exports of Palestinian cotton had dropped by more than 90 percent both in total quantity and in price per pound, and, except for a brief rise in prices during the American Civil War and the resulting world "cotton famine," the era of profitable trade that had begun in the era of Dahir al-Umar was over. A new age was about to begin.

The farmers of the Galilee, now having no guaranteed, steady source of income, gradually returned to subsistence farming. New crops, such as sesame and sorghum, were sold to European traders but only on a limited scale. Many villages in the Galilee were abandoned, and fields formerly planted with cotton now lay uncultivated, often presenting a grim and desolate landscape to the increasing numbers of Europeans who came to the country in the later 19th century. But because those Western explorers, archaeologists, and travelers were interested primarily in the remains of the biblical and classical periods—and had only passing interest in the recent history of the region—they ascribed this sad state of affairs to *centuries* of Mamluk and Ottoman misrule. And an archaeological tradition was firmly established, as scholars delineated a long period in the history of the country that could safely be ignored.

The situation was, of course, far more complex. The Ottoman period, like all the others in the country's history, witnessed eras of *both* prosperity and decline. And the end of that last era of prosperity paved the way for the next stage of development. The depopulation of certain agricultural regions of the north of the country and the willingness of large landowners to sell off large tracts of the once highly productive farmland were two of the factors that made possible the settlement of a new population in the region—a mass movement that would ultimately result in the establishment of the State of Israel.

So the archaeological remains of the rise and fall of Dahir al-Umar's cotton kingdom could provide not only a fruitful field of study, they might also provide the final link between the country's present and its past. There seemed to be no reason to maintain a scholarly separation between "ancient times" and the "modern era," when the abundant archaeological remains revealed the fact of their continuum. If projects of a regional nature could discern long-range patterns of settlement and economy from the Stone Age to the time of the Crusaders, there was no apparent reason to stop at an arbitrary date such as 1700—and to fail to examine the modern economic and social roots of this part of the Middle East.

That change seemed, in fact, to be coming. A small group of archaeologists born and educated in the country was beginning to investigate the remains of this forgotten period in order to establish a new link to the land. At the village of Ta'annek on the West Bank, about 25 miles southwest of Deir Hanna, an expedition of the Department of Archaeology of Bir Zeit University—the most prominent Palestinian university—was digging. From several rows of neat excavation squares in and around the modern village, the archaeological team of students and teachers was carefully uncovering a latticework of pavements, mud ovens, and foundations of ruined walls. Like the Austrian and American archaeologists who had previously excavated the ruins of the biblical city of Taanach, whose high mound loomed above the village, they carefully recorded and analyzed every artifact uncovered and struggled to understand the site's complex stratigraphy. But in their use of other clues—such as the fragments of clay tobacco pipes, detailed Ottoman tax records, and extensive interviews with elderly village residents—this attempt to trace the history of the modern village of Ta'annek was unlike any archaeological project undertaken in the country before.

It wasn't going to be easy to begin a new field of study, especially if the old field—as if planted with cotton—had always produced a standard yield. But to understand the Ottoman period was an essential archaeological challenge. For while the cultural changes in other, more remote periods of the country's history were certainly no less significant, the economic and social developments that took place during the Ottoman period had continuing effects today. The archaeology of the Ottoman period would not miraculously transform the historical image of the last few centuries from a period of desolation into a new "golden age," but in the systematic examination of the remains of that period, *both* Palestinian and Israeli archaeologists might someday come to recognize a shared heritage in that era of dramatic social change.

NOTES

On the ruins and present state of the village of Deir Hanna, see Menachem Zaharoni (ed.), *Israel Guide*, Vol. 3: *Lower Galilee and Kinneret Region* (Jerusalem, 1978), pp. 57–60 (in Hebrew). On the history of Deir Hanna and the Zaydani family, see Amnon Cohen, *Palestine in the 18th Century: Patterns of Government and Administration* (Jerusalem, 1973) and Uriel Heyd, *Dahir al-Umar, Ruler of the Galilee in the 18th Century* (Jerusalem, 1942) (in Hebrew).

For surveys of the recent developments in historical archaeology and historical preservation, see Mark P. Leone and Parker B. Potter (eds.), *The Recovery of Meaning: Historical Archaeology in the Eastern United States* (Washington, DC, 1988); Robert L. Schuyler (ed.), *Historical Archaeology: A Guide to Substantive and Theoretical Contributions* (Farmingdale, NY, 1978); Susan Porter Benson, Stephen Brier, and Roy Rozenzweig, *Presenting the Past: Essays on History and the Public* (Philadelphia, 1986); and Jo Blatti (ed.), *Past Meets Present* (Washington, DC, 1987).

Among the few recent excavations in Israel to include clay tobacco pipes in their reports is Tel Yoqne'am in the western Jezreel Valley. See, for example, Amnon Ben-Tor and Renate Rosenthal, The First Season of Excavation at Tel Yoqne'am: Preliminary Report, *Israel Exploration Journal* 28 (1978):70, where they were, however, initially misdated to the Mamluk period. The published reports of the recent excavations at the Jerusalem Citadel, where pipes were found in abundance, do not mention this class of artifacts and touch on the Ottoman period only briefly. Compare Hillel Geva, Excavations in the Citadel of Jerusalem, 1979–1980: Preliminary Report, *Israel Exploration Journal* 33 (1983):55–71.

On the early archaeological use of tobacco pipes in America and England, see Ivor Noël Hume, *Martin's Hundred* (New York, 1982), pp. 119–122; J. C. Harrington, Dating Stem Fragments of Seventeenth and Eighteenth Century Clay Tobacco Pipes, *Quarterly Bulletin of the Archaeological Society of Virginia* 9 (1954):9–13; and Lewis Binford, A New Method of Calculating Dates from Kaolin Pipe Stem Samples, *Southeastern Archaeological Conference Newsletter* 9 (1961):19–21.

Rebecca Robinson's articles include Tobacco Pipes of Corinth and the Athenian Agora, *Hesperia* 54 (1985):149–203 and Clay Tobacco Pipes from the Kerameikos, *Mitteilungen des Deutschen Archäologischen Instituts*, Athenische Abteilung, 98 (1983):265–285.

For the history of tobacco and its spread, see, for example, Count Corti, *A History of Smoking* (London, 1931); Alfred Dunhill, *The Pipe Book* (London, 1924); B. Laufer, The Introduction of Tobacco into Europe, *Field Museum Anthropology Leaflets* 19 (1924) and 29 (1930); and Fernand Braudel, *Civilization and Capitalism: 15–18th Century*, Vol. 1: *The Structures of Everyday Life* (London, 1981), pp. 160–265.

The significance of pipe forms in tracing their origins and diffusion was first noted in Thurstan Shaw, Early Smoking Pipes: In Africa, Europe, and America, *Journal of the Royal Anthropological Institute* 96 (1960):272–305. Among the recent important studies of tobacco pipes in the Ottoman Empire is John Hayes, *Turkish Clay Pipes: A Provisional Typology, The Archaeology of the Clay Pipe, IV*, published in *British Archaeological Reports* International Series 92 (1980):3–10.

On the documentary sources for the history of early Ottoman Palestine, see Uriel Heyd, *Ottoman Documents on Palestine, 1552–1615* (Oxford, 1960); Amnon Cohen, Some Notes on the Marseilles Archives as a Source for the History of Palestine, in *Studies on Palestine During the Ottoman Period*, Moshe Ma'oz (ed.) (Jerusalem, 1975), pp. 578–582; Wolf Hütteroth and Kamal Abdulfattah, *Historical Geography of Palestine, Transjordan, and Southern Syria in the Late 16th Century* (Erlangen, 1977); and Amnon Cohen and Bernard Lewis, *Population and Revenue in the Towns of Palestine in the 16th Century* (Princeton, 1978).

For the rise and fall of the cotton economy of the Galilee, see Uriel Heyd, *Dahir al-Umar, Ruler of the Galilee in the 18th Century* (Jerusalem 1942) (in Hebrew); Amnon Cohen, *Palestine in the 18th Century: Patterns of Government and Administration* (Jerusalem, 1973) and his article Ottoman Rule and the Re-emergence of the Coast of Palestine, *Cathedra* 34 (1985):55–74; and Shmuel Avitsur, Cotton Growing in Israel, *Nofim* 3 (1976):7–35 (in Hebrew). The statistics for the dramatic drop in the export of Galilean cotton are quoted in Avitsur, pp. 16–18.

Among the many recent studies of the complex technological, economic, and demographic transformations of Palestine in the late 19th sentury, see Fred M. Gottheil, Money and Product Flows in Mid-19th Century Palestine: The Physiocratic Model Applied, *Palestine in the Late Ottoman Period*, David Kushner (ed.) (Jerusalem, 1986), pp. 211–230; Shmuel Avitsur, The Influence of Western Technology on the Economy of Palestine During the Nineteenth Century, and Gabriel Baer, The Impact of Economic Change on Traditional Society in Nineteenth Century Palestine, in *Studies on Palestine During the Ottoman Period*, Moshe Ma'oz (ed.) (Jerusalem, 1975), pp. 485–494, 495–498; Iris Agmon, Foreign Trade as a Catalyst of Change in the Arab Economy in Palestine, *Cathedra* 41 (1986):107–132 (in Hebrew); and Simon Schama, *Two Rothschilds and the Land of Israel* (New York, 1978).

DATE DUE

DEC 2 0 2000	
ILL : 48054050	Due : 12/9/08
TW : 54485	
ILL 5403573	due 3-27-08
TN # 58 327	
93019	

DEMCO, INC. 38-2931